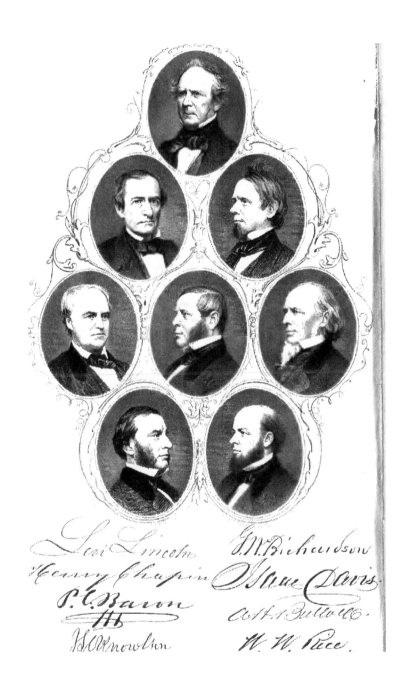

HISTORY

OF

WORCESTER,

MASSACHUSETTS,

FROM ITS EARLIEST SETTLEMENT TO SEPTEMBER 1836

WITH

VARIOUS NOTICES RELATING TO THE HISTORY OF
WORCESTER COUNTY.

BY WILLIAM LINCOLN.

'These local annals are full of *little things*, names, dates, and facts and rumors of every sort, which seem, at first sight, almost too trifling to be noticed and yet, not only is it true, that the general historian must essentially depend on the local, to a very considerable extent, for the mass of loose seeds from which the spirit of *his* narrative should be laboriously distilled but it is also true, that there is almost always a good deal of that spirit already made in such materials at his hand Many of these little things which we speak of, are little only in size and name They are full of rich meaning They are graphic and characteristic in a high degree. They suggest far more than they say They illustrate classes of men, and ages of time They are small but brilliant lights on the walls of the past, pouring floods of splendor from their little niches on the vast abysses around them.'
AMERICAN QUARTERLY REVIEW, June, 1836

WORCESTER:
PUBLISHED BY CHARLES HERSEY.
HENRY J HOWLAND, PRINTER.
1862

TO THE REV AARON BANCROFT, D D

Except for the warm encouragement of the general design of this history, without nowledge of the manner of its execution, it would have perished. If there is any merit 1 the preservation of the facts it contains, it is yours the errors are those of the comiler. On the completion of the work, his highest gratification is derived, from the pportunity of expressing veneration for the character of the beloved pastor, and gratiude for the communications, which, rightly used, would have given value to the volume ow respectfully dedicated to you, who have contributed more than all others to perpetate the memory of the events and men of Worcester in past times.

PREFACE.

—

There are few employments of industry more humble than in the compilation of local
annals. It should be permitted to him who has finished his task, to explain why it was
undertaken, and how it has been accomplished.

In 1792, a memoir of four pages, by Timothy Paine, William Young, Edward Bangs, and
Samuel Stearns, relating to Worcester, was communicated to the Massachusetts Historical Society, and published in the volume of their collections for that year. The materials furnished by these gentlemen, were transferred by the Rev. Peter Whitney to his
history of the County. The sermons of the Rev. Dr. Bancroft in 1811, 1825, and 1836,
and the Address of Hon. John Davis, May 2, 1825, with their appended notes and documents, contain many facts illustrative of civil and ecclesiastical condition. These were
the only printed narratives of the settlement and progress of Worcester. It seemed
desirable, while it was yet possible, to gather the fast fading traditions and scattered records of the past, and preserve more full view of our local history, than was permitted
by the limits of religious discourse and festival address, or accorded with the plan of former writers.

To accomplish this object, the files and records of the colonial and provincial governments, of the original proprietors, of the town, and its parishes, churches, and societies,
of the county courts and registries, and the series of newspapers from their commencement, have been examined: private journals and papers, the recollections of the aged
inhabitants, the treasures of the garrets, and the knowledge of the race in active life,
have been collected, with some labor. In the execution of the work, the result of these
examinations, there has been no effort for literary excellence, and none can be expected:
the primary purpose has been accuracy. In the multitude of facts and dates there will
doubtless be found many and great errors; it will be consolation when they are discovered, that they have not resulted from want of disposition or exertion to be correct.
Reliance has seldom been placed on tradition when it was not confirmed by better evidence, or corroborated by the concurrent testimony of records. Wherever it has
been practicable, reference has been made to the authority for statements, that their truth
might be tested.

The work has been extended diffusely, and probably tediously and unprofitably. The
events of the history of the town were closely interwoven with those of the county, and
seemed to demand detailed notice from this connection; and at every step, matters of
various interest, which it seemed impossible to reject, arose to seduce from the direct
path of narrative, until the annals of the village have become as voluminous as the records of an empire.

The language of original papers has been constantly preferred, wherever it could be
used to the words of the compiler, lest by changing forms of expression, something of
the fidelity of delineation and vividness of description of the actors in the scenes of the

past, should be lost. The modes of spelling, which were erroneous in the days when they were used, have not been retained ; but the ancient documents transcribed, except those copied in the appendix, have been made to conform to modern orthography. Names of persons and places have been printed as they were found written in the manuscripts consulted, or books quoted ; although by following this rule, the same word has been made to assume various and sometimes strange forms, on different pages.

The general plan of arrangement, affording convenience in tracing the course and connection of events, and facility of reference, has been imitated from Mr. Shattuck's History of Concord. It would have been greatly desirable that the excellence of this model could have been more fully copied.

The comparative length of the biographical memoirs will be found sometimes to have been determined more by the means of information than the merits of the subjects of the sketches. In relation to living persons, the dates of birth have, with few exceptions, been intentionally omitted.

The pleasant duty of acknowledgment for kindness remains. Some, to whom heavy debt of gratitude was due for aid, have gone down to the grave while these sheets have been in preparation, with the rich mines of their recollections unexhausted.

There is scarcely an individual named in the succeeding pages, who has not contributed good wishes or useful information. The compiler has been under great obligations to Rev. Dr. Bancroft, Mr. Thomas Rice, Edward D. Bangs, Esq., Hon. Nathaniel Paine, Samuel Jennison, Esq., Dr. John Green, Isaac Davis, Esq., to the clerks of the town and parishes ; and to Joseph Willard, Esq., Mr. Samuel G. Drake, and Rev. Joseph B. Felt of Boston, for many courtesies, communications, and valuable papers.

CONTENTS.

—

GENERAL HISTORY.

HISTORY OF WORCESTER.

GENERAL HISTORY.

—

CHAPTER I

First Period, from 1664 to 1675 first settlement Grants to Increase Nowell and Thomas Noyes. Report of exploring Committee, 1668 Petition of Committee of settlement, 1669 Project for settlement Difficulties with Ephraim Curtis, 1671 Indian Deed Grants of lands to settlers, 1675 View of the plantation, in 1675 Hostilities with the Indians Settlement abandoned

Few years elapsed after the first settlement of Massachusetts before the outposts of cultivation were advanced far and fast into the wilderness The stream of emigration soon began to flow westward from its fountain Eight years after the landing of the Pilgrims, in 1628, Salem was planted The next year. Lynn was inhabited In 1630, Boston was founded, and Cambridge and Watertown occupied Concord was purchased of the natives and commenced in 1635. Sudbury, begun in 1638, sent out colonies to Marlborough, incorporated in 1660 The swelling population pushed farther onward the frontier of improvement The fertile country around Worcester early attracted attention When the title of the vast region, acquired from the defeated savage, vested, by undisputed right, in the whole people, the wise policy of government encouraged settlement, while it rewarded patriotic exertions in the public service, and aided objects and institutions of general utility, by gratuities of portions of the forest In 1657, May 6, a grant of 3200 acres of land was made to Mr Increase Nowell, of Charlestown [1] May 6, 1662,[2] 1000 acres were bestowed on the church in Malden, to be forever appropriated to the use of its ministry Oct 19, 1664, 250 acres were given to Ensign Thomas Noyes, of Sudbury, who had served under Capt Hugh Mason [3] These were

[1] Colony Records, iv 240.   [2] ib. iv. 397.   ib iv 461

2

all, subsequently, located in the vicinity of Quinsigamond.[1] The favorable impression from the surveys, excited enterprise to undertake that plantation, which long retained the original name, borrowed from the beautiful sheet of water spreading in the neighborhood of the settlement.

John Haynes and Josiah Haynes, of Sudbury, and Nathaniel Treadaway, of Watertown, with Thomas Noyes, purchased the right of Increase Nowell, of his executors, and, on the 18th of May, 1664, having procured the acceptance of a return, became proprietors of a wide tract, extending along the east side of Quinsigamond, including two of its southern islands, near 'the going out of Nipnapp River.'[2] They petitioned the Great and General Court for the appointment of a Committee, to view the country. In compliance with their request, Capt. Daniel Gookin, Capt. Edward Johnson, Lt. Joshua Fisher and Lt. Thomas Noyes, were commissioned, Oct. 11, 1665,[3] to make survey, to determine if there be a 'meet place for a plantation, that it may be improved for that end, and not spoiled by granting of farms,' and directed to report the results of their examination to the next Court of Elections.

The death of Thomas Noyes, which occurred soon after, and the difficulties arising from the disturbed state of the country, having prevented the execution of this order, the attention of the colonial legislature was again directed to the contemplated settlement, in 1667. On the 15th of May[4] of that year, Capt. Daniel Gookin, Capt. Edward Johnson, Mr. Samuel Andrew, and Andrew Belchar, senior, were empowered, as a Committee,[5] 'to take an exact view, as soon as conveniently they can, to make true report whether the place be capable to make a village, and what number of families, they conceive, may be there accommodated. And if they find it fit for a plantation, then to offer some meet expedient how the same may be settled and improved for the public good.'

Gookin, Johnson, and Belchar, discharged the duty assigned them, in the Autumn of the following year, and presented a report on the 20th Oct. 1668,[6] which exhibits an interesting outline of the views entertained in former times, and of the general principles adopted in the formation of towns.

'The Committee's return about a new plantation near Quandsigamond Ponds. Boston, 20 Oct. 1668.

We have, according to the Court's order, bearing date 15th May, 1667,[7]

---

[1] The orthography of Indian names is quite uncertain. The same word is not only written in different manner by contemporary authors, but assumes various shapes in the same instrument. The ancient name of Worcester appears in them, among other forms: Quansiggemuck, Quinsigamug, Quansicamoag, Quansitamud, Quonsiquamon, Quansigamon, Quansiquanog, Quanciggugug, Quonsogogong. Quinsigamond, has been established by most general use, and is therefore adopted. The true reading was probably *Quonsigamoag*.

[2] Nipmuck, now Blackstone River.   [3] Colony Rec. iv. 562.   [4] ib. iv. 587.

[5] Notices of the committees of settlement, and of some of the early planters, will be found in the succeeding pages.

[6] Col. Rec. iv. 624.   [7] Col. Rec. iv. 587.

viewed the place therein mentioned, and find it to be about twelve miles westward from Marlboro', near the road to Springfield, and that it contains a tract of very good chesnut tree land ; a large quantity : but the meadow we find not so much ; because a very considerable quantity of meadow and upland, about five thousand acres, is laid out unto particular persons, and confirmed by this Court, as we are informed, which falls within this tract of land : viz ; to Ensign Noyes deceased and his brethren, three thousand two hundred acres : unto the church of Malden, one thousand acres, unto others, five hundred acres, bought of Ensign Noyes ; but, all this notwithstanding, we conceive there may be enough meadow for a small plantation, or town, of about thirty families : and if those farms be annexed to it, it may supply about sixty families. Therefore, we conceive it expedient, that the honored Court will be pleased to reserve it for a town, being conveniently situated, and well watered with ponds and brooks, and lying near midway between Boston and Springfield, about one day's journey from either : and, for the settling thereof we do offer unto the Court that which follows ; viz :

That there be a meet proportion of land granted and laid out for a town, in the best form the place will bear, about the contents of eight miles square :

That a prudent and able committee be appointed and empowered to lay it out : to admit inhabitants, and order the affairs of the place, in forming the town, granting lots, and directing and ordering all matters of a prudential nature, until the place be settled with a sufficient number of inhabitants and persons of discretion, able to order the affairs thereof, in the judgment of the Court :

That due care be taken by the said Committee, that a good Minister of God's word be placed there, as soon as may be : that such people as may be there planted may not live like lambs in a *large* place :

That there be two or three hundred acres of land, with a proportion of meadow, in some convenient place, at the discretion of the Committee, reserved, and laid out for the Commonwealth ; and the Committee to have power and liberty to settle inhabitants thereupon, for lives or times, upon a small rent, to be paid after the first seven years.'   Daniel Gookin.
                                                                 Edward Johnson.
                                                                 Andrew Belchar.

This report was approved and accepted, its recommendations confirmed, and Capt. Daniel Gookin, Capt. Thomas Prentice, Mr. Daniel Henchman, and Lt. Richard Beers, appointed a Committee to carry them into execution.

At the distance of more than a century and a half, when we see the hills and vallies of the ' *very good chesnut tree land* ' explored by the committee, thickly dotted with the homes of the husbandman and the villages of the manufacturer, traversed by canal and railway, and supporting a dense population, their estimate of the capacity of the tract, eight miles square, to maintain thirty or sixty families, furnishes strong contrast between their humble anticipations and our overflowing prosperity.

At the period when the examination took place, meadow lands were esteemed of high value, and were, indeed, essential for the support of the new settlements. The low grounds, cleared of woods by the industry of the beaver, erecting dams to flood their surfaces : by the waste of fires kindled by the hunter ; or the action of streams ; afforded the only pasturage that could be obtained, until the forest had been hewn away, and the herbage rose upon the cultivated fields.

Notwithstanding, the Great and General Court, by their order, May 15, 1667, had prohibited the laying out of lands within the new plantation, a location had been subsequently made, in right of Ensign Noyes. His heirs had sold their lands to Ephraim Curtis, of Sudbury, afterward distinguished for his gallantry and good conduct in the war with the Indians. The Committee, embarrassed by the selections made by the claimants under the old grants, on the 27th of May, 1669,[1] presented the following petition for relief from the difficulties which had arisen, to retard the progress of settlement.

'We, the Committee of the General Court, whose names are subscribed, being appointed and empowered to lay out, settle and manage a plantation, at or about Quansigamond pond, twelve miles beyond Marlborough, in the road way to Springfield and Hadley, which place is very commodious for the situation of a town, the better to unite and strengthen the inland plantations, and, in all probability, will be advantageous for travellers, it falling near midway between Boston and Springfield, and about a day's journey from either ; we, having lately been upon the place, to make an exact discovery and survey thereof, accompanied with sundry honest and able persons that are willing forthwith to settle themselves there : but finding some obstructions in the work, which, unless this Court please to remove, and, we conceive, they may justly do it, the proceeding will be utterly hindered ; and, therefore, we shall humbly offer them unto the honored Court, desiring help therein :

1. We find, that, though the place contains a tract of good land, yet, it is much straitened for meadow. We cannot find above three hundred acres of meadow belonging to it, within several miles : but, there are swamps and other moist lands. that, in time, with labor and industry, may make meadow.

2. We find, that there is a grant of one thousand acres to the ministry of Malden, May the 7th, 1662, which grant is laid out in this place. This farm contains a choice tract of land, and swallows up about one hundred acres of the aforesaid meadow ; but the condition of the grant, as the record will declare, is, that it be improved, within three years after the grant, for the ends wherefore it was granted ; but that being not done ; for it is now above six years since, and no improvement made ; we apprehend, the grant is void : but yet, if the Court please to renew it, in any other place, we speak not to oppose it : but if it be continued and confirmed in this place, it will utterly hinder the settling of a plantation here.

[1] Col. Rec. iv. 426.

3. There is another grant of land, unto Ensign Noyes, deceased, laid out in this place, containing two hundred fifty acres of choice land, with a considerable quantity of meadow, lying in the heart of this place; and by him was sold to one Ephraim Curtis, a young man living in Sudbury. We desire that the Court will please to make void this grant; being not laid out regularly for quantity or quality, as we conceive, and it will very much prejudice this town. The person concerned may have his land in another place, bordering upon this town, where there is sufficient to accommodate it, and also may have a lot in this town, if he desire it.

4. Whereas, the Court, in their grant of this town, hath reserved two or three hundred acres of land, with a proportion of meadow, to be laid out for the Commonwealth; if it please the Court, because of the straitness for meadow, to abate that reservation, so far as concerns meadow, it will greatly encourage the work.

If the honored Court please to remove these obstructions, we hope it will not be long before this place be settled in a good way, for the honor of God and the public good.

The Committee, in their journey, having discovered two other places beyond this to the westward, that will make two or three towns, the one place called Pamaquesset, lying upon the head of Chequabee River, the other place called Swquakeag,[1] upon Connecticut River, nearer to Boston than Hadley, we desire the Court will please to order that these places be reserved to make towns, the better to strengthen those inland parts, and the laying out of particular grants prohibited in the said places.'

Daniel Henchman,   Daniel Gookin,

Richard Beers,   Thomas Prentice.

The reservation to the public in the meadow was released, but the petition, in relation to the private grants, was refused.

The progress of the Committee of settlement in the discharge of their duties was, necessarily, slow, and, for a long time, their efforts were defeated by calamitous circumstances. Their first meeting was held in Cambridge, July 6th, 1669, when a plan was formed for the projected plantation. The foundation principles and rules they matured are entered on their original book of records, in the hand-writing of the venerable Gookin, and indicate the wisdom and forecast of their authors. It was proposed, that the territory, including the whole of Worcester and Holden, and a large part of Ward, should first be divided into ninety twenty five acre house lots, and, in the apportionment of these to the settlers, 'respect should be had to the quality, estate, usefulness, and other considerations of the person and family to whom they were granted:' that the most convenient place, nearest the middle of the town, should be set apart and improved for placing the meeting house, for the worship of God: a convenient lot of fifty acres for the first minister, should

[1] Northfield.

2*

be laid out as near to it as might be : another lot, in the next convenient place, not far from thence, for the ministry that should succeed in all future times : that twenty acres, should be reserved, near the centre, for a training field, and to build a school house upon : that a lot, of twenty five acres, should be appropriated for the maintenance of a school and school master, to remain for that use forever : and that two hundred and fifty acres, should be for the use of the country. Provision was made for the equal apportionment of common charges upon the proprietors of lots, for erecting mills, opening and repairing ways, and for the equitable division of the remaining lands.[1] Subsequent events prevented the practical effects of these regulations from being felt in the affairs of the inhabitants, excep in the example and aid they might have afforded to those who directed their prudential concerns in more prosperous days.

The exertions of the committee to procure settlement, seem, for a long period, to have been unavailing. At length, brighter prospects opened before them. In the year 1673, a company of thirty persons were engaged to commence the plantation, and, in the following spring, thirty house lots were laid out, and they began to build and cultivate. Ephraim Curtis of Sudbury had, probably, previous to this time, taken possession of the rich tract of land near the centre of the present town of Worcester, and had erected a house on the 'Connecticut road,' west of the head of Quisnigamond. So great was the obstruction encountered from his claims, that the Committee were compelled, again, to ask the aid of the legislature, in removing the vexatious incumbrance arising from his rights and pretentions. The following petition, subscribed by those who proposed to become inhabitants, was presented by them, on the 27th of May, 1674.[2]

' To the Hon'ble the Governor, Deputy Governor, Assistants and Deputies, assembled in the General Court of the Massachusetts Colony in New England, this 27th of May, 1674.

The humble petition of Daniel Gookin senior, Thomas Prentice, Richard Beers, and Daniel Henchman, a committee, appointed and authorized by the General Court, to order and manage a new plantation granted by this Court, lying and being upon the road to Springfield, about twelve miles westward from Marlborough, together with divers other persons hereunto subscribed, who have lots granted and laid out there, humbly sheweth :

That, whereas, your petitioners have been at a very considerable expense, both of time and estate, in order to settle a plantation there ; which, they conceive, when it is effected, will more conduce to the public good of the country than their particular advantage ; and have so far advanced in that work, as to lay out about thirty house lots, and engage the people to settle them speedily : also have begun to build, plant, and cut hay there ; but now, meeting with an obstruction and hinderance, by a young man called Ephraim Curtis, of Sudbury, who does lay claim unto two tracts of land, containing about five

[1] Proprietors' Records, 3.   [2] Colony Files, 1674.

hundred acres, lying in the centre of this plantation, especially one of the parcels, being about 250 acres, in which place the committee have laid out a minister's lot, a place for a meeting house, a mill, and ten other particular men's house lots, so that if this place be taken from us, this town is not like to proceed, to the damage of the public and your petitioners · now, although we cannot grant that the said Curtis hath any legal right to debar our proceeding, yet, for peace sake, we have offered him a double share in the plantation, viz two house lots, and accommodations to them, which will, in the end, amount to much more land than he pretends unto, but all offers he declines. Therefore,

Our humble request unto the Court is, that you will be pleased to order, that the said Curtis may be sent for and that both him, and your Committee, may be [*examined*] either before some Committee of the Court, thereunto to report the matter, or by the whole Court · for the substance of the case will as we conceive, turn upon this hinge, whether an order of the General Court, dated in May 1667, prohibiting the laying out any particular grants in this place, in order to reserve it for a village, shall be of force and efficacy to nullify the acceptance of a particular grant laid out in this place, as is pretended, a year after, namely, at a Court held Anno 1668, the untying of this knot, which none can do but the General Court, will resolve the matter of controversy one way or other, so that this town will proceed or cease, and that your Committee, and others concerned, may not be wrapt up in trouble and contention about this matter, whose scope and aim is, the public good, and that the good of many may be preferred before one, wherein we have no cause to doubt of this honored Court's favor and encouragement.

And so your petitioners desire in all humility to pray &c, for you.

Phinehas Upham,	Daniel Whittamore,	Jona Treadaway,
Richard Dana,	Palatiah Whittamore,	Joseph Dana,
John Damond,	John Richards,	Thomas Brown,
Philip Atwood,	Joseph Richards,	William Hersy,
Thomas Tewksbury,	William Reed,	Jno. Provender,
Symon Meylin,	Samuel Lee,	Edward Wildes,
Lazarus Grover,	Thomas Pratt,	Jno Wilder,
Thomas Grover,	Thomas Skinner,	Theophilus Thornton,
Stephen Grover,	Henry Swillaway,	Thomas Thornton,
Lyman Grover,	John Starkey,	
Daniel Gookin, sen	Thomas Prentice,	Ric Beers.'
D. Henchman,		

In compliance with this petition, the parties were heard before the deputies and magistrates, their evidence and arguments considered, and the controversy determined, by the equitable decision expressed in the following order June 5, 1674.

'In answer to the petition of Capt. Daniel Gookin, Capt. Prentice, Lieut. Richard Beers and Mr. Henchman, and as a full issue of the case between the said petitioners and Ephraim Curtis; The Deputies judge meet, that the said Curtis shall have fifty acres of the land that is already laid out to him, where he hath built, so it be in one place, with all manner of accommodation appertaining thereto as other inhabitants have. And also, that he shall have liberty to take up the 250 acres of land without the bounds of said place, provided it be near adjoining thereunto: and to be in lieu of the land formerly granted to Mr. John Norton: and all this with reference to the consent of our honored Magistrates hereto.   William Torrey, Cleric.

'5. 4. 1674.[1] The Magistrates consent hereto, provided that the 250 acres to be laid out, without the bounds of the place, be understood without the bounds of the town; and that the fifty acres where he hath built, be laid out and ordered by the Committee for said plantation as other lots there are.
John Pynchon, p. order.'

'June 5, 1674. Consented to by the Deputies.   Wm. Torrey, Cleric.'[2]

The adverse claim of Curtis having been thus quieted, the grant of the future town secured, and the rules for conducting the settlement established, the next care of the Committee was to extinguish the title of the Indians, then numerous in the vicinity, that neighbors so dangerous and powerful might be propitiated. A deed of eight miles square, for the consideration of 'twelve pounds in lawful money of New England, or the full value thereof in other specie to the content of the grantees, within three months after the date to be paid and satisfied,' was executed, with great formality, on the 13th of July, 1674, by Solomon, alias Woonaskochu, sagamore of Tatacsit, and John, alias Hoorrawannonit, sagamore of Packachoag.[3] The receipt of part of the purchase, viz. two coats and four yards of trucking cloth, valued at

---

[1] 5th month, 4th day: June 15, 1674, new style.

By Stat. 24. Geo. II. Colony Laws 579, for regulating the commencement of the year and correcting the calendar, the style was changed. It was enacted that from the last day of December, 1751, the year should be considered as beginning on the first day of January, and that the day following the *second* of September, 1752, should be called the *fifteenth*, omitting eleven intermediate nominal days.

Previous to this act, the year was considered as commencing on the 25th of March, the Lady day, or Annunciation of the church. According to the ancient reckoning, March was the first, and February the last month.

The correction of the calendar, made by Pope Gregory XIII, in 1582, was immediately adopted in catholic countries. Although not established in England until 1752, it was customary to indicate the change by double dates, between the first of January and the 25th of March: thus, March 24, 1674-5, would have been written; the day being after the commencement of 75, new style, and before the end of 74, old style.

To adjust the difference of style, eleven days are to be added to all dates previous to Sept. 2, 1752.

[2] Colony Files, 1674.   [3] Middlesex Registry of Deeds, Lib. 8, Fol. 317.

twenty six shillings, as earnest, in hand, was acknowledged   The conveyance
was in fee, to the Committee, and the rest of the people admitted, or to be
admitted, to be inhabitants   The terms, included all and every part of the
natural or civil right of the native chiefs, in all and singular the broken up
land and wood land, woods, trees, rivers, brooks, ponds, swamps, meadows,
minerals, or things whatsoever, lying and being within the eight miles square
Covenants were inserted that the lands should be held without any let, molestation, or disturbance by the grantors or their kindred, or people, or any
claiming under them , and that full and ample deeds and writings should be
made according to law on finishing the payment   From a marginal note,
attested by the venerable Gookin, it appears, that the full consideration was
discharged, Aug 20th, 1676, one half being advanced by himself, and the
other moiety furnished by an assessment of one shilling the acre on the house-
lots of the proprietors

The acknowledgment of this deed was before Gookin himself, though one
of the grantees; a circumstance not remarkable in times of purity, when the
interest of the man was not considered as affecting the uprightness of the
magistrate

The following persons attested the instrument as subscribing witnesses

Onnomoq, sagamore of Occonomesset,[1] now Marlborough   He is mentioned Dec 1671,[2] ' as lately deceased about two months since, which is a
great blow to that place   He was a pious and discreet man, and the very soul,
as it were, of that town '   He was the last ruler of his tribe

Nomphow, sagamore of Wamessit, now Tewksbury, said by Gookin,[4] to be
' of the blood of the chief sachems '   His son Samuel was teacher of the
praying Indians, ' A young man of good parts, and who can speak, read and
write English and Indian competently   He is one of those that was bred up
at school at the charge of the Corporation for the Indians '

Joseph Thatcher, of Chabanakonkomon,[4] now Dudley, who was a teacher
Nosoonowit   a christian of Pakachoag

In 1673, the work of settlement was prosecuted with vigor   About the
middle of April, surveys were made of the lands by David Fisk of Cambridge and John Flint of Concord.[4]   The lines and boundaries of the lots
were established by actual admeasurement, and grants were made, confirmed
and registered   Fifty acres were laid out to Gookin and Prentice, and twenty

----

[1] This word is written by Gookin, 1 Mass Hist Col 1 185, Okommakamesit   by Hutchinson, quoting from Elliot, Hist Mass 1, 156, Ogguonikongquamesut   by Rev Mr Allen,
Wor Mag 11 141, Ockueangansett · and is said to have been corrupted to Agogingga-
missit

[2] 1 Mass Hist Col 1, 185

[3] Written Chabanakongkamun, 1 Mass Hist Col 1 189   On Carleton's map of Massachusetts, it is called Chargoggagoggmanchugg igogg   This collection of syllables is divided into two words, on Keach's map of Dudley, 1831, and bestowed on Slater's Pond

[4] Prop Records, 7—12

five to Henchman, of the Committee. A lot granted to Phinehas Upham,[1] July 8, 1673, was now described and located, 'and although it should contain more than fifty acres, yet the Committee have confirmed it to him for a fifty acre lot, more or less; and this they did upon a rule of justice and equity, in consideration of the labor, travel, and activity of the said Upham, from time to time, in furthering, advancing, and encouraging the settlement of the plantation.'[2] In pursuance of the order of Court, fifty acres were assigned to Ephraim Curtis 'where he had begun to build a small house.'[3] A lot of forty acres was appointed for the use of the 'first learned, pious, and orthodox minister.'[4]

At this time the grants to the following persons were surveyed, confirmed, and recorded. The figures express the number of acres in each lot.

In the west squadron or division on the north side of Connecticut road: Thomas Hall, 25, of Woburn: Daniel Gookin, 50: Samuel Gookin, 25, of Cambridge: Simon Meyling, 25; Ephraim Curtis, 50, of Sudbury: Daniel Henchman, 25, of Boston: Dr. Leonard Hoar, 25, of Concord.

In the west squadron or division on the south side the Country road: Phinehas Upham, 50, of Malden: Philip Atwood, 50, of Concord: Trial Newbury, 25, of Woburn.

In the middle squadron or division on the north side of the Country road: Thomas Brown, 50, of Sudbury: Richard Dana, 50; Jacob Dana, 25, of Watertown: Joel Jenkins, 100, of Malden.

In the middle division, on the south side of the Country road, east side mill brook: Thomas Prentice, 50, of Woburn: Benjamin Webb, 50, of Marlborough: First Minister, 40: Benjamin Crane, 50, of Sudbury; Thomas Hall, 25, of Woburn.

In the eastern squadron, lying next to the Country road to Boston; Joseph Waigh, or Wayt, 25, of Marlborough: John Provender, 25, of Malden: Samuel Brigham, 25; John Fay, 50, of Marlborough: Gershom Eames, 25, of Framingham: Thomas Grover, 25; John Paul, 50; John Shaw, 25, of Malden: John Curtis, 44; Simon Meyling, 55, of Sudbury.

Another squadron in the way to Lancaster: Michael Flagg, 25; Joshua Bigelow, 25; Joseph Beamis, 25; all of Watertown.

Other lots granted and Indian purchase money paid but not laid out: Wm. Taylor, 25, of Malden: Jonathan Treadaway, 25, of Sudbury: Wm. Adams, 25, of Concord or Sudbury.

In 1675, 'the Country road to Connecticut'[5] as it was called, the highway

---

[1] Phinehas Upham afterwards distinguished himself in the War with Philip as Lieutenant of Infantry. He was mortally wounded in the attack on the Narraganset Fort, Dec. 19, 1675, and died, soon after, in Boston.

[2] Prop. Rec. 8.   [3] ib. 7.   [4] ib. 10.

[5] This was the new road from Marlborough, through what is now Northborough, Shrewsbury, and Worcester to Connecticut. The Nipmuck, or old road, passed through the east part of Northborough, over Rock hill, east of Great and Little Chauncey Ponds, into

of communication between Boston and the western settlements, entered the town near the head of the Pond, and following along the course of the present Shrewsbury road to its intersection with that to Lancaster, passed westward of the route now traveled, and crossed the stream nearly a quarter of a mile above the bridge. It then traversed the plain and ascended the hill west of the modern Court House, near where a private lane now exists. It was merely a path cut through the woods, practicable for passengers on foot and with horses.

On this road, south of the fording place, was erected, at a very early period, one of those edifices called block, or garrison houses, and denominated on the records, 'the old Indian Fort.' The structures for defence against the tribes prowling in the forest, so far as specimens have survived the waste of time, or descriptions been preserved by tradition, had great uniformity in construction. They were built of timbers hewn on the sides in contact with each other, firmly interlocked at the ends, and fastened together with strong pins. They were generally square in form and two stories in height. The basement was furnished with a single thick door of plank. The walls were perforated with narrow loop holes for the use of musketry against an approaching foe. A ladder, easily drawn up if the lower floor was forced, ascended to the next room, which projected two or three feet over on each side, having slits for infantry and wider port holes for cannon. The gentle slope of the roof afforded an elevated position to overlook the surrounding country, and was sometimes crowned with a little turret for an observatory. These watch towers, impervious to ball or arrow, were of abundant strength to resist an enemy unprovided with artillery, and might defy any attack, except that by fire on the combustible materials. To these wooden castles, in the infancy of the country, the inhabitants repaired on the alarm of danger, and found ample protection within the rude fortresses, seldom reduced by the savage, of too fierce temperament to await the lingering progress of seige.

The lands eastward of Main Street, in the centre of the town, had been flooded by the Beavers, who had established their hamlet and built a dam

Westborough, and thence through Grafton. The first house built on the new road west of Marlborough, was that of Col. James Eager of Northborough. In 1674, there was no human habitation on its route between Marlborough and Brookfield, except the wigwams on Pakachoag. Wor. Mag. ii 152.

In the agreement of the Committee with Capt. Henchman, in 1684, it is said ' the country road is to lead up where carts have gone towards the north west corner of the citadel, and so pass into the street, next on the westerly side, where the mills are to stand, that carts as well as horse may pass therein.'

The way to Lancaster went northward from the town nearly on the route followed by the present old Boston road.

In Wor. Mag. ii 112, it is supposed that the village of Pakachoag was on the Connecticut road. The account of Gookin shows that it was about three miles distant, at this time. A highway was subsequently located, south of the ancient path, which passed near the foot of Pakachoag.

across the stream near the bridge on Front Street. It is probable, the tract around the head of the Blackstone Canal then spread like a fair prairie, free from trees and covered with the herbage of the meadows.

There were tracts which had been occupied by the Indians as planting grounds ; and their simple husbandry, if it did not improve by tillage, admitted the rays of the sun through the thick foliage of the primeval woods, to warm the soil enriched by the decayed vegetation of ages. The 'Indian broken up lands' are frequently mentioned in the proprietary records. The fires of the hunter, anticipating the work of the axe, had prepared fields for the plough.

These are the only vestiges of improvement which can be traced as existing when the first settlers of Worcester commenced their labors.

Most of those who had expressed intention to become planters and joined in the petition of the Committee in May, 1674, discouraged by difficulties or delay, had abandoned their purpose. Of the persons who obtained grants, many did not discharge the purchase money of one shilling the acre, and but few actually removed. It required stout hearts to penetrate the depth of the wilderness and maintain residence in the immediate vicinity of the savage.

Ephraim Curtis, who had already built, Thomas Hall, Simon Meyling, Phinehas Upham, Thomas Grover, Philip Atwood, Joseph Waight, John Provender, and perhaps some others, had arrived in the month of April, 1675. Six or seven houses were erected. Neither record nor tradition, affords information of the position of the habitations. The neighborhood of the Fort, the convenient proximity of water and meadow, would, it may reasonably be conjectured, have induced to the selection of the northern part of the present central settlement.

To the edition of Hubbard's Narrative published in 1677, is prefixed a map of New England, being, as the title expresses, ' the first map here cut,' framed to illustrate the events of the war with Philip. The places 'assaulted by the Indians during the late awful revolutions of Providence ' are indicated upon this rude specimen of the origin of the arts in our country. The town of Worcester is thus distinguished. In the work it is described, as ' a village called Quonsigamog, in the middle way between Marlborough and Quabaog, consisting of about six or seven houses.'[1]

The settlement was prosperously advancing, and the inhabitants, in the language of the record, ' had built after the manner of a town,' when the war with Philip of Mount Hope broke out in Plymouth colony. The conspiracy to crush the white men by a general massacre, if, as has been asserted by the early annalists, such a combination existed, was disclosed before it had ripened to its sanguinary maturity, and the Indians were driven unprepared into the conflict ending in the extermination of their tribes. The influence of the great native warrior extended widely through the tributary nations. The confederation he planned to expel the invader, who grew stronger day by day, and

[1] Hubbard's Nar. 135.

like the serpent, though crushed at one point was alive at another, with renovated power to injure, though defeated of its primary object, was the commencement of a series of hostilities that desolated the frontier settlements Although remote for a time, the war soon approached the plantation of Quinsigamond   The son of Matoonus had been executed in 1671, for the murder of an Englishman, and his head placed on a pole, where it long remained, as the terrific memorial of justice.   The father, a grave and sober Indian, appointed by Gookin constable of Pakachoag, in his profession of Christianity had not forsaken the vindictive principle so deeply cherished by his people   July 10, 1675,[1] he visited Mendon, and revenged the loss of his offspring by the death of five of its inhabitants [2]

This was the signal for the commencement of a desperate contest.   Common danger produced that efficient union of the northern colonies cemented by the necessity of self preservation   The war was not of long continuance.

Energetic and rapid excursions laid waste the resources of the hostile tribes, the allies, enticed to their support, foreseeing their fate, grew cold towards ancient friendships . their supplies were destroyed · their wigwams consumed . and Philip and his forces, hunted from post to post, deserted their homes and took refuge among the Nipmuck villages, where they received shelter and reinforcement.   Unable to maintain open fight, they continued an unsparing predatory warfare upon the exposed hamlets and garrisons   Alarm prevailed through New England   None knew when to expect the visitation of the foe, lurking unseen in the solitude of the forest, until the blow fell, as sudden as the lightning, and left its effects traced with fire and blood   The husbandman went forth to cultivate the field, armed as if for battle; the musket and the sword rested by the pillow, whose slumbers were often broken, as the war whoop rose on the watches of the night   The planters of Worcester, placed hard by the seat of the enemy, remote from friendly aid, with no dwelling of civilized man nearer than Marlborough on the east, Lancaster towards the north, and Quabaog, now Brookfield, westward, to afford assistance and support, were compelled to desert their possessions, and dispersed among the larger towns   The silence of desolation succeeded to the cheerful sounds of industry, and the village was abandoned to the wild beast and the fiercer foe

[1] Hubbard's Nar   31

[2] This event is thus noticed by Mather   'July 14, the Nipnep, or Nipmuck Indians, began their mischief at a town called *Mendam* (had we *amended* our ways as we should have done, this misery might have been prevented), where they committed *barbarous murders*   This day deserves to have a *Remark* set upon it, considering that blood was never shed in *Massachusetts colony* in a war of hostility before this day   Moreover, the Providence of God herein is the more awful and tremendous, in that this very day the church in *Dorchester* was before the Lord humbling themselves by fasting and prayer on account of the *day of trouble* now begun among us.

The news of this bloodshed came to us at Boston, the next day, in Lecture time, in the midst of the sermon   the Scripture then improved being that, Isai 42 24   Who gave Jacob to the spoil, and Israel to the robbers?   Did not the Lord?   He against whom we have sinned'   Mather's Hist 5

3

CHAPTER II.

King Philip's war, 1675, 1676. The Nipmuck country. Indian Settlements. Visit of Gookin and Eliot. Attack on Quaboag. Ephraim Curtis. Phinehas Upham. Hench-man's expedition. Quinsigamond burnt. Henchman's second expedition. Sagamore John surrenders. Matoonus shot. Executions in Boston. Destruction of the Indians.

The natives of Quinsigamond were of the Nipmuck or Nipnet Indians. The territorial jurisdiction of this tribe is not accurately defined by the early historians. Gookin, high authority on such subjects, includes within ' the Nipmuck country,' as it was called, ten villages of Christian converts : Has-sanamisset in Grafton ; Manchoag, now Oxford ; Chabanakongkamon, now Dudley ; Maanesit, Quantisset and Wabquisset in Woodstock ; Packachaog in Worcester and Ward ; Waentug, now Uxbridge ; Weshakim, now Sterling ; and Quabaog in Brookfield.[1] From the position of these places, the domain of the nation must have extended over all the south, and part of the north, of the County of Worcester, and included a portion of Connecticut. On the south were the fierce Pequots ; the Massachusetts, inhabiting from the bay of that name to the interior, were on the east ; North, were the Pawtuckets, dwelling along the Merrimack and its tributary waters. The western bound-ary is uncertain. It is possible that it was as remote as the Connecticut River and the possessions of the warlike Maquas or Mohawks. Eliot, in 1651, speaks of Nipmuck, as ' a great country lying between *Connectacot* and the Massachusetts, called Nipnet, where there be many Indians dispersed.'[2] The Nipmucks enjoyed a wide region, abounding with lakes and rivers for fishing, forests for the hunter, and soil favorable for their rude tillage. Their character was more gentle and peaceful than generally belongs to savage life. Surrounded by powerful and ferocious tribes, they had lost national independ-ence. The chiefs and sagamores of the scattered hamlets were subordinate and tributary to their strong neighbors. When the planters first arrived, Wattasacompanum was nominally ruler. But his authority was controlled, and his efforts to preserve the friendly relations which had always subsisted between his people and the English, were rendered ineffectual, by the superior influence and bolder spirit of the Sachems, who held their subjects by para-mount allegiance to their wild governments, and they were drawn, reluctantly and unwillingly, into hostilities.

The principal settlement of the Indians in Worcester, was on the hill rising in the south part of the town, and extending into Ward, called by them Pak-achoag, now known as Bogachoag. It is thus described by Gookin, in his ' Historical Collections of the Indians in New England,'[3] written in Dec. 1674. ' This village lyeth about three miles south from the new road way that leadeth from Boston to Connecticut ; about eighteen miles, west-south-erly, from Marlborough ; and from Boston about forty four miles. It consists

---

[1] 1 Mass. Hist. Col. i. 189. [2] 3 Mass. Hist. Col. iv. 170. [3] 1 Mass. Hist. Col. i. 192.

of about twenty families, and hath about one hundred souls therein   This town is seated upon a fertile hill, and is denominated from a delicate spring of water that is there '

The western hills, bearing originally the appellation of Tataesset, corrupted, in common use, into Tatnuck, were occupied by similar hamlets

Wigwam Hill, on the western shore of Quinsigamond, was probably a favorite place of residence for the people who ranged along its waters for fish and game.   The name given by the planters indicates that it was once the site of the bark tents of the aborigines

The remains of rude workmanship frequently discovered around these eminences, and the vestiges of primitive agriculture formerly scattered over our territory, show that the tribe once roving through our forests was numerous

The benevolent exertions of self-devoted teachers in diffusing the light of Christianity, had been extended to these villages, and as early as 1672, they had been here instructed in the doctrines of religion and the ceremonial of the church.

On the 17th of September, 1674, John Eliot, well styled the apostle of the Indians, visited Pakachoag, accompanied by Gookin, who then held the office of Superintendent, on his return from an excursion among the nations intrusted to his paternal guardianship   The description, left by the latter, affords a view of the condition of the population previous to the commencement of that war whose exterminating edge soon fell on their kindred

' We took leave of the christian Indians at Chabanakongkomun, and took our journey, 17th of the seventh month,[1] by Manchage to Pakachoog, which lieth from Manchage, north-west, about twelve miles   We arrived there about noon '

, ' We repaired to the sagamore's house, called John, alias Horowanninit, who kindly entertained us   There is another sagamore belonging to this place, of kindred to the former, whose name is Solomon, alias Wooanakochu. This man was also present, who courteously welcomed us   As soon as the people could be got together, Mr Eliot preached unto them, and they attended reverently   Their teacher, named James Speen, being present, read and set the tune of a psalm that was sung affectionately   Then was the whole duty concluded with prayer '

' After some short respite, a Court was kept among them   My chief assistant was Wattasacompanum, ruler of the Nipmuck Indians, a grave and pious man of the chief sachem's blood of the Nipmuck country.   He resides at Hassanamisset   but, by former appointment calleth here, together with some others   The principal matter done at this Court, was, first, to constitute John and Solomon to be rulers of this people and co-ordinate in power, clothed with the authority of the English government, which they accepted   also to allow and approve James Speen for their minister   This man is of good parts, and pious   He hath preached to this people almost two years, but he yet resides at Hassanamisset, about seven miles distant   Also they chose, and

[1] 28 September, 1674, N S.

the Court confirmed, a new constable, a grave and sober Indian, called Matoonus.   Then I gave both the rulers, teacher, constable and people, their respective charges, to be diligent and faithful for God, zealous against sin, and careful in sanctifying the Sabbath.'

Having sent a grave and pious Indian to be a teacher at Nashaway, near Lancaster, with a letter of advice and exhortation, written and dated at Pakachoag, and nominated one of that tribe, who was present, as constable, with power, ' to apprehend drunkards, take away their strong drink, and bring the offenders before himself for punishment;' an office which the candidate refused to accept until he could consult his friends; the exercises were concluded with singing a psalm and offering prayer, and they retired to rest.   The next morning early they passed to Marlborough, and thence returned to their homes.[1]

While the flame of war spread through the whole jurisdiction of Massachusetts, Quinsigamond was distinguished as the central point in a territory depopulated by hostilities, and as a post for military movements.   Some of the christian Indians, during this gloomy period, repaired to Marlborough : but most of them, enticed by the persuasions and awed by the lofty spirit of Philip, united themselves with him.   As early as July, 1675, this bold and sagacious warrior was at Pakachoag, and was accompanied westward by sagamore John, who participated in the attack on Quabaog.   When this John surrendered himself at Boston, the year after, ' he affirmed ' says Hubbard, ' that he had never intended any mischief to the English at Brookfield, but that Philip, coming over night among them, he was forced, for fear of his own life, to join with them against the English.'[2]   Many of our Indians went with him.

While the natives of Pakachoag were attempting the destruction of Brookfield, Ephraim Curtis, who may be considered as the first settler of Worcester, distinguished himself as a gallant soldier in repelling their attacks.   Having actively engaged in military service, he received the commission of Lieutenant. The government, desirous of reclaiming the Nipmucks to their fidelity, repeatedly sent messengers to their chiefs.   On the 24th of July, 1675, Curtis held a conference with four of their sachems, and received assurances of their peaceful intentions.[3]   Induced by deceptive promises, Capt. Edward Hutchinson, and Capt. Thomas Wheeler, were sent into the interior ; the former, commissioned to negociate a treaty, and the latter, in command of a military force of 20 men, for the protection of the embassy.   Commencing their march from Cambridge, July 28, and passing the forsaken wigwams of the savages, who fled before them to concentrate power for a heavy blow, they arrived near Brookfield, August 2.   Having been amused by delusive appointments for meetings, they were led into a narrow defile, between a steep hill

[1] 1 Mass. Hist. Col. i. 192.

[2] Hubbard's Narrative, 101.   ' One eyed John accuses sagamore John to have fired the first gun at Quabaog, and killed Capt. Hutchinson.'   Sewall's Journal.

[3] Hub. Nar. 35.

and deep swamp. Two or three hundred Indians rose suddenly from their ambuscade, and, with the first fire, killed eight and wounded five men, including both the commanders. The survivors of the ill-fated company, with difficulty, effected a retreat to the town, where they fortified one of the largest houses.

'Within two hours after our coming to the said house, or less,' says Wheeler, in his narrative,[1] 'the said Capt. Hutchinson and myself posted away Ephraim Curtis of Sudbury, and Henry Young of Concord, to go to the honored council, at Boston, to give them an account of the Lord's dealing with us, and our present condition. When they came to the further end of the town, they saw the enemy rifling of houses, which the inhabitants had forsaken. The post fired upon them, and immediately returned to us again ; they discerning no safety in going forward, and being desirous to inform us of the enemies actings, that we might the more prepare for a sudden assault by them.'

This assault followed with great violence, but was bravely resisted. During the night, the attack continued, and the Indians attempted to fire the house, with combustibles. 'I,' says Wheeler, 'being desirous to hasten intelligence to the honored Council of our present great distress, we being so remote from any succor, it being between 60 and 70 miles from us to Boston, where the Council useth to sit, and fearing our ammunition would not last long to withstand them, if they continued so to assault us, I spake to Ephraim Curtis, to adventure forth again on that service, and to attempt it on foot, as the way wherein there was most hope of getting away undiscovered : he readily assented, and, accordingly, went out ; but there were so many Indians everywhere thereabouts, that he could not pass, without apparent hazard of life ; so he came back again ; but, towards morning, the said Ephraim adventured forth the third time, and was fain to creep on his hands and knees for some space of ground, that he might not be discerned by the enemy, who waited to prevent our sending, if they could have hindered it. But, through God's mercy, he escaped their hands, and got safely to Marlborough, though very much spent, and ready to faint, by reason of want of sleep before he went from us, and his sore travel, night and day, in that hot season, till he got thither, from whence he went to Boston.'

Intelligence had reached Marlborough before the arrival of Ephraim Curtis, and Major Simon Willard, whose memory has been unhappily slandered by tradition, had marched for the relief of the little band surrounded by more than three hundred Indians.

On the 1st of September 1675, another of the early settlers of Worcester, Lt. Phinehas Upham, advanced, with a force of 100 men under the command

---

[1] See the very interesting tract, reprinted in the New Hampshire Historical Society's Collections, ii. 5, written by Captain Thomas Wheeler, entitled 'A True narrative of the Lord's providences in various dispensations towards Capt. Edward Hutchinson and myself, and those who went with us, into the Nipmug country, and also to Quabaog, alias Brookfield.'

of Capt. Gorham, into the Nipmuck country. The object of the expedition was to destroy the planting fields and burn the wigwams of the Indians, to deprive them of shelter and food during the winter. Gookin complains that they attacked only the villages of the praying converts, while Pakachoag, where there was abundance of corn, was left untouched.[1]

In November following, the enemy's forces captured the people of Hassan-amisset, while employed about their harvest. Wattasacompanum, the chief ruler and assistant, who had held court with Gookin in 1674, was prevailed with to unite with Philip, and his example drew after him most of his sub-jects. When information of this movement reached the Council, Capt. Hench-man and Capt. Sill were immediately dispatched to range the country with two companies. Having visited Grafton, and rescued some captives ' they marched,' says Gookin in his Narrative of the sufferings of the christian Indians,[2] ' to a place called Packachoage, about ten miles distant from Hassan-amisset, towards the north-west, where was plenty of good indian corn, and in this place they hoped to meet some of the enemy. Coming to the place, they saw signs of Indians, that had been lately there, but it seems, were withdrawn upon the approach of the English. Here our forces took up their quarters one night, there being two wigwams, which were good shelter for our soldiers, the weather being wet and stormy. The next morning, our forces searched about the cornfields, to find the enemy, but could not discover them, though, in all probability the enemy saw them in all their motions, and con-cealed themselves ; for this is their ordinary way ; to lie hid in thick swamps and other secret places, and to move as our men do scatter themselves, in small parties, and lie close, observing all our men's motions. The English, in their search, found above 100 bushels of Indian corn newly gathered, and a great quantity of corn standing. About 10 o'clock in the forenoon, the English Captains and their soldiers marched back to Hassanamisset. Being gone about two miles on their way, Capt. Henchman, missing, as he apprehended, his letter case, wherein his writings and orders ere, he sent back two En-glishmen, and the Indian Thomas, on horseback, to see at the wigwam where he lodged, to find his papers : these messengers, accordingly, going back, the Indian led them the way, and ascending up a steep hill, at the top whereof stood the wigwam, as soon as ever he discovered it, being not above six rods distant, he saw two Indian enemies, standing at the wigwam door, newly come out, and four more, sitting at the fire, in the house. At which sight he be-stirred himself, and, looking back, called earnestly (as if many men were be-hind, coming up the hill,) to hasten away and encompass the enemy. One of the enemy, thereupon, presented his gun at our Indian ; but, the gun mis-sing fire, (probably the moist rainy weather had put it out of case,) where-upon, the rest of them, that were in the wigwam, came all out, and ran away as fast as they could, suspecting that the English forces were at hand. And then Thomas, with his two comrades, having thus prudently scared away the

[1] Gookin's Hist. Christian Indians, in American Antiquarian Society's Collections.
[2] American Antiquarian Society's Collections.

enemy, they thought it seasonable also to ride back again to their company as fast as they could And, indeed, there was good reason for it , because Thomas, the Indian, had only a pistol . one of the Englishmen, who was their chirurgeon, a young man, had no gun · the third had a gun, but the flint was lost so that they were in ill case to defend themselves, or offend the enemy · but God preserved them, by the prudence and courage of the Indian which deliverance, one of the Englishmen directly acknowledged to me, attributing their preservation, under God, to this fellow so they got safe to their captain, who, in the interim, searching diligently, had found his letter case, and staid for these messengers ’[1]

The buildings, deserted by the planters of Worcester, were destroyed by the Indians. Dec 2, 1675 an event in which Mather discovers a special admonition of the displeasure of divine Providence The expedition against the Narragansets was then about to march ' But before they set out,' says the annalist, ' the churches were all upon their knees before the Lord, the God of armies, entreating his favor and gracious success in that undertaking. This day of Prayer and Humiliation was observed December 2d . when, also, something happened, intimating as if the Lord were still angry with our prayers for, this day, all the houses in Quonsukamuck were burnt by the Indians ’[2]

During the winter, the hostile Indians were scattered through the country between Marlborough and Brookfield A large body gathered round Wachuset. Philip having visited Canada, they remained for the most part inactive. On his return, the tomahawk was again lifted, and torture and death resumed their work On the first of February, 1675,[3] the Nipmucks destroyed the house of Thomas Eames in Framingham Three of the men of Pakachoag were afterwards executed in Boston for this burning. A curious inventory of the loss sustained by the sufferer was afterwards presented to the General Court, in which a wife and five children are included among the articles of furniture and items of property for reimbursement

The Nipmucks were engaged in the attack on Lancaster, Feb'y. 10, 1675,[4] rendered memorable by the simple narrative of Mrs. Rowlandson's captivity ; and, probably, participated in the depredations on other towns. The troops of Prentice, Savage, Mosely, and the other distinguished leaders of the time, frequently traversed the territory along the Connecticut road, to seek or pursue the foe Parties were sometimes stationed at Quinsigamond, to await reenforcements or watch the operations of the enemy.

In April, 1676, three companies of infantry, under Captains Sill, Cutler and Holbrook, and three of cavalry, with Capts Brattle and Prentice, and Capt. Henchman, who was commander-in-chief, were sent out towards Hassanamisset. Having been released for a time from service, on the 30th of May Henchman was again despatched from Boston, to meet a corps from Connecticut, to scour the forest on both sides Connecticut River, to distress the enemy and prevent their fishing in those waters. The two parties were to unite

[1] See Hubbard's Nar 45 [2] Increase Mather's History, 19
[3] Feb. 12, 1676, New Style. [4] Feb. 22, 1676, N S.

at Brookfield, but Henchman turned aside to attack a party at Weshakim ponds. This service successfully performed, he proceeded westward and met the troops of the neighboring colony at Hadley. The object of the campaign accomplished, the men of Massachusetts returned. The instructions of the Council, dated June 10, state that Philip, with several sachems, but with few fighting men, had then planted at Quabaog and Pakachoag. On arriving near the last-named place, they found that Philip and the Narragansets were gone several days before. On the 30th of June, Henchman, having halted at Marlborough, made a report, from which the following passages are extracted.

' By advice, I drew out a commanded party, under the conduct of Capt. Sill, viz. sixteen files of English, all my troop, and the Indians, excepting one file, being all we could make provision for ; for what with the falling short of the bread promised us, and a great deal of that we had proving mouldy, the rest of the men had but one biscuit a man to bring them to this place. This party we ordered towards Wachuset, and so to Nashaway, and the Weshakim Ponds, and so to return to this place. The commanded party we left at *Quonsiquomon*, where they intended to stay awhile for the last scout we sent out. Eleven prisoners we had in all ; two of the eldest, by counsel, we put to death, the other nine the commissary is ordered to convey to Boston.'[1]

From this time the fortunes of Philip rapidly declined. The spirit of disaffection spread among his allies, and the formidable confederacy his genius had formed was parted. The confidence he had inspired was lost, and the dread of the English power revived as unsparing vengeance was visited on the hostile tribes.

Sagamore John, alarmed at the dangerous condition of affairs, prudently sought safety by timely submission. In the early part of July, he opened a negociation for peace with the government in Boston.

A curious letter, composed by a christian Indian who had learned to write, supplicating mercy in very imperfect language, is preserved in one of a series of tracts, first printed in London in 1676.[2] John subscribed this paper, as a highland chieftain would have done, with the name of his clan. It was signed by other Nipmuck sagamores, and sent by a party with a white flag, July 6, 1676, from Nashaway.

' Mr. John Leveret, my Lord, Mr. Waban, and all the chief men our brethren, praying to God.[3] We beseech you all to help us ; my wife she is but one, but there be more prisoners, which we pray you keep well : Mattamuck his wife, we entreat you for her ; and not only that man, but it is the request of two Sachems, *Sam* Sachem of *Weshakim* and the *Pakashoag* Sachem.'

' And that further you will consider about the making peace. We have

---

[1] Hubbard Nar. 86.

[2] ' A true account of the most considerable occurrences that have happened in the warre between the English and Indians in New England,' reprinted in Drake's Indian Chronicle, 131.

[3] The letter is intended to be addressed to Gov. Leveret, Mr. Waban, and the christian Indians who prayed to God.

spoken to the people of Nashobah (viz. *Tom Dubler and Peter*) that we would agree with you and make a covenant of peace with you. We have been destroyed by your soldiers: but still we remember it now, to sit still; do you consider it again: we do earnestly entreat you that it may be so, by *Jesus Christ*. O! let it be so! *Amen. Amen.*'

> Mattamuck, his mark N.
> Sam. Sachem, his mark ⅄.
> Simon Pottoquam, Scribe ‡
> Uppanippaquem, his (mark) C.
> Pakaskoag, his mark ⌇.[1]

Soon after this letter was written, about July 13,[2] sagamore John ventured to visit Boston, to deliver himself to the Magistrates and make terms for his men. The Governor and Council, with policy equally wise and humane, had issued proclamations offering pardon to the Indians who voluntarily came in and surrendered. John expressed sincere sorrow for taking part against the English, engaged to be true to their interests in future, promised to give some testimonials of fidelity, received assurances of security and protection, and was permitted to depart. On the 27th of July, he returned, bringing with him an hundred and eighty of his followers. To propitiate favor, and purchase peace by an acceptable offering, he had treacherously seized that Matoonus, who had shed the first blood in Massachusetts on the beginning of the war at Mendon, with Nehemiah his son, both probably natives of Pakachoag, and brought them down bound with cords, to be given up to justice. Matoonus, having been examined, was condemned to immediate death. Sagamore John, with the new-born zeal of the traitor, to signalize his devotion to the cause he adopts by extraordinary rancor against that he deserts, entreated for himself and his men the office of executioners. Matoonus was led out, and being tied to a tree on Boston common, was shot by his own countrymen, his head cut off, and placed upon a pole opposite to that of his son, who formerly suffered on the same spot for a real or supposed murder committed in 1671.

The historians of the period heap upon Matoonus a load of abusive and uncharitable epithets. The great injury he received, the deepest the heart of savage or civilized man can suffer, affords, in their view, no apology for acts of violence, which although cruel, were according to the custom of war among his people. 'Sagamore John,' says Hubbard, 'that he might more ingratiate himself with the English, whose friendship he was now willing to seek after, did by a wile, get into his hands one Matoonus, *an old malicious villain*, who was the first that did any mischief within the Massachusetts Colony, July 14, 1675, bearing an old grudge against them as is thought, for justice

---

[1] The name of the residence of sagamore John was spelt by different early writers thus: Pakachoge: Packachooge: Pakchoog: Pakachage: Pakachauge: Poppachaug: Poquebaug: Pakachewog: Pakashooge: Packashoag: Pakaskoag: Pacachoog. The best authority is for *Pakachoag*.

[2] Drake's Indian Chronicle, 137. I. Mather's Hist. 43. Hub. Nar. 101.

that was done upon one of his sons, 1671, whose head since stands upon a pole near the gibbet where he was hanged up: the bringing in of this *malicious caitife* was a hopeful presage that it would not be long before Philip himself, the grand villain, would in like manner receive a just reward of his wickedness and murders.'

Increase Mather, another minister of that gospel which inculcates the forgiveness of injuries, adds his testimony with equal bitterness, in a sermon preached in 1677.[1]

'How often have we prayed that the Lord would remember the cruelty, treachery, and above all the blasphemy of these heathen! The prayer hath been heard in Heaven . . . . . . Matoonus, who was the first Indian that treacherously shed innocent English blood in Massachusetts colony, he some years before pretended something of religion, being a professor in general, (though never baptized, nor of the inchurched Indians,) that so he might the more covertly manage the *hellish design* of revenge, that was harbored in his *devilish heart:* but at last sagamore John, with some of his Indians, unexpectedly surprised him and delivered him to justice.'[2]

Sagamore John, with nineteen of those who surrendered with him, were placed under the charge of Capt. Thomas Prentice, in Cambridge. During the succeeding winter, they escaped to the woods, and although closely followed, eluded pursuit. Three of the company were executed, with some of their associates, for burning the house of Thomas Eames. Of their fate Sewall makes this brief record in his journal: 'Sept. 13, eight Indians shot to death on the (Boston) common.' Thirty were sold as slaves, under the milder name of putting out to service. The residue of the captives were confined to Deer Island, where many died by famine and exposure without suitable food or shelter from cold.

The assistant Wattasacompanum, better known in the annals of the time by the appellation of Capt. Tom,[3] was made prisoner, June 11, 1676, with his daughter and two young children. Henchman, announcing the capture, reports that this man was said to have left the enemy early in the spring, intending to give himself up to the English, but dared not come in for fear of their scouts. The minutes of his trial allege, that 'Capt. Tom was not only an instigator to others over whom he was made a captain, but also was actually present and an actor in the devastation of some of our plantations.' Although the company of friendly Indians, who had done good service to the colony, petitioned for his release, he was executed June 22. 'He was,' says Gookin,[4] 'a prudent, and, I believe, a pious man, and had given good demonstration of it many years. I had particular acquaintance with him, and cannot, in charity, think otherwise concerning him in his life, or at his death:

---

[1] Historical discourse on the prevalence of prayer, 6.

[2] Mather states that one of the sons of Matoonus was brought in with him, which is confirmed by the following entry in Sewall's MS. Journal, 'July 27, 1676. Sagamore John brings in Matoonus and his son: shot to death the same day.'

[3] Shattuck's Concord, 62.   [4] Hist. Christian Indians, in Am. Ant. Soc. Col.

though possibly he was tempted beyond his strength , for had he done as he
ought, he should have rather suffered death than have gone among the wicked
enemies of God's people '

During the summer, military executions were frequent in Boston   Thirty
Indians were shot in one day on the common   The return of troops from victorious expeditions into the interior, was often followed by judicial slaughter,
only to be defended on the ground of necessity   The captives were sometimes
treated as traitors, and blood profusely shed   The heads of the sufferers,
exposed near the spot where they fell, were ghastly memorials of the stern
character of vindictive justice

An order of Council, August 30, 1675, directed that all Indians desirous of
proving their fidelity should repair to Natick, Punkapaug,[1] Wamesit,[2] Nashobah,[3] and Hassanamisset, to be confined within a circle drawn at the distance
of a mile from the centre of the dwellings   The christians of Quinsigamond
about this period went to Grafton, where they were afterwards surprised by a
large force and compelled to join the enemy, as is stated, although it is not
probable strong compulsion was needed to induce them to take part with their
countrymen   Some were at a fort occupied by the converts of Marlborough.
Measures of severity were adopted, involving innocent and guilty in common
suffering, scarcely admitting defence   The friendly Indians were principally
transported to Deer Island   Taken away from their cornfields without being
permitted to gather the harvest, without the resources of hunting, with slender
provision for their support, many died for want of food and shelter from the
inclemency of winter   The change of residence was sometimes effected without regard to the feelings or convenience of the victims   Those of Marlborough, surrounded by a company under Capt Mosely, who had been
commander of a privateer by sea before he became captain of soldiers, were
taken into custody, their hands tied behind them, and fastened to a cart rope,
they were driven away.[4]   The act was disclaimed as unauthorised, but the officer
was not punished nor the captives released

With the death of Philip, the animating spirit of the hostile confederacy,
Aug 12, 1676, the war ended   Its progress arrested the earliest efforts for
settlement, and destroyed the little village beginning to rise in Quinsigamond
its termination left the soil almost without a relic of the aboriginal population
When the white settlers commenced building here, there were between two
and three hundred of the natives   They possessed extensive planting fields,
and had set appletrees obtained from the English. The light of christianity
had dawned upon them, and some advance had been made in civilization. By
the sword, by famine, by violent removal, and by flight, they were nearly
exterminated   When the second plantation was attempted, only superannu-
ated old men, women and children, remained of the red people   those able to
bear arms had been slain, or dispersed, seeking refuge in Canada among the
French, or migrating far westward beyond the reach of the power they had too

[1] Stoughton.   [2] Lowell.   [3] Easterly part of Littleton
     [4] Allen's Northborough, in Wor Mag. ii. 147. Biglow's Natick, 36

much provoked for their own safety. The whole nation perished, leaving no monuments of their existence on our lands, and no remains except little articles of ornament, rude utensils of culinary art, and rough weapons of stone, discovered in their former dominion.

CHAPTER III.

1677 to 1713. Second settlement. Indian deed, 1677. Meeting of planters, 1678. Henchman's agreement, 1684. Citadel. Survey. Mills built. Name of Worcester. Lots laid out. New Committees. Capt. Fitch's letter. Queen Anne's war. Town abandoned. Digory Serjent killed. Elisha Ward. Indian hostilities. Petition for resettlement refused, 1709.

Peace having been reestablished, the Committee earnestly endeavored to procure the settlement of the town. The little remnant of the Indians, who survived the perils and sufferings of war, had returned to their homes. On the 6th of Dec. 1677,[1] the right of Pannosunet, a sagamore who had not subscribed the former instrument of conveyance, was purchased of his heirs and relatives. The deed[2] was executed by Anthony, or Wannashawakum, otherwise, Wannoshanohannawit, and Abagail, his wife, ' daughter and only heir of Pannasunet :' Nannaswane, the widow ; Sasomet, and his wife Quassawake, sister of the deceased proprietor ; who are described as ' all natives and inhabitants, they and their ancestors, of Quinsigamound,' and who covenanted that they had good and just title, and natural right and interest in the territory, and that they would warrant its enjoyment. The same good faith and equity governed in this as in the former contract. The receipt of full satisfaction for this release of dower and inheritance, in trucking cloth and corn, is acknowledged.

Although the storm of war had passed over, the recollection of its destructive visitation was still fresh. No serious fears could be entertained of immediate disturbance of the repose of the Colony, by the dispersed and defeated enemy. In the interval of peace, the Committee, in 1678, directed the Planters to return before the year 1680, and build together so as to defend themselves : but, in their own words, ' there was no going by any of them, or

---

[1] Middlesex Registry of Deeds. Lib. 8, Page 318.

[2] The subscribing witnesses to this deed were the apostolic John Eliot, Nathaniel Gookin of Cambridge, son of Daniel Gookin, James Speen, Waban and Simon Betoghan.

James Speen was of Natick, and distinguished for fidelity to the English.

Thomas Waban was of Natick, the son of the earliest convert to Christianity, for a long time Clerk, Justice of the Peace, and constable of the Indian town.

Simon Betoghan was probably the scribe by whom the letter of the sagamores was written.

The grantors probably lived on Wigwam Hill.

hope that they would so do : for divers of them being importuned to go, would not.' The exposed and remote situation of the place, affords sufficient explanation of the refusal.

A meeting of those interested in the plantation was held in Cambridge, March 3, 1678.[1] Gookin, Henchman, and Prentice of the Committee were present, with Joel Jenkins, Richard Dana, Philip Atwood, Thomas Brown, John Paul, Thomas Groves, John Fay, Thomas Hall, Thomas Skinner, John Bemis, Richard Tree, Miscal Flagg, John Upham, William Taylor, Benjamin Webb, and Simon Meyling, whose names are entered on the margin of the original record. The following paper expresses the result of their deliberations.

1. 'It is agreed by all the persons named in the margent, that, God willing, they intend and purpose, if God spare life, and peace continue, to endeavor, either in their persons, or by their relations, or by their purses, to settle the said plantation sometime the next summer, come twelve month, which shall be in the year of our Lord 1680.

2. 'They do engage to build in a way of a town, according to a model proposed by Major Gookin and Major Henchman, or some model equivalent thereunto, for the attaining these six ends ; 1st, security from the enemies in case (of alarm) : 2d, for the better *convenity* of attending God's worship : 3d, for the better education of their children in society : 4th, for the better accommodation of trades people : 5th, for better helps to civility : 6th, for more convenient help in case of sickness, fire or other casualty.

3. 'That the most convenient place is to be chosen and pitched upon to build the town, sometime this next summer, by the committee, or the major part of such of the people as go up to view the place, which is intended this next May, if God please.

4. 'That after the place is chosen and pitched upon, others that are not present, do engage to submit and settle there.'

The resolutions of settlement unanimously adopted, like other good intentions, seem to have ended with the formation, as no evidence remains of any practical attempt to carry them into execution.

The General Court, at their October session, 1682, gave notice to the Committee, that the grant would be considered forfeit and be lost, unless measures were taken to form a plantation.

The necessity of immediate exertion to preserve the rights of those who had procured the title of the soil, incurred much expense, and performed no inconsiderable labor, in efforts for settlement, having been thus officially presented to the Committee, after long negociation, they accepted proposals offered by Capt. Henchman and his associates for accomplishing their purpose. An agreement was entered into, April 24, 1684,[2] evidenced by a formal instrument of that date. The inducements to this arrangement are stated to be : ' that the plantations might be secured : the first planters prevailed with to

---

[1] March 14, 1679, N. S. [2] Proprietors' Records, 13.

resettle; others encouraged to plant; public occasions provided for; recompense made to those who have labored therein; those rewarded that shall forward the place; manufactures promoted; the country advantaged; travellers accommodated; and not any damnified that are concerned.' The quantity of meadow being estimated at 180 acres, it was proposed to divide the whole township into that number of lots: 200 for the planters: 80 for public uses or specific appropriations; and the remaining 200 to be laid out on the northern extremity, forming a division, afterwards known as North Worcester, and subsequently rendered permanent by the incorporation of Holden.

Among other arrangements for mutual safety and provisions for social happiness, it was stipulated, that 'land for a citadel should be laid out, on the Fort River, about half a mile square, for house lots, for those who should, at their first settling, build and dwell thereon, and make it their certain place of abode for their families: to the end the inhabitants may settle in a way of defence, as enjoined by law,[1] and formerly ordered by the committee for divers reasons, and each one so doing, to have a house lot there, at least six rods square.'

This citadel, or central station, was on the stream flowing by the present town, then called Fort River, from the ancient fortress which had been thrown up on its bank: soon after named Mill Brook, from the works moved by its waters; and sometimes denominated Bimeleck. From references at a subsequent period, it may be inferred, its northern line was parallel with the town way north of the Court House, and that it included the greater part of the village of Worcester.

The contractors were required 'to build two fire rooms in the citadel, to shelter such as shall come to settle, and travellers, until there be an ordinary: for accommodation of whom,' it is said, 'was one reason of granting the plantation.'

There is traditional evidence that a fortified house was erected a little east from Main street;[2] it was surrounded with a palisade. The inhabitants resorted to its defence by night, and maintained a guard to secure their slumbers.

It was enjoined, 'that care be taken to provide a minister with all convenient speed; and a schoolmaster in due season; and, in the interim, that the Lord's day be sanctified by the inhabitants meeting together thereon, to worship God as they shall be' (able).

The territory without the citadel was divided into lots of ten and twenty five acres: ample reservations were made for public uses and common benefit; for the support of teachers of religion, and the instruction of youth, as well as for the encouragement of useful arts and trades. Lands were appropriated for building saw, corn and fulling mills. Four lots were assigned to the Commonwealth, as our ancestors loved to style the colony, in lieu of those

---

[1] In 1635, the General Court ordered, that 'no new building shall be built more than half a mile from the meeting house, in any new plantation.'

[2] This garrison was a few rods east of the head of the street now (1836) called Columbian avenue, on land over which the street passes.

reserved for the country by the original grant. The zealous exertions of
Gookin to promote the prosperity of the infant town were acknowledged by a
donation of eight lots. Each of the Committee were to be entitled, in their
official capacity, to four lots, ' for their care and pains.'

The principles for conducting settlement being fixed, the work of improvement was soon commenced. A general survey was made by Samuel Andrews
of Watertown, May 16, 1683 ; the plan, on which the boundaries were deli-
eated, was presented, on the 7th of May, 1684, and allowed and confirmed.
The township was estimated to contain 43,020 acres, an allowance of two in
the hundred being made for the inaccuracy of measuring the wilderness.[1]

A vacancy in the committee, occasioned by the death of Lt. Richard Beers
of Watertown, killed in the defeat of the English near Northfield, in Sept.
1675, was supplied, on the application of the survivors, by the appointment
of Capt. John Wing of Boston.

Many persons made contracts with Capt. Henchman, and some became
residents. Corn and saw mills were erected by Capt. Wing, a short distance
above the bridge at the north end of Main street, where the remains of the
dam are still visible in the little island that divides the stream. His house
and barn were placed in their vicinity.[2]

Upon the motion and desire of Gookin, Prentice and Henchman, on the
10th of Sept. 1684, the Great and General Court granted their request, ' that
their plantation at Quansigamond be called Worcester.'[3]

Partial surveys were made in May, 1685. A lot was laid out for Gookin,
of 100 acres, on the east side of Pakachoag Hill, and another lot of 80 acres
on Raccoon Plain. There were present at this time Gookin himself, Capt.
Henchman, Nathaniel Henchman his son, David Fiske, the surveyor, Digory
Serjent, Will, a mulatto, Christopher Reed, and Benjamin Eaton.

[1] Prop. Records, 2.

[2] On land now [1836] of Stephen Salisbury, Esq., north of Lincoln square.

[3] The reasons for the selection of the name of Worcester cannot now be ascertained. It
was probably adopted from the place of residence of some of the committee or planters in
England.

The word *Worcester* is said, Henry's England, ii. 558, to have been derived from the Saxon
Wegera-ceaster, meaning *war castle*, and descriptive of the military character of the place
to which it was originally applied by the martial clans of remote antiquity.

In England, one place only bears this name. The city of Worcester, the capital of a
shire, situated on the banks of the Severn, contained in 1824 a population of about 20,000,
supported a flourishing trade in gloves and the manufacture of fine china ware, held
three market days the week, and returned two members to Parliament. It is noted in
history as the scene of a sanguinary battle in 1651, between Cromwell and the Pretender,
afterwards Charles II., which crushed for a time the hopes of the Stuart.

In the United States, the rapid birth of new towns has multiplied the name. It had
been given to the following places, in 1832 :

1. Worcester, post town, Otsego county,	New York,	pop. in 1830,	2093.
2. ————, post town, Montgomery co.	Pennsylvania,	"	"	1155.
3. ————, town, Washington co.	Vermont,	"	"	432.
4. ————, township, Wayne county,	Ohio,	"	"	1953.
5. ————, town, Wayne county,	Ohio,	"	"	977.
6. ———— county, chief town, Snow Hill,	Maryland,	"	"	18271.

A tract of 80 acres was assigned to Capt. John Wing, around his mills, and on the west side of the brook, with the exclusive privilege of its waters.

George Danson, who was a baker, of Boston, obtained a grant of 200 acres on the same side of the stream, north of the citadel, and extending to North Pond.

Thomas Hall occupied the meadow below the mills.

At this distance of time, without the aid of full records, ill supplied by the scattered fragments of history and tradition which have descended, it is not possible to ascertain the names or number of the actual settlers of the new town which rose from the ashes of the former plantation.

In addition to those already mentioned, the following were probably among the inhabitants :

Thomas Atherton,	George Rosbury,	James Daniel,
Peter Goulding,	Isaac George,	Matthew Tomlin,
Isaac Bull,	Thomas Brown,	Daniel Turell,
William Weeks,	Jacob Leonard,	Isaac Tomlin,
Enos Salter,	John Cowell,	James Dutton.

The Committee suffered the loss of one of its most energetic members by the death of Capt. Henchman, 1686, who had personally aided and superintended the allotment of lands.

The President and Council, administering the affairs of the Province in the stormy period of the Revolution following the abrogation of the charter, on the 10th of June, 1686, upon the application of the proprietors of Worcester, reappointed Gen. Gookin and Capt. Prentice of the old Committee, and added Mr. William Bond of Watertown, Capt. Joseph Lynde and Deacon John Haynes of Sudbury, as new members, with general powers to order and regulate all matters concerning the settlement.[1]

For a time we lose sight of the town and its inhabitants. From 1686 to 1713, no record is preserved on the proprietary book of any transactions. Neither history nor tradition informs us of the labors, dangers and sufferings of the earlier planters, or discloses particulars to measure the advance of population under the salutary regulation and prudential guardianship of able and discreet committees, or the difficulties interposed by public embarrassments. Gen. Gookin, the early and faithful friend of the plantation, was called to the rewards of a long life, characterized by fervent piety, enlightened benevolence, incorruptible integrity, and the practice of every manly virtue, in March, 1687. The office he held in relation to the town was filled by the appointment of Capt. Adam Winthrop, who had become proprietor of extensive tracts.

Other vacancies having occurred, Dec. 23, 1691, Capt. Penn Townsend, Capt. Ephraim Hunt, and Mr. John Haynes, were added to Capt. Prentice, Capt. Winthrop and Capt. Wing, for the ordering of affairs :[2] a circumstance rendering it certain that the number of settlers had not so increased as to prevent the necessity of relying on others for the direction of their municipal concerns.

[1] Proprietors' Records, 23.   [2] Province Records, vi. 210.

On the 23d of August, 1696, a house in Oxford was assaulted by the Albany or Western Indians, and Goodman Levenz and three children of its inmates killed. Mr Johnson, who was returning to the place, was shot in the road. On the intelligence of these outrages and of the appearance of hostile parties near Woodstock, Major James Fitch marched to that town. On the 27th, a party was sent out of thirty eight Norwich, Mohegan and Nipmuck Indians, and twelve soldiers. to range the woods towards Lancaster, under Capt Daniel Fitch. On their march they passed through Worcester, and discovered traces of the enemy in its vicinity. The following letter of their commander gives an account of their expedition.

'To the Rt Honorable William Stoughton, Esq., Lieut. Governor and Commander in chief, &c.

'Whereas we were informed of several persons killed at Oxford on Tuesday night last past, (23d) and not knowing what danger might be near to Woodstock and several other frontiers towards the western parts of the Massachusetts Province several persons appearing volunteers, both English and Indians, to the number of about 50, (concerning which this bearer, Mr James Corbin, may more fully inform your Honor,) all which were willing to follow the Indian enemy, hoping to find those that had done the late mischief, in prosecution whereof we have ranged the woods to the westward of Oxford, and so to Worcester, and then to Lancaster, and are freely willing to spend some considerable time in endeavoring to find any of the enemy that may be upon Merrimack or Penicook Rivers, or any where in the western woods. to which end we humbly request your Honor would be pleased to encourage said design, by granting us some supply of provisions and ammunition, and also by strengthening us as to anything wherein we may be short in any respect, that so we may be under no disadvantage nor discouragement

'They may further inform your Honor, that on the sabbath day (28), coming at a place called Half Way River, betwixt Oxford and Worcester, we came upon the fresh tracks of several Indians which were gone towards Worcester, which we apprehend were the Indians that did the late damage at Oxford ; and being very desirous to do some service that may be to the benefit of his majesty's subjects, we humbly crave your Honor's favorable assistance Herein I remain your Honor's most humble servant, according to my ability.

Lancaster, 31 August, 1696.　　　　　　　　　　Daniel Fitch '

On the commencement of the eighteenth century, the peace of the country was again disturbed by renewed outrages of the savages, always capricious in friendship, treacherous in alliance, and unrelenting in enmity. Although Worcester suffered less in Queen Anne's war, which began in 1702, by loss of life, than many towns, it shared in the alarm and participated in the miseries of the final struggles of the red men to reclaim their possessions and avenge the wrongs inflicted by our ancestors

When the same danger which had once before pressed on the planters, became extreme, and the Indians again kindled the slumbering flame of mur-

4*

derous hostility, the second attempt to build a town here was abandoned. The inhabitants fled; the place of their residence was delivered up to decay; the traces of cultivation were effaced; and the silence of ruin was again over the forsaken farms and deserted homes

Among those who attempted the settlement of Worcester after the first unsuccessful enterprise, was Digory Serjent, who had built his house on Sagatabscot Hill, south-eastward of the present town. He was a native of Sudbury, and had been a carpenter by occupation before his removal. A will made by him in 1679 is preserved on the Middlesex Records. As the list of goods and effects, strangely mingled together, presents example of the humble personal possessions of former times, and the style affords specimen of quaint peculiarity, it will not be uninteresting.

'March, the 17th day, 1696. The last Will and Testament of Digory Serjent.

'I Digory Serjent, being in my health and strength, and in my perfect memory, blessed be the Lord for it; these few lines may satisfy whom it may concern, that I, Digory Serjent, do freely give unto my Daughter Martha Serjent, my house and land with all its rights and privileges thereunto belonging: this house and four score acre lot of land lieth within the township of Worcester: I likewise do give unto her all my goods; one flock bed and boulster, with one rugg, and two blankets and two coverlets; six froes; one broad ax and one falling ax and one handsaw; one frying pan; one shave; one drawing knife; one trunk and a sermon book that is at Mrs. Mary Mason's, widow, at Boston; with one pewter pint pot; one washing tub; one cow and calf; one mare; three iron wedges; two beetle rings: And if in case the Lord should see good to take away the said Digory Serjent by death, then I, the said Digory Serjent, do leave these things above written unto George Parmeter of Sudbury, to be disposed of as he shall see good, to bring up the said Digory Serjent's child; and if in case that this child should die likewise, then I do freely give my house and land with all the goods above mentioned unto George Parmeter forever, and to his heirs, to look after these things and to dispose of them as he shall see cause. In witness whereof I have hereunto set my hand and seal, the day and year above named. There is one gun too.

Digory Serjent.

Witnessed by John Keyes, John Wetherby.'

Having afterwards been married to the sister of Parmeter, (as I think,) his family became more numerous, and afforded more victims to be involved in the miseries of death and captivity.

Long after the other planters had fled from the perils of the conflict that raged around them, Serjent remained with his children, the solitary occupants of the town, resisting all importunity to seek safety by desertion, and resolving with fearless intrepidity to defend from the savage the fields his industry had redeemed from the waste.

During the summer of 1702,[1] his residence was unmolested. As winter approached, the committee, alarmed by his situation on the frontier of danger, sent messengers to advise his removal to a place of security. As their admonitions were disregarded, they at length dispatched an armed force of twelve men under Capt. Howe, to compel compliance with the order. At the close of day the party arrived at a garrison near the mills. Here they halted for the night, which grew dark with storm and snow, and kindling their fires, laid down to rest, while one of the band watched the slumbers of his comrades. In the morning they went onward, and reached the house of Serjent on Sagatabscot, at the distance of nearly two miles from the post where they had halted. They found the door broken down, the owner stretched in blood on the floor, and the dwelling desolate. The prints of many mockasins leading westward, still visible through the snow, indicated that they had been anticipated by a short time only in the object of their mission. Having pursued the trail of the murderers a little way, they returned and buried Serjent at the foot of an oak, long since decayed. On retracing their course to the spot of their repose, they found the prints of feet going from the fort towards Wachuset. After the war was ended, the Indians, when they revisited the settlers, declared that six of them had entered the building for shelter from the tempest, when the near advance of the English was discovered, too late to permit escape from a force so considerable, and they secreted themselves in the cellar. The soldiers had spread their blankets and laid down over the trap door, thus securing their foes, until the morning march gave opportunity for flight.

It was soon found that the children of Serjent were living in Canada. On the release of the eldest, she related the particulars of the fearful catastrophe they had witnessed. When the Indians, headed by sagamore John, as is said, surrounded the house, Serjent seized his gun to defend his life, and was fired on. As he retreated to the stair way, a ball took effect and he fell. The savages rushed in, with their tomahawks completed the work of death, and tore off the scalp from his head, as the trophy of victory. They seized the mother and her children, John, Daniel, Thomas, Martha and Mary, and having discovered the neighborhood of the white men, commenced a rapid retreat westward. The wife of Serjent, fainting with grief and fear, and in feeble circumstances, faltered and impeded their progress. The apprehension of pursuit induced the Indian to forego the terrible pleasure of torturing his victim. As they ascended the hills of Tataesset, a chief stept out from the file, and looking around among the leafless forests as if for game, excited no alarm in the exhausted and sinking captive, and awoke no cry of horror to betray their course. When she had passed by, one merciful blow from the strong arm of the sachem removed the obstruction of their flight. The children, they carried away, reached the northern frontier in safety, and were a long

_____
[1] This is the date given in the brief account in 1 Mass. Hist. Col. i. 112, copied by Whitney and subsequent writers. It is probable the death of Serjent was in 1703 or 1704, at the period when Northampton, Lancaster and other towns were attacked by the French and Indians.

time in Canada. Daniel and Mary, preferring the wild freedom of their captors to the restraints of civilized life, adopted the habits and manners of the Indians. They never again resided with their relatives, although they once made them a visit, when Miss Williams, taken at Deerfield, was restored.

In 1715, Thomas was at Boston. John had been liberated in 1721. Martha was probably redeemed earlier than her brothers. She married Daniel Shattuck, and returned to dwell on the spot so fatal to her family, as may be inferred from the following order, to the commissioners appointed in 1721, to make partition of the inherited lands in Worcester.

'If D. Shattuck's hovel, made of the stuff of the said deceased's old house, needs consideration, his brother John must allow for it, if you in your good discretion think good: and also for any labor which the said Daniel has done on the mother lot: it proves equal that he should have for this year liberty to enjoy the fruits of his own labor: so do what is right and equal, as you must be sworn.'   'Francis Foxcraft, J. Pro. for Middlesex.'

The approach of Capt. Howe's party, whose night's rest was at the expense of lives and suffering, probably prevented the conflagration of the house and the destruction of property. A full inventory of the goods and effects collected, was returned into the Probate Office by George Parmeter, who seems to have taken administration by virtue of the will, although its provisions were inoperative.[1]

Although the power of the savage was crushed, predatory bands visited the town. In August, 1709, Elisha Ward, sent on an express from Marlborough to Hadley, having stopped to examine his deserted farm, was killed. After the permanent settlement in 1713, no lives were lost, but the quiet of the inhabitants was frequently disturbed. On one occasion, three Indians were discovered lurking near the stream below the upper canal lock. The alarm was given and the townsmen extended themselves along the meadow, then a dark and tangled swamp, and explored its thickets. One of them discharged his musket at an object he supposed to be an Indian, but as the company who gathered to the spot discerned no trace of a foe, it was concluded that he had been deceived. It was afterwards ascertained that the shot took effect, and that the knee of one of the warriors was broken by the ball. Being on the margin of the brook, he dropped down the bank, and crawled into an opening fortunately large enough to conceal his person. When the pursuit was over, his companions returned and carried him into the heart of a deep morass west of Pakachoag Hill, where they built a wigwam to shelter him until his wound healed, and renovated strength enabled them to depart forever from the land of their ancestral heritage.

Tradition tells that William Taylor, a bold and fearless man, discovering

[1] Relation of Thomas Rice. Rev. Dr. Bancroft's Sermon, 11. Davis's Address, 15. Whitney Hist. 26. 1 Mass. Hist. Col. i. 115. Middlesex Probate Records. Proprietors' Records.

an Indian approaching his house, shot him to death. The son watched an opportunity of revenge. He was observed by Taylor, stretched behind a log on the margin of the field he cultivated, and the same gun which had been fatal to the father sent a bullet to the heart of the descendant.

The last of the race who here died by the hand of the white man, is said to have fallen on the plain, north of the first mill place.

Fortunately, none of the posterity of the Indian *here* remain, to contrast their degradation with the lofty and in some points noble character of the ancient tribes.

The following Petition was presented to the Legislature in 1709, by those interested in the township, for aid in the resettlement.

' To his Excellency Joseph Dudley, Esq., Capt. General and Governor in chief in and over her Majesty's province of the Massachusetts Bay in New England, and to the Honorable the Council and Representatives in General Court assembled :

' May it please your Excellency and Honors. We, the subscribers, presuming that the resettlement of Worcester would be beneficial to the Province, have taken the boldness to trouble your Excellency and Honors with a few lines, humbly informing that if we may have a firm foundation of a settlement laid and a fort built, and needful protection, we are willing to inhabit and settle the place. We humbly intreat your Excellency and Honors' approbation and direction in the matter ; that so we may take such proper methods as are needful, and as you shall direct us unto : And that your Excellency and Honors would promote this business speedily, before the season be past, and so the settlement be deferred till another year. Thus, in short, we take the boldness to subscribe, your Excellency's and Honors' most humble servants,

Joseph Sawyer,	Thomas Barrett,	Richard Wiles,
William Ward,	James Caly,	Benjamin Headley,
John Perry,	John Wheeler,	James Atherton,
Benjamin Bellows,	Thomas Smith,	John Sawyer,
Jonathan Whitcomb,	Ebenezer Perry,	Abiel Bush.'
Elias Sawyer,		

The Council ordered, that Elisha Hutchinson, Samuel Sewall, and Nathaniel Paine, Esquires, should be a Committee to consider the expediency of granting the request, and the course to be adopted. The House refused to concur, as the disturbed condition of the times rendered the enterprise too dangerous to be sanctioned by legislative approbation.[1]

[1] Province Files, 1709. Province Records, ix. 5.

CHAPTER IV.

1713 to 1722. Third settlement to incorporation. Petition, 1713. New Committee. Report, 1714. First Settlers. James Rice. Gershom Rice. Nathaniel Moore. Garrisons. Mills. Roads. View of the town, 1718. Grants to proprietors. Scotch and Irish emigrants. Town incorporated, 1722.

More favorable prospects having opened in 1713, the proprietors, undiscouraged by former failure, attempted to rebuild the town. On the 13th of Oct. Col. Adam Winthrop, Gershom Rice and Jonas Rice of Marlborough, addressed the General Court in behalf of themselves and others interested; [1] They represented their desire ' to endeavor and enter upon a new settlement of the place from which they had been driven by the war,' and prayed ' for the countenance and encouragement of the Court in their undertaking : for such directions and regulations as should be thought fit to make them defensible in case of a new rupture with the Indians : and for a proper Committee to direct in ordering the prudentials of the plantation till they come to a full settlement.'

The prayer of this petition was granted, and Hon. William Taylor, Col. Adam Winthrop, Hon. William Dudley, Lt. Col. John Ballantine and Capt. Thomas Howe were appointed a Committee.

On the 14th of June, 1714, a detailed report was presented by this Committee of their proceedings in adjusting the claims of the former settlers and promoting the prosperity of the future plantation. After giving notice to all interested, and making a journey to Worcester, they had allowed thirty one rights of ancient inhabitants, and admitted twenty eight persons more to take lands on condition of paying twelve pence per acre for their planting or house lots only, being the amount collected of the original planters, and of building and dwelling on each right, whether acquired by purchase, grant or representation. It was recommended that the provision made for support of the ministry and schools be accepted instead of the reservation to the Commonwealth in 1668.

The Committee asked, as they had spent much time in receiving claims for grants of lands, made journeys to effect adjustment of controversies, advanced sums of money, and expected to have the care and trouble of the affairs of the town for many years, that a lot of forty acres should be assigned to each, with just proportions in future divisions, as compensation for services.

This report was accepted, and received the approval of Gov. Dudley, June 14, 1714.

Jonas Rice, who had been a planter during the second settlement, returned Oct. 21, 1713. From this day is dated the permanent settlement of the town. He built on Sagatabscot hill, and his farm included some of the lands once cultivated by Serjent. The selection of residence was probably made with

[1] Prop. Records.

reference to fertility of soil, proximity to extensive meadows, and it may be, from prior occupation by himself[1] He remained with his family alone in the forest, the solitary inhabitant of Worcester, until the spring of 1715

The union of cool intrepidity and resolute firmness with good sense and integrity in the character of Mr Rice, commanded the respect and secured the confidence of his fellow citizens when the town he had founded rose from its ashes in renovated beauty to commence that steady progress of prosperity which has brightened its advance   He was often elected to municipal offices, was frequently representative to the General Court, and was one of the Justices of the Court of Common Pleas at the time of his decease, Sept 22, 1753, at the age of 84 years

The first male child born in Worcester, Nov 7, 1711, was Adonijah, son of Jonas Rice On arriving to manhood, year after year, his name is entered on the rolls of the provincial troops during the French wars. after each summer campaign was finished, he returned to his home, and the quiet of domestic and agricultural life He removed to Shoreham, Vt , where he died, Feb 1802, aged 88.

The second settler appears from the records to have been Gershom Rice, who came in 1715, to join his brother Jonas, the hardy pioneer of population, maintaining his post for nearly two years unsupported by assistance and uncheered by associates.[2]

The third settler was Nathaniel Moore, of Sudbury, a man of exemplary character, who was deacon of the first church from its foundation   He died Nov 25, 1761, aged 84 years [3]

[1] Jonas Rice's house stood near that of his descendant, Mr Sewall Rice, on the town way between the Sutton and Grafton roads

[2] These families of the Rices removed from Marlborough Their distant ancestor, Richard, was one of the early proprietors of Concord in 1635 Edmund, admitted to the freeman's oath in 1640, was, in that year, representative from Sudbury and one of the petitioners for the grant of Marlborough

These families were remarkable for longevity The father of Gershom died at the age of 70 his mother 84 They had 14 children three died in infancy: the others lived to advanced age 1, Peter 97 2, Thomas 94· 3, Mary 80 4, Nathaniel 70· 5, Ephraim 71 6, James 72 7, Sarah 80 8 Francis 96 9, Jonas 84 10, Grace 94 11, Gershom died Dec 29, 1769, aged 101 his wife died at the age of 80 they lived together in marriage nearly 65 years and left seven children, some of whom, on the decease of their father, were upwards of 70 Boston Gazette, 1769

[3] His son, Nathaniel Moore, came into the town at the age of three months He lived respected, and died July 24, 1811, aged 96 The following notice of his character is from the Massachusetts Spy

'He was a man of exemplary piety and benevolence He resided in Worcester more than 95 years, being a member of the third family that began the settlement of the town He lived in the marriage state with the same wife nearly 69 years, but left no descendants

'He saw this town rise from a state of uncultivated nature to its opulent improvement, witnessed the ordination of five ministers of the Gospel within the town, four of them over the same society in succession saw three houses erected for public worship, three court houses rising on the same spot, one after another, for the administration of justice, and three gaols as a terror to evil doers Thus has ended the life of an honest man, the noblest work of God'

Capt. Thomas Howe and Lt. David Haynes were appointed by the Committee to give certificates for such of the inhabitants as had built upon their lots and performed. the conditions of their grants. On the 23d of April, 1718, they returned a list, which has unfortunately perished in the lapse of time. The record of surveys, made in the same year, partially supplies the deficiency, and enables us to determine the progress of settlement. Well authenticated traditions, preserved in the memory of descendants of early planters, connected with, and confirmed by this source of information, afford materials for delineating a picture of the condition of Worcester, which though imperfect, may be considered as presenting a faithful outline of the prominent objects.

The first labor of the inhabitants had been to erect a garrison house, on the west side of the Leicester road, not far distant from the old south church. It was reared by the united labors of all, and those residing near, gathered by night to its walls, during the first year.

Another of these fortresses of logs was near the head of the street called Columbian avenue, [1836] constructed by Dea. Daniel Heywood. A patriarchal pear tree, planted by him, still stands, at the end of a century, on ground he once owned, a venerable example of vegetable longevity.

The third of the wooden castles, was a large building on the Connecticut road, north of Lincoln square, affording shelter to the traveller and defending the mills erected on the stream.

Eastward from the intersection of the Lancaster and Boston roads, near the modern Adams square, in the north part of the town, was a structure which exhibited marks of fortification until an advanced old age.

A regular block house was placed north of Adams square, where a long iron cannon was subsequently mounted to give the alarm of coming danger. During the French war, this gun was removed to the green near the meeting house. On the commencement of the revolution, it was posted west of the Court House, and its voice called our citizens to arms when the tidings of the march to Lexington roused the land. Since, it has rested with the other artillery of the town.

Many of the scattered houses were protected by outworks, as well as guarded by the bold spirit of the inmates. Joshua Rice held his garrison a mile westward of the old mill place, where a cellar still remains to carry back the memory to days when a man's house was literally his castle, when the musket was laid on the plough beam, and the sword was by the side while the hand was on the sickle. From the remote position of Jonas Rice and his brother planters of Sagatabscot hill, it is probable some fortified structure there afforded them security.

On Mill brook, over the western sluice, where the stream is parted by the little island above the bridge, was a saw mill erected by Capt. John Wing, then owned by Thomas Palmer and Cornelius Waldo of Boston, and John Oulton of Marblehead, copartners of extensive commercial business, and proprietors of wide tracts of land. The pond, overflowing the valley above, extended its eastern margin to the present Boston road.

Obediah Ward had built a saw mill above the works long known as the Red Mills, near the upper canal lock, which he devised by his will, dated Dec 16, 1717, to his son Richard.

The first corn mill was erected by Elijah Chase, near the Quinsigamond Paper Mills, on the Blackstone river. For many years it was the only accommodation of the kind.

The traveller of 1718, on entering the town from the head of Quinsigamond, following the Connecticut road, first passed the houses of Benjamin Crosbee and Isaac Miller, on opposite sides of the way, where the buildings of the town farm now stand

Westward, about half a mile, was the land granted to Ephraim Curtis, where his son then lived, still owned by his descendants.

Next, was the house of Thomas Haggat, whose daughter was the first female born in Worcester [1]

Passing his residence, the Connecticut road followed the little way leading to the Lancaster road, by the dwelling of Ichabod and Thomas Brown, to the corner north of Adams square, where Henry Lee, Esq , then resided

Turning south, the path went through the valley a few rods westward of the highway now used, to the house of Nathaniel Henchman, a son of that distinguished officer who was one of the founders of the town.[2]

The Country road crossed Mill brook, by a fording place about a fourth of a mile north of the present bridge After passing the fort and mill, it turned west and ascended the hill, to the settlement of Joshua Rice. It was continued by a circuitous route to New Worcester.

The Lancaster way, coming from the north, along the present Boston road, went through Main street, then shaded by primeval forests, to the garrison house of Deacon Daniel Heywood [3] Moses Rice had thus early opened an ordinary or tavern,[4] a few rods north of the Town Hall Daniel Ward had

[1] Haggat, among other occupations, manufactured wooden shovels With the mechanical ingenuity, he possessed the trading propensity of a Yankee Having set off on an excursion, to dispose of a stock of wooden wares, he was induced to exchange horses frequently, always giving some part of his own merchandize to equalize the pretended difference of value. This trade was conducted with so little profit, that the shovel merchant, at the conclusion, was glad to regain his original steed by parting with all his remaining property is wood work. On returning with the same animal with which he had commenced his journey, without any of his stock in trade, he gravely remarked that ' he had saved his horse though he had lost his shovels '

[2] Henchman was an eccentric man, having even stronger peculiarities of manner than are usual attributes of celibacy. He constructed his coffin and hollowed his grave with his own hands many years before his decease. Willing to derive benefit while living from the first of these tenements of mortality, the box was deposited in the garret, and annually filled with the productions of his garden, until he took personal possession. A stone long marked the spot where his remains reposed amid the fields he cultivated , but no memorial now indicates the place of his rest Several aged apple trees, planted by him near his dwelling, on the farm of the late Levi Lincoln, still survive. On his decease, the land descended to the family of the late Gov John Hancock.

[3] On the site of the Central Exchange　　　　　　[4] Now United States Hotel.

built nearly opposite the old south meeting house. The house of Jonathan Hubbard, the first man who died after the resettlement, and that of James Rice, more south, completes the enumeration of edifices where population has become most crowded.

After Jonas Rice became a resident of the town, a road was made from the head of the pond, passing by the houses of James Taylor, Moses Leonard, Palmer Goulding, Richard Flagg, running along the grass-grown path east of the Grafton road, and through the fields, by Deacon Nathaniel Moore's to Jonas Rice's ;[1] thence it was carried westward, in a direct course, across Raccoon Plain to Halfway river, where it joined the Connecticut path.

These were the two great highways of the town. A log placed over the stream where the canal bridge now stands on Front street, accommodated those who passed by the house of James Holmes, to that of Gershom Rice, on the south side of the Grafton road, where the first orchard was planted. This way led into the old Connecticut road through Hassanamisset to Springfield.

A path along Summer street went to the first burial place, situated north of the junction of Thomas street. A beautiful grove of oaks waved over the graves of the forefathers of the hamlet, emblems of the sturdy characters and hardy virtues of those whose narrow beds they shaded. In the recollection of many living inhabitants, little piles of stone and mouldering heaps of turf marked the last homes of the early settlers. The hillocks and the trees have disappeared in the progress of improvement, and the cemetery is no longer distinguishable from the green spots unhallowed by the rest of the dead.[2]

The house of Gershom Rice, was the place where meetings for religious worship were first held. A building was soon erected for devotional exercises on Green street, north of the union of Franklin street, where the inhabitants assembled on the Sabbath, until a more spacious meeting house was reared in 1719, on the site of the old south church.

There were in Worcester in 1718, if the evidence of the proprietary records is to be credited, fifty eight dwelling houses. Tradition says they were humble edifices, principally of logs, one story high, with ample stone chimneys. Some were furnished with windows of diamond glass, where the resources of the proprietor afforded means for procuring such luxury ; the light was admitted in many, through the dim transparency of oiled paper. It is hardly necessary to add, that all have long since sunk in decay, or been removed to give place to the more splendid habitations of modern times.

Worcester, probably, contained at this period, about two hundred souls.

Certificates, entered by direction of the Committee, on the books of the proprietors, show that the individuals named below, had complied with the order of the Court, by erecting houses upon the lots granted, and occupying

[1] The position of these buildings is indicated on H. Stebbins' Map of Worcester, published by C. Harris, 1833.
[2] This spot is enclosed [1836] within the play ground of the Brick School House, on Thomas and Summer streets.

them three years.　The figures indicate the number of acres assigned to each, on the first division of lands.

Jonas Rice, 80 : James Rice, 100 : Gershom Rice, 80 : all of Marlborough : Joshua Rice, 30 : Elisha Rice, 30 : Thomas Gleason, 30 : Obediah Ward, 30 : Aaron Adams, 30 : David Haynes, 30 : Richard Ward, 30 : Ephraim Curtis, 50 : George Parmeter, 60 : Josiah Rice, 30 : Ephraim Rice, 30 : Ephraim Rice, jun. 30 : Rev. Benjamin Allen, 40 : Nathaniel Moore, 40 : all of Sudbury : John Elliot and John Smith, 180 : Daniel Henchman, 150 : Jonathan Tyng, 40 : Stephen Minot, 20 : William Paine, 20 : Thomas Palmer, Cornelius Waldo, (with John Oulton of Marblehead,) 213 : Peter Goulding, 50 : Nathaniel Jones, 40 : George Danson, 200 : all of Boston : Jacob Leonard, 40 : Moses Leonard, 30 : Isaac Leonard, 40 : all of Bridgewater : Isaac Wheeler, 40 : of Medfield : Thomas Brown, 30 : Ichabod Brown, 30 : Thomas Prentice, 60 : of Newton : James Taylor, 30 : Daniel Livermore, 40 : of Malden ; Thomas Haggat, 20 : of Andover : James Holmes, 40 : of Woodstock : Leonard Hoar, 30 : Henry Lee, 30 : Daniel Heywood, 40 : Josiah Heywood, 30 : of Concord : Thomas Binney, 40 : John Barron, 50 : James Butler, 40 : Benjamin Fletcher, 30 : Benjamin Barron, 30.

Lots of 40 acres each were assigned for the use of schools, the minister and the ministry, and to Col. Adam Winthrop, Col. John Ballantine, Col. William Dudley, Col. William Taylor, and Capt. Thomas Howe, of the Committee. Other lots were granted very early to Benjamin Flagg, David Bigelow and John Stearns, of Watertown : Peter King, Henry Knapp, James Knapp, of Sudbury : John Gray, Jonathan Marble, Isaac Miller, Joseph Crosbee, Martha Serjent and Andrew McFarland.

Such is the account which record and tradition afford of the appearance of the town in its infancy: not uninteresting from the comparison of vigorous maturity with early feebleness.[1]

---

[1] When the Indian foe disappeared and the inhabitants became strong, a warfare was commenced and long continued, with the ferocious animals and poisonous reptiles infesting the township.　Large bounties were offered for their destruction.　In 1728, the sum of 3 pence was voted for the death of a rattlesnake, and a draft of £1 on the treasury was accompanied with 80 rattles as vouchers.　The gratuity was annually increased in amount as the common enemy diminished.　In 1734, Mr. Jonas Moore claimed payment for 72 in his own right.　The last demand was as recent as 1758, when 16 serpents were paid for at the rate of 1d. each.

The young settlements were much harassed by the incursions of troops of wolves.　In 1734, it is recorded, ' that notwithstanding the law of the Province giving encouragement for the destruction of wolves, they still continue very troublesome and mischievous, especially among young cattle and sheep : whereby people were discouraged from keeping sheep, so necessary for clothing,' and a reward of £4 was voted for their capture.　In 1733, so great injury was done by these marauders, that the price of their heads was raised to £8.

The precipitous cliff still called Rattlesnake rocks, was the favorite resort of wolves, bears, wild cats and serpents, in those days, rendering the steep dangerous to man.

The winged depredators on the husbandman's harvests were early proscribed.　A bounty of 3d. thinned the armies of blackbirds, jays, and other feathered plunderers.

The town of Worcester shared liberally in the accession to the population of New England, by the emigration, in the early years of the past century, of the descendants of a colony of Scots, who removed from Argyleshire, in the reign of James I., and formed a plantation in the north of Ireland, near Londonderry, in the province of Ulster. Adhering with conscientious fidelity to the presbyterian tenets, they endured the persecution which pressed on the protestants during successive reigns. The accession of William, although it lightened their burdens, did not relieve dissenting christians from galling exactions. Allowed to retain their form of worship, they were compelled to contribute from their resources, to the support of another church. Loaded with tythes of the harvests of lands held by tenancy under exorbitant rents, they embarked for a country where religious freedom was united with civil liberty, and neither tythingman nor taxgatherer had oppressive jurisdiction. In 1718, about one hundred families arrived in Boston, and twenty others landed at Casco, afterwards followed by new colonies, dispersed through the country.[1]

A company of the Scots early settled in Worcester, and here suffered illiberal opposition, and even active hostility. Having formed a religious society, they commenced the erection of a meeting house on the west side of the Boston road.[2] The timbers had been raised and the building was in the progress of construction, when the inhabitants gathered tumultuously by night, and demolished the structure. Persons of consideration and respectability aided in the riotous work of violence, and the defenceless foreigners were compelled to submit to the wrong. Many, unable to endure the insults and bitter prejudices they encountered, joined their brethren of the same denomination, who, under the charge of the Rev. Mr. Abercrombie, commenced the settlement of the town of Pelham, in the county of Hampshire.

They were industrious, frugal, and peaceful, contributing to the prosperity of the province, by the example of diligence and the introduction of useful arts. 'They brought with them,' says the faithful historian of New Hampshire,[3] 'the necessary materials for the manufacture of linen : and their spinning wheels, turned by the foot, were a novelty in the country. They also introduced the culture of potatoes, which were first planted in the garden of Nathaniel Walker of Andover.' The characteristic of the age in which they lived was not charity. Differences of language, habits, and ceremonial, laid

[1] The grant by Massachusetts of unappropriated lands at the East, not affording a place suited to the wishes of the emigrants, alter exploring the wilderness, they selected a township in New Hampshire, then called Nutfield, from the abundance of its forest fruits, and afterwards named Londonderry, from the city of their sojourning in Ireland, where sixteen families assembled beneath a venerable oak, on the 11th of April, 1719, to unite in devotional exercises. Belknap. Parker's Century Sermon, 1819.

The society that visited Boston under the spiritual guidance of the Rev. James Moorhead, in 1727, formed the Federal street church in that city. Dr. Channing's sermon, on the ordination of Mr. Gannet, 1824.

[2] North of the house of Frederic W. Paine, Esq.

[3] Belknap's New Hampshire, i. 193. Farmer's edition.

the foundation of unreasonable hatred, and the strangers were not treated with common decency by their English neighbors Their settlements, in other places, were approached by bodies of armed men, and their property, in some instances, wantonly destroyed They were every where abused and misrepresented as Irish, a people then generally but undeservedly obnoxious ; a reproach peculiarly grievous to the emigrants ' We are surprised,' writes the Rev Mr McGregoire, the pastor of Londonderry, in a letter to Gov Shute, bearing date in 1720, as quoted by Belknap, ' to hear ourselves termed Irish people, when we so frequently ventured our all for the British crown and liberties against the Irish papists, and gave all tests of our loyalty which the government of Ireland required, and are always ready to do the same when required ' The jealousy with which they were first regarded, finally yielded to the influence of their simple virtues and sterling worth [1]

Abraham Blair, an ancestor of some of our present townsmen, distinguished himself in the memorable siege of Londonderry, in 1689 After a series of bloody battles, the besieged were reduced to such extremity by famine ' that a dog's head was held dog cheap at half a crown ' Blair, William Caldwell, and a few others, as an honorary testimonial of their services, were made free of taxation throughout the British provinces.

The Scotch were accompanied by a few of the native Irish, with whom they had contracted relationship during their long residence, or been attached by community of sentiment and suffering.

Among those deriving nativity from Ireland, were the ancestors of the Young family, who first introduced and planted here the useful potato [2] John

---

[1] Among those who remained in Worcester, after the removal of their countrymen, were the following persons, whose names are collected from the records of the town and county

James McGregoire,	William McHan,	John Duncan,	John McClentick,
James Furgerson,	John Batley,	Duncan Graham,	James Glasford,
John Clark,	Andrew Fairand,	Hugh Kelso,	James Hambleton,
Alexander McKonkey,	William Caldwell,	James Forbush,	Robert Lorthog,
James McClellan,	William Young,	Andrew McFarlard,	James Thornington,
William Gray,	Robert Crawford,	Patrick Peables,	John McKonkey,
Robert Gray,	Robert Peables,	John Peables,	Abraham Blair,
Matthew Gray,	Robert Barbour,		

Matthew Thornton, who, as delegate to the Continental Congress from New Hampshire, signed the declaration of Independence, is said, by his biographer, to have resided when a child among the emigrants in Worcester

[2] It is remarkable that the esculent, now considered essentially necessary for table and farm, should have been introduced at a period so late It is related, that some of our early inhabitants, after enjoying the hospitality of one of the Irish families, were each presented with a few potatoes for planting Unwilling to give offense by refusing the present, they accepted the donation but suspecting the poisonous quality, they carried the roots only to the next swamp, and there threw them away, as unsafe to enter their homes.

Young died June 30, 1730, at the great age of 107 years: his son David, died Dec. 26, 1736, aged 94.[1]

The toils and dangers of original settlement being passed, the plantation advanced with vigorous and rapid growth. The swelling population and expanding resources required municipal powers for the management of the common interests of the inhabitants. In 1721, the freeholders and proprietors presented a petition to the General Court for incorporation, which was intrusted to John Houghton, Esq. of Lancaster, and Peter Rice of Marlborough, with the following letter from Jonas and Gershom Rice, the 'fathers of the town,' dated May 31, 1721.

'Gentlemen: Whereas sundry of the freeholders and proprietors of Worcester, having preferred a petition to the General Assembly, on several heads, as appears by said petition, have empowered us to take care that it be seasonably entered and moved; inasmuch as it is a difficult time, by reason of a contagious distemper now raging in Boston, we know not where the session will be; we, therefore humbly crave the favor of you, Gentlemen, to take the trouble upon you, to enter said petition and to move it in the court as there is opportunity.

'So, craving your serious thoughtfulness for the poor, distressed town of Worcester, we subscribe ourselves your humble servants,'

Gershom Rice,
Jonas Rice.'

Other petitions of similar import were subsequently presented, and, on the 14th of June, 1722, a resolve passed the Legislature, vesting the inhabitants of Worcester with the powers and privileges of other towns within the province, and directing that the freeholders and inhabitants be assembled on the last Wednesday of September then next, to choose all town officers, as by law accustomed for towns to do at their annual meetings in March.

Under the authority of this resolve, a warrant was issued by Francis Fulham, Esq. of Weston: and on the 28th day of September, 1722, the inhabitants convened in their first town meeting. Municipal officers were chosen, and from that day, Worcester, then in the County of Middlesex, assumed her place among the regularly organized towns of the Commonwealth.

---

[1] The following inscriptions are chiselled on the common head stone placed over their graves in the old burial place:

'Here lies interred the remains of John Young, who was born in the Isle of Bert, near Londonderry, in the kingdom of Ireland. He departed this life, June 30, 1730, aged 107 years.'

'Here lies interred the remains of David Young, who was born in the parish of Tahbeyn, county of Donegal and kingdom of Ireland. He departed this life, December 23, aged 94 years.'

'The aged son and the more aged father Beneath (these) stones, Their mould'ring bones Here rest together.'

CHAPTER V.

The peace of the country was disturbed by the renewal of hostilities by the eastern Indians, in 1722, when that war broke out which derives its distinctive appellation from Lovell, its hero and martyr. The native tribes of Massachusetts had long ceased to be formidable; but the incursions of the allies of the French from Canada spread alarm along the exposed frontier, and rendered military force necessary for the security of the settlements. Worcester, in 1722, furnished five men for the country's service, in the company of scouts under Major John Chandler. Two were posted at Leicester.[1] Two others,[2] in an independent party, commanded by Benjamin Flagg, with the rank of serjeant, kept garrison in this town or ranged the woods.

In the autumn of 1723, seven of the inhabitants of Worcester enlisted as soldiers, and served during the winter. Five[3] were posted at Rutland under Capt. Samuel Wright: Two[4] were in Capt. Joseph Kellog's company.

In the spring of 1724, the safety of the town was endangered by numerous parties of hostile Indians lurking in the woods; May 3, 1724, the selectmen presented the following petition for aid.

'To his Honor, the Lieut. Governor and Commander in chief, in and over his Majesty's Province of the Massachusetts Bay in New England.

'The petition of the subscribers, humbly sheweth: Whereas, the town of Worcester is very much exposed to the Indian rebels in the present war, there being a great distance between the towns of Lancaster and Rutland, in which we lie open to the enemy, we do therefore, at the desire of the principal part of our inhabitants, humbly lay our difficulties before your honor; earnestly entreating that you would be pleased, in your great wisdom, so far to commiserate our distressed state, as to send us some soldiers to strengthen our front garrisons and scout our woods: otherwise we fear the sad effects which may happen; there being no scout in our woods, or soldiers to guard our defensible places, or inhabitants most exposed, and very much disheartened by reason of the present danger they apprehend themselves to be in; and if your honor will be pleased to afford us some relief, it will be a means to cause our front garrisons to keep their stations; otherwise, we humbly conceive, it

---

[1] John Gray and Robert Crawford.   [2] Ephraim Roper and James Knapp.
[3] Zebediah Rice, Phineas Jones, John Crawford, Uriah Ward, Moses Rice.
[4] John Serjent, Daniel Shattuck.

is morally impossible they should: and for that great privilege to your honor's poor petitioners, as in duty bound shall ever pray.

Nathaniel Moore,   Benjamin Flagg, jr. } Selectmen of
James McLellan,   James Holden,   } Worcester.[1]

The greater pressure of danger on other towns, scattered over the wide territory in the rapid advance of cultivation, prevented immediate relief being afforded. A letter addressed to Col. Chandler, June 21, 1724, exhibits vivid description of the condition of the inhabitants of Worcester.

'Honored Sir: With all due submission, these are to lay before your honor, the distressed condition of this poor place. Through God's goodness the Indians have made no attack upon us as yet, but we are constantly under surprising fears of it. We received the caution from your honor, with the late intelligence of the Indians coming over the lake: also we hear of the late mischief done at Hatfield; and just now we have a post from Rutland with an account of the continual discoveries of the enemy, and the last night our town was alarmed by (as one of our inhabitants says) discovering an Indian: so that this day (Sunday) we have but a thin meeting: the more because some dare not stay from home. I have been but very loth to trouble your honor, being sensible of the pressure of business: but waiting so long and having no help, and being so very much exposed, your honor will excuse me. Our town is not only very much exposed, being so open to the enemy, but we are no way capable of defending ourselves; nor can we expect much help from one another. A small number of Indians, according to appearance, might overcome the whole place. Further, my house, though near the centre, is almost an outside. I have no fort about it: nor if I were able to build have I now sufficient strength to keep it myself. I have began to get some timber to fortify, but am too weak handed to go through, and understanding the backwardness of the country to support us, we are very much disheartened. We have an expectation upon your honor to be a father to us, and we hope the country will not see us stand here waiting to be a prey to our enemies. We are informed that it is objected against our having assistance, that Brookfield, Rutland and Leicester defend us; but let any one consider that understands the ground. It is affirmed to me by those that should be best able to know, that it is fourteen miles from Brookfield to Rutland, and that a line drawn from Brookfield to Rutland will be fifteen miles of our settlement. As to Leicester, the people there more need help from us than are able to render us any, as likewise do Shrewsbury and Hassanamisset. Rutland and Brookfield being well garrisoned and manned, what is more common than for them (the enemy) to go a little further for advantage in weaker spots? The late instance at Hatfield, as well as many others formerly and lately, are sufficient witnesses. If we cannot be supported now about our harvest, we must be starved out of necessity. Instead of assistance, we cannot but remind

[1] Province Files, 1724.

your honor, that we now have five of our soldiers at Rutland in the service; we are informed by rumor, we are allowed ten soldiers, for which we are thankful; but pray, it be possible that the number might be doubled, and that they might be sent as speedily as possible I am ashamed I detain your honor so long. I shall conclude by wishing you all prosperity I am your honor's to command,   Gershom Rice '

' Sundry of our principal inhabitants being present, send their humble duty to your honor, and pray that your honor would take what is here written unto your serious and thoughtful consideration, and move herein unto the honored Lieut Governor and the Council ' [1]

The expectation of immediate reenforcement was disappointed. Col Chandler, then in Watertown, writes June 22, to the Governor and Council ' I am sorry that the poor people of Worcester, Leicester, and Brimfield, find themselves mistaken in having men allowed them to scout and guard said towns. I pray your honor's consideration of the distressed circumstances of the poor people of these towns, as well as other the frontiers · for the encouragement of whom I shall always be ready to obey such orders as your honors shall be pleased to give '

In July, orders were issued to Col. Chandler, to impress twenty men for the frontier service   Subsequently, other detachments were made from other regiments, and nineteen soldiers were stationed at Worcester, where they remained until the 29th of October, 1724, when they were dismissed.[2]

On the 3d of August, 1724, Uriah Ward, who enlisted in the country's service, from Worcester, was killed at Rutland The following account of the transaction is given by Capt. Wright, commanding at that post.

' About twelve o'clock, five men and a boy being in a meadow in the middle of the town making hay, a number of Indians surrounded them, and shot first at the boy, which alarmed the men , they run to their guns, but the Indians shot upon them, and kept them from their guns, and shot down three of the men and scalped them, wounded another in the arm, a flesh wound, who got home without other injury   the first got home without any damage; the boy is not yet found.   The action was hardly over before Col. Tyng came into town with thirty men, but was a little too late · but we joined him, and

---

[1] American Antiquarian Society's Manuscripts

[2] July, 1724. The company of Capt. William Chandler of Woodstock was stationed at Leicester and Rutland The following are the numbers of men posted in the exposed towns at this time ·

| Shrewsbury, | 10 | Brookfield, | 10 | Leicester, | 29 |
| Lancaster, | 14 | Rutland, | 38 | Lunenburg, | 12 |

In Worcester, there were 19 · viz Ephraim Roper, Jonathan Rugg, Samuel Rice, Daniel Coney, Jesse Taylor, William Gibbs, Abraham Joslin, John Death, William Harris, Ephraim Whitcomb, John Demorris, Jesse How, Joseph Woods, Samuel Fletcher, John Holland, Robert Hunt, Samuel Cobley, Samuel Rumlymarsh, Peter Lawrence

Those at Worcester, Shrewsbury and Leicester, were posted as independent guards to the inhabitants, without commissioned officers

divided our men, one party with the Colonel to follow, the other with me to head them : but they got away.

'Since Col. Tyng went from us, we have made a more particular discovery of their number and contrivance in waylaying the meadow where they (the Indians) killed the people. There being in number about thirty, as near as can be thought, by their squatting places or seats when they sat to watch. By what we can learn, they might be near half the company that lay in ambush to shoot down those who come to the relief, so that if there were but a small party of men had gone, they would likely have shot them down before they had seen the Indians.'

From a letter of Col. Chandler, it may be inferred, that the presence of the soldiers saved Worcester from desolation. On the 7th of August, ' an Indian was discovered from a garrison house and fired on by the guard. A soldier and a boy being out near a meadow, spied an Indian nearer to the garrison than they were. The boy ran away. The soldier presented his gun and was ready to fire, when two more rose up by his side ; whereupon he did not venture to fire, but fled : and both came safe to the garrison. During the night their noises were heard crying as wolves, the people made an alarm, and the Indians beat upon a deserted house, drumming violently upon the sides, and so went off.'

The season for the attempts of the enemy having passed, the forces were reduced, and those posted at Worcester were dismissed in the end of October.

Early in April, 1725, Col. Chandler was directed to send orders to the officers in the several frontier towns within his regiment, including Worcester, ' to keep the soldiers and inhabitants upon a strict duty, and to see that they be not off their guard, but well prepared to receive the enemy, who they may expect will attack them ; and especially that no man go abroad without his arms, and in places of hazard that they do not go out except in companies.'

On the 8th of April, Gov. Dummer communicated information to Col. Chandler that several parties of Indians were on their way from Canada, and ordered him ' to visit the exposed towns in his regiment, and charge the people to be vigilant and careful in their duty, and not expose themselves by going abroad unarmed and in small numbers, lest the enemy gain some great advantage over them by such stupid neglect as many of our people have been guilty of on such occasions.'

Parties of the Indians having made their appearance in the vicinity, the inhabitants petitioned the government for succor. The following letter was addressed to Gov. Dummer, April 30, 1725.

' To his Honor the Lt. Governor : With all dutiful respect, these are to acquaint your honor, that news hath just now come unto us of two companies of Indians discovered between us and Wachuset ; and whereas, we the last summer labored under great difficulties, and hardships severe to be borne, by reason of the war with the Indian enemy, not being able to raise corn so much as was needful, or to procure sufficiency of other provision, so as it was rendered very difficult to subsist ourselves and families and, we apprehend, that without your honor's pleased to afford us some relief in our present distressed state, by strengthening our hands, that the corn cannot be planted, the earth tilled, the harvests gathered, or food provided, and that the settlements in the town will be entirely broken up . wherefore, we humbly entreat your honor, that if it may be, we may have some speedy assistance of soldiers, to defend us and scout the woods Our numbers are but small, and many disheartened by reason of the exposed situation of the town. We are the more earnest in our entreaty for the present relief, as it was so late last summer before we had soldiers that we are exceeding behind with our needful business

   'Craving your thoughtfulness of these matters, we are in all gratitude and respect your humble petitioners,

Nathaniel Moore,	Benjamin Flagg, jr.
Moses Leonard,	James Holden,
James McLellan,	Selectmen.'

   The following letter from Capt Samuel Wright to Col Chandler,[1] May 24, 1725, shows that the request was complied with, although not until after some delay

   ' Honored Sir :   These are to inform your honor that I have received the men from your regiment for Worcester   Though some, at least two not so able and effective as I could be glad they were, viz . Ebenezer White and John Field, both from Capt. Thayer of Mendon, who are not able to travel. His honor's the Lt Governor's order to me was, that I should put suitable officers over the men, and that they should scout and guard.   But inasmuch as my orders are not so clear as that I dare venture to put one of the inhabitants officer over them, I have left them under the care and conduct of Capt Pond's son at present   but inasmuch as he, nor any of the men, have not any knowledge of the woods, so are not like to do much service in scouting, unless there be an inhabitant put an officer over them, I desire therefore you would get his honor's leave to put Moses Rice and Benjamin Flagg to be the officer over them alternately, when one comes in, the other to go out, to have but one man's pay   which will be likely to have the duty better performed, and is the mind of the town.   . . .   Your honor's very humble and dutiful servant,

                                                Samuel Wright '

   Another letter from Capt Wright, sent from Worcester by Moses Rice, and dated in May, 1725, is too curious to be omitted

   ' May it please your honor . I give your honor thanks for care of us in sending a new recruit of twelve men. Your honor's directions were, to scout, but at present we have business. The Indians are among us, and have dis-

      [1] American Antiquarian Society's Manuscripts.

covered themselves several times, and we have had several pursuits after them, and have been very vigilant in prosecuting all methods to come up with them by watching and ranging the swamps and lurking places, and by watching a nights in private places without the garrisons: but they are so much like wolves that we cannot yet surprise them, but hope we shall by some means *trepan* them. We have now taken a method to hunt them with dogs, and have started them out of their thickets twice, and see them run out, but at such a distance we could not come at them. Having an opportunity, thought it my duty to acquaint your honor with it: but having but a minutes time to write could but only give you an account in short, and remain your honor's dutiful and obliged servant,   Samuel Wright.'

The names and numbers of those posted at Worcester within this year cannot now be ascertained. An incident which occurred during the period of their service is related in a letter, July 17, 1725, from Benjamin Flagg.

'Honored Sir: These are to inform you that we this day went out as a guard to those that worked in the meadow to gather in their hay, of fourteen men, with those that worked, who wrought in two or three places near to one another. As we scouted the swamps round the meadow, we did discover Indian tracks, in the morning, in the swamp by the meadow side, which made us very strict upon our guard, but made not any more discovery until the middle of the day, we sat to eat victuals upon a knoll where we thought we might be safe; but while we were eating, a dog that was with us barked and ran out from us. I immediately sent three men to discover, who ran, and immediately we heard a running among the brush: which was Indians, who had crawled up the brush to make a shot at us. We ran so fast upon them that the grass rose up under their tracks, but could not see them, the brush being so thick. We pursued them where we heard them whistle one to another in the thicket, but they scattered and scampered so we could not find them: but found where they had sat down and just gone. We pursued on after the enemy: but it is as easy to find a needle in a wood, as find them when scattered. So we returned. This I have thought meet to acquaint your honor of, and so I remain, your honor's humble and obliged servant. These with care and speed.   Benjamin Flagg.'

The sufferings of the frontier settlements were terminated by the treaty concluded with the Indians in the following winter, (Dec. 15,) and ratified in the spring of 1726.

Although relieved from the danger and alarm of hostile invasion, the progress of the town in population and wealth was slow during the succeeding years.[1]

[1] In May 1724, the town had received an amount proportioned to its taxation, of the bills of credit or stock of the Public Bank, and applied the depreciating paper currency to finish the meeting house. In March, 1728, trustees were appointed to obtain the sum of £170, 15 s. granted to Worcester from the emission of £50.000, and make loans to the inhabitants from this fund, not exceeding £10 nor less than £5 to each.

The act erecting the County of Worcester passed April 2, 1731, to take effect from the 10th of July following. Its provisions included Worcester, Lancaster, Westborough, Shrewsbury, Southborough, Leicester, Rutland, Lunenburg, and the south town laid out to the Narraganset soldiers,[1] now Westminster, taken from Middlesex: Mendon, Woodstock, now in Connecticut, Sutton, including Hassanamisset, now Grafton, Uxbridge, the land granted to the petitioners of Medfield, now Sturbridge, from Suffolk: and Brookfield, from the County of Hampshire.

The location of the shire town of the new county occasioned much debate and diversity of opinion. For many years, Sutton, Lancaster, Mendon, and Brookfield, stood higher in rank, graduated on population and valuation, than Worcester. The central position of the latter town, gave it advantage over its competitors for the honor of becoming the capital. The proposition to make Lancaster and Worcester half shires, having the sessions of Court held alternately in each, would have prevailed, except for the opposition of Joseph Wilder, Esq., who remonstrated against the administration of justice in Lancaster, lest the morals of its people should be corrupted. His influence decided a question of so much importance to its prosperity, in favor of the present metropolis.

The first Court of Probate was held in the meeting house, July 13, 1731, and the Common Pleas and General Sessions of the Peace 10th of August following, by the Hon. John Chandler, then of Woodstock, Chief Justice of both tribunals. A sermon was preached on the occasion by the Rev. John Prentice, of Lancaster. The Superior Court of Judicature was held on the 22d of September. The centennial anniversary of its session was commemorated October 4th, 1831, when an address was delivered by the Hon. John Davis, of Worcester.

Capt. Nathaniel Jones and Ensign Moses Leonard were trustees of the first loan: Nathaniel Moore, Daniel Heywood and John Hubbard of the second.

May, 1726, the inhabitants voted, that thanks be returned to Hon. Adam Winthrop, for his bounty in bestowing upon the town a *cushion* as furniture for the pulpit, and that the town clerk present his honor a copy of said vote.

March, 1729: voted that the constable warn town meetings in future by going from house to house. 1735, the selectmen were directed to erect a suitable sign post, at the town's charge, near the meeting house, and the constable to serve notices by posting them thereon.

May 17, 1732, John Chandler, Esq., Capt. Jonas Rice and Mr. Benjamin Flagg, jr., were of a committee to return thanks to Mr. Wigglesworth Switcher of Boston, for the present (of £5 towards completing the meeting house) he lately made the town, and on the receipt of the same to dispose of it to the best advantage.

[1] In 1728 and 1733, seven townships were granted by the General Court to the descendants of the soldiers in the Narraganset war. The grantees assembled on Boston common in 1733, and formed themselves into seven societies of 120 persons entitled to one township. On the 17th of October, a committee of three from each company elected at this meeting, made an allotment of lands. Amoskeag, then called Narraganset No. 4, was assigned to those from Worcester and 40 other towns. The number of grantees in each must necessarily have been very small; their names are not preserved.

One term of the Superior Court was held annually in October.

The Inferior Court had its sittings in May, August, November and February. The General Sessions of the Peace was composed of all the justices within the county, who commonly attended and decided the matters presented for adjudication by vote.[1]

When public festivals were few, and anniversaries unfrequent, the terms of court were the great holidays of the county; and its population assembled in Worcester, as on a general exchange, for the transaction of business, or pursuit of amusement in the rude sports of the period. The judicial proceedings, now forsaken except by parties, witnesses and officers, were generally attended by a multitude that thronged the streets. Wrestling, fighting, and horse racing were common exercises. The stocks, pillory, and whipping post crowned the summit of Court hill, then sloping with steep declivity to the highway, and partially covered with bushes. Frequent exhibitions of discipline attracted crowds of spectators.[2]

Governor Belcher, with the members of the Council, on their way to Albany to hold a conference with the Six Nations, visited Worcester, 21st of August, 1735. The Justices of the General Sessions[3] with a delegation of citizens, waited on the executive officers of the government. Their complimentary address is preserved on the public records, and affords evidence that the controversy between the royal prerogative and the representatives of the people, then directed against grants for permanent salary, had not extended to a community who offered such loyal salutations.

' May it please your excellency : We, his majesty's justices of the Court of General Sessions of the Peace, now held in this place, for the county of Worcester, by adjournment, humbly beg leave to congratulate your excellency's safe arrival in this part of your government. It is with hearts full of joy that we now see your excellency's face, together with the honorable Council, in the shire town of this county, which has received its being and constitution by the favor of your excellency, under the Divine conduct and benediction, and by whose wise, mild and just administration, this whole province enjoys

[1] General Ruggles, the Chief Justice, in stern derision of the constitution of this court, on one occasion, reprimanded a dog who had taken his seat beside his master, for appearing on the bench before he had been qualified as a Justice of Peace, and directed him to go and be sworn before he came to vote there.

[2] The common practice of racing in Main street during the terms of the courts having become a nuisance, the following prohibitory vote was passed, September 19th, 1745. ' Whosoever shall for the future, during the space of three years from the 15th day of November next, in the times of the sittings of the superior court of judicature, court of assize and general jail delivery, the times of the sitting of the inferior court of common pleas and general sessions of the peace in this town, presume to run races on horseback, or pace their horses for trial in the country road, from the house of Mr. Joshua Eaton to the house where Mr. Richard Wheeler now lives, shall forfeit the sum of 20 s. lawful money to the use of the poor of the town.'

[3] The Justices present, were John Chandler, Josiah Wilder, William Ward, William Jennison, John Chandler, jr., Josiah Willard, Nahum Ward, Henry Lee, Samuel Willard and John Keyes.

,reat quietness, which, we trust, will be continued and accepted in all places with all thankfulness   We are also sensibly affected that your excellency has condescended, and is now pursuing, a very necessary, although a very difficult and tedious, journey, to visit the western frontiers, and meet with the Cagnavaga Indians, and such tribes as may be desirous to renew their friendship with his government, in order to preserve and perpetuate the happy peace subsisting with them   May your excellency and the honorable gentlemen of the Council, and such of the honorable House of Representatives who attend you, be encompassed with the Divine favor as with a shield, and in due time returned in safety to your respective habitations '

The Hon John Chandler having read this Address to the Governor, in the language of the record, ' his excellency was pleased to return the following answer.'

'Gentlemen: I thank you very kindly for the welcome you give me, with the hon gentlemen of his majesty's Council and the gentlemen of the House of Representatives, into this part of his majesty's province.   I take this opportunity of assuring you that I shall always cheerfully join my power with yours, that justice and judgment may flourish in the county of Worcester, which will greatly contribute to the happiness and welfare of the people '

After this reply, the justices returned, and immediately adjourned without day.

William Jennison, Esq and Mr Gershom Rice, were appointed as a committee, in March, 1737, ' to repair to the Great Falls at the head of Providence river, or where Blackstone's river falls into the salt water, to see if it be possible for the falls to be made practicable for fish to come up : provided the towns lying on said river, or near adjoining, join in sending committees also ' It is noted that ' these gentlemen offered to go upon free cost ' Although they reported that the stream could be made navigable for fish, and £30 were appropriated for the purpose, no benefit resulted from the examination or grant, and the fund was restored to the treasury

The town contributed liberally to the defence of the province during the wars with the French, sent its men, and expended its means freely for the reduction of the fortresses of Nova Scotia and Canada   The voluntary exertions of the inhabitants in support of the government, and in aid of its military expeditions, would seem incredible, if they were not verified by authentic rolls, rendered on oath, by officers in command, and by the testimony of history to the ardor of the patriotic spirit pervading the community.

The quota of Worcester, in the army of Sir William Pepperell, for the conquest of Cape Breton, is not exactly ascertained   Benjamin Gleason, who enlisted in that service, died before the walls of Louisbourg, in 1745, before its surrender   Adonijah Rice, the first born of our native citizens, was in a company of rangers in the seige

In 1746, an alarm of a French invasion spread through the country.   The express sent by Governor Shirley arrived Sept. 23d, when the inhabitants were assembled in town meeting.[1] Abandoning their municipal affairs, they immediately adjourned and took up arms. Before sunset the whole military force was mustered, and ready to march with a week's provisions to meet the enemy. A second messenger arrived seasonably to prevent their departure.

Fort Massachusetts had been erected by the province at the beginning of the war, in 1744, at Hoosick, now Williamstown, to guard the western frontier. After its capture by Vaudrieul,[2] in August, 1746, it was strengthened and defended by a sufficient garrison, partly from Worcester. Eight of our men[3] were stationed there from Dec. 1747 to March 1748.

The depredations of the Indians were so injurious in the summer of 1748, that 200 volunteers were enlisted from Col. Chandler's regiment, with some from Hampshire, to drive them back to Canada. Brigadier Dwight was entrusted with the command. One company of fifty three, all from Worcester, marched on the eighth of August, and returned after a campaign of seventeen days, having accomplished their object without loss, the enemy retiring without giving battle. The officers were Daniel Heywood, Major commandant: John Stearns, Captain: Tyrus Rice, Lieutenant: Richard Flagg, Ensign.

In 1754, a bill was proposed, imposing an excise on wines and spirits, containing an extraordinary provision, obliging every householder, when required by a collector or deputy, to render an account under oath of the quantity of such liquors consumed in his family, not purchased of a licensed person, and to make payment of the duty. Gov. Shirley refused his assent, and procured the printing of the bill for the consideration of the people. Sept. 2, it was unanimously voted ' to be contrary to the mind of the town that the act relating to the excise on the private consumption of spirituous liquors be passed into a law; and that John Chandler, the representative of the town, use his utmost endeavor to prevent the same.' This is the earliest instance on our records of the instructions of the constituents to their representative.

Thirteen soldiers were in service this year under Capt. John Johnson, and were employed at forts Western and Halifax, near Augusta and Waterville, on the Kennebec river.

In May, 1755, it appears from the returns of Gen. John Winslow, seventeen men from Worcester were in his majesty's service in Nova Scotia under his command: seventeen more were posted at Fort Cumberland. John Walker, after having served in a provincial regiment in different grades, was commissioned as a captain in the king's army.

Adonijah Rice and another soldier, engaged in the expedition against Crown Point, in August. In September, orders were issued to Col. Chandler to impress troops for the reinforcement of the army. Sept. 17, fourteen volunteers were returned from Worcester.

[1] Town Records.   [2] Williams' Vermont, i. 333.
[3] Abraham Bass, William McLellan, Silas Pratt, Abner Roberts, John Crawford, Samuel Brewer, Abraham Peck and Hezekiah Ward. These were under Capt. Elisha Hawley.

On the 21st of October, the inhabitants instructed Col Doolittle, the representative, to join in no measure countenancing a stamp act

In the autumn of 1755, that cruel measure of policy, the darkest blot on our history, the removal of the inhabitants of Nova Scotia and their dispersion through the provinces, was executed by General Winslow. About a thousand of the French Neutrals, as these unfortunate people were called, arrived in Boston at the beginning of winter, and were distributed among the several towns designated by a committee The proportion assigned to Worcester was eleven They were received and supported by the selectmen, at the expense of the province The following description is annexed to an account rendered for their subsistence

'Eleven French persons, an aged man and woman 65 or 70 years old, past labor; the female very weak, a girl about seventeen years old, who employs her whole time in taking care of the old people They have four sons who support themselves In this family are Jean Herbert and Monsieur Lebere Justin White and his wife, aged about thirty, both very feeble, the man inclining to a consumption and unfit for labor, they have three small children, the eldest but about five years old, all chargeable, one of the children has been born very lately, so that the whole number now is twelve.'

These families, torn from their homes, reduced from comparative affluence to desolate poverty, thrown among strangers of different language and religion, excited pity for their misfortunes Their industrious and frugal habits, and mild and simple manners, attracted regard, and they were treated here with great kindness They cultivated a little tract of land, were permitted to hunt deer at all seasons, and aided in their own support by laboring as reapers and by manufacturing wooden implements Although they tilled the fields, they kept no animals for labor The young men drew their fuel and materials for fencing on the ground, with thongs of sinew, and turned the earth with a spade So deep was the feeling of their sufferings in their violent removal, that any allusion to their native country drew from them a flood of tears. The aged persons died broken hearted In 1767, the remnant removed to Canada among their countrymen The town then granted £7 to lay in stores and pay the passage of John Lebere to Quebec, and authorized the selectmen to raise that sum by loan

The year 1756 was marked by increased exertions of the inhabitants to fill the ranks of the army destined to act against Crown Point Our own citizens freely volunteered in the expedition, whose success, it was confidently expected, would terminate the war which pressed so heavily on the resources and population of the province. A company of 43 men was raised under Capt Aaron Rice of Rutland, on his death in camp, he was succeeded in the command by Lieut Jacob Hemmenway. Forty-four other soldiers were returned by other officers in Col Ruggles' regiment, in the service of the country. Some of these troops suffered in the reverses of the campaign Daniel Stearns was made prisoner near Fort Edward, Edward Hair, at the capitulation of Oswego and Jonathan Child in the vicinity of Fort William

6*

Henry. They were detained in captivity at Montreal until the exchange in 1758. Many died of epidemic diseases at Lake George.

Regimental head quarters were established at Worcester, which was appointed the rendezvous of troops to be mustered into service. The town was often filled with military detachments waiting orders to march, and the neighboring hills whitened with tents.

A depot of munitions of war was formed for the armament of the levies as they advanced towards the scene of operations on the western frontiers. A report of the commissary shows a total of 403 arms complete, 7 boxes of guns, 403 bayonets, 212 blankets, 151 bandoliers, 80 cartouch boxes, 1 cask of powder.

Earl Loudon, successor of Gen. Shirley, in expectation of an attack from the enemy, ordered Col. Chandler, on the 30th of September, to detach one hundred and fifty men for the reenforcement of his army. The militia companies of the town, with the former levies from the regiment, promptly marched under James Putnam, the distinguished counsellor, bearing the military rank of Major. After waiting at Westfield for the troops of Hampshire, finding the necessity for their services had passed, the forces of Worcester county, amounting to 300, were dismissed and returned.

Intelligence of the siege of Fort William Henry, Aug. 4, 1757, induced the Governor to order the colonels of all the regiments to hold each man in readiness to march at a moment's warning.

The following report, July 20, 1757, shows the preparation of Worcester, then included in the first regiment under the command of Col. John Chandler, jr.

'Agreeably to an order of the honorable, his majesty's council, of the fifth of July last, requiring me to take effectual care that every person, both upon the alarm and train band lists, within my regiment, and the several stocks in said regiment, be furnished with arms and ammunition according to law, if not already provided : immediately on the receipt of said order, I forthwith sent out my warrant requiring a strict view into the state of the respective companies and town stocks in my regiment, and returns have since been made to me that they are well equipt.

'And agreeably to an order of the honorable, his majesty's council, of the 6th of June last,[1] requiring me, in case of an alarm being made, or notice given of the approach of an enemy by sea, to cause my regiment to appear complete in arms, with ammunition according to law, and each man to be furnished with seven days provision of meat. I also sent out my warrant, requiring the several companies, in such case, with the utmost expedition to march to Boston, and further to act agreeably to such orders as they shall receive. Agreeably to the order aforesaid, return has been made from the respective companies that they are each ready to march at an hour's warning.

John Chandler, jr., Colonel.'

[1] A French fleet having appeared off the coast, alarm and dismay spread through the country, in apprehension of an invasion of New England. These orders were issued to meet the danger from this source.

Fort William Henry having surrendered, and advices having been received of the advance of the French to attack Gen Webb, orders were issued to Col Chandler ' to march the regiment of militia under his command into the extreme parts of the province on the western frontier, there to receive such further orders as shall be necessary for the aid and assistance of his majesty's troops ' The country, which had been resting on its arms during the whole summer, roused itself at the summons The whole militia of the town marched on the 10th of August One company mustered 56 men, with Col Chandler himself at the head, James Goodwin, was Captain, Noah Jones, Lieut, David Bancroft, Ensign, and Nahum Willard, Surgeon Another company, 54 strong, was under Major Gardner Chandler, with Capt John Curtis, Lieut Luke Brown, and Ens Asa Flagg They reached Sheffield, 105 miles distant as the roads then were, where they were met by orders from Gen Webb, and intelligence that the enemy remained contented with his acquisition. On the 8th of August they were disbanded, except a few men detached to Stockbridge.

Eight of our men, in the troop of cavalry under Lieut Jonathan Newhall of Leicester, reached the army at Fort Edward Ten soldiers, regularly enlisted, served during the campaign

On the 17th of September, Gen Amherst halted for a day here, on his march westward, with an army of 4500 men Capt Samuel Clark Paine commanded a company, principally raised in Worcester, in this body, and served during the winter There are nine soldiers under Gen Abercrombie in the unfortunate attack on Ticonderoga.

This company continued in service in the splendid campaign of Gen Amherst, during 1759 Daniel McFarland was Lieutenant, and the late Samuel Ward of Lancaster, Ensign Twenty-three non-commissioned officers and privates are returned from Worcester as doing duty in its ranks Fourteen men more were in other companies of Gen Ruggles' regiment William Crawford officiated as Chaplain of Col Abijah Willard s regiment Benjamin Stowell was Lieutenant of Capt. Johnson s company. Many returned laboring under the diseases contracted by residence in the region of fever and ague.

Capt Paine having died in December, Lieut Daniel McFarland was elected to the command of the company, in Feb 1760 William Ward is returned as Lieut Samuel Ward, the Ensign, was promoted to be Adjutant of Col. Willard's regiment William Crawford, the former Chaplain, became Surgeon in Gen Ruggles' regiment Thomas Cowden served as Lieutenant in Capt. Jeffeids company, and twelve privates are borne on the rolls. as from Worcester.

In 1761, Thomas Cowden was commissioned as Captain : twenty-five men from Worcester were in the army from May to November, principally under his command. He remained in service till the end of the following year. Nine soldiers only appear to have enlisted with him

The peace of 1763 terminated exertions, which, in reference to the population and resources of the province, may well be deemed extraordinary. The whole number of men furnished by this town alone, during the French wars, for defence and conquest, as derived from the well-authenticated rolls still preserved, exceeded 450, as appears from the following summary.

1748,	. . . . . 69.		1758,	. . . . . 20.
1754,	. . . . . 13.		1759,	. . . . . 43.
1755,	. . . . . 34.		1760,	. . . . . 17.
1756,	. . . . . 93.		1761,	. . . . . 26.
1757,	. . . . 130.		1762,	. . . . . 8...453 men.

In these numbers are not included those who enlisted into the regular army : nor, except in 1748 and 1757, the occasional service of the militia companies. It is probable that many names have been omitted in the examination of voluminous papers in the archives of the state, and as the series is not perfect, many may have been lost.

Worcester furnished to the provincial service during this period, 1 colonel, 1 lieutenant colonel, 2 majors, 6 captains, 8 lieutenants, 7 ensigns, 27 serjeants, 2 surgeons, a chaplain, and an adjutant.

The same patriotic spirit, which was the moving spring of efforts so considerable, pervaded the province. 'Nearly one third of the effective men,' says Minot, 'were in military service in some mode or other, and all this zeal was manifested after the most depressing disappointments, and a burden of taxes which is said to have been so great in the capital, as to equal two thirds of the income of the real estate.'

The advantages from the sessions of courts, the erection of buildings, and the residence of public officers, having become apparent in the prosperity of Worcester, attempts were made to transfer these benefits to the towns who had once declined their enjoyment.

In 1764, Timothy Paine, James Putnam, John Chandler, were a committee to give reasons to the General Court, why the petition of Abel Lawrence and others, praying for a new county from the northern part of Worcester and the western part of Middlesex, should not be granted.

This project was urged during several sessions of the Legislature. Remonstrances were presented from towns in both counties against the dismemberment. After orders of notice had been issued, and several committees had taken the expediency of division into consideration, the petitioners abandoned their object, in 1766.

Lancaster having petitioned for the sessions of some of the courts there, it was voted, 'that by removing any of them from the town of Worcester, the shire of the county, to Lancaster, three fourths of the inhabitants of the county will be obliged to travel farther than they now do.' Mr. Joshua Bigelow, then representative, was instructed to use his utmost endeavor to prevent the removal, and procure the establishment here of another term of the Superior Court. In the former he was successful.

CHAPTER VI.

1765 to 1775   American Revolution   Instructions, 1766, 1767   Resolutions, 1768   Covenant, 1768   Tea   Votes, 1773   Committee of Correspondence, 1773   Political Society   Peter Oliver.   Address of Grand Jury, 1774   Report on grievances, 1774   Instructions   Protest of royalists   Town Meeting   Record expunged   Non consumption covenant and oath   Mandamus counsellors   Assembly of the people   Alarm   Minute men   Courts stopped   County Convention   Sheriff Chandler   William Campbell   Instructions   Blacksmiths' Convention   Depot of military stores

We have now reached the period of deepest interest in our history. The middle of the century had scarcely past, before the shadows of oppression began to darken the land, and the first tremulous motions of the revolution, which finally upheaved the colonial government, were felt   The collision of popular privilege with royal prerogative, maintained during successive years by the representatives, had prepared the people for the investigation of the principles on which their connection with the mother country rested, and waked their vigilance for the protection of chartered and inherited rights   The long series of wars we have reviewed, were useful schools, diffusing military spirit, and imparting knowledge of strength and skill, and confidence for repulsing encroachments

When the appeal to arms approached, many of the inhabitants of Worcester most distinguished for talents, influence, and honors, adhered with constancy to the king   In the hostility of party and the struggles of warfare, they were driven into exile and loaded with reproach   At this distance of time, when the bitterness of the controversy has long subsided, while we do justice to their memories, a warmer glow of gratitude springs in our hearts for the patriots whose prophetic forecast saw, beyond the dangers and sufferings of the contest, the prosperity and happiness that brighten over our republican institutions   The royalists here, were those who had sustained with equal fidelity and ability, the highest civil and military offices, enjoyed the confidence of their fellow citizens, and given testimony of their love of country by earnest exertions in its service

Standing as they did, and knowing how scanty were the resources for resistance, they might well entertain doubts whether the period had arrived, when it was possible to secure independence, and refuse to hazard all that was dear on the uncertain issue of a war with the most formidable nation of Europe   Educated with sentiments of veneration for the sovereign to whom they had sworn fealty, indebted to his bounty for the honors and wealth they possessed, loyalty and gratitude alike influenced them to resist acts, which, to them, seemed treasonable and rebellious   However much they erred in judgment and feeling, we may respect the sincerity of motives, attested by the sacrifice of property, the loss of home, and all the miseries of confiscation and exile   Some among them, it is known, were ardently attached to the principles of liberty. but, in their view, the opposition to the measures of government was premature in its advance to extremities. The times did not admit of a middle course. The crisis had indeed arrived, although they misunderstood the progress of events, and became involved in indiscriminate denunciation.

It is not for the purpose of wantonly drawing from oblivion those, whose descendants have been among our worthiest citizens, that the names of the royalists are mentioned in the following narrative. To understand the transactions, it is necessary to know the persons who were engaged in them, and to whom they applied. By changing even slight features, the resemblance of the picture would be destroyed. The annals would be worthless, which impaired confidence by the suppression of truth, even though unpleasant and unwelcome. There is no discretion entrusted to the historian to select among the events of the past. It is his task to relate with fidelity the incidents of the times he reviews, that he may place loyalty and patriotism in their just contrast.

The earliest expression of opinion, on the records of the town, in relation to revolutionary measures, was on the 21st of October, 1765, when Capt Ephraim Doolittle, the representative, was instructed to join in no measure countenancing the stamp act.

Soon after the destruction of the property of Gov. Hutchinson and other officers of the crown, in August 1765, at the Superior Court, the Grand Jury expressed to the Chief Justice, in strong terms, the disapprobation of the people of the riotous proceedings in Boston.

In May following, the town refused to give instructions respecting restitution to those who had suffered from the disgraceful violence.

The instructions to the representative[1] 19th of May, 1766, are, generally, marked by singular good sense and moderation.

' 1. That you use the whole of your influence and endeavor, that no person holding any fee or military office whatsoever, especially Judges of the Superior Court, Judges of the Probate, Registers of Probate, Secretary, Clerk of either of the Courts, Sheriffs, or Province Treasurer, be chosen into his majesty's Council of this province, and that you attend at the election of Counsellors, and give your vote accordingly.

' 2. That you endeavor, that, for the future, the General Court of this province be held in an open manner, that such as are so minded and behave agreeable to good order, may see and hear how affairs are conducted in said court, and if the desired end be obtained, that a proper and convenient house, both for the court and spectators, be forthwith prepared.

' 3. That you endeavor, that the present fee table of this province be made null and void, and that a new fee table be made and established instead thereof, which shall be more equal and impartial; not giving to any officer in the government, except the Governor, more nor less than you would be

[1] Ephraim Doolittle. The instructions were reported by Jonathan Stone, Benjamin Flagg, and Nathan Baldwin.

willing to do the same service for yourself, and that you observe this rule in granting pay for contingencies and occasional services

'4 That you endeavor, that there be no monopoly of public offices in this government, and that one man be not invested with more than one office at one time, except it be compatible with the true interests of the people in general.

'5 That you endeavor, that there be a law made, that whenever any representative shall receive any office or commission from the Governor, he shall be dismissed the house, and not be allowed to act as a member thereof, without he should be chosen anew by his constituents, and that the said constituents be forthwith served with a new precept to call a meeting for the choice of some meet and suitable person to represent them in the Great and General Court

'6 That you endeavor, the excise act be repealed, and that there be no excise laid upon any commodities of trade, but that all lawful trade be encouraged, and free of duty or excise: and that all the public charge be paid directly by a rate, except such money as shall be raised by fines for the breach of the good, wholesome laws of this province.

'7 That the law for keeping of Latin grammar schools be repealed, and that we be not obliged to keep more than one grammar school in a county, and that to be at the county charge, and that each town be obliged by law to keep good and sufficient schools for the education of their youth in the art of reading, writing and arithmetic, and that the schoolmasters for the said purpose shall be such as shall be approved of by the selectmen of each respective town

'8. That you use your utmost endeavor, that a law be made to prevent bribery and corruption in the several towns in this province in the choice of representatives

'9 That you give diligent attendance at every session of the General Court of this province this present year, and adhere to these our instructions, and the spirit of them, as you regard our friendship, and would avoid our just resentment'

The instructions, reported by Ephraim Doolittle, Nathan Baldwin, and Jonathan Stone, on the 18th of May, 1767, breathe a similar spirit, and are, in many respects, applicable to the present times

'To Mr. Joshua Bigelow · Sir · As we have devolved upon you the important trust of representing us at the Great and General Court, the year ensuing, we, your constituents, therefore, think it our duty and interest to give you the following instructions relative to some of your conduct in said trust

'1. That you use your influence to maintain and continue that harmony and good will between Great Britain and this province [which] may be most conducive to the prosperity of each, by a steady and firm attachment to English liberty and the charter rights of this province, and [that] you willingly suffer no invasions, either through pretext of precedency, or any other way whatsoever· and if you find any encroachments on our charter rights, that you use your utmost ability to obtain constitutional redress

'2 That you use your influence to obtain a law to put an end to that unchristian and impolitic practice of making slaves of the human species in this province and that you give your vote for none to serve in his majesty's Council, who, you may have reason to think, will use their influence against such a law, or that sustain any office incompatible with such trust and in such choice, prefer such gentlemen, and such only, who have distinguished themselves in the defence of our liberty.

'3. That you use your influence that the fee table of this province be established more agreeable to the rules of justice. Set not to the sheriff, as fees, double as much pay as the service may be done for, and in general is by the deputy sheriffs, neither oblige jurymen, &c , to do service at the expense of their own private estates, or be subjected to large fines or penalties , but subject all, or none at all, by penalties, and appoint so much fees and no more, as may be agreeable to each service ; and that you observe this rule, in granting pay for occasional and contingent charges

'4 That you use your endeavor to relieve the people of this province from the great burden of supporting so many Latin grammar schools, whereby they are prevented from attaining such a degree of English learning as is necessary to retain the freedom of any state

'5 That you make diligent inquiry into the cause of such general neglect of the Militia of this province, and endeavor a redress of such grievance , without which, we apprehend, in time, we may be made an easy prey of, by the enemies of Great Britain

'6 Take special care of the liberty of the press.

'And, Sir, we hope and trust, that in all matters that may come before you, you will have a single eye to the public good, have a watchful eye over those who are seeking the ruin of this province, and endeavor to make this province reciprocally happy with our mother country '

The indignation of the people on the promulgation of the act of Parliament imposing duties on paper, tea, and other articles imported into the colonies, was first manifested in Boston.   In October, 1767, a meeting was held there, and resolutions to encourage domestic manufactures and refrain from purchasing the taxed articles, were passed and transmitted to the selectmen of every town

At the next session of the Legislature, resolves of similar import were adopted, which are recited in the papers and copied below

On the 14th of March, 1768, a town meeting was held in Worcester, when the subject was presented   The following extract from the record exhibits the proceedings of the inhabitants

'The article in the warrant being read relative to promoting industry and economy, Mr. Joshua Bigelow, our representative, moved to the town, that before they came to a vote he might read the vote of the hon. House of Representatives of this province, passed the 26th of Feb last, relative to the promoting industry, economy and good morals, and for the discountenancing the use of foreign superfluities, and to encourage the manufactures of this province which was granted him it was also moved and seconded, that the reasons given by the Hon Timothy Ruggles, the representative of Hardwick, on his dissenting answer to the vote aforesaid, might be read also [1] which accordingly was done, and the question was put whether the town would buy any British manufactures more than they could pay for, and it passed in the affirmative '[2]

The sentiments of the inhabitants are more easily deduced from subsequent events, than understood from the concluding expressions of the record The town clerk, a gentleman of strong royalist attachments, was not probably desirous of correcting any absurdity in the motions of his political adversaries

Soon after this meeting, the patriotic party procured the subscriptions of many of the inhabitants to the following paper.

' Whereas the Hon. House of Representatives of this province, on the 26th day of February last, did declare, that the happiness and well-being of civil communities depend upon industry, economy, and good morals, and taking into serious consideration the great decay of trade, the scarcity of money, the heavy debt contracted in the late war, which still remains on the people, and the great difficulties to which they are by these means reduced, did resolve, to use their utmost endeavors, and enforce their endeavors by example, in suppressing extravagance, idleness, and vice, and promoting industry, economy, and good morals and in order to prevent the unnecessary exportation of money, of which the province hath, of late, been drained, did further resolve, that they would, by all prudent means, endeavor to discountenance the use of foreign superfluities, and encourage the manufactures of this province , and whereas, the Parliament of Great Britian has passed an act imposing duties

[1] Brigadier Ruggles alone opposed the passage of these resolutions His reasons for dissenting were offered in writing, but it was voted that they should not be entered on the journal His objections to the encouragement of manufactures were these

1   Because in all countries manufactures are set up at the expense of husbandry, or other general employment of the people, and if they have not peculiar advantages over husbandry, they will, by discouraging the latter, have an injurious effect

2   That manufactures here must encounter insurmountable obstacles from the thin population and high price of labor and would be detrimental, by taking hands away from agriculture and the fisheries

Other objections were deduced from the colonial relation of the province and the mother country, and the injury which might result to the interests of England

[2] One of the earliest woolen manufactories of Massachusetts is thus noticed in the Boston Evening Post, October 10, 1768

' We hear from Brookfield, that Mr. Joshua Upham of that town, a gentleman in the law, and his two brothers, with a number of other gentlemen, have lately erected a building 50 feet in length and two stories high, for a manufactory house, and are collecting tradesmen of several sorts for the woolen manufactory, and they propose to keep a large number of looms constantly at work.

on sundry articles for the purpose of raising a revenue on America, which is unconstitutional, and an infringement of our just rights and privileges; and the merchants of this province have generally come into an agreement not to import goods from Great Britain, a few articles excepted, till that act is repealed; which in our opinion is a lawful and prudent measure: therefore, we the subscribers, do solemnly promise and engage, each with the other, to to give all possible encouragement to our own manufactures: to avoid paying the tax imposed by said act, by not buying any European commodity but what is absolutely necessary; that we will not, at funerals, use any gloves except those made here, or purchase any article of mourning on such occasion, but what shall be absolutely necessary; and we consent to abandon the use, so far as may be, not only of all the articles mentioned in the Boston resolves, but of all foreign teas, which are clearly superfluous, our own fields abounding in herbs more healthful, and which we doubt not, may, by use, be found agreeable: we further promise and engage, that we will not purchase any goods of any persons who, preferring their own interest to that of the public, shall import merchandize from Great Britain, until a general importation takes place; or of any trader who purchases his goods of such importer: and that we will hold no intercourse, or connection, or correspondence, with any person who shall purchase goods of such importer, or retailer; and we will hold him dishonored, an enemy to the liberties of his country, and infamous, who shall break this agreement.'

The execution of resolutions against tea, required the aid of those to whose care the fragrant herb was entrusted in the household. A female convention assembled in Boston, and agreed to discontinue the use of the taxed leaf and substitute a native shrub,[1] an inhabitant of our meadows. In imitation of this example, a meeting was held here by the patriotic ladies, who cordially concurred with the good resolutions of their sisters of the metropolis. The royalists, who loved their tea and their king, and were equally averse to the desertion of the social urn or the sovereign, had influence enough to convene another assembly, and procure the reconsideration of its approbation of the American plant, and a renewal of allegiance to the exotic of India.

A paragraph in the Boston Evening Post, alludes to the doings of the fair partizans.

'Worcester, Nov. 11, 1768. We hear that the ladies have discovered the most malignant quality in the Labrador tea, which, by vote of the daughters of liberty within the metropolis, was substituted, to be used in the room of the Indian shrub called Bohea: that they find it to be of so debilitating a quality, and that it produces such a total frigidity in their warmest friends of the other sex, that at a later convention, to deliberate on matters of the greatest consequence, it was agreed, by a majority greater than that of 92 to 17,[2] to rescind their former vote in favor of the detested plant, as being clearly

---

[1] *Ledum Palustre,*   Labrador Tea.

[2] Alluding to the vote on the question of rescinding the resolutions of the House of Representatives.

nconstitutional, and tending to rob us of our dearest privileges and deprive
s of our most sacred and invaluable rights

As the nonconsumption agreement prevented the sale by the merchants of
he obnoxious article, the gardens and fields were laid under contributions to
upply the table urn   The cup was filled with odoriferous infusions of Mint
nd Sage, and those who ventured to acknowledge the abstract right of tax-
tion, by the use of tea indulged in the luxury, as if they were committing
rime, with the utmost secresy, drawing bolt and bar, and closing every crev-
~e which might betray the fragrance of the proscribed beverage

From this period to 1773, no doings of the inhabitants in their corporate
apacity mark the progress of the spirit of independence   The influence of
he loyalists prevented public expression of the high-toned patriotism radi-
ted from the metropolis to every village, and growing day by day more fervid
nd intense

A petition of Othniel Taylor and forty others, called the attention of the
own, at the annual meeting in March, 1773, to the grievances under which
he province labored   After debate, the celebrated Boston Pamphlet was
ead   A committee was appointed[1] to consider its contents, who presented
n elaborate report at the adjournment in May following   Going back to the
oundation of civil society, they deduce the principles, that mankind are by
ature free, and that the end and design of forming the social compact was,
hat each member of the state might enjoy liberty and property, and the
nrestrained exercise of civil and religious rights   Tracing the history of
he pilgrims, they derive illustrations of the sacredness of the charter,
lighted by loyal faith   Appealing to the long series of services rendered by
he province as testimonials of fidelity, they declare, ' the fond affection that
ver has subsisted in our hearts for Great Britain and its sovereign, has ever
nduced us, to esteem it above any other country, and as fond children speak
f a father's house we have ever called it our home, and always [have been
eady to] rejoice, when they rejoiced, to weep when they have wept, and
vhenever required, to bleed when they have bled, and in return, we are
orry to say, we have had our harbors filled with ships of war, in a hostile
nanner, and troops posted in our metropolis, in a time of profound peace ·
ot only posted [in a manner] greatly insulting, but actually slaughtering the
nhabitants   cannon levelled against our senate house, the fortress or key of
he province taken from us. and as an addition to our distress, the com-
nander in chief of the province [has declared] he had not power to control
he troops, &c   Nevertheless we are ready and willing to stand forth in
lefence of the king of Great Britain, his crown and dignity, and our noble
·onstitution, and, when called to it, risk our lives, and in that day let him
hat hath no sword, sell his garment and buy one '

It was recommended ' that there be a committee of correspondence chosen,
o correspond with the committees of correspondence in the other towns in
his province, to give the earliest intelligence to the inhabitants of this town,

---

[1] William Young, David Bancroft, Samuel Curtis, Timothy Bigelow, Stephen Salisbury

of any designs that they shall discover, at any time, against our natural and constitutional rights.'

The recommendations of the report were adopted, and William Young, Timothy Bigelow, and John Smith, were elected a committee of correspondence.

The spirit of discontent, repressed in public, was actively working in the minds of men, and the doctrine of resistance, branded by one party as the theory of treason, preparing the way for events the brightest of history. In the peculiar situation of the town, an efficient and firm union among the friends of freedom was necessary. On the 27th of December, 1773, the leading whigs assembled, and formed a Society, which became a powerful instrument of revolutionary action, directing the proceedings of the town, and extending a controling influence to some of its neighbors. Its organization and doings, illustrative of the feeling of the times and the mode of political operation, are worthy of extended notice.

The constitution and rules of proceeding, reported by Nathan Baldwin, Samuel Curtis and Timothy Bigelow, exhibit the purposes of the association. The former recites, ' that at the then present time the good people of the county, and with respect to some particular circumstances, the town of Worcester especially, labor under many impositions and burdens grievous to be borne, which, it is apprehended, could never have been imposed upon us had we been united and opposed the machinations of some designing persons in this province, who are grasping at power and the property of their neighbors : for preventing these evils and better securing liberty and property, and counteracting the designs of enemies, the associates incorporate themselves into a society, by the name of The American Political Society, to meet at some public house, at least once in every other month, to advise with each other on proper methods to be pursued respecting common rights and liberties, civil and religious.' The members covenanted, that no discourse or transaction in any of the meetings should be communicated to any person without common consent ; that they would avoid all lawsuits as much as possible, and particularly with each other : and if differences should arise between members, which they were unable to adjust, they should be referred to the determination of the society ; that each would, as he had opportunity, promote the interest of the other, in all honest ways within his power, without injury to himself ; and that each member would give information in the meetings; of any infringement of the common rights of mankind which might come to his knowledge. Penalties were established for absence, provision made for regular monthly meetings, the elections, admissions, and order of debate, usual in similar associations. It is expressed, ' that each particular member, reposing special trust and confidence in every other member of the society, looks upon himself bound, and does bind himself, by the ties of honor, virtue, truth, sincerity, and every appellation dear to him in this life, faithfully and truly to keep and perform its articles.' Thirty one persons were original subscribers, and thirty two others were, from time to time, admitted, making the whole number of members during the two years of its existence sixty three.

The objects of the society, as expressed in its constitution, were extensive. The associates, practically, limited their views to the circle of their own corporation, and instead of proceeding in the task of reforming the world, confined their exertions to secure the rights of that portion of mankind in their own neighborhood   They erected themselves into a supreme authority, not only assuming advisory superintendence of local concerns, but claiming to direct in absolute terms   Sessions were held previous to the meetings of the inhabitants, and votes passed, afterwards confirmed by the town   To show how important was their agency, it will be necessary to anticipate the regular progress of the narrative, to examine their records

The first debate, Feb 4, 1774, was had on the impropriety of choosing any person to office, who was not an open and professed friend to constitutional liberty   Feb 25, the business of the society was, to agree on a plan of proceedings for March meeting   In April, it was voted ' that the chairman of the committee of correspondence be directed to send circular letters to the committees of correspondence in the several towns in the county, advising them that the votes for County Treasurer had not been counted by the Court of Sessions of the Peace, as had been usual, and of the danger consequent thereon, that the whole people of the county may be on their guard against fraud and deception '   A committee was appointed to prepare instructions for the representative to be chosen in May following

Among the boldest of its acts, was its instruction to the Grand Jurors to refuse being sworn if Judge Oliver was present at the Superior Court in April

The act of parliament for raising revenues, by taxation of the colonies, authorized appropriations from them, for the salaries of the judges of the Superior Court, rendering the judicial officers dependants of the crown   The Governor had refused his assent to legislative grants for their support, and the Representatives remonstrated with spirit, against the invasion of charter rights   After ineffectual negociations with Mr Hutchinson, the inflexible assertor of loyal prerogative, at the termination of the first session of 1773, it was resolved ' that any of the judges, who, while they hold their offices during pleasure, shall accept support from the crown, independent of the grants of the General Court, will discover, that he is an enemy to the constitution, and has it in his heart to promote the establishment of arbitrary government.'   In Feb 1774, four of the judges, Trowbridge, Hutchinson, Ropes, and Cushing, on the appeal being made by the Assembly, replied that they had received no part of the allowance from the king, which was deemed satisfactory   Chief Justice Oliver alone, dared to brave popular sentiment, and answered that he had accepted his Majesty's bounty, and could not refuse it in future, without royal permission.   The concentrated weight of indignation fell upon him.   The House immediately voted that he had rendered himself obnoxious to the people as an enemy of the constitution   A petition was presented for his removal, and articles of impeachment for high crimes and misdemeanors exhibited, which the Governor refused to countenance

Such was the relation of Peter Oliver to the people, when the term of the

7*

Superior Court for the county of Worcester drew near. The political society, as guardians of popular rights, took the subject into consideration. After much treasonable debate, as the expression of opinions which would have endangered life, might be termed by those who could have claimed its forfeiture, the determination was expressed in the following vote, unanimously adopted, April 4.

'This society will each one bear and pay their equal part of the fine and charges that may be laid on Messrs. Joshua Bigelow and Timothy Bigelow, for their refusal to be empanneled upon the Grand Jury at our next Superior Court of Assize, for the county of Worcester, if they shall be chosen into that office, and their refusal is founded upon the principle, that they cannot, consistently with good conscience and order, serve, if Peter Oliver, Esq., is present on the bench as chief justice, or judge of said court, before he is lawfully tried and acquitted from the high crimes and charges for which he now stands impeached by the honorable House of Representatives, and the major part of the grand jurors for the whole county join them in refusing to serve for the reasons aforesaid.'

So little apprehension was entertained of the concurrence of their fellows, or of the return of the two gentlemen named, that they were provided with a remonstrance for presentation to the court. The exact circumstances, modestly designated as contingent and conditional, were made certain by the influence and exertions of the society. Messrs. Joshua Bigelow and Timothy Bigelow *were* chosen, and the majority of the jurors *did* join with them at the opening of the court in offering this paper, April 19, 1774.

' To the honorable, his majesty's justices of the Superior Court of Judicature now sitting at Worcester, in and for said county.

We, the subscribers, being returned by our respective towns to serve as jurors of inquest for this court, beg leave humbly to inform your honors, that it is agreeable to the sense of those we represent, that we should not empannel, or be sworn into this important office, provided Peter Oliver, Esq., sits as chief justice of this court; and we would further add, that our own sentiments coincide perfectly with those of our constituents respecting this matter; so, to whatever inconvenience we expose ourselves, we are firmly resolved not to empannel, unless we are first assured that the above gentleman will not act as a judge in this court, for the following reasons:

1. Because the honorable House of Commons of this province, at their last session, among other things, resolved, that Peter Oliver, Esq., hath, by his conduct, rendered himself totally disqualified any longer to hold and act in the office of a justice of this court, and ought, forthwith, to be removed therefrom.

2. Because the House of Commons, in their said session, did impeach the said Peter Oliver, Esq., of high crimes and misdemeanors; the particulars of which impeachment, we apprehend, are known to your honors, which will excuse us from reciting them at large; to which impeachment the said Peter Oliver, Esq., hath not been yet brought to answer; and therefore, we apprehend, that the veniri bearing test, Peter Oliver, Esq., is illegal.

But, if we should be mistaken, nevertheless, we remonstrate and protest, against the said Peter Oliver. Esq , acting as judge on any of the bills we may find at this session, unless he is constitutionally acquitted of said impeachment because, we apprehend it would be highly injurious, to subject a fellow countryman to trial at a bar, where one of the judges is not only disqualified as aforesaid, but, by his own confession, stands convicted, in the minds of the people, of a crime more heinous, in all probability, than any that might come before him   These, with other reasons that might be offered, we hope your honors will esteem sufficient to justify us for presenting the foregoing remonstrance '

Joshua Bigelow,	John Fuller,	William Henshaw,
Thomas Robinson,	John Tyler,	Nathaniel Carrel,
Phinehas Heywood,	Daniel Clapp,	Moses Livermore,
Nathan Walker,	Silas Bayley,	Timothy Bigelow,
Ephraim Doolittle,	John Sherman,	William Campbell

After consultation, this paper was received by the court, and publicly read by the clerk   One of the judges then informed the jurors, that it was altogether improbable that the Chief Justice would attend to take his seat [1] and being assured that the sheriff had, as usual, been a number of miles out of town, in order to meet and escort him to his lodgings, and had returned without him, the jurors retired to determine what course to pursue   On considering the personal and public inconvenience resulting from their refusal to proceed to business, and finding no sacrifice of principle from compliance, they returned, were sworn, and received the charge.

[1] Judge Oliver, in a letter to Gov Hutchinson, May 15, 1774, published in Edes' Gazette, Sept. 18, 1775, expresses his anger at the conduct of his associates of the bench in strong terms

' As to the affair of the Grand Jury's libel at Worcester court, I did not know of their conduct until I saw it in the newspapers; and had any of my brethren charged in so infamous a manner, I would forever have quitted the bench rather than have suffered such indignity to them to have passed unnoticed   How it is possible to let a brother judge, a friend, or even a brute, be treated in so ignominious a manner, I have no conception in my ideas of humanity. But so it is   and if the Supreme Court is content with such rudeness, inferior jurisdictions are to be exculpated in suffering the commonwealth to be destroyed '

Oliver sought consolation under popular odium, from the sympathy of the representative of the king without communicating to his associates the indignation breathing in his letter   The existence of this document seems to have remained unknown to his judicial brethren, long after the publication   Judge Trowbridge in a letter to the late Levi Lincoln Dec 27, 1780, says, ' this letter was wrote by Chief Justice Oliver, as I suppose, to the governor, at the castle , and the court referred to, must be the Superior Court at Worcester, on the third Tuesday of September, 1773 , for the chief justice was not at that court   I don't know that I ever saw what he calls the libel. I can't find it in Edes & Gill's Gazette printed that year, and therefore conclude it was published in the Spy, soon after the court   I hear Mr Thomas lives in Worcester, and suppose he has those papers by him. If you would be kind enough to know of him, if he printed the account of the proceeding which, I suppose, the judge calls a libel, and favor me with a copy thereof, you will much oblige me

' I was at Judge Oliver's house, on May 15, 1774, (the day of the date of his letter) but he never said a word to me about that matter, as I remember ; which I think he might have done, before he wrote that letter to the governor '

It is said to have been resolved by the Society, that they would rescue the jurors by force, if they should be committed for contempt, in presenting the chief justice to the court as a criminal. No written evidence of such purpose can be supposed to exist, and the removal of the difficulty, threatening interruption of the administration of justice, fortunately prevented more solemn testimony from being furnished.

At the monthly meeting in June, it was voted to sign a covenant, not to purchase any English goods, until the port of Boston was opened, and to discontinue intercourse with those declining to subscribe. A committee was appointed to prepare an instrument for this purpose, and obtain the signatures of the citizens, and to draft a similar agreement to be signed by the women.

In August, it was voted, 'that Nathan Perry be moderator of our next town meeting, if he should be chosen : in case he should refuse, then Josiah Pierce shall preside.'

The selectmen were directed, forthwith, to examine the town's stock of ammunition, and ascertain its quality and quantity.

A committee was chosen to present to the inhabitants an obligation to be completely armed, and to enforce its execution.

Sept. 5. A committee was commissioned ' to inspect the tories going to and coming from Lancaster, or any other way,' and it was subsequently entered of record, that it was contrary to the mind of the society that the tories should vote in town meeting.

Oct. 3. The instructions to be reported at the next town meeting for the representatives in the Provincial Congress and General Court, were read, paragraph by paragraph, and accepted.

A respectable merchant of the town was summoned before the association, to exhibit the certificate of an oath not to purchase English goods, made by Artemas Ward, Esq., afterwards General in the Continental Army. The form not being considered satisfactory, a new oath was required and taken.

We have traced the society far enough in the detail of its acts, to show the control it assumed and exercised over committees of correspondence, the grand jury, the town, its selectmen and citizens.

Its career is interesting, as indicating the spring by whose impulse the complex machinery was moved, and as illustrative of the manner in which the government of opinion acted on the people, when the authority of the established officers tottered, the tribunals of justice were silent, and self-constituted magistracies took the guardianship of the general welfare, and the lead in the municipal republics.

It remains only to notice the dissolution of this remarkable body. Many of the members having been called into the military service of the country, much of its energy was lost. In 1776, it is stated, that unhappy differences had arisen and divisions grown up in the town. It was voted, to institute an enquiry into their origin, and endeavor to suppress contention and reestablish harmony. Each member was desired to give intelligence of misbehavior, and answer truly and fully to any question proposed by a committee, formed from both parties, to investigate the causes of the difficulty. It was resolved,

' that the society, in its corporate capacity, should pass no votes relative to the choice of town or public officers, or for the management of town meetings, until a report was made and acted on '

The committee, composed of discordant materials, was unable to effect a compromise The last meetings of the Society appear to have been passed in unavailing struggles to prolong its existence, in jealous rivalship of the committees of correspondence and safety, who had wrested away its power, and in stormy discussion of the deviations from the original principles of its constitution. It lingered until the first Monday of June, 1776, when, by mutual consent, it was suffered to expire, after a life of two years and a half.

The struggle between the patriotism of the people and the loyalty of a minority, powerful in numbers, as well as in talents, wealth and influence, arrived to its crisis in this town early in 1774, and terminated in the total defeat of the adherents of the king

At the annual meeting, March 7, a committee[1] was formed, to take into consideration the acts of the British Parliament for raising revenue from the colonies, who soon presented the following report, matured by the Society, whose acts we have noticed, which was accepted.

' We, the freeholders and inhabitants of Worcester, think it our duty, at this important time, when affairs of the greatest consequence to ourselves and posterity are hastening to a crisis, after due consideration, to offer our sentiments on the many grievous impositions, which are laid upon us we would particularize some of the most intolerable ones, viz

' 1 Courts of Admiralty, wherein that most inestimable privilege, trial by jury, is destroyed Boards of commissioners, with their numerous trains of dependents, which departments are generally filled with those who have proved themselves to be destitute of honor, honesty, or the common feelings of humanity , those who are known to be the greatest enemies of the people and constitution of this country, even those who have murdered its inhabitants For a recent instance of their consummate insolence, and of their barbarously harassing the subject from port to port, at the expense of time and money, and unjustly detaining property, we would mention the case of Capt Walker, commander of the Brigantine Brothers

' 2 The Governor and Judges of the Superior Court, rendered independent of the people of the province, for whose good only they were appointed, for which service they ought to depend on those they serve for pay and, we are constrained to say, that to have these who are to determine and judge on our lives [and] property paid by a foreign state, immediately destroys that natural dependence which ought to subsist between a people and their officers, and [is,] of course, destructive of liberty. For which reason, we are of opinion, that we [are] not in the least bound in duty submit to the ordering and determining of such officers as are not dependent on the grants of the people for their pay, and we have the satisfaction to hear that four of the superior judges, to their immortal honor, have refused the bribe offered them.

[1] William Young, Josiah Pierce, Timothy Bigelow.

' But, as we have had an opportunity heretofore, jointly, to express our minds respecting our many grievances, we, principally, shall confine our observations to the East India company's exporting teas to America, subject to a duty laid thereon by the British Parliament, to be paid by us, not so much as mentioned for the regulation of trade, but for the sole purpose of raising a revenue : in consequence of which, we take it upon us to say, that it is an addition to the many proofs, that the British ministry are determined, if possible, to enslave us : but, we rest assured, that however attached we may have been to that truly detestable herb, we can firmly resist the charm, and thereby convince our enemies in Great Britain and America, that however artful and alluring their snares, and gilded the bait, we have wisdom to foresee and virtue to resist.

' Therefore, resolved ; that we will not buy, sell, use, or any way be concerned with India teas of any kind, dutied or undutied, imported from Great Britain, Holland, or elsewhere, until the unrighteous act imposing a duty thereon be repealed ; the former on account of the aforesaid duty ; the latter, because we still maintain such a regard for Great Britain as to be unwilling to promote the interests of a rival.

' Resolved ; that we will break off all commercial intercourse with those persons, if any there should be, in this or any other place, who should act counter to these, our resolutions, thus publicly made known : that the tea consignees, and all those that have been aiding or assisting in introducing the East India company's tea among us, have justly merited our indignation and contempt, and must be considered, and treated by us, as enemies and traitors to their country : that we contemptuously abhor and detest all those, whether in Great Britain or America, that are not content with their own honest industry, but contrary to known principles of justice and equity, attempt to take the property of others in any wise without their consent.

' Resolved ; that we have an indisputable right, at this time, and at all times, boldly to assert our rights, and make known our grievances ; being sensible that the freedom of speech and security of property always go together. None but the base tyrant and his wicked tools dread this liberty. Upright measures will always defend themselves. It is not only our indubitable right, but a requisite duty, in this legal and public manner, to make known our grievances. Amongst the many benefits that will naturally result therefrom, [will be] we hope, that important one of undeceiving our gracious sovereign, who from the wicked measures practiced against us, we have just reason to suppose, has been artfully deluded ; in defence of whose sacred person, crown and dignity, together with our natural and constitutional rights, we are ready, at all times, boldly to risk our lives and fortunes.'

Twenty-six of the royalists dissented from these resolutions, and their protest was entered of record, although rejected by the town.

Mr. Joshua Bigelow was chosen representative, with the following instructions,[1] May 20, 1774.

[1] The committee who reported these instructions, were Josiah Pierce, Timothy Bigelow,

'As English America is in a general alarm, in consequence of some late unconstitutional stretches of power, we are sensible this is the most difficult period that hath ever yet commenced since the first arrival of our ancestors into this then unexplored, uncultivated and inhospitable wilderness. and being fully sensible that the wisest head, uprightest heart, and the firmest resolution, are the necessary qualifications of the person fit and suitable to represent us in the Great and General Court of this Province the present year, [we] have honored you with our suffrages for that important office Notwithstanding our confidence in your virtue and abilities, we think it necessary to prescribe some certain rules for your conduct And first as there is a late act of the British Parliament, to be enforced in America, with troops and ships of war [on] the first [day] of June, in order to stop the port and harbor of Boston, thereby depriving us of the winds and seas, which God and nature gave in common to mankind, we are induced to believe that [the ministers] of Great Britain, through misinformation, are led to a prostitution of that power which has heretofore made Europe tremble, to abridge us, their brethren in this province, of our natural and civil rights, notwithstanding, exclusive of our natural rights, we had all the privileges and immunities of Englishmen confirmed to us by our loyal charter And as we view this hostile manoeuvre of Great Britain as a blow aimed, through Boston, at the whole of American liberties, being emboldened through a consciousness of the justice of our cause, we, in the most solemn manner, direct you, that whatever measure Great Britain may take to distress us, you be not in the least intimidated, and thereby induced, that whatever requisitions, or ministerial mandate there may be, in order to subject us to any unconstitutional acts of the British Parliament, to comply therewith But to the utmost of your power, resist the most distant approaches of slavery But more particularly, should the people of this province, through their representatives, be required to compensate the East India company for the loss of their tea, we hereby lay the strictest injunction on you not to comply therewith As the destruction of the tea was not a public act, we cannot see the justice of a public demand As the civil law is open to punish the offenders, we rather think, instead of an equitable compensation, it would be the means of encouraging riots and robberies, and, of consequence, render the courts of justice of no use

'We also earnestly require that a strict union of the colonies be one of the first objects in your view, and that you carefully and immediately pursue every legal measure that may tend thereto ; viz. that committees of corespondence be kept up between the several houses of assembly through the colonies , and that you by no means fail to use your utmost endeavors, that there be a general Congress formed of deputies from the same : that so we may unite in some safe and sure plan, to secure and defend the American liberties, at this important crisis of affairs.

'Also we direct you, as soon as may be, to endeavor that Peter Oliver,

Stephen Salisbury, Samuel Curtis, Edward Crafts, John Kelso, and Joshua Whitney. They had been prepared by Mr. Nathan Baldwin, the ablest writer of the party here, and matured by the political society.

Esq. be brought to answer to the impeachment against him, preferred by the Representatives of this province, in the name of the whole people.

'There are a number of other matters respecting the internal policy of this province, that, in our opinion, at this season, require the attention of the legislator: but, at a time like this, when Britain in return for the blood we have, on every needful occasion, so freely shed in her cause, has reduced thousands, through a wanton exercise of power, in our metropolis, to the most [distressing] circumstances, which, at first view, is sufficient to excite in the human breast every tender and compassionate feeling, [this] is enough to engross your whole attention. Should other matters come under your consideration in the course of the present year, relative to the common and ordinary exigencies of government, we make not the least doubt, you will, on your part, make the peace and prosperity of the whole province your ultimate aim and end, and by that means honor yourself and us, your constituents, in the choice we have made.'

Language so strong and decided, could not but be offensive to the royalists. The acceptance was strenuously opposed; Col. Putnam, the distinguished counsellor, exerting the whole force of his eloquence to prevent the cooperation of the town in acts of rebellion, but without success. Thus defeated, measures were taken to procure the reconsideration of the votes. A petition, signed by 43 freeholders, was presented to the selectmen, requesting them to issue their warrant for a meeting, in the expectation, by concentrating the whole strength of the opposition, that the early efforts of freedom could be crushed.

A meeting called in conformity with the prayer of the petition, which is recited at length in the warrant of the selectmen, was held on the 20th of June. After long and violent debate, the whigs prevailed, and it was voted not to act, in any manner, on any of the matters contained in the petition. Nothing remained to the defeated party but the right of protesting. A spirited and most loyal paper was offered and refused. The Town Clerk, influenced more by feeling than prudence, entered a copy on the records, afterwards sent to Boston for publication. This production is one of the boldest and most indignant remonstrances of the friends of royal government among the productions of the time. It is inserted in the Boston Gazette, printed on the 4th of July, 1774. The entry on the record was afterwards entirely obliterated.

'At a meeting of the inhabitants of the town of Worcester, held there on the 20th day of June, A. D. 1774, pursuant to an application made to the selectmen by 43 voters and freeholders of the same town, dated the 20th day of May last, therein, among other things, declaring their just apprehensions of the fatal consequences that may follow the many riotous and seditious actions that have of late times been done and perpetrated in divers places within this province: the votes and proceedings of which meeting are by us deemed irregular and arbitrary:

'Wherefore we, some of us who were petitioners for the said meeting, and others inhabitants of the town, hereunto subscribing, thinking it our indispensable duty, in these times of discord and confusion in too many of the towns within this province, to bear testimony in the most open and unreserved manner against all riotous, disorderly and seditious practices, must therefore now declare, that it is with the deepest concern for public peace and order that we behold so many, whom we used to esteem sober, peaceable men, so far deceived, deluded and led astray by the artful, crafty and insidious practices of some evil-minded and ill-disposed persons, who, under the disguise of patriotism, and falsely styling themselves the friends of liberty, some of them neglecting their own proper business and occupation, in which they ought to be employed for the support of their families, spending their time in discoursing of matters they do not understand, raising and propagating falsehoods and calumnies of those men they look up to with envy, and on whose fall and ruin they wish to rise, intend to reduce all things to a state of tumult, discord and confusion

'And in pursuance of those evil purposes and practices, they have imposed on the understanding of some, corrupted the principles of others, and distracted the minds of many, who, under the influence of this delusion, have been tempted to act a part that may prove, and that has already proved, extremely prejudicial to the province, and as it may be, fatal to themselves, bringing into real danger, and in many instances destroying, that liberty and property we all hold sacred, and which they vainly and impiously boast of defending at the expense of their blood and treasure

'And, as it appears to us, that many of this town seem to be led aside by strange opinions, and are prevented coming to such prudent votes and resolutions as might be for the general good and the advantage of this town in particular, agreeably to the request of the petitioners for this meeting :

'And as the town has refused to dismiss the persons styling themselves the committee of correspondence for the town, and has also refused so much as to call on them to render an account of their past dark and pernicious proceedings

'We therefore, whose names are hereunto subscribed, do each of us declare and protest, it is our firm opinion, that the committees of correspondence in the several towns of this province, being creatures of modern invention, and constituted as they be, are a legal grievance, having no legal foundation, contrived by a junto to serve particular designs and purposes of their own, and that they, as they have been and are now managed in this town, are a nuisance And we fear, it is in a great measure owing to the baneful influence of such committees, that the teas of immense value, lately belonging to the East India company, were, not long since, scandalously destroyed in Boston, and that many other enormous acts of violence and oppression have been perpetrated, whereby the lives of many honest, worthy persons, have been endangered, and their property destroyed

'It is by these committees also, that papers have been lately published and are now circulating through the province, inviting, and wickedly tempting, all persons to join them, fully implying, if not expressly denouncing the destruc-

8

tion of all that refuse to subscribe those unlawful combinations, tending directly to sedition, civil war, and rebellion

' These, and all such enormities, we detest and abhor   and the authors of
them we esteem enemies to our king and country, violators of all law and
civil liberty. the malevolent disturbers of the peace of society, subverters of
the established constitution, and enemies of mankind '

The whole number of voters of the town at this time could not have exceeded two hundred and fifty   Fifty two inhabitants subscribed the protest
The first intimation received by the whigs, of the existence of sentiments
so loyal, on the same pages with the narrative of their own patriotic declarations, was derived from the publication   Immediately after its appearance,
a petition was presented to the selectmen, describing the protest as a false
and scandalous attack on the inhabitants, the committee, and their doings,
charging the town clerk with a violation of his trust, and requesting them to
convene a meeting to consider the subject   The town assembled on the 22d
of August, and referred the matter to a Committee,[1] to report at the adjournment to the 24th   Before that time, many of the protesters, shrinking from
the violence of the storm they had roused, and under the compulsion of
force, sought safety by submission, and signed penitential confessions of error.
When the people reassembled, the following counter statement and the
accompanying resolutions were adopted

' Whereas, the publication in the Massachusetts Gazette of June 30, was
made, as a protest of the signers of it against the proceedings of the town of
Worcester, and contains in it a number of groundless reflections and aspersions
against the inhabitants of the town, viz : it seems to be implied in the direction to the printer, published at the front of the protest, that the signers were
the only persons in the town who were friends to truth, peace and order, and
that they only were the persons, that had any just apprehensions of the ill
consequences arising by mobs, riots, &c , and that all the rest of the inhabitants acted irregularly and arbitrarily , notwithstanding the matters [voted]
in said meeting were fairly considered . and that they were so destitute of understanding as to be led astray, by evil minded persons, who were endeavoring
to reduce all things to a state of disorder and confusion , thereby making
themselves the sole judges of what is rule and order, and what is not   and
proceed to stigmatize the inhabitants as holding to such bad opinions, as to
prevent the town's acting prudently and for the general good   It is also implied in the publication, that this town allows a number of persons in it, to
assume the character of a committee of correspondence for the town, and to
act darkly and perniciously with impunity, contrary to rule and good order,
and in violation of the truth , after, with unparalleled arrogance, representing
themselves as the only friends to it, [they] assert that the town has refused
to dismiss the persons styling themselves a committee of correspondence for

1 The committee were Joshua Bigelow, Jonas Hubbard, David Bancroft, Samuel Curtis,
Jonathan Stone, Benjamin Flagg, Iosiah Pierce.

the town. when, setting aside the inconsistency of the town's dismissing persons who had arrogated the character of a committee, and consequently [were in fact] not chosen by the town, they well knew that the town had not been requested, either to dismiss persons styling themselves a committee, or those gentlemen so denominated by the town : neither was there an article in the warrant for calling said meeting, to dismiss any persons whatever from office, nor so much as proposed in the meeting   There is also a malignity cast upon committees of correspondence in general through the continent, and in particular against the committee chosen by this town, without any reason assigned for the same but the opinion of the protesters, too slender a foundation to asperse the character of town officers upon, and [they] have endeavored to insinuate into the minds of the public, that the men of which committees of correspondence are composed through the province, are a parcel of unprincipled knaves, who are endeavoring to destroy the lives and property of the peaceable and well-disposed, and also alleging that it is by these committees that papers have been lately published, and [that they have] wickedly tempted all persons to sign them, which they call an unlawful combination, tending directly to civil war and rebellion   This town knows of no such paper if it be the non-consumption agreement, entered and entering into through this and the neighboring provinces, that is pointed at, we take it upon us to say, that we much approve of the same, that if strictly adhered to it will save our money, promote industry, frugality, and our own manufactures, and tend directly to prevent civil war and rebellion.

‘ After offering their opinions of mobs, riots, tumults and disorder, and the proceedings of the town, so cruelly and with such temerity, as shows them to be destitute of that humanity and christian charity which we in all duty owe one to the other, they brand all that do not join with them, with the characters of enemies of the king and country, violators of all law and civil liberty, the malevolent disturbers of society, subverters of the established constitution, and enemies to mankind   And as it appears by the said publication, that the same is recorded in the town book, notwithstanding the many aspersions it contains against the people of this town, and without the liberty or knowledge of the town ; therefore,

‘ Voted, that the town clerk do, in presence of the town, obliterate, erase, or otherwise deface the said recorded protest, and the names thereto subscribed, so that it may become utterly illegible and unintelligible

‘ Voted, that the method taken by the leaders, in protesting, and procuring a very considerable number to sign the protest who are not voters in the town, we think was a piece of low cunning, to deceive the public, and make their party appear more numerous and formidable than it was in reality

‘ Voted, that the signers of said protest, on some of whom the town has conferred many favors, and consequently might expect their kindest and best services, be deemed unworthy of holding any town office or honor, until they have made satisfaction for their offence to the acceptance of the town, which ought to be made as public as the protest was

‘ Voted, that as it is highly needful that those of the signers who have not

made satisfaction as aforesaid, should be known in future: it is therefore necessary that their names should be inserted as follows, viz.

| James Putnam, | Isaac Moore, | Joshua Johnson, |
| William Paine, | John Walker. | |

' Voted, that the following admonition be given to the town clerk:

' Mr. Clark Chandler : Whereas, this town, at their annual meeting in March
last, as well as for several years before, honored you by choosing you for their
clerk, relying on your fidelity, that you would act for the honor of the town,
and find themselves much disappointed, by your conduct in recording on the
town book the scandalous protest of William Elder and others, filled with
falsehood and reflections against the town, we have just reason to fear you was
actuated in the matter by unjustifiable motives, and, at this time, exhort you
to be more circumspect in the execution of [the duties of] your office, and
never give this town the like trouble, of calling a town meeting again on
such an occasion. The town wish to see your behavior such as may restore
you to their former good opinion of you.

' Whereas, the committee of correspondence for this town willingly laid all
their proceedings before the town, when requested, and it thereby appears,
notwithstanding the ungenerous abuse heaped on them by the protesters, that
they have acted with care, diligence and caution, therefore, voted, that the
thanks of this town be given to the committee for their circumspection, and
that they be directed to go on, with their [former] vigilance, in corresponding
with the other committees of the several towns in this province.'

These resolves were directed to be entered on record, and forwarded for publication in the Massachusetts Gazette and Spy. They did not appear in the
latter newsprint till Dec. 8. From an acknowledgment in the paper of Sept.
13, it appears that the recantation of forty-three of the protesters had been
received by the publisher, the late Isaiah Thomas, but was not inserted for
want of room, nor was it afterwards placed in his columns.

In pursuance of this vote, the clerk, in open town meeting, and in the presence of the inhabitants, blotted out the obnoxious record, and the work of the
pen in defacing its own traces not being satisfactory, his fingers were dipped in
ink and drawn over the protest. The pages still remain in the town book, so
utterly illegible as to bear full testimony of the fidelity of the recording officer, in the execution of the singular and unwelcome duty of expunging, thus
imposed upon him.

The selectmen were appointed as a committee, to receive any articles of provisions the inhabitants should contribute, for the poor of the town of Boston.

A committee [1] was raised, to offer the following covenant, for subscription,
to the inhabitants of the town.

' As the distresses of the people loudly call on [all] inhabitants of this
province, to use their utmost efforts to free themselves from that bondage in-

[1] Aug. 22. Jonathan Stone, David Bancroft, Josiah Pierce, Jonathan Rice, David Chadwick.

tended for them by the late acts of the British Parliament, and, as we apprehend, nothing will better conduce to such purpose than the following agreement we, whose names are hereunto subscribed, promise, we will not ourselves, or any for or under us, directly or indirectly, buy or cause to be
bought, and as far as we are able by advice and command, will prevent our
children or servants from buying any article, except drugs and medicines, that
may be imported into this, or any other province or colony on this continent,
that was manufactured, or came from Great Britain or Ireland, or that may
come from thence to the West Indies, or any where else, that may be imported into this, or any other colony or province on the continent, from and after
the first day of September next, nor buy any article made or brought as aforesaid of any person whatsoever, who shall not be furnished with an oath in
writing, taken before a magistrate in the town where they dwell, or that next
adjoining, that the articles shewn were bona fide imported before the said first
day of September . and we, in the same manner as aforesaid, for ourselves,
our children and servants, promise we will not buy of any chapman or pedler
any articles whatever These promises and agreements we religiously promise to observe, in a sacred manner, until the port of Boston shall be opened
as usual, the troops withdrawn, the castle restored, all revenue acts annulled,
all pensions to governors. judges, &c . cease, and in one word, until the liberties of this people are restored, and so secured that every one may have legal
security for the safety of his person and property, and again feel, and be, in
the full enjoyment of those blessings which we are entitled to as men and
those rights and privileges which the charter of this province gives us right to
expect, demand and strive for And to determine when this is done, the majority of the signers then alive shall determine and be the judges '

This paper was not only subscribed, but a solemn oath for its performance
was taken in the following form

'In the presence of the Great God, that Being who liveth forever and ever,
who knoweth the secrets of all hearts, we acknowledge that the agreement
here subscribed is our free act, and solemnly swear that we will, by His grace
assisting us, strictly perform the same, in its true and literal meaning, without any equivocation or mental reservation So help us God.'

Oct 25, A committee of inspection [1] was elected, to examine, from time to
time, the merchants and traders of the town, and prevent their offering for
sale any goods imported or purchased contrary to the spirit and intent of the
'solemn league and covenant,' as it was styled

The system of coercive measures adopted as vindictive expedients for the
punishment of past misdemeanors and the suppression of future opposition,
had roused the free spirit of the country into intense action. The practical
operation of the celebrated bills, following each other in rapid succession, for
the imposition of duties, closing the port of Boston, altering the charter, cre-

---

[1] John Kelso, Nathan Baldwin, Ebenezer Lovell.

8*

ating officers of the crown independent of the people, transporting persons accused for trial, prohibiting town meetings,[1] and vesting the government of the province in the dependents of the king, aggravated the irritation and urged to acts of personal violence. The weight of public indignation fell on those appointed to offices under the new acts, and they were soon compelled to lay aside their obnoxious honors.

Timothy Paine, Esq., had received a commission as one of the mandamus counsellors. High as was the personal regard and respect for the purity of private character of this gentleman, it was controlled by the political feeling of a period of excitement, and measures were taken to compel his resignation of a post, which was unwelcome to himself, but which he dared not refuse, when declining would have been construed as contempt of the authority of the king by whom it was conferred. The committee of correspondence summoned the friends of liberty in the neighboring towns to appear at Worcester, on the 22d of August. Companies, headed by their own officers, marched into the town in military order, but without arms, and formed in lines on the common before 7 o'clock of the morning. When reenforced by our own inhabitants the number exceeded three thousand men. A committee, of two or three persons from each company, was delegated to wait on Mr. Paine and demand his resignation as counsellor. The representatives proceeded to his residence, and easily effected their object. A declaration was prepared and subscribed by him, expressing his sense of obligation to his fellow citizens, reluctance to oppose their wishes, regret for having been qualified for the new office, and a solemn promise that he would never exercise its powers. The committee returned to their constituents, who had moved from the common and extended their lines through Main street, from the court house to the meeting house. The acknowledgment was considered satisfactory: but the confirmation was required in the presence of the whole body. A sub-committee was commissioned to invite Mr. Paine's attendance. Requests from such a source were not to be declined, and he accompanied the gentlemen who delivered the message.

The signers of the protest had been informed by the committee of correspondence, that apology for their opposition would be required from them. Forty three of them had met the evening previous to this visitation at the King's Arms tavern,[2] and having subscribed an acknowledgment of error and repentance, and received an instrument purporting to restore them to favor, and ensuring protection, they had mixed in the crowd. unsuspicious of any act of insult. Those who appeared, were collected by the revolutionary magistrates, and on the arrival of Mr. Paine, were escorted through the ranks, halting at every few paces to listen to the reading of their several confessions

---

[1] The provision was in the Regulating Bill, that no town meetings should be held without permission in writing from the governor or lieutenant governor, after August 1, 1774, except the annual meeting in March, for the election of municipal officers, and that in May, for the choice of representatives. Gordon, i, 250.

[2] This tavern was then kept by Mrs. Sternes, with the royal arms as the sign. It stood on the site of the Worcester House.

of political transgression   Having thus passed in review, and suffered some wanton outrage of feeling, in addition to the humiliation of the procession, they were dismissed

The objects of assembling being accomplished, the majority of the convention disbanded and retired to their homes   A party of about five hundred, with the Worcester committee of correspondence, repaired to Rutland, to ask the resignation of Col. Murray, another of the new council   Before their arrival, they were joined by nearly a thousand men from the western towns A committee visited his house, and being informed of his absence from home, reported the fact   This was voted unsatisfactory, and a most strict search was instituted   After convincing themselves of the truth of the representation made by the family, they addressed a letter to Col Murray, informing him that unless he published the resignation of his office in the Boston newspapers, before the 10th of September, they would wait on him again

Some of the royalists of Worcester, alarmed at these proceedings, and fearful of danger to themselves, when those who had been most respected were treated with indignity, retired to Stone House hill, within the boundary of Holden, with their arms, and made some additions to the natural defences of the situation they selected, which afterwards received the appellation of the Tory Fort   They carried such provisions as could conveniently be collected to this retreat, and derived some supplies from friends, expecting safety from concealment, rather than from capacity to resist storm or seige   They remained two or three weeks in their rocky fortress, when their apprehensions had subsided, they returned

A band of the king's troops having made an excursion by night up the Mystic river, and carried off a quantity of gunpowder deposited in the arsenal in the northwest part of Charlestown, the intelligence spread rapidly through the country, and was magnified as it went, into a report, that the soldiers on the neck had slain the inhabitants, and that the fleet and army were firing on Boston   The effect was electric.   The bells rang out from the spires, beacon fires flamed from the hills· alarm guns echoed through the villages, and the people rose spontaneously on the summons   It is stated in the prints of the day, that before the next sun went down, 6000 men from the county of Worcester were on their way to fight or fall with their countrymen, if need were and the venerable Dr Stiles records in his diary, that the succeeding morning would have shone on an array of 30,000 men, concentrated at the point of supposed danger, had not their movements been countermanded   The alarm reached Worcester in the afternoon   The committee of correspondence immediately despatched messengers with warrants to the military to assemble. The early part of the night was spent in changing pewter platters and leaden window frames into musket bullets, and in preparation for immediate engagement   As soon as these arrangements could be completed, a large company marched, and reached Shrewsbury, before the return of messengers from Boston assured them their further advance was unnecessary

It has been supposed the occasion had been seized to try the temper of the people, and ascertain the extent and strength of the resolution of resistance.

The highways, thronged with citizens bearing such weapons as the enthusiasm of the hour supplied, are described as presenting scenes the counterparts to the display of the military establishment of the Dutch dynasty of New York, so ingeniously delineated by its faithful annalist ' There came men without officers and officers without men, long fowling pieces and short blunderbusses, muskets of all sorts and sizes, some without locks, others without stocks, and many without lock, stock, or barrel ; cartridge boxes, shot belts, powder horns, swords, hatchets, snickersees, crow bars, and broom sticks, all mingled together ' Yet such was the spirit animating the community, that men who had never seen the tents of the enemy, left the plough in the furrow and the sickle in the harvest, and went out, without discipline, equipments, or munitions, to encounter the trained veterans of foreign lands. Ample evidence was afforded of stern determination to meet even the terrible appeal to war, and a pledge was given of the support every town might hope from its neighbors, in extremity

One beneficial result from this excitement, was the admonition of the necessity of better preparation for the result which it was now apparent was hastening On the 4th of July, the Political society had subscribed to purchase two pounds of gunpowder for each of its members: and, in August, had voted a covenant for the signature of each citizen, to bind him to provide arms and ammunition The company of minute men were enrolled, under the command of Capt Timothy Bigelow, and met, each evening, after the labors of the day were past, for drill and martial exercise Muskets were procured for their armament from Boston Four cannon were purchased by the town, secretly conveyed out of the metropolis,[1] and mounted at an expense of £38 A train of artillery was organized under Capt. Edward Crafts.

The purity of the administration of justice having been corrupted by the act of Parliament, it was resolved that its tribunals should be suspended A body of about six thousand men assembled on the invitation of the committee of correspondence, on the 6th of September, and blocked up the passage to the Court House The Justices of the Inferior Court of Common Pleas were compelled to make a declaration in writing, that they would not attempt to exercise their authority, or appear officially, in opposition to the will of the people The Court, thus interrupted, never resumed the exercise of its functions A term was commenced, but immediately adjourned, without transacting business. No trials were had, or judgments rendered, until July, 1776, when the courts were again opened under the new government

A convention of all the committees of correspondence, was held in Worcester, on the 21st day of September This assembly assumed legislative powers, and in the interregnum of royal prerogative and constitutional authority, its orders were obeyed as laws

The first object which engaged the attention of this county congress, in

---

[1] £2 12s. 10d were voted to Mr Jonathan Rice, for his trouble and expenses in getting these cannon out of Boston ; £2 to Jonathan Stone for similar services to Edward Knight, £1 6s. 8d , and to William Dana and Samuel Whitney, £1 13s 4d. each, for transportation from Brookline

onsidering the situation of public affairs, and devising measures for the com-
ion safety, was the organization of the militia   It was voted and recom-
iended, that all subordinate officers surrender up the commissions given by the
oyal governors, to their colonels, and those of higher rank publish their
esignations in the newspapers.   A new arrangement of the military force was
irected to be made, by division into regiments   the first, to include Worces-
r, Leicester, Holden, Spencer and Paxton , the primary elections of com-
any officers to be made by the soldiers   and those who should be chosen in
us manner, to meet and designate the regimental staff.   One third of the
en, able to do duty, between the ages of eighteen and sixty, were to be en-
illed, formed into companies, and be ready to march at a *minute's* warning,
id committees were to be elected to supply their wants should they be
lled to service.

A standing committee of correspondence of the convention was formed, by
e union of the committees of Worcester and Leicester, and the addition of
homas Denny, Joseph Henshaw, and Joshua Bigelow, and authorized to call
eetings, communicate with towns in the county, and persons abroad, and
esent subjects for consideration

Civil officers holding commissions in June, were directed to continue in the
scharge of their duties, excepting Timothy Ruggles, John Murray, and
mes Putnam.

It was voted, ' as the opinion of this body, that the sheriff do adjourn the
iperior Court to be held this day, and that he retain such as are or may be
mmitted as criminals in his custody, until they have a trial '

' Resolved   That as the ordinary courts of justice will be stayed, in conse-
ience of the late arbitrary and oppressive acts of the British parliament, we
uld earnestly recommend to every inhabitant of this county, to pay his just
bts as soon as possible, without dispute or litigation , and if any disputes
nceining debts or trespasses should arise, which cannot be settled by the
rties, we recommend it to them, to submit all such causes to arbitration ,
d if the parties, or either of them, shall refuse to do so, they ought to be
nsidered as cooperating with the enemies of the country '

It was recommended to the several towns, to instruct their representatives,
refuse to be sworn by any officers except such as were constitutionally
pointed , to decline acting with any others not conforming to the charter :
d not to attend at Boston, while garrisoned with troops and invested by
ets · but should any thing prevent their acting with a governor and council
pointed according to the charter, to repair to the town of Concord, and
ere join in a provincial Congress

The towns were requested to provide and mount field pieces, obtain proper
imunition, and put themselves in a posture of defence   Sheriff Chandler[1]
d presented an address from the Justices of the Court of Common Pleas,
its June session, congratulating Gen Gage on his appointment as first

The Court appointed Hon Timothy Ruggles, John Chandler, Esq , James Putnam,
el Willard, and Gardner Chandler, Esq'rs to wait upon His Excellency Gen. Gage, and
esent this Address   It was delivered however by the Sheriff.

magistrate of the province, lamenting the disturbed condition of the times, bearing testimony against all riots, combinations, and unwarrantable resolves, denouncing the circulation of inflammatory papers by order of certain persons, calling themselves a committee of correspondence for the town of Worcester, which they represent as stimulating the people to break off all connections with Great Britain, and having a tendency to alienate the affections of the people from the mother country, and to create discord and confusion, concluding with the assurance of their exertions to discountenance such proceedings, to support the execution of the laws, and render the administration successful and prosperous   The convention voted, ' to take notice of Mr. Sheriff Chandler, for carrying an address to Gov Gage,' and appointed a committee to wait on him and require his attendance   That gentleman presented himself before this remarkable body, whose jurisdiction seemed supreme, and with some hesitation subscribed the following declaration

' Whereas, the convention of committees have expressed their uneasiness to the sheriff of this county, now present before them, for presenting, with others, an address to Gov Gage, he frankly declares it was precipitately done by him · that he is sorry for it, and disclaims an intention to do anything against the minds of the inhabitants of this county, and had he known it would have given offence, he would not have presented that address

Gardner Chandler.'

A copy of the resolves of the convention, certified by the clerk, Col. William Henshaw, was published in the Massachusetts Spy [1]

Resolutions adopted at an earlier session were copied into the London Journals, as evidence of the feelings of the people   The editor subjoined the significant inquiries, ' doth this look like submission ? doth it carry the face of acquiescence ? '

The royalist party had long before been prostrated in this town. Most of the protesters had been induced to make submission. Some who refused, were waylaid and cruelly beaten   A few remained obstinate, and finally retired into exile   Others, unable to separate themselves from their friends and country, and to sacrifice all they held dear, were persecuted into compliance with the public will, and at length purchased safety for person and property by soliciting forgiveness in terms more humiliating in proportion to

---

[1] From the Massachusetts Spy of Sept 15. ' We have received from Worcester, the recantation of John Chandler, Esq, and forty two others of the protesters against the proceedings of that town, which gave such just cause of offence to the public, as also the acknowledgment of six justices of that county, for having aspersed the people in an address to Gen Gage. Want of room prevents their being inserted in this paper '

These recantations were extorted by a force too powerful to admit of refusal   Resistance would have been martyrdom.

Some of the confessions, published in the prints of the day, are expressed with ludicrous energy   For example

' Whereas, I, the subscriber, signed an address to the late Gov Hutchinson, I wish the Devil had had said address before I had seen it   Marblehead, Oct 24, 1774

John Prentice.'

the time it was deferred   The records of the town afford a specimen, Oct 5, 1774, of the self abasement of these tardy 'recantations '

'To the inhabitants of the town of Worcester   Gentlemen . Whereas, I, the subscriber, with a number of others, signed a protest, against the proceedings of the town, and the same was published in the Boston Gazette of June last, wherein the inhabitants were unjustly reflected upon in general, and also the whole body of committees of correspondence throughout this whole province, for which I am heartily sorry, and ask the forgiveness of all the inhabitants of the town, and the justly offended public, and also for any other offence that I may have given by any means, whether in word or action   I heartily request your acceptance of this sincere acknowledgment, and that if either of the inhabitants hath any other charge against me, for any particular of my conduct, that he would make it known, that I may have an opportunity of giving christian satisfaction, which I ever shall stand ready to afford   Witness my hand   William Campbell '

Joshua Bigelow was elected, Oct 1, representative to the General Court, to be held in Salem, and Timothy Bigelow delegate to the provincial Congress, to assemble at Concord   The former was directed, not to recede from the most rigid virtue in recovering and defending the rights and liberties of the people , to refuse to be sworn by any officer not appointed according to the charter, or to act with any branch of the legislature not constituted and supported in conformity with its provisions   to decline attending in Boston, while it should be invested with armies and fleets , and if prevented from acting with a constitutional Governor and Council, to repair to Concord, and join the provincial Congress   The instructions to the latter, require, that he should endeavor, in the most peaceable manner, to obtain redress of grievances ; to procure the opening of the port of Boston , restoration of free trade , removal of the king's troops , resignation of the command of the fortress at the south end of Boston, prohibition from erecting entrenchments by the royal forces , restitution of the military stores forcibly taken from the arsenals and magazines , the resignation of the mandamus counsellors, or their impeachment as traitors   the mission of an agent to Canada to treat with its inhabitants, and express grateful recognition of friendly donations ; and the appointment of a commander-in-chief for the whole militia.   Strict observance of the advice of the Continental Congress was enjoined

It is said, 'If all infractions of our rights, by acts of the British Parliament, be not redressed, and we restored to the full enjoyment of all our privileges, contained in the charter of this province, granted by their late majesties, King William and Queen Mary, *to a punctilio*, before the day of your meeting, then, and in that case, you are to consider the people of this province as absolved, on their part, from the obligation therein contained, and to all intents and purposes reduced to a state of nature   and you are to exert yourself in devising ways and means to raise from the dissolution of the old constitution, as from the ashes of the Phenix, a new form, wherein all officers shall be dependent on the suffrages of the people for their existence as such, whatever unfavorable constructions our enemies may put upon such procedure. The exigency of our public affairs leaves us no other alternative from a state of anarchy or slavery.' [1]

A more explicit declaration of independence can scarcely be found in the splendid document, which in 1776, in more glowing words proclaimed the dissolution of all ties of colonial relation.

Gov. Gage, alarmed by the spirit of the instructions, and the stormy aspect of the times, issued his proclamation, Sept. 28, declaring, that it was expedient, the session of the General Court summoned for the fifth of October, should not then be held; discharging the members from attendance at that time; and announcing his intention not to meet the assembly. The current of popular feeling was not thus to be diverted. The representatives elect convened at Salem, resolved themselves into a provincial Congress, elected John Hancock, President, and Benjamin Lincoln, Secretary, and immediately adjourned to Concord.

The Committee of Worcester county waited on Gen. Gage, Oct. 20, and presented a well-written remonstrance against the oppressive acts of the ministry, to which, they say, ' this people are determined, by the Divine favor, never to submit, but with their lives ' The military governor returned a very brief and unsatisfactory answer.

The patriotic resistance of invasions of liberty was not confined to municipal corporations or general assemblies of citizens. The fervid enthusiasm, pervading the whole fabric of society, manifested itself in varied forms. Meetings of artisans and craftsmen, as distinct bodies, were held, and spirited resolutions adopted. One specimen, selected from many, will afford example of their proceedings.

A convention of the Blacksmiths of the County, was held at Worcester, Sept. 8, and continued by adjournment to Nov. 8, 1774. Ross Wyman, of Shrewsbury, presided, and Timothy Bigelow, of Worcester, was clerk. The result of their session, subscribed by forty three members, was widely distributed in handbills. It was as follows:

' Whereas, at a meeting of the delegates from the counties of Worcester, Middlesex and Essex, with the committee of correspondence of the town of Boston, in behalf of the county of Suffolk, holden at Boston, the 26th day of August, 1774, it was resolved: That all such officers or private persons as have given sufficient proof of their enmity to the people and constitution of this country, should be held in contempt, and that those who are connected with them ought to separate from them; laborers to shun their vineyards, merchants, husbandmen and others to withhold their commerce and supplies:

' In compliance, therefore, to a resolution of so respectable a body as aforesaid, so reasonable in its contents, and so necessary at this distressing day of

---

[1] These instructions were reported by David Bancroft, Jonathan Stone, Nathan Baldwin and Stephen Salisbury. They have been printed at length in the appendix to the address of the Hon. John Davis, at the dedication of the town hall, 1825.

trial, we, the subscribers, being deeply impressed with a sense of our duty to our country, paternal affection for our children and unborn millions, as also for our personal rights and liberties, solemnly covenant, agree and engage, to and with each other, that from and after the first day of December, 1774, we will not, according to the best of our knowledge, any or either of us, nor any person by our direction, order, or approbation, for or under any or either of us, do or perform any Blacksmith's work, or business of any kind whatever, for any person or persons whom we esteem enemies to this country, commonly known by the name of tories, viz. all counsellors in this province appointed by mandamus, who have not publicly resigned said office, also every person who addressed governor Hutchinson at his departure from this province, who has not publicly recanted, also every officer exercising authority by virtue of any commission they hold tending to carry any of the late oppressive acts of parliament into execution in America; and in particular, we will not do any work for Tim Ruggles of Hardwick, John Murray of Rutland, and James Putnam of Worcester, Esq'rs, nor for any person or persons cultivating, tilling, improving, dressing, hiring or occupying any of their lands or tenements Also we agree to refuse our work of every kind as aforesaid, to all and every person or persons, who shall not have signed the non-consumption agreement, or have entered into a similar contract or engagement, or that shall not strictly conform to the association or covenant agreed upon and signed by the Continental Congress lately convened at Philadelphia

'We further agree, that we will not do any work for any mechanic, tradesman, laborer, or others, that shall work for, or in any ways or by any means whatever, aid, assist, or promote the business, or pecuniary advantage, pleasures, or profits of any of the said enemies to this country

'Resolved, That all lawful ways and means ought to be adopted by the whole body of the people of this province, to discountenance all our inveterate political enemies in manner as aforesaid Therefore, we earnestly recommend it to all denominations of artificers, that they call meetings of their respective craftsmen in their several counties, as soon as may be, and enter into associations and agreements for said purposes and that all husbandmen, laborers, &c do the like And that whoever shall be guilty of any breach of any or either of the articles or agreements, be held by us in contempt, as enemies to our common rights.'

A volume might be collected from the instructions resolutions, memorials, and addresses spread on the records of the town, and scattered through the documents of its committees, conventions, and political associations The same decision, intelligence, and independence, woven into the papers which have been copied, were continually embodied in language, always forcible and energetic, usually simple and correct, often eloquent and elegant. Many of the productions of later periods were marked by distinguished ability It is only possible to select a small portion from the great mass of materials the omissions are less to be regretted, as action soon gave stronger illustration of feeling, than could be derived from written declarations In the primary

movements of the revolution, Worcester was the central point from which
animating influences were diffused over the surrounding country If the first
impulses were derived from the metropolis of the state, the motion was communicated and wonderfully accelerated by the vigorous exertion of the capital
of the county If the impressions made by that capital on her neighbors
were less distinct during the progress, than at the commencement of the struggle, it was not because the flame of patriotism burned less bright, but that
the most ardent of her citizens had down the pen to take up the sword, and
the efforts to produce union and excite resolution in the assemblies of the
people, were exchanged for demonstrations of their practical effects in the
camp and on the battle field

Towards the close of the year, efforts were made to establish a depot of
provisions and munitions of war, at Worcester. Beef, pork, grain, and flour
were collected from the inhabitants, and probably from other sources, as subscriptions for the purpose were made by some of the patriotic leaders in Boston A quantity of lead was obtained, and some of the committee of correspondence exhibited so much zeal, as to solicit the gift of the broad pewter
platters of family use, to be converted into bullets As compared with the
collections which gave to Concord the glory of the visit of the British troops
on the nineteenth of April following, the deposites here were very inconsiderable.

CHAPTER VII.

On the commencement of the year 1775, was a period of intense interest
The difficulties between the mother country and the colonies were fast hastening to a decision by the appeal to battle The whigs, who might at the outset
have been contented with the redress of grievances, and by reasonable con-
cessions, now looked forward to the accomplishment of independence. The
royalists, driven by the course of events into a position from which they could
not recede, were separated from their countrymen. The inflexible perseverance of the ministry left no hope of conciliation The language of moderation was still on the lips of men, but stern determination in their hearts
was like the pause on the eve of fight, when the signal for engagement is impatiently awaited

Preparations for the conflict were actively, though silently made In January, 1775, it was recommended to the company of minute men, to exerci-

requently and perfect themselves in discipline, and payment was promised
or their services Efforts were strenuously made to procure a supply of arms
and munitions The collectors of taxes were instructed, as all public moneys
ought to be appropriated for the greatest benefit, and the Provincial Congress
had appointed Henry Gardner, Esq receiver general, to pay over to him all
sums which might come to their hands from assessments, and it was voted,
to indemnify them from the consequences of obedience to this injunction

A committee of inspection was elected, to carry into direct execution the
resolves of the Continental Congress against the consumption of teas and the
importation of foreign goods

The instructions [1] to Timothy Bigelow, reelected delegate to the Provincial
Congress, attest the reluctance which was felt to become aggressors After
commenting on the violations of rights and soliciting ' the advice of the general Congress, as to what measures are most proper for the province to adopt
respecting civil government, which at this day we are deprived of,' they say,
and we determine to rest quietly in this situation, however perplexing, agree-
ibly to the recommendation of our late Continental Congress, until the opera-
ion of their petition to his majesty be known excepting the commencement
of hostilities against us, should require the adopting a form of civil government for the defence of our lives and property And under such exigency,
you are to conduct yourself accordingly, and endeavor that the best form pos-
ible be adopted, for the support of good order and the liberties of the people,
which, we think, make every servant of the public dependent upon the suffrages of the people for their authority

The severity of the winter prevented any movements of the British troops
rom Boston, to repress the revolutionary spirit manifesting itself in military
arrangements, as well as in municipal resolutions. Preparations were, however, made for the march of the forces, in the spring, into the counties of
Worcester and Middlesex, to inflict vengeance on those styled rebels Capt
Brown of the 52d, and Ensign De Bernicie, of the 10th regiment, were
ordered by Gen Gage, to make an expedition, examine the roads, note the
distances from town to town, sketch the positions of the streams, heights,
passes, and posts, and collect such topographical information as would be use-
ul for the advance of a detachment The report of their journey, made by
he latter officer, was found after the evacuation of the metropolis [2] They
left Boston disguised as countrymen, without uniform, and passed through
Cambridge, Watertown, and by Framingham to Shrewsbury, on the old road.
The following is the account of their visit in Worcester

' We came into a pass, about four miles from Worcester, where we were
obliged to stop to sketch We arrived at Worcester at five o'clock in the
evening, very much fatigued the people in the town did not take notice of
us as we came in, so that we got safe to Mr Jones' tavern [3] on our entrance

[1] Reported by Nathan Baldwin and Jonathan Stone, Jan 24 1775
[2] This paper was first printed in 1779, and republished in 2 Mass Hist Col iv 204
[3] A few rods south of the Old South Church

he seemed a little sour, but it wore off by degrees, and we found him to be
our friend, which made us very happy: we dined and supped without any
thing happening out of the common run. The next day being Sunday, we
could not think of travelling, as it was contrary to the custom of the country:
nor dare we stir out until the evening, because of meeting: and nobody is
allowed to walk the streets, during divine service, without being taken up
and examined: so that, thinking we could not stand the examination so well,
we thought it prudent to stay at home, where we wrote and corrected our
sketches. The landlord was very attentive to us, and on our asking what he
could give us for breakfast, he told us, tea, or any thing else we chose; that
was an open confession what he was: but for fear he might be imprudent, we
did not tell him who we were, though we were certain he knew it. In the
evening, we went round the town, and on all the hills that command it,
sketched every thing we desired, and returned to the town without being
seen. That evening about eight o'clock, the landlord came in and told us
there were two gentlemen who wanted to speak with us. We asked him who
they were? On which he said, we would be safe in their company: we said
we did not doubt that, as we hoped two gentlemen, who travelled merely to
see the country and stretch our limbs, as we had lately come from sea, could
not meet with any thing else but civility, when we behaved ourselves properly. He told us he would come in again in a little time, and perhaps we
would change our minds, and left us. An hour after, he returned, and told
us the gentlemen were gone, but had begged him to let us know, as they
knew us to be officers of the army, that all their friends of government at
Petersham were disarmed by the rebels, and that they threatened to do the
same at Worcester in a very little time: he sat and talked politics, and drank
a bottle of wine with us; and also told us, that none but a few friends to
government knew we were in town: we said, it was very indifferent to us
whether they did or not, though we thought very differently: however, as we
imagined we had staid long enough in that town, we resolved to set off at day
break the next morning, and get to Framingham. Accordingly, off we set,
after getting some roast beef and brandy from our landlord, which was very
necessary on a long march, and prevented us going into houses where, perhaps,
they might be too inquisitive. We took a road we had not come, and that
led us to the pass four miles from Worcester. We went on unobserved by
any one, until we passed Shrewsbury, when we were overtaken by a horseman, who examined us very attentively, and especially me, whom he looked
at from head to foot, as if he wanted to know me again: after he had taken
his observations, he rode off pretty hard, and took the Marlborough road, but
by good luck, we took the Framingham road again, to be more perfect in it,
as we thought it would be the one made use of.'

The horseman was Capt. Timothy Bigelow, sent by the committee of correspondence to observe the officers, whose martial bearing, notwithstanding
their caution and disguise, betrayed their military character. Having followed the Framingham road to its intersection with the highway through Sudbury

they turned back to Marlborough   There they were in great danger of being seized and detained , but, by the aid of the friends of government, they escaped and reached Boston in safety   Soon after they explored the road to Concord and the country round

It was, unquestionably, the purpose of Gen Gage, to have marched troops to Worcester, to capture the stores reported to be collected here in great quantities although really inconsiderable in amount   A plan of the village, with the outline of military works, and notes indicating the position of two regiments, was seen by a citizen of the town, [1] among the papers left by the British after the evacuation   Possibly it might have been proposed to canton a part of the army in the interior   Whatever disposition of troops had been contemplated, the result of the April movements prevented the execution

In March, the company of minute men were directed to train half a day in each week , payment of one shilling was allowed to each for this service, and a penalty provided, equal in amount, for absence   This company had met almost daily for months   When the weather permitted, they paraded on the common, or occupied the streets   In the storms of winter they were drilled in some hall   Under the instruction of Capt Bigelow , they had attained great proficiency in military science, and when afterwards mustered at Cambridge, received commendations from the superior officers, for good discipline and celerity of evolution   Captain Bigelow was soon promoted, and was succeeded in the command by Lieutenant Hubbard.   When new enlistments were made, this company was virtually disbanded, although the men served in the new corps which were formed

Their services were soon to be required for the defence of the country   Before noon, on the 19th of April, an express came to the town, shouting, as he passed through the street at full speed, ' to arms ' to arms ' the war is begun ' ' His white horse, bloody with spurring, and dripping with sweat, fell exhausted by the church   Another was instantly procured, and the tidings went on [2] The bell rang out the alarm, cannon were fired, and messengers sent to every part of the town to collect the soldiery   As the news spread, the implements of husbandry were thrown by in the field, and the citizens left their homes with no longer delay than to seize their arms   In a short time the minute men were paraded on the green, under Capt Timothy Bigelow , after fervent prayer by the Rev Mr Maccarty, they took up the line of march   They were soon followed by as many of the train bands as could be gathered, under Capt Benjamin Flagg   On that day, 110 men marched from the town of Worcester for Concord   Intelligence of the retreat of the enemy, met them after they advanced, and they turned towards Boston.   When Capt Bigelow

---

[1] The late Isaiah Thomas   An extensive encampment, with a fortress, was projected on Chandler hill, the eminence commanding the town on the east

[2] The passage of the messenger of war, mounted on his white steed, and gathering the population to battle, made vivid impression on memory   The tradition of his appearance is preserved in many of our villages   In the animated description of the aged, it seems like the representation of death on the pale horse, careering through the land, with his terrific summons to the grave

reached the ancient Howe tavern, in Sudbury, he halted to rest his men. Capt. Benjamin Flagg, who had commenced his march an hour or two later, came up, and insisting on pushing forward without loss of time, both officers moved on to Cambridge.

The rolls of these soldiers of patriotism have fortunately been preserved in the office of the Secretary of State, where they were returned in compliance with a resolution of the Provincial Congress.[1]

The organization of the army which had spontaneously collected at Cambridge, was immediately made. Timothy Bigelow was appointed Major in Col. Jonathan Ward's regiment. A company of fifty-nine men, enlisted on the 24th of April, under Capt. Jonas Hubbard, with John Smith and William Gates, lieutenants, all from Worcester.

Seventeen other soldiers joined the companies of Capts. Washburn, Fay and Jones, in Cols. Ward's and Doolittle's regiments of infantry.

About twenty more were enrolled in the regiment of artillery under Col.

---

[1] ' Muster roll of a company of minute and militia men, which marched from the town of Worcester to Cambridge, on the alarm, April 19, 1775, under the command of Capt. Timothy Bigelow, in the regiment of which Artemas Ward, Esq., was Colonel.'

Timothy Bigelow, captain; Jonas Hubbard, John Smith, lieutenants; William Gates, Nathaniel Harrington, John Kannaday, William Dana, serjeants; John Pierce, Cyprian Stevens, Joel Smith, Nathaniel Heywood, corporals; Eli Putnam, drummer; John Hair, Joseph Pierce, fifers.

Peter Boyden,	John Hall.	Joseph Ball,	Daniel Willington,
Benjamin Bennet,	Artemas Knight,	Jonathan Stone,	William Curtis,
David Chadwick,	John Knower,	Samuel Wesson,	William Treadwell,
Eli Chapin,	Ephraim Miller,	Thomas Nichols,	Edward Swan,
Philip Donehue,	William Miles,	Thomas Knight,	Joseph Curtis,
Benjamin Estabrook,	Joseph Morse,	Joseph Miller,	Samuel Cook,
Josiah Flag,	Jonas Nichols,	Samuel Harrington,	Samuel Dunham,
Phineas Flagg,	Josiah Pierce,	Thomas Lynde,	Asa Ward,
Nathaniel Flagg,	Solomon Smith,	Joseph Cunningham,	Elisha Fuller,
Josiah Gates,	Ithamar Smith,	Joshua Harrington,	John Totman,
Thomas Gates,	Phinehas Ward,	Robert Crawford,	Joseph Thorp,
Jonathan Gleason,	Ebenezer Wiswall,	Moses Hamilton,	George Walker,
James Taylor,	James Wiser,	Samuel Bennett,	Thomas Drury,
William Griggs,	Daniel Haven.	Samuel Hemmenway,	Samuel Brown,
Gideon Griggs,	William Trowbridge,	William Walker,	Adam Hemmenway,
Edward Hair,	John Cole,	Nicholas Powers,	Josiah Perry.
Asa Harrington,			

' Muster Roll of Capt. Benjamin Flagg's company, in the Colony service, on the alarm, April 19, 1775.

Benjamin Flagg, captain; William McFarland, lieutenant; Ebenezer Lovell, ensign; Daniel Beard, Benjamin Flagg, Jr., serjeants.

Eleazer Holbrook,	Isaac Gleason,	Gershom Holmes,	Samuel Whitney,
Isaac Morse,	Robert Smith,	Simon Gates,	Benjamin Whitney, Jr.
Abel Holbrook,	Samuel Sturtevant,	Isaac Knight,	Josiah Harrington, Jr.
Jacob Holmes, Jr.,	Daniel Stearns,	Ezekiel Howe, Jr.	Samuel Whitney, Jr.
Simeon Duncan,	Edward Crafts,	Abel Flagg.	Jonathan Stone,
Samuel Clark,	Samuel Gates,	Levi Houghton,	Oliver Pierce.
Eleazer Hawes,	David Richards,		

Thomas Crafts, Edward Crafts served with the rank of captain, William Dana and William Treadwell were lieutenants in his company.

While the military strength of the town was arrayed in arms against the troops of the king, the committee of correspondence were dealing with the internal enemies of the country. On the intelligence of the commencement of the war, many of the protesters abandoned their families, their homes and possessions, and took refuge in Boston. Those who remained were summoned before the revolutionary tribunal, on the 21st of April, and were compelled to give assurances that they would not go out of the town without permission from the selectmen. On the 8th of May, Mr William Campbell, charged with a violation of this agreement, and Mr Samuel Paine, accused of circulating reports injurious to the honor of the provincial army, were arrested, and sent under guard to the Congress, at Watertown by order of the town. An opportunity was offered to the royalists of redeeming their character by joining the American troops, 'under penalty of being considered unworthy of the future confidence of their countrymen and willing to join an unlawful banditti, to murder and ravage.' As the proposal was not complied with, the committee issued their precept to the sheriff, to notify twenty nine persons to appear before them with their muskets and ammunition. The order was obeyed, and the remains of the party thus summoned, were disarmed, and then permitted to retire.

The negroes of Bristol and Worcester having petitioned the committee of correspondence of the latter county, to assist them in obtaining their freedom, it was resolved, in a convention held at Worcester, June 14. 'That we abhor the enslaving of any of the human race, and particularly of the negroes in this country, and that whenever there shall be a door opened, or opportunity present for anything to be done towards the emancipation of the negroes, we will use our influence and endeavor that such a thing may be brought about.'

In September, 1775,[1] the company from Worcester, stationed at Dorchester, with the officers of Col. Ward's regiment, presented to the General Assembly at Watertown, a remonstrance against indulgences to the royalists, representing, 'that as some of these vermin, or worse, emissaries of tyranny, are crawling out of Boston to their forfeited seats in Worcester, there is reason to suspect, that either their expectations fail, and therefore they would gladly return to their former seats and profits, until a more favorable opportunity presents to carry their evil machinations into execution, or, they are contriving, by degrees, to slide back to their seats, and there to avail themselves of the good opinion of the people, in order to play their parts, to divide and subdivide, or by some method weaken our union, or to form some diabolical plan for the ministry to save the supremacy of parliament, under some soft, sophistical, reconciliatory terms.

'Wherefore, we, your humble memorialists, entreat your honors not to suffer any of those who return, however humble and penitent they may appear, to go at large, or return to their former seats, or even to be so far favored as to be confined within the limits of Worcester, but treat them as they deserve, enemies in a superlative degree; confine them close, and render them incapable of doing harm, or return them to Boston, their favorite asylum'   .

The refugees in Boston addressed Gen Gage, on his departure from the capital, in respectful terms   Among the subscribers of the paper presented, were some who had been among the most distinguished citizens of Worcester [1]

The dealings of the committee of correspondence with those who had incurred the displeasure of the patriotic, were of no gentle character   One gentleman, having expressed censure of the doings of the revolutionary bodies, was compelled to make atonement   Having been summoned to appear for an investigation of his conduct, at its conclusion, he was requested to affix his signature to a paper prepared for the purpose, afterwards printed in the Spy   The proposal could not be resisted, and the following humiliating 'confession,' as it was termed, was subscribed, Aug, 21, 1775.

'Whereas I, the subscriber, have from the perverseness of my wicked heart, maliciously and scandalously abused the characters and proceedings of the Continental and Provincial Congresses, the selectmen of the town, and the committees of correspondence in general

'I do hereby declare, that at the time of my doing it, I knew the said abuses to be the most scandalous falsehoods, and that I did it for the sole purpose of abusing those bodies of men, and affronting my townsmen, and all the friends of liberty throughout the continent, being now fully sensible of my wickedness and notorious falsehoods, humbly beg pardon of those worthy characters I have so scandalously abused, and of my countrymen in general, and desire this confession of mine may be printed in the American Oracle of Liberty, for three weeks successively'

Having read this declaration of political sin in public, at the meeting house and in the streets, and paid the expenses for printing, the confessor was liberated, and immediately fled to seek asylum from such administration of justice

Mr Clark Chandler had left Worcester in June, and reached Boston by way of Newport   After a voyage to Nova Scotia and a journey to Canada, he returned in September, and directly surrendered himself and was committed as a prisoner to the common jail, by order of the committee, on suspicion of having held intercourse with the enemy   His health becoming impaired by confinement, he petitioned the committee, and the General Assembly, for liberation, under such restrictions as should be prescribed; but without avail   The unwholesome air and privations of his situation, having brought on dangerous sickness, on the fifth of December, consent was obtained for his removal to his mother's house, sufficient bonds being filed, that he would not depart from his home, and on the recovery of health would await the orders of the municipal authority claiming power so absolute

[1] Hon John Chandler, Col James Putnam, William Campbell, William Chandler, Samuel Paine, James Putnam Jr, Adam Walker, Nathaniel Chandler, were those who subscribed the address from Worcester.

over personal freedom on the 15th of December, an order of council passed, granting him permission to reside in Lancaster, on furnishing security that he would not go out of the limits of that town

As an incident of the jurisdiction exercised by the committee, was the preservation of its own dignity. We find, in December, they had committed to prison ' one John Holden,' a paper maker, for insolent behavior towards its members The punishment of this contempt was confirmed by a resolve of the General Assembly, ordering his detention in jail, until farther directions from the Court

These facts are curious, as indicating how unlimited was the control of the little bodies, invested by the towns with the care of the public safety, and acknowledging no superior, except the Congress of the state or the continent

Early in May, 15 prisoners from the British army were sent to Worcester During the residue of the year the prison was crowded by the successes of of the American arms The captives were enlarged on parol, when employment could be obtained among the inhabitants, and provision was made for their support and clothing by the General Assembly

On the 1st of May, a resolve of the Continental Congress provided for the removal of the indigent inhabitants of Boston, estimated to number 5000, and their distribution among the towns of the interior The proportion of Worcester county was 1633 Lancaster 103 Brookfield 99 Sutton 98 : Worcester 82 Difficulties arose about the removal to other towns, and not more than half the number assigned, were supported here

The selectmen were required to furnish the soldiers of the town with blankets, which were promptly delivered

June 15, a requisition was made upon the towns for fire arms and bayonets for the use of the army The quota of Worcester county was 514 Worcester, 30

June 29, all of the towns in Worcester county were earnestly requested to deliver their powder to a committee, except a small quantity left for emergency. Worcester supplied three barrels, retaining only half a cask from its stock

Another requisition was made on the same day, for blankets, and for clothing for the men in the service

The two largest cannon owned by the town were delivered to the Board of War, in November, for the defence of Gloucester

In the autumn of 1775, that expedition against Quebec, alike memorable for boldness of conception, chivalrous daring of execution, and melancholy failure in its result, was projected Among the volunteers, under the command of Arnold, who engaged in the winter march through the wilderness, were Major Timothy Bigelow, Capt Jonas Hubbard, and twelve soldiers from Worcester In the attack on the strongest fortress of the north, on the 31st of December, Capt Hubbard received a severe wound, beneath the ramparts of the lower town. refusing to be removed, he perished in the snow storm which raged with unusual violence Serjeant Silas Wesson was slain Timothy Rice, mortally wounded, died in the hospital Major Bigelow and our other citizens were made prisoners, and remained in captivity until November of the following year, when they were liberated on parol, and afterwards exchanged

Civil government having ceased to exist in its usual form, and the operation of the judiciary being suspended, in January 1776, two persons were elected as magistrates,[1] to exercise the powers of justices of the peace, for the preservation of order and the punishment of crime

Subsequently, May 8, an officer was elected,[2] to take acknowledgments of debt, where the amount did not exceed twenty pounds

A requisition was made on the towns, at the request of Gen Washington, for blankets. The quota of the county was 598 Brookfield, 30 , Sutton, 30 : Lancaster, 33 Worcester, 27

Men were drafted for the reenforcement of the army investing Boston, in January, by the officers of the militia and the selectmen. Of 749 assigned to Wo cester county, there were levied in Worcester 32 Brookfield 49 , Lancaster 46 Sutton 39 Mendon 33

On the 23d of May, ' a motion was made, to see if the town would support Independence, if it should be declared , and it was voted unanimously, that if the Continental Congress should declare the American colonies independent of Great Britain, we will support the measure with our lives and fortunes.' A copy of this vote was transmitted to the representative,[3] for his direction

A resolution of the General Court was passed June 25, in compliance with the request of the Continental Congress, to raise 5000 men to cooperate with the continental troops in Canada and New York Worcester county was required to furnish 1136 men from the alarm and train band lists of the towns, to be formed into companies of 59, and embodied in two battalions destined for New York. The quota of Lancaster was 72 Brookfield 69 Sutton 67 . Worcester 56 The bounty allowed to each man was £3, with 18s more for the use of arms and equipments furnished by each

It was voted to augment the bounty of the soldiers from this town to nine pounds, in addition to the allowance from the colony, and £186 were assessed for that purpose.

On the 10th of July, a new order was passed by the General Court, for detaching every twenty fifth man on the train band and alarm list, exclusive of those already ordered to be raised, to form two regiments, in companies of 77 each, to support the army in the northern department

On Saturday, the fourteenth of July, 1776, the Declaration of Independence was received. This instrument, the eloquent echo of sentiments as boldly expressed, in less splendid form, from almost every village of New England, long before they were promulgated in that paper which has been reverenced as the Magna Charta of Freedom, was hailed with enthusiasm It was first publicly read, by the late Isaiah Thomas, from the porch of the old south meeting house, to the assembled crowd On Sunday, after divine

[1] Samuel Curtis, William Young.   [2] Nathan Baldwin.   [3] David Bancroft.

service, it was read in the church. Measures having been adopted for a celebration of the event which separated the colonies from the mother country,
with formal solemnity, on Monday following, the earliest festive commemoration of the occasion, since hallowed as the national anniversary, took
place The following account of the ceremonies is from the Spy The
homely style of the sentiments, furnishes curious contrast with the elaborate
exercise of more modern times

' On Monday last, a number of patriotic gentlemen of this town, animated
with a love of their country, and to show their approbation of the measures
lately taken by the Grand Council of America, assembled on the green, near
the liberty pole, where, after having displayed the colors of the thirteen con-
federate colonies of America, the bells were set ringing and the drums a
beating After which the Declaration of Independence of the United States
was read to a large and respectable body. among whom were the selectmen
and committee of correspondence, assembled on the occasion, who testified
their approbation by repeated huzzas, firing of musketry and cannon, bonfires,
and other demonstrations of joy When the arms of that tyrant in Britain,
George the III, of execrable memory, which in former times decorated, but of
late disgraced the court house in this town, were committed to the flames and
consumed to ashes, after which, a select company of the sons of freedom,
repaired to the tavern, lately known by the sign of the King s Arms, which
odious signature of despotism was taken down by order of the people, which
was cheerfully complied with by the innkeeper, where the following toasts
were drank, and the evening spent with joy, on the commencement of the
happy era

' 1. Prosperity and perpetuity to the United States of America 2 The
president of the Grand Council of America 3 The Grand Council of
America 4. His excellency General Washington 5. All the Generals in
the American army 6 Commodore Hopkins 7 The officers and soldiers
of the American army 8 The officers and seamen in the American navy.
9 The patriots of America 10 Every friend of America 11 George rejected and liberty protected 12. Success to the American arms. 13. Sore
eyes to all tories, and a chestnut burr for an eye stone 14 Perpetual itch-
ing without the benefit of scratching, to the enemies of America 15 The
Council and Representatives of the State of Massachusetts Bay 16 The
officers and soldiers in the Massachusetts service 17 The memory of the
brave General Warren 18 The memory of the magnanimous General Mont-
gomery 19 Speedy redemption to all the officers and soldiers who are now
prisoners of war among our enemies 20 The State of Massachusetts Bay.
21. The town of Boston. 22 The selectmen and committees of correspondence for the town of Worcester 23 May the enemies of America be laid
at her feet 24 May the freedom and independency of America endure, till
the sun grows dim with age, and this earth returns to chaos

'The greatest decency and good order was observed, and at a suitable time
each man returned to his respective home [1]

[1] Mass Spy, July 24, 1776

On the 10th of September, one fifth part of the militia of the state were called out immediately to march to New York, to prevent the enemy from cutting off the communication between the American army in the city and on the Island of New York and the country   One fourth part of the residue of the military, were ordered to be equipped and ready to march at a moment's warning   Frequent calls were made for troops for the defence of Boston and other exposed places. Worcester answered each demand, following in quick succession, to the utmost extent of her means

In September, it was submitted to the people to determine, whether they would consent, that the House of Representatives and Council in convention, should adopt such constitution and frame of government, as, on the most mature deliberation, they should judge would most conduce to the safety, peace, and happiness of the state in after successions and generations   The town, considering the importance of the object, and the propriety of all the freemen having opportunity to express opinion, declined acting, as so many of the citizens were absent in the public service   Opposition was made by other towns, to the assembly proposing the measure, assuming this high duty, as the representatives had not been elected with a view to such object

The selectmen and committee of correspondence, having been authorized by an act to prevent monopoly and oppression, to fix and establish prices, in November, reported regulations for the sale of articles of common use and consumption   They recommended to the good people of the town, to use their utmost endeavors, by example, precept and legal exertions to support the laws of the country in general, and called upon them, ' in the name of the government and people of Massachusetts Bay, in the name of the passing soldier, in behalf of widows and orphans, as they regarded the credit of the currency, the establishment of an army, and the support of the authority of government, which alone renders war successful and gives dignity to peace, to prevent monopolies and oppression, by vindicating their act against the lawless violence which should dare to trample upon it ' [1]

The beneficial results of the regulations established throughout the commonwealth, were defeated by the fluctuations of the currency, unsustained by a metallic basis, which finally depreciated to worthlessness

[1] The following are the prices of some articles, as fixed in November, 1776. Labor in summer, 3s per day   Wheat, bushel, 6s 8d . Rye, 4s 6d   Indian Corn, 3s   Peas, 7s   Beans, 6s   Potatoes, Spanish, 1s 6d   Oats, 1s 9d   Apples, winter, 1s   Fresh Pork, pound, 4d, Salt Pork, 7d   Beef, grass fed, 3d   Beef, stall fed, 4d   Cheese, 6d   Butter, 9d   Pork, salted, 220 lbs barrel, £4, 6s   Beef, salted 240 lbs barrel, £3 8s 6d   Flour, £1 3s . Milk, quart, 2⅟   Cider, at the press, barrel, 4s   Mutton or Veal, pound, 3½d   Dinners at taverns, of boiled meat or equivalent, 8d   Suppers or breakfasts, of tea, coffee or chocolate, 8d   Lodgings, (soldiers sleeping on the floor not to be considered such,) 4d   Flip or toddy, made with New England rum, mug, 9d   Cotton and linen homespun cloth, yard wide, best common sort, yard, 3s 6d   Tow cloth, good quality and a yard wide, 2s 3d   Shoes, men's of neat's leather, best common sort, pair, 7s 6d   Breeches, of best deer's leather, for men, £2 2s   Beaver hats, best quality, £2 2s. Felt hats, 7s   Making a full suit of clothes, full trimmed, £1 4s   Wood, good oak, delivered at the door, cord, 8s   Boards, best white pine, at the mill, per thousand, £2 8s   Hay, English, best quality, cwt 3s

In December, Governor Cooke, of Rhode Island, by express, forwarded letters, addressed to ' all the brave inhabitants of New England,' earnestly entreating instant assistance to repel apprehended invasion   The whole of Col Wood's and Col Holman s regiments, were ordered to march to the relief of the sister state   Many volunteers from Worcester, promptly entered the ranks on the alarm, and remained in service during a portion of the winter

The company under Capt. William Gates, in Col Holman s regiment, was principally formed of men from Worcester.   Lieutenant Nathaniel Heywood and thirty-five privates, were in its ranks, and served in New York   Light were slain in battle or died in camp.

In Col Thomas Craft's regiment of artillery were twenty four of our citizens

The year 1777 had scarcely commenced, when a requisition was made on Worcester, for 32 blankets , followed, on the 26th of January, by a draft of every seventh of the male inhabitants, over 16 years of age, to complete the quota of Massachusetts in the continental army and to serve for eight months at least

The act of the General Court changing the ratio of representation, had excited discontent in the community   The town of Sutton invited a county congress, to convene at Worcester, in February, to deliberate on existing grievances, and adopt measures for redress   The committees of correspondence, in their general meeting, about the same time, recommended petitions and instructions for the repeal of the law   At the meeting of the inhabitants of Worcester, in March, they remonstrated against its provisions, as impolitic, unnecessary, unconstitutional, and attended with consequences injurious to the inland parts of the state

In February, each town was required to purchase and deliver shirts, stockings, and other clothing for the Massachusetts troops in the continental army, in the proportion of one set to every seven males over 16 years of age of the population   Worcester supplied sixty-two sets, for which compensation was afterwards made

A committee was directed, March 18, to ascertain how much each person had contributed towards the support of the war, and how much those deficient should pay to render the burden equal.   A bounty of £20 in addition to the grants from the state and continent, was offered to every soldier who should enter the army to fill the quota of the town.

The sum of £1656 2s 2d was levied to defray the expenses of the war, and for the payment of bounties

Upon representation of the great suffering for salt in the interior, 115 bushels were granted to Worcester, to be paid for by the selectmen, at the rate of 20s per bushel, and was distributed

The selectmen presented to the town a list of persons, esteemed by them to be internal enemies   More were nominated and elected in town meeting, June 16, and the names of 19 were finally accepted as dangerous   A committee was appointed to collect evidence against them preparatory to prosecution   Doubts arose of the justice and equity of this extemporaneous process of conviction of high crimes, without trial or opportunity for defence, and the

clerk was directed to suspend his return of the accused with some exceptions
A few months after, on the petition of the suspected, it was voted, ' to restore
the majority to the town's favor,' and on payment of the costs of the proceedings instituted against them, they were to be considered innocent of treasonable designs against the republic

Money was raised by loan, to purchase 100 muskets and bayonets, and a
quantity of powder to be delivered to the militia on payment of reasonable
price

The prisoners of war, long confined in the common jail, or permitted to
labor among the inhabitants for support, were removed in June, to Ipswich.
The rooms of the prison were soon again crowded with captured refugees,
suspected enemies, deserters, and criminals

Every sixth man in Worcester county was drafted, under the resolve of
August 9, to join the northern army for three months

On the alarm occasioned by the successes of Burgoyne, and the march of
the British army on Bennington, a company, under Lt Col Benjamin Flagg,
with Capt. David Chadwick, Lts Abel Holbrook and Jonathan Stone, and 68
non commissioned officers and privates, advanced to Hadley, August 28, on
their way to Albany Counter orders, received there, directed their return,
as the danger had ceased

The General Court, September 22, strongly recommended to the militia of
Worcester, and the western counties, that at least one half should march forthwith, to reenforce Gen Gates, and payment was promised.

An invitation was given by Sutton, November 3, to the neighboring towns,
to send delegates to a convention, to be held for the purpose of taking into
consideration an act providing for the payment of interest on state debts and
securities, and restraining the circulation of bills of lower denomination than
£10. The circular letter represents the law to be cruel, oppressive, and unjust, and remonstrates against its operation in angry terms. Delegates were
elected by Worcester The deliberations of the body, which met on the 13th
of November, resulted in a petition to the legislature for repeal of the obnoxious statute, and redress of grievances.

A committee was elected in December, to provide for the families of the
soldiers, and considerable disbursements were made in this and succeeding
years for their support

From the return of the selectmen it appears, that 68 men from Worcester
were in service in the continental line, on terms of enlistment for 8 months,
3 years, or during the war, who received their clothing principally from the
town

From Capt. Ebenezer Lovell's company, thirty seven enlisted in February,
for three years, and from Capt Joshua Whitney's twenty six for the same
period

The inhabitants expressed their approbation of the articles of Confederation
of the United States, in January, 1778, and their determination to support
the government by their utmost exertions

A requisition for clothing was made March 13, and Worcester furnished 62 ets of shirts, shoes, and stockings, for the army A colonel and 522 privates were detached from the brigade of the county, for service on the North river and in Rhode Island Worcester furnished 15 men for this battalion, in April At the same time, a draft was made to complete the state line in the continental army. Twelve were returned from Worcester to serve for nine months

A constitution for the State, reported by a committee of the General Court, in December, 1777, and approved by that body in January following, was submitted to the people, and rejected by a great majority. Of 58 votes given here, eight only were in favor of acceptance

Six of our citizens were drafted, under the resolve of June 12, for raising 80 men for an expedition to Rhode Island On the 23d of June, four more were required, as guards for the captured troops of General Burgoyne. In November, £736 were granted for bounties to soldiers and the support of their families

The names of six inhabitants of Worcester[1] are included in the banishment act, forbidding the return of the former citizens of the State who had joined the enemy, requiring them, if they once revisited their native country, forthwith to depart and denouncing the penalty of death if they should be found, second time, within the jurisdiction. One thus designated, had afterwards permission to reside in the town, regained the confidence, and long enjoyed the respect and esteem of the community

In March, 1779, the sum of £2000 was assessed to support the war, and the militia officers were directed to engage men for the public service, by enlistment or draft. In April, three teams were furnished for the transportation of warlike stores to Springfield Ten soldiers were raised, in June, to reenforce the army, and sixty-two sets of articles of dress supplied A voluntary contribution of £78 was taken up, in the church, after divine service, for the distressed inhabitants of Newport. The town obtained, on loan, £5200 for the payment of bounties

The anniversary of the Declaration of Independence was commemorated on the 8th of July, by the ringing of bells in the morning, the discharge of 13 cannon at noon, illumination and the display of 13 rockets at night.

Severe distress was experienced, from the depreciation of the currency, the exorbitant price of the necessaries of life, and the distrust of public credit A convention assembled at Concord, by the invitation of Boston, on the 14th of July, composed of delegates from all parts of the State, for the purpose of consulting on measures to give effect to the recommendations of Congress for the relief of the people Worcester was represented by David Bigelow and Joseph Barber Prices were regulated by a moderate appraisal of the value of articles of produce and merchandise, loans to government, provision for the support of the clergy, and attention to schools, as the means of good education, were earnestly recommended Another convention was proposed, in October, and an address was adopted

[1] John Chandler, James Putnam, Rufus Chandler, William Chandler, Adam Walker, William Paine

The town, at a meeting in August, expressed cordial approbation of these proceedings, and joined a committee to the standing board of correspondence and safety to enforce their execution.

Resolutions[1] were adopted at the same time, which indicate the condition and spirit of the country. Some extracts follow

'As many of the respectable merchants and fair traders have retired from business, their places have been supplied by an augmented number of *locus's* and *canker worms*, in human form, who have increased, and proceeded along the road of plunder, until they have become odiously formidable, and their contagious influence dangerously prevalent Therefore, Resolved, That such persons ought not to be admitted to bear a part in any mercantile consultation, but should be considered pestilential mushrooms of trade, which have come up in the night of public calamity, and ought to perish in the same night

'Whereas, regrators in the public markets, forestallers, engrossers of the produce of the country, and higlers, have had a great share in depreciating the public currency by their pernicious practices Resolved, That all such persons are guilty of a dangerous opposition to the measures necessary to promote the well being and prosperity of this country, and ought to be subjected to the resentment and indignation of the public, whether their conduct proceeds from a general disaffection to public measures, and the independence of these states, or from private motives of sordid interest

'Resolved, That whoever refuses to sell the surplus of the produce of his farm, and retains the same to procure a higher price by means of an artificial scarcity, is very criminally accessory to the calamities of the country, and ought to be subjected to those penalties and disabilities which are due to an inveterate enemy.'

Delegates from Worcester attended a county convention, on the eleventh of August, when a scale of prices was fixed, and resolutions adopted to adhere to and execute the regulations[2]

The same gentlemen were deputed to attend the second State Convention at Concord, Oct. 12, where a more detailed regulation of prices was made, resolutions passed, and an address framed, not essentially different from those of the former meeting.

---

[1] Not having been entered of record, by a singular omission, they have been preserved by their publication in the Massachusetts Spy, Aug 12, 1779. They were reported by William Stearns, Nathan Baldwin, and Joseph Allen

[2] The following prices stated August, 1779, on comparison with those of November, 1776, will show the depreciation of the currency in the interval

Corn, bushel, £3 12s Rye, £5 2s Wheat, £8 2s Oats, £1 16s Cider, barrel, £4 Hay, cwt £1 10s Labor in husbandry, day, £2 14s Women's labor, week, £2 Beef, pound, 5s 6d Mutton, Veal, 3s 6d Butter, 11s Cheese, 5s 6d Wool, £1 4s · Men's shoes, pair, £6 Stockings, £3 12s . Shirts, tow cloth, £4 16s. In June, 1779, farmers' produce had advanced in the ratio of 36½ to 1 West India goods as 41 1-9 to 1 Labor as 15 to 1 of the price in March of the same year

In August, Levi Lincoln, Joseph Allen, and David Bigelow, were elected delegates to the convention for framing a constitution

On a requisition for blankets, Sept 11, Worcester supplied 31

The selectmen being required to report the expenditures for raising soldiers, made return of 48 persons then in service, who had received $1906, for bounties on enlistments of three years. The supplies furnished for nine of their families, requiring public assistance, during the year, amounted to £599 0s. 6d. at the current price : reduced to the stated convention price, £39 17s. 6d. In August, £892 was granted to pay for clothing.

Eight soldiers were raised, Sept. 21, at an expense of £638, for the Rhode Island department, and thirteen under the resolve of Oct. 9, to join Gen. Washington, at Claverack, on Hudson's river, they received a bounty of £30 each, and were supported by the town, at a charge, in the aggregate, of £2515 10s. These sums were advanced by individuals, and the credit of the own pledged for payment

The exertions of preceding years had almost exhausted the money, men, and means of the country The difficulty of complying with the increased requisitions for public defence, was severely felt, and the burdens of the war rested with heavy pressure on the community Yet redoubled efforts were made o sustain the army, and meet the frequent demands of the government

In compliance with a resolve of May 4th, 1780, Worcester furnished 43 sets of blankets, shirts, shoes and stockings. On the 5th of June, 3954 men were levied for the continental army, to remain in service 6 months The quota of the county was 636 Worcester supplied 22 : Lancaster 40 Sutton 36 Brookfield 35 Mendon 29 Each soldier enlisting for the town, received £27 in agricultural produce, at the prices of 1774. In July, 12 horses were provided for transportation and cavalry service The quota of 4726 men for three months, under the resolve of June 22, was raised with great labor. Worcester county was required to enlist 766 Worcester 28 Lancaster 48 : Brookfield 42 Sutton 12 Mendon 35 The sum of £30,000, of continental currency, was assessed, as a tax, for the payment of the troops of the own A further requisition for men was made, on the same day, to be levied n the proportion of one to every four detached on the 5th of June, to march .o Springfield and await orders Worcester raised 5 soldiers Provisions being needed for the army, Worcester was called on to deliver 17,640 pounds of beef, purchased for £529 On the 4th of December, another assessment of 33,871 pounds was provided for, at the cost of £1270, 3s 3d

In May, the Bill of Rights and Frame of Government was submitted to the people, and accepted. The town disapproved of the 3d article of the Bill of Rights, relating to the support of religious worship and instruction, and the 20th, providing that the power of suspending the execution of the laws should only be exercised by the legislature the first was supposed to interfere with the rights of conscience, and the latter to restrict too much the authority of the executive department Some articles of the constitution were not accepted The 4th article of the 1st section, chapter 1st, investing the General Court with powers deemed too extensive for the legislative branch : the 1st

10*

article of the 3d section of the same chapter, containing the principle of representation the 9th article following, fixing the quorum of representatives for the transaction of business the 7th article, section 1st, of the 2d chapter, defining the power of the Governor the 3d article of the 6th chapter, establishing the value of money, and thereby determining the amount of salaries : and the 7th article, prohibiting the suspension of the privilege of the writ of habeas corpus, except upon most urgent occasion, and for a limited time, were all negatived Our citizens were desirous of strengthening the executive, and giving more efficiency to government This course, in conflict with the prevalent principles before the revolution, was founded on the necessity of an energetic administration, as it was made apparent by the progress of the war, and the embarrassments of the times.

The first elections under this constitution, ratified by the people, took place in September. The votes of Worcester were divided Hancock received 56, and Bowdoin 20, for Governor. James Warren 23, and Artemas Ward 28, for Lt. Governor.

On the 2d of December, 1780, 29 men were required as the town's proportion of 4240, to be enlisted for 3 years, or during the war The usual means of procuring the quota were employed without effect The companies of militia furnished no volunteers ; drafts had become unpopular, committees to seek recruits in other states had been unsuccessful, and, at length, a system of conscription was resorted to, as the only remaining resource for maintaining the army.

The citizens were divided into twenty nine classes, according to the valuation and amount of taxes paid by the individuals. Each class was required to furnish a soldier, and provide for his wages and support Each member contributed to this expense, in proportion to his property, ascertained by the returns of taxation. The delinquents were reported to the assessors, and the sums due from each to his class was included in the next tax and demanded by the collector. By this strong measure, the men were procured in February, and mustered into service

The inhabitants of Sutton, who seem to have been alike discontented at the passing or repeal of acts, in March, addressed letters to the towns, inviting a convention, to remonstrate against the resolve of the Legislature, suspending the tender of the depreciated paper in payment of debts at the rate of 40 for 1. Three delegates from this town were elected The assembly was small, and no important consequence followed from the meeting

Although the line of the continental army had been filled by permanent enlistments, troops were required for occasional service In June, a detachment of 500 men was ordered to march to Rhode Island, and Worcester granted £414, in hard money, for the payment of its troops in the expedition June 22, the town was required to procure 13,980 pounds of beef, and appropriated £400 in gold and silver for that purpose. On the same day, another resolve levied on the town 29 blankets, and 59 sets of articles of clothing. On the 30th, 23 men, for three months service, were raised. The supplying of soldiers had become so difficult, that they were only procured by exorbitant bounties, and the most zealous exertions [1]

In anticipation of an attack on New York, Gen Washington asked for re-enforcements, and one quarter part of the militia were ordered to hold them-selves in readiness to move   The town voted to grant pay to them, should they march, in the same proportion with the regular troops

The surrender of Cornwallis diffused general joy throughout the country, as the omen of a triumphant termination of the war. The event was commemo-rated here, on the 7th of November, by the usual festive observances of days of rejoicing 'In consequence of this glorious intelligence,' says the Spy, with singular extravagance of expression, 'the morning was ushered in by ringing of bells, discharging of cannon, displaying of colors, attended with the shouts of a grateful populace, and *even Aurora advanced and unlocked the ruddy gates of the morning with a sympathetic smile !'*

In January, 1782, the town expressed strong disapprobation of an act im-posing duties on spirituous liquors, teas and other articles of luxury   The in-structions to the representative, reported by Timothy Paine, Esq , Nathan Baldwin, and Cornelius Stowell, illustrate the change of principles with times The denunciations of tea in the votes, resolutions, and solemn covenants of 1774, had been forgotten, and opinions of the value of spirits are expressed which have been demonstrated to be entirely unsound by the philanthropists of recent days

'Whereas, the town, at a meeting held on the 21st of January, 1782, dis-approved of a late act of this commonwealth, laying an excise on wine, rum,

---

[1] The amount of money raised by the inhabitants for the support of the war, was really very great The depreciation of the paper currency rendered the nominal amount of tax-ation excessive The true value of grants and appropriations may be estimated by ref-erence to the subjoined scale The figures indicate the number of dollars, in continental currency, equivalent to one hundred, in gold or silver To April, 1780, the value was fix-ed as stated below, by the act of Massachusetts From that date, it has been ascertained by taking the average depreciation through the month

	1777.	1778	1779	1780
January,	105	325	742	2934
February,	107	350	868	3322
March,	109	375	1000	3736
April,	112	400	1104	4000
May,	115	400	1215	5450
June,	120	400	1342	6650
July,	125	425	1477	6900
August,	150	450	1630	7000
September,	175	475	1800	7100
October,	275	500	2030	7200
November,	300	545	2308	7250
December,	310	634	2595	7400

In 1781, one dollar of specie was equal to 187 cents in new emission bills, from Feb 27 to May 1 , 225 to May 25 , 300 to June 15 , 400 to Oct 1 Below these dates, the depreci-ation approached total worthlessness

The whole expenses of the Revolutionary war to the States were, in paper money, $359,-547,027 , estimated in specie, $135,193,703

wheel carriages, &c., and did then vote to instruct Samuel Curtis, Esq, their representative, to use his utmost endeavors to have that act repealed.

'The town now, January 25, taking the matter again into consideration, do give the following reasons why said act ought to be repealed

'1. It is an indirect method of levying monies; as those who defray those duties cannot know what sum they pay, which is contrary to the genius of a free government, which should equalize burdens

'2 It multiplies oaths, and subjects a great number of persons to be sworn, in matters wherein they are deeply interested, and, consequently, instead of suppressing immorality, has a contrary tendency.

'3. If it is necessary to lay duties for the support of government and the suppression of extravagance, such duties ought to be levied on such articles as are merely luxurious, and not on some of those mentioned in this act; spirituous liquors being absolutely necessary for our seafaring brethren, coasting along our shores in boats and lighters, at all seasons of the year, to supply the markets with wood, lumber and fish, also for the farmer, whose fatigue is almost unsupportable in hay time and harvest and for the beginners in bringing forward new townships where they have nothing to drink but water, and are, perhaps, exposed to more hardships than any other persons, nor on Bohea Tea, which, in populous towns, and in many places in the country, is substituted, by many poor persons, in the room of milk, which is not to be had, and they find it to be a cheap diet; nor on common chaises and other carriages, such as are kept in the country, for the necessary conveyance of families to meeting, &c the use of them very often saves the keeping of a horse extraordinary, and enables the farmer to keep more cattle and sheep, which are more profitable; and all carriages being manufactured among ourselves, laying a duty upon them has a tendency to discourage all those mechanics who are employed in making them

'4. The mode pointed out in the act, for collecting duties, is much more expensive than necessary, however small the commissions allowed the collector may appear, for if the collector can afford to ride into every town in the county for three per cent., the common collector of taxes in each town can afford to collect the same in his own town for one per cent; and convey the money to the treasury with his other public money.

'5. All consumers of spirituous liquors at taverns, will pay about eight times as much as the duties amount to: for it is well known that the tavern keeper sells his mixed liquors for two pence more in a mug than before the excise was laid, when, in fact, the duties on each mug do not amount to more than a farthing

'6 All persons living upon the borders of this government, will purchase liquors for their own consumption of the neighboring governments, and thereby avoid paying any of said duties.

'7. The act laying an excise upon tea, exempts all persons from paying a duty who buy at one time fifty pounds or more of Bohea tea, or twenty five pounds or more of other India tea, which appears to be calculated to lay a tax upon the poor and exempt the rich.

'8 The consumers of spirituous liquors are charged by the retailer and tavern keeper with the whole of the excise, and they are obliged to pay it, when, at the same time, the seller is allowed ten per cent for leakage and waste, which, with three per cent allowed the collector, amounts to nearly thirteen per cent out of the duties intended to be raised by said act · as also a further allowance to be made to the seller for as much more as he shall see cause to swear that he may have lost by extraordinary leakage or other casualty

'9 There is no check upon the collector s accounts, nor anything to prove that the whole money he shall collect is contained in the accounts he shall render to the Receiver General when, by former excise acts, the collector, when he received any duties, was obliged to give two receipts of the same tenor and date, one of which was to be lodged with clerk of the Sessions, and the clerk was obliged to transmit the same or copies, to the Treasurer, in order to compare with the accounts of the Collector

' Lastly The act is attended with many difficulties, and has a direct tendency to embarrass and obstruct trade, and, it is the opinion of this town, if continued, it will create great uneasiness among the good people of this Commonwealth, and not answer the design of government in passing the same

'The town clerk is, therefore, hereby directed, to furnish Samuel Curtis, Esq, our representative, with a copy of our vote of the 21st inst and the foregoing reasons and the said Samuel Curtis is directed to use his endeavors, not only to cause the said act to be repealed, but to prevent in future any excise or duty being laid upon the necessaries of life

The last requisition for men to join the army was in March, 1782, when 6 were drafted, for three years [1]

The minute recital we have followed seemed necessary, as the only means of giving adequate idea of those municipal exertions, whose merit has almost passed from remembrance, in the triumphant results they aided to accomplish

The supplies, and expenditures of the towns, were charged to the commonwealth, and allowed by the United States But, as they only went to discharge taxes and assessments, they were, in reality, uncompensated gratuities to the public

Worcester furnished a large proportion of her male population to the army of the revolution The exact numbers in service cannot be ascertained with certainty If we include with the troops of the regular line, those called out for short periods of duty, the following may be considered as a correct statement of the numbers of men from Worcester in military service during seven years of war

1 colonel, 2 lieutenant colonels, 2 majors, 7 captains, 10 lieutenants, 5 ensigns, 20 serjeants, and 389 privates

---

[1] Quota of Worcester county 217 Brookfield 12 Sutton 12 : Shrewsbury 9 · Lancaster 7 (Sterling having been taken off) Mendon 5, (Milford being set off) This and some earlier requisitions for men clothing, and provisions, were apportioned, not on the basis of population, but property according to valuation which explains the difference in relative proportions

A letter from the committee of correspondence of Boston, in relation to the absentees and refugees, was received in May, and a committee[1] elected to express the sentiments of the town in reply.

The following, selected from many votes reported to and accepted by the citizens, May 19, 1783, contains the substance of their doings

'Voted, That this town consider every country, in times of invasion, as having equally a right to the assistance, personal services and property of all its subjects, in opposing its assailants That this country, more than eight years since, was invaded, and has been scourged by a war, which, for the purpose of reducing it to the servile subjection of foreign domination, has been, by sea and land, wasting, and by every species of barbarity, distressing its innocent inhabitants · a war that has desolated and burned whole towns, and rendered wretched and turned out thousands of virtuous Americans, destitute, despoiled, and unprovided for by the treaty of peace, which leaves them dependent on the gratitude and generosity of the country . a war promoted, encouraged, and invited by those, who, the moment the bloody banners were displayed, abandoned their native land, turned parricides, and conspired to involve their country in tumult, ruin, and blood

'Voted, That, in the opinion of this town, it would be extremely dangerous to the peace, happiness, liberty, and safety of these states, to suffer persons of the above description to become the subjects of and reside in this government that it would be not only dangerous, but inconsistent with justice, policy, our past laws, the public faith, and the principles of a free and independent state, to admit them ourselves, or have them forced upon us without our consent

'Voted, That, in the opinion of this town, this commonwealth ought with the utmost caution, to naturalize, or in any other way admit as subjects, a common enemy, a set of people who have been, by the united voice of the continent, declared outlaws, exiles, aliens, and enemies, dangerous to its political being and happiness

'Voted, That while there are thousands of the innocent. peaceable and defenceless inhabitants of these states, whose property has been destroyed and taken from them in the course of the war, for whom no provision is made, to whom there is no restitution of estates, no compensation for losses, that it would be unreasonable, cruel, and unjust, to suffer those who were the wicked occasion of those losses, to obtain a restitution of the estates they refused to protect, and which they have abandoned and forfeited to their country

'Voted, That it is the expectation of this town, and the earnest request of their committee of correspondence, inspection and safety, that they, with care and diligence, will observe the movements of our only remaining enemies that until the further order of government, they will, with decision. spirit and firmness, endeavor to enforce and carry into execution, the several laws of this commonwealth respecting these enemies to our rights, and the rights of man

[1] Levi Lincoln, William Stearns, Joseph Allen, David Bigelow, Isaiah Thomas, Joseph Wheeler, Jonathan Rice.

kind   give information should they know of any obtruding themselves into
any part of this state, suffer none to remain in this town, but cause to be confined immediately, for the purpose of transportation, according to law, any
that may presume to enter it '

CHAPTER VIII.

1782 to 1787   Insurrection   Distresses of the people   County Conventions, 1782, 1784,
   1786   Court stopped, Sept 1786   Spirited conduct of Judge Ward   Proceedings of the
   insurgents   Convention, Sept 1786   Town meeting, Oct. 1786   Court of Sessions
   interrupted   Sheriff Greenleaf   Insurgents occupy the town, Dec 1786   Militia of
   Worcester appear in arms for the government   Capt Howe.   Consultations of the insurgents   Distresses of their retreat   Gen Lincoln's army.   Affair at New Braintree
   Dispersion of the insurgents

The struggles of the Revolution had scarce terminated, before disturbances
arose among the people, which, in their progress, brought the commonwealth
to the very verge of ruin.

Could the existence of insurrection and rebellion be effaced from memory,
it would be wanton outrage to recall from oblivion the tale of misfortune and
dishonor   But those events cannot be forgotten : they have floated down in
tradition · they are recounted by the winter fire-side, in the homes of New
England . they are inscribed on roll and record in the archives and annals of
the state   History, the mirror of the past, reflects with painful fidelity, the
dark as well as the bright objects from departed years, and although we may
wish to contemplate only the glowing picture of patriotism and prosperity,
the gloomy image of civil commotion is still full in our sight, shadowing the
background with its solemn admonition

The investigation ot the causes of the unhappy tumults of 1786, does not
belong to the narrative of their local effects on one of the principal scenes of
action   But it would be great injustice to omit the statement, that circumstances existed, which palliate, though they do not justify, the conduct of
those who took up arms against the government of their own establishment.
After eight years of war, Massachusetts stood, with the splendor of triumph,
in republican poverty, bankrupt in resources, with no revenue but of an expiring currency. and no metal in her treasury more precious than the continental copper, bearing the devices of union and freedom   The country had
been drained by taxation for the support of the army of independence, to
the utmost limits of its means , public credit was extinct, manners had become
relaxed, trade decayed, manufactures languishing, paper money depreciated to
worthlessness, claims on the nation accumulated by the commutation of the
pay of officers for securities, and a heavy and increasing pressure of debt
rested on commonwealth, corporations and citizens   The first reviving efforts
of commerce overstocked the markets with foreign luxuries and superfluities,

sold to those who trusted to the future to supply the ability of payment
The temporary act of 1782, making property a tender in discharge of pecuniary contracts, instead of the designed remedial effect, enhanced the evils of
general insolvency, by postponing collections   The outstanding demands of
the royalist refugees, who had been driven from large estates and extensive
business, enforced with no lenient forbearance, came in to increase the embarrassments of the deferred pay day   At length, a flood of suits broke out.
In 1784, more than 2000 actions were entered in the county of Worcester,
then having a population less than 50,000, and in 1785, about 1700   Lands
and goods were seized and sacrificed on sale, when the general difficulties
drove away purchasers   Amid the universal distress, artful and designing
persons discerned prospect for advancement, and fomented the discontent by
inflammatory publications and seditious appeals to every excitable passion and
prejudice   The constitution was misrepresented as defective, the administration as corrupt, the laws as unequal and unjust   The celebrated papers of
Honestus directed jealousy towards the judicial tribunals, and thundered
anathemas against the lawyers, unfortunately for them, the immediate agents
and ministers of creditors   Driven to despair by the actual evil of enormous
debt, and irritated to madness by the increasing clamor about supposed grievances, it is scarcely surprising that a suffering and deluded people should
have attempted relief, without considering that the misery they endured was
the necessary result from the confusion of years of warfare [1]

Before the close of the revolutionary contest, whose pressure had united
all by the tie of common danger, indications of discontent had been manifested   The acts of the legislature had excited temporary and local uneasiness in former years, as the operation of laws conflicted with the views of
expediency or interest entertained by the village politicians   But in 1782,
complaints arose of grievances, springing from the policy and administration
of government, of more general character   On the 14th of April of that
year, the delegates of twenty six towns of the county assembled in convention, and attributing the prevailing dissatisfaction of the people, to want of
confidence in the disbursement of the great sums of money annually assessed,
recommended instructions to the representatives, to require immediate settlement with all public officers entrusted with the funds of the commonwealth,
and if the adjustment was delayed or refused, to withdraw from the General

1 Could we roll back the tide of time, till its retiring wave left bare the rocks on which
the commonwealth was so nearly wrecked, it is not improbable, we should discover, that a
loftier and more dangerous ambition, and wider, deeper, and more unhallowed purposes,
urged on and sustained the men who were pushed into the front rank of rebellion than
came from the limited capacity of their own minds   We might find that the accredited
leaders of 1786, were only humble instruments of stronger spirits, waiting in their concealment the results to the tempest they had roused.   Fortunately, the energy of government, gave to rising revolution the harmless character of crushed insurrection, saved to
after years the inquiry for the Catalines of the young republic, and left to us the happy
privilege of receiving the coin impressed with the mark of patriotism, at its stamped value, without testing its deficiency of weight, or assaying the metal to determine the mix-
ture of alloy.

Court, and return to their constituents, to reduce the compensation of the
members of the House, and the fees of lawyers, to procure sessions of the
Court of Probate in different places in the county, the revival of confessions
of debt; enlargement of the jurisdiction of justices of the peace to £20,
contribution to the support of the continental army in specific articles instead
of money and the settlement of accounts between the Commonwealth and
Congress At an adjourned session, May 13, they further recommended, that
account of the public expenditures should be annually rendered to the towns,
the removal of the General Court from Boston, separation of the business of
the Common Pleas and Sessions, and inquiry into the grants of lands in
Maine in favor of Alexander Shepherd and others Worcester was represented in these assemblies, and in the instructions to Samuel Curtis, Esq., framed
in accordance with their resolutions, on the 8th of June, the town represented
as additional grievances, that the Treasurer held the office of Justice of the
Common Pleas in Middlesex, interfering with the discharge of his general
duties, and the proposition for the allowance of half pay for life to the officers
deranged on the new organization of the army, and not in service Some of
the complaints were quieted by legal provisions, and when the convention
was appointed to be again held by adjournment, in August, the few discontented persons in attendance dispersed without transacting business [1]

The murmurs of the coming storm were first heard here, early in 1784
On the invitation of Sutton to each town of the county, the capital sent delegates to a convention, held in March of that year, of which Ebenezer Davis,
Esq. was President. Although assembled for the professed purpose of considering the expediency af an excise duty alone, the inquiries of this body
were more extensive in pursuit of existing evils When the result of its
deliberations was communicated to the inhabitants of Worcester, they adopted
for themselves the petition prepared for general acceptance, representing as
grievances, the grant to Congress of an impost for twenty-five years to discharge the interest accruing on state securities, the payment from the treasury of the expenses of festive days of rejoicing, large compensation to officers
of the continental army ; neglect to redeem the paper currency ; the want of
a circulating medium ; and the impaired state of credit The representative
of the town was instructed to endeavor to procure the removal of the General
Court from Boston to some country town, where it would be secure from im-
proper influences, and to cause an account of the debts, revenues and charges
of government to be published annually These complaints, unnoticed by
the Legislature, seemed to be hushed and quieted by the very neglect they
experienced.

But the spirit of discontent, though stilled, was not extinct. It spread
wider and deeper, and grew stronger in the minds of men, and its voice was

[1] ' While the great body of the people desired only escape from impending suits, without premeditated malice against the Commonwealth or its institutions, every trivial cause
was magnified and perverted to increase the existing irritation, till, under the influence
of delusion, a deadly blow was struck at both.' MSS. Centennial Address of Hon John
Davis.

again heard   In May, 1786, another invitation from Sutton, for a general
meeting, was circulated, and passed over here without attention   The delegates of 17 towns, however, formed a convention at Leicester, and elected
Willis Hall, of Sutton, its President.   As the attendance was thin, letters
were addressed to Worcester, and the other towns of the county unrepre-
sented, requesting their participation, and an adjournment took place to the
15th of August following   Our inhabitants, at a meeting held on this application, determined, by a great majority, not to comply , on the grounds, that
the body from which it emanated was not recognized by the constitution,
and that its session was unnecessary and illegal   Thirty seven towns, appeared by their representatives when the convention was reorganized at Leicester   It is not uninteresting to notice the gradual increase of alleged evils
in its doings   In 1784, the list was brief   In 1786, without essential change
in policy or condition, it had swelled to voluminous extent   In addition to the
grievances already stated, they enumerated among the sources of uneasiness,
abuses in the practice of the law , exorbitance of the items in the fee bill ·
the existence and administration of the Courts of Common Pleas and Sessions , the number and salaries of public officers ; grants to the Attorney
General ; and to Congress, while the state accounts remained unliquidated.
    A committee was instructed to report a memorial, at another session, to be
had, by adjournment, in Paxton, on the last Tuesday of September
    Thus far, redress had been sought by the constitutional appeal of the citi-
zen to the Legislature. The recorded proceedings of the convention are of
pacific character, expressing disapprobation of combinations, mobs, and riots
yet, it is probable, that during the period of its consultations, the bold design
was originated by the most violent of its members, of resisting the execution
of the laws and suspending the operations of courts. Soon after the first
meeting, it was stated in the paper of the town printed by Mr Thomas, that
apprehensions existed of obstruction to the Common Pleas in June. The first
open act of insurrection followed close upon the adjournment of the convention in August
    Although warning of danger had been given, confiding in the loyalty of the
people, their love of order, and respect for the laws, the officers of government had made no preparations to support the court, to be held in Worcester,
in September, 1786   On Monday night, of the first week in that month, a
body of eighty armed men, under Capt Adam Wheeler of Hubbardston
entered the town, and took possession of the Court House   Early the next
morning, their numbers were augmented to nearly one hundred, and as many
more collected without fire arms   The Judges of the Common Pleas had
assembled at the house of the Hon. Joseph Allen   At the usual hour, with
the Justices of the Sessions and the members of the bar, attended by the clerk
and sheriff, they moved towards the Court House   Chief Justice Artemas
Ward, a general of the revolution, united intrepid firmness with prudent
moderation. His resolute and manly bearing on that day of difficulty and
embarrassment, sustained the dignity of the office he bore, and commanded
the respect even of his opponents   On him devolved the responsibility of a

occasion affecting deeply the future peace of the community and it was supported well and ably

On the verge of the crowd thronging the hill, a sentinel was pacing on his round, who challenged the procession as it approached his post Gen Ward sternly ordered the soldier, formerly a subaltern of his own particular regiment, to recover his levelled musket The man, awed by the voice he had been accustomed to obey, instantly complied, and presented his piece, in military salute, to his old commander The Court, having received the honors of war, from him who was planted to oppose their advance, went on. The multitude, receding to the right and left, made way in sullen silence, till the judicial officers reached the Court House. On the steps was stationed a file of men with fixed bayonets on the front, stood Captain Wheeler, with his drawn sword The crier was directed to open the doors and permitted to throw them back, displaying a party of infantry with their guns levelled, as if ready to fire. Judge Ward then advanced, and the bayonets were turned against his breast. He demanded, repeatedly, who commanded the people there, by what authority, and for what purpose, they had met in hostile array. Wheeler at length replied: after disclaiming the rank of leader, he stated, that they had come to relieve the distresses of the country, by preventing the sittings of courts until they could obtain redress of grievances The Chief Justice answered, that he would satisfy them their complaints were without just foundation He was told by Capt Smith of Barre, that any communication he had to make must be reduced to writing Judge Ward indignantly refused to do this he said, he ' did not value their bayonets they might plunge them to his heart but while that heart beat he would do his duty when opposed to it, his life was of little consequence if they would take away their bayonets and give him some position where he could be heard 'by his fellow citizens, and not by the leaders alone who had deceived and 'deluded them, he would speak, but not otherwise' The insurgent officers, 'fearful of the effect of his determined manner on the minds of their followers, interrupted They did not come there, they said, to listen to long speeches, 'but to resist oppression they had the power to compel submission and they 'demanded an adjournment without day Judge Ward peremptorily refused to 'answer any proposition, unless it was accompanied by the name of him by whom it was made. They then desired him to fall back the drum was beat, and the guard ordered to charge The soldiers advanced, until the points of 'their bayonets pressed hard upon the breast of the Chief Justice, who stood 'as immovable as a statue, without stirring a limb, or yielding an inch, although the steel in the hands of desperate men penetrated his dress Struck 'with admiration by his intrepidity, and shrinking from the sacrifice of life, the guns were removed, and Judge Ward, ascending the steps, addressed the assembly In a style of clear and forcible argument, he examined their supposed grievances, exposed their fallacy explained the dangerous tendency of their rash measures, admonished them that they were placing in peril the liberty acquired by the efforts and sufferings of years, plunging the country in civil war, and involving themselves and their families in misery:

that the measures they had taken must defeat their own wishes ; for the government would never yield that to force, which would be readily accorded to respectful representations : and warned them that the majesty of the laws would be vindicated, and their resistance of its power avenged. He spoke nearly two hours, not without frequent interruption. But admonition and argument were unavailing : the insurgents declared they would maintain their ground until satisfaction was obtained. Judge Ward addressing himself to Wheeler, advised him to suffer the troops to disperse : ' they were waging war, which was treason, and its end would be,' he added, after a momentary pause, ' the gallows.' The judges then retired, unmolested, through armed files. Soon after, the Court was opened at the United States Arms Tavern,[1] and immediately adjourned to the next day. Orders were despatched to the colonels in the brigade to call out their regiments, and march without a moment's delay, to sustain the judicial tribunals : but that right arm on which the government rests for defence was paralyzed : in this hour of its utmost need, the militia shared in the disaffection, and the officers reported, that it was out of their power to muster their companies, because they generally favored those movements of the people directed against the highest civil institutions of the state, and tending to the subversion of social order.

In the afternoon of Tuesday, a petition was presented from Athol. requesting that no judgments should be rendered in civil actions, except where debts would be lost by delay, and no trials had unless with the consent of the parties : a course corresponding with the views entertained by the court. Soon after, Capt. Smith of Barre, unceremoniously introduced himself to the judges, with his sword drawn, and offered a paper purporting to be the petition of ' the body of people now collected for their own good and that of the Commonwealth,' requiring an adjournment of the courts without day. He demanded, in a threatening manner, an answer in half an hour. Judge Ward, with great dignity, replied, that no answer would be given, and the intruder retired. An interview was solicited, during the evening, by a committee, who were informed that the officers of government would make no promises to men in hostile array : an intimation was given that the request of the people of Athol was considered reasonable : and the conference terminated. A report of the result was made to the insurgents, who voted it was unsatisfactory, and resolved to remain until the following day.

During the night, the Court House was guarded in martial form : sentinels were posted along the front of the building, and along Main street : the men not on duty, bivouaced in the hall of justice, or sought shelter with their friends. In the first light of morning, the whole force paraded on the hill, and was harangued by the leaders. In the forenoon, a new deputation waited on the court, with a repetition of their former demand, and received similar reply. The justices assured the committee, if the body dispersed, the people of the county would have no just cause of complaint with the course the court would adopt. The insurgents, reenforced with about two hundred from Holden and Ward, now mustered four hundred strong, half with fire arms, and

[1] On the site of the Exchange Coffee House, 1836.

the remainder furnished with sticks They formed in column, and marched through Main street, with their music, inviting all who sought relief from oppression to join their ranks, but receiving no accession of recruits from our citizens, they returned to the Court House Sprigs of evergreen had been distributed, and mounted as the distinctive badge of rebellion, and a young pine tree was elevated at their post as the standard of revolt.

The court at length, finding that no reliance could be placed on military support, and no hope entertained of being permitted to proceed with business, adjourned, continuing all causes to the next term. Proclamation was made by the sheriff to the people, and a copy of the record communicated After this, about two hundred men, with sticks only paraded before the house of Mr Allen, where the justices had retired, and halted nearly an hour, as if meditating some act of violence. The main body then marched down, and passing through the other party, whose open ranks closed after them, the whole moved to the common, where they displayed into line, and sent another committee to the court

The sessions, considering their deliberations controlled by the mob, deemed it expedient to follow the example of the superior tribunal, by an adjournment to the 21st of November When the insurgent adjutant presented a paper, requiring it should be without fixed day, Judge Ward replied, the business was finished and could not be changed.

Before night closed down, the Regulators, as they styled themselves, dispersed ; and thus terminated the first interference of the citizens in arms with the course of justice Whatever fears might have been entertained of future disastrous consequences, their visit brought with it no terror, and no apprehension for personal safety to their opposers Both parties, indeed, seemed more inclined to hear than strike The conduct of Judge Ward was dignified and spirited, in a situation of great embarrassment His own deprecation, that the sun might not shine on the day when the constitution was trampled on with impunity, seemed to be realized Clouds, darkness, and storm, brooded over the meeting of the insurgents, and rested on their tumultuary assemblies in the county at subsequent periods

The state of feeling here, was unfavorably influenced by the success of the insurgents. At a meeting of the inhabitants, on the 25th of September, delegates were elected to the county convention at Paxton, with instructions to report their doings to the town The list of grievances received some slight additions from this assembly The delay and expense of Courts of Probate, the manner of recording deeds in one general office of registry, instead of entering them on the books of the town where the land was situated ; and the right of absentees to sue for the collection of debts, were the subjects of complaint in a petition, concluding with the request that precepts might be issued for meetings, to express public sentiment in relation to a revision of the consitution, and if two thirds of the qualified voters were in favor of amendment, that a state convention might be called. The existence of this body was continued by an adjournment to Worcester The petition was immediately forwarded to the General Court A copy was subsequently submitted to the

11*

town, at a meeting held October 2, for the purpose of receiving a report from
the delegates.   It was then voted, 'that Mr Daniel Baird be requested to
inform the town whether this petition was according to his mind, and he
informed the town it was but that he did not approve of its being sent to
the General Court before it had been laid before the town.'   The petition was
read paragraph by paragraph, rejected, and the delegates dismissed.

On the 16th of October, in compliance with the request of 34 freeholders,
another town meeting was called after long and warm debate, the former
delegates were reelected, to attend the convention, at its adjourned session.
A petition had been offered, praying consideration of the measures proper in
the alarming situation of the country, and for instructions to the representative to inquire into the expenditure of public money, the salaries of officers,
the means of increasing manufactures, encouraging agriculture, introducing
economy, and removing every grievance.   Directions were given to endeavor
to procure the removal of the Legislature from the metropolis to the interior ,
the annihilation of the Inferior Courts . the substitution of a cheaper and
more expeditious administration of justice ; the immediate repeal of the sup-
plementary fund granted to congress ; the appropriation of the revenue arising
from impost and excise to the payment of the foreign debt , and the withholding all supplies from Congress until settlement of accounts between the
Commonwealth and Continent.   Resolutions, introduced by the supporters of
government, expressing disapprobation of unconstitutional assemblies, armed
combinations, and riotous movements, and pointing to the Legislature as the
only legitimate source of redress, were rejected.   The convention party was
triumphant by a small majority   While the discussion was urged, a consid-
erate citizen enquired of one of the most zealous of the discontented, what
grievances he suffered, and what were the principal evils among them ?
' There are grievances enough, thank God " was the hasty reply, 'and they
are all principal ones '

The jurisdiction of the sessions was principally over criminal offences, and
its powers were exercised for the preservation of social order   No opposition
had been anticipated to its session, on the 21st of November, and no defensive preparations were made   On that day, about sixty armed men, under
Abraham Gale of Princeton, entered the north part of the town   During the
evening, and on Wednesday morning, about one hundred more arrived, from
Hubbardston, Shrewsbury, and some adjacent towns   A committee presented
a petition to the court, at the United States Arms tavern, for their adjournment until a new choice of representatives, which was not received   The
insurgents then took possession of the ground around the Court House.
When the Justices approached, the armed men made way, and they passed
through the opening ranks to the steps   There, triple rows of bayonets presented to their breasts, opposed farther advance   The Sheriff, Col William
Greenleaf of Lancaster, addressed the assembled crowd, stating the danger to
themselves and the public from their lawless measures.   Reasoning and warning were ineffectual, and the proclamation in the riot act was read for their
dispersion   Amid the grave solemnity of the scene, some incidents were

interposed of lighter character   Col Greenleaf remarked with great severity,
on the conduct of the armed party around him   One of the leaders replied,
they sought relief from grievances : that among the most intolerable of them
was the Sheriff himself and next to his person were his fees, which were
exorbitant and excessive, particularly on criminal executions   ' If you consider fees for executions oppressive,' replied the sheriff, irritated by the attack,
' you need not wait long for redress , for I will hang you all, Gentlemen, for
nothing, with the greatest pleasure   Some hand among the crowd, which
pressed close, placed a pine branch on his hat, and the county officer retired,
with the Justices, decorated with the evergreen badge of rebellion. The clerk
entered on his records, that the court was prevented from being held by an
armed force, the only notice contained on their pages that our soil has ever
been dishonored by resistance of the laws.

   To this period, the indulgence of government had dealt with its revolted
subjects as misguided citizens, seduced to acts of violence from misconception
of the sources of their distress. Conciliatory policy had applied remedial
statutes wherever practicable, and proffered full pardon and indemnity for past
misconduct   Reasonable hopes were entertained that disaffection, quieted by
lenient measures, would lay down the arms assumed under strong excitement,
and that reviving order would rise from the confusion   But the insurgents,
animated by temporary success, and mistaking the mildness of forbearance for
weakness or fear, had extended their designs from present relief to permanent
change   Their early movements were without further object than to stay that
flood of executions which wasted their property and made their homes desolate   That portion of the community, who condemned the violence of the
actors in the scenes we have described, sympathized in their sufferings, and
were disposed to consider the offences venial, while the professed purpose of
their commission was merely to obtain the delay necessary for seeking constitutional redress   All implicated, stood on safe and honorable ground, until
the renewal on the 21st of November, of the opposition to the administration
of justice. Defiance of the authority of the state, could no longer be tolerated
without the prostration of its institutions   The crisis had arrived, when government, driven to the utmost limit of concession, must appeal to the sword for
preservation, even though its destroying edge, turn d on the citizen, might be
crimsoned with civil slaughter   Information was communicated to the executive of extensive levies of troops for the suppression of the judiciary, and the
coercion of the legislature. Great exertions were making to prevent the approaching session of the Court of Common Pleas, in Worcester, in the first week
of December. Gov Bowdoin and the council, resolved to adopt vigorous measures to overawe the insurgents   Orders were issued to Major General Warner,
to call out the militia of his division, and five regiments were directed to hold
themselves in instant readiness to march   Doubts, however, arose, how far
reliance could be placed on the troops of an infected district   The sheriff
reported, that a sufficient force could not be collected   The first instructions
were therefore countermanded, a plan having been settled to raise an army
whose power might effectually crush resistance, and the Judges were advised

to adjourn to the 23d of January following, when the contemplated arrangements could be matured to terminate the unhappy troubles

The insurgents, unapprised of the change of operations, began to concentrate their whole strength to interrupt the courts at Worcester and Concord. They had fixed on Shrewsbury as the place of rendezvous. On the 29th of November, a party of forty from Barre, Spencer and Leicester, joined Capt Wheeler, who had established his head quarters in that town during the preceding week, and succeeded in enlisting about thirty men. Daniel Shays, the reputed commander in chief, and nominal head of the rebellion, made his first public appearance in the county soon after, with troops from Hampshire. Reenforcements came in, till the number at the post exceeded four hundred. Sentinels stopped and examined travellers, and patrols were sent out towards Concord, Cambridge, and Worcester. On Thursday, Nov 30, information was received, that the Light Horse, under Col Hitchborn, had captured Shattuck, Parker and Paige, and that a detachment of cavalry was marching against themselves. This intelligence disconcerted their arrangements for an expedition into Middlesex, and they retreated, in great alarm, to Holden. On Friday, Wheeler was in a house passed by the horsemen, and only escaped from being captured by accident. Another person, supposed to be commander, was pursued, and received a sabre cut in the hand. The blow was slight, but afforded sufficient foundation for raising the cry that blood had been shed, and raising passion to vengeance. The wounded insurgent was exhibited and bewailed as the martyr of their cause. As the light horse retired, it was discovered they did not exceed twenty. About an hundred of Shay's men rallied, and returned to Shrewsbury, following a foe whose celerity of movement left no cause to fear they could be brought to an encounter. Search was made for the town stock of powder, removed by the vigilance of one of the selectmen, Col Cushing, whose house they surrounded, and whose person they endeavored to seize, but he escaped. Consultation was held on the expediency of marching directly to Worcester, and encamping before the Court House. Without clothing to protect them from cold, without money, or food to supply the wants of hunger, it was considered impracticable to maintain themselves there, and on Saturday, th y marched to Grafton, and went into quarters with their friends

The party left at Holden, found one object of their meeting, the junction with the insurgents at Concord, frustrated. Those who belonged to the neighboring towns were therefore dismissed, with orders to assemble in Worcester on Monday following. Shays retired to the barracks in Rutland, and sent messengers to hasten on the parties from Berkshire and Hampshire, in anticipation of meeting the militia of government at Worcester

On Sunday evening, the detachment from Grafton entered the town, under the command of Abraham Gale of Princeton, Adam Wheeler of Hubbardston, Simeon Hazeltine of Hardwick, and John Williams, reputed to be a deserter from the British army, and once a serjeant of the continental line. They halted before the Court House, and having obtained the keys, placed a strong guard around the building, and posted sentinels on all the streets and avenues

of the town to prevent surprise. Those who were off duty, rolling themselves in their blankets, rested on their arms, on the floor of the Court room

However the fidelity of Worcester might have wavered, its citizens had
now become aware of the peril of their rights, when the mustering power of
rebellion was attempting to upheave the foundations of government The
whole military strength of the town rallied to its support Two full companies of our militia, enrolling one hundred and seventy rank and file, paraded
on Monday, at the South Meeting House, under the senior captain, Joel Howe.
In the afternoon, they formed in column, and marched down Main street.
On approaching the United States Arms tavern, the head quarters of the insurgents, the drums beat to arms, and their lines were formed across the road
Capt Howe, advancing in slow time, sent forward an adjutant to demand by
what authority the highways were obstructed A contemptuous answer was
returned, that he might come and see Another officer was detached, to order
them to remove, as the militia intended to pass over the ground they occupied the reply was, they might pass if they could Capt Howe then halted,
and addressed his men in an animating tone, expressing his determination to
proceed, and his reliance on their intrepidity The bayonets were fixed, and
the company then advanced in a few paces they came to the position for a
charge. The front rank of the insurgents stood in readiness to use their
muskets, while the band of Capt Howe moved steadily down upon their line.
For a moment, civil war seemed about to drench our streets in blood Veterans of the revolution were arrayed on both sides, who had been too often
amid the shot of battle to shrink from danger in any form Fortunately, the
insurgents were not prepared to stain their cause by the slaughter of their
brethren Their line wavered, and breaking, by a rapid wheel, gained a new
position on the hill. The militia went by their post, to the Hancock Arms,[1]
beyond the north square It was doing no injustice to their gallantry to believe, their congratulations were sincere on the innocent result of appearances
so menacing. After brief rest, they returned, and were dismissed, until the
next morning, with merited commendations Their spirited conduct was productive of salutary effects It ascertained, that their opponents were too
apprehensive of consequences to support their demands by force, and the dread
their formidable array might have inspired, was changed to contempt and
derision of their pretensions

As the evening closed in, one of the most furious snow storms of a severe
winter commenced One division of the insurgents occupied the Court
House another sought shelter at the Hancock Arms. The sentinels, chilled
by the tempest, and imagining themselves secured by its violence from attack,
joined their comrades around the fire of the guard room The young men of
the town, in the spirit of sportive mischief, contrived to carry away their muskets, incautiously stacked in the entryway, and having secreted them at a
distance, raised the alarm that the light horse were upon them The party
sallied out in confusion, and panic struck at the silent disappearance of their

[1] This building was afterwards the Brown & Butman Tavern, and destroyed by fire, Dec
24, 1824.

arms, fled through the fast falling snow to the Court House, where their associates had paraded. The guns were discovered, at length, and the whole force remained, ready for action, several hours, frequently disturbed by the fresh outcries of their vexatious persecutors.

The increasing fury of the storm, and the almost impassable condition of the roads, did not prevent the arrival of many from Holden, and the vicinity, on Tuesday, swelling the numerical force of malcontents to five hundred. The Court was opened at the Sun Tavern,[1] and in conformity with the instructions of the Governor, adjourned to the 23d of January, without attempting to transact business. Petitions from committees of Sutton and Douglas, that the next session might be postponed to March, were disregarded.

Worcester assumed the appearance of a garrisoned town. The citizens answered to the frequent challenges of military guards : the traveller was admonished to stay his steps by the voice and bayonet of the soldier. Sentries paced before the house of Mr. Allen, the clerk, where Judge Ward resided, and the former gentleman was threatened with violence on his own threshold. Mr. Justice Washburn of Leicester, was opposed on his way, and two of his friends, who seized the gun presented to his breast, were arrested and detained in custody. Justice Baker, on his return homeward, was apprehended in the road, and some of his captors suggested the propriety of sending him to prison, to experience the corrective discipline, to which as a magistrate, he had subjected others.

On Tuesday evening, a council of war was convened, and it was seriously determined to march to Boston, and effect the liberation of the state prisoners, as soon as sufficient strength could be collected. In anticipation of attack, the Governor gathered the means of defence around the metropolis. Guards were mounted at the prison, and at the entrances of the city : alarm posts were assigned ; and Major General Brooks held the militia of Middlesex contiguous to the road, in readiness for action, and watched the force at Worcester.

During the evening of Tuesday, an alarm broke out, more terrific to the party quartered at the Hancock Arms, than that which had disturbed the repose of the preceding night. Soon after partaking the refreshment which was sometimes used by the military, before the institution of temperance societies, several of the men were seized with violent sickness, and a rumor spread, that poison had been mingled with the fountain which supplied their water. Dr. Samuel Stearns of Paxton, astrologer, almanac manufacturer, and quack by profession, detected in the sediment of the cups they had drained, a substance, which he unhesitatingly pronounced to be a compound of arsenic and antimony, so deleterious, that a single grain would extinguish the lives of a thousand. The numbers of the afflicted increased with frightful rapidity, and the symptoms grew more fearful. It was suddenly recollected that the sugar used in their beverage, had been purchased from a respectable merchant of the town,[2] whose attachment to government was well known, and the sickness around was deemed proof conclusive that it had been adulterated for their destruction. A file of soldiers seized the seller, and brought him to answer for

[1] United States Hotel, 1836.   [2] The late Daniel Waldo (sen.) Esq.

the supposed attempt to murder the levies of rebellion   As he entered the house, the cry of indignation rose strong   Fortunately for his safety, Dr Green of Ward, an intelligent practitioner of medicine, arrived, and the execution of vengeance was deferred until his opinion of its propriety could be obtained. After careful inspection of the suspected substance, and subjecting it to the test of different senses, he declared, that to the best of his knowledge, it was genuine, yellow, scotch *snuff*. The reputed dying raised their heads from the floor   the slightly affected recovered   the gloom which had settled heavily on the supposed victims of mortal disease was dispelled, and the illness soon vanished   Strict enquiry furnished a reasonable explanation   a clerk in the store of the merchant had opened a package of the fragrant commodity, in the vicinity of the sugar barrel, and a portion of the odoriferous leaf had, inadvertently, been scattered from the counter into its uncovered head   A keg of spirit was accepted in full satisfaction for the panic occasioned by the decoction of tobacco so innocently administered.

Bodies of militia anxious to testify their reviving zeal, were toiling through the deep snow drifts   Gen Warner, finding that no benefit could be derived from their presence, sent orders for their return to their homes, and the insurgents enjoyed the triumph of holding undisputed possession of the town

On Wednesday, December 6, they went out to meet Shays, who arrived from Rutland with 350 men. As they reentered the street, the appearance of the column of 800 was highly imposing   The companies included many who had learned their tactics from Steuben, and served an apprenticeship of discipline in the ranks of the revolution   war worn veterans, who in a good cause, would have been invincible. The pine tuft supplied the place of plume in their hats. Shays, with his aid, mounted on white horses, led on the van   They displayed into line before the Court House, where they were reviewed and inspected. The men were then billeted on the inhabitants   No compulsion was used   where admittance was peremptorily refused, they quietly retired, and sought food and shelter elsewhere. Provision having been made for the soldiers, Shays joined the other leaders in council   At night, he was attended to his quarters, at the house of the late Col Samuel Flagg, by a strong guard, preceded by the music of the army, with something of the state assumed by a general officer. Precautions against surprise were redoubled   Chains of sentinels were stretched along the streets, planted in every avenue of approach, and on the neighboring hills, examining all who passed. The cry of ' all's well,' rose on the watches of the night, from those whose presence brought danger to the Commonwealth

Committees from some of the neighboring towns, and many of the prominent members of the conventions, assembled with the military leaders, on Thursday, the 6th of December   Their deliberations were perplexed and discordant   The inclemency of the weather had prevented the arrival of the large force expected   The impossibility of retaining the men who had assembled, without munitions, subsistence, or stores, compelled them to abandon the meditated attack on Boston, then put in a posture of defence, and more pacific measures were finally adopted   A petition was prepared for circulation, remonstrating against the suspension of the habeas corpus writ; asking for the pardon and release of the prisoners, a new act of amnesty, the adjournment of courts until the session of the new Legislature in May; and expressing their readiness to lay down their arms on compliance with these demands In the afternoon, Shay's men and part of Wheeler's, to the number of 500, began their march for Paxton, on their way to the barracks in Rutland About an hundred more retired to the north part of the town.

Friday was spent in consultation Aware that public sentiment was setting against them with strong reaction, the mercy which had been rejected was now supplicated Letters were addressed to each town of the county, inviting the inhabitants to unite in their petitions Shays himself, in a private conference with an acquaintance, made use of these expressions · For God's sake, have matters settled peaceably, it was against my inclinations I undertook this business, importunity was used which I could not withstand, but I heartily wish it was well over ·

In the evening, the Court House was abandoned, but sentries were posted at almost every door of the outside and interior of the public house, where the leaders remained in consultation.

Another snow storm commenced on Saturday morning Luke Day, with 150 men from Hampshire, reached Leicester, but was unable to proceed in the tempest About noon, all the insurgents in Worcester paraded before their head quarters, and were dismissed The companies of Ward, Holden, Spencer, Rutland, Barre, and Petersham, after moving slowly through Main street in distinct bodies, took up the line of march for their respective homes, through roads choked with drifts

The condition of these deluded men during their stay here, was such as to excite compassion rather than fear Destitute of almost every necessary of life, in an inclement season, without money to purchase the food which their friends could not supply, unwelcome guests in the quarters they occupied, pride restrained the exposure of their wants. Many must have endured the gnawings of hunger in our streets yet, standing with arms in their hands, enduring privations in the midst of plenty, they took nothing by force, and trespassed on no man's rights by violence some declared they had not tasted bread for twenty four hours; all who made known their situation, were relieved by our citizens with liberal charity

The forlorn condition of the insurgents was deepened by the distresses of their retreat. Their course was amid the wildest revelry of storm and wind, in a night of intense cold Some were frozen to death by the way. others, exhausted with struggling through the deep and drifted snow, sunk down, and would have perished but for the aid of their stouter comrades when relief was sought among the farm houses, every door was opened at the call of misery, and the wrongs done by the rebel were forgotten in the sufferings of him who claimed hospitality as a stranger

The whole number assembled at Worcester never exceeded a thousand The spirit animating the first movements had grown cold, and Shays expressed to an acquaintance here, the impression that the cause had become gloomy and hopeless In conversation with an officer of government, he disclaimed being at the head of the rebellion ; declared he had come to the resolution to have nothing more to do with stopping courts : that if he could not obtain pardon, he would gather the whole force he could command, and fight to the last extremity, rather than be hanged When asked if he would accept pardon were it offered, and abandon the insurgents, he replied, ' Yes, in a moment ' [1]

The delay of government, while it afforded time to circulate correct information among the people, left the insurgents at liberty to pursue their measures The Court at Springfield, on the 26th of December, was resisted, and intelligence was received of active exertions to prevent the session of the Common Pleas, at Worcester, on the 23d of January Longer forbearance would have been weakness, and vigorous measures were adopted for sustaining the judiciary An army of 4400 men was raised from the counties of Suffolk, Essex, Middlesex, Hampshire, and Worcester, for thirty days service General Benjamin Lincoln, whose prudence and military skill peculiarly qualified him for the important trust, received the command Voluntary loans were made by individuals for the armament, pay, and subsistence of the troops

On the 21st of January, the army took up the line of march from Roxbury The inclemency of the weather, and the condition of the roads, rendered a halt necessary at Marlborough The next day, the troops reached Worcester, notwithstanding the effects of sudden thaw on the deep snow, and were quartered on the inhabitants, the houses being thrown open for their shelter and comfort. Here they were joined by the regiments of the county. The town contributed its quota liberally In the company under Capt. Joel Howe, were 27 non commissioned officers and privates In the artillery, under Capt William Treadwell, were enrolled 13 of our citizens Nineteen served under Capt Phinehas Jones Seven dragoons were embodied in a legionary corps Lt Daniel Goulding was at the head of a troop of cavalry The late judge Edward Bangs, Timothy Bigelow, afterwards Speaker of the house of Representatives of Massachusetts, and Theophilus Wheeler, Esq , served as volunteers

Detachments of insurgents collected at Rutland, New Braintree, Princeton, Sterling, and Sutton, but, intimidated by the military, hovered at a distance, while the courts proceeded On the 25th of January, Gen Lincoln hastened westward for the relief of Shepard, and of the arsenal at Springfield, invested by Shays and Day

Major General Warner was left in command at Worcester, with a regiment

---

[1] The retreat of Shays not only afforded the friends of order occasion for triumph but sport for wit An epigram, from one of the prints, affords a specimen of the poetry and jest of the time The name of the common carriage, the chaise, and that of the insurgent leader, had then the same spelling as well as sound

' Says sober Will, well *Shays* has fled,
  And peace returns to bless our days
Indeed ' cries Ned, I always said,
  He'd prove at last a *full back Shays*,
And those turned over and undone,
  Call him a worthless *Shays to run.*'

of infantry, a corps of artillery, including Capt. Treadwell's company, two
field pieces, and a party from the legionary battalion of volunteer cavalry.   Information having been given that a body of about two hundred insurgents
had assembled at New Braintree, intercepting travellers and insulting the
friends of government, twenty horsemen, supported by about 150 infantry in
sleighs, were sent out, on the night of the 2d of February, to capture or disperse
the disaffected.   Upon approaching the place of their destination, the cavalry
were ordered to advance at full speed to surprise the enemy.   The insurgents,
apprised of the expedition, had abandoned their quarters at the house of Micah
Hamilton, and taken post behind the walls of the road side, and having fired
a volley of musketry upon the detachment, fled to the woods : Mr. Jonathan
Rice of Worcester, a deputy sheriff, was shot through the arm and hand :
Doct. David Young was severely wounded in the knee : [1] the bridle rein of
Theophilus Wheeler, Esq., was cut by a ball.   Without halting, the soldiers
rapidly pursued their way to the deserted head quarters, where they liberated
Messrs. Samuel Flagg and John Stanton of Worcester, who had been seized
the day previous, while transacting private business at Leicester.   Having
dispersed those who occupied the barracks at Rutland, the next day, the companies returned with four prisoners.

The career of Shays was fast drawing to its close.   Driven from post to
post, he suddenly retired from Pelham to Petersham, where he expected to
concentrate the forces of expiring rebellion, and make his final stand.   Intelligence of this change of position reached Gen. Lincoln at Hadley, February
3d, and he determined, by prompt and decisive action, to terminate the warfare.   When the troops took up the line of march, at 8 o'clock, the evening
was bright and mild.   Before morning the cold became intense : the dry and
light snow, whirled before a violent north wind, filled the paths and rendered
them almost impassable.   The severity of the cold prevented any halt for rest
or refreshment.   At a distance from shelter, without defence against the
inclemency of the weather, it became necessary to press on, without pausing,
to the camp occupied by men possessing all martial advantages, except courage and a good cause.   The heavy sufferings of the night were terminated, by
the arrival of the troops in the very center of Petersham.   The followers of
Shays, trusting to the violence of the storm and the obstructions of the highways, rested in careless security.   The first warning of danger was from the
appearance of the advanced guard of the forces of government, after a journey
of thirty miles, in the midst of their cantonment.   Had an army dropped
from the clouds upon the hill, the consternation could not have been greater.
Panic struck, the insurgents fled, without firing a gun, or offering resistance
to soldiers exhausted by fatigue, with frozen limbs, and almost sinking under
the privations and hardships of the severe service.

Thirty of the citizens of Worcester were in this expedition, and shared in
the movement, called by Minot ' one of the most indefatigable marches that
ever was performed in America.'   Gen. Lincoln writes from Petersham, Feb.

[1] Dr. Young afterwards recovered £1000, in a civil action, against those by whom he
was wounded.

4, 'we arrived here about nine o'clock, exceedingly fatigued by a march of thirty miles, part of it in a deep snow, and in a most violent storm When this abated, the cold increased, and a great part of our men were frozen in some part or other , but I hope none of them dangerously so, and that most of them will be able to march again in a short time' The insurgents never again collected in force independent parties appeared in different parts of the western counties : but they were soon compelled to seek safety by submission, or flight into the neighboring states. Two or three only, of our townsmen, bore arms with Shays

The rebellion being terminated, the infliction of some punishment for the highest political crime was deemed expedient Some of those who had been in arms against the laws, were brought to trial convicted of treason, and sentenced to death. Henry Gale of Princeton was the only insurgent found guilty of capital offence, in this county [1] On the 23d day of June, at the hour fixed for his execution by the warrant, he was led out to the gallows erected on the common, with all the solemn ceremony of such exhibitions A reprieve was there read to him, and afterwards full pardon was given [2] Proceedings for seditious practices, pending against several prisoners, were suspended The mercy of government was finally extended to all, who had been involved in the difficulties and disorders of the time, upon taking the oath of allegiance to the commonwealth, after some temporary civil disqualifications [3]

---

[1] The court assigned as his counsel, Levi Lincoln, sen and James Sullivan The warm support of government by the former had rendered him obnoxious to the insurgents. During their occupation of the town, they sent parties to seize his person, who surrounded and searched his house Seasonably informed of their intentions, he was able to disappoint them

[2] Six were convicted of treason in the county of Berkshire, six in Hampshire, one in Worcester, and one in Middlesex all of whom received sentence of death, but were subsequently pardoned The only public punishment actually inflicted, except limited disqualifications from civil or military office was on a member of the house of representatives, guilty of seditious words and practices, who was sentenced to sit on the gallows with a rope about his neck, pay a fine of £50, and to be bound to keep the peace and be of good behavior for five years

[3] The facts stated in the foregoing chapter have been derived, from the Worcester Magazine, published by Isaiah Thomas, 1786, 1787, Independent Chronicle, Columbian Centinel, Minot's History of the Insurrection, Files in the office of the Secretary of State, Correspondence of Levi Lincoln, sen American Antiquarian Society's MSS Some notice of Daniel Shays will be found in the appendix

CHAPTER IX.

Reception of Washington, 1789.   Memorial on the treaty with England, 1797.   Volunteers, 1798.   Funeral honors to Washington, 1800.   Militia volunteer, 1807.   Boston Memorial, 1808.   War of 1812.   British prisoners.   Troops called into service, 1814. Visit of Lafayette, 1824.   Amendments of the Constitution.   Benefactions of Isaiah Thomas.   Incorporation of Holden and Ward.   Proposed division of the county.

In the progress of the narrative, we have arrived to that period, when the events of the past are so closely connected with the feelings of the present, as to impose painful restraint on the course of minute recital.   The faithful review of the incidents of local history from the adoption of the federal constitution, embracing the struggles of the great parties dividing the community, executed in the spirit of independence and impartiality, would be alike useful and interesting.   But the time has not yet come when the details of the contest agitating every village of the country, and kindling strife in the relations of social life, can be recorded with freedom and frankness.   The embers of political controversy, long covered over, have not been so extinguished, that the annalist may tread with safety over the spot where they once glowed. The sons may not hope to render unbiassed judgment of the measures of the sires, in scenes of intense excitement.   When another generation shall have passed away, and the passions and irritation of the actors shall exist in memory alone, the story may be told faithfully, without fear that inherited partiality or prejudice may lend undue coloring to the picture delineated.

Some particulars of the history of the last half century, insulated from those dissentions which have long been quieted and which it is not desirable now to recall to recollection, are scattered through the space remaining to be traversed.

In 1789, President Washington visited New England, and was received with those demonstrations of gratitude and respect due to his eminent services and exalted virtues.   The notice of his arrival at Worcester, in the Spy, is characteristic of the style of the times.

' Information being received on Thursday evening, [Oct. 22] that *his Highness* would be in town the next morning, a number of respectable citizens, about forty, paraded before sunrise, on horseback, and went as far as Leicester line to welcome him, and escorted him into town.   The Worcester company of artillery, commanded by Major Treadwell, were already assembled ; on notice being given that *his Highness* was approaching, five cannon were fired, for the five New England States ; three for the three in the Union ; one for Vermont, which will speedily be admitted ; and one as a call to Rhode Island to be ready before it be too late.   When the President General arrived in sight of the meeting-house, eleven cannon were fired : he viewed with attention the artillery company as he passed, and expressed to the inhabitants his sense of the honor done him.   He stopped at the United States Arms, and breakfasted, and then proceeded on his journey.   To gratify the inhabitants, he politely passed through the town on horseback, dressed in a brown suit, and pleasure glowed in every countenance, eleven cannon were again fired.   The gentlemen of the town escorted him a few miles, when they took their leave

Acceptable as the testimonials of the enthusiastic joy of his fellow citizens must have been to the great patriot, the extravagant epithets of description comported little with the simplicity and unostentious plainness of his character.

On the request of a number of the principal inhabitants, a meeting was convened, May 2, 1796, for the expression of sentiments in relation to the commercial treaty with England, a memorial, reported by a committee [1] was adopted and transmitted to the Hon Dwight Foster, representative of the district in Congress for presentation.

'To the honorable House of Representatives of the United States The inhabitants of the town of Worcester, in the county of Worcester, and state of Massachusetts, sensible that it is not wise in the people in their primary assemblies, to decide confidently on important and difficult political questions, or even to use their right of petitioning with design to impose their particular opinions, yet, on the present occasion, when the voice of the people appears to be called for, and is going forth to your honorable body from all parts of the union, leaving all questions concerning the merits of the treaty with Great Britain, take the liberty to suggest, as our opinion, that, considering the present state of the treaty already ratified by the President and Senate we believe from a serious impression of duty, and considering the happy advantages of peace and neutrality now enjoyed by this country, and the alarms, the anxieties, and interruptions to business, if not war, that may be the consequences of delaying to carry the treaty into effect, it would be best, and we, therefore, beg leave to express our wishes, that your honorable house would not delay to make appropriations to carry the same into effect '

The hostile attitude of France, in 1798, required energetic preparations for defence   Congress authorized the President, to raise troops for the war establishment, and to organize volunteer corps in a provisional army, to be called out in case of apprehended invasion, or on pressing emergency, but not to receive pay unless in actual service   A company of sixty, rank and file, was formed here, under Capt. Thomas Chandler, called the Worcester Volunteer Cadet Infantry, holding themselves in readiness to march on the reception of orders   A standard was wrought, and presented to this corps by the ladies, with the usual complimentary and patriotic address, and received with the accustomed chivalrous expressions of gratitude   The company of artillery joined the forces collected in the south part of the county, and was in the bloodless campaign of ' the Oxford Army.'   A rendezvous was opened here, during the differences with the French republic   Some of our citizens enlisted, and encamped with the 14th regiment, commanded by Lieut Col. Rice   No opportunity of distinction was afforded by land, the laurels were exclusively gathered from the ocean.

[1] Edward Bangs, Isaiah Thomas, Samuel Chandler, Benjamin Heywood, and William Caldwell.

12*

The town joined in the national honors paid to the memory of Washington, on the 22d of February, 1800, the anniversary of the birth of the father of his country. The company of cavalry, the artillery, cadets, militia, the youth of the schools, and a great concourse of citizens, moved with solemn music to the old south church, which was hung with black and with emblems of mourning. An eloquent eulogy was pronounced by the Rev. Doct. Bancroft, on the virtues of the departed soldier, statesman, and patriot.

During the political controversies, which, for nearly thirty years, divided public opinion in the United States, a decided majority of the inhabitants of Worcester were of the democratic party, when the name marked well-defined distinction of principles. The leading men of the times were ardent politicians, and there were periods of excitement when diversity of sentiment impaired the harmony of social intercourse, separated those closely allied by the ties of kindred, and dissolved the bonds of ancient friendship. When the feuds and animosities of the past have subsided, it excites surprise, that the surface, now so tranquil, should ever have been agitated by commotions as angry as were those which once disturbed its repose.[1]

Conventions of the antagonist parties constantly assembled here, and embodied, in their resolutions, the feelings of the times.

In 1807, after the attack on the Chesapeake, when it was apprehended that hostilities with England would immediately ensue, the Worcester Light Infantry, then commanded by Capt. Enoch Flagg, tendered their services in defence of the union. At a meeting of that military corps, August 4, 1807, it was resolved, unanimously, ' That in the present exigency of our country, the characters of the citizen and the soldier are inseparable ;' and with the same unanimity, it was voted, ' that we are ready, at a moment's warning, to march wherever the executive authority may direct, in defence of the independence and integrity of our country, in repelling and chastising insult or invasion ; and that, for this purpose, we will constantly hold ourselves in a state of preparation.' Soon after, the company of artillery under Capt. Curtis, two companies of infantry, under Capts. Harrington and Johnson, and the company of cavalry of Worcester and the adjacent towns, under Capt. Goulding, volunteered to serve as occasion might require.

The selectmen of Boston, on the 10th of August, 1808, transmitted a petition, adopted by the citizens of that place, addressed to President Jefferson, praying the suspension of the embargo laws ; or, if doubt existed of the competency of the executive for affording relief from measures that pressed heavily on commerce, requesting that congress might be convened for the purpose of taking the subject into consideration. The communication was accompanied with an invitation to call a meeting of the inhabitants of the town to obtain their concurrence in the sentiments expressed by the capital. The municipal officers declined compliance with the proposition. In their reply they say : ' we deferred returning an answer, because we thought we had reason to believe, that there would be found ten of our own freehold-

[1] The state of political sentiment will be sufficiently indicated by the list of votes for executive officers, in successive years, in the appendix.

ers, knowing our sentiments and differing from us, who, by signifying their desire in writing, would make it our duty to call such meeting. We can delay no longer a civility due to our fellow citizens of the respectable town of Boston. We will, therefore, with that friendly freedom which becomes citizens whose interests are the same, expose the reasons and sentiments, which forbid us to act, in our official capacity, according to your proposal.' Assenting to the constitutional right of the citizens to assemble and consult for the common good, cordially concurring in respect for the constituted authorities of the country, they depart widely from the views of policy entertained by the petitioners, and conclude by declaring, that, ' fully persuaded we have expressed the sentiments of a large majority of the inhabitants of this town, in expressing our own, we cannot believe it would be satisfactory to them, on this occasion, at this season of the year, to be called together in town meeting.'[1]

In the same year, the town voted bounties to the soldiers, detached in conformity with the act of Congress, March, 30, 1808, as a part of the state s quota of 100,000 men, and the Light Infantry again tendered their services.

On the declaration of war with England, in 1812, an act of Congress authorized the President to require of the governors of the several states and territories, to take effectual measures to arm, organize, and hold in readiness to march on the shortest notice, their respective proportions of 100,000 militia. Massachusetts was called on to furnish men for the fortresses on the maritime frontier. The executive declined compliance with the requisitions, on the ground of constitutional objections, and the troops of the state were not called to the field. The town voted, Nov. 9th, 1812, to allow each soldier detached, when mustered and ready to march, ten dollars bounty, in addition to the wages. Recruiting officers were stationed here, and some of the citizens enlisted in the regular army, or entered the navy, and served with various fortune.

In the summer of 1813, several British officers, captured on the northern frontier, were quartered here, on parole. Sir George Prevost, commanding in Canada, with the sanction of his government, selected from the American prisoners of war, and sent to Great Britain, for trial as criminals, a number of individuals, who had emigrated from the king's dominions long previous to the war between the two nations, become naturalized, and were taken fighting under the banners of their adopted country. For the protection of these citizens, charged with violation of their duties of allegiance to the land of their nativity, an equal number of English subjects were ordered into confinement, to endure the same fate which might befall those for whom they were hostages. The effect of this stern measure of retaliation was, to induce the enemy to commit to prison two American officers, for every one of the British soldiers confined by the President, to suffer death if vindictive punishment should be inflicted on the latter. Forty-six British officers, prisoners of war, were immediately placed in the prisons, and the Prince Regent was informed of the determination of

---

[1] The letter is subscribed by Ephraim Mower, Edward Bangs, Nathaniel Harrington, Nathan White, Thomas Nichols, Selectmen, and was published in the National Ægis, Aug 24, 1808.

the government to deal with his subjects in the same manner in which our citizens in captivity should be treated. On the 2d of December, ten of those who had resided here,[1] on parole, were committed by the marshal of the district, to the jail in Worcester, to abide the issue of this deplorable contest. On the 12th of January, nine of these persons succeeded in making their escape, by overpowering and binding the attendant, who had entered their room between 10 and 11 o'clock of the evening, to secure them for the night. The turnkey was so loosely confined, that he extricated himself in about fifteen minutes, and communicated information of the flight of the prisoners. Actual invasion could scarcely have produced greater commotion : the bells were rung and cannon fired at midnight. Vigorous search was prosecuted in the vicinity, and hot pursuit extended in all directions. In the excitement of the time, houses were entered without the formality of warrants, and domiciliary visits paid without the justification of judicial process, to detect the supposed concealment of the fugitives. About two o'clock the next morning, one of the prisoners was apprehended in Holden, nearly exhausted by the labor of travelling on foot, in an inclement season, after long confinement : four more were apprehended the succeeding evening in Barre ; and four succeeded in eluding capture, and reached Quebec in safety. After this event, the prisoners were removed. The returning sense of justice of their own government, permitted the liberation of gallant but unfortunate enemies, from the gloomy prospect of execution, in accordance with that necessary, but cruel policy, which holds the innocent subject to expiate the sins of the sovereign, and would have forfeited life to a contested point of international law.

In the summer of 1814, two companies of militia were drafted from the county, and served on the forts in the vicinity of Boston.

The capture of Washington, the violations of our territory by the British forces, the menace of destruction to the cities and villages of the sea board, by the naval commander on the American station, while they spread alarm, roused the patriotic spirit of the people to vigorous action. Governor Strong, by general orders, September 6, 1814, directed the whole of the militia of the state to hold themselves in readiness to march at a moment's warning, and called the flank companies of the seventh division into immediate service for the defence of the coast. The Worcester Light Infantry and Worcester Artillery, commenced their march for the metropolis, on Sunday, September 14th.[2] They were stationed at South Boston, and remained in camp until

---

[1] Lt. Col. William Grant, of the Beauharnois militia : Maj. Charles Villette, Capt. Francis Decenta, Lt. David Duvall, Lt. Albert Manuel, of the Waterville regiment : Lt. William A. Steel, Adjutant, Lt. Joseph F. Green, Commissary, 89th regiment : Lt. Arthur Carter, of the Royal Artillery : Lt. Charles Morris, of the Halifax Volunteers.

[2] The Officers of the Light Infantry were John W. Lincoln, Captain ; Sewall Hamilton, Lieutenant ; John Coolidge, Ensign : Of the Artillery, Samuel Graves, Captain ; Simeon Hastings, 1st Lieutenant, Nathan Heard, 2d Lieutenant. The forces at South Boston were under the command of Major General Joseph Whiton, of Lee. Light companies were detached from the 1st, 2d, 3d, 4th, 5th, 7th and 9th divisions, and the artillery of the 3d, 4th, 5th, 7th and 8th divisions, to form the army for the defence of Boston. The troops of the seventh division, including Worcester county, now in the sixth division, were in the regiment under Col. Salem Towne, jr., of Charlton.

the 31st of October following, when they were discharged and returned. On the Sabbath following their arrival at their homes, the members of both corps attended divine service, in full dress, agreeably to the recommendation of the General in command, and offered public acknowledgments for restoration to their friends

The town voted to procure complete camp equipage for the militia, to be kept in readiness for use in actual service, to provide for the families of soldiers where assistance was needed, and to furnish any inhabitant detached, with arms and equipments, if unable to procure them himself

As the sound of war went through the land, the veterans of the revolution, persons exempted from military duty by age or office, and the youth, formed themselves, in many towns of the county, into volunteer corps, and prepared to strike for their homes and their rights　The step of an invader on the New England soil, would have found her yeomanry as prompt to answer the summons to battle, as in the glorious days of old

The ratification of the treaty of peace was celebrated with festive rejoicing.

Gen. Lafayette, during his visit to America, in the journey which resembled a triumphal progress through the land, arrived at Worcester, September 2d, 1824　He was received on the northern boundary of the town by a deputation from the committee of the citizens, and escorted by two companies of cavalry, a regiment of the light troops of the division, and a great concourse of the people of the county　From hoary age to lisping childhood all were eager to manifest affection and respect for the guest of the nation　He passed through crowded streets, between lines of the children of the schools, ranged under the care of their teachers, who scattered laurels in his path, beneath arches inscribed with his own memorable words and with the names of the scenes of his signal services, amidst companions who had borne arms with him in the army of independence, and through the multitudes who had gathered from the vicinage to greet the return of the friend of their fathers.

Abraham Lincoln, Levi Lincoln, and Edward D Bangs, were elected delegates to the convention which was convened in 1820, for the amendment of the state constitution　Of the articles adopted by this body, November 15, 1820, and submitted to the people, nine were approved and adopted, April 9, 1821. The inhabitants of Worcester refused to ratify the 5th article, relating to the organization of the council and senate, providing that every town, having a population of 1200, should be entitled to one representative, and establishing 1200 as the ratio of increased representation and the 10th, concerning the rights and privileges of Harvard College [1]

[1] The votes of the town on the several amendments were as follows

Art.	Yeas	Nays.	Art	Yeas	Nays.
1	106	99	8	191	12
2	161	41	9	161	11
3	177	34	10	61	140
4	155	46	11	161	41
5	61	139	12	166	37
6	148	39	13	166	37
7	133	70	14	156	46

The amendment numbered as the 10th in the Revised Statutes, changing the commencement of the political year from the last Wednesday of May, to the first Wednesday of January, adopted by the legislatures of 1829 30, and 1830-31, was accepted by the people, May 11, 1831   The votes here, were, 146 for, 11 against

The amendment numbered as 11 in the volume referred to, modifying and altering the third article of the bill of rights, having passed the legislatures of 1832, 1833, was accepted by the citizens, Nov 11, 1833   Two hundred and forty six votes were given by the inhabitants of Worcester in the affirmative ; fifty five in the negative

By his last will, Doct Isaiah Thomas, devised to the town of Worcester, a lot of land on Thomas street, on the conditions, ' that the town should erect, within three years from the testator's decease, a Charity House, and pay annually to the overseers of the poor, twenty dollars, to be appropriated towards providing for poor persons who might be there maintained, on thanksgiving days, a good and liberal dinner suitable for the occasion, and to furnish on that day, half a pint of common but good wine for each person, or a reasonable quantity of such other liquors as any of them might prefer, that they might have the means of participating with their more affluent neighbors in some of the essential good things of life bestowed by a bountiful Providence, and be enabled to unite in grateful orisons for the peace and felicity of our country '   If the whole sum should not be required for the kind purpose indicated by the donor, the residue was to be expended in the purchase of books for the children of poor parents, or otherwise appropriated at the discretion of the trustees   The inhabitants, having already provided, at great expense, ample accommodations for the indigent, although duly appreciating the benevolent intentions of the testator, were compelled to decline the acceptance of the benefaction, Nov 14, 1831, on the condition imposed of erecting new buildings

The donation by the same liberal individual, of a lot, extending 172 feet on the north side of Thomas street, and 169 feet on Summer street, including the ancient burial place, for the erection of a large school house, was accepted, and the condition of the bequest complied with, by the completion of a suitable edifice

The sum of $2500 was granted by the town, April 21, 1830, to be appropriated for the purchase of the site of the Lunatic Hospital, and given to the Commonwealth.

In the narrative of events in the civil and municipal history of the town, notice of the divisions made during the period we have passed, has been reserved for the purpose of collecting the territorial changes into a connected view.

The plantation of Quinsigamond, as originally granted and surveyed, extended nearly twelve miles from north to south, and six miles from east to west [1]   It was designed to include within the boundaries established, the

1 As stated on the original plan, the north and south lines were 1920 rods each   the east line 3815   the west 3760   The Rev Mr Whitney, History of Worcester County, 25, says, ' Worcester is part of a tract of land called by the aborigines, Quinsigamond which

same quantity of land which would have been comprehended in a tract eight miles square. Extreme liberality of admeasurement greatly enlarged the proposed area. In 1684 it was directed, that the whole township should be divided into 480 lots, 200 to be set off adjoining the northern boundary. A line was drawn corresponding with this arrangement, separating the town. The north part of the lots long remained unoccupied. In 1722, a meeting of the owners, holding as tenants in common, was convened by the warrant of Stephen Minot, Esq., and a distinct proprietary erected, called North Worcester. It was determined to make partition of the lands. surveys were commenced in 1724. tracts were reserved for public uses. and grants to settlers registered. It was provided, that Col. Adam Winthrop, 'for his good services done the town, shall have the first pitch.' The planters, in 1730, were exempted from town rates in the south part, for seven years, on condition of making and maintaining their own highways. The town voted, in 1740, to consent to the incorporation, 'if it be the pleasure of the Great and General Court, in consideration of the great distance from the place of public worship.'

An act of the Legislature, giving corporate powers, passed November 2, 1740, and North Worcester became a town, by the name of Holden, in honor of the Hon. Samuel Holden, a director of the Bank of England, whose elevated character and beneficent exertions to promote the interests of literature and religion, well merited the token of respectful and grateful recollection. The first town meeting was held, May 4, 1741.

Between Worcester and that part of Sutton now Grafton, a tract of land intervened, called the Country Gore, beyond the jurisdiction of either municipality. The owners and inhabitants of this territory petitioned to be annexed to Worcester. It was voted, March 3, 1743, ' that the town cheerfully accept of this offer, and pray they be joined to, and for the future be accounted as a part of the town of Worcester, to do duty and enjoy equal privileges with us, if it may be consistent with the wisdom of the Great and General Court to grant their request.' A resolve of Massachusetts, April 5, 1743, united the petitioners and their estates to this town.[1]

Another accession of inhabitants was gained, June 2, 1758, when James Hart, Thomas Beard, James Wallis, and Jonathan Stone were set off from Leicester.

The slight additions to population were more than balanced by another dis-

territory was esteemed by them to bound, easterly partly on Quinsigamond pond and partly on Hassanamisco, now Grafton : southerly, on the Nipnet or Nipmug country, where Oxford and some adjacent towns now are westerly on Quaboag, now Brookfield, and lands in that vicinity and northerly on Nashawog, now Lancaster, Sterling, &c.' No evidence now remains to verify the assertion that Worcester was *part* of this territory. On the contrary, all the memorials which exist at this day, show that the aboriginal name was applied to the waters of the lake and the country immediately adjacent, and that it was borrowed by the committee of settlement, and bestowed upon the plantation, afterwards Worcester. The venerable father of county history was mistaken in Indian geography, when he limited the Nipmug country to the southern towns. The best authorities declare that its boundaries were much wider.

[1] The petitioners were, John Barber, Thomas Richardson, Daniel Boyden, Jonas Woodard, Ephraim Curtis, Jabez Totman, Matthias Rice, Timothy Green.

membeiment   June 23, 1773, a precinct was erected, extending three miles
into Worcester, three into Oxford, three into Leicester, and one mile and a
half into Sutton, measured from the place designated for the new meeting
house, along the roads then travelled   This district, which was denominated
the South Parish of Worcester, was incorporated, April 10, 1778, as the town
of Ward, receiving its name from Artemas Ward, Esq, a brave general of the
revolution, member of the Council of the Provincial Congress, judge of the
County Courts, and representative in Congress   About thirty families were
thus separated from Worcester   The boundaries of the parish and new town
were nearly, though not precisely, coincident   The act provided, that certain
individuals, included by the latter, but not within the limits of the former,
might retain their relations to the towns of their original settlement, until it
was their pleasure to express, in writing, intention to unite with the new corporation   Ten persons,[1] by this exception, were permitted to continue their
former connections   In 1826, Thaddeus Chapin and ten others petitioned
the Legislature to reannex the territory in which their estates were situated to
Worcester; their request was refused   and this town still has citizens exercising rights and subject to duties within the lines of Ward

The erection of a precinct, and the incorporation of a town, were strenuously resisted   Long and earnest remonstrances opposed the proceedings in each
stage, and the separation was effected by persevering efforts, renewed and
pressed in successive years

In 1785, a petition of James Ball and others was presented to the General
Court, praying for the erection of a new county, of which Petersham should
be the shire town   Hardwick, Barre, Hubbardston, Petersham, Templeton,
Winchendon, Athol, and Royalston, were to be separated from the county of
Worcester, and Warwick, Wendell, New Salem, Shutesbury, the district of
Orange, and Greenwich, from Hampshire   Orders of notice were issued, but
the proposition shared the fate of similar projects to diminish the integrity of
our territory

A memorial of the delegates of Templeton, Barre, Petersham, Athol,
Winchendon, Hubbardston, Oakham, Gerry, Gardner, Royalston, and Warwick, at the January session of the Legislature in 1798, prayed for the incorporation of those towns into a new county   The people, in April, voted that
it was inexpedient to divide Worcester into two distinct counties.

At the annual meetings in April, 1828, the question was submitted, by the
Legislature, to the people of Worcester and Middlesex, shall a new county be
formed of the towns of Royalston, Winchendon, Athol, Templeton, Gardner,
Westminster, Ashburnham, Fitchburg, Leominster, Lunenburg, Princeton,
Hubbardston, Philipston, Lancaster, Bolton, and Harvard, from the county
of Worcester, Groton, Shirley, Pepperell, Ashby, and Townsend, from the
county of Middlesex, as was prayed for in a petition bearing the name of Ivers
Jewett at the head?   The decision was in the negative, by a great majority of
the voters

[1] Samuel Curtis, Mary Bigelow, William Elder, Daniel Bigelow, John Elder, Jonathan
Fiske, Benjamin Chapin, Eli Chapin, Joseph Clark, Moses Bancroft,

ECCLESIASTICAL HISTORY.

—

CHAPTER X.

First Parish   First meeting houses   Rev Andrew Gardner   Difficulties on his dismission.   Mr Bourne   Rev Isaac Burr   Visit of Whitefield   Church Covenant, 1716   Rev. Thaddeus Maccarty   Controversy about Church music   Seating the meeting house   Difficulties ending in the separation of the Second Parish   Mr Story   Rev. Samuel Austin   Church Covenant   Rev Charles A Goodrich   Rev Aretius B Hull   Rev Rodney A Miller.   Presbyterian Church, 1719   Rev. Edward Fitzgerald   Rev William Johnston

No records of the early days of the church in Worcester have descended to our times. The knowledge possessed in relation to its organization and proceedings, previous to 1722, is derived from tradition   Subsequent to that period, some information of the prominent events in our ecclesiastical history, may be collected from the votes of the inhabitants concurrent with the acts of the church : for it was the ancient usage of all our towns, before they had been divided into parishes, to manage their parochial concerns in the general meetings

The committee of grantees, in their covenant with the first planters, provided, that care should be taken to procure a teacher of morality and religion, as soon as might be, and until regular instruction should be obtained, directed, that the Lord's day should be sanctified, by assembling together for devotional exercises. Liberal grants of land were made for the support of the ministry, and a lot appropriated for the first learned, pious, and orthodox teacher of religion

Meetings for worship were held at the dwelling houses most convenient in regard to central situation. Each man repaired to the assembly with his gun, and joined in the peaceful exercises as completely armed as if prepared for instant military service.[1] Sentinels were stationed around to give warning of approaching danger. The well-known custom of the Indians, whose prowling bands selected the rest of the Sabbath, in many instances, for their murderous invasions, rendered vigilance and precaution necessary for safety. Tradition relates, that the devotions of the planters were sometimes disturbed by alarms of the coming foe   On one occasion, an arrow, directed against the dwelling where they had assembled, entered the loop hole which served for window   The protecting Providence of God averted its point from his servants, and gliding over the congregation, it struck deep in the timbers of the opposite wall.

---

[1] In 1675, the colony court ordered, ' that every man that comes to meeting on the Lord's day, bring with him his arms with at least six charges of powder and shot   also, that whosoever shall shoot off a gun, at any game whatsoever, except at an Indian or a wolf, shall forfeit 5s   on such default until further order '

13

Soon after the last permanent settlement, a church was gathered, and Deacons Daniel Heywood, and Nathaniel Moore, elected its officers.

A plain and rude structure of logs was erected for the public meetings of the inhabitants, in 1717, eastward from the Baptist meeting house, at the junction of Franklin and Green streets, and was occupied during a few years for worship.

In 1719, a more spacious and commodious house was commenced, on the common, near the site of the present edifice.

In the autumn of the same year, the Rev. Andrew Gardner, ordained as the first settled minister of the Gospel, formed that connection with the town, terminating in acrimonious controversy, and embittering the harmony of the people of his charge. On his settlement, a gratuity of £60 was voted. The amount of salary can only be inferred from the fact, that in 1722, taxes of £40, of the then currency, were levied, for support of public worship in that year. Difficulties between the church and pastor soon arose. Complaints, probably reasonable, were made by him of neglect in the payment of his annual stipend, and of refusal to discharge the grant made on his acceptance of the office. He was accused of remissness in the performance of duty, and of too ardent love for the chase of the deer, and the sports of the hunter. The dissatisfaction so much increased, that some, who had united in the invitation to Mr. Gardner, withdrew from attendance on his preaching, and declined contributing to his maintenance. Petitions were presented to the Legislature for direction and relief, but without effect. In September, 1721, an ecclesiastical council was convened from seven churches: but its result was ineffectual for the settlement of the unhappy differences which existed. Recourse was afterwards had to other advisers, with as little beneficial influence. New petitions having been presented, a resolve was passed by the General Court, June 14th, 1722, 'that it be earnestly recommended to that council only of the seven churches which did meet at Worcester, in September, 1721, to whom the contending parties submitted their differences, relating to the Rev. Andrew Gardner, that the said council proceed and go to Worcester, on or before the first Wednesday of September next, to finish what is further necessary to be done for the procuring and establishing of peace in the said town, according to the submission of the parties.'

On the 10th of August following, the inhabitants represented, 'that the elders and messengers of the several churches, appointed to meet at Worcester, for deciding the differences in that church, decline going thither by reason of the rupture with the Indians, it being a frontier place: it was therefore recommended that the ministers meet at Dedham, for the affair aforesaid.'

The council met, pursuant to this direction, and after mature deliberation, advised that the relations of Mr. Gardner be dissolved, 'his temporal interest being secured,' and on the 31st of October, 1722, he was dismissed from the ministerial office in Worcester. Soon after, a suit at law was instituted by Mr. Gardner, for the arrears of salary. The irritation occasioned by the long controversy was increased by this unfriendly act at parting, and a vote was passed, against the remonstrance and protest of many of the elder inhabitants, not to allow the grant of sixty pounds formerly bestowed as a gratuity, which he had 'left to the generosity of the town' An accommodation was at length effected by mutual arbitrators

The Rev Andrew Gardner was a native of Brookline, Mass., and graduated at Harvard University, 1712 His name is last on the list of the class, in the period when the pupils of the venerable institution at Cambridge were entered on its catalogue according to the honors and station in society of the parents After his removal from Worcester, he was installed as the first minister of Lunenburg, Mass , May 15, 1728 This connection was as unfortunate in its termination as his earlier engagement He was dismissed, February 7, 1731-2, 'because,' says the Rev Mr. Adams, 'he was unworthy.' Mr Gardner then retired to one of the towns on Connecticut river, where he died at an advanced age [1]

The errors of Mr Gardner seem to have been more of the head than heart. Eccentricities, resulting from secluded habits, and ignorance of the ways of the world, united with that independence of spirit regardless of its opinions, diminished his usefulness Less mindful of clerical dignity than of the exhibition of wit in its practical sports, the strict sense of propriety was sometimes shocked by acts in themselves innocent Tradition relates, as illustrative of manner, that he once secretly substituted a large stone for the better food in the pot of a friend who had invited him to dine, and consoled himself for the loss of his dinner, by the gratification of witnessing the astonishment created by the appearance of the unusual dish of boiled granite Whatever imperfections marred his reputation, his benevolence and charity should be permitted to spread their mantle over his errors. Pecuniary embarrassment sometimes arose from generosity that would not hesitate to count cost An instance of its extent is preserved A poor parishioner having solicited aid in circumstances of distress, the clergyman gave away his only pair of shoes for his relief, and as this was done on Saturday, appeared the next day in his stockings, at the desk, to perform the morning service, and, in the evening, officiated in borrowed slippers, a world too wide for his slender members [2]

January 6, 1724, an invitation was given to the Rev Shearjashub Bourne to become the minister of the town, with a settlement of £100, and a salary of £75 for five years, afterwards to be raised to £80. Although the offer was declined, he continued to preach for a few months.

This gentleman was the son of Hon Melatiah Bourne, of Sandwich, and descended from the first emigrant to that town He graduated at Harvard College in 1720, and was married to Abigail, the daughter of Rev Richard Cotton of Sandwich. He was ordained in Scituate, Mass Dec 1724. His health becoming impaired by paralytic affections, he was dismissed in 1761. From an inscription on the head stone over a grave in the east burial place in Roxbury, it appears that he died there, Aug 14, 1768, aged 69 [3] His character is briefly delineated in the following lines on the time-worn monument

[1] Whitney's History of Worcester County, 144, 150   [2] Relation of Mr Daniel Goulding.
[3] MSS of Samuel Jennison, Esq Town Records 2 Hist Col iv 231

> 'Cautious himself, he others ne'er deceived,
> Lived as he taught, and taught as he believed.'

Between the dismission of Mr. Gardner and the settlement of his successor, the Rev. Samuel Jennison, son of Hon. William Jennison of Worcester, who died in that part of Sudbury now Wayland, October 14, 1729, aged 29, Mr. Fitzgerald, and Mr. Richardson, were employed to preach occasionally. The sum of £2. 3s. was paid to them for the services of the sabbath.

On the 24th of August, 1724, the church elected the Rev. Thomas White to be their pastor: the town, however, did not concur in the choice, but appointed a committee, ' to address Mr. White for his further assistance in the work of the gospel.' He was afterwards ordained minister of the first church in Bolton, Conn. Oct. 25, 1725, where he died, Feb. 22, 1763.

Soon after, the Rev. Isaac Burr was engaged to supply the pulpit, and on the 10th of February, 1725, was invited to assume the sacred office, with a settlement of 200 pounds in money, or the value in land, and the annual salary of 80 pounds. The call having been accepted, he was ordained on the 13th of October following. The churches in Hartford, Framingham, Marlborough, Lancaster, Leicester, Sudbury, Weston, and Shrewsbury, were requested to render their assistance at the ceremony; and the sum of ten pounds was appropriated for the entertainment of the elders, messengers, and delegates attending.

The ministry of Mr. Burr was long, and peaceful, until near its close. The votes in relation to pecuniary supplies, evince the cordial regard of his parishioners. The taxes not being regularly paid, it was voted, September 25, 1727, ' That the inhabitants contribute, once a month, on the Lord's day, after divine service, for the support of the minister, until a rate can properly be made; each person to paper up his money, and subscribe his name on the paper; so that an account may be taken of each person's money, to be allowed on his rate, when made.' The paper currency of the province, having depreciated in the fluctuations which diversify its history, frequent voluntary contributions were made for the minister. In answer to the petition of Mr. Burr, it was voted, October 24, 1732, ' that the town cheerfully grant him £20, and earnestly desire he would lay the same out in purchasing an addition to his library.' Successive grants of money were made, as is expressed, ' to encourage him.' The salary had been raised to £140, in bills of credit. The instability and depreciation of this medium, rendered a more certain standard of compensation necessary. In 1741, the inhabitants voted, ' to make his salary equal to what money was at the time of his settlement, having regard to the difference between silver and paper:' 29 shillings of the latter being estimated as equivalent to an ounce of the former.

The celebrated Whitefield, whose splendid eloquence seemed almost the gift of inspiration, controlling the judgment, and swaying the feelings of men at pleasure, went through New England, during his second visit, preaching to congregations gathering by the acre, beneath the open sky, in numbers no house could contain. On his way to New York, this powerful exhorter arrived in Worcester, Oct. 14, 1740, accompanied by Gov. Belcher, whose mind had been deeply impressed by the glowing elocution which had roused thousands The account of their reception is in Whitefield's continuation of the journal of his evangelical labors

'1740 Tuesday, Oct 14. Got to Marlborough, eight miles from Sudbury, about 4 : preached in the meeting house, to a large congregation At first, my heart was dead, and I had little freedom ; but before I had finished, the word came, with such a demonstration of the spirit, that great numbers were much melted down When I came into the meeting house, I turned about, and, to my surprise, found Gov Belcher there He was affected, and though it rained, and he was much advanced in years, yet he went with us as far as Worcester, 15 miles from Marlborough, whither we got about 8, at night Here we were kindly entertained, at the house of Col Chandler We spent the remainder of the evening very agreeably, with the governor, and after prayer, retired to rest Oh, that I may approve myself a disciple of that master, who, while tabernacling here on earth, had not where to lay his head

'Wednesday, Oct. 15 Perceived the governor to be more affectionate than ever After morning prayer, he took me by myself, kissed me, wept, and exhorted me to go on stirring up the ministers , 'for,' said he, 'reformation must begin at the house of God' As we were going to meeting, says he, 'Mr Whitefield, do not spare me any more than the ministers , no, not the chief of them.' I preached in the open air, on the common, to some thousands , the word fell with weight indeed , it carried all before it After sermon, the governor said to me, 'I pray God I may apply what has been said to my own heart. Pray, Mr. Whitefield, that I may hunger and thirst after righteousness' Dinner being ended, with tears in his eyes he kissed and took leave of me Oh, that we may meet in heaven. I have observed that I have had greater power than ordinary whenever the governor has been at public worship A sign, I hope, that the Most High intends effectually to bring him home and place him at his right hand. . . . . Was enabled much to rejoice in spirit. . . Preached at Leicester, in the afternoon, 6 miles from Worcester, with some, though not so much power as in the morning.'

The health of Mr. Burr having become impaired, and differences having arisen, he was desirous of relinquishing the office he had held during twenty years. In Nov 1744, a mutual council was convened The result, advising separation, met with the almost unanimous acquiescence of church and parish, and Mr Burr was dismissed, in March, 1745

The Rev. David Hall, of Sutton, seems to have been instrumental in originating the difficulties which led to the dismission of Mr Burr The following passages from his diary,[1] throw much light on the subject Dr Hall was a follower of Whitefield.

'Jan. 22, 1742, O S Preached this week twice at Worcester, in private houses. Mr Burr gave his consent before I went ꞏ but seemed not pleased at my coming, as I was informed I am grieved at my heart, to observe the violent opposition made against the work of God in the land, by those that are called his servants. But this I know, that wherein they deal proudly, the

[1] American Antiquarian Society's MSS.

13*

Lord is above them. I find much deadness of heart, for the most part: but when preaching the blessed gospel, my soul hath, of late, by times, felt all on fire: and I humbly trust the fire is from God's altar. 'Feb. 7. I am in great concern about religious matters, Mr. Burr of Worcester, refusing the urgent request of some people of Worcester, to hear me preach again with them. God seems to have blessed my poor labors lately among them, for the awakening of some of them. But oh! the prejudice of Mr. B. who is, I fear, too much a stranger to the power of godliness, or otherwise, surely, he would rejoice in having his people in concern about their souls, and in the help of such ministers as wish their salvation. Oh that the Lord would forgive him and open his eyes, and strengthen me, his poor unworthy worm, to be valiant in following the rules of my dear Redeemer.

'Nov. 30, 1744. This week Mr. Burr and the church part, under the direction of a council. The Lord stir up ministers to faithfulness by such providences.'

Mr. Bliss of Concord, one of the most distinguished of the clergy, who, in that day, were denominated *new lights*, occasionally preached to the separatists at Worcester, 'where he had been requested by a multitude of souls,' in the bold, zealous, and impassioned style he had adopted.[1]

The Rev. Isaac Burr, a graduate of Yale College, in 1717, was born in Fairfield, Conn. in 1698, and descended from an ancient family. His father, Hon. Peter Burr, of Harvard College, 1690, was in the magistracy from 1703, twenty one years; judge of Probate for Fairfield county; judge of the Superior Court of Connecticut, from the first establishment in 1711, to 1717, and from 1722 to his death, Dec. 25, 1724.[2] After his dismission, Mr. Burr removed from Worcester to Windsor in Vermont.

The difficulty experienced in procuring a successor to Mr. Burr is apparent from the instructions of the town to the committee appointed to supply the pulpit. Dec. 1744, they were directed ' to intercede with the reverend Elders of the late council to preach, each one day.' March, 1745, they were charged ' to use their utmost endeavor that the town be not destitute of preaching on the Lord's day; to procure Mr. Townsend if to be had; if not, to consult with the Rev. President Holyoke, of Harvard College, Professor Appleton, and Dr. Wigglesworth, who to engage in a probationary way.' In May, they were desired to procure two more gentlemen for the same purpose, with the advice of the Rev. President and Professors; and it was voted, ' that when they had been heard, the church should proceed to the choice from them and the three gentlemen who had already preached, Mr. Stephens, Mr. Marsh, and Mr. Phillips, and that the town will hear no more persons before a choice is made.'

On the 29th of August, 1745, Mr. Nathaniel Gardner of Harvard College, 1739, received an invitation to settle on a salary of £60 in bills of credit,

[1] Shattuck's Hist. of Concord, 175.

[2] The Rev. Aaron Burr, born in Fairfield, 1714, of Yale College, 1735, the learned President of the College at Princeton in New Jersey, was son of Judge Peter Burr. He died 1757, aged 43, leaving one daughter, who married the Hon. Tappan Reeves, a distinguished jurist, and one son, the celebrated Aaron Burr, late Vice President of the United States. MSS. Letter of Rev. Dr. Harris.

and with a gratuity of £100 of the same currency, which was declined

In the state of uncertainty and doubt which prevailed, it was voted to request the Rev Mr Peabody, and Mr Rogers of Littleton, to assist ' in carrying on a day of fasting and prayer, Feb. 28, 1746, to implore the divine direction in the church's leading in the choice of a person to be ordained ' On the 9th of May following, unanimous and earnest desire was expressed, that the Rev Mr Appleton of Cambridge, Mr Williams of Waltham, and Mr Turell of Medford, give their best advice, ' who they may judge proper to hear in order for a gentleman's being settled among us in case he can be obtained , and to advise whether all those male persons who are in full communion with other churches, and have removed hither, should be permitted to vote in the choice, provided there be no just objection.' A committee was delegated to wait on the selected advisers, ' and desire they would condescend to serve us herein ' In the interval between asking and obtaining counsel, having arrived at conclusions of their own, the opinions they had formed were adopted instead of those they obtained , on the 17th of October, ' the vote was put, whether the church would adhere to the advice of the Rev Mr Appleton, Mr Williams, and Mr Turell, and it passed in the negative '[1]

The following covenant, prepared by the Rev Mr Campbell of Oxford, and the Rev. Mr Stone of Southborough, was adopted, Sept 22, 1746, and afterwards subscribed by fifty members of the church [2]

' We, whose names are hereunto subscribed, being inhabitants of the town of Worcester, in New England, knowing that we are very prone to offend and provoke God, Most High, both in heart and life, through the prevalency of sin that dwelleth in us, and the manifold temptations from without us, for which we have great reason to be unfeignedly humble before him, from day to day, do, in the name of our Lord and Savior, Jesus Christ, with dependence upon the gracious assistance of his Holy Spirit, solemnly enter into covenant with God, and with one another, according to his holy direction, as follows ,

' First That having chosen and taken the Lord Jehovah, Father, Son, and Holy Spirit, to be our God, we will fear him, cleave to him in love. and serve him in truth, with all our hearts, giving up ourselves to him, to be his people, in all things to be at his direction and sovereign disposal. that we may have and hold communion with him, as members of Christ's mystical body, according to his revealed will, to our lives' end

' Secondly We bind ourselves to bring up our children and servants, in the knowledge and fear of God, by his instructions, according to our best abilities, and, in special, by orthodox catechisms, viz the Assembly's at Westminster larger and shorter catechisms, that the true religion may be maintained in our families while we live , yea, and among such as shall survive us, when we are dead and gone

---

[1] Sept 22, 1746. It was voted ' that the church will esteem it an offence, if any member there f, shall hereafter countenance itinerant preachers '
[2] Church Records of Rev Mr Maccarty.

'Thirdly We furthermore promise, to keep close to the truth of Christ, endeavoring with lively affections of it in our hearts, to defend it against all opposers thereof, as God shall call us at any time thereunto ; which, that we may do, we resolve to use the Holy Scriptures as our directory, whereby we may discern the mind and will of Christ, and not the new found inventions of men.

'Fourthly· We also engage ourselves, to have a careful inspection over our hearts, so as to endeavor, by virtue of the death of Christ, the mortification of our sinful passions, worldly frames, and disorderly affections, whereby we may be withdrawn from the living God

'Fifthly We furthermore oblige ourselves, in the faithful improvement of all our abilities and opportunities, to worship God, according to the particular institutions of Christ for his church, under gospel administrations; to give a reverent attention to the word of God , to pray unto him ; to sing his praises ; and to hold communion with one another, in the use of both the sacraments of the New Testament, viz Baptism and the Lord's supper

'Sixthly We likewise promise, that we will submit ourselves unto the holy discipline appointed by Christ in his church, for offenders, obeying, according to the will of God, them that rule over us in the Lord.

'Seventhly We also bind ourselves, to walk in love one towards another, endeavoring our mutual edification, visiting, exhorting, comforting, as occasion serveth, any brother or sister which offends , not divulging private offences irregularly, but heedfully following the several precepts laid down by Christ for church discipline, in xviii of Matthew, 15, 16, 17,; willingly forgiving all that manifest, unto the judgment of charity, that they truly repent of all their miscarriages

' Now, the God of peace, which brought again from the dead our Lord and Savior Jesus Christ, the Great Shepherd of the sheep, through the blood of the everlasting covenant, make us all perfect in every good word and work, to do his will, working in us that which is well pleasing in his sight, through Jesus Christ, to whom be glory forever and ever   Amen.

' Worcester, Sept 22, 1746   This church this day renewed covenant with God and with one another, and unanimously signified their assent to the above-written instrument, declaring, at the same time, their readiness to subscribe the same, at the next meeting of the church   Present, at their desire, John Prentice, Pastor of Lancaster, John Campbell, Pastor of Oxford.'

In the period of nearly two years, subsequent to the dismission of Mr Burr, many candidates were heard. Among them, the son of Rev Mr. Williams of Lebanon, the son of Rev. Mr. Williams of Springfield, Mr. Brown, Mr Emerson, Mr Marsh, Mr Benjamin Stevens, Mr Walley, Mr. Lawrence of Groton were invited to officiate   On the 17th of October, 1746, the committee were instructed, to request the Rev Thaddeus Maccarty of Boston, and the Rev Jonathan Mayhew of Martha's Vineyard, afterwards pastor of the West Church in Boston, and distinguished as one of the most intrepid champions of civil and religious liberty, and ablest divines of New England, to preach four sabbaths each.

On the 27th of November, 1746, Mr Maccarty preached his first sermon, on the public annual thanksgiving and continued to officiate very acceptably, until the day was fixed for the election of a minister, on the 19th of January, 1747

The sabbath preceding the determination between the candidates, Mr Mayhew, who had previously been heard by the people, officiated in the forenoon, and Mr. Maccarty performed the afternoon service. The latter was elected, by 42 of the 44 votes given by the church three only dissented, in town meeting, on the question of concurrence. On the 10th of June, 1747, he was installed as pastor of the religious society. The introductory prayer at the ordination was offered by Rev John Campbell of Oxford the sermon was preached by Mr Maccarty himself, from 1 Thess ii 13, and afterwards published Rev Mr. Williams of Weston, delivered the charge, and Rev Mr Cotton of Newton, gave the right hand of fellowship. The concluding prayer was by Rev Mr Appleton of Cambridge After singing Psalm lxxviii 2 to 7 verses, the benediction was pronounced by Mr Maccarty [1]

The town voted a salary of £100 in last emission money, 'having special regard to the small value of bills of credit, but if the future circumstances of Mr. Maccarty's family should call for it, they would cheerfully and willingly make him such further addition as may be judged proper from time to time' From 1750 to 1759, the annual stipend was 80 pounds, in lawful money. After the latter year, the sum of 20 pounds was bestowed by the name of gratuity

On the 23d of March, 1747, the inhabitants voted to raise the sum of £300, and appointed a committee to make sale of 100 acres of the ministerial lands in the town, for the purpose of purchasing a parsonage A resolve of the General Court, passed June 3, 1747, authorized the sale, provided the proceeds were invested in real estate for the use of the ministry The house of Dr. Samuel Breck, situated on the common, south east from the meeting house, was purchased for £187 10s and conveyed, by deed dated Sept 25, 1747, with about two acres of land adjoining, to John Chandler, treasurer, to and for the use of the town This property was granted to Mr Maccarty, on his release of all expenses for repairs, and conveyed March 4th, 1765

The history of these transactions, has, unfortunately, become matter of judicial record, [2] a suit having been instituted, April 30th, 1811, by Rev. Samuel Austin, to recover, in right of the parish, the tract of land from the tenant, claiming under the conveyance of the executors of Mr. Maccarty, in which it was finally determined that the deed of the town, in its parochial capacity, passed no title, and a judgment was rendered for the demandant, afterwards released by the Parish

On the commencement of the revolution, which Mr Maccarty had promoted by his influence, although feeling the pressure of declining years, and having a numerous family dependent upon him, he relinquished a portion of his allowance.

The feebleness of Mr. Maccarty prevented his regular performance of cler-

[1] First Church's Records, 1 1.   [2] 14 Mass Reports, 333 Austin vs Thomas

ical duties during the last years of his life. His long and useful ministry of 37 years was closed by death, July 20, 1784.

The Rev. Thaddeus Maccarty, son of Capt. Thaddeus Maccarty, an experienced commander and skillful navigator in the merchant service, was born in Boston, 1721. Early destined to a seafaring life, he accompanied his father in several voyages,[1] but the delicateness of his constitution, rendered him unable to endure the hardships and exposure of the ocean, and his attention was directed to the more quiet pursuits of a profession. His preparatory studies were in the town school of Boston, and he graduated at Harvard College, in 1739.

Soon after completing his theological education, he received and accepted an invitation to settle in Kingston, in Plymouth county, where he was ordained as the pastor of that town, Nov. 3, 1742. At the expiration of three years, the connection was dissolved, under peculiar circumstances. The enthusiastic eloquence of Whitefield had stirred up the slumbering spirit of piety, and his bold attacks on the regular clergy, alarmed the friends of the church. The unguarded bitterness of expressions, and the neglect of conciliatory policy on the part of that celebrated itinerant, changed mere disapprobation of his measures into determined hostility. The inhabitants of Kingston, apprehensive of the disturbance of their peace by his visit, and fearful of his power to excite commotion, appointed a committee, Jan. 29, 1745, to prevent the intrusion of roving exhorters. An unfounded report was circulated that Mr. Maccarty, who was supposed to be attached to Whitefield, then in Plymouth, had invited him to preach the sacramental lecture. Much excitement arose, and effectual care was taken to prevent the exercises of the obnoxious individual, by closing and fastening the meeting house, nailing the doors, and covering the windows with boards. Mr. Maccarty, indignant at the personal insult and violation of his rights, omitted attending at the time appointed for the lecture, and immediately asked dismission. A council was convened, and, although, it is said, he had become desirous of withdrawing his request, it was granted, against his wishes, and the result, advising separation, accepted by the town. On the 3d of November, 1745, three years to a day from his ordination, he preached a farewell sermon, from the appropriate text, Acts xx. 31. ' Therefore watch, and remember that by the space of *three years*, I ceased not to warn every one, night and day, with tears. And now, brethren, I commend you to God, and to the word of his grace, which is able to build you up, and to give you an inheritance among all them that are sanctified.' A copy of the discourse was left in Kingston, and sixty years after the delivery, and long after the decease of the author, it was published, with a preface, containing a brief statement of the transaction, and remarks reproachful to the people of Kingston.[2]

His character is faithfully delineated in the following inscription on the monument erected to his memory.

' Beneath this stone are deposited the remains of the Rev. Thaddeus Mac-

[1] MS. note on a sermon, in hand writing of Rev. Mr. Maccarty.
[2] 2 Mass. Hist. Coll. iii. 209.

carty, for thirty seven years pastor of the church in Worcester   Through the
course of his ministry, he uniformly exhibited an example of the peaceable
and amiable virtues of christianity   Under a slow and painful decline, he
discovered an ardent love to his master, by a cheerful attention to his service,
and at the approach of death, he patiently submitted, in the full hope of a
glorious resurrection from the grave.   In testimony of his fidelity, the people
of his charge erect this monument   Obiit, July 20, 1784, Ætatis 63.'

Mr. Maccarty was tall in stature: in person slender and thin, with a dark
and penetrating eye   a distinct and sonorous, though somewhat harsh-toned
voice.   His address was impressive and solemn.   In sentiment he was strictly
calvinistic [1] in politics decided and firm, ranking however with the moderate
whigs   His printed sermons are more characterized by judicious thought,
good sense, and piety, than elegance or eloquence   After preaching a convention sermon, a contemporary clergyman remarked, that he had never heard
him preach either a very low, or a very brilliant discourse [2]

[1] President John Adams, in a letter to the Rev. Dr. Bancroft, says; 'when I removed to
Worcester, in 1735, I found that county hot with controversy between the parties of Mr
Buckminster and Mr. Mellen   I became acquainted with Dyer, Doolittle, and Baldwin,
three notable disputants.   Mr Maccarty, though a calvinist, was not a bigot, but the town
was a scene of disputes all the time I lived there '   Mass. Spy, April 23, 1823

Joseph Dyer, attorney and merchant, Ephraim Doolittle, merchant and afterward colonel
of a regiment, Nathan Baldwin, Register of Deeds, were all deists   Of the two former,
some notice will be found in succeeding pages   The latter was an ardent politician, and
the author of many of the addresses and documents of our revolutionary annals   He
died at Worcester, July 21, 1784.

[2] The following list contains all the publications of Mr Maccarty   1 Farewell sermon,
preached at Kingston, Nov 3, 1745, printed, Boston, 1804   2 The success of the preached
gospel matter to faithful ministers of continual thankfulness to God   sermon at the author's installation to the pastoral office in Worcester, June 10, 1747   1 Thes xi 13   3
The advice of Joab to the Host of Israel going forth to war, considered and urged . in two
discourses delivered in Worcester, April 5, 1759, being the day of the annual fast, and
the day preceding the general muster of the militia throughout the province for the enlisting soldiers for the intended expedition against Canada   4 The power and grace of
Christ displayed to a dying malefactor   sermon, Oct 20, 1768, the day of the execution of
Arthur, a negro, at Worcester   5 The most heinous sinners capable of the saving blessings of the gospel   sermon, Oct 25, 1770, on the execution of William Lindsey for burglary, at Worcester.   6 Praise to God, a duty of continual obligation   sermon, Nov 23,
1775, public thanksgiving   7 The guilt of innocent blood put away   sermon, July 2, 1778,
on the execution of Buchannan, Brooks, Ross, and Mrs Spooner, for murder, at Worcester.
Most of the manuscripts of Mr. Maccarty were destroyed at his decease, in compliance
with his wishes   Among them, was the historical discourse, of whose contents the following memorandum was entered by him on the church records

'Thursday, Dec 8, 1763   This day, being the public thanksgiving throughout the province, and the day also of this congregation's assembling in their new meeting house, which
began to be erected on June 21st preceding, exactly 16 years from the time of my instal-
ment to the pastoral office, I preached a sermon from 1 Chr xxix 16, 17, in which some
brief account was given of the original settlement of this town, the gathering of this
church, its pastors, admissions, baptisms, &c and some proper notice taken of the solemnity of thanksgiving'

Rev Thaddeus Maccarty married Mary Gatcomb, Sept 8, 1743   Their children were
1 Thaddeus, b July 29, 1744. 2 John, b Aug 16, 1745 . both died in Kingston   3.
Thaddeus, b Dec 19, 1747, graduated at Yale College, 1766 . married Experience, d of

A singular controversy in relation to the form of conducting the musical portion of public worship in our churches, growing out of attachment to ancient customs and resistance of innovations, arose at an early period. In its progress, it converted the harmony of christians in the house of prayer into discord, and though trifling in its origin, became of so much importance, as to require the frequent directory interference of town meetings, and only arrived at its conclusion when the great revolutionary struggle swallowed up all minor objects.

Anciently, those who joined in singing the devotional poetry of religious exercises, were dispersed through the congregation, having no place assigned them as a distinct body, and no privileges separate from their fellow worshippers. After the clergyman had read the whole psalm, he repeated the first line, which was sung by those who were able to aid in the pious melody : the eldest deacon then pronounced the next line, which was sung in similar man-

Thomas Cowdin, Esq. of Fitchburg, Jan. 16, 1775 : physician, practiced sometime in Worcester, then in Keene, N. H. where he died Nov. 21, 1802. 4. Thomas, b. Sept. 24, 1749 : d. March 14, 1750. 5. Mary, b. Oct. 30, 1750 : married Hon. Benjamin West, of Charlestown, N. H. in 1781 : d. Aug. 1803. 6. John, b. Jan. 10, 1752 : d. June 19, 1752. 7. Elizabeth, b. Jan. 7, 1753 : d. March 25, 1823. 8. William Greenough, b. Dec. 20, 1753, quarter master, in Col. Bigelow's, 15th Mass. regiment, died at Billerica, Aug. 13, 1791 : he married Hannah Soley of Charlestown, Mass. who after his decease married Nathan Adams of the same town, and is now his widow. 9. Samuel, b. March 23, 1755 : d. July 21, 1755. 10. Thomas, b. and d. Dec. 5, 1755. 11. Francis, b. Sept. 28, 1756 : d. June 7, 1757. 12. Nathaniel, b. July 10, 1758 : learned the trade of a printer, with Isaiah Thomas, afterwards merchant in Petersham, died in Worcester, Oct. 14, 1831. 13. Lucy, b. June 25, 1760 : d. June 23, 1813. 14. Lucretia, b. July 15, 1762 : d. Jan. 1810. 15. Francis, b. Aug. 8, 1763 : d. Sept. 9, 1764. The mother died, Dec. 28, 1783, at Worcester.

Mary Gatcomb was daughter of Francis Gatcomb, an emigrant from Wales, who became a wealthy merchant of Boston, where he died, July 20, 1744, aged 51 ; his wife, Rachel, died, Nov. 20, 1752, aged 51. The marriage of one of their four daughters with one Winter, was full of the romance of real life. He had worked as a wood sawyer at her father's door, and it was not known to the family that she even spoken to him. One afternoon, she put on her bonnet and shawl, and said she was about to visit a place she named. Her sister observed, ' stop a few minutes, and I will go with you.' ' No,' she replied, ' I am in a hurry ;' and immediately went out. Night coming on, the family became greatly alarmed by her absence, and made ineffectual search in all directions. The next morning revealed the mystery of her disappearance ; she had become the lawful wife of Winter. Her parents were much incensed, and forbade her the house ; but afterwards, on his death bed, her father became reconciled, received her again to favor, and in the division of his estate, which was large for those days, made her share equal to that of his other children. Winter proved a kind, but thriftless husband. They embarked for Halifax, were shipwrecked, lost all their effects, and narrowly escaped with life. Finding nothing but poverty and distress at Halifax, they returned to Boston. Winter did the best he could to support his family by day labor, and was ever kind and affectionate to the woman he had led from the affluence of her former home to the penury of his own lot. Misfortune followed him, and his exertions were unsuccessful. His wife, at length, fell into consumption. The Rev. Mr. Maccarty, who married her sister, went to Boston to visit her in distress, and found her in a bare hovel, on a straw bed, destitute of every thing. He administered all the consolation in his power, gave to her a guinea, a large present for him to make at that time, knelt down by her and prayed, and, commending her to the protection of heaven, departed. She died, in about six weeks after, without issue. MS. Letter of John W. Stiles, Esq.

ner, and the exercises of singing and reading went on alternately. When the advantages of education were less generally diffused than at present, the custom was established, to avoid the embarrassment resulting from the ignorance of those who were more skilful in giving sound to notes than deciphering letters   The barbarous effect produced by each individual repeating the words to such tune as was agreeable to his own taste, became apparent   The first attempt at the reformation of this 'usual way,' as it was termed, was made March, 1726, when a meeting of the inhabitants was called for the purpose of considering 'in which way the congregation shall sing in future, in public, whether in the ruleable way, or in the usual way,' and the former was adopted, though not without strong opposition at the time and great discontent after [1] Ineffectual application having been made to the selectmen, to convene the people, for the purpose of again discussing the subject, a warrant was procured from John Minzies, Esq of Leicester, calling a meeting, 'to see if the town will reconsider their vote concerning singing, it being of an ecclesiastical nature, which ought not to stand on our town records ' but the article was dismissed.

The next step was, the attempt to procure the aid of some suitable person to lead and direct in the performances   It was voted, May, 1769, 'that the elder's seat be used for some persons to lead the congregation in singing' The adherents of old usage possessed sufficient influence to negative a proposition for raising a committee to invite a qualified individual to perform this office   In March, 1770, 'it was voted, that Messrs James McFarland, Jonathan Stone, and Ebenezer Flagg, sit in the elder's seat to lead, and on a motion made and seconded, voted unanimously, that Mr William Swan sit in the same seat, to assist the aforesaid gentlemen in singing '   It remained, to gather the musicians to one choir, where their talents in psalmody could be better exerted than in their dispersion, and in 1773, 'the two hind body seats, on the men's side, on the lower floor of the meeting house,' were assigned to those who sat together and conducted singing on the Lord's day

The final blow was struck on the old system, by the resolution of the town, Aug 5, 1779   'Voted, That the singers sit in the front seats in the front gallery, and those gentlemen who have heretofore sat in the front seats in said gallery, have a right to sit in the front seat and second seat below, and that said singers have said seats appropriated to said use   Voted, That said singers be requested to take said seats and carry on singing in public worship. Voted, That the mode of singing in the congregation here, be without reading the psalms, line by line, to be sung '

The sabbath succeeding the adoption of these votes, after the hymn had been read by the minister, the aged and venerable Deacon Chamberlain, unwilling to desert the custom of his fathers, rose, and read the first line according to his usual practice   The singers prepared to carry the alteration into effect, proceeded, without pausing at its conclusion   the white-haired officer

---

[1] Its execution was defeated by the resistance of the deacons, who, on the ensuing Lord's day, read line by line as usual, without regard to the vote   Respectful regard to the feelings of these venerable men prevented the contemplated change

of the church, with the full power of his voice, read on, until the louder notes of the collected body overpowered the attempt to resist the progress of improvement, and the deacon, deeply mortified at the triumph of musical reformation, seized his hat, and retired from the meeting house, in tears. His conduct was censured by the church, and he was, for a time, deprived of its communion, for absenting himself from the public services of the sabbath.

The mode of reading prevailed in Boston, and throughout New England, until a few years prior to the last mentioned date, and in some places beyond it. A relic of the old custom probably still survives, in the repetition of the first line of the hymn by clergymen of the present day.

The improved version, by President Dunster, of the translation attempted by Rev. Mr. Weld, Rev. Mr. Eliot of Roxbury, and Rev. Richard Mather of Dorchester, according to the agreement of the ministers in 1639, was used in the church here until 1761, when it was voted, ' that it would be agreeable to change the version of the Psalms, and to sing the version composed by Tate and Brady, with an appendix of scriptural hymns of Dr. Watts', and this was begun to be used Nov. 29, of that year. The hymns of Dr. Watts were substituted for the book before used, Jan. 20, 1790.

The public reading of a lesson from the Scriptures, as a stated portion of the service, was not introduced into New England until near the middle of the last century. The following extract from the church records shows the period when it was first commenced here. ' 1749, Sept. 3. Voted, that thanks be given, by the pastor, publicly, to the Hon. John Chandler, Esq. for his present of a handsome folio Bible for the public reading of the Scriptures, which laudable custom was very unanimously come into, by the church, at one of their meetings some time before.'

The assignment of places in church was formerly matter of grave consideration, and frequently claimed the attention of the town. In 1724, a large committee was instructed to seat the meeting house, ' taking as the general rule the two last invoices of ratable estate, saving liberty to have due regard to principal builders as they shall see cause.' After long lapse of time, they were directed in 1733, ' to proceed and finish the meeting house, and that the rule they principally guide themselves by, be a person's usefulness, or the station he holds in age and pay, not having regard to plurality of polls, but to real and personal estate.' In 1748, it was directed, that the men's seats in the body of the house be enlarged to the women's seats, that a man and woman be placed in each of the pews to be constructed, and a seat for the children be made in the body before the seats.' An article was inserted in the warrant of April, 1750, ' to give directions that people may sit in the seats assigned to them, to prevent discord, and that they do not put themselves too forward,' and at the meeting it was voted, ' that the selectmen give tickets to such people as have not taken their seats properly, according to the last seating, directing them to sit where they ought, so as to prevent disorder, and that they fill up properly any pews lately built.' In the house erected in 1763, the right of selection of pews was given ' in the order of amounts paid for building.'

The declining health of Mr Maccarty, during the last years of his life, had prevented his constant ministration, and rendered aid necessary for the pulpit In March, 1781, a committee was instructed to engage the temporary assistance of clergymen

In July, 1783, the increasing infirmities of the pastor, made it apparent that the days of his usefulness were drawing near their close   With the view to provide an assistant, or successor, it was voted, to settle a colleague, and to invite candidates to officiate on probation   Gentlemen whose labors in other towns were afterwards crowned with distinguished success, were heard, but failed to produce such impression as to unite the members of the parish in the selection from the number   Among others, the Rev Aaron Bancroft preached eight sabbaths in the autumn of 1783   On the termination of his engagement, Mr Maccarty was so far restored to health, as to be able to resume the discharge of his duties for a short period

In July 1784, the pulpit was left vacant by his decease   In October following, Mr Bancroft again preached five or six times   Differences of opinion on religious doctrine had sprung up, which in their progress, produced division in the parent parish, and are stated on the record, to have disturbed the peace of the town and the intercourse of society

In November, 1784, a day was set apart by the town, for humiliation, prayer, and supplication of the divine assistance for the reestablishment of the Gospel ministry

Mr Bancroft returned to Worcester, under a third engagement to preach, in January 1785   A meeting was convened in March of that year, on the request of 48 petitioners   A motion was made to settle Mr. Bancroft as the minister   The opposition of the majority arose from diversity of religious sentiment,[1] and not from objection to the character or ability of the candidate.   It was proposed, as a means of compromise, that he should be called to settle   that those opposed should be at liberty to settle a colleague of their own choice · and that the salaries of both be paid from the common treasury, but this was rejected   The friends of Mr Bancroft, next requested the assent of the town to the formation of another society, which was refused   They then withdrew, voluntarily associated themselves together, and although the legal connection was not dissolved until an act of incorporation was obtained, long afterwards, they maintained public worship separate from the parish

The division springing from this source, and extending its distracting influence over civil, municipal, social, and private affairs, continued to impair harmony.   Those who seceded, still remained liable to taxation, and while

---

[1] ' On application for an incorporating act, a committee of the legislature was appointed to report on the prayer of the petition, of which the venerable Charles Turner, once a distinguished clergyman, was chairman   He was liberal in his opinions, but much opposed to the ecclesiastical division of towns and parishes, and he demanded the reasons, which rendered it expedient that the town of Worcester should thus be divided   Judge Lincoln, chairman of the parish committee, replied, ' The majority of our inhabitants are rigid Calvinists, the petitioners are rank Arminians ' Dr Bancroft's Half Century Sermon, 42.

charged with the support of their own minister, were compelled to contribute their proportion of the parochial expenses of their opponents. The members of the new society claimed a share in the funds arising from the sale of lands appropriated for religious purposes, and of the property which had been held in common for ministerial use. During two years, continual but ineffectual attempts were made to secure equitable adjustment. Meeting after meeting was held. Propositions to exonerate the new society from taxation in the parish from which they had separated ; to distribute the ministerial funds and property ; to submit the determination of the whole matter to the arbitration of the Justices of the Supreme Judicial Court, or of referees mutually chosen ; with all varieties of modifications, were successively rejected. The petitions for incorporation were opposed ; all terms of accommodation denied ; and the meetings were disturbed by the conflict of the contending parties, until the act of the Legislature defined the rights of the minority, and all the controversy subsided.

While this warfare of brethren was going on, attempts were made to settle a minister in the elder society.

May 15, 1786, an invitation was given to Rev. Daniel Story for this purpose, with an offer of £300 settlement, and £120 annual salary, and accepted by him. His ordination was postponed, with the hope that an amicable settlement of the controversies of the societies could be effected. October 15, 1787, the last Wednesday of November was fixed for the ceremony, and a committee charged with the proper preparations. Before the time appointed for his installation arrived, another meeting was held, and the former vote reconsidered. Adjournments took place from month to month, without final action on the subject, until March 10th, 1788, when the invitation was recalled, and the relation which had commenced between pastor and people was dissolved, after Mr. Story had preached about two years. This measure was adopted, probably in compliance with his wishes, and was induced by his reluctance to remain permanently, where his means of usefulness would be limited, and restrained by the existing divisions.

Rev. Daniel Story, son of William Story of Boston, who held the office of Commissioner of Stamps, was a graduate of Dartmouth College in the class of 1780. After his removal from Worcester, he preached as a candidate for the ministry in Concord, New Hampshire. Although an acceptable preacher, the Arminian sentiments he was said to entertain, prevented his settlement. He removed to Ohio, and was settled as the first minister of Marietta, where he died in 1813.[1]

Nov. 13, 1787, the New Society was incorporated by the legislature. From this time, the first parish commenced its legal existence distinct from the municipal corporation, and the support of worship ceased to be provided for by the inhabitants in their general meetings.

The Rev. Abiel Flint, Israel Evans, Elijah Kellog, Enoch Pond, Joshua Cushman, William F. Rowland, and Ebenezer Fitch, supplied the desk, after the retirement of Mr. Story.

[1] J. Farmer, in New Hampshire Hist. Coll. iii. 248.

On the 22d of March, 1790, the Rev Samuel Austin of New Haven, was invited to settle on a salary of £130 After the acceptance of the call by that gentleman, disapprobation was expressed by an individual For the purpose of ascertaining the precise extent of opposition, and to avoid the painful consequences of discontent a second meeting was held, when there were found to be seventy three for, and only two against the candidate.

Mr Austin was installed, Sept 30, 1790. The Rev Samuel Spring of Newburyport, introduced the solemnities with prayer : Rev Samuel Hopkins of Hadley, delivered the sermon Rev Ebenezer Chaplin of Sutton, made the ordaining prayer : Rev Joseph Sumner of Shrewsbury, gave the charge Rev Nehemiah Williams of Brimfield, bestowed the right hand of fellowship Rev Nathaniel Emmons of Franklin, offered the concluding prayer

As a substitute for the old articles of faith and covenant, the following were unanimously adopted by the church, to be used in the admission of members [1]

'1 I believe that there is one, only, living, and true God, a Being independent and eternal in his existence and glory, unchangeable in his purposes, possessed of infinite power, wisdom, and justice, goodness and truth, and who is the Creator, Benefactor, Preserver, and sovereign righteous Governor of the universe

'2 I believe that the Scriptures of the Old and New Testament were given by inspiration of God, are clothed with divine authority, and are a perfect rule of faith and manners

'3 I believe that the Scriptures teach, that God exists, in a manner incomprehensible to us, under a threefold distinction or Trinity of persons, as the Father, Son, and Holy Ghost, and that to these three persons, as the one God, all divine perfections are to be equally ascribed

'4 I believe that every individual of the human race, is, by connection with the first man, and in consequence of his apostasy, natively dead in trespasses and sins, at enmity with God, and must be regenerate in heart, and sanctified by the agency of the Holy Ghost, in order to final salvation.

'5 I believe that God hath, from the foundation of the world, ordained some, by an election purely of grace, unto everlasting life, who, and who only, will be finally gathered into the kingdom of the Redeemer

'6 The only Redeemer of sinners, I believe, is the Lord Jesus Christ, who is strictly and properly a divine person, who, by the assumption of the human nature in union with the divine, became capable of making a meritorious and effectual sacrifice for sin, by giving himself up to the death of the cross, that by this sacrifice he became the propitiation of the sins of men ; that, as risen from the dead, ascended and glorified, he is the Head of the Church, and the final Judge of the world, and that all who are saved, will be entirely indebted to the sovereign Grace of God, through his atonement.

'7 I believe that those who are regenerated and united to Christ by a true faith, will never finally fall away, but will be preserved by divine power,

---

[1] These articles were not entered on the church records until May 23, 1815 They were then revised, but it stated, were varied in phraseology only, and not in sentiment

14*

and in fulfillment of God's eternal purpose of Grace, unto final salvation.

'8. I believe that those who die in a state of impenitency and unbelief are irrevocably lost.

'9. I believe in the resurrection of the dead and a general judgment, in the issue of which the righteous will be received to the perfect and endless enjoyment of God in heaven, and the wicked will be sentenced to be everlastingly punished in that fire which was prepared for the devil and his angels, which sentence I believe will be fully executed.

'10. I believe in the sacraments of the Gospel dispensation, baptism and the Lord's Supper, as the two ordinances instituted by Christ, for the edification of his body the church : that visible believers only, who appear to receive the truth in the love of it, and to maintain a conversation becoming the Gospel, have a right of admission to the Lord's Supper, and that they, with their households, are the only proper subjects to whom baptism is to be administered.'

The following Covenant was subscribed.

'You do now, in the presence, of God, angels, and men, avouch the Lord Jehovah, Father, Son, and Holy Ghost, to be your God, the object of your supreme love and your portion : You receive, trust in, and desire to obey, the Lord Jesus Christ as your only Redeemer ; You choose the Holy Spirit as as your Sanctifier : You give up yourself and all that you have to God, to be his, desiring above all things to be an instrument of his glory in that way which he shall see best ; and promising, through the help of divine grace, without which you can do nothing, that you will deny ungodliness and worldly lusts, and that you will live soberly, righteously, and godly, even unto death, you cordially join yourself, as a brother, to this church, as a true church of our Lord Jesus Christ, and engage to be subject to its discipline, so far as it is comformable to the rules which Christ has given in the Gospel, and that you will walk with the members thereof, in all memberlike love, watchfulness, and purity.'

Upon assent to this covenant, on occasion of admission, the church respond, 'Then doth this church receive you into its bosom, promising you our prayers and christian love, and we severally engage, with the help of divine grace, that we will walk with you in all brotherly watchfulness and kindness, hoping that you and we shall become more and more conformed to the example of our divine Master, till we at last come to the perfection of holiness in the kingdom of his glory. Amen.'

During the war, and amid the violence of party contention, Dr. Austin expressed his political sentiments strongly, in sermons preached on the special fasts.[1] Many took offence at this course. A meeting was called, to ascer-

---

[1] The sermon preached on occasion of the special fast, July 23, 1812, was published, with the following characteristic imprint on the title page : ' Published from the press, by the desire of some who heard it, and liked it ; by the desire of some who heard it, and did not like it ; and by the desire of others, who did not hear it, but imagine they should not have liked it, if they had.'

tain the views of the parish in relation to these discourses, and to consider the
expediency of dissolving the existing connection   The minister was sustained
by a great majority, and the meeting dissolved without action. The disaffected withdrew from his congregation, and many united in forming the Baptist
Society.

In 1815, Mr Austin accepted the presidency of the University of Vermont,
and solicited dismission ; but, on the request of the church and parish,
assented to their concurrent votes, June 12, giving him leave of absence until
the first of September then following, that he might have time and opportunity to obtain the information necessary for final decision, and that candidates
might be invited to supply the pulpit, with a view to the settlement of colleague or successor. Having determined to remain in Burlington, it was considered desirable that his pastoral relations should still be retained, on account
of the civil process instituted in his name by the parish against the town, for
the recovery of ministerial lands   An adjudication was had in the legal controversy, at the distance of about two years from his change of residence.
Regard for the wishes of a minority, influenced him in longer preserving the
original connection, which was finally terminated by the result of a mutual
council, Dec 23, 1818.

Dr Samuel Austin was born in New Haven, Nov 7, 1760 [1]   When the
revolutionary war commenced, he entered the army, and served in New York
when the British took possession of the city, and, occasionally, for short periods, in other campaigns   After having devoted some time to the instruction
of youth, he applied himself to the study of law with Judge Chauncy of
Connecticut   Feeling the necessity of higher classical attainments, he fitted
himself, and was admitted to the Sophomore class of Yale College, in 1781,
where he was distinguished as an accomplished linguist, and received the first
appointment in the commencement exercises of 1784. Under the theological
tuition of Dr Edwards, he was prepared for the ministry   For four succeeding years, while a candidate, he was at the head of an academy in Norwich.

During the period of this employment, one unanimous invitation to settle
in Hampton, Connecticut, and another, to become colleague with Dr. Livingston, in the pastoral care of the Middle Dutch Church in the city of New York,
were declined   The religious sentiments of Dr. Austin were decidedly calvinistic, of the school of the Edwardses, and he required a stricter creed than
that of either society   In 1787, he accepted the call of the church of Fair
Haven, in the city of New Haven. During the next year, he was married to
Jerusha, daughter of Dr. Samuel Hopkins of Hadley.   Strong disapprobation
of the *halfway covenant*, as it was called, induced him to seek the dissolution
of the connection with the society of his settlement, which had continued two
years. Before the ceremony of dismission, as soon as his intention to leave
New Haven became known, he was earnestly solicited to become minister of
the first parish in Worcester   Yielding personal wishes to sense of duty, he
was installed, Sept 30, 1790, and retained the relation, thus commenced,

---

[1] His father, Samuel Austin, married Lydia Walcot   they had two sons and a daughter,
of whom Dr Austin was the eldest.

twenty five years. Having been elected President of the University of Vermont, in 1815, he removed to Burlington The operations of that institution had been suspended for three years by the war, and its buildings occupied as barracks for troops The whole permanent income little exceeding one thousand dollars annually, its prosperity suffered by the derangement and depression of the times. Feeling that his expectations of usefulness and happiness could not be realized, after discharging the duties of his appointment six years, with fidelity, Dr Austin resigned The labors of his station had impaired his health, and its anxieties probably, pressed heavily on his mind. He resumed occupations more congenial to his tastes and habits, than were the government and support of the college, and selecting a people at Newport, in Rhode Island, unable to afford full support, went among them as on a missionary charity, and was installed in 1822 Increasing infirmity of body and depression of spirits, compelled him to retire, in 1826, and he returned to Worcester He afterwards preached in Millbury, and was solicited to resume the ministry by a new society in that place, but declined. The death of a nephew and adopted son, John W. Hubbard, Esq , and the separation of a family, where he might have expected to make a peaceful home, cheered by the kindness which soothes the heavy hours of sickness and despondency, involved him in affliction and engaged him in entangled affairs of business. Under the perplexities and beneath the oppressive burden of unaccustomed transactions, his mental energies gave way, and were, at length, prostrated. Occasional aberrations of reason terminated in deep religious melancholy, and sometimes, paroxysms of hopeless despair clouded his declining days with gloom After passing a year in the family of his brother in law, Mr Hopkins of Northampton, he removed to that of a nephew, the Rev. Mr Riddel of Glastenbury, Connecticut, where he died, in an apoplectic fit, Dec. 4, 1830, aged 71.

He was one of the founders, with Drs Emmons and Spring, of the Massachusetts Missionary Society ; active in originating the General Association of Massachusetts ; member of the American Board of Commissioners for Foreign Missions : one of the projectors and a contributor of the Panoplist, an able religious periodical ; and promoted with energy and zeal the objects of many public charitable institutions. In 1808, he collected and published the works of the elder President Edwards, the first and only complete and accurate edition of the writings of that celebrated theologian He received the degree of Doctor of Divinity from Williams College During his whole life he was an industrious and voluminous author.[1]

[1] The printed works of Dr Austin are the following 1 Funeral oration in the chapel at Yale College, on the death of David Ripley, a classmate, July 11, 1782 2 Sermon on disinterested love, New York 3 Funeral sermon, Exeter, N H. April 10, 1790 4 Sermon on the sabbath following the author's installation, Worcester, Sept 1790 5 Sermon on the sabbath following the death of Miss Hannah Blair, 1792. 6 Thanksgiving Sermon, Worcester, Dec 15, 1796 7. Sermon on the Ordination of Rev Samuel Worcester, at Fitchburg, Mass. Sept 27, 1797, and again preached at the Ordination of Rev. Nathaniel Hale, Oct 4, 1797, at Granville N Y 8 Oration, July 4, 1798, at Worcester. 9 Sermon at the ordination of Rev. Leonard Worcester, Oct. 30, 1799, at Peacham, Vt, 10. Ser-

A funeral discourse was pronounced at the interment of Dr Austin, by his friend, the Rev Dr Caleb J Tenney of Wethersfield from which many of these particulars have been abstracted ' His intellect,' says that biographer, ' was superior Its operations were marked by rapidity, vigor and general accuracy His classical attainments and extensive general knowledge, secured him a respectable standing among the learned in our country   . As a writer for the pulpit, his mind was original and fertile, his style at once copious and discriminating ... In delivery, he was animated and vehement   .. while, occasionally, he rose to high and powerful eloquence '

Dr Austin was of commanding stature An austere air and severe countenance, were united with ardent feelings, and constitutional susceptibility to external incidents and influences In appearance, he might be supposed to resemble, as in fearless spirit and firmness he would have imitated, had occasion called to the trial, one of the reformers and martyrs of old.

On the 15th of July, 1816, the Rev. Charles A Goodrich was invited to settle, as colleague with Dr Austin until the latter should be regularly dismissed from office, and thenceforward as sole pastor, by 64 of 66 members of the parish, and this was confirmed, August 26, 88 to 2 A salary of $900 was offered. The ordination took place, Oct 9. The prayer was by the Rev Benjamin Wood of Upton sermon by Rev Samuel Goodrich of Berlin, Conn, father of the pastor consecrating prayer by Rev Edmund Mills of Sutton charge by Rev Mr Smith of Durham, Conn exhortation to church and people by Rev Joseph Goffe of Millbury address and right hand of fellowship by Rev. John Nelson of Leicester : concluding prayer by Rev Mr. Whittlesey of Washington, Conn

mon at the ordination of Rev Samuel Worcester April 20, 1803, at Salem 11 Sermon in a volume, ' Sermons Collected,' published at Hartford, 1803 12 Sermon before Massachusetts Missionary Society, May 24, 1803, Boston 13, 14 Two Sermons in the Columbian Preacher, published at Catskill, N Y 1308 15 Examination of the representations and reasonings contained in seven sermons by Rev. Daniel Merrill 12mo pp 108 1805 16 Mr Merrill's defensive armor taken from him, a reply to his twelve letters to the author, on the mode and subjects of Baptism 12mo pp 58 1806 17 View of the economy of the church of God, as it existed under the Abrahamic Dispensation and the Sinai Law, and as it is perpetuated under the more luminous Dispensation of the Gospel, particularly in regard to the Covenants 8vo pp 328 1907 18 Sermon at the ordination of Rev John M Whiton, Sept 28, 1808, at Antrim, N H 19 Sermon at the dedication of a new meeting house, Nov. 3, 1808, at Hadley, Mass. 20 Sermon at the ordination of Rev Warren Fay, Nov 1808, at Brimfield, Mass 21 Fast Sermon, April 11, 1811, Worcester 22 Sermon at the ordination of Rev John Nelson, March 11, 1812, at Leicester. 23 Sermon on the Special Fast, July 23, 1812 Worcester 24 The apology of patriots; or the heresy of Washington and peace policy defended Sermon on the National Fast, Aug 20, 1812 Worcester 25 Sermon at the ordination of Rev Gamaliel S. Olds, Nov 13, 1813, at Greenfield 26 Inaugural Address on induction into office as President of the University in Vermont, July 26, 1816, Burlington, Vt 27 Election Sermon, Oct 10, 1816, at Montpelier, Vt 28 Protest against proceedings of first church in Worcester, June, 1821 29 Oration, July 4, 1822, at Newport, R I. 30 Sermon on the dedication of the Calvinist Church, Oct 13, 1823, at Worcester 31 Discourse at the 15th annual Meeting of the American Board of Commissioners of Foreign Missions, Sept 15, 1824, at Hartford 32 Address, July 4, 1825, at Worcester 33. Dissertations upon several fundamental articles of Christian Theology 8vo pp 260 Worcester. 1826

The opposition manifested to the call of Mr. Goodrich, grew stronger after his ordination, and was much increased by the dismission of his colleague. Twenty eight members of the church protested, before the ecclesiastical council convened by the assent of Dr. Austin, Nov. 18, 1818, against the dissolution of the then existing relations. That body, on the 23d of December, separated the connection of the senior pastor. Objections of a personal nature to the ministration of Mr. Goodrich, and to the discipline and proceedings of the church, led to long and acrimonious controversy. The disaffected, and those who considered themselves aggrieved, withdrew, or were dismissed, and joined the Baptist Society, or united themselves to other religious associations, and were finally formed into the Calvinist Church. The troubles of this period have too recently been laid before the public in voluminous tracts, to require repetition of the narrative.[1]

Mr. Goodrich asked and received dismission, Nov. 14, 1820.

The Rev. Charles A. Goodrich, was a native of Berlin in Connecticut, son of the clergyman of the parish of Worthington, in that town, and graduated at Yale College, in 1815. After his removal from Worcester, he returned to his native place, and has since been engaged in literary labors.

The Rev. Aretius B. Hull, invited to settle as the successor of Mr. Goodrich, by a vote of 101 to 3, was ordained May 23, 1821. Rev. Dr. Reuben Puffer of Berlin, made the introductory prayer: the sermon was preached by Rev. Nathaniel W. Taylor of New Haven: the consecrating prayer offered by Rev. Daniel Tomlinson of Oakham: the charge given by Rev. Joseph Avery of Holden: right hand of fellowship extended by Rev. John Nelson of Leicester: address to the church delivered by Rev. Thomas Snell of North Brookfield: and the concluding prayer pronounced by Rev. Micah Stone of Brookfield. The venerable Dr. Sumner of Shrewsbury, presided in the Council.

The Rev. Aretius B. Hull, descended from a respectable family emigrating from the vicinity of Liverpool, in England, to New Haven, at an early period, was born at Woodbridge, in Connecticut, October 12, 1788. Having been fitted by the Rev. Dr. Eli, he graduated at Yale, in 1807. Adopting the usual resource of young men indigent in circumstances, to acquire the pecuniary means of professional education, he taught the academy at Wethersfield, for a short space after completing his collegiate course. The seeds of consumption were implanted in his constitution, and he sought relief from the genial climate of the Southern states. Returning with improved health, he accepted the appointment of tutor in his own college, in 1810, and remained

[1] The full history of these difficulties, and discussions of their leading points, are contained in a series of publications: 1. Origin and Progress of the late difficulties in the First Church in Worcester, containing all the documents relating to the subject. 2. Remarks on the late publication of the First Church in Worcester, relating to the origin and progress of the late difficulties in that church. 3. Result of a Mutual Ecclesiastical Council, Nov. 14, 1820, to consider the expediency of granting the request of Rev. Charles A. Goodrich to be dismissed. 4. Protest against the proceedings of the First Church in Worcester, by Samuel Austin, D. D. 5. Communication from the Brookfield association, to the Ecclesiastical Council who ordained Rev. Loammi Ives Hoadly, over the Calvinist Church, in Worcester.

in that station until the autumn of 1816, when he was licensed to preach
Although still suffering from the lurking complaint, he officiated in Brookfield,
Connecticut, and in other places, until his ordination in Worcester, in 1821.
The disease, which medical skill has not been yet able to arrest, in May 1825,
interrupted his labors, and, on the 17th of May, 1826, terminated his exis-
tence, at the age of 38

'He possessed,' says the Rev Mr Nelson,[1] ' a mind of a very high
order, and that mind was enriched with uncommon attainments of general as
well as professional knowledge. His conceptions were clear, just, and discriminating At the same time, a highly cultivated taste, a refinement of
thought and feeling, as pleasing as it was genuine, pervaded all his writings
and all his conversation '

After the death of Mr Hull, Mr. Joseph Whiting was invited to settle as
his successor, Nov 16, 1826, but as there was apparent want of unanimity
in the election, the call was declined

The Rev Rodney A Miller, the present clergyman, received an invitation,
with a single dissenting voice only, to become Pastor of the First Parish,
Feb 19, 1827

Mr Miller, descended from a puritan family emigrating from Devonshire,
in England, and settling near Hampton, on the east end of Long Island, son
of Mr Uriah Miller of Troy, New York graduated at Union College, 1819,
pursued the usual course of professional studies at the Theological Seminary
in Princeton, N. J and was ordained at Worcester, June 7, 1827 The exercises were these . introductory prayer by Rev Edward Beecher of Park
Street Church, Boston sermon by the Rev Warren Fay of Charlestown .
consecrating prayer by Rev Micah Stone of Brookfield charge by Rev
Thomas Snell of North Brookfield right hand of fellowship by Rev George
Allen of Shrewsbury address to the people by Rev John Fiske of New
Braintree concluding prayer by Rev Dr Codman of Dorchester [2]

PRESBYTERIAN CHURCH.

A church was gathered of the Scotch emigrants, soon after their arrival in
this town in 1719 They were accompanied, it is said, by the Rev Edward
Fitzgerald, from Londonderry, in Ireland, who preached to the society during
some months They assembled for religious worship in the old garrison house,
near the intersection of the Boston and Lancaster roads. As the meeting
house they attempted to rear was destroyed, it is probable they continued to
occupy this humble edifice.

[1] Sermon delivered at his funeral, May, 1826, by Rev John Nelson, Pastor of the Church
in Leicester Mr Nelson was a native of Hopkinton, whence he removed with his father,
Deacon John Nelson, sometime resident in Milford, to Worcester He graduated at Williams College, 1807, was subsequently tutor there, afterwards pursued theological studies
with the Rev Dr Austin, was ordained in Leicester, March 4, 1812, and still remains in
that town, having the praise in the churches of an able and faithful minister, and enjoying
the respect and affection of his people

[2] Rev Mr Miller has published a thanksgiving sermon, at Worcester, Nov 29, 1832, on
the importance of religious influence to national prosperity.

Little care was taken to preserve the memorials of this unoffending but persecuted people, whose history discloses only the injustice and intolerance of our ancestors. Few facts can now be ascertained of their struggle with prejudices and hostility, which finally drove them away to seek asylum in other states.

The number of Presbyterian communicants is said to have been nearly equal to those of the Congregational church. Mr. Fitzgerald, being unable to procure proper maintenance, removed, before the settlement of Mr. Burr. The members of the first parish had proposed an union, and the Presbyterian clergyman had once been invited to occupy the pulpit vacated by the dismission of Mr. Gardner, for a single sabbath, when no candidate could be procured. The request was not repeated, and no encouragement was held out to him to remain.

On the settlement of Mr. Burr, it was understood, that if the Presbyterians would aid in his support, they should be permitted to place in the pulpit, occasionally, teachers of their own denomination, and the foreigners united with the other inhabitants. After some time, finding their expectations would not be realized, they withdrew, and the Rev. William Johnston was installed as their minister.

It has been already stated, that they commenced the erection of a meeting house on the Boston road; after the materials had been procured, the frame raised, and the building was fast rising, a body of the inhabitants, assembled by night, hewed down and demolished the structure. The riotous act was sustained by the intolerant spirit of the day, and the injured foreigners were compelled to mourn in silence over the ruins of the altar, profaned by the hand of violence.

Being compelled to contribute to the support of the Rev. Mr. Burr, an appeal was made to the justice of their fellow townsmen, in 1736, for relief from a tax inconsistent with their religious privileges, but without avail. The recorded answer to their application, furnishes a curious specimen of mingled subtlety and illiberality.

'In answer to the petition of John Clark and others, praying to be [released] from paying towards the support of the Rev. Isaac Burr, pastor of the church in this town, or any other except Mr. Johnston, (or the ministry carried on after the Congregational way by the said minister of the church, according to the establishment of the Province, in this town) &c. the town, upon mature consideration, think that the request is unreasonable, and that they ought not to comply with it, upon many considerations:

'1. That it doth not appear in the petition, who they are that desire to be set off, only from the names of the subscribers; [therefore] it would be for the town to act too much at random, to set them off on such a general request:

'2. That it doth not appear, that the petitioners, or others joining with them, have been actuated by just reasons, or any such principles of conscience as should at all necessitate their forsaking the assembling themselves with us: for, as to the Westminster confession of faith, which they say they promised their adherence to at their baptism, it is the same which we hold, maintain, and desire to adhere to   And as to the worship, discipline, and government of the church, as set forth by the assembly of divines at Westminster, they are not substantially differing from our own professed principles As they themselves well know, they may enjoy the same worship, ordinances, and christian privileges, and means of their spiritual edification, with us, as in the way which they call Presbyterian, and their consciences not be imposed on in any thing ·

'3 Inasmuch, also, as a number of those now withdrawing from us, were jointly concerned in the settlement of the Rev Isaac Burr, our present minister, and joined with us in church fellowship and communion, and we know not why it should be contrary to their consciences to continue with us in communion and worship, but have rather reason to suppose that their separation from us is from some irregular views and motives, which it would be unworthy of us to countenance

'4   We look upon the petitioners and others breaking off from us as they have done, [as] being full of irregularity and disorder; not to mention, that the ordination of their minister was disorderly, even with respect to the principles which they themselves pretend to act by, as well as with respect to us, to whom they stand related, and with whom they cohabit, and enjoy with us in common all proper social, civil, and christian rights and privileges their separating from us being contrary to the public establishment and laws of this province, contrary to their own covenant with us, and unreasonably weakening to the town, whose numbers and dimensions, the north part being excepted by the vote from paying to Mr Burr, will not admit of the honorable support of two ministers of the gospel, and tending to cause and cherish divisions and parties, greatly destructive to our civil and religious interests, and the peace, tranquility and happiness of the town

'Upon all which, and other accounts, the town refuse to comply with the request,' and it was voted, by a great majority of the inhabitants, that the petition be dismissed.

All efforts to obtain justice, and protection for religious freedom, having proved unavailing, many of the Presbyterian planters removed. Some joined their brethren of the same denomination, who under the pastoral charge of the Rev Mr Abercrombie, founded the town of Pelham, in Hampshire county, others united themselves with the society in Londonderry, N H and many emigrated to the colony on the banks of the Unadilla, in New York

The Rev Mr Johnston was settled in Londonderry in 1747. His connection was dissolved in July, 1753,[1] not on account of impropriety of conduct or disaffection of the people; but because poverty prevented them from affording proper support.

By the persuasion of the Rev Mr. Dunlop, about thirty persons had been induced to remove from Londonderry, in 1741, to Cherry Valley, in Otsego county, New York After the dismission of Mr Johnston, he emigrated, with a little colony, to Unadilla, on the east side of the Susquehannah, in what was then called the Old England district The unfortunate foreigners were des-

[1] Rev Mr Parker's Century Sermon Londonderry, April 22, 1819.

15

tined to endure suffering every where. Escaping from persecution, they encountered the horrors of Indian warfare. The celebrated Brant visited the
plantation, in 1777, and having called together the military officers, with Mr.
Johnston, demanded supplies of provisions. The power of the red warrior enforced compliance. The inhabitants, plundered of their cattle, soon after
abandoned the town, and with their families took refuge in places of greater
security. Some of them were involved in the massacres which desolated the
ancient county of Tryon.[1]

It is probable, Mr. Johnston was accompanied by some of his former parishioners, and that the town of Worcester, at the south east corner of Otsego
county, derives its name from their recollections of the place of their first
American settlement.

CHAPTER XI.

Second Congregational Society. Separation from the first Parish. Difficulties. Church
formed. Covenant. Rev. Aaron Bancroft ordained, 1786. Society incorporated, 1787.
Rev. Alonzo Hill ordained, 1827. Votes of Parish and Church. Memoir of Rev. Dr.
Bancroft.

The history of the second congregational society is more remarkable for
strong principles than striking incidents.[2] It was formed by the secession of
members of the first parish. Difficulties, springing from efforts to settle a
colleague with the Rev. Mr. Maccarty, multiplied and increased in the selection of a successor after his decease. Fixed differences of sentiment, diversity
of taste, and discordant and conflicting opinions, interposed insuperable obstacles to union. Those embracing the doctrinal views of Mr. Bancroft, and
desirous of attending his ministrations, after ineffectual attempts at reconcilia-
tion, withdrew from the religious community where the law had bound them.
In a memorial to the legislature, they represented, that ‘ town meeting after
town meeting was productive of heat, contention, and unchristian struggles
for a major vote : the division reached in its influence to private affairs, and
to the civil and prudential concerns of the town. This being matter of notoriety, respectable persons in the neighborhood urged, from the largeness of
the town, the number of its inhabitants, their ability, and the extensive duties
of a minister, the expediency and necessity of settling two [clergymen.] Your
petitioners readily agreed to, and pressed the proposal, in the March meeting
of 1785, which was then rejected by a majority of votes, as was, also, a request for the liberty of forming into a separate religious society by themselves.
Under these circumstances, seeing no prospect of union, desirous of a minister whose sentiments they approved, wishing the same indulgence to those

[1] Campbell's Annals of Tryon, 21. 27. 68.
[2] Free use has been made of two historical sermons of Doct. Bancroft, April 8, 1827, and
January 31, 1836, in the notice of the second society.

A. Bancroft.

who differed from them, weary of unprofitable contention, and finding every
thing was to be carried by a major vote, without any attention to the wishes
or feelings of the minor part, your petitioners judging it for the peace and
happiness of the town, by a separation, to put an end to disputes that might
embroil for years, withdrew '   A voluntary association was formed, in March,
1785, for the support of public worship   Sixty-seven individuals, by a written
instrument, agreed to form a religious society, under a proper covenant, to
endeavor to procure an act of incorporation, to apply to Mr Bancroft to settle
with them, as their minister, and severally, to pay their respective proportions of the sum of £150 annually, each according to the assessment of town
rates, as salary

To this period, the inland parishes of Massachusetts had been marked out
by geographical boundaries. The inhabitants within prescribed territorial
limits, were united by the existing laws, with the society established within
the precinct of their residence   Conscience was circumscribed by lines drawn
on the map and its exercise restrained by the monumental stakes and stones
of civil jurisdiction   Voluntary association for religious worship, unsanctioned
by the authority of government, was bold innovation, conflicting with the
prejudices, as it violated the usages of the times [1]   The erection of a poll parish, bringing together those of similar opinions, without regard to local habitation, almost, if not entirely unprecedented, except in the metropolis, was
strenuously resisted   The founders of the second society went forward, by
one long stride, years in advance of public opinion   They grasped firmly, and
wrested from opposition, those rights, which, after the lapse of time, have
been accorded as common privileges [2]   It is to their honor, to have taken the
first step in establishing those principles of religious freedom, of which their
venerable pastor, from youth to age, has been the fearless asserter

Meetings commenced on the third Sunday of March, 1785, in the Court
House, and were held in that place until Jan. 1, 1792   The Rev Mr Bancroft was invited, and consented to become the minister, June 7, 1785. Of
the associates, two men, and three or four females only, had been communicants   It became necessary to organize a church   For this purpose, the following covenant was prepared by the pastor elect, which has been retained,
unchanged, for half a century.

' In the first place, we humbly renew the dedication of ourselves and offspring to the great God, who is over all, blessed forever .

And we do hereby profess our firm belief of the Holy Scriptures contained
in the Old and New Testaments   And taking them as our sole and sufficient
rule of faith and practice, we do covenant to and with each other, that we will
walk together as a Christian Society, in the faith and order of the Gospel

---

[1] In 1757, a few families left the old parish in Leominster, and formed a society under
Mr John Rogers   The seceders were incorporated, as individuals, into a poll parish, without succession as a corporation   This body was dissolved on the death of the minister in
1789

[2] Among those most influential in the formation of the new society, were Levi Lincoln,
sen Joseph Allen, Edward Bangs, Timothy Paine, Timothy Bigelow, and Isaiah Thomas

And we do hereby engage, as far as in our power, for all under our care, that we will live as true disciples of Jesus Christ, in all good carriage and behavior, both towards God and towards man. Professing ourselves to be in charity with all men who love the Lord Jesus Christ in sincerity and truth. All this, we engage faithfully to perform, by divine assistance, for which we are encouraged to hope, relying on the mediation of Jesus Christ for the pardon of our manifold sins, and praying the God of all grace, through him, to strengthen and enable us to keep this, our covenant, inviolate, and to establish and settle us, that at the second coming of Jesus, we may appear before his presence with exceeding joy.'

Such was the instrument circulated among the families, deliberately considered, and fully approved. A public lecture was appointed for the formal and solemn expression of assent. Two ministers, from neighboring towns, were invited to participate in the devotional exercises, but neither thought proper to attend. Such was the state of feeling existing in that period, that countenance or aid could not be expected or obtained, from the clergy or congregations of the vicinity. Standing thus isolated amid society, if a religious community was then formed, it must be founded, like the social compact of the May Flower, framed by the pilgrim fathers of New England, on the basis of original rights underived from human authority. At the time appointed, Mr. Bancroft preached on the constitution of the christian church and the nature and ends of gospel rites. The covenant was read to the people, and subscribed, in the presence of all who had assembled, by twenty seven of those disposed to assume its obligations.

On the first day of February, 1786, the Rev. Aaron Bancroft was ordained. So general was the opposition to a mode of organization then unprecedented, and, in the view of many, irregular and disorderly, now authorised by liberalized legislation, that two churches only, in the county of Worcester, could be requested to assist in the solemnities, without strong probability of refusal. A council was formed with difficulty. The introductory prayer was offered by Rev. Dr. Simeon Howard, of the west church in Boston : the sermon preached by the Rev. Thomas Barnard of the north church in Salem : the charge given by Rev. Timothy Harrington of Lancaster : the right hand of fellowship presented by Rev. Zabdiel Adams of Lunenburg : the concluding prayer made by the Rev. Dr. John Lathrop, of the north church in Boston : and the benediction of Heaven implored, by the Rev. Timothy Hilliard of Cambridge.[1]

Great difficulties were overcome by the formation of the church and society, but formidable obstacles remained to impede its progress. So deep was the feeling of hostility to both, that the members were subjected to unpleasant and injurious effects in the concerns of social and civil life.

1 ' The members of the old church who joined the new society, had applied to that body for dismission, and their request had been denied : their case was, therefore, presented to the consideration of the ordaining council. The council advised the newly organized church, not formally to admit the members of the old church into their body, but, by a special vote, to grant them all the privileges of members in regular standing. This was done.' Dr. Bancroft's Discourse, April 8, 1827.

The constitutional provisions, as then applied by the statutes, failed to afford perfect protection to the exercise of private judgment The boundaries of the first parish, coextensive with those of the town, embraced the estates of the associates, and while they contributed to the support of their own teacher, they were compelled to pay ministerial rates in the same manner as before the separation At the period when pecuniary distress, decayed currency, and the pressure of public burdens and private debts, had driven the people into rebellion, the double taxation was peculiarly onerous To assess the annual salary, or enforce the collection, in the usual manner, was impracticable Monthly contributions were made, and the sums thus advanced, by individuals, credited in the final settlement of proportional payments On the 13th of November, 1787, an act of incorporation was obtained, providing that any inhabitant might change his relations from one parish to the other, by leaving his name with the town clerk for the purpose The first meeting of the parish was convened on the warrant of Levi Lincoln, sen March 9, 1789 The associates, from the commencement, by a written agreement, had bound themselves to pay the sum of five hundred dollars as salary After the incorporation, it was still deemed inexpedient to attempt the assessment of taxes The amount due from each subscriber, for three years salary was apportioned, and the pastor requested to settle personally with each individual A mode of compensation so troublesome and painful to the clergyman, was resorted to from necessity alone

In 1789, for the purpose of aiding in the erection of a meeting house, the Rev Mr Bancroft relinquished one third part of his annual salary, not, in the language of his letter from a supposition that the whole was more than adequate to decent support, but from readiness to bear full proportion of all burdens [1] It was voted, to erect a house for worship, provided it could be done without expense to the corporation Subscriptions were obtained, the site fixed south of Antiquarian Hall, and the work commenced On the first day of January, 1792, the edifice was completed and dedicated A sermon was preached on the occasion, by the Rev Zabdiel Adams of Lunenburg The pews were sold, subject to an annual tax of four dollars each, to be appropriated towards the salary

Until this period, the expenses of the support of worship had been defrayed by voluntary payments In 1797, for the first time, and afterwards, in successive years, a tax of $232 was levied, making, with the amount derived from the owners of pews, the salary of $500 In 1806, in consequence of the enhanced prices of commodities, an additional grant of $200 was made to Mr Bancroft In 1810, $300 was voted, and for five years after, $100 annually appropriated for the same purpose From 1816 to 1827, the salary was $800 ; subsequently $500, according to the original contract [2]

[1] Records of 2d Parish, i 4

[2] The uninterrupted harmony of the society, and its peaceful relations with its neighbors after the troubles of organization had subsided, has been the occasion of great satisfaction to its members The following pleasant anecdote, related in one of the notes appended to Dr Bancroft's Half-Century Sermon, has the merit of wit if not of truth

' A stranger of distinction, having occasion to pass some weeks in Worcester, became ac-

On the first day of January, 1827, the Rev. Alonzo Hill was invited to become colleague with Dr. Bancroft, and a salary of $800 was voted. His ordination took place, on the 28th of March following. The exercises were the following: Introductory prayer and reading of the Scriptures, by Rev. Alexander Young of the New South church, Boston; prayer by Rev. Dr. Thaddeus M. Harris of Dorchester: sermon, by Rev. John Brazer of Salem: ordaining prayer, by Rev. Dr. John T. Kirkland, President of Harvard University: charge, by Rev. Dr. Bancroft: right hand of fellowship, by Rev. George Ripley, of the Purchase street church, Boston: address to the people by Rev. Dr. Nathaniel Thayer of Lancaster: concluding prayer, by Rev. Isaac Allen of Bolton.

Mr. Hill, the present junior pastor, a native of Harvard, in the county of Worcester, is the son of Mr. Oliver Hill, a respectable farmer of that town. He graduated at Harvard College, was assistant instructor at Leicester Academy from 1822, to the spring of 1824, and then pursued his studies in the theological institution at Cambridge.[1]

The new brick church, erected by the society on Main street, south from the Court House, was dedicated August 20, 1829, when an appropriate discourse was preached by the senior pastor.

After the election of the Rev. Mr. Hill, Dr. Bancroft relinquished, in future years, the sum of three hundred dollars, which he had for a long time previous, statedly received. The parish, Jan. 29, 1827, unanimously resolved, ' that while we deem superfluous any encomiums upon the character and standing of him, whose praise has long been in all the churches, where christianity, freed from human inventions, is inculcated in its purity, we cannot forbear to express the deep sense which this society entertains, of the watchful care over its welfare, and readiness, at all times, to sacrifice personal interest to its advancement, which, in all past years of the history of the society, have distinguished the ministry of its pastor, and which, as the present act of unsolicited liberality affords evidence, are still exhibited, in all his ministerial relations, with force unabated by time.[2]

The church, at a meeting, March 5, 1836, expressed their sense of the fidelity of the senior pastor.

' Resolved, that this church, in reviewing its history from its first organization, feel deep cause of gratitude to God for its long continuance as a church of Christ, for its harmony, unanimity, and uninterrupted prosperity.

' Resolved, that this church is much indebted, under God, to the prudence,

quainted with the internal state of the two societies, then existing in this town; and he observed to a member of the first parish, ' How does it happen that you, who profess to be in possession of the true faith, and claim an exalted standing in piety, are frequently in contention, while the second society, whom you denominate heretics, live in peace and harmony?' The reply was, ' the members of the second society have not religion enough to quarrel about it.' '

[1] Rev. Mr. Hill married Frances Mary Clark, daughter of Hugh Hamilton Clark, formerly merchant of Boston, Dec. 29, 1830. Mr. Hill has published: sermon at the ordination of Rev. Josiah Moore, at Athol, Dec. 8, 1830: Reports of the Worcester Sunday School Society for 1835, 1836: sermon in Liberal Preacher, Aug. 1836.

[2] Second Parish Records, ii. 46.

zeal, fidelity, and untiring labors of its senior pastor, the Rev Dr Bancroft, under whose influence it was first gathered, and by whom it has been ever watched over, guided, and instructed, with the tenderness of a father, and the earnestness and solicitude of a devoted christian minister   Therefore

'Resolved, That the church tender to their rev senior pastor their grateful acknowledgments of his past labors, and their christian sympathies under the growing infirmities of a weight of years spent in their service, and the assurance of their prayers for his continued life and usefulness

'Resolved, That the treasurer of the church be, and he hereby is directed, to present to the Rev Dr Bancroft, two hundred dollars, out of any monies in the treasury not otherwise disposed of, in testimony of their affectionate regard for his person, his character, and ministerial labors '

In a letter to the church, March 10, 1836, Dr Bancroft writes, in answer to a communication of these votes, ' With you, I join in returns of gratitude to God, for the peace and prosperity which have attended us to the present time   Your approbation of my services is grateful to my heart   your pecuniary donation has intrinsic value , but its highest estimation in my mind, is, the evidence it bears of the feelings you cherish towards me.'

The Rev Aaron Bancroft, D D born at Reading, Mass , Nov 10, 1755, was son of Samuel Bancroft, formerly an extensive landholder, deacon of the west church of that town, field officer of militia, magistrate, and a useful and respected citizen   Engaged in the cultivation of the fields acquired by successful industry, the father considered agriculture as the best employment for his children, in times of political commotion, but yielded his own preference to the desire of the son for collegiate education.   Mr Bancroft commenced the study of the languages, in the moving grammar school of his native place, and followed an incompetent instructor in his migrations through the districts. During the year, while the school was temporarily suspended, he labored, at intervals, on the paternal farm.   The settlement of a new minister, afforded a more capable teacher than the former   But during the few months of his tuition, the engagements of courtship and of building occupied so much of the attention of the master, that the pupil, after the daily walk of a mile, was left with the half-recited or postponed recitation, to explore his way unaided through the elementary difficulties of literature.   Mr Bancroft entered Harvard College in 1774.   The revolutionary movements of April, 1775, dispersed the students, and he went to his home, and worked steadily on the farm until the next October, when the scholars were called together at Concord, and in March of the following year, reassembled at Cambridge.   The din of arms rose around the halls of the university   The great affairs of the country and the events of war, had deep interest for the government of the institution, and the student was compelled to rely more on his own exertions for improvement than on the information imparted by the professors   Having graduated, in 1778, Mr. Bancroft taught the town school of Cambridge for a few months, and then commenced his theological course with Mr Haven, minister of his father's parish, a gentleman of fine intellect.   In the Autumn of 1779, he first preached, for three or four sabbaths, for the occasional assistance of clerical friends. The severity of the succeeding winter, and the excessive depth of snow, almost suspended travelling, and he remained in the family of Mr. Haven, sometimes supplying his desk. A proposal from Mr. Barnard, of Yarmouth, Nova Scotia, to visit that province, was accepted in the spring of 1780. Mr. Bancroft obtained permission from the executive council of Massachusetts, to leave the state, and resided in Yarmouth, Horton, Cornwallis, Annapolis, and for a few weeks in Halifax, during an absence of three years. Peace having been restored, he returned from the British dominions in 1783, landed at Salem in July, and the next week was invited to Worcester, to supply the pulpit during the illness of Mr. Maccarty. Here, where his labors have been so long continued, Mr. Bancroft first appeared as a candidate for settlement. After eight sabbaths, the temporary restoration of declining health enabled the minister to resume his duties. Mr. Bancroft was immediately engaged in vacant parishes. In the spring of 1784, he was solicited to become pastor of the church in that part of Stoughton, now Canton, but felt constrained to decline. In the same year, he officiated in East Windsor, Connecticut. In October, 1784, he again visited Worcester, and after conducting the religious services of five or six sabbaths, went to Sandwich, in the county of Barnstable, where the desire of the most influential members of the society to secure his permanent residence, was prevented from public and formal expression, by his own reluctance to receive a call. On a third invitation, he returned to Worcester, in Jan. 1785, and in March following, that connection was formed with the second congregational society, which has continued for more than fifty years.

Unitarian sentiments, explicitly avowed, separated Mr. Bancroft from that friendly communication with professional neighbors, which lightens and cheers the labors of the clergyman, and for seven years, he stood almost alone. Within this period, he exchanged once a year with the Rev. Messrs. Harrington and Adams, occasionally with some ministers in Boston, and with one in Salem, and twice only with others of the vicinity. Efforts of some liberal members of the clerical association of the county, to procure his admission, opposed by those who were unwilling to hold intercourse with one entertaining opinions they deemed heretical, drove the more tolerant from that body, and led to its temporary dissolution. It was afterwards reestablished on foundation less exclusive. In some years, when the enhanced prices of the necessaries of life rendered a moderate salary inadequate for comfortable maintenance, the deficiency of income was partially supplied by the emolument of instruction to young men, and to the daughters of parishioners, the reception of boarders, and literary labors. Most men would have yielded to depression of spirits under circumstances so disheartening, and sought easier task, and more peaceful position. The society, in its early days, embarrassed by difficulties, and pressed by angry opposition, would, in all probability, have been dissolved, if unsustained by his perseverance and firmness. Much of the prosperity of later years was derived from his pecuniary sacrifices, and unwearied exertions, or resulted from the independence and prudence of his course [1]

The Life of Washington, in one volume octavo, came from the press in 1807 The popular and familiar style and faithful narrative of this work, gave it extensive sale. A stereotype edition, in two volumes, 12mo, was published in Boston, in 1826, as one of the series of Bedlington's Cabinet Library

In 1821, Dr Bancroft delivered a series of doctrinal discourses, which were printed on the request of the hearers. In relation to these sermons, the late President John Adams, thus expresses himself, Jan 24, 1823 'I thank you for your kind letter of Dec 30th, and above all, for the gift of a precious volume It is a chain of diamonds set in links of gold I have never read, nor heard read, a volume of sermons better calculated and adapted to the age and country in which it was written How different from the sermons I heard and read in the town of Worcester from the year 1755 to 1758 '   'You may well suppose, that I have heard controversies enough but, after all, I declare to you, that your twenty-nine sermons have expressed the result of all my reading, experience, and reflections, in a manner more satisfactory to me, than I could have done in the best days of my strength '[2]

---

[1] One of his parishioners addressed the minister thus 'Well, Mr. Bancroft, what do you think the people of the old society say of you now?' 'Something good, I hope,' was the reply 'Why, they say, it is time to let you alone, for if they find fault with you, you do not regard it, and if they praise you, you do not mind it, but keep steadily on in your own way '

[2] The publications of Dr Bancroft are the following 1 Sermon at the ordination of Rev. Samuel Shuttlesworth, June 23, 1790, at Windsor, Vt. 2 Sermon before the Grand Lodge of Massachusetts, June 11, 1793, at Worcester 3 Sermon on the execution of Samuel Frost, for murder, July 16, 1793, at Worcester 4 Sermon at the installation of Rev Clark Brown, June 20, 1793, at Brimfield. 5 Eulogy on General Washington, Feb 22, 1800, at Worcester 6 Election Sermon, May 27, 1801 7. Address on the importance of education, at the opening of a new building at Leicester Academy, July 4, 1806 8 Life of General Washington, Worcester, 1807 8vo pp 552 Stereotype, Boston, 1826 2 vols 12mo 9 Sermon at the ordination of Rev Nathan Parker, Sept 14, 1808, at Portsmouth, N H 10. Sermon before Society for promotion of christian knowledge, piety and charity, May 29, 1810, at Boston 11 New Year's Sermon, Jan 6, 1811 12 Nature and worth of Christian Liberty, sermon, June 28, 1816, at Worcester, with an appendix, containing the history of Consociation ; 2 editions 13 Duties of the Fourth Commandment, sermon, Jan 1817, at Worcester, 2 editions 14 Vindication of the result of a mutual council at Princeton, March, 1817 15 Discourse on Conversion, April, 1818 16 The Leaf an emblem of Human Life, sermon on the death of Mrs Mary Thomas, Nov 22, 1818 17 The Doctrine of Immortality, Christmas sermon, 1818 18. Sermon at the installation of Rev Luther Wilson, June 23, 1819, at Petersham 19 Sermon before the Convention of Congregational Ministers, June 1, 1820 20. Sermons on the Doctrines of the Gospel, Worcester, 1822, 8vo pp 429 21 Mediation and ministry of Jesus Christ, sermon, Aug. 15, 1819, at Keene, N H 22 Moral purpose of Ancient Sacrifices, of the Mosaic Ritual, and of Christian Observances, sermon, Aug 15, 1819, at Keene, N H 23 Sermon at the installation of Rev Andrew Bigelow, July 9, 1823, at Medford 24 Duties of Parents, sermon, Aug 10, 1823, at Worcester. 25. Sermon before the Auxiliary Society for meliorating the condition of the Jews, April 23, 1824, at Worcester. 26 Sermon at the funeral of Rev. Dr Joseph Sumner, Dec. 30, 1824 27 Sermon on the death of Prest John Adams, July 19, 1826 28 Sermon on the Sabbath following the ordination of Rev. Alonzo Hill,

On the 31st of January, 1836, Dr. Bancroft delivered a discourse on the termination of fifty years of his ministry, afterwards printed in compliance with the request of the society, with interesting and valuable historical notes 'If the question of improvement has respect to the members of the Society,' he says, ' who are the individuals to whom I can appeal? They, who with me began their course of Christian improvement are removed from life, but one man remains, of those who invited me to settle with them as their minister, and but two women now live, who at that time were heads of families. I am the oldest man in the parish, with one exception, and his connection with us was but of yesterday   I have been longer in a married state with one wife, than any other living member of our community   I have outlived my generation; and in the midst of society, may be considered a solitary man '

Doct Bancroft, was member of the Board of Trustees of Leicester Academy for thirty years, and long its President ; President of the Worcester County Bible Society ; of the American Unitarian Association, from its organization in 1825 to 1836 ; and of the Society for Promoting Christian Knowledge, Piety, and Charity ; Vice President of the Worcester and Middlesex Missionary Society, afterward merged in the Evangelical Missionary Society , and of the American Antiquarian Society, from 1816 to 1832   Fellow of the American Academy of Arts and Sciences, and member of other societies   His long-continued and persevering exertions in the cause of education, contributed greatly to the introduction and establishment of the improved school system of the town   In 1810, he received the degree of Doctor of Divinity from Harvard University

The oldest clergyman in the county of Worcester, and one of the most aged ministers of Massachusetts, Dr Bancroft continues to officiate in the pulpit May that period be yet far distant, when biography shall speak fully of the merits of his works, the worth of his character, and the virtues of his life.

April 8, 1827   29 Sermon at the dedication of the New Unitarian Meeting House, Aug. 20, 1829   30-1-2 Sermons in Liberal Preacher   Office of Reason in the Concerns of Religion, July, 1827   Female Duties and Trials, Aug 1828   Importance of Salvation, August 1830   33 End of the commandments, sermon in Christian Monitor   34 A Glance at the past and present state of ecclesiastical affairs in Massachusetts, in Unitarian Advocate, Jan 1831.   35. Moral Power of Christianity, in Western Messenger, i 350   36 Sermon on the termination of fifty years of his ministry, Jan 31, 1836

Dr Bancroft was married to Lucretia, daughter of Judge John Chandler, Oct. 1786

1797   A clock for the tower was presented by Isaiah Thomas, Esq to the Second Society, and an elegant folio Bible in two volumes, for the pulpit, by his lady   In 1817, the same liberal individual made a donation of two cups for the communion service , the old furniture of the table was given by the church to the Evangelical Missionary Society, to be by them bestowed on some new church gathered under their auspices 1829 A donation of a baptismal basin was made by F W Paine, Esq 1832 Nathaniel Maccarty, Esq bequeathed to the church $75

CHAPTER XII

First Baptist Society, Formation, 1812   Rev William Bentley   Articles of Faith   Rev
Jonathan Going   Rev Frederic A Willard   Rev Jonathan Aldrich   Elm Street Socie
ty, 1836   Calvinist Society   Separation from fir-t church, 1820   Formation of Society,
1822   Rev Loammi I Hoadley   House and Fund bestowed by Hon Daniel Waldo
Rev John S C Abbott   Rev David Peabody   Catholic Society, 1834   Rev James Fitton.   Methodist Episcopal Society, 1834.   Protestant Episcopal Society, 1835   Rev.
Thomas H Vail   Union Society, 1836

Previous to 1795, there were three persons, only, of the Baptist denomination in Worcester [1]   In the spring of that year James Wilson, Esq.,[2] emigrating from Newcastle-upon-Tyne, in England, took up his residence here
During the long period intervening between 1795 and 1812, meetings for
religious worship were sometimes held in his own house, when the casual visits of teachers offered opportunity of obtaining the ministration of instructors
of the order   Those of similar sentiments were successively removed by
death , their places were not filled   and for a time he remained the solitary
advocate and supporter of those views of Christian ordinances asserted by the
church with which he was united   But, although alone, he cherished the
leading purpose of his life, and became the founder of the Baptist society
By his zealous and persevering exertions, an association was formed under
favorable circumstances   Some discourses of Di Austin, on national and
state fasts, gave offence to many of the eldest parish   The facilities for procuring ministers had increased   Accessions of numbers were derived from
the swelling population   In 1812, lectures and devotional exercises were had,
regularly on the Sabbath, and on other days of the week, in different places
of the town.   The Hall in the School House of the Centre District was
rented, and opened for stated worship on the Lord's Day, July 30, 1812.
Opposition gave that excitement desirable to strengthen and cement union,
even if higher feelings had not rendered the connection of the associates permanent   On the 28th of September, Elder William Bentley, on the unanimous request of the members of the association, entered into an engagement
to preach for them on a salary of $300 per annum, and an allowance of four
Sundays of the year for visits   The sum appointed for his compensation was
defrayed by the contribution of individuals, parties to an agreement to pay
the amount in proportions fixed by the terms of their subscriptions   On the
5th of November, a meeting of those who held church membership was had,
and it was voted, ' to form a church, by the name of " the Baptist Church in
Worcester," and the following confession of faith was adopted [3]

[1] Dr John Green, son of Thomas Green, founder of the Baptist church in Leicester,
Mr. Amos Putnam, an aged member of the church in Charlton, and Mrs Dolly Flagg, a
female advanced in years, connected with the first Baptist church in Boston.

[2] James Wilson, Esq Postmaster of Worcester from 1801 to 1833, deacon of the first
Baptist church here from its foundation, removed, with his family, to Cincinnati, Ohio, in
1833

[3] The same articles had been adopted by the First Baptist Church, in Portland, Maine

'As the church of Christ is made up of a number of persons, who are renewed by divine grace, and united in the fellowship of the Gospel; and as that fellowship consists in a unison of sentiments, interest and affection; and as two cannot walk together, except they be agreed, we think it our duty to make the following declaration of our views of divine truth: for the satisfaction of any who may wish to unite with us in church fellowship; which declaration is as follows:

'We believe the Scriptures of the Old and New Testament were written by men divinely inspired, and that God requires of us, to believe in, and embrace them as our only rule of faith and practice, and that among others they contain the following all-important truths.

'1. The existence of one only, living, and true God, infinite in all excellence, immutable, eternal, self sufficient, and independent, who created all things, and who upholds, governs, and disposes of them for his own glory.

'2. That in one God there are three persons, the Father, Son, and Holy Ghost; the same in essence, and equal in every divine perfection.

'3. That all God's works of creation, providence, and grace, ever have been, still are, and ever will be accomplished, according to his own will; which he purposed in himself before the world began.

'4. That man was created holy, but, by wilfully violating the law of his Maker, he fell from his first rectitude; and as Adam was the father, and representative of all his posterity, we, in him, became wholly defiled and dead in trespasses and sins: so that by nature we are indisposed to all good, and wholly inclined to all evil: and are children of wrath, and subjects of death, and of all other miseries, temporal, spiritual, and eternal.

'5. That the only way of salvation from this state of guilt and condemnation, is, through the righteousness and atonement of Jesus Christ, who as the good shepherd, laid down his life for his sheep; that he might redeem them from all iniquity, and purify to himself a peculiar people, zealous of good works: and those only who receive the gift of repentance and faith in him, will be finally saved by the atonement.

'6. That all, who ever have been or will be brought to repentance and faith in the gospel, were chosen in Christ to salvation, before the foundation of the world; and that, in consequence of the eternal love of God to them, through the atonement, the Holy Ghost is sent to effect the work of regeneration in their hearts, without which regenerating influence, none would ever repent or believe.

'7. That the perfect righteousness of Christ, which he wrought out by his obedience and death, is reckoned or imputed to those who believe, as the alone matter of their justification.

'8. That nothing can separate true believers from the love of God, but they will be kept by his power, through faith unto salvation.

'9. That the only proper subjects of the ordinances of baptism and the Lord's Supper, are professed believers in Christ; and that baptism is properly administered, only by immersing the whole body in water, in the name of the Father, Son and Holy Ghost: and is by Scripture example, a prerequisite to communion at the Lord's table.

' 10. That the true church of Christ on earth, is made up of those, who are renewed by grace, partake of the Spirit of life in Christ Jesus, united in the fellowship of the truth, and are as lively stones built up in a spiritual house, to offer spiritual sacrifice, holy and acceptable to God by Jesus Christ That the only officers to be ordained in the church, are Bishops or teaching Elders, and Deacons That those officers have no more power to decide matters for the church, than any other members Yet we believe, so far as their gifts and graces may enable them to lead the church to a right judgment according to the Scriptures, we are to submit to them, for they watch for our souls, as they that must give an account in the day of judgment.

' 11 That God hath appointed a day, in which he will judge the world in righteousness, by Christ Jesus, and that the bodies of both the righteous and the wicked will then be raised from their graves and again united to their souls, and appear before God to be judged according to the deeds done in the body , at which time the wicked will be sentenced to endless punishment, and the righteous be received into eternal glory and happiness, where they will be ever with the Lord.'

The 9th of December was fixed for the constitution of the church, the reception of fellowship from others, and the installation of the pastor elect. The use of the old south meeting house was formally solicited, and obtained from the selectmen and assessors The clergyman of the first and second societies were courteously invited to attend on the occasion On the evening previous to the ceremonies, a note was sent by Dr Austin, refusing to be present , declining to countenance proceedings which, in his view, indicated hostility to union, and interference with endeavors to promote the kingdom of Christ in the world , declaring that Mr. Bentley, ' originally excited by some, seconded by others, whose sectarian zeal carried them beyond a regard to several of the primary precepts of the Gospel, had commenced and was prosecuting a partizan warfare against the harmony and prosperity of the church and congregation under his care;' complaining that the occupation of his pulpit would be ' against full expression of personal feeling, the rights of the christian ministry, the order of Christ's house, and the laws of the land ·' and expressing ' determination not officiously to interrupt,' and ' wish not to be interrupted, in the prosecution of a work, consigned to him, as he hoped, by the Redeemer of Zion ' This communication rendered a change of place necessary. Application was made to Dr. Bancroft for leave to occupy his desk, which was freely given, and the exercises of installation were in the meeting house of the second parish The first church in Providence, and the churches in Leicester, Charlton, Grafton, and Sutton, by their elders or delegates, were represented in council. Discourses were preached, in the forenoon, by the Rev. Joseph Cornell, and in the afternoon, by Rev Stephen Gano of Providence The right hand of fellowship was tendered by the latter elder The church, at this time, numbered fourteen males, and fourteen females, among its members.

The erection of a meeting house was commenced, May 29, 1813. It was placed on the slight eminence, eastward from the burial place, adjoining the com-

16

mon. The site was purchased for the consideration of $100, by subscription of the church, and conveyed to their committee, in trust for the society. The building was completed, Dec. 13, of the same year, at an expense of $2459, principally defrayed by the sale of pews. It was dedicated, Dec. 23, 1813, when a sermon was preached by Elder Bentley.

Elder William Bentley first followed the business of a baker in Boston. He received ordination, and settled in the ministry, at Tiverton, R. I. Well fitted to be the pioneer of a religious enterprise, he was called thence by the society founded in Worcester, in its infancy. He removed to Wethersfield, in Connecticut, after a few months : was pastor of the church there : and has since been much employed in missionary exertions.

On the 30th of June, 1815, Mr. Bentley asked and received dismission. On the third of November following, the Rev. Jonathan Going accepted a call to settle as successor, on a salary of $400 annually. Having been previously ordained as a minister of the Gospel, there were no public ceremonies on assuming the office in Worcester. The stipend was increased by occasional grants. In 1819, it was $500 : in 1820, $600 : the next year, $550 : from 1823 to 1826, the original compensation of $400 was paid ; afterwards $500.

An act of incorporation was obtained, June 8, 1819, and the first meeting of the parish held, August 16, under the warrant of Hon. Daniel Waldo.

In April, 1831, the Rev. Mr. Going had leave of absence from parochial and pastoral duties, to enable him to prosecute a journey to the West, for the restoration of health, and for missionary labors. In January, 1832, he requested dismission. During a ministry of sixteen years, the society had increased from a handful to a large congregation. The connection of pastor and parish had been one of uninterrupted harmony. The intimation of his intention to remove, was received with ' an expression of regret by words and tears, that circumstances had led to this result.' ' Do you then,' he says, in a communication to the church, ' ask me, why leave us ? My answer is ; not that I love the Baptist church and society in Worcester less ; but that I love the body of Baptists, and the multitudes who are destitute in the United States, more. During my whole ministry, I have felt constrained by a sense of duty, to devote much attention to works of religious charity, and, especially, for several years past, more time than is consistent with the highest advantages of a particular church. Besides, I have felt a deep solicitude, for some years, in the moral condition of the West. And my late tour has settled that solicitude, in full conviction of my duty to devote myself to the interests of home missions, particularly in the Valley of the Mississippi. Plainly, a mighty effort must be made ; and by the body of evangelical christians in the Atlantic States ; and made soon ; or ignorance and popery, heresy and infidelity, will entrench themselves too strongly to be repulsed. And, in that case, it is morally certain, that our republic will be overturned, and our institutions, civil and religious, will be demolished.' . . . . ' To the existence and success of the projected Baptist Home Mission Society, it is indispensa-
°ble, that the whole time and energies of some man should be devoted ; and

our friends, whose opinions ought to determine questions of this sort, have
said this work belonged to *me* '

In complying with the request of Mr Going, and dissolving his connection,
church and parish strongly expressed affection for his person, respect for his
character, and gratitude for his services

The Rev Jonathan Going, was born at Reading, in Windsor county, Vt
March 7, 1786. After brief attendance on the common schools of a country
then recently planted, he commenced preparations for college, in 1803, at the
academy of New Salem, Mass. ; entered Brown University in 1805, graduated in 1809, and read divinity with the late president of that institution,
the Rev. Dr Asa Messer. In May, 1813 he received ordination, as the first
settled minister of Cavendish, in his native county, where he resided until
December, 1815. He then assumed the pastoral charge of the Baptist church
in Worcester, which was retained for sixteen years In January, 1832, it was
resigned, for the purpose of accepting the office of Corresponding Secretary
of the American Baptist Home Mission Society He has since resided in the
city of New York, in the discharge of its duties.

In the early part of his ministry here, Mr Going instructed the Latin
Grammar school during one year In the arduous labors which matured the
improved system of education, and superintended its operations in elevating
the common schools of the town to high excellence, he bore active and efficient
part The registers, indicating the degree of fidelity in the teacher and assiduity of the pupils, were introduced by him One of the first Sabbath schools
of the county was established, under his direction, in the Baptist society in
Worcester

Mr Going received the degree of Master of Arts, at Brown University and
the University of Vermont, in 1818, and that of Doctor of Divinity from
Waterville College, Me in 1832 In addition to the preparation of reports,
addresses, and papers for periodicals, he has been, two years, editor of the
American Baptist, a religious newspaper published weekly in New York

The paternal ancestors of Mr Going were from Scotland. the maternal,
from England. Robert Going, or Gowing, came from Edinburgh, settled in
Lynn, Mass at an early period, and was admitted freeman, in Dedham, Mass
in 1644 The father of the subject of this notice, Capt. Jonathan Going,
born in Lunenburgh, Mass 1761, and still living in the state of New York,
married Sarah Kendall of Dunstable, Mass. in 1785 [1]

The Rev Frederic A. Willard, who had supplied the pulpit three months
previously, was elected pastor, without dissenting voice, January 2, 1832, and
a salary of $500, was voted The first Baptist church in Boston, the church-
es of Leicester, Spencer, West Boylston, Grafton, Sutton, Northampton, and
the Newton Theological Seminary, attended in council at the ordination, on
the 18th of the same month. The Scriptures were read by Rev John Green
of Leicester, the introductory prayer offered by Rev Otis Converse of Grafton the sermon preached by Professor Henry J Ripley of the Seminary in
Newton. the church and people addressed by Rev. Jonathan Going. the

[1] Rev. Jonathan Going married Lucy Thorndike, of Dunstable, Mass. August 1811.

right hand of fellowship offered by Rev. William Hague of Boston ; and the concluding prayer made by Rev. John Walker of Sutton.

Regarding the evils of intemperance, and its desolating effects on the happiness of individuals, public and private virtue, and the welfare of the community, it was declared, May 22, 1834, to be the strong and deliberate conviction of the church, that the time had arrived, when no professed disciple of Christ, could manufacture, buy, sell, or use, ardent spirit, as a drink, without being guilty of immorality, and violating his profession as a christian : and it was resolved, that entire abstinence from the manufacture, use, and sale of this article, should be an invariable condition for membership and good standing.[1]

The father of Rev. Frederic A. Willard, Benjamin Willard, formerly of Lancaster, an elder of the Baptist Church, now resident in Northampton, personally conducted the early literary education of the son : the closing portion of studies preparatory to entering college, was pursued under the direction of Rev. Abiel Fisher, then of Bellingham, Mass. He graduated at Amherst college, 1826. During the year following, Mr. Willard was connected with the Clinical School of Medicine, at Woodstock, Vt. : in 1827, was matriculated as member of the Newton Theological Institution, and received a professional diploma in 1830. In 1831, an appointment by the trustees of Waterville College in Maine, to the Professorship of Chemistry, was declined. After leaving his official station in Worcester, he accepted an invitation to become pastor of the first Baptist church, in Newton, Mass. where he now resides.[2]

On the 30th of July, 1835, Mr. Willard resigned his office. On the 17th of October following, the Rev. Jonathan Aldrich was elected his successor. The annual salary has been $700.

The services at the public recognition of this gentleman, Oct. 27, 1835, were : reading of Scripture by Rev. George Waters of Holden : prayer by Rev. Charles O. Kimball of Methuen : sermon by Rev. Baron Stow of Boston : charge by Rev. Abisha Sampson of Southborough : hand of fellowship by Rev. Frederic A. Willard : address to the church and society by Rev. Charles Train of Framingham : prayer by Rev. John Walker of Sutton : benediction by Rev. Mr. Aldrich.

Rev. Jonathan Aldrich, son of Asquire Aldrich, a worthy farmer of St. Johnsbury, Vt., prepared for college in the Academy of Peacham, Vt. and under the tuition of Rev. Mr. Fisher of Bellingham : received his degree from Brown University, 1826 : pursued theological studies in the Newton Seminary : was ordained at Dedham, Mass. in December, 1827, where he remained nearly three years : installed at Beverly, Mass. May 1830 : and at East Cambridge in June 1833.[3]

It had been considered expedient to form a second society. Mr. John Flagg, Isaac Davis, Esq. and Deacon Daniel Goddard, were incorporated,

[1] Oct. 2, 1827. A bequest of $1000 was made to the society by the last will and testament of Mr. John Goodale, who died May 2, 1827, aged 82, and it was voted to erect a monument to his memory, with a suitable inscription.

[2] Mr. Willard married Mary, daughter of Seth Davis, Esq. of Newton, May 1, 1835.

[3] Mr. Aldrich married Catherine P. daughter of Mr. Asa Lewis, formerly of Boston, since of Worcester, April 2, 1828.

April 6, 1836, with their associates and successors, as proprietors of the Elm Street Baptist meeting house A site was purchased for the building, westward from the Worcester house. After the destruction of the place of worship of the first Baptist church by fire, the members of the new association reunited with the original parish, in rearing another edifice on the spot before occupied with that which had been burned

CALVINIST SOCIETY.

About the period of the settlement of the Rev Mr. Goodrich, difficulties arose in the first parish, increased and extended upon the separation of Rev. Dr Austin, and by the disciplinary measures instituted against the disaffected Deacon David Richards, and four other members, retired from the watch of the church, and from the support of the society, and on the 16th of January, 1819, asked to be dismissed and recommended to other churches The request was granted, so far only as related to dismission, but recommendation was refused Five applicants, at the same time, for similar purposes, had leave to withdraw their petitions Nine individuals more, soon after, united with the former, in soliciting the dissolution of their relations, and the customary credentials of good standing, with the expressed intention of forming a new society. The reason assigned by all, in substance, was, that they could not experience edification and improvement from the ministrations of the pastor The church declined compliance with the request Those who considered themselves aggrieved by its decision, immediately invited an ecclesiastical council, to consider their situation, determine the propriety of establishing a separate and distinct church, and effect its organization if deemed expedient By their ministers and delegates, the Old South Church in Boston, and the churches of Charlestown, Northbridge, Millbury, Upton, Ward, and Sutton, met, on the 17th of February, 1819 The Rev. Jedediah Morse was elected moderator Their result recommended those who had already been dismissed, to the fellowship of churches, to which they were afterwards united The council paused here, and awaiting further light from future events of Providence, adjourned their session, but were not again called to assemble. On the 18th of March succeeding, seventeen persons asked dismission and recommendation. The first church proposed to submit the regularity of their anterior proceedings, and the propriety of granting the pending application, to the decision of a mutual council, which was declined It was subsequently voted, that the church did not feel able to comply with the request, nor willing to reject it, but were in doubt, and wished for advice A final answer was waived; the members did not renew their petition, but joined the Baptist Society in April, although they continued to commune with the first church On the 2d of June, 1820, acting on the principle, that uniting and worshipping with another denomination, and withholding pecuniary support, was virtual separation, it was declared, that the individuals not dismissed, had, by their own acts. cut themselves off from the privileges of the first church Thus parted from all relations with any religious association, they invited an ecclesiastical council, which convened, Aug 16, 1820, from the churches in

16*

Franklin, Northbridge, Sutton, Upton, Wrentham, Ward, and Park Street in Boston. Rev. Nathaniel Emmons of Franklin, was elected moderator. The result, expressed approval of constituting a regular church from the applicants, and it was accordingly organized.[1]

Subsequently, proposals were made by the first church, on conditions which were considered exceptionable, to submit to a mutual council the whole subject of the subsisting difficulties. Conferences were held by committees of the two bodies, terminating, after long negotiation, in the conclusion, that it was possible only to agree to remain separate.

On the 8th of February, 1822, a meeting of the Calvinist church, and of those associating with them for religious purposes, was held, for the organization of a society, according to the laws of the Commonwealth. Daniel Waldo, David Richards, William McFarland, John W. Hubbard, Moses N. Child, Samuel Taylor, Benjamin Goddard, and Jonas Parker, bound themselves, to defray, out of their private property, the expenses of supporting public worship for five years, deducting such sums as might be voluntarily contributed by others.

Regular worship was commenced, on the first Sabbath of April, 1822, in the Court House. The pulpit was supplied by Rev. Thomas J. Murdock, then late of Portland; Mr. Washington Smith of Hadley, since ordained in St. Albans, Vt.; Mr. Elam Clark, afterwards settled in Providence, R. I.; Mr. Joseph Torrey of Salem, subsequently minister of Royalston, Vt. and thence called to be Professor of Languages in the University of Vermont.

The Rev. Loammi Ives Hoadley preached his first sermon to the congregation, Oct. 20, 1822, under an engagement for two or three sabbaths. He was afterwards induced to remain, reserving liberty to retire at pleasure. In March, 1823, he was invited to Taunton. The church immediately requested his permanent settlement as their pastor. The concurrence of the society was given to this call, on the 14th of April following. The stated salary was $800 : and provision was made, that pastor or parish might dissolve the contract, after one year's previous notice of desire to separate. The ordination services took place October 15, 1823. The introductory prayer was offered by Rev. Joel Hawes of Hartford, Conn.: the sermon preached by Rev. Lyman Beecher of Litchfield, Conn.: ordaining prayer made by Rev. Edmund Mills of Sutton, moderator of the council: the charge delivered by Rev. Elisha Fiske of Wrentham; the right hand of fellowship presented by Rev. Baxter Dickinson of Long Meadow: the address to the people was by Rev. William B. Sprague of West Springfield : and the concluding prayer by Rev. Benjamin Wood of Upton.

A committee of the first church had appeared before the council, instructed to object to proceedings conforming to the request of 'those persons styling themselves the Calvinist Church.' Most of them, it was stated, in a protest

---

[1] Full narrative of the proceedings, elaborate discussions of their regularity, and ample exposition of the views of the contending parties, are contained in a series of publications enumerated on page 162. The whole are contained in an octavo volume in the Library of the American Antiquarian Society.

offered by the chairman, held such attitude that they could not, with propriety, be recognized as a regular church of Christ they were considered as under censure having rejected proposals of settling controversy by the intervention of mutual council, they could not, consistently with the objects of discipline, be held in fellowship, collectively or individually, until proofs of penitence for the fault of separation, or the judgment by which they had been sent forth should be overruled by a competent tribunal The council determined, that the official result constituting the Calvinist church, was evidence of its regular existence, disclaimed authority to reverse the acts of the ecclesiastical body for its organization ; and declined receiving the remonstrance

A meeting house had been erected by the Hon Daniel Waldo, at the cost of about $14,000, on Main street The dedication was had on the same day with the ordination, and the society removed from the Court House, to their permanent place of worship. Selections from the Scriptures were read by Rev. Benjamin B Wisner of the Old South church in Boston , prayer offered by Rev Samuel Green of the Essex street church in Boston , and the sermon delivered by Rev Dr Samuel Austin, then of Newport, R I

The house, and the land upon which it was built, were conveyed, July 9, 1825, by Mr Waldo, for the use and benefit of the church and society A donation of five thousand dollars was added to this great benefaction The income and interest were secured to be appropriated towards the payment of the salary of such pastor as should have been elected, ordained, and settled, conformably to the rules and usages of congregational calvinistic churches and societies in this Commonwealth ' The Trustees of the Parochial Funds of the Calvinist society in Worcester,' were incorporated, Feb 2, 1827, by an act of the Legislature, to hold the property upon the trusts declared in the instruments of conveyance Vacancies in the corporation are filled by the votes of owners of pews

On the 28th of June, 1828, several of the most honored among the calvinistic clergymen of Massachusetts, visitants of the town on occasion of special devotional exercises, in view of the difficulties so long existing, and of their unhappy consequences to the parties and cause of religion, by letter of advice, expressed the opinion, that the controversies should, without delay, be adjusted. Although they considered the doings of the First church, in the discipline of the persons organized as the Calvinist church, and those of the latter association, in rejecting proposals for a mutual council, as erroneous, and not, in all respects, in accordance with strict ecclesiastical rule, yet they considered, that each might, consistently with duty, acknowledge the other as a church of Christ. In compliance with their earnest recommendation, on the following day, the members of both churches united in participating the sacrament of the Lord's Supper, as a public testimonial of intention to reestablish and maintain christian fellowship

The illness of Mr Hoadley requiring temporary relinquishment of labor, his request for dismission was granted, June 5, 1829, and the sum of $500 voted, to aid him in defraying unavoidable expenses while seeking means of support in some mode less detrimental to health than ministerial duties

The Rev. Mr. Hoadley, a native of Northford, New Haven county, Conn. graduated at Yale College in 1818, and studied at the Theological Seminary, in Andover, with which he was connected after his removal from Worcester. He now resides in Charlestown, Mass.

On the 9th of December, 1829, the Rev. J. S. C. Abbott accepted the unanimous invitation to become successor to Mr. Hoadley, with a salary of $900. The churches of Millbury, Paxton, Leicester, Hartford, Shrewsbury, Holden, West Boylston, Sutton, Boylston, Ward, Cambridge, Cambridgeport, Grafton, the church in the Theological Seminary at Andover, the Old South and Union churches in Boston, the Presbyterian church in Millbury, and the first church in Worcester, were represented in the ordaining council, January 28, 1830. These were the exercises: prayer by Rev. John Nelson of Leicester; sermon by Rev. Joel Hawes of Hartford, Conn.: ordaining prayer by Rev. Samuel Green, of the Union church, Boston; right hand of fellowship by Rev. Nehemiah Adams of Cambridge; concluding prayer by Rev. John Boardman of West Boylston.

The articles of faith, originally adopted in 1820, were copied from those of the first church. In 1831, a confession, more brief in form and simpler in language, expressing, substantially, the same views of Christian doctrine, was adopted.

'1. We believe that there is one God, the Creator, and rightful disposer of all things, existing as Father, Son, and Holy Ghost, and that to these three persons, as the one God, all divine perfections are to be equally ascribed.

'2. That the Bible was given by inspiration of God, as the only unerring rule of faith and practise.

'3. That mankind are fallen from their original rectitude, and are, while in a state of nature, wholly destitute of that holiness which is required by the divine law.

'4. That Jesus Christ, the Eternal Word, became man, and by his obedience, sufferings, and death, made an atonement for the sins of the world.

'5. That they, and they only, will be saved in consequence of the merits of Christ, who repent of sin and believe in him.

'6. That although the invitations of the gospel are such that all who will may come, and take of the waters of life freely: yet the wickedness of the human heart is such, that none will come, unless drawn by the special influence of the Holy Spirit.

'7. That the sacraments of the New Testament are Baptism and the Lord's Supper: baptism to be administered only to believers and their households, and the supper only to believers in regular church standing.

'8. That God has appointed a day in which he will judge the world, when there will be a resurrection of the dead, and when the righteous will enter on eternal happiness, and the wicked will be sentenced to eternal misery.'

In consequence of the earnest exertions of philanthropists to promote temperance, the church, Feb. 28, 1833, by resolutions, declared, that dealing in ardent spirits was considered an immorality; and that it was the duty of the members to abstain totally from the use and traffic, except in case of necessity and as medicine.

The health of Mr Abbott declined, and he was compelled to solicit dismission January 17, 1835. The records bear testimony of the reluctance with which both church and parish acquiesced in the dissolution of a connection of uninterrupted harmony, and to their deep sense of the merits of their pastor

The Rev John Stevens Cabot Abbott, second son of Mr Jacob Abbott, was born in Brunswick, Maine Having resided with his father's family in Hallowell, he entered Bowdoin College 1821, and they returned to dwell in the place of his nativity He graduated in 1825, and was assistant teacher in the Academy at Amherst, Mass during the succeeding year The regular course of studies was pursued at the Theological Seminary in Andover, and soon after leaving that institution, he was invited, in 1830, to Worcester. His fidelity, social, moral, and religious worth, talents and usefulness, secured affection as they commanded respect. Impaired health rendered it necessary to ask dismission, to the great regret of his people Having partially recovered, he was installed pastor of the Eliot church, in Roxbury, Nov 25, 1835, where he now resides.

In the spring of 1833, Mr Abbott published 'The Mother at Home,' and in November of the same year, 'The Child at Home' Both these works have been republished in England, and have passed through numerous editions here. In September, 1836, 'The Path of Peace' was issued from the press. He has also printed two or three smaller works without his name [1]

In May 1835, Rev David Peabody, the present clergyman, was elected pastor, and a salary of $1000 annually granted At the installation, July 15, the exercises were these. record of the proceedings of the council read by the scribe, Rev. Wm P Paine of Holden; introductory prayer by Rev David Perry of Hollis, N H , sermon by Rev Dr Thomas H Skinner of the Theological Institution at Andover, installation prayer by Rev John Nelson of Leicester, fellowship of the churches by the Rev Wm P Paine of Holden, charge by Rev Osgood Herrick of Millbury, address to the people by Rev. John Wilde of Grafton; concluding prayer by Rev Elijah Paine of West Boylston

Rev David Peabody, born in Topsfield, Essex county, Mass graduated at Dartmouth College, 1828 commenced his theological studies in the institution at Andover, Mass , which were completed at the Union Seminary, Va. and was first settled over the First Congregational Church in Lynn, Mass. Nov 15, 1832 [2]

Nineteen members of the church, considering the rapid increase of the

[1] Mr Abbott married Jane Williams Bourne, daughter of Abner Bourne, Esq of Boston, Aug 17, 1830 Four of the brothers of Mr Abbott are in the ministry, or nearly closing their preparatory studies

[2] Mr Peabody married Maria Brigham of Cambridgeport, Sept 11, 1834 His father, John Peabody, descended in the fourth generation from Francis Peabody, who derived family ancestry from Wales, emigrated about 1680 from England, and became a land holder in Topsfield, The name was anciently written Pabodie

population of the town and the necessity of providing greater facilities for public worship, asked to be dismissed, for the purpose of forming a third orthodox congregational society. Consent to their request, Jan. 8, 1836, was accompanied with the expression of christian sympathies, and of an earnest desire that the Great Head of the Church would bless and prosper them, and the enterprise in which they were engaged.

ROMAN CATHOLIC SOCIETY.

When the Blackstone Canal was commenced, many catholic emigrants were brought into the vicinity. Religious exercises were occasionally held during the construction of that work. In 1834, the Rev. James Fitton commenced visiting the town, once each month. In April of that year, the catholics in Worcester, were four families and about twenty unmarried persons. To afford them the means of assembling for divine worship, he laid the foundations of a small church on Temple Street, July 7, 1834. The execution of great undertakings of public improvement, and other causes, have since greatly increased the number. Accessions of individuals, uniting themselves to the society, and coming from other places, rendered it necessary to enlarge the church. Those who attend its services from Worcester and its vicinity are nearly three hundred.

The Rev. James Fitton, is a native of Boston. His early studies were pursued in that city until 1822, when he visited Canada, to acquire the languages and other branches of education, under private tuition. Returning to Boston, he studied theology with the Rt. Rev. Bishop Fenwick. In December 1827, he was ordained, and appointed to official duty in the church of the Holy Cross. In 1828, he held the twofold office of pastor and teacher to the Indians of Maine. He was in 1830, designated as pastor of Trinity Church in Hartford, Conn. and employed in that city, and on missionary circuits through the neighboring country for the distance of an hundred miles, till a church and resident minister were obtained in New Haven, and an assistant in Hartford. Soon after, his monthly visits to Worcester began, and, in May 1836, he removed to this town.

Since his residence here, Mr. Fitton has established two schools, one in the basement of the church for children, the other for higher branches of education, for boys exclusively, called Mount Saint James Seminary, on the ancient Pakachoag hill.[1]

METHODIST EPISCOPAL SOCIETY.

The Methodist Episcopal church in Worcester was commenced in the winter of 1834. Eight or ten persons who had become inhabitants of the town, attached to the Methodist institutions, formed a class, according to the regulations of that denomination. In the spring of the same year, with their

[1] The works translated and compiled by Rev. Mr. Fitton, beside a number of pamphlets, are: Youth's directory: Boston. 18mo. pp. 250. Triumph of religion: Baltimore. 2 vols: 18mo. History of Palestine: Baltimore. 2 vols, 18mo. Companion to the Sanctuary: Hartford. 18mo. pp. 220.

associates, they organized a religious society for the purpose of supporting public worship

The use of the Town Hall was obtained for meetings. The Rev J A Merrill preached for the first three months   At the June session of the New England Conference of the Methodist Episcopal church for 1834, Rev George Pickering was stationed in Worcester, and continued in the pastoral charge of the society for one year. He was succeeded by Rev John T Burrill, who still continues to officiate as the regular minister [1]

During this period, the society has increased with rapidity. They have now about one hundred church members, and a numerous congregation   In September 1836, a house for worship was erected on the street called Columbian Avenue

PROTESTANT EPISCOPAL SOCIETY.

The establishment of an Episcopal Society in Worcester, had been frequently subject of consideration with those directing the domestic missionary organization of the church, in Massachusetts   No distinct effort for its accomplishment was made, until the close of 1835   The first regular services according to the liturgy of the Protestant Episcopal church, were performed by Rev Thomas H. Vail, on the 13th of December of that year   Since that time they have been continued in the South Hall of the Town House   At the commencement, only two families were known to be attached to the society   Twelve were connected with it, in Sept 1836. the communicants were about sixteen   The rite of baptism had been administered, once privately, twice publicly, and there had been one confirmation

Wardens and vestry, officers corresponding to the deacons and trustees of congregational societies, have not yet been elected. A subscription of $6000 was raised in Worcester for the erection of a church, in March and April, 1836   The execution of the work was suspended, on account of disappointment in obtaining aid from abroad, but measures are in progress to procure the construction of an edifice for worship during 1837

The Rev Mr Vail was born in Richmond, Va. where he resided until 1822   Subsequently, his home was in Norwich, Conn until his removal to Worcester   He graduated at Washington College, Hartford, Conn in 1831 : was afterwards connected with the General Protestant Episcopal Theological Seminary in the city of New York, four years   was ordained deacon by Bishop Brownell, in New Canaan, Conn in July 1835 · and officiated a short time, in Philadelphia and Boston, under temporary arrangements

---

[1] The Catholic, Methodist, and Episcopal Societies, embracing the distinctive general tenets of the denominations to which they severally belong, have no articles of faith peculiar to the individual local churches

A summary of the doctrines and discipline of the Methodist Episcopal Church in the United States, will be found in the appendix to Kay's edition of Buck's Theological Dictionary

As the Methodist ministers cannot retain the particular stations assigned, for a longer period than two years, the connection of those gentlemen who have visited the society here, has not been considered sufficiently permanent to justify biographical notice

UNION SOCIETY.

In the Autumn of 1834, meetings were held, preparatory to the formation of a third orthodox society. In December, it was resolved to take measures to erect a building for worship, and subscriptions for that purpose were obtained. On the 11th of March, 1835, the Proprietors of the Union Meeting House were incorporated. Proceedings for the organization of a church, commenced Dec. 25, 1835. Members of the First and Calvinist Churches united in adopting the following confession of faith.

'1. We believe in one God, who possesses in an infinite degree, all natural and moral perfections : who is the creator, upholder, and governor of the universe, who is revealed to us as Father, Son, and Holy Ghost.

' 2. We believe that the Scriptures of the Old and New Testaments, were written under the inspiration of God, and clothed with divine authority, and are a perfect rule of faith and practice.

' 3. We believe that mankind are fallen from a state of rectitude, and are, while in a state of nature, wholly destitute of that holiness, which is required by the divine law.

' 4. We believe that all who are saved, will be saved by the sovereign mercy of God, through the atonement, which was effected by the obedience, sufferings, and death of Christ.

' 5. We believe in the necessity of regeneration, through the Holy Spirit.

' 6. We believe there are properly belonging to the Christian religion two, and only two, sacraments, Baptism and the Lord's Supper.

' 7. We believe that God has appointed a day, in the which he will judge the world in righteousness, when the dead shall arise from their graves, and, together with the living, shall stand before the judgment seat of Christ, and be adjudged, the righteous to everlasting life, and the wicked to shame and everlasting contempt.'

An ecclesiastical council convened, agreeably to the letters missive of Alfred D. Foster and others, a committee of invitation, Feb. 3, 1836, from the churches in Hubbardston, Leicester, Rutland, Shrewsbury, East Douglas, Holden, Paxton, Boylston, West Boylston, Oxford, Eliot church in Roxbury, and the First and Calvinist churches in Worcester.

Twenty seven individuals had been dismissed and recommended from the First church, and nineteen from the Calvinist Church. Sixty three persons in all, were constituted the Union Church. The public exercises were thus assigned : introductory prayer by Rev. John Boardman of East Douglas : sermon by Rev. Josiah Clark of Rutland : constituting of the church by Rev. Samuel Gay of Hubbardston : consecrating prayer by Rev- John S. C. Abbott of Roxbury : right hand of fellowship by Rev. John Nelson of Leicester : the Rev. Rodney A. Miller of Worcester, and Rev. George Allen of Shrewsbury, administered the Lord's Supper.

The first meeting of the Union Society, in its parochial capacity, was convened, on the warrant of Emory Washburn, Esq. March 5, 1836.

The dedication of the meeting house took place July 6, 1836 . the invocation of the Divine Presence was by Rev Jonathan Aldrich of the first Baptist church , lessons from the Scriptures were read by Rev David Peabody. of the Calvinist church the dedicatory prayer was offered by Rev. George Allen of Shrewsbury a sermon preached by Rev John Nelson of Leicester. and the exercises concluded with prayer by Rev John T Burnll of the Methodist church.

The Rev Jonathan Edwards Woodbridge was invited to settle as pastor, August, 1836.

The following list shows the succession of Deacons of the Churches. The dates prefixed indicate the time of election to office

FIRST CHURCH

1716	. . .	Daniel Heywood	1791 Nov 15	John Chamberlain
1716		Nathaniel Moore	1797 Oct 19.	Leonard Worcester
1748	Jan 14	Jonas Rice, jun	1801. Nov 23	David Richards,
1748	" "	Thomas Wheeler	1807 June 18	Moses Perry
1751	Dec 16.	Jacob Chamberlain.	1812 April 16	John Nelson
1751.	" "	Samuel Miller	1833 Jan 30	Lewis Chapin
1783.	Nov 5.	Nathan Perry	1833. " "	Moses Brigham
1793.	" "	Thomas Wheeler		

SECOND CHURCH.

1786	May 17.	Samuel Bridge.	1817. Oct 3	Jeremiah Robinson.
1786	" "	David Bigelow.	1827 Oct 29.	Benjamin Butman
1799	Sept 7	Nathan Heard	1817. " "	Alpheus Merrifield
1807	June 29	William Trowbridge.		

BAPTIST CHURCH

1812	Dec 4,	James Wilson	1823 March.	Daniel Goddard
1822.	March	Nathaniel Stowell.	1836 May.	Zebina E Berry

CALVINIST CHURCH

1824	June 11	Samuel Taylor	1830 Nov 10.	John Coe

UNION CHURCH.

1836	Feb 23	Moses Perry	1836. Feb 23,	Ichabod Washburn
1836	" "	Alfred D Foster.		

The number of communicants, Sept. 1836, as they are stated by the Clerks, are as follows

First church,	about 350	Baptist church,	434	Methodist church, about 100
Second church,	about 150	Calvinist church, about 200		Union church,	63

BIOGRAPHICAL NOTICES.

CHAPTER XIII.

Professional Men.[1] Biographical notices of the Practitioners, Counsellors and Attorneys at Law, and Physicians, before and since the Revolution.

The professional gentlemen who have been or are resident in Worcester, have been arranged, in the following pages, as nearly as possible, in the order in which they commenced business here, without regard to age, standing, or other principle of priority. Those in practice in September, 1836, are distinguished by *italics*.

The capital letters following the names, are the initials of Harvard and Brown Universities, Yale, Dartmouth, Williams, Union, Bowdoin, and Amherst Colleges.

LAWYERS.[2]

JOSHUA EATON was the first lawyer of Worcester, in point of time. He was born in that part of Watertown, now Waltham, Dec. 15, 1714. The only son of honest and well respected parents, who bestowed upon him a liberal education, with the sole view to preparation for the ministry, after graduating at Harvard University, in 1735, he disappointed their hopes and wishes, by preference of the legal to the clerical profession. The noviciate was short in early times. Having spent two years with Judge Trowbridge, in the study of the law, Mr. Eaton commenced the practise in Worcester, in 1737, not long after the establishment of the county. Simplicity and sincerity united in his character with ardor and zeal: at the foundation was a substratum of pious devotion pervading his whole life. He acquired the reputation of a faithful and honest practitioner. Although his talents could not entitle him to eminence, he obtained extensive employment. While his worldly prospects grew brighter, his attention was awakened to his spiritual condition, and prospects of higher usefulness opened. The captivating and energetic eloquence of Whitefield diffused a contagious enthusiasm on religious subjects. The spirit was imbibed by Eaton, and cooperated with his own inclinations and the recollections of the earnest desire of his parents, to induce

[1] Notices of the clergymen of the town should properly be inserted in the division of biography. The connection of the lives of the pastors with the history of their parishes is so intimate, that it has been deemed most convenient to place the brief memoirs of the ministers with those of the societies of their settlement.

[2] In compiling the sketches of lawyers, much has been derived from the excellent address to the Bar of Worcester County, Oct. 2, 1829, by Joseph Willard, Esq. sometime of Lancaster, now of Boston. Higher authority could not be desired, than the antiquarian accuracy and fidelity of the author of that production. The reader will find occasion to regret, that the classic elegance of his composition could not be adopted, as easily as the materials gathered by his diligence have been appropriated.

him to abandon the profession he had adopted, and to seek the service of the
altar. After five years practice at the bar, he commenced the study of theology. The fervor of his exercises was deemed fanatical, and he incurred the
censure of the church in Worcester. Feeling aggrieved by their disciplinary
measures, redress was sought by appeal to an ecclesiastical council. In a
private diary is entered, under date Oct. 23, 1743, 'This day detained from
the house of God, and I think to forbear preaching any more, until after the
council. I hope I even long again to go up to the house of God, and to tread
his courts.' Three days were dedicated by him to fasting, humiliation and
prayer, on account of the difficulties. The troubles of his spirit were at length
removed, by his restoration to christian communion. It was noted, Nov. 25,
'The church was pleased to restore me to christian privileges without any
acknowledgment, and gave as a reason for what they had done in censuring
me, that they looked upon me, as being actuated by an overheated brain.'
The next Sabbath he resumed his clerical occupation, and preached so acceptably in the South Precinct of Leicester, now the town of Spencer, that he was
soon after invited to settle there, and ordained, Nov. 7, 1744. Zeal in the
performance of duty overcame infirmity of body, and habitual depression of
mind. The enjoyments and honors of his former situation never elicited regret for desertion. He writes, Feb. 7, 1744, 'Attended court at Worcester
upon business. but, oh! the tumult, and dissipation, and snares, that attend
the courts. I think, I would not return to the practice of the law on any consideration.' A faithful ministry was finished by death, April, 1772. The
fragments of his diary are replete with indications of deep humility, ardent
piety, and conscientious regard to duty. The successive decease of his children and consort, the sufferings of long sickness, and the afflictions of his lot,
exemplified his resignation and patience. After his death, a volume of plain
and judicious discourses, not remarkable either for brilliancy or force, were
published by his friend, Rev. Eli Forbes of Brookfield, who pronounced his
funeral discourse, and received the custody of his papers [1]

STEPHEN FESSENDEN, a native of Cambridge, was graduated at Harvard
University in 1737, studied with Judge Trowbridge, and probably succeeded
Eaton in the practice of the law in Worcester. Specimens of instruments
drafted by him, exhibit remarkable neatness and accuracy. A crowd of irregular practitioners, pressing into business, seem to have cut off his supplies,
and finally driven him away [2]

JOSEPH DYER was a person of another description. Not bred to the profession, he came here in 1736, and commenced business as office and shop-
keeper. Law and merchandise he treated as equally matters of trade. With
some ingenuity and acuteness, he fell, at length, victim to the litigious spirit
he encouraged in others. Having worked himself into the belief of the valid-
ity of a peculiar view of the qualifications of voters, the opposition of others
to his own construction, produced a degree of monomania. It was his pleas-

[1] The biographical sketch prefixed to this volume, and Willard's Address, have furnished materials for this notice.

[2] Willard's Address, 51.

ure to interpose exceptions to all municipal proceedings until he became the common nuisance of the inhabitants. For more than twenty years he protested either verbally or in writing, against acts specially or doings generally of the town. No taxes could be collected from him, unless by levy of warrants of distress on his chattels. Year after year, the people resolved to sustain their officers in the execution of coercive process for payment of his share of common charges. At length, it seems to have been determined to silence the voice of continual remonstrance, and subdue resistance to legal assessments, by deprivation of liberty. In 1759, Dyer was committed to the common jail, for neglect to discharge a fine incurred by absence from a military muster, nominally of £16 in the depreciated currency, really of small amount in specie. The remedy was ineffectual. He entered his cell protesting against the law, its process, and the prison. Protesting he would never come out by submission to the payment of a farthing, he settled himself down in the house of the government as a home. His beard, permitted to grow unshorn, gave him the aspect of an ancient philosopher in retirement. The little emolument of professional business, and the income of the shop managed by his family, gave food for his subsistence. Two years went by, and the citizens, alarmed lest his obstinacy should bring upon them the support of himself and his children, held a meeting to consider his situation, and proposed to release the two thirds of the fine given by the statute to the corporation, if the residue was paid. The offer was rejected. Three years longer, Dyer persisted in remaining under confinement, probably sweetening the solitude by the compilation of a dictionary of the English language, afterwards published. A subscription was raised, against his will, by the charitable ; the sum necessary for liberation was advanced, and he was told that he was free. The habit of resisting was so inveterate, that he objected to this benevolence ; refused to remove from his rooms, and was, at length, only ejected by force. Dyer left the jail, as he entered it, protesting against the right to put him in or out The first use of liberty, was to commence a suit against the keeper for false imprisonment : the failure of the action contributed to the recovery of mental sanity, impaired on a single point only. He afterwards removed to Newfane, Vt.[1]

In the same low class of pettifoggers, was NATHANIEL GREENE, a shop-keeper, who attended courts, made writs, drew wills and deeds, and did business in the humbler walks of the profession, from 1746 to 1760.

JAMES PUTNAM, H. U. 1746, attained and deserved the highest rank of professional distinction. He was born in that part of Salem, now Danvers, in 1725, studied with Judge Trowbridge, and commenced the practise of the law in Worcester in 1749. Strong native power was increased by extensive acquirement and unwearied cultivation. His ability and learning soon gave him a flood of clients, and enabled him not only to contest, but to hold, possession of the best business, while Trowbridge, Hawley, Gridley, Pratt, and the other celebrated counsellors who attended the terms of our courts, were competitors. The highest encomium which can be bestowed upon professional qualification,

---

[1] Ebenezer Dyer is mentioned in Thomson's Gazetteer of Vermont, as one of the first settlers of Newfane in 1766. He was probably son of Joseph.

was pronounced, in after life, by an associate, who well knew his worth [1] ' Judge Putnam was an unerring lawyer, he was never astray in his law He was, I am inclined to think, the best lawyer of North America ' His arguments were marked by strong and clear reasoning, logical precision and arrangement, and that sound judgment whose conclusions were presented so forcibly as to command assent A well-read lawyer, skilful pleader, safe adviser, and successful advocate, his extending fame gave him wide sphere for action and usefulness Retained in Middlesex and Hampshire, he attended the courts of those counties constantly, and, in important cases, assisted in those of Suffolk, where then, as now, the best talents of the state were gathered At a time when military rank was given as the real distinction of merit, and had not become worse than an empty title, he was Colonel of a regiment When Jonathan Sewall was raised to the bench of the Court of Admiralty, James Putnam was appointed his successor, as Attorney General of the province. When the revolution commenced, having given the whole weight of his high character and great influence, to sustain the royal government, he was compelled to take refuge in Boston

He accompanied the British army to New York, thence he went to Halifax, and embarked for England in 1776, where he remained until the peace of 1783. In 1784, he was appointed member of the Council of New Brunswick, and Judge of the Supreme Court of that province In the discharge of the duties of his judicial office, he obtained the highest praise which human ambition should desire, that of inflexible justice The sternness and austerity of official demeanor, and the reserved habits of social life, were relieved by flashes of wit which are described as irresistible. He resided in the city of St. John, and retained the office of Judge till his death, Oct 23, 1789

Among those who received legal education from him, were President John Adams, Joshua Atherton of Lancaster, Rufus Chandler, and Nathaniel Chandler of Worcester.

RUFUS CHANDLER, H U. 1766, son of the second judge John Chandler, was born at Worcester, May 18, 1747, and died in London, Oct 11, 1823 He studied with James Putnam, was admitted to the bar in 1768, and practised in Worcester until the Courts were closed, in June, 1774. Inheriting the loyalty of the family which shared so freely in the bounty of the king, he left the country on the commencement of hostilities, and resided in England as a private gentleman

He was more remarkable for accuracy and method, than for high mental endowments Fidelity in business, and purity of life, secured the confidence of his clients He was economical in his habits from principle, and most punctiliously neat in personal appearance

LEVI LINCOLN, born May 5, 1749, was third son of Enoch Lincoln, a strongminded and substantial farmer of Hingham, member of the revolutionary committees, and frequently representative of that town. Unable to afford liberal education to all his children, and unwilling to bestow peculiar advantages

[1] Cited in Willard's Address, 61.

17*

on one, the son was bound apprentice to an ironsmith.[1] Indications of talent,
and of strong inclination for literary pursuits, were early exhibited. While
he yet wrought at the anvil, he indulged the taste for reading in the hours allotted for sleep, and devoted a portion of the night to the study of the Latin
and Greek languages. Sedate and thoughtful manner, and diligence and capacity in the acquisition of knowledge, interested others in his welfare. Assistance and encouragement were derived from Mr. Lewis, long master of the
Grammar School, and from the Rev. Dr. Gay, for whom his pupil cherished
enthusiastic veneration. As the love of literature increased, he abandoned the
forge, and after six months preparation, entered Harvard University, where he
was graduated in 1772. Originally intending to adopt the clerical profession,
his purpose was changed by an accidental visit to the courts, when the eloquence of the elder Adams threw its power over the pending cause. He commenced the study of law with Daniel Farnham, Esq. in Newburyport, where
he staid a year, and then completed his noviciate in the office of Joseph Hawley of Northampton, distinguished as jurist, statesman, and patriot. In April,
1775, he marched as volunteer with the minute men to Cambridge : as the
emergency of danger which called for the service had passed, and the army
settled down in their entrenchments for protracted siege, he returned; was
admitted to practise in regular course in Hampshire, and immediately established himself in Worcester. A wide and clear field for the exertion of talent
was presented. The principal men of the county had espoused the cause of
the royal government, and been driven from their homes, or deserted their
country. Two lawyers only remained at the bar when the temples of justice
were reopened, in 1775, after having been closed by the tumult of arms for a
year.[2] Decision of character and energy of purpose capacity to lead and popular address, soon gave him prominent station. Introduced into extensive
business, he still devoted his talents to the cause of independence, and immediately became an active member of the committees of the revolution. Animated appeals to patriotism in written addresses, and printed communications
to the newspaper of the town, attest the ardor of his devotion and the powerful expression of his pen. When the courts commenced, after their suspension, in Dec. 1775, he was appointed Clerk. In Jan. 1777, on resigning, he
was commissioned by the executive council, Judge of Probate, and held the
office till 1781, when it was relinquished, in consequence of interference with
professional engagements.

In 1779, he was specially designated to prosecute the claims of government
to the large estates of the refugees, confiscated under the Absentee Act : and
was Commissioner to expedite the payment of the Continental tax. He was
delegate of the town to the convention in Cambridge for framing a state constitution. In Feb. 1781, he was elected by the Legislature, under the Con-

---

[1] Jeremiah Lincoln of Hingham, who had been a soldier in the French wars, and escaped
from the massacre of Fort William Henry. He died at Lunenburg, Mass. Another of his
apprentices, Dr. Peter Hobart of Hanover, left his work shop for the University. Solomon
Lincoln's History of Hingham, 90. 127.

[2] The late Judge John Sprague of Lancaster and Joshua Upham of Brookfield.

federation, representative in the Continental Congress, but the honor was declined In 1783, he was called by the Supreme Court to the degree of Barrister at law, a judicial distinction only conferred on himself and Judge Sprague in the county, after the revolution.[1] In 1796, he was representative in the General Court in 1797, member of the Senate of the Commonwealth: and excited strong influence in the legislative action, particularly in the modification of the judicial and school systems. In the autumn of 1800, although his democratic principles were known to be opposed to those of a majority of the electors, he was returned representative to the seventh Congress, and was chosen to supply the vacancy occasioned by the resignation of Hon Dwight Foster at the then next session. He was selected, soon after taking his seat, by President Jefferson to form one of his cabinet On the 5th March, 1801, he was appointed Attorney General of the United States, and was provisional Secretary of State, until the arrival of Mr Madison at the Federal city, in May following The duties of the former charge separating him from his family, it was resigned, after nearly four years service 'I received, last night,' writes Mr Jefferson, Dec. 28, 1804, 'your letter, proposing to resign your office. and I received it with real affliction It would have been my greatest happiness, to have kept together to the end of my term our executive family; for our harmony and cordiality have really made us but as one family Yet, I am a father, and have been a husband I know the sacred duties which these relations impose, the feelings they inspire; and that they are not to be resisted by a warm heart. I yield, therefore, to your wishes You carry with you my entire approbation of your official conduct, my thanks for your services, my regrets on losing them, and my affectionate friendship' In the spring of 1806, he was elected member of the Council of Massachusetts In 1807, and 1808, he was Lieutenant Governor of the Commonwealth On the decease of Gov Sullivan, in Dec 1808, he discharged the duties of Chief Magistrate for the remainder of the term of office. He was nominated for election as Governor, in 1809, but, in the revolution of party, his competitor, Gov Gore, prevailed He afterwards declined being candidate, when the ascendency of the political principles to which he adhered, would have rendered success more sure In 1810, and 1811, he was again councillor In 1811, he was appointed Associate Justice of the Supreme Court of the United States 'You will see,' writes President Madison, 'by the commission which will be forwarded from the Department of State, that I have taken the liberty of nominating you to the Senate as successor to Judge Cushing, notwithstanding your remonstrances against a recall into the national service. I was induced to this

---

[1] The following precept is an example of the form in which the honorary legal distinction, now obsolete, was conferred

To Levi Lincoln, of Worcester, Esquire, Greeting. We, well knowing your ability, learning, and integrity, command you, that you appear before our Justices of our Supreme Judicial Court next to be holden at Boston, in and for our county of Suffolk, on the third Tuesday of February next, then and there, in our said Court, to take upon you the state and degree of Barrister at Law Hereof fail not Witness William Cushing, Esq our Chief Justice at Boston, this 26th day of December, A. D. 1783, and in the eighth year of our independence. By order of Court   Charles Cushing, Clerk

step, not only by my personal wishes, but by those of others, between whom
and yourself exists all the reciprocal respect that can add weight to them, and
particularly by their persuading themselves, that your patriotism would ac-
quiesce in an appointment, however contrary it might be to your previous inclinations. I venture to flatter myself that in this we may not be disappointed : and that, in every event, you will regard the liberty I have taken in
imposing the dilemma upon you, with the indulgence due to my motives, and
to the great esteem and sincere friendship of which I pray you to accept my
renewed assurances.' Weakness of sight, terminating in almost total blind-
ness, rendered it necessary to decline even such solicitation, and to retire from
public life.[1] Partial restoration of vision, enabled him to resume the cultivation of the farm and the classical studies, both objects of passionate attachment, and among the fields and with the pages of his favorite Latin authors,
to alleviate the infirmities of decaying health and pressing age. He died
April 14, 1820, aged 71.

'For a period of nearly forty years,' says Mr. Willard, ' he was in active
life, and bore leading part amid vast and important changes in our community,
such as none of the present generation can be called on to witness. He was
without question, at the head of the bar, from the close of the Revolution till
he left our courts at the commencement of the present century. His professional business far exceeded that of any other member of the bar. He was retained in every case of importance, and for many years, constantly attended the
courts in Hampshire and Middlesex, [and frequently those of the neighboring
states.] His great command of language, his power in searching out the truth
from unwilling witnesses, in analysing, arranging, and presenting to the mind
the evidence of the case, rendered him a highly popular advocate, and gave
him great success in jury trials. Wide reading and extensive practise constituted him a learned jurist.' The arbitrary encroachments of the royalist
clergymen, claiming the sovereign right of veto, were successfully resisted by
him. His love of religious freedom, broke through the ecclesiastical usurpa-
tions of early time, and contributed to establish the conflicting interests of
church, parish, and ministers on sure distinctions. The fetters of negro bondage were broken in Massachusetts, by the decision, in a case, in which his
whole energies were exerted, that the relation of master and slave could not
justify assault. The ' Farmer's Letters,' published in 1800, and 1801, were
widely circulated, produced powerful sensation in the political world, and
busied the press, for a long time, with efforts to answer their arguments, and
personal attack on their author.

He was one of the original members of the American Academy of Arts and
Sciences, Trustee of Leicester Academy, first President of the Worcester Agricultural Society, and associate of many useful institutions.

It is not for the partiality of filial reverence to attempt to delineate the pri-

[1] Mr. Jefferson writes ; ' be assured your place is high among those whose remembrance
I have brought with me into retirement, and cherish with warmth. I was overjoyed when
i heard you were appointed to the supreme bench of national justice, and as much mortified when I heard you had declined.'

vate character of a venerated sire   All that is permitted by the plan of this work, is to indicate the public and professional standing of our citizens, where neither space nor ability afford hope of doing justice to their merits

WILLIAM STEARNS, H. U. 1770, was born in Lunenburg, Mass   He first commenced the study of divinity, and preached for a short time, but was not settled as a clergyman   He then devoted himself to the law, was admitted to practise, Dec. 1776, and established himself in Worcester.   During one year he was connected with Daniel Bigelow, Esq   in the publication of the Massachusetts Spy   His professional business was considerable until his early death, in 1784   He possessed good sense, respectable learning, lively wit, and much kindness of feeling

EDWARD BANGS was born in Harwich in the county of Barnstable, Sept. 5, 1756   He prepared for college at Dummer Academy, in Newbury, under the instruction of the celebrated Master Moody, and entered Harvard University, in 1773   He remained in Cambridge during the spring vacation of 1775, when the British troops marched to Concord   On the 19th of April, as soon as intelligence of the hostile movement was received, he hastily equipped himself from the armory of the college company, repaired to the scene of action, and fought gallantly during the day   He saved the life of a British soldier, severely wounded, who had been overtaken in flight, and was about to be sacrificed to the vengeance of his captors   The events of the war dispersed the students, and interrupted, for a time, the course of instruction   Mr Bangs continued his studies at home, until the halls were again opened   He graduated in 1777, in the same class with the late Rufus King, James Freeman, William Bentley, Thomas Dawes, and others, who became eminent as learned divines, or able civilians   He immediately entered the office of Chief Justice Parsons at Newburyport, and was admitted to the bar, in Essex, in 1780. The same year he removed to Worcester, and commenced business in partnership with William Stearns.   This connection continued about two years   After its dissolution, he pursued the profession alone, and with good success. When the insurrection broke out, he engaged with great ardor in defence of the constitution   His pen was exerted in the cause of order with ability   In January, 1787, he joined the army of Gen. Lincoln, as a volunteer   In that brief campaign, he suffered so much from exposure and hardship, that his health was impaired, and the foundation of disorders laid, from which he never recovered   In 1805, he formed a partnership with William E Green, who had just removed from Grafton to Worcester, which subsisted until 1811 He was appointed Attorney of the Commonwealth for the County of Worcester, on the resignation of Hon Nathaniel Paine, by the Court, and soon after reappointed by the Governor and Council, Oct 21, 1807   He was removed to the bench, as Associate Justice of the Court of Common Pleas for the western circuit, Oct. 8, 1811, on the first organization of that court   This office he retained till his death, June 28, 1818, at the age of 62.

He was representative of Worcester, in the General Court, from 1802 to 1811 inclusive · for many years one of the board of selectmen ; was on many important committees , and sustained various town offices.   Without seriously interrupting his professional avocations, he took a prominent part in political transactions. In 1801, he was nominated for member of Congress from Worcester south district, but declined the honor. During the stormy period of party controversy, he was induced to become a candidate for the same station, but his competitor was elected.

He practised successfully, as a lawyer, for thirty years. He was a good classical and general scholar, and possessed taste for mathematical science. Deep and conscientious regard to sincerity and truth was manifested in his whole transactions. However erroneous he might have been considered, by those who differed from him, none doubted his honesty. He was of ardent temperament, and warm in attachment to friends, and the opinions or party he adopted. His love of nature was enthusiastic, and he contemplated her works with intense admiration. His leisure was devoted to the cultivation of a garden, ornamented with singular elegance, and filled, by his care, with rare exotics, beautiful native plants, and choice fruits.

He possessed taste for poetry. Although he did not distinguish himself for that talent, some of his compositions were extensively circulated in the journals of the day. A humorous song, called 'the Somerset on shore,' attained considerable degree of popularity. His odes for public festive occasions were of respectable merit.[1]

WILLIAM SEVER, H. U. 1778, son of Hon. William Sever, was born in Kingston, in Plymouth county. He studied with Levi Lincoln, sen. was called to the bar in 1781: practised two years in Kingston: in 1785, removed to Worcester; where he died, October 31, 1798, leaving the reputation of fine talents, which with greater assiduity, might have given high professional distinction.

Nathaniel Paine, H. U. 1775, son of Hon. Timothy Paine of Worcester, studied with Hon. John Sprague of Lancaster. Immediately upon admission, Aug. 1781, he commenced practise in Groton, Mass. and after four years residence there, returned to Worcester. He succeeded Daniel Bigelow, Esq. as County Attorney. In 1798, 1799 and 1800, he represented the town in

---

[1] Edward Bangs, m. Hannah Lynde, d. of Joseph Lynde, Esq. sometime of Charlestown, afterwards of Worcester, Sept. 18, 1788. He left two children. 1. Edward Dillingham. 2. Anna L. b. 1800; d. Feb. 14, 1823.

The ancestor of the family was Edward Bangs, a native of Chichester in England, who arrived in Plymouth in July, 1623, by the Ann, the third ship which brought the pilgrim emigrants, having been preceeded by the Mayflower and the Fortune. In the division of the live stock, to 12 companies, that to which Edward Bangs belonged received ' the great white-backed cow, which was brought over with the first in the Ann; also two she goats.' In 1627, he was member of a commission with Gov. Bradford, to make a new division of lands. He was a shipwright, and is said to have superintended the construction of the first vessel built at Plymouth. He removed with Gov. Prince, and others, to Eastham, in 1644, where he died in 1678, a. 86. 2. His son Jonathan, born at Plymouth, 1610; m. Mary Mayo, July 16, 1664; d. at Harwich, now Brewster, 1728. 3. Edward, son of Jonathan, b. at Eastham, Sept. 30, 1665, d. May 22, 1746. 4. Edward, son of Edward, b. 1694; d. June 3, 1755. 5. Benjamin, son of Edward, b. 1721; m. Desire Dillingham, d. 1769. He was father of Judge Edward Bangs. Farmer's Genealogical Register. Willard's Address, 90. MS. of Edward D. Bangs, Esq.

the Legislature   He was appointed Judge of Probate, Jan 24, 1801, and held
that office thirty five years   His resignation was accepted Jan 18, 1836

TIMOTHY GREEN, B U. 1786, a native of Worcester, was son of the first
Dr John Green, and grandson of Hon. Timothy Ruggles   He studied with
Levi Lincoln, sen and practised two years in Worcester   He then removed
to the city of New York, where he engaged successfully in land trade   After
a visit to the South, his preparations had been completed for an overland
journey home, when he was prevailed on to take passage by sea   He embarked, in 1812, on board a privateer-built vessel at Charleston, in company
with Mrs Alston, the accomplished lady of the governor of South Carolina,
and daughter of the celebrated Aaron Burr.   The ship sailed, and no tidings
of her fate were ever afterwards heard.

JOSEPH ALLEN, H U 1792, eldest son of Hon   Joseph Allen, born in
Leicester, commenced practise in Worcester, removed to Western. Mass now
Warren, where he remained to 1805   He afterwards went to Charlestown,
N H and died in that town.

SAMUEL A FLAGG, H U 1794, was born in Mendon, Mass . studied with
Hon Nathaniel Paine   established himself in Worcester, 1797, and died here,
March 5, 1825, aged 50

ANDREW MORTON, B U 1795, of Freetown, Mass studied with Levi Lincoln, sen . practised in Worcester from 1802 to 1804   then settled in Hampden, Maine, where he died, Oct 26, 1805

FRANCIS BLAKE, H U. 1789, fifth son of Joseph Blake, was born October
14, 1771.   His father, a native and eminent merchant of Boston, for several
years anterior and subsequent to the commencement of the revolution, was engaged in extensive trade in Rutland, Mass and removed to Hingham, in 1779
His son was in the principal school of the town, then under the tuition of
Rev Joseph Thaxter, afterwards clergyman of Martha's Vineyard, and distinguished for the eloquence of his address in prayer on the semi-centennial anniversary of the battle of Bunker Hill   Under the instruction of this gentleman, of his successor, Mr Howard, and of Dr Barker, he was fitted for college   Although prepared for admission to the freshman class at the age of
eleven, he did not enter the University until 1787.   After having graduated,
he read law with the Hon John Sprague, and was twenty years of age when
called to the bar in 1794.   He commenced practise in his native town of Rutland, and his fine genius soon raised him to high professional standing   In
1802, he removed to Worcester.   In 1810, 1811, he was in the Senate of
Massachusetts.   In 1816, he was appointed Clerk of the courts, and held that
office until his death, Feb 23, 1817

   The highest efforts of the great advocate rear no enduring monument to his
name   The reputation of his eloquence is entrusted to the generation that
witnesses its display   Few memorials of the splendid talents of Mr Blake
survive, except in the admiration of his contemporaries   An Oration at Worcester, July 4, 1796 , an examination of the constitutionality of the embargo
laws . and an oration at Worcester, July 4, 1812, are the only publications
which preserve permanent testimonials of magnificent intellectual action

His character is thus delineated by the elegant writer so often quoted. ' Mr. Blake possessed all the constituent properties of a great orator. He was of an ardent temperament, the usual companion of fine intellect, and of a character that dwelt with satisfaction and delight upon whatever was lofty and honorable. His was the nicely modulated voice, all whose cadences were musical; and though, like the harp of Memnon, in unrestrained inspiration, they sometimes breathed wildly, they breathed eloquently. His was the classic elegance of language, poured out in rich profusion from a never failing source. His was the vivid imagination, that threw over all, the crimson flush of light, and dazzled by its brilliancy. He brought to his aid the advantages of wide reading, and commendable scholarship, that served to increase his power of expression. He was often vehement and impassioned, and that, probably, was the prevailing tone of his eloquence, especially when he detected and brought to light the hidden things of chicanery and deceit; but his vehemence and his warmth never caused him to forget himself, nor to lose that harmony and measure of expression that were peculiarly his own.'[1]

LEVI THAXTER, of Hingham, son of Jonathan Thaxter, studied with Levi Lincoln, sen. commenced practise in Worcester in 1803. He was the first cashier of the Worcester Bank, which office he resigned in 1805, and removed to Watertown, where he now resides. He was Senator of Massachusetts from 1822 to 1826.

LEVI LINCOLN, H. U. 1802, son of Levi Lincoln, sen. of Worcester, read law in the office of his father, then Attorney General of the United States, and necessarily absent in the discharge of official duty. He was admitted to the bar in 1805, and commenced practise here. In 1812, he was member of the Senate of Massachusetts, and drew, and with Hon. Benjamin Crowninshield, presented, the answer of that body to the speech of Gov. Strong. In 1814, he was elected to the House of Representatives, and prepared and offered the protest of the minority against the act authorizing the famous Hartford Convention. In succeeding years, from 1814 to 1822, he represented the town, with the exception of three intervals, when he declined being candidate. In 1820, he was in the convention to revise the state constitution, and afterwards one of the Commissioners, under the act for the separation of Maine, to make partition and apportionment of the public property. In 1822, he was chosen Speaker of the House of Representatives, when a majority of that assembly differed from his political sentiments. He was Lieutenant Governor, in 1823, and, in February, 1824, appointed Associate Justice of the Supreme Judicial Court. In April, 1825, upon the nomination of the two great parties, he was Governor of the Commonwealth, and continued in this office by nine successive reelections, until, having declined being candidate, he retired upon the induction of his successor, in January, 1834. In February of that year, he was elected to supply the vacancy in the representation of the district, occasioned by the transfer of Hon. John Davis to the Executive chair, and, in November following, was chosen member of the twenty fourth Congress.

The degree of LL. D. was conferred upon him by Williams College and by

1 Willard's Address, 93.

Harvard University. He was for several years member of the Board of Trustees of Leicester Academy, some time its Treasurer, and afterwards President ; President of the Worcester Agricultural Society from 1823, Fellow of the American Academy of Arts and Sciences, member of the Board of Overseers of Harvard College, and Councillor of the American Antiquarian Society.

WILLIAM E GREEN, B U 1798, son of the first Dr. John Green, studied with Judge Edward Bangs, was admitted in 1801, and practised in Grafton to 1805 He then returned to Worcester, and was in partnership with Mr Bangs until the appointment of that gentleman to the bench in 1811, and afterwards, until Oct. 9, 1816, connected with Edward D Bangs, Esq

JOSEPH B. CALDWELL, H U. 1802, son of William Caldwell, Esq sheriff of Worcester County from 1793 to 1805, was born in Rutland, studied with Hon. Nathaniel Paine, practised in Grafton to 1809, Worcester in 1810, Rutland to 1812 He returned to Worcester in 1813, and died here in that year

Samuel M Burnside, D C 1805 son of Thomas Burnside, was born at Northumberland, Coos co N H His early education was in the common schools of a new-planted country, except nine months at an academy preparatory to admission at college After having graduated, he passed two years in superintending a female academy at Andover, Mass In October, 1807, he commenced the study of law in the office of Hon Artemas Ward, the present Chief Justice of the Court of Common Pleas. No one was more able or willing to afford aid to his students Familiar acquaintance with the principles of the common, merchant, and statute law, unsurpassed skill as conveyancer and special pleader, with uniform kindness and liberality, justified their affectionate reverence for the character of that able jurist and excellent man. His business was immense He was, consequently, much from home at this period, and his pupils were left to follow principally the dictates of their own judgment in regard to their course of reading Mr Burnside was admitted to practise in March, 1810, and was first sworn at the bar of the Supreme Judicial Court upon examination, being one of the few persons who have been suffered to pass to that court without having previously been admitted at the lower tribunal He commenced business in Westborough in the spring of 1810 In the autumn of that year, he removed to Worcester, and has since resided here [1]

---

[1] His father, Thomas Burnside, was a descendant of that colony of Scots, settling in the north of Ireland about 1650, many of whom emigrated to New England in 1719. Among them, was Rev James McGregore, his maternal grandfather, ordained first minister of Londonderry, 1719, who died March 5, 1729, leaving three sons, 1 David, succeeding in the ministry in 1737, 2 James, who became merchant in Londonderry, and 3, Alexander, who settled in Warwick, R I Susannah, only daughter of Alexander on the death of her father, was adopted and educated by her uncle James, himself childless, inherited with her brother his considerable estate, and married Thomas Burnside

Thomas Burnside was brought up in Londonderry as a merchant, took active part in the French wars from 1755 to 1763, was in many bloody battles on the frontier, and fought by the side of Wolfe on the plains of Abraham On the restoration of peace, he was engaged several years in mercantile pursuits He yielded to the flattering overtures of Gov Wentworth, to establish settlements in the northern parts of New Hampshire, within

18

Rejoice Newton, D. C. 1807, a native of Greenfield, Mass., son of Isaac Newton, commenced his studies with Hon. Richard E. Newcomb, at Greenfield, which were concluded with Hon. Elijah Mills, at Northampton. He was admitted attorney in Hampshire county, in 1810; immediately formed connection in professional business with Hon. Francis Blake of Worcester, which continued until April, 1814. On the decease of William C. White, he was appointed County Attorney, having discharged the duties a year previous. This office he resigned in 1824. He represented the town in the General Court in 1829, 1830, and 1831, and was elected Senator of Massachusetts in 1834. Since 1826, he has been connected in business with William Lincoln.

JAMES ELIOT. He was Representative in Congress from Vermont from 1803 to 1809. He was invited to Worcester to assume the editorial management of the Spy, in October, 1810, which he relinquished in February following, and soon afterward removed. He has since been Clerk of the Courts of Windham County, Vt., and resides at Newfane.

LEVI HEYWOOD, D. C. 1808, son of Seth Heywood, was born in Gardner, Mass., June, 1784. The study of law, commenced with Hon. Nathaniel Paine of Worcester, was finished with Hon. Elijah Mills of Northampton. Admitted to the bar in 1811, he began practise here in that year. In October, 1818, he removed to Pinckneyville, Louisiana, where he engaged in teaching school. Having kept an office in New York for a short period, he became Principal of the Academy in Hackensack, N. J. He again resumed practise in the city of New York, where he died, Nov. 22, 1832.

WILLIAM CHARLES WHITE, player, poet, advocate, and author, possessed versatility of talents, which gave some distinction in each of his various occupations. His father, William White of Boston, extensively engaged in commerce and trade, destined his eldest son to mercantile pursuits. His education for business was commenced, as the clerk of Mr. Joseph Cooledge, and diligently followed for a few years. At length, avocations more congenial to the taste of the young man, seduced his attention from the employments of the counting house, and the journal and ledger gave place to books of lighter literature. In 1796, at the age of nineteen, he had written ' Orlando,' a tragedy,

the valley of the Connecticut, whose fertile intervals had been traversed in his military campaigns. Animated by a bold spirit of enterprise, he left lucrative business and devoted friends, removed sixty miles above Haverhill, then the most northern settlement, into the wilderness, inhabited only by the red man, its ancient proprietor, and became the first planter of Northumberland, then called Stonington. For two or three years, he had no neighbor within sixty miles, and no direction to an English village but the line of *spotted trees.* In 1775, while busied in the labors of the harvest, a friendly Indian came running into the field in urgent haste, to warn him to flee for life, assuring him that a body of hostile savages were within two or three hours march. Immediately, he and his family were on horseback, hastening to a place of safety. The mother, then unaccustomed to hardship, rode with her infant in her arms, swam her horse across the Connecticut in the flight, and after extreme difficulties reached Haverhill in safety. Within the short time mentioned by his savage friend, the house, buildings, and crops of Mr. Burnside were destroyed by the enemy. Undiscouraged by such perilous escape, with the courage of a soldier, he soon returned to his desolate farm, and until the close of the war, divided his time between the peaceful avocations of the husbandman, and the martial enterprises required for the defence of the country. He died Nov. 3, 1798. MS of S. M. Burnside, Esq.

subsequently printed with the head of the author. The father, a formal and correct person, devoted to practical matters, seems to have contemplated the intellectual acquisitions of his son with little satisfaction.[1] Of the theatre, he entertained profound horror, regarding its pretensions to be the school of virtue as the mask of profligacy, and its occupations as the lowest degradation. His mortification was extreme, on finding the attachment of young White for the drama growing into a passion, too strong to be controlled by reason, and when excited by opposition, becoming so intense as to affect the sanity of mind and health of body In the winter of 1796, the elder White found it necessary to make a long visit to the city of New York He writes to a friend at home, ' William had, for some time, discovered his propensity for theatric exhibitions, and by all opportunities, I discountenanced in him this inordinate passion. During my absence from Boston last summer, he wrote a play which, on my return, some of the family mentioned to me Although I was not pleased with his study and writings in this style, yet I supposed it a good opportunity to turn his attention, and destroy gradually his predilection for the stage About a month previous to my leaving Boston, he grew sick, and was, apparently, in a decline I was very anxious, and postponed my journey for some time A few days before I left home, he seemed to be in better spirits, and declared himself to feel essentially better than he had been, and when I came away, opened himself, in a very dutiful and respectful manner, by observing that his illness arose from his insatiable thirst for the stage, but that his resolution had gained the ascendency of his desires, and entreated me not to have the least uneasiness respecting him in that particular, for he had determined not to give way to that inclination ' However sincere was the promise, it was soon broken The conflict of filial duty with passionate desire was so violent, as to bring its victim to the verge of distraction Unable to resist his dramatic love, he made his first appearance at the Federal Street Theatre, Dec 14, 1796, in the character of Norval, in the tragedy of Douglas, and was received with great applause, by an audience of indulgent friends In a letter of apology, written the next day, to his father, he says, ' I am sorry I was compelled by violence of inclination, to deviate from my promises to you ; but life was one series of vexation, disappointment and wretchedness Pray let this consideration have some weight with you But, for Heaven's sake, for your own sake, and for my sake, do not tear me from a profession, which, if I am deprived of, will be attended with fatal consequences.' Never did parent mourn more inconsolably for the worst follies or darkest crimes of his offspring, than did the father of the actor, over this example of perversity in his family His epistles are filled with expressions of distress, so extravagant, that they are only redeemed from being ludicrous, by the deep sorrow they breathe He thus addresses the tragedian ' Dear William ' for so I will still call you my beloved son' stain not the memory of your amiable and tender mother by your folly . break not the heart of your father . bring not down his gray hairs with sorrow to the grave · but rouse

[1] ' A son his father's spirit doomed to cross,
By penning stanzas while he should engross '

yourself, from this seeming state of insanity. . . . Your youth will excuse you for once. . . . . But for God's sake, and every thing you hold dear, I pray you to refrain, and be not again seen upon a common stage.' The temporary success of the aspirant for theatric fame, alleviated the sufferings of the distressed parent, and he reluctantly yielded to the advice of friends, and consented that Charles might occasionally tread the boards, but only in the elevated walks of tragedy. 'Let me enjoin it on you,' he writes, 'never to appear, no, not for once, in any comic act, where the mimic tricks of a monkey are better fitted to excite laughter, and where dancing, singing and kissing, may be thought amusement enough for a dollar. No, William, I had, much as I love you, rather follow you to the grave, than to see you, and myself, and my family, so disgraced.'

Mr. White appeared as Orlando, in his own tragedy, Dec. 20 ; Tancred, in Thompson's Tancred and Sigismunda, Jan. 2, 1797. Romeo, in Romeo and Juliet, Feb. 6 : and Octavian, in the Mountaineers, April 7, on the Boston stage. The ebb of popular favor effected, what parental admonition and entreaty failed to accomplish. Controversy with the manager arose ; the applause which followed his first efforts grew fainter : the fit of romantic enthusiasm exhausted itself : and the earliest exertion of reflection, resulted in the determination to adopt the profession of the law. In July, 1797, he entered the office of Levi Lincoln, sen. in Worcester, as a student. In July, 1800, he removed to Providence, where he completed his professional noviciate, under the instruction of Judge Howell. When admitted to practise, in Rhode Island, in September following, a partnership was proposed by that gentleman, on terms which were declined. Mr. White opened an office in Providence, but did not obtain employment or fees.

The want of business led directly to the want of money. The pressure of pecuniary embarrassment drove him again to the stage, in New York. 'On the 19th of January, 1801,' says Dunlap,[1] 'Mr. White, a young man from Worcester, Massachusetts, was brought out with some promise of success, in Young Norval. Curiosity was excited, and a house of $614 obtained. He had performed in Boston, when quite a boy, with that applause so freely, and often so injudiciously bestowed on such efforts : had since studied law, and was at this time a tall, handsome youth ; but not destined by nature to shine. He attempted Romeo, and gave hopes of improvement, but much improvement was wanting to constitute him an artist.' He played Alonzo in Columbus ; Aimwell in the Beaux Stratagem : Theodore in the Court of Narbonne ; Elvirus in the Christian Suitor : and Altamont in the Fair Penitent. In the play of ' the Abbé de l'Epée,' he failed altogether in the part of St. Alme, was hissed, and withdrawn by his own consent, as it was announced to the public, on ' finding the character too difficult.' About this time was begun, and nearly completed, a drama, with the title, ' the Conflict of Love and Patriotism, or the Afflicted Queen,' still preserved in manuscript, and never finished. A visit to Richmond, Va , where he played a few nights, was crowned with such success, that he contemplated devoting life to the theatre.

[1] History of the American Theatre. 281, 286.

The reverse of fortune in some of his efforts, again cured the dramatic mania. In the summer of 1801, he returned to the bar, and established himself in Rutland, in Worcester county, where some of his relatives then resided, and where his father, who had been unfortunate in business, soon after removed He was married to Tamar Smith, daughter of a respectable farmer of that town The degree of eminence and emolument he attained as counsellor, did not content his ambition, and he sought wider field. In May 1809, he had contracted to compile ' a Compendium of the Laws of Massachusetts ' printed in the same and the next following year, a work useful at the day of its publication, but soon rendered useless by revisions of the statutes More industry than talent was required for the compilation [1] To superintend the execution of this work, Mr White removed to Boston in 1810, and formed a professional connection with David Everett, Esq of brief continuance On the resignation of Judge Bangs in 1811, he was appointed County Attorney, which office he retained till his death He established himself in Grafton, in 1812 the next year he resided in Worcester. In 1814, he removed to Sutton, where he married Susan Johannot, daughter of Dr Stephen Monroe, August 13, 1815 He returned to Worcester in 1816, and died May 2, 1818. He had been long in declining health An organic disease, the dropsy, during the last years of his life, spread ' mortal paleness ' over his countenance

Through his whole career, the suppressed love of the drama was working on his mind The Clergyman s Daughter, a play founded on McKensie's Man of the World, was first presented on the Boston stage, Jan 1, 1810, and obtained remarkable success In December of that year, he produced the Poor Lodger, a comedy, adopting the incidents of Miss Burney's novel of Evelina Mr White was a frequent correspondent of the National Ægis, while that paper was under the direction of the late Francis Blake, and afterwards became editor In 1813, he published a pamphlet in vindication against the charge of apostasy from democratic principles His odes and poetical productions obtained some celebrity [2]

He possessed that high grade of talent, which is called genius. In his addresses at the bar there were passages of splendid eloquence. but they were unequal, although parts were strong, they were not connected with logical method and clearness His taste was refined and correct Greater constancy and perseverance might have raised him to a high rank in any of the departments of forensic exertion, literary effort, or dramatic exhibition

SAMUEL BRAZER, son of Samuel Brazer, was born at Worcester, in 1785

---

[1] The severe but witty comment of a distinguished jurist on this work was, that it resembled the tessellated pavement in Burke's description, ' here a little *black stone*, there a little *white*.

[2] MS of Samuel Jennison, Esq White MSS in Am Antiq Society's Collections

The publications of William Charles White are these 1. Orlando, or Parental Persecution tragedy Boston, 1797, 12mo. 2 The Clergyman's Daughter tragedy Boston, 1810, 12mo 3 The poor Lodger comedy Boston, 1811, 12mo 4 Compendium and Digest of the Laws of Massachusetts Boston, 1809-10, 2 vols 8vo 5 Avowals of a Republican Worcester, 1813, 8vo 6 Oration Rutland · July 4, 1802 7 Oration Worcester, July 4, 1804 8 Oration before the Bunker Hill Association Boston, July 4, 1809 9. Oration, Hubbardston, July 4, 1810.

His early education was received in the common schools. He was placed in a store in Boston, preparatory to engaging in mercantile business. Discovering no aptitude for the employment, and a decided inclination for literary avocations, he was sent to Leicester Academy to be prepared for college. There he remained long enough to be fitted for the junior class of Harvard University; but owing to some difficulty with the instructor, who often felt the lash of his playful satire, he failed of being presented for admission. Although overfond of amusement, apparently idle in the habits of study, and foremost in schemes of frolic, he easily took and maintained the highest place of his class in the academy. Disappointed in going to college, he entered the office of Hon. Francis Blake. The tone of party politics was, at that time, high and angry. With characteristic impetuosity he rushed into the midst of the conflict, and became one of the most distinguished contributors to the National Ægis, established in support of Mr. Jefferson's administration. The literary department of that print derived aid, in verse and prose, from his pen, in many essays and poetical papers distinguished for facility, point, and caustic vein of humor. He was frequently called on to deliver political orations on public anniversaries, and acquitted himself with great reputation. The first effort of this kind, was an Address in commemoration of the purchase of Louisiana, in 1804, at the age of eighteen, which was extremely popular with his party friends. He entered into the practise of the profession in New Salem, Mass. But he did not love the law, and the enjoyments of festivity seduced him from the pursuit of that distinction his talents would have won. In 1812, he was resident in Worcester. Subsequently he removed to Baltimore, Md., where he conducted the newspaper called the Baltimore Patriot. Its editorial articles, during his connection, indicate his industry and consistency, and are marked by the vigor of his nervous style. He died in that city, Feb. 24, 1823.

ENOCH LINCOLN, [B. C. 1821, A. M.] son of Levi Lincoln, sen., was born at Worcester, Dec. 28, 1788. He entered the Sophomore class of Harvard College in 1806. One of those unhappy commotions, which have disturbed the repose of the ancient seat of learning in Cambridge, occurred in 1808, and he voluntarily withdrew from the University during his senior year. His professional studies were pursued in the office of his brother, Levi Lincoln. He was admitted attorney in 1811, and commenced business in Salem, Mass. In 1812, he returned to Worcester, and practised here until the spring of 1813, when he settled in Fryeburg, Maine. While resident there, he published 'The Village,' a poem descriptive of the beautiful scenery of the fairest town on the stream of the Saco, of the wild and romantic region around, and of the social condition of the population of the youthful state. In 1815, he was appointed deputy by Hon. William P. Preble, then District Attorney of the United States. In 1819, he was elected to Congress, and removed to Paris, the capital of the county. He continued to represent the district of Oxford in the national Legislature until 1826. He was elected Governor of Maine for three years succeeding that date, with the approbation of the two political parties, and with unanimity almost unprecedented in times of feverish excitement. In the spring of 1829, he declined being again candidate, intending,

in retirement, amid the pursuits of agriculture, dear to him from education, in the cultivation of the natural sciences, with the flowers and fields he loved, and the literary avocations he delighted to follow, to seek means of usefulness and happiness In the autumn, induced by ardent desire to promote the cause of education, he visited Augusta, to address the Female Academy, founded there by a philanthropic citizen Suffering from severe sickness, the performance of the task exhausted his strength, and he became a martyr to the effort He retired from the exercises to the house of a friend, where he died, three days after, Oct 11, 1829, at the age of forty years.

His proclamations were marked with purity and expansive liberality of sentiment, and terse felicity of expression Official correspondence, vindicating, with decision and dignity, the rights of the state, was published among the documents of the contested north eastern boundary His contributions to the press were characterized by singular elegance of style, masculine energy of thought, and comprehensive views. An extended work, illustrative of the history and resources of Maine, was left unfinished, in manuscript

In his moral constitution there were elements brighter than gifts of genius Overflowing kindness of disposition, ready to do good to every human being, was associated with rectitude of judgment, and united to qualities giving to benevolence its highest value. The steadfast sense of justice was never debased by personal interest or feeling, or darkened by sectarian or party prejudice Manly intrepidity, fearing nothing but the consciousness of doing wrong, was unshaken by the dread of undeserved censure or popular excitement

EDWARD D BANGS, [H U. 1827, A M] son of Hon Edward Bangs of Worcester, studied with his father, and, on being admitted to practice in 1813, entered into partnership with William E Green, which continued four years In 1816, 1817, 1820, and 1824, he was representative of the town In 1824, he was appointed successor to Rejoice Newton, as County Attorney, and soon after, was elected Secretary of the Commonwealth The duties of this office were discharged for twelve years with fidelity and ability which commanded the respect, and courtesy and urbanity securing the good will of all Mr Bangs declined reelection, in January, 1836, on account of the impaired state of his health.[1]

JOHN DAVIS, Y C 1812, son of Isaac Davis, of Northborough, Mass (a respectable farmer, and for more than forty years deacon of the church of that town,) studied with Hon. Francis Blake, came to the bar in Dec 1815, and established himself in Spencer, in the county of Worcester, a place then of small business, and affording narrow sphere for the exertion of talent In May, 1816, he removed to Worcester, and soon attained high professional eminence From 1823 to the time of the appointment of Levi Lincoln to the bench of the Supreme Court in 1824, he was partner of that gentleman, afterwards connected with Charles Allen, Esq from 1824 to 1831 ; and subsequently with Emory Washburn, Esq to 1834.

[1] The unwearied kindness of Mr Bangs, in full and frequent communications, and in permitting free access to the rolls and files among the precious treasures of the past, heretofore in his official custody, has essentially aided in the preparation of this work, and deserves the most grateful acknowledgment.

In the autumn of 1824, he was chosen Representative of the south district of Worcester county in the Congress of the United States, and held his seat by successive reelections until January 1834. He was distinguished as the advocate of the 'American System' of protection to home industry: his speeches on the bill to increase the duties on wool and woolens of 1827; on the Tariff bill of 1828; upon the bill for the more effectual collection of imposts of 1830; and in answer to Mr. McDuffie of South Carolina in 1832; were widely circulated in newspapers and pamphlets. In 1830, he was appointed by the Executive, special Agent, to attend at Washington the adjustment of the claim of Massachusetts, for services rendered by her troops during the war with England. He was elected Governor of the Commonwealth, for the year beginning January 1, 1834, and reelected for the succeeding political term. In 1835 he was chosen by the Legislature, Senator of the United States for the period expiring in 1841. He received the degree of LL. D. from Harvard University, in 1834. He was elected President of the Worcester County Historical Society in 1826, and Vice President of the American Antiquarian Society in 1832.

JOHN W. HUBBARD, D. C. 1814, son of Roswell Hubbard, was born at Brookfield, Vt., and adopted and educated by Rev. Samuel Austin, his relative by marriage. His professional studies were pursued partly with Gov. Van Ness, at Burlington, Vt., and partly with Samuel M. Burnside, Esq. From his admission to the bar in 1817, until his death, September 17, 1825, he practised here. He possessed a strong and well-cultivated mind, and had given evidence of talents and acquirements which, with health and longer life, would have ensured distinction.

Pliny Merrick, H. U. 1814, son of Hon. Pliny Merrick of Brookfield; studied with Levi Lincoln; opened an office in Worcester, after admission to the bar in 1817: practised here to May 1818; in Charlton, Mass for three months following: in Swansey, Bristol county, to Aug. 1820; and in Taunton, where he was partner of Hon. Marcus Morton, during one year, to 1824. In June of the latter year, he removed to Worcester; on the 6th of July, 1824, was appointed County Attorney, by Gov. Eustis, succeeding Edward D. Bangs, Esq.: and Attorney for the Middle District, by Gov. Lincoln, May 24, 1832, upon the organization of the criminal courts distinct from the civil tribunals. He represented the town in the Legislature in 1827; and in 1827, 1828, 1829, 1835, was one of the board of Selectmen.

AUSTIN DENNY, son of Daniel Denny, was born in Worcester, Dec. 31, 1795. Although possessing a vigorous constitution, an accident at early age, occasioned a painful disease, which followed him to a premature grave. He graduated at Yale College in 1814, and commenced the study of law in the office of Hon. Nathaniel Paine. The malady preying on his system, deprived him of the use of his right arm, and so debilitated another member, that the exercise of walking was attended with difficulty. Fortitude and perseverance mitigated the pressure of misfortunes so severe. In December, 1817, he was admitted to the bar of the Court of Common Pleas, and commenced practise in Harvard, in this county. In 1819 he returned to Worcester. For several years he was editor of the Massachusetts Spy, and in 1823, established the Massachusetts Yeoman, and continued proprietor and conductor of that print until his decease, July 1, 1830

He was a well-read lawyer, industrious and faithful in the transaction of business, and a vigorous and able writer ' Of his intellectual powers,' says one who knew him well, ' the distinguishing feature was clearness and strength of comprehension His views were distinct, his knowledge exact, his reasonings just and candid his expressions forcible and pertinent He was not one of the few, who could astonish by the vastness of the efforts, or the splendor of their achievements He belonged to a larger, and not less useful class, who give life and health and vigor to society, by bringing to its service practical talents, useful knowledge, and blameless morals [1]

Charles Allen, [Y C 1836, A. M] son of Hon Joseph Allen, born in Worcester, Aug. 9, 1797, entered Yale College, but soon withdrew from that institution He studied with Samuel M Burnside, Esq · was admitted in August, 1818, and practised in New Braintree to July, 1824. In that year he removed to Worcester, and was partner of Hon. John Davis to 1831 He was elected representative of the town in 1829, 1833, and 1834, of the Board of Selectmen in 1832, and Senator of the Commonwealth in 1835, 1836

ALFRED DWIGHT FOSTER, H U 1819, son of Hon Dwight Foster, born in Brookfield, studied in the office of Samuel M Burnside, Esq, was admitted in 1822, and resided in his native town to 1824. He settled in Worcester in 1825, was professional partner of Mr Burnside until 1827, and has since retired from practise He was representative in 1831, 1832, 1833, and selectman in 1832 He has been one of the Trustees and Treasurer of the State Lunatic Hospital from 1833

WILLIAM S ANDREWS, H U 1812, son of William Andrews, born in Boston, studied at the Law School in Litchfield, Conn, and with Hon Francis Blake He was in business in Spencer, Mass. in 1817, afterwards practised in Maine. and in Worcester in 1824 and 1834 He is now resident in Boston, and has been author of several theological treatises

Isaac Davis, B U 1822, son of Phinehas Davis, was born in Northborough, Mass, studied with Hon John Davis and settled in Worcester, upon being admitted in 1825 He was one of the Visitors of the Military Academy at West Point in 1833, Vice President of the Massachusetts Sabbath School Union from 1832, of the Massachusetts Baptist Convention from 1833 of the New England Sabbath School Union from its organization in 1835 and President of the Board of Trustees of the Worcester Manual Labor High School from 1834

Thomas Kinnicutt, B U 1822, son of Thomas Kinnicutt, was born in Warren, R I ; studied with Hon Francis Baylies at Taunton, Mass, at the Law School in Litchfield, Conn, and with Hon. John Davis, and practised in Worcester from 1825 He was in the House of Representatives of Massachusetts in 1835; Trustee of the State Lunatic Hospital in 1835, 1836, and selectman in 1836.

[1] Massachusetts Spy, July 7, 1830

William Lincoln, H. U. 1822, son of Levi Lincoln, sen.

RICHARD H. VOSE, B. C. 1822, born at Augusta, Maine, son of Solomon Vose, Esq. grandson of Rufus Chandler, studied with Levi Lincoln and Hon. John Davis, practised here about a year in partnership with Pliny Merrick, Esq. and removed to Augusta in 1826.

CHRISTOPHER COLUMBUS BALDWIN, son of Eden Baldwin, was born in Templeton, Mass. August 1, 1800; entered Harvard University in 1819; and withdrew from that institution, with many of his classmates, May 1823. He entered the office of Levi Lincoln and Hon. John Davis, and on the retirement of the former from the bar, completed his legal studies with the latter gentleman; was admitted in June 1826, and commenced practise in Worcester. In May 1830, he removed to Barre, Mass., and in November following, to Sutton, Mass., where he formed a connection with Jonas L. Sibley, afterwards Marshal of Massachusetts. In the autumn of 1831, he was elected Librarian of the American Antiquarian Society, and relinquished a profession he never loved. The duties of this office were discharged with singular zeal and fidelity. While on a journey for the recovering of impaired health, and with the purpose of exploring the mounds and memorials of the perished nations of the West, he was killed, in Norwich, Ohio, by the overturn of a stage coach, August 20, 1835, at the age of thirty five years.

He possessed lively wit, antiquarian taste and knowledge, kindness of disposition and benevolence of feeling, and remarkable sincerity and simplicity of character.

In the autumn of 1825, Mr. Baldwin became one of the editors and proprietors of the Worcester Magazine and Historical Journal, published by himself and William Lincoln, in monthly numbers, during a year, forming two octavo volumes. He furnished the history of Templeton, many essays, biographical sketches, and selections of revolutionary papers, for that work.

ISAAC GOODWIN, son of William Goodwin, long postmaster and cashier of a bank in Plymouth, was born in that ancient town, June 28, 1786. Educated in the common schools, he early entered the office of Hon. Joshua Thomas, a counsellor of good reputation, and was admitted to practise in 1808. He opened an office in Boston, but removed, August 16, 1809, to Sterling, in Worcester county. There he remained to April, 1826; and then he became resident in Worcester, where he died, of dropsy of the heart, Sept. 17, 1832.

One nurtured fast by the pilgrim's rock, on the soil they first trod, could not fail to imbibe the antiquarian's love of old times. Such taste, combined with studious habits and facility in the acquisition of knowledge, led him to familiar acquaintance with the traditionary lore and recorded narratives of New England's history. Diligent inquiry into the origin and progress of our social and beneficent institutions, with lively interest in their objects, enabled him to extend their usefulness. Readiness in assuming and transacting business of a public character, made him a valuable member of the community. Writing with ease and grace, he was frequent contributor to the periodical press. The general view of the county, and the detailed account of Sterling, in the Worcester Magazine of 1826, were from his pen. He published ' The

Town Officer,' in 1826, which has been through three editions . and ' The New England Sheriff' in 1830 , useful compilations of the duties of municipal and civil officers Of the many occasional addresses delivered by him, the following were printed address before the American Antiquarian Society, Aug 24, 1820 : address before the Worcester Agricultural Society, Oct 13, 1821 Oration on the one hundred and fiftieth anniversary of the destruction of Lancaster by the Indians Feb 21, 1826

Emory Washburn, W C 1817, son of Joseph Washburn of Leicester , studied with Nathaniel P Denny, Esq and Bradford Sumner, Esq in his native town , in the Law school of Harvard University , and with Charles Dewey, Esq , then of Williamstown and was admitted attorney at Lenox, in March, 1821 He practised at Charlemont, in Franklin County, for six months , in Leicester, to March, 1828 , and since in Worcester

In 1826, he was representative of Leicester, Master in Chancery from 1830, and Trustee of the State Lunatic Hospital in 1836.

EDWARD J VOSL, B C 1825, brother of Richard, studied with Hon John Davis and Charles Allen, Esq , was admitted in 1828, opened an office here in 1829, and died June 1831

Henry Paine, son of Hon Nathaniel Paine of Worcester, entered Yale College in 1820, but soon left that institution on account of ill health , studied with Samuel M Burnside, Esq , and was admitted and began practise here, in June 1827.

William N Green, son of William E Green, a native of Worcester, pursued his professional studies with Samuel M Burnside, Esq , and commenced practise here in 1828

WILLIAM M. TOWNE, A C 1825, son of Hon Salem Towne, born in Charlton, Mass , studied with Hon John Davis and Charles Allen, Esq and commenced practise here in 1828 In 1831, he formed a partnership with Joseph W. Newcomb , and in the autumn of 1835, relinquished the profession, and engaged in manufacture

Jubal Harrington, B U. 1825, son of Fortunatus Harrington, born in Shrewsbury, Mass , studied in the Law School at Northampton, Mass , under the instruction of the late Hon. Samuel Howe and Elijah H Mills, and with Pliny Merrick, Esq He commenced practise here in 1828 , was editor of the ' Worcester Republican ' from the establishment of that print, March 4, 1829 representative in 1831, and 1836 , and postmaster from Nov 9, 1833.

Charles G Prentiss, born in Leominster, Mass., was son of Charles Prentiss. He studied with Rejoice Newton, and practised in Oxford, Worcester county, from his admission in 1821 to 1829. He then removed to Worcester, and has been town treasurer from 1832.

OTIS C. WHEELER, son of Daniel G Wheeler, born in Worcester, studied with Hon John Davis and Charles Allen, Esq , and was admitted to the bar in 1830 Consumption had fastened upon him and he died, of that disease, while on a journey, at St Augustine, Florida, Feb 6, 1831, aged 23.

DANIEL HENSHAW, H U. 1807, son of Col William Henshaw, born in Leicester, Mass , studied with Hon Nathaniel Paine , practised at Winchendon, in Worcester county, to 1830, in Worcester during the succeeding year; removed to Boston in 1832 ; and afterwards to Lynn, Mass.

David T. Brigham, U. C. 1828, son of Edmund Brigham ; born in Shrewsbury, Mass. ; studied with E. C. Southerland of Orange County, N. Y.; and Pliny Merrick, Esq. ; was admitted and began business here in 1831.

Maturin L. Fisher, B. U. 1828, son of Rev. Lewis Fisher, born at Danville, Vt. ; studied with Isaac Davis, Esq. ; was admitted 1831 ; and entered into practise here. Since the decease of Mr. Baldwin he has been acting Librarian of the American Antiquarian Society.

George Folsom, H. U. 1822, of Saco, Maine, studied with Ether Shepley, Esq. and commenced practise here in 1832.

Benjamin F. Thomas, B. U.1830, son of Isaiah Thomas, jun., and grandson of Dr. Isaiah Thomas ; studied in the Law School of Harvard University, and with Pliny Merrick, Esq., and was admitted to practise in 1833.

Edwin Conant, H. U. 1829, son of Jacob Conant, born in Sterling, Mass , studied with Rejoice Newton and William Lincoln, and at the Law School in Cambridge ; practised in Sterling to 1833 ; and since in Worcester.

Jesse W. Goodrich, U. C. 1829, son of Jesse Goodrich, born in Pittsfield, Mass. ; studied with Jonathan Jenkins of Rensselaerville, N. Y.; and R. M. Blatchford in the city of New York. In 1833, he was admitted at the bar of Worcester county, and formed a copartnership with David T. Brigham, which continued to June, 1836.

Abijah Bigelow, D. C. 1795, son of Elisha Bigelow, born in Westminster, Mass. ; studied with Hon. Samuel Dana in Groton ; and for a short time with Hon. Samuel Dexter in Charlestown : and practised in Leominster to 1817, On the decease of Hon. Francis Blake, he was appointed Clerk of the Courts, which he resigned in the spring of 1834, and opened an office in Worcester, in connection with George Folsom, Esq. This partnership continued about a year.

Mr. Bigelow was member of the House of Representatives in the 11th and 12th Congress, from 1810 to 1813.

Ira Barton, B. U. 1819, born in Oxford, Mass. ; studied with Samuel W. Bridgham, Esq. in Providence, R. I.; Sumner Barstow, Esq. in Sutton ; Levi Lincoln in Worcester ; and in the Law School at Cambridge ; and practised in Oxford to 1834. He represented that town in the Legislature of the Commonwealth, in 1830, 1831, 1832 ; and was Senator of Massachusetts in 1833, 1834. In 1834, he removed to Worcester, and, in Jan. 1836, was appointed Judge of Probate for the county of Worcester, on the resignation of Hon. Nathaniel Paine.

George W. Richardson, H U. 1829, son of John Richardson, now of Newton, born in Boston ; studied with John H. Richardson, Esq. and Pliny Merrick, Esq.: was admitted, and began practise here, in 1834.

Andrew Jackson Davis, son of Phinehas Davis, born in Northborough, Mass. ; studied with his brother, Isaac Davis, Esq. and after admission to practise, in September, 1834, was connected in business with him for a year.

Daniel Waldo Lincoln, H. U. 1831, son of Levi Lincoln, born in Worcester, studied with Rejoice Newton and William Lincoln, and was admitted to practise in 1834

Joseph W Newcomb, W C 1825, son of Richard E Newcomb, born in Greenfield, Mass studied with his father and with Rejoice Newton and William Lincoln, practised in Templeton to 1830, Salisbury, Mass to 1834 and since in Worcester He removed to New Orleans in the autumn of 1836.

William Pratt, B U 1825, son of Col Nymphas Pratt, born in Shrewsbury, Mass , studied with Pliny Merrick, Esq , and practised in his native town, until April, 1835 when he came to Worcester, and formed professional connection with Mr Merrick

ANDREW D. McFARLAND, U C 1832, son of William McFarland, born in Worcester, in 1811, studied with Hon John Davis and Emory Washburn, Esq ; commenced practise here in 1835 and died in Worcester, June 23, 1836

John H Richardson, H. U 1825, brother of George W. Richardson, born at Concord, Mass · studied with Hon Levi Thaxter, of Watertown, Hon William Prescott and Franklin Dexter, Esq. of Boston ; and commenced practise in Newton, Mass He removed to Worcester, April, 1836, and entered into partnership with his brother

George Ticknor Curtis, H U. 1832, son of Benjamin Curtis of Boston, born in Watertown , studied in the Law School at Cambridge , in the offices of Wells and Alvord at Greenfield ; and of Charles P Curtis in Boston ; was admitted in Suffolk, August, 1836, and established himself in Worcester soon after

PHYSICIANS

It is not now practicable to trace with exactness the succession of physicians of the town Of the professional life of the early medical men, no public record remains of their personal history, little has been preserved The few memorials of their useful labors which can be gathered, are derived principally from tradition The following list, accurate so far as it extends, cannot be considered full or complete

ROBERT CRAWFORD, was probably the first practitioner of medicine in Worcester He emigrated from Ireland with the colony of Scottish extraction, planting here in 1718. From his employment in the military expeditions of the period, in the capacity of surgeon, it may be inferred that he sustained respectable professional standing

WILLIAM CRAWFORD, united the clerical and medical offices, and served in the French Wars, sometimes as chaplain and sometimes as surgeon He was in the campaigns in Nova Scotia and on the northern frontier [1]

SAMUEL BRICK, son of Rev Robert Breck, second minister of Marlborough, who married Elizabeth Wainwright of Haver'hill, in 1707, was probably here

---

[1] A branch of the Crawford family, was early settled in that part of Rutland called Dublin several brought testimonials of their church fellowship in Ireland Hon William H. Crawford, formerly secretary of the Treasury of the United States, and Judge of the Supreme Court of Georgia, is said to have descended from the planters of Rutland. Reed's Rutland, 155.

in 1730. He too was surgeon in the provincial army. He removed to Windsor, Conn. about 1747, and died in Springfield, Mass. in 1764.

NAHUM WILLARD, son of Col. Abijah Willard, of Lancaster, was born April 22, 1733, and probably settled here about 1755. He was surgeon of Capt. Goodwin's company, marching with Col. Chandler's regiment for the relief of Fort William Henry in 1757 : and was in extensive practise. He removed to Uxbridge, Mass. after the revolution, and died there, April 26, 1792, aged 59.

JOHN GREEN, (sen.) son of Dr. Thomas Green,[1] was born at Leicester, Aug. 14, 1736. Educated by his father, and inheriting peculiar talents, he came into the profession early, and settled in Worcester about 1757. Tradition bears ample, though very general, testimony of his worth. Fortunate adaptation of natural capacity to professional pursuits, gave an extensive circuit of employment and high reputation. Habits of accurate observation, the action of vigorous intellect, and the results of experience, seem to have supplied the place of that learning, deriving its acquirements from the deductions of others, through the medium of books. Enjoying great esteem for skill and fidelity, hospitality and benevolence secured personal regard. He was a leading and influential whig, member of the revolutionary committees, representative in 1777, and selectman in 1780. He died Oct. 29, 1799, aged 63 years.[2]

ELIJAH DIX, son of James Dix of Waltham, studied with the elder Dr. Green, and commenced practise about 1770. Managing extensive concerns, and having much employment as physician and druggist, he was in active business more than thirty years. He died at Dixmont, Me. June 7, 1809.

WILLIAM PAINE, H. U. 1768, eldest son of Hon. Timothy Paine, was

1 Thomas Green, ancestor of a family distinguished through successive generations for medical skill, was a native of Malden, Mass. The surgeon of a British ship, a casual visitor of his father, probably gave direction to the taste of the son, by the donation of a volume on medicine. Active, energetic, and enterprising, he set forth into the wilderness to seek fortune, with the outfit of an axe, a gun, a cow, and his whole library of one book, and became an early settler of the plantation, called by the natives *Towtaid*, by the English *Strawberry-bank*, now Leicester. His first dwelling was formed under a shelving rock, which stretched a natural roof over his cabin. The severe labor of hewing away the forest brought on a fever. Feeling the premonitory symptons of the disease, he provided for subsistence during impending sickness in the solitude, by tying the calf of the single animal he owned, near his primitive habitation, and when the mother returned to feed her offspring, he was enabled to obtain the nourishment feeble condition prevented him from seeking abroad, and thus, alone and unassisted, he preserved a valuable life through severe illness.

The Indians were near neighbors of the white settler. From their communicated knowledge of roots and herbs, from the science drawn from a few books, and, more than all, from the action of a vigorous mind, he soon became skilful as a physician. While he exercised the cure of bodies, he assumed the care of souls, as clergyman, an union of professions not remarkable in early times. His success as a preacher, was scarcely less considerable than his reputation as doctor. A respectable Baptist society was gathered, and a meeting house built, through his agency. A life of persevering industry and extensive usefulness, terminated, October 25, 1773, at the age of 73 years. Thatcher's Medical Biography, 274. Washburn's Leicester in Wor. Hist. Mag. ii. 92.

2 Dr. Green married Mary Osgood, and afterwards Mary, daughter of Brigadier Timothy Ruggles, who died June 16, 1814, aged 74 years.

born in Worcester, June 5, 1750   One of his early instructors was President John Adams, who taught a school while reading law in the office of James Putnam   His medical studies were under the direction of the late venerable Dr Edward A Holyoke, at Salem   After the usual period of novitiate, he commenced practise here, in 1771   A partnership was formed with Drs Levi Shepherd and Ebenezer Hunt of Northampton, for the sale of drugs and medicines, and the first apothecary's shop of the county opened here, about 1772   For the purpose of facilitating the negotiations of this business abroad, and of perfecting his medical education, Dr Paine visited Europe, long previous to the commencement of hostilities   Sailing from England, in the spring of 1775, he found, on his arrival at Salem, that war had broken out   The proceedings of the revolutionary tribunals, were summary   On the evidence that he was an absentee, he was denounced as loyalist   Return to his family and home being precluded, he took passage back to Liverpool, designing to avail himself of the advantages and means of improvement afforded by foreign institutions, until the conflict should terminate   His property, thus abandoned, suffered confiscation, and his name was inserted on the list of those designated as enemies of their country   After a year's attendance on the hospitals, having received the diploma of Doctor of Medicine from Marischal College, Aberdeen, Nov. 1, 1775, as the contest still continued, he accepted the commission of Apothecary to the forces in America, entered the army in that capacity, and served in Rhode Island and at New York   In January, 1781, in attendance on his patient, Lord Winchelsea, he again crossed the Atlantic. Driven from her course by storms, the ship entered the port of Lisbon   After some stay there, he went to England, and in October, was admitted licentiate of the Royal College of Physicians, and, for a long time, his name was enrolled among those of the practitioners of London   Returning to New York, in March, 1782, he was appointed by Sir Guy Carlton, in October following, Physician to the army, and soon was ordered to Halifax, where he remained on duty, until the troops were reduced, in 1783, when he was disbanded on half pay   In June, 1784, he took possession of Le Tete Island, in the Bay of Passamaquoddy, granted by the government for services, and erected a house, with a view to permanent residence.   The solitude of the wild situation not proving agreeable to his family, he removed, and entered into practise in the city of St Johns   In 1785, he was elected member of the assembly of New Brunswick, from the County of Charlotte, and appointed Clerk of that body   The office of deputy, was conferred by his friend, Gov Wentworth, Surveyor General of the King's Forests, and retained until the summer of 1787, when, by permission from the War Office, he went to Salem   With good professional business, and occasionally writing marine policies there, after the death of his father, July 17, 1793, he returned to his native place, and occupied the paternal estate until his decease, April 19, 1833, at the age of 83 years.

Dr Paine was fellow of the American Academy of Arts and Sciences, and member of the Medical, Agricultural, Linnean, Essex Historical, and American Antiquarian Societies.   He possessed extensive professional learning and refined literary taste, and was equally respected as a physician and citizen.

JOSEPH LYNDE, son of Joseph Lynde,[1] born at Charlestown, Mass. Feb. 8, 1749, commenced practise about 1774, and was for a time connected with Dr. Dix; superintended the hospital for the small pox in 1775, and had the reputation of a first-rate physician and an excellent man. He removed about 1783, and established himself as druggist in Hartford, Conn., and died in that city, Jan. 15, 1829, aged 80.

Among other physicians in practise here before the revolution were these: EBENEZER WHITNEY, in the inventory of whose estate, March 7, 1744, the library is appraised at 4s. 6d. and the drugs at £6. 18s.: ZACHARIAH HARVEY, whose medical title is preserved on the records, with the fact that he slew sixty seven rattlesnakes in 1740: JOHN FISKE, who died here in 1761; THOMAS NICHOLS of Danvers, who came from Sutton about 1765, and died Dec. 17, 1794, at the age of 82 years: WILLIAM and GEORGE WALKER, sons of that Capt. John Walker, who commanded a company of foot in the provincial service during the French wars.

THADDEUS MACCARTY, Y. C. 1766, son of the Rev. Thaddeus Maccarty, was born in Worcester, Dec. 19, 1747. Under the instruction of Dr. John Frink of Rutland, an eminent physician of the county, he received his medical education, and commenced practise in Dudley, in 1770, entering into partnership and extensive business with Dr. Ebenezer Lillie. On the termination of three years, this connection was dissolved. Removing to Fitchburg, Mass. he found there full and laborious employment. The small pox made fearful ravages in the country about this period. Dr. James Latham, managed this terrible disease, once the scourge of the race, with great safety in the Suttonian method.[2] To acquire the art of resisting the prevalent malady, in 1775, Dr. Maccarty left his family, repaired to a hospital in Great Barrington under the superintendence of this practitioner, and learned the mode of cure by suffering its operation. In the following year, having obtained the right to extend the remedy, and the license required by law from the Court of Sessions, with Dr. Israel Atherton of Lancaster, he conducted a hospital in Fitchburg,

---

[1] Joseph Lynde, H. U. 1723, born at Charlestown, Mass. Jan. 7, 1703, married Mary Lemmon, Feb. 24, 1736. After the destruction of Charlestown by the British troops in 1775, he resided in Worcester till his death. Four of his daughters married here: 1. Sarah, b. Feb. 21, 1743, m. Andrew Duncan: 2. Dorothy, b. May 23, 1746, m. Dr. Elijah Dix: 3. Elizabeth, b. Oct. 1, 1756, m. Theophilus Wheeler, Esq. d. March 7, 1833: 4. Hannah, b. July 4, 1760, married Hon. Edward Bangs, d. Sept. 10, 1806.

[2] The remedy was kept secret by the inventor, Dr. William Sutton, of Surry, in England, except from those who purchased knowledge. It is hinted in a publication of the time, that, in obtaining his patent, he veiled his discovery by a false specification. Dr. Latham, surgeon in his majesty's 8th regiment of foot, partner and agent of Sutton, who introduced the system in America, resided at Livingston Manor, in New York. He licensed physicians to administer the medicines prepared and furnished by himself, within certain towns and limits, they contracting to pay over to him one half of all monies received, until his portion should amount to three hundred pounds, and afterwards, one third of all further sums obtained in the business: and covenanting not to attempt, by analysis or otherwise, to discover the composition of the medicines. Different innocent drugs were mixed in the preparation, to defeat any examination which might be made. MS. of John W. Stiles, Esq.

with such success, that of eight hundred patients, five only were lost by death. The earnest solicitations of his father, the venerable clergyman of Worcester, then fast declining to the grave, induced the son, at great sacrifice, to return to his native town, in June, 1781. In June, 1785, he was elected Fellow of the Massachusetts Medical Society. Not receiving adequate patronage here, and his own health being much impaired, he took up his permanent residence in Keene, N H in June, 1789, and engaged in mercantile business, practising physic occasionally. In the spring of 1793, he again made use of Dr Sutton's medicine, in a small pox hospital at Charlestown, N H. In 1796, he applied Dr Perkins' once famous Metallic Tractors, with singular efficacy. For some time, wonderful cures were wrought, and these fanciful agents, in his hands, enjoyed signal reputation. But the warm faith so essential to their usefulness subsided, and the Tractors sunk beneath the merciless satire of Fessenden. In February, 1797, Dr Maccarty was commissioned Justice of the peace for the County of Cheshire, and in February, 1802, of the Quorum, and officiated extensively in the capacity of magistrate. He was Chairman of the Selectmen of Keene for many years. He died in that town, Nov 21, 1802 [1]

JOHN GREEN, the second of like name and fame, born in Worcester, March 18, 1763, came to the practise of medicine at the early age of eighteen years. 'From his childhood,' writes his biographer,[2] 'the natural bias of his mind led him to that profession, which through life, was the sole object of his ardent pursuit. To be distinguished as a physician, was not his chief incentive. To assuage the sufferings of humanity by his skill, was the higher motive of his benevolent mind. Every duty was performed with delicacy and tenderness. With these propensities, aided by a strong, inquisitive, and discriminating mind, he attained to a preeminent rank among the physicians and surgeons of our country.' It has been the high privilege of few of our community to enjoy so much of confidence and respect, to be so loved while living, and so mourned when dead. A life whose events were acts of usefulness, skill and charity, affords few incidents for narrative, it was terminated Aug 11, 1808.

SAMUEL PRENTICE, a man of talents and eminent as a surgeon, came from Stonington, Conn in January, 1783. A Medical Society was formed in the County in 1785, but not sustained. Of this association he was Secretary. He removed to Keene, N H about 1786, and afterwards settled in Saratoga, N Y.

OLIVER FISKE, H U 1787, son of Rev Nathan Fiske, was born in Brookfield, Mass. Sept 2, 1762. His early education was superintended by his father, whose productive farm, during most of the revolutionary war, was, from necessity, principally confided to his management. In the summer of

---

[1] Dr Maccarty married Experience, daughter of Thomas Cowdin, Esq of Fitchburg, Jan. 1775. she died at Worcester, Jan 29, 1789. His only daughter married, Nov. 1801, John W Stiles, Esq sometime of Templeton, who died at Worcester, Sept 1836.

Although the Rev Thaddeus Maccarty had a numerous family of fifteen children, there now survive of his posterity only one grand child, two great-grandchildren, and three great-great grandchildren.

[2] Hon. Oliver Fiske, in Thatcher's Medical Biography

19*

1780, a requisition for recruits was made. The quotas of men had, thus far, been furnished without compulsory process; but levies had been so frequent, that none would enlist freely, at a season so busy. The company, then commanded by the late Major General John Cutler, was ordered to meet for a draft. Exempted, by the courtesy extended to clergymen, from military duty, and never having been enrolled, Dr. Fiske offered himself as volunteer, with the approbation of his father, who applauded the patriotic spirit, while the personal sacrifice it involved was severely felt. Animated by the example, the requisite number came from the ranks on the parade. The regiment, in which they were embodied, was ordered to West Point, and was stationed in the vicinity of that post, at the defection of Arnold and the capture and execution of Andre. On being discharged, he returned to the farm, and was employed in its cultivation until the close of the war, in 1783, when he entered Harvard College. At the breaking out of Shay's Insurrection, he was instrumental in reorganizing the Marti-Mercurian Band of the University, in obtaining an order from Gov. Bowdoin for sixty stands of arms at Castle William, and was second officer of the company. When the court commenced at Concord, he was the organ of a petition from this corps, to march in support of government, which was properly declined by the authorities of the institution. In the winter vacation of 1786-7, he took a school at Lincoln, but hearing of the threatened movements of the malcontents to stop the judicial tribunals at Worcester, he procured a substitute to assume his engagement, exchanged the ferule for appropriate weapon, and hastened to this place. Finding the enemy dispersed, and the troops on their way to Springfield, he set out to visit his father. On the heights of Leicester, the report of Gen. Shepherd's Artillery diverted him from his course. Uniting himself to a body of light horsemen, then on their route, he joined Gen. Lincoln's army. When the rebellion was suppressed, he resumed his studies, without censure for the long absence, and graduated in 1787. After the usual preparation, under the tuition of Dr. Atherton, of Lancaster, he commenced business in this town, in October, 1790. He was active in forming a County Medical Association, and in obtaining the establishment of the present district organization of the Mass. Medical Society. Soon after the formation of the last named body in the second medical district, he was elected President, and held the offices of Councillor and Censor until he retired from the profession. In February, 1803, he was appointed special Justice of the Court of Common Pleas. During five years succeeding 1809, he was member of the Executive Council. The commissions of Justice of the Peace, of the Quorum, and throughout the Commonwealth, were successively received, and the latter has been renewed to the present time. Dr. Fiske was Corresponding Secretary of the Linnean Society of New England in 1815; of the Worcester Agricultural Society from 1824; and Councillor of the American Antiquarian Society. He was Register of Deeds during the triennial term from 1816 to 1821. From this period, an increasing defect in the sense of hearing, induced him to retire from busy life, and devote himself to the pursuits of horticulture and agriculture, those employments, in his own graceful language, ' the best substitute to our pro-

John Green

genitors for their loss of Paradise, and the best solace to their posterity for the evils they entailed ' The results of that taste and skill in his favorite occupations, early imbibed, ardently cherished, and successfully cultivated, have been freely and frequently communicated to the public in many essays, useful and practical in matter, and singularly elegant in manner.

John Green, B U 1801, son of the second Dr. Green, born in Worcester, studied with his father, and succeeded to his practise in 1807 He has received the degree of M. D. from Harvard and Brown Universities, and been Councillor and Censor of the Massachusetts Medical Society, President of the Worcester District Medical Society, and Councillor of the American Antiquarian Society

BENJAMIN CHAPIN, son of Thaddeus Chapin, was born at Worcester, May 29, 1781. He studied with the second Dr John Green, and first entered into practise in Marlborough, Mass. In 1808, he returned, was elected town clerk from 1818 to 1833, and died here Jan. 15, 1835, aged 54 years

Benjamin F Heywood, D C 1812, son of Hon. Benjamin Heywood, a native of Worcester, attended the lectures of Dr Nathan Smith in the Medical schools of Dartmouth and Yale Colleges, received the degree of M D at the latter institution in 1815, and formed partnership in practise with Dr. John Green, which continued twenty years. He is Councillor and Censor of the Massachusetts Medical Society.

Oliver Hunter Blood, H U 1821, son of Gen. Thomas H Blood of Sterling, was born at Bolton, Mass. His studies were pursued with Dr. Lemuel Capen in Sterling, and in the Medical Institution of Harvard University, where he received his degree in regular course. He practised in Worcester from 1825 to 1828 : resided in Brookfield, Mass from April, 1829, to Feb. 1831, when he returned to Worcester

John Simpkins Butler, Y C 1825, son of Daniel Butler, born in Northampton, Mass · pursued his professional studies in the Medical College in Boston, and the Jefferson Medical School in Philadelphia, and received the degree of M D. at the latter institution, in 1828 He commenced practise in Worcester, in 1829.

George Chandler, son of Maj John Wilkes Chandler, born in Pomfret, Conn , pursued his preparatory studies in Brown University and Union College, read medicine with Dr H Holt, and received the degree of M D at Yale College, March 4, 1831 ; commenced practise in Worcester, Nov 3, 1831 ; and since March 28, 1833, has resided in the State Lunatic Hospital, in the capacity of Assistant Physician and Apothecary.

SAMUEL BAYARD WOODWARD, [Y. C 1822, M D] son of Dr Samuel Woodward,[1] an eminent physician of Torringford, Conn is a native of that town Having received a good academic education, he pursued medical stud-

---

[1] Dr Samuel Woodward, born at Watertown, Conn 1750, was not only distinguished in his profession, but in political life From 1800 to 1810, he was the candidate of the democratic party, then a minority, for member of Congress ; was long member of the Legislature of Connecticut , and, for many years, as the oldest representative, ' father of the house.' He died, Jan 26, 1835, aged 84

ies, and entered into practice, with his father, in his birth place. Removing
to Wethersfield, Conn. in November, 1810, extensive engagements of business attended his high professional reputation. During his residence there,
he was elected Secretary of the Connecticut Medical Society, Vice President
of the Hopkins Medical Association, and one of the Medical Examiners of Yale
College. In 1827, he was appointed Physician of the State's Prison in
Wethersfield, and held this office six years. In the spring of 1832, he was
chosen Senator in the Legislature of Connecticut from the first district. In
the foundation of the Retreat for the Insane, at Hartford, he bore leading part.
One of the first by whom the project of that noble charity was presented to
the public, by his efforts, the funds of the Medical Society of the State were
bestowed for this most worthy purpose. Of the committees to obtain subscriptions, to assist in the foundation of the institution, determine its location,
and superintend the erection of buildings, and one of the Visitors, the great
weight of his personal exertions and influence were devoted to its prosperity.

By a selection most fortunate for Massachusetts, Dr. Woodward was appointed Superintendent of the State Lunatic Hospital, and became resident in
Worcester in January, 1833,[1] bringing to that establishment, on its commencement, those high qualifications desirable for its success.

Since his residence here he has become member of the Massachusetts Medical Society, of the Ohio Historical, Philosophical and Medical Society, President of a Temperance Society, and connected with other literary, medical, and
useful associations.

The heavy and increasing labors of his official situation, preclude him from
exercising, beyond the walls of the hospital, except in consultation, the skill
and experience acquired by wide practice. Yet the relation he holds, justifies,
while his high character renders desirable, the claim, to number among *our*
physicians, one of whose name any community might be proud.

Aaron Gardner Babcock, son of Amos Babcock, born at Princeton, Mass.:
studied with Dr. Chandler Smith in that town; attended the lectures, and received medical degree at Bowdoin College, in 1830; commenced and continued business in Holden for three succeeding years; and began practise here
in May, 1834.

William Workman, son of Daniel T. Workman, born in Coleraine, Mass.
studied with Dr. Seth Washburn at Greenfield, and Dr. Flint at Northampton, and received the degree of M. D. at the Medical College of Harvard University in 1825. He practised in Shrewsbury from 1825 to 1835, and in
April of the latter year, removed to Worcester.

Chandler Smith, son of Calvin Smith, born in Peru, Berkshire county,
studied with Dr. John M Smith of West Boylston, received his professional
diploma from the Berkshire Medical Institution in 1825: and practised in
Princeton, Mass. from Nov. 1826, until his removal to Worcester in June, 1836.

---

[1] On the removal of Dr. Woodward from Wethersfield, a card was transmitted to him,
subscribed by 670 persons, expressing warm personal regard, high respect for his talents,
worth and usefulness, and the sincere regret, which would be understood by all who enjoy
his acquaintance, for his departure. Mass. Spy, Jan. 16, 1833.

Among the physicians since the revolution, not included in the foregoing list, were GEORGE HOLMES HALL, a native of Medford, who practised here nearly three years from 1788, married a daughter of Gardner Chandler, and removed to Brattleborough, Vt. where he remained in his profession and in the business of apothecary. SAMUEL WILLARD of Harvard, who was resident of this town about two years after 1790; and JOHN HOMANS, afterwards of Brookfield, now of the city of Boston, who was of Worcester a few months in 1815.[1]

CHAPTER XIV.

Graduates of Colleges, and natives of the town who have received liberal education. Distinguished citizens. John Chandler. Capt. Jonas Hubbard. Col. Timothy Bigelow. Col. Ephraim Doolittle. David Thomas. Benjamin Heywood. Joseph Allen. Isaiah Thomas.

JOSEPH ALLEN is the first person borne on the records of Harvard College from Worcester. His father was the Rev. Benjamin Allen, an early settler,

[1] The kindness of that accurate antiquarian the Rev. Dr. T. M. Harris, by a communication since the last sheet went through the press, has furnished materials for correcting and extending the very brief notice of Dr. Dix, on page 214.

Doct. Elijah Dix, was born at *Watertown*, Aug. 24, 1747. Enjoying few advantages of early education, such was his desire to become qualified for respectable station in society, that, when a young man, he went to live with the Rev. Aaron Hutchinson of Grafton, engaging to do sufficient work for him to pay for board and instruction. With this eccentric man, who was a thorough scholar, he made good proficiency in the elements of literature and science. His circumstances in life precluding the attainment of collegiate education, he entered himself as medical student with Dr. John Green. On commencing the practise of the profession in Worcester, he connected with it an Apothecary's store, having been qualified for this business by being sometime with Dr. William Greenleaf of Boston, and by careful attention to the most approved Dispensatories. In the spring of 1784, having unsettled accounts with Dr. Sylvester Gardner, who went, at the commencement of the revolution, from Boston to England as a loyalist, Dr. Dix, with an honorable sense of responsibility, made a voyage thither, with the means to liquidate the outstanding claims. An adjustment was effected to the mutual satisfaction of the old friends. The visit afforded opportunity, not only of enlarging his knowledge of mankind, but establishing correspondence, for trade, with the houses of eminent chemists and druggists in London. Besides a choice assortment of medicines, he brought back some valuable books and philosophical and chemical apparatus. Returning to Worcester, he formed the plan of an Academy here, and uniting with him a number of gentlemen, the institution was commenced, and for some time flourished. Attentive to public improvement, he was the first to set trees himself, and induce others to plant them, on the borders of Main Street. He was one of the most efficient and zealous promoters of the Worcester and Boston Turnpike, a work affording, at the period of its establishment, great facilities to travel. Having built a house in Boston, and a store for wholesale druggist's trade, he removed there in 1795. After that part of Dorchester, now South Boston, was set off from the metropolis, and connected with it by a bridge, he erected there an edifice with furnaces and ovens, for refining Sulphur, and a laboratory for clarifying camphor, and other preparations, proofs alike of chemical science and energetic spirit.

He was of strong natural powers of mind, of active industry and ardent enterprise. As a physician, skill, improved by study, observation, and experience, rendered his services useful and successful. MS. of Rev. T. M. Harris.

to whom land was granted at the south east corner of the town. He was born Feb. 14, 1720, entered the University, but was not graduated, and, it seems, died early.

TIMOTHY PAINE, H. U. 1748, son of Hon. Nathaniel Paine of Bristol, R. I. removed to Worcester at the age of eight years, and was long one of our most respected and useful citizens. Soon after leaving college he was engaged in the public service. The number and variety of offices he held, exhibit the estimation in which he stood. He was clerk of the Courts from 1750 to 1774: Register of Probate from 1756 to 1767: Register of Deeds from 1761 to 1778: Member of the Executive Council of the Province from 1766 to 1773; in 1774, was appointed one of his Majesty's Mandamus Councillors, a station which was declined in compliance with public will, expressed in the manner related in preceding pages; Selectman from 1753 to 1763, and from 1765 to 1774: Town Clerk for ten years from 1753: and Representative in 1788 and 1789.

Solid talents, practical sense, candor, sincerity, affability, and mildness, were the characteristics of his life, which closed July 17, 1793, at the age of 63 years.

RUFUS CHANDLER, H. U. 1766. See Lawyers.

SAMUEL WILLARD, H. U. 1767, son of Dr. Nahum Willard, born April 13, 1748, studied medicine with Dr. Israel Atherton of Lancaster, and established himself in Uxbridge in 1770. He was particularly distinguished for his treatment of the insane.[1]

WILLIAM PAINE, H. U. 1768. See Physicians.

NATHANIEL CHANDLER, H. U. 1768, son of Hon. John Chandler, born Nov. 6, 1750, a student of James Putnam, was called to the bar in 1771, and commenced business in Petersham, which he continued until the courts were closed. Almost necessarily a royalist, he became a refugee, and, for a time, commanded a corps of volunteers in the British service. From New York he went to England. Returning, in 1784, he engaged in trade in Petersham. Sickness compelled him to relinquish the shop. He removed to Worcester, where he died, March 7, 1801.[2]

SAMUEL PAINE, H. U. 1771, son of Hon. Timothy Paine, born Aug. 23, 1754; was associated with his father as Clerk of the Courts and Register of Probate, before the revolution. He left the country, and visited New York, Nova Scotia, and England. He received a pension of £84 per annum, from the British government, as an American Loyalist. After the war he returned home, and died in Worcester, June 21, 1807.

WILLIAM CHANDLER, H. U. 1772, son of Hon. John Chandler, born Dec. 5, 1752, left the country at the commencement of the revolution, and re-

---

[1] He married Olive, daughter of Rev. Amariah Frost, of Milford, by whom he had two sons: 1. Abijah, born Feb. 16, 1782, practised medicine in Uxbridge, and died April 12, 1816. 2. George, physician in Uxbridge, and representative of that town in the Legislature. Levi Willard, brother of Samuel, son of Nahum, born in Worcester, Nov. 24, 1749, studied with his father, and went into the practise of medicine and surgery in Mendon; acquired good reputation in both departments; and died there Dec. 11, 1809.

[2] Willard's Address, 77.

mained with the British during that contest. He returned, and died in Worcester.

JAMES PUTNAM, H. U. 1774, son of James Putnam, Esq. born Nov. 16, 1756, retired to Nova Scotia immediately after leaving the University; became a favorite with the Duke of Kent; accompanied him to England, obtained the office of Marshal; was member of the household of his patron, and one of the executors of his will.

DANIEL BIGELOW, H. U. 1775, son of Daniel Bigelow, was born April 27, 1752. After leaving college, he instructed the town school to the spring of 1776. Then he formed connection with William Stearns, Esq. in the publication of the Spy. On the return of Mr. Thomas from Salem, in 1777, the newspaper was surrendered to its original proprietor. He then entered the office of Mr. Stearns, as student at law, was admitted June, 1780, and opened an office in Petersham, where he died Nov. 5, 1806. He was representative of that town from 1790 to 1795; senator of the county from 1794 to 1799; member of the executive council in 1801; and was successor to Judge Sprague and predecessor of Judge Paine, as county attorney.[1]

NATHANIEL PAINE, H. U. 1775. See Lawyers.

SAMUEL CHANDLER, son of John Chandler, born Feb. 25, 1757, was merchant, for some time connected with his brother Charles in Worcester, afterwards engaged in trade in Putney, Vt. and was in extensive business. He died Oct. 26, 1813, in Woodstock, Vt. He entered Harvard College in 1771, but soon left the University.

TIMOTHY BIGELOW, H. U. 1786, was born in Worcester, April 30, 1767. His father, Col. Timothy Bigelow, engaging in the primary movements of the revolution, was soon called into military service. The early education of the son, necessarily devolving on maternal care, was commenced in the public schools of his native place. This then imperfect source of instruction was soon disturbed by the troubles of the times, and he entered the printing office of Isaiah Thomas, where he was occupied during two years.[2] The passion for books and the strong love of literature, were manifested amid the employments of the press, by the devotion of leisure hours to the acquisition of the elementary branches of English, and the rudiments of Latin. In 1778, he was placed as pupil under the charge of the Rev. Joseph Pope of Spencer. The spring of 1779 found him in the quarters of the Continental Army, posted to watch the British forces on Rhode Island, gaining the manly accomplishments a camp affords, and enjoying the frank courtesies of military life. When the regiment of Col. Bigelow marched South, he returned to his home, and pursued his studies for two years under the kind superintendence of Benjamin Lincoln, son of the revolutionary general, then student at law; and when this gentleman left Worcester, they were continued, under the direction of another law student, of great eminence in after life, the late Hon. Samuel

[1] Willard's Address, 88.

[2] Hon. Benjamin Russell, long editor of the Columbian Centinel, and Senator and Councillor of Massachusetts, was apprentice of Mr. Thomas, while Mr. Bigelow was in the printing office. Warm friendship arose, and was cherished, between these gentlemen, until the death of the latter.

Dexter, who accompanied his scholar, and presented him for admission at the University, in 1782. In college, Mr. Bigelow took prominent rank in a distinguished class,[1] excelling in the exact sciences, and particularly in mathematics. Leaving Cambridge he adopted the profession of the law, and entered the office of Levi Lincoln, sen. When the insurrection broke out, in 1787, he joined the army and aided in sustaining the government against the wild designs of its internal enemies. When a company of colonists was formed by Gen. Rufus Putnam, from the inhabitants of Worcester and Essex, for the first settlement of Ohio, he entered into the plan of emigration, but was reluctantly induced to relinquish the execution by domestic considerations. Admitted to the bar in 1789, he commenced in Groton, Mass. the practise of a profession, whose duties and labors were sustained, for more than thirty years, by a constitution never robust, against the pressure of bodily infirmity. In 1806, he removed to Medford, and while resident there had an office in Boston. His business was widely extended. Attending the Courts of Middlesex and Worcester, and those of Hillsborough and Merrimack, N. H., he became one of the prominent counsellors at the bar of Suffolk, and, in the latter years of his life, was retained in many of the important causes in Essex and Norfolk. Among able competitors and eloquent advocates, the broad range and multiplicity of his engagements are indications of standing not to be mistaken. A fluent speaker, well versed in his profession, enjoying the reputation of a good general scholar, he possessed the nobler merit of high moral and religious principles.

Mr. Bigelow early entered the Legislature of the Commonwealth. From 1792 to May, 1797, he was representative from Groton: during the four succeeding years, Senator: in 1802, Councillor: in 1804, he was again elected representative: for eighteen ensuing years was returned member of the house; in 1805, he was chosen its speaker; and in 1808 and 1809, and subsequently, from 1812 to 1819 inclusive, presided over this branch of the legislative department with signal ability and popularity. Entering warmly into the politics of the times, and entertaining the views of the opponents of the policy and measures of the General Administration, he was a prominent member of the Federal party; and in December 1814, as delegate from Massachusetts, attended the Hartford Convention, with his colleagues, Hon. George Cabot, Hon. Harrison G. Otis, and Hon. William Prescott, of Boston.[2] In 1820 he was at the Council board; but, before the term had expired, he had ceased from earthly cares and laid down the burden of mortality. He died at Medford, May 18, 1821, aged 54 years.

Endowed with ready apprehension, of active and inquisitive mind, gathering knowledge with remarkable facility, exact method and system enabled him, under the pressure of a load of labors, to compass a vast amount of reading.

---

[1] Among his classmates, were the late lamented Chief Justice Parker, Christopher G. Champlin, U. S. Senator from Rhode Island, Thomas W. Thompson, U. S. Senator from New Hampshire, Alden Bradford, Secretary of Massachusetts, John Lowell of Roxbury, and William Harris, President of Columbia College. With such competitors, excellence was high merit.

[2] Of this famous political assembly, Hon. Daniel Waldo of Worcester, was a member.

Exploring almost every branch of liberal science, he was peculiarly conversant with Theology   Resting on scripture truth as the basis of faith and the guide of practise, the better to resolve the dubious texts of the Bible, in his latter years, he added to familiar acquaintance with Greek, sufficient proficiency in Hebrew, to enable him to read the Old and New Testaments in their original languages   With rare colloquial talents, he freely poured forth the stores of diversified information, and the treasures of retentive memory, enlivened by illustrative anecdote, and a vein of sparkling humor   He was a member of the American Academy, and Vice President of the American Antiquarian Society [1]   He was active in establishing and conducting the association of the ' Middlesex Husbandmen '   Taste for Horticulture, led him to execute a systematic plan of ornamental gardening around his home, which his liberal spirit made the seat of hospitality, and where were exercised the social and domestic virtues, rendering his private life as excellent, as his public course was eminent [2]

THOMAS CHANDLER, H U. 1787, son of the third Hon John Chandler, born Jan. 11, 1768, was merchant, and died here

GARDNER L CHANDLER, H U. 1787, son of Col Gardner Chandler, born Nov. 29, 1768, studied law with Levi Lincoln, sen. and discovered distinguished talent and capacity for a profession, which he soon abandoned and devoted himself to merchandise, in Boston

JOSEPH ALLEN, H U 1792   See Lawyers

WILLIAM DIX, H U 1792, son of Dr Elijah Dix, born July 25, 1772, studied medicine with Dr Waterhouse in Cambridge, and took his medical degree in 1795, when he delivered an inaugural dissertation on dropsy, which was printed   He died at the Island of Dominica, in the West Indies, April 4, 1799

ELIJAH DIX GREEN, B. U 1793, son of the second Dr. Green, born July 4, 1769, was physician in Charleston, S C where he died, Sept 21, 1795

[1] While Free Masonry was in its palmy state in New England, Mr Bigelow presided, for two triennial terms, over the Grand Lodge of Massachusetts, and, in that capacity, with a splendid cortege of craftsmen, in 1805, made a journey to Portland, to instal the officers of the Grand Lodge of Maine

[2] Hon Timothy Bigelow married, Sept 1791, Luey, daughter of Judge Oliver Prescott of Groton, one of the founders of the American Academy and of the Mass Medical Society His children were   1 Katherine, m Hon Abbott Lawrence of Boston   2. Andrew, settled in the ministry, first in Medford, afterwards over the first Congregational Church, in Taunton   3 John Prescott, Secretary of the Commonwealth   4 Edward, residing at Medford   5 Helen   6 Francis, merchant in Boston   7 Elizabeth Prescott, living at Medford

The publications of Hon Timothy Bigelow, were   1 Oration before the Phi Beta Kappa July 21, 1796, at Cambridge   2 Funeral Oration on Hon Samuel Dana, April 4, 1798, at Amherst, N H   3 Eulogy on Washington, Feb 11, 1800, at Boston   4 Address before the Washington Benevolent Society, April 30, 1814, at Boston

The materials for this sketch have been derived from a Memoir, kindly furnished by the Rev Andrew Bigelow   Could the pen of that ripe scholar and elegant writer have been borrowed, ample justice might have been rendered to the worth of his father   In the Centinel of May 19, 1821, is a tribute to the memory of Mr Bigelow, traced by his early associate, Maj Russell, with the glowing pen of friendship.

SAMUEL BROWN, H. U. 1793, born Dec. 9. 1768, was son of Luke Brown, commenced the study of physic with the elder John Green, which was completed with Dr. John Jeffries, to whose daughter he was united in marriage, and established himself in Boston. An inaugural dissertation on the bilious malignant fever, July 10, 1797, of extraordinary merit, gave him, at once, distinguished reputation, well sustained by rare skill and science. As a testimonial of approbation of the high merit of his essay, a silver plate was bestowed by the Massachusetts Medical Society, of which he was a member. A disease of the knee so impaired his constitution, that he submitted to the amputation of the limb. The result did not restore health. He died, at Bolton, Aug. 4, 1800, while on a visit to his mother, who had married William Osborne, an innkeeper of that town.[1]

ASA MCFARLAND, D. C. 1793, son of James McFarland, was born April 19, 1769. He was tutor in Dartmouth College two years; and appointed Trustee of that institution; which office he resigned in 1821. He was ordained minister of Concord, N. H. March 7, 1798, officiated twenty-seven years, and died, Feb. 18, 1827. He was President of the N. H. Domestic Missionary Society, and connected with many other charitable associations. The Doctorate of Divinity was conferred upon him by Yale College, under the presidency of the venerable Dr. Dwight, in 1809.[2]

JOHN CURTIS CHAMBERLAIN, H. U. 1793, son of John Chamberlain, born June 5, 1773, read law with Hon. Benjamin West of Charlestown, N. H. was admitted to practise in 1796, opened an office in Alstead, and held prominent place at the bar of Cheshire county. He was representative in Congress from 1809 to 1811. In 1826, he removed to the Western part of the state of New-York, and died at Utica, Nov. 15, 1834, at the age of 62.

LUKE BROWN, H. U. 1794, son of Luke Brown, jun. born Nov. 29, 1772, read law and entered into its practise in Hardwick, Mass. where he married a daughter of Gen. Jonathan Warner, and for a time pursued the profession with indifferent success, but he soon abandoned his office.

HENRY VASSALL CHAMBERLAIN, son of John Chamberlain, born Jan. 11, 1777, entered Harvard College in 1794. He withdrew from the University, studied law with Hon. Nathaniel Paine, and with his brother, John C. Cham-

[1] Luke Brown, grandfather of Dr. Samuel, removed from Sudbury about 1750, opened, and long kept, a public house, north of Lincoln square, near the site of the ancient jail, and acquired wealth by speculation in wild lands. While on a journey to New York, undertaken for negociating the purchase of a township in Vermont, now Newfane, he contracted the small pox, and died soon after his return, April 14, 1772, aged 58. He was succeeded in the business of innkeeper, by his son Luke, who died Nov. 6, 1776, aged 31, leaving four sons, Luke, Arad, John, and Samuel.

[2] The ancestor of this family here was Daniel McFarland, who emigrated from Ulster, in Ireland in 1718. His son Andrew, grandfather of Asa, left three sons; William and James, both dying at Worcester; and Daniel, who removed to Pennsylvania, about the commencement of the revolution, and settled on the Monongahela, where his descendants remain. Duncan, brother of the first Daniel, planted in Rutland. By his last will, Aug. 14, 1746, he devised 'to Daniel, my well beloved son, whom I likewise constitute, make, and ordain my sole executor, the one half of all my lands that I enjoy at present, on the strict condition that he will never marry Betty Harper.'

berlain, was admitted in 1801 at the bar of Cheshire, N. H. practised in Farmington, Me. a few years ; about 1810, removed to the South, and has resided for twenty years in Mobile, Ala. where he has acquired wealth and reputation. He has there held the offices of Port Warden, Alderman, Sheriff of the County of Mobile, Judge of the Orphan's Court, and Chief Justice of the Court of Common Pleas.[1]

WILLIAM E. GREEN, B. U. 1798. See Lawyers.

MOSES MILLER, B. U. 1800, son of Moses Miller, who married Sarah Gray, born Nov. 23, 1776 : was fitted for college, principally in the town school, under the instruction of Mr. Andrew Morton. He was tutor in Brown University three years, while acquiring theological education, and was ordained minister of Heath, Mass. Dec. 26, 1804, where he has since remained the sole pastor of the Congregational Society.[2]

TYLER BIGELOW, H. U. 1801, son of David Bigelow, studied law with Hon. Timothy Bigelow, in Groton, opened an office in Leominister, and removed to Watertown, Oct. 4, 1804, where he has since resided. having received ample share of the confidence of clients and the emoluments of the profession.[3]

LEVI LINCOLN, H. U. 1802. See Lawyers.

DANIEL WALDO LINCOLN, H. U. 1803, son of Levi Lincoln, sen. born March 2, 1784, read law with his father, established himself in Portland, Me. was appointed by Gov. Sullivan, County Attorney of Cumberland; was in practise in Boston from April 1810, to July 1813 ; resumed business in Portland ; and died April 17, 1815, at the age of 31 years. An Oration delivered at Worcester, July 4, 1805, and one before the Bunker Hill Association, July 4, 1810, are the only printed memorials of the splendid genius he possessed.

LEVI CHAMBERLAIN, son of John Chamberlain, entered Williams College in 1804, but after two years, took up his connections with that institution, and became student at law, first in the office of his brother John, and afterwards in that of Levi Lincoln ; came to the bar in Worcester, Dec. 1813 ; practised in Fitzwilliam and Keene, N. H.: was Clerk of the Courts and County Attorney of Cheshire: and from 1821 to 1833, member of the Legislature of New Hampshire, as representative and senator.

---

[1] His only child, Henry Chamberlain, a lawyer of good standing, has been member of the legislature of Alabama.

[2] The Rev. Mr. Miller married Bethiah, daughter of Dr. Samuel Ware, of Conway, and has had nine children, of whom six are living. The oldest son was member of Amherst College in Sept. 1836. His grandfather Moses, was for many years, deacon of the old South Church in Worcester, held many civil offices in the town during the revolution, was a man of firm patriotism, unusual soundness of judgment, strict integrity, and liberal benevolence. His great grandfather, was a soldier of Capt. Church in the Indian wars, was wounded severely, and carried a musket ball, received in fight, to his grave.

[3] The ancestors of this family of Bigelow, came to Worcester from Watertown. David Bigelow, father of Tyler, an ardent whig, was member of the revolutionary committees, and delegate to each of the Conventions, at Concord, Cambridge, Boston, and within the county, in which the town was represented, from 1774 to 1789. In the convention of 1787, to consider the Federal Constitution, he voted with the minority, from jealousy of delegated power. He died May, 1810, aged 80.

JOHN GREEN, B U. 1804. See Physicians.

FREDERICK W. PAINE, [H. U. 1819, A. M.] son of Dr. William Paine, entered Harvard College in 1803, but soon left the University for commerce. He was representative in 1829 ; chairman of the Board of Selectmen in 1831, and President of the Worcester County Mutual Insurance Company from 1832.

JOHN NELSON, W. C. 1807, son of Deac. John Nelson, born in Hopkinton, Mass. became resident here at an early age. He studied with Rev. Dr. Austin, and was settled in Leicester, March 4, 1812.'[1]

ALEXANDER REED, D. C. 1808, son of Deac. Ebenezer Reed, born at Milford, Mass. July 10, 1786, became an inhabitant of Worcester with his father, (who died here May 21, 1823, aged 82,) in 1794. Under the tuition of the celebrated Dr. Nathan Smith, he studied medicine, received medical diploma in 1811, and has since practised in New Bedford, Mass. The degree of Doctor of Medicine was conferred by Yale College, in 1816. Dr. Reed has been, for several years, the oldest councillor of the Mass. Medical Society for the Bristol county district.

GARDNER BURBANK, B. U. 1809, a native of that part of Sutton, now Milbury, was son of Elijah Burbank, who came to Worcester about 1798; he studied law with Hon. Francis Blake ; was admitted to the bar ; but immediately engaged in the manufacture of paper, and in 1835, removed to Sharon, Vt.

THOMAS GARDNER MOWER, H. U. 1810, son of Thomas Mower, studied medicine with Dr. Thomas Babbet of Brookfield ; received the degree of M. D. from the University of New York ; entered the army as surgeon in 1813 ; served in the campaigns on the Canadian frontier during the war with England ; and has since resided in the city of New York.

BENJAMIN FRANKLIN HEYWOOD, D. C. 1812. See Physicians.

JOHN BRAZER, H. U. 1813, son of Samuel Brazer, succeeded Gov. Edward Everett as Latin Tutor in Harvard University, in 1815 ; was Professor of the Latin language in that institution, from 1817 to 1820; and was ordained Pastor of the North Church in Salem, Nov. 14, 1820; he was elected Fellow of the American Academy in 1823: one of the Overseers of Harvard University in 1829 ; and received the degree of Doctor of Divinity from that college in 1836.

DANIEL KNIGHT, B. U. 1813, son of Edward Knight, studied law with Levi Lincoln, practised in Spencer, and afterwards in Leicester, where he died, Aug. 16, 1826.

GEORGE ALLEN, Y. C. 1813, son of Hon. Joseph Allen, studied theology with Rev. Dr. Andrew Yates, Professor in Union College, and was ordained minister of Shrewsbury, Nov. 19, 1823.

HENRY ELIJAH DIX, H. U. 1813, son of Dr. Elijah Dix, born Feb. 6, 1793, studied medicine with Dr. John Warren of Boston, entered the United States Navy, and died in the Hospital at Norfolk, Va. Jan. 21, 1822.

AUSTIN DENNY, Y. C. 1814. See Lawyers.

[1] Of this gentleman a notice was inserted in the note to page 163.

STEPHEN SALISBURY, H. U. 1817, son of Stephen Salisbury, studied law with Samuel M. Burnside, Esq. and was admitted to the bar, but did not enter into the practise of the profession.

FRANCIS ARTHUR BLAKE, H. U. 1814, son of Hon. Francis Blake, born in Rutland, April 4, 1794, but early resident here, adopted the profession and entered the office of his father. Admitted to the bar 1817, he settled in Cincinnati, Ohio, removed to the city of New York in 1823, where he died March 22, 1824, immediately after a favorable exhibition of talent as counsel in the trial of a capital case.

GEORGE BANCROFT, H. U. 1817, son of Rev. Dr. Aaron Bancroft, visited Europe in the autumn of 1818; was two years in the University of Gottingen in Germany, where he was admitted Doctor of Philosophy; spent 15 or 18 months in a tour on the continent; was tutor in Harvard College from 1822 to 1823; afterwards opened a high school at Northampton: and has resided for some years past in Springfield. In 1834, he published the first volume of the History of the United States; and has been greatly distinguished as a fine scholar and elegant writer.

BAXTER PERRY, H. U. 1817, son of Deac. Moses Perry; born April 16, 1792: studied theology in the Andover Seminary; settled in the ministry at Lyme, N. H.; where he died, Jan. 18, 1830.

ROBERT TREAT PAINE FISKE, H. U. 1818, son of Dr. Oliver Fiske, is now practising physician in Hingham, Mass.

WILLIAM LINCOLN, H. U. 1822. See Lawyers.

CLARK PERRY, H. U. 1823, son of Deac. Moses Perry, studied theology at Andover, and was ordained at Newbury, Mass. Oct. 1828.

DAVID PERRY, D. C. 1824, son of Deac. Moses Perry, of the Andover Theological seminary, was settled as clergyman, in Cambridgeport, in 1829.

ISAIAH THOMAS, H. U. 1825, son of Isaiah Thomas, jun. has been proprietor and editor of the ' American,' a newspaper in Cincinnati, Ohio, and merchant of that city; and is now resident in New York.

ANDREW BIGELOW, son of Walter Bigelow, entered Harvard College in 1825, but was compelled to leave his class by ill health. He became assistant instructor at Garrison Forest Academy, and died at Worcester, April 1, 1826, aged 24.

BENJAMIN F. THOMAS, B. U. 1830. See Lawyers.

WILLIAM S. LINCOLN, B. C. 1830, son of Levi Lincoln, read law with Rejoice Newton and William Lincoln, was admitted Attorney in 1833, and has since been in the profession in Millbury, Mass.

DANIEL WALDO LINCOLN, H. U. 1831. See Lawyers.

HARRISON GRAY OTIS BLAKE, H. U. 1835, son of Hon. Francis Blake, is student of theology in the Divinity School at Cambridge.

HENRY BIGELOW, H. U. 1836, son of Lewis Bigelow, is student of medicine.

JOHN HEALY HEYWOOD, H. U. 1836, son of Levi Heywood, is engaged in instruction.

John Chandler

cease of his father, he succeeded to the higher offices of Judge, Colonel, and
Councillor. His talents were rather brilliant and showy than solid or profound. With manners highly popular, he possessed cheerful and joyous disposition, indulging in jest and hilarity, and exercised liberal hospitality.
While Judge of Probate, he kept open table, on court days, for the widows
and orphans who were brought to his tribunal by concerns of business. He
died at Worcester in 1763.

JOHN CHANDLER, son of the last mentioned John and of Hannah Gardner,
described as 'daughter of John Gardner, Lord of the Isle of Wight, in the
Province of New York, born Feb 26, 1720, as he succeeded to the military,
municipal, and some of the judicial offices of his father, inherited the characteristic traits of his ancestors. He was cheerful in temperament, engaging in
manner, hospitable as a citizen, friendly and kind as a neighbor, industrious
and enterprising as a merchant, and successful as a man of business. Leaving
the country at the commencement of the revolution, he sacrificed large possessions to a chivalrous sense of loyalty. In the schedule exhibited to the
British Commissioners appointed to adjust the compensation to the Americans, who adhered to the loyal government, the amount of his real and personal estate which was confiscated, is estimated at £11,067, and the losses, of
the income of offices, from the destruction of business, and by other causes, at
nearly £6,000 more. So just and moderate was this computation ascertained
to be, at a time when extravagant claims were presented by others, that he
was denominated in England, 'the honest refugee.' He died in London in
the autumn of 1780.

CAPTAIN JONAS HUBBARD. The son of an early settler, he was born in
Worcester. Previous to the revolution, he was engaged in the cultivation of
his patrimonial estate, and in the management of extensive concerns of business. The first sounds of coming war found him an Ensign in one of the
three militia companies of the town. A few months before hostilities commenced, Captain Rufus Chandler, a decided royalist, afterwards a refugee,
and an active and influential man, paraded his troops before some British officers who had visited him from Boston, and boasted to his guests of that loyalty among his men, which the king vainly expected would sustain his as-
sumptions of power amidst a bold and intelligent yeomanry, knowing their
rights and willing to defend them.

When the volunteer company of minute men was raised, Hubbard was elected Lieutenant, and actively participated in the evening drills, after the labors
of the day were over, and in the preparations made by the busy industry of
the martial spirit of the times, for immediate action.

Soon after this gallant corps marched to Cambridge, he was appointed Captain. When the expedition through the Kennebeck wilderness, against Quebec, was planned, volunteers were enlisted from the army at large. The object of the service, or the destination of the troops, was known only to the superior officers. It was understood that it would be attended with danger, labor, and suffering. Hubbard, brave and energetic, did not shrink from peril
or hardship in the cause to which he had devoted himself, and, at his own re-

quest, was appointed to the command of a company, in the detachment of Arnold. While the troops halted at Fort Weston, on the Kennebeck, he wrote to his wife, in terms worthy of a patriot martyr. 'I know not if I shall ever see you again. The weather grows severe cold, and the woods, they say, are terrible to pass. But I do not value life or property, if I can secure liberty for my children' Captain Hubbard shared in the extreme sufferings of the march, and probably more than his proportion, as acting under a commission, among those who had no reverence for artificial distinctions, beyond that yielded to the legitimate authority of courage and wisdom.

On the arrival of Arnold before Quebec, the golden opportunity when he might have entered its gates triumphantly was lost. The attack was made by the way of the lower town, at midnight of the last day of December, 1775, in a fierce tempest. In storming a barrier, Capt Hubbard fell, at the head of his company, severely wounded. Respected for his fearless intrepidity and loved for his personal worth, his men wished to remove him to a place of shelter from the fast falling snow, and of safety from the vollies of balls poured down from the ramparts. But he peremptorily refused. 'I came here to serve with you, I will stay here to die with you,' were his last words to a comrade who survived. Bleeding and stretched on a bed of ice, exposed to the bitter influence of a winter storm, life soon departed. It was a glorious time and place for the gallant soldier to yield up his breath, beneath the massive walls of the impregnable citadel, with the death shot flashing fast, and the thunder of battle swelling round him

The history of many families of New England is told in that of Capt Hubbard. The ancestor, hardy and enterprising, went out from the cultivated country to redeem new tracts from the waste. The father, animated by a noble patriotism, exchanged the sickle for the sword, the peaceful pursuits of agriculture for the privations of military life. The sons, inheriting his adventurous and manly spirit, emigrated to Maine, where the eldest ranks among the founders of towns [1]

COL TIMOTHY BIGELOW, was born in Worcester, August 12, 1739. His father, Daniel Bigelow, was of that class of substantial farmers who have been distinguished here for independence, good sense, industry and probity.[2] The youngest son, the subject of this sketch, was first apprenticed to a mechanic trade, and afterwards prosecuted the business of a blacksmith with diligence.[3]

[1] Gen Levi Hubbard, the first settler of Paris, in Maine, has borne many offices with honor. He was representative of Oxford District, in Congress, from 1813 to 1815

[2] Daniel Bigelow married Elizabeth Whitney, and with his wife moved from Watertown to Worcester, and resided in that part of the town then called Bogachoag, now Ward, where he died at the great age of 92 years. He had five children, David, Nathaniel, Daniel, Timothy and Silence · the latter was for many years a school mistress; the former, with a single exception, have been before mentioned. His paternal ancestors early emigrated from England. The first recorded notice of any of the family in this country, is of John Bigelow, an inhabitant of Watertown, who in 1636, served as Grand Juror, at a term of the Court held at Newton, now Cambridge. He was possessed of extensive tracts of land, cultivated a farm, and 'was well to live' The name was formerly written *Biglo*, by corruption from *Bedloe*, the more ancient orthography.

[3] He built a forge before the war on the south side of Lincoln Square. After returning

He was soon ranked among the most energetic and prosperous of the young men of the village. With strong native power, and shrewd observation of men and things, he labored to supply the want of the advantages of education: he collected a small but well-selected library, became acquainted with some of the best English authors, and gained the art of speaking with directness and force, and of writing with point and accuracy. These acquisitions were soon called into full exercise. As the clouds of the revolution gathered, he was placed in prominent position among the whigs of the town. Our best educated and most influential men were decided tories. Mr. Bigelow, espousing with ardor the opposite party, as early as March 1773, was elected of the local Committee of Correspondence, and, in December, organized the Political Society[1]. Meetings of these bodies were often held at his dwelling, and measures were there conceited in secret, which broke the control of the adherents of the king. The recital of his exertions would be but repetition of the narrative of that struggle between the patriots and royalists, with which he was identified, already spread through former pages. The bold and then treasonable resolutions of the town, in 1774, were resisted in the public meeting of the inhabitants by Col Putnam, who remonstrated against the adoption, in an appeal of solemn and lofty eloquence: they were sustained vigorously, by Mr Bigelow, and carried triumphantly. From that day the 'sons of liberty' were victorious, where toryism had possessed its strongest hold in the interior. Member of the famous 'Whig Club' assembling in Boston, he was associated with Warren, Otis, and other eminent movers of the springs of 'rebellion.' He was delegate in the Provincial Congress during its first and second sessions[2]. When the company of Minute Men was formed, he was chosen, by unanimous vote, to be its commander. Under his unwearied instruction, this corps attained such excellence in military exercises, as to draw from Washington, on the first review, the expression, 'this is discipline indeed.' On the day preceding the Concord fight, he had been engaged in preparations for the removal of the military stores to a place of safety, and returned, in good time to place himself at the head of his men, when they took up the line of march, on the 19th of April, 1775. Arriving at Cambridge, on the following day, he joined the army, as Captain, and soon after, by commission from Congress, was promoted to the rank of Major. In September 1775, he engaged, as volunteer, in the expedition against Quebec. Had that winter march through the wilderness been the exploit of a Grecian phalanx, or Roman legion, the narrative of sufferings and dangers, severe as were ever endured or encountered, would have been celebrated in song and story. One of the three divisions penetrating through the forest, by the route of the Kennebeck, was

from the army, he erected a triphammer and other iron works, on the site of the Court Mills, now owned by Stephen Salisbury, Esq.

[1] An account of this society and of the political exertions of Col Bigelow will be found in the sixth and seventh chapters of this work.

[2] Col Bigelow, with other leading whigs, desirous of the establishment of a press in Worcester, had made proposals to Isaiah Thomas to issue a newspaper here. An arrangement was effected for this purpose at the commencement of 1775. The removal of the Spy from Boston, took place immediately after the battle of Lexington.

commanded by Major Bigelow.[1] In the attack on Quebec, during the night
of the 31st of December, in the assault on the fortress, exposed to a shower
of balls from the barriers and ramparts, he was made prisoner, and remained
in captivity until the summer of 1776   An exchange having been negotiated,
he returned, and was soon after called into service with the rank of Lieutenant Colonel. The commission of Colonel was received Feb 8, 1777, and he
was appointed to the command of the 15th Regiment of the Massachusetts
line in the Continental Army, then forming, principally of the men of Worcester county   Remaining in Worcester, until the ranks were filled and the
new troops drilled, he marched to join the Northern Army under Gen Gates,
and arrived on the scene of action in season to assist in the capture of Burgoyne   With his regiment, we afterwards trace him, at Saratoga, in Rhode
Island, at Verplank's Point, Robinson's Farms, N. J Peekskill, Valley Forge,
and West Point   A braver band never took the field or mustered to battle.
High character for intrepidity and discipline, early acquired, was maintained
unsullied to the close of their service.

After the army was disbanded, Col Bigelow was stationed for a time at
West Point, and afterwards assigned to the command of the national arsenal
at Springfield   When he left military life, it was with the reputation of a
meritorious officer, but with straightened purse. The pay of the soldiers of
freedom had been irregularly advanced, in depreciated currency,[2] and large
arrears were withheld   With a frame physically impaired by long hardship,
toil and exposure, with blighted worldly prospects, with the remains of private property, considerable at the outset, but seriously diminished by the many
sacrifices of his martial career, he returned to his home. With resolute spirit
he set to work to repair his shattered fortunes, and resumed the old occupations of the forge and work shop   But times had changed since the fires of
the furnace had been last kindled. If the products of his skill were in as
quick demand as in former days, responsible customers were diminished.

[1] During a day's halt of the troops, on this memorable march, Major Bigelow ascended a
steep and rugged height, about 40 miles northwestward from Norridgewock, in Somerset
County, Maine, for the purpose of observation   This eminence still bears the name of
Mount Bigelow.

A faithful and most interesting narrative of the campaign against Quebec, was published by John Joseph Henry, a soldier in the expedition, afterwards President of the Second
Judicial District of Pennsylvania   the journal of Major Return J Meigs is printed in 2
Mass Hist Coll ii 227 some original letters of Arnold, are inserted in the Maine Historical Society's Collections, i 341. From these sources may be derived full detail of the
memorable expedition

[2] The following extracts of a letter from Mrs Bigelow to her husband, Feb 26, 1780,
show the depreciated state of the currency.

'On account of the heavy fall of snow, there is not a possibility of getting wood from
the farm at present, no one who does not live on the great road can bring any with a sled.
The common price is *fifty dollars*, and it has been sold for *fifty six dollars* the load '   .   .
' The money you sent me was very acceptable, for I was in debt for Andrew's pair of shoes,
forty dollars, and also for mending in the family, which made the account almost *seventy
dollars*. I paid the servant, *fifty eight dollars* for what money he had expended on the road
[in a journey of about 60 miles] A bushel of malt now sells for *thirty dollars*, and a pound
of hops for *six dollars*.

Hard money had ceased to circulate; credit existed only in name; and public confidence was destroyed. Change too had come over the war-worn veteran himself. The stirring occupations of the field, the habits formed by eight years of active service, the tastes acquired by residence in the camp, and action in the exciting events of the revolution, and disuse of old avocations, had produced inaptitude for a course of business so long discontinued. Still, he bore up against circumstances of discouragement, and contrived to maintain his family in comfort and in respectable position. With others, he obtained a grant of a township of land in Vermont, containing 23040 acres, Oct. 21, 1780, upon which he founded a town and bestowed the name of Montpelier, now the capital of the State. A severe domestic affliction, in 1787, the loss of his second son, Andrew, who fell a victim to rapid consumption, uniting with other disappointments, depressed his energy, and cast over his mind a gloom presaging the approaching night of premature old age. He died March 31, 1790, in the 51st year of his age.[1]

Col. Bigelow was of fine personal appearance. His figure was tall and commanding. In stature he was more than six feet in height. His bearing was erect and martial, and his step was said to have been one of the most graceful of the army. With taste for military life, he was deeply skilled in the science of war, and the troops under his command and instruction, exhibited the highest condition of discipline. He possessed vigorous intellect, ardent temperament, and a warm and generous heart.

COL. EPHRAIM DOOLITTLE. Although Worcester was not the place of the birth or decease of this gentleman, his long residence here entitles us to

[1] Col. Bigelow married Anna Andrews, a young orphan lady of Worcester, born April 11, 1747, and at the time of her marriage, July 7, 1762, heiress of a fortune considerable in those days. The union was a love match, and was contracted at Hampton, N. H. the Gretna Green of the Old Bay State. She died at Groton, July, 1809. She was the only child of a connection formed under somewhat romantic circumstances. Her father, Samuel Andrews, at a late period of youth, having fitted himself for college, and passed the customary examination, was admitted to Harvard University. Returning to visit his friends, before commencing his classes, he saw and became enamored of Anna, youngest daughter of James Rankin and Rachel Irving, his wife, emigrants from Ireland with the Scotch Presbyterians of 1718. His suit, prosecuted with ardor and assiduity, was successful, and the bridal was soon solemnized. Abandoning the plan of obtaining a liberal education, he purchased and cultivated a small farm on the western shore of Quinsigamond. Diligence, prudence, and sobriety, brought the reward of prosperity. He removed to the village, erected a house on the site of the jail, lately pulled down, established a tannery north of the bridge on Lincoln square, and in 1749, built the old Bigelow mansion, opposite to the Court House, on the spot where the large brick dwellings of Stephen Salisbury, Esq. now stand, where he died. On his decease, the estate descended to his only daughter Anna.

Col. Bigelow had six children, 1. Nancy: born Jun. 2, 1765, married Hon. Abraham Lincoln, long Selectman and Representative of the town, and Member of the Council at the time of his death, July 2, 1824. 2. Timothy: b. April 30, 1767, (See page 223.) 3. Andrew, b. March 30, 1769, d. Nov. 1787. 4. Lucy: b. May 13, 1774: m. Hon. Luther Lawrence. formerly of Groton, now of Lowell. 5. Rufus: b. July 7, 1772: he was merchant in Baltimore, and died unmarried in that city, Dec. 21, 1813. 6. Clara: b. Dec. 29, 1781, m. Tyler Bigelow, Esq. of Watertown.

The materials for this sketch have been derived from an excellent memoir of Col. Bigelow, kindly communicated by the Rev. Andrew Bigelow of Taunton.

claim him among our citizens. From 1760 to 1772, he was an inhabitant, and during that period was engaged in business as a merchant. In 1763, he was selectman: in 1766, representative. Taking active part in the political transactions of the times, he was placed on important municipal committees. From the commencement of the difficulties preceding the revolution, he was a decided and ardent whig. In 1772, he removed to Petersham; in December of that year, he reported a spirited answer to the circular from Boston, distributed through the country. In 1773, he was selectman, and representative in the General Court. The year following, he was delegate to the Provincial Congress convened at Concord. He was elected captain of a company of militia by the town, in the autumn of 1774, and soon after was colonel of the regiment of minute men in the county. The troops under his command marched on the 19th of April, were mustered into service, and stationed in Cambridge. On the organization of the army, he retained his rank in the Massachusetts line. His regiment was engaged in the battle of the 17th of June. Col. Doolittle being confined to his bed by an accidental injury, they were led by Major Moore of Paxton, who found a soldier's honorable grave on Bunker Hill.

For many years he was chairman of the committee of correspondence of Petersham: in 1778, of the committee reporting against the form of constitution proposed by the general court, and almost unanimously rejected by the people: in 1779, delegate in the convention at Cambridge, to frame a new constitution. He participated in almost every act of a public character in Worcester and Petersham, during his residence in either town.

Soon after the close of the war, he removed to Shoreham in Vermont, where he remained until the period of his decease, in 1802, at an advanced old age.

He was more distinguished for sound judgment and accuracy, than brilliancy or extent of talent; for the scrupulous practise of common virtues, rather than the exercise of extraordinary powers.

A curious implement was invented by him, to supply the deficiency of muskets in the armament of his regiment. When the long shaft, of heavy material, was held levelled towards an advancing enemy, two stout blades, eight inches long, united to a strong head, projected forward like the prongs of the hay fork: two other blades of equal length extended laterally, and another was turned downwards, to give a descending blow. Five little swords, whetted on both edges, were thus provided, to attack an assailant on any exposed point. The handle was lined, for two or three feet from the end, with sharp steel plates set in the wood to defend it from sabre cuts, and to lacerate the hand which should grasp the weapon to wrest it from the owner. The lower extremity terminated in a rounded iron point, to be fixed in or against rampart or masonry. The formidable instrument of warfare, after short trial, was laid aside.

HON. DAVID THOMAS. About 1718, David Thomas, an emigrant from Wales, arrived in Worcester, purchased, cleared, and afterwards cultivated, a tract of woodland on the summit of Tatnuck hill, in the western part of the town,

where he lived to a good old age   Land and name were inherited by his son
David, born in 1710, who bestowed the latter on *his* son, David, the subject
of this notice, born in Worcester, June 11, 1762   From the early age at
which the children of New England begin their lessons of industry until fifteen, he labored on the farm, attending in winter the common school of the
district   In 1777, he served as a volunteer, with the troops raised for the
relief of Rhode Island , at one time for the term of three months , at another
for two.   Soon after, he was bound apprentice to the shoemaker's trade.   In
1781 the town was required to furnish twenty nine soldiers for the army of
the revolution, and the inhabitants were divided into the same number of
classes, each to furnish, pay, and maintain one man during three years   Mr.
Thomas entered into an agreement with Capt Palmer Goulding, with whom
he lived, and who was head of a class, to cancel the indentures, and enlisted
in the service as a soldier for that class.   He joined the fifth Massachusetts
Regiment, under Col Rufus Putnam, at West Point, and was appointed to be
corporal   on the preliminary articles of peace being signed, he was transferred
to the third regiment of the state line, and promoted to be serjeant   When
the army was disbanded, he returned to Worcester   His residence in his native place was short   In the spring of 1784, he emigrated to Salem, in
Washington county, New York, and engaged in agriculture, as a day laborer.
Industry, frugality, and capacity, earned then just rewards   He was enabled
to become the owner of the farm upon which he had hired   Military offices
were showered fast upon him   He rose, step by step, through the gradations
of captain, major, colonel, and brigadier, to the rank of Major General of a
division of militia.   Civil honors flowed scarcely less rapidly   He was magistrate, county judge, and representative in the state legislature many years
In 1800, he was elected representative in Congress, when New York was entitled to ten members only, from a district composed of the counties of Washington, Saratoga, Warren, Essex, Clinton, and Franklin   This office he held
until 1808, when he was appointed Treasurer of the State of New York and,
ex-officio, Commissioner of the Land Office, and trustee of Union College.
To discharge these duties, it became necessary for him to remove to the city
of Albany   There he resided until 1813, when he resigned all public trusts,
in consequence of domestic troubles.   After his retirement to private life, he
removed to Providence, where he remained till his decease, in 1834, at the
age of 72

Hon BENJAMIN HEYWOOD was son of Phinehas Heywood, a respectable
farmer of Shrewsbury.   At the common age, he was bound apprentice to a
housewright   Having completed the term prescribed by his indentures, he
began business as carpenter, and worked at that trade one or two years
Love of letters, and confidence of capacity for usefulness, induced him to
throw aside the hammer and chisel, and devote himself assiduously to preparations for collegiate education   He entered Harvard College in 1771
There is cotemporary evidence of his sobriety of conduct, diligent application,
and proficiency in mathematical science.

The martial spirit pervading the country, penetrated even the seats of learning

21

The young men of the institution formed a military company, under the designation of the Marti-mercurian Band, a name descriptive of the union of the soldier and scholar in its ranks. Mr. Heywood was ensign of this corps, on the nineteenth of April, 1775, and, with some of his comrades, participated in the perils of that memorable day. Amid the tumult of arms, the quiet pursuits of literature were suspended; the students were dismissed, and the halls occupied by troops. The senior class, of which Mr. Heywood was member, did not again return to the seminary, although their degrees were conferred in course.

Mr. Heywood immediately entered the service of his country, and received the commision of Lieutenant, in May, 1775. In 1776, he was promoted to the rank of Captain, which he retained through the whole war. His habits of order and accuracy qualified him for the office of paymaster, to which he was soon appointed and attached to Col. Nixon's regiment.[1] He was at the capture of Burgoyne, partook of the sufferings, and shared in the victories of the army, during the long period of its service. When the soldiers were about to be disbanded, a dangerous state of feeling arose. The tedious postponement of payments meritoriously earned, the pressure of want, and the anticipation of future poverty, excited discontents, artfully fomented by inflammatory publications. Gen. Washington, apprehensive of serious violence from exasperated troops, feeling the injustice of the country and conscious of the power of numbers, discipline and arms, to avenge, if not redress, the real or supposed wrongs, convened an assembly of the officers, addressed them on the disastrous consequences of the course to which they had been directed, and left them to their deliberations. Gen. Knox, Col. Brooks, and Capt. Heywood were appointed a committee, to consider and recommend proper measures to be adopted in the impending crisis. By their prudence and energy, the rising disorders were quieted.

Another proof of the confidence of his companions in arms in the honor and capacity of Capt. Heywood, was his election on a committee to adjust the accounts of the officers and soldiers of the Massachusetts line. He was associated with Major Fernald, Capt. Hull, and Capt. Learned. The duty of the committee led to long negociation with the Legislature of the state, resulted in provision for equitable settlement, and was concluded by voluminous reports prepared by Capt. Heywood.

When the army was disbanded, he was retained, for some months, in the office of the General Superintendent, and afforded valuable aid in arranging the complicated concerns of the department charged with the settlement of the affairs of the war.

After the restoration of peace, he returned to his home, and married an adopted daughter of Mr. Nathaniel Moore, an early settler and respectable farmer of Worcester. Activity of disposition, and facility in business, enabled him, in addition to the management of a farm, to devote much time to the concerns of his neighbors, and to public affairs. The reliance on his in-

---

[1] The entire series of rolls and accounts of his office, preserved in the Am. Ant. Society's Collections, afford proof of his fidelity in this trust.

tegrity and good judgment, was testified by frequent selection as arbitrator, executor, and guardian In 1802, he was appointed Judge of the Court of Common Pleas, and held that office until Sept 1811, when, by a new arrangement of the judicial system, the seats of all the judges of that tribunal were vacated For many years he was an acting magistrate of the county, and member of the Board of Trustees of Leicester Academy. He was twice chosen an elector of President and Vice President of the United States By the General Court, he was appointed Trustee of the Hassanamisset Indians and was an officer of many charitable and religious associations

He died Dec 6, 1816, aged 71, leaving the reputation of unstained integrity and extensive usefulness [1]

Hon Joseph Allen, a native of Boston was born Sept 2, 1749 [2] Attending through the regular term of seven years, from the age of seven to that of fourteen, on the Grammar School, he was a favorite pupil of the celebrated master Lovell. About 1770, after regular mercantile apprenticeship, he entered into business in Leicester A firm whig, he was active in the preliminary movements of the revolution, and with Col William Henshaw, Col Thomas Denny, and other patriotic citizens of the place of his residence, drafted, circulated, and supported, the spirited resolutions, memorials, and addresses of the citizens in their primary meetings, and conventions [3] Soon after the change of the government he was appointed, in 1776, to succeed Levi Lincoln, sen as Clerk of the Courts, and removed to Worcester The duties of this office he discharged for thirty three years with singular accuracy and fidelity It was relinquished in 1810, against the wishes of the judicial officers He occasionally accepted those public honors conferred as testimonials of esteem and confidence. On the death of Mr Upham, he was chosen Representative to the 11th Congress, and at the expiration of the term declined reelection. From 1815 to 1818, he was of the Executive Council: and twice of the College of Electors of President. One of the founders and patrons of Leicester Academy, he was long Treasurer of the corporation, and was first President of the Worcester County Bible Society ' His mind and manners,' writes one of the best of our portrait painters of character, ' were alike formed on the best models ; in addition to his classical attainments, he was distinguished for

[1] These facts have been derived from the venerable Dr Bancroft, to whom the men of Worcester have been indebted for many an obituary memorial of their fathers The notices of our distinguished citizens from his pen have been remarkable for felicitous expression, fidelity, accurate discrimination, and all the excellences of biography

Benjamin Heywood married Mehitable Goddard, d of Elisha Goddard of Sutton Their children were, 1 Mehitable 2 Nathaniel Moore, merchant, b July 1788 m Caroline Sumner of Boston, Sept 16, 1816, died at Richmond, Va 3 Elizabeth 4 Benjamin Franklin, physician in Worcester, m Nancy Green, d of Doct John Green of Worcester : 5. Joseph 6 Lucy b April, 1796, d Nov. 1796 7. Nancy, b Feb 7, 1798; d Aug 30, 1814

[2] His father, James Allen, a merchant of Boston, married the sister of Samuel Adams

[3] A little circumstance, illustrative of the influence of the unsettled condition of the times on the relations of private life, is related At one time, Mr Allen had his knapsack packed with the soldier's blanket, and his trunk with his nuptial suit, uncertain whether he should be earliest called to the bridal or the battle

that politeness and gracefulness of deportment, which was, in some degree, peculiar to the men of his generation. Through his whole course, strict integrity,[1] unblemished honor, and undisguised detestation of whatever was base and unworthy, were predominant traits in his character. A native generosity of disposition prompted him to deeds of beneficence. He was familiar with the best English writers, and had stored his mind with their beauties, which his refined and discriminating taste taught him to appreciate with singular accuracy and apply with the happiest effect.' He died Sept. 2, 1827, aged 78.

ISAIAH THOMAS,[2] a native of Boston, was the descendant of ancestors of good repute, emigrating from England, soon after the foundation of the town, and engaging in mercantile business. His father, Moses Thomas,[3] soldier, mariner, trader, and farmer, at different periods, after sharing and escaping the perils of the unfortunate expedition against Cuba, in 1740, when pestilence destroyed most of the provincial forces spared by the sword, lived a few years on Long Island. Revisiting his early home, reverses of fortune wasted his share of a good inheritance. Driven abroad, he died in North Carolina, about 1752, leaving a widow in destitute condition, with five small children. The energy and fertility of invention, so often manifested by females in similar circumstances, soon provided resources for the support of her family. The

[1] The following example may serve as an illustration of his honorable sense of integrity, more scrupulous than is usually found among men In the negociation of business, Mr. Allen had become indebted to John Smith, 2d Lieutenant of Capt. Bigelow's company of Minute men. The account was deliberately adjusted, the balance carefully ascertained to the mutual satisfaction of both parties, payment made, and full and ample discharges given. Some years after, when Smith was passing through town, he was met by Mr. Allen, who informed him that he had then recently discovered an error in the settlement favorable to himself, which he desired to correct by a further payment. The creditor, declaring his entire satisfaction with the former computation, and his conviction that no mistake could have occurred, declined an examination. With reluctance he was induced to review the accounts, and on revision, still expressed content. Mr. Allen then explained to him, by reference to the scale of depreciation, that he had received a less amount than he was entitled to have, and delivered to him the sum of money, which he long refused to believe he had lost on the original liquidation.

[2] In the History of Printing, i. 368, is a narrative of the life of Mr. Thomas from his own pen. In the Massachusetts Spy, April 13, 1831, are published portions of an address containing beautiful delineation of his character, delivered by Isaac Goodwin, Esq. before the American Antiquarian Society, and transferred to the 2d volume of their Transactions. The first writer was under the restraints imposed on the autobiographer; the last, felt those resting on the public speaker. Neither space nor ability permit the attempt here, to do justice to the services of one of our most eminent citizens. The duty of raising worthy memorial, remains for more fortunate hands. The materials of the notice of Mr. Thomas in these pages, are taken from the memoirs before mentioned. The few facts which have been added, are stated on the authority of his personal relation, were obtained from the diaries of interleaved almanacs, or are derived from official papers.

[3] The earliest of the name, mentioned by John Farmer, the most faithful and accurate of the antiquarians of the age, in his Register of the First Settlers, is Evan Thomas, vinter, of Boston, admitted freeman in 1641, who died Aug. 25, 1661. George Thomas, and Rebecca his wife, had three sons: 1. Peter, b. Feb. 6, 1682; 2. George, b. March 16, 1685; 3. Maveric, b. March 19, 1694. Peter, the eldest, was a merchant in Boston, and acquired good estate; his children were; George, Peter, Elias, *Moses*, mentioned in the text, Mary, Mercy, Elizabeth, and William, who lived to mature years.

ISAIAH THOMAS LL.D

FROM THE MARBLE BUST BY B.H.KINNEY

IN POSSESSION OF THE AMERICAN ANTIQUARIAN SOCIETY

profits of a little shop, added to the other gains of industry and ingenuity, and the savings of frugal thrift, afforded comparative comfort and independence She was, at length, able to purchase a small estate in Cambridge, afterwards lost, on sale, by the depreciation of the continental currency [1]

The youngest son, Isaiah, was born Jan 19, 1749, at the age of less than six years, he was bound apprentice to Zechariah Fowle, a printer of single sheets, small tracts, and pamphlets, described in the History of Printing, as honest, but eccentric, irritable, effeminate, and better skilled in domestic cares than the mysteries of the printing house It reflects no credit on the sense or taste of the master, that the first essay of his almost infant workman, who required the elevation of a high bench to reach the case, should have been directed to the composition of a licentious ballad [2] The pupil, deprived of the usual advantages of schools and of good instruction in the art, was compelled to rely on his own resources to supply the deficiencies of education Earnest desire of improvement found or made the way. A tattered dictionary and ink stained bible were the whole library of the office Two or three books, purchased with the savings of trifling perquisites, and a few more borrowed from friends, were added to this slender collection of literature. Diligent study and persevering assiduity, enabled him, unassisted, to possess himself of the elementary branches of learning, and to acquire such facility of expression as to be able to put his thoughts in type without the aid of writing, and the expertness in printing which made him principal manager of a business extended under his supervision After eleven years of apprenticeship and employment with Fowle, Mr Thomas went to Nova Scotia and entered the office of Anthony Henry, proprietor of the Halifax Gazette, the government paper, a good-humored and indolent man The willing assistant was allowed to assume the management Although Henry's labors were diminished, his responsibilities directly increased It was the period of the Stamp Act, and the Boston boy brought with him the spirit kindled in his birth place The appearance of an article in opposition to the obnoxious measure which roused the colonies to resistance, was followed by citation before the authorities, and Henry escaped punishment, only on the ground that the paragraph had been inserted by his journeyman without his knowledge On the repetition of the offence, the young man himself was called before the Secretary of the Province, and received reprimand, admonition, and threats, alike ineffectual. Not long after this interview, the whole year's stock of paper arrived from England, stamped according to the act · by night, the brand of oppression was cut off from the sheets the effigy of the commissioner appointed to collect the impost, was found suspended from the gallows The very correct opinion prevailed, that Mr Thomas was principal in these and other acts of defiance of government. The sheriff, sent for the purpose of intimidating the young

---

[1] She married a person named Blackman, and died Jan 17, 1798, aged 73 years

[2] The composing stick first used by Mr. Thomas, an impression of ' The Lawyer's Pedigree,' and the very press upon which it was worked, which afterwards sent out the glowing words of the patriots of the Revolution, were given to the Antiquarian Society by its founder, and have been scrupulously preserved, in accordance with his wishes

printer by threats, or extorting confessions, was met with so much firmness and intrepidity, that the fruitless mission was abandoned [1]

In March, 1767, Mr. Thomas went from Nova Scotia to Portsmouth in New Hampshire, and four months afterwards, returned to the employment of Fowle in Boston. Active and enterprising spirit led him to accept the invitation of a shipmaster to try the fortune of a voyage to Wilmington in North Carolina. Negotiations for an establishment there were frustrated, and he embarked for the West Indies, intending to seek passage thence to London. Again his expectations were defeated, and he repaired to Charleston in South Carolina. After a residence of two years, with impaired health, he retraced his steps, and came again to the home of his fathers. Entering into partnership with Zachariah Fowle, they published a little newspaper, discontinued in December of the same year. The connection was of brief duration. It was dissolved in three months, and Mr. Thomas, having purchased the printing apparatus, issued another paper, bearing the name of its predecessor, ' The Massachusetts Spy,' March 7, 1771. The early professions of neutrality in the great contest then impending, could not long be maintained against the decided inclination of the conductor to the popular cause, and the print soon became the leading advocate of whig principles. Managed with great ability, in some departments, by Mr. Thomas himself, the strongest of the patriot writers gave the power of their pens to its support, and the Spy became the favorite channel for the diffusion of high-toned sentiment. Its influence was felt and feared by the royalists, and they endeavored to avert the danger of a free press. Overtures to the editor, with promises of honors, office, patronage and reward, on espousing the cause of government, were rejected, and threats of vengeance for resistance, disregarded. A man too independent to be bought by gain or controlled by power, must be crushed. The debt contracted for the purchase of the establishment was suddenly and sternly demanded : the aid of friends discharged the sum and defeated the attempt to ruin by pecuniary pressure. The publication of a bold essay, written by Joseph Greenleaf, with the signature of Mucius Scævola, afforded pretext for fresh persecution. Mr Thomas was summoned to appear before the Governor and Council. Obedience to the executive mandate, three times repeated, was as often fearlessly refused. Hutchinson was too good lawyer to issue process for compulsion, where no authority existed for its execution. The punishment of the offender, was entrusted to the judicial arm, and the

---

[1] The Philadelphia Journal arrived, dressed with mourning pages; decorated with death's heads, crossed bones, and other emblems of mortality; and announcing its own decease, by a complaint called the Stamp Act. To imitate this patriotic typography required no little boldness. It was done by Mr Thomas, with equal courage and adroitness. The columns of the Halifax Gazette were surrounded with heavy black lines, the titlewas surmounted by the skull, a death's head placed as substitute for stamp; and a large figure of a coffin laid at the end of the last page ; accompanied by the following notice . ' We are desired, by a number of our readers, to give a description of the extraordinary appearance of the Pennsylvania Journal of the 30th of October [1765] We can in no better way comply with this request, than by the exemplification we have given of that Journal in this day's Gazette.'

Attorney General directed to institute prosecution for libel. Indictment and information, though pushed forward by the united efforts of the officers of the
crown, alike failed. The Spy held on its way, vindicating the liberty of the
press and of the citizen, against ministerial usurpation Renewed attempts at
coercion, only served to call forth testimonials of the ardent interest felt by the
leading men of the time for the welfare of the establishment, and pledges of protection and defence [1] Such course, rendered Mr Thomas obnoxious to the administration His name was placed on the list of the suspected · his printing
house received the honorary appellation of ' sedition factory ' and threats of
personal violence were frequent in the mouths of the soldiery. Having been
solicited by the whigs of Worcester, to establish a newspaper, he made contracts and sent out proposals for subscriptions in February, 1775 , and with
the assistance of Col Bigelow, under the care of Gen Warren, he privately
conveyed a press and cases of types, over the river to Charlestown, thence
transported to this town, a short time previous to the Lexington Fight The
movements of the British troops for an expedition into the country, being discovered, Mr Thomas was active in spreading the alarm, and at day break of
the memorable 19th of April, joined the militia in arms against the ' regulars '
Laying aside the musket after the fight, to put in action a more powerful engine of freedom, and journeying almost all the next night, he reached Worcester the following day The first printing done in any inland town of New
England, was performed in Worcester The Spy reappeared, after a suspension of three weeks, May 3, 1775, and was distributed by posts and messengers The publications of the Provincial Congress were executed here,
until presses were put in operation in Cambridge and Concord, the places of
its session

Although the acquisitions of five years toil had been abandoned to be plundered, with the exception of the little remnant saved by the fortunate arrangements of early removal, the better capital of industry, capacity, and enterprise,
was undiminished, and was brought into full exertion. He was appointed
Postmaster, by Benjamin Franklin, Sept 25, 1775, and the commission was
renewed for triennial terms, by Ebenezer Hazard, Samuel Osgood, Timothy
Pickering, and Joseph Habersham, the heads of the department in succeeding
years In 1776, having leased his property to Messrs. Bigelow and Stearns,
and afterwards to Anthony Haswell, he went to Salem While on a visit
here, the declaration of independence was received, and first read to the citizens, by Mr Thomas, July 14, 1776, from the porch of the Old South
Church. Returning for permanent residence, in 1778, he resumed the management of the Spy [2] At that period, trade was disordered , in the fluctuating currency, the representative paper had no constituent specie ; manufactures were in infancy ; materials were deficient , difficulties sprang up on all
sides ; and the print was only sustained through the war, by the unyielding
resolution of the proprietor The restoration of peace opened the channels

[1] It is stated by Mr Goodwin, that the celebrated James Otis, ' then withdrawn from
active life in consequence of the malady which prostrated the energies of his mighty
mind,' proffered his professional services to Mr. Thomas

[2] ' In the indulgence of a peculiar poetical fancy, his papers were generally ornamented

of commerce; new types and apparatus were obtained, and his business expanded itself on a great scale. Uniting the employments of printer, publisher, and bookseller, establishing the first bindery and building the second paper mill in the county, the relations of a business which may well be called vast, as they extended to almost every part of the union, were conducted with that systematic and methodical arrangement which gave successful action to the complex machinery. At one period, under his own personal direction and that of his partners, sixteen presses were in constant motion, seven of them working here; three weekly newspapers and one monthly magazine, issued: and five bookstores in Massachusetts, one in New Hampshire, one in New York, and one in Maryland, almost supplied the literary sustenance of the community. One of the most liberal publishers of the age, he produced and distributed works, whose titles formed a voluminous annual catalogue. The great folio edition of the bible in 1791, illustrated with the copperplates of native artists, was unrivalled, at the period, for neatness, accuracy, and general elegance and excellence of execution; the whole types for smaller copies of the Holy Scriptures were kept standing and often used.

Previous to the revolution, Mr. Thomas commenced the Essex Gazette, at Newburyport, in 1773; in January of the next year, he began the Royal American Magazine, the last of the periodicals of Boston under the provincial governors. After the war, in 1793, he founded the Farmer's Museum, enlivened with the spirit of Prentiss, Dennie, Fessenden, and the coterie of wits gathered at Walpole, N. H.; established the Farmer's Journal in Brookfield, Mass. in 1799; in connection with Ebenezer T. Andrews, junior partner of a house existing thirty one years, he printed the Massachusetts Magazine, in Boston, from 1783 to 1795. The Spy was suspended, in consequence of the resemblance of an Excise Act to the Stamp duty, for two years. The Worcester Magazine, in 1787 and 1788, supplied the place of that paper. Mr. Thomas was partner of Dr. Joseph Trumbull, in the business of druggist in this town for some time after Aug. 31, 1780.

In 1802, Mr. Thomas relinquished a prosperous business at Worcester, to his son Isaiah, and retired from the pressing cares of wide concerns to the enjoyment of fortune honorably won and liberally used.

The evening twilight of a day of intense activity was not given to the repose of idleness. Enjoying personal acquaintance with some of the early conductors of the press in this country, familiar by their narrations with their predecessors, himself a prominent actor through an important period, greater advantages could not have been desired for the undertaking, on which he entered, of compiling the annals of American typography. 'The History of Printing,' published in 1810, in two octavo volumes, bears internal evidence,

with curiously significant devices and appropriate mottoes. In 1774, they bore a dragon and a snake, the former representing Great Britain, and the serpent this country. The latter was separated into p rts to represent the different colonies. The head and tail were furnished with stings for defence against the dragon, which was placed in the posture of making attack. The device extended the whole width of the paper, with the motto over the serpent, in large capitals, JOIN OR DIE.' Goodwin's Memoir in Mass. Spy, April 13, 1831.

in the fulness and fidelity of its narrative, that neither toil, research, nor money was spared for its preparation. Containing notices of the antiquities and progress of the art, the biography of printers and newspapers, the work received the approbation of criticism, and the rank of standard authority While this good enterprise advanced, Mr Thomas had gathered rare treasures of literature and rich relics of the past Collected, they were of inestimable value each fragment if dispersed, would have been desirable, but less precious than if fixed in its place as a connecting link of the chain of events. With an elevated benevolence, contemplating in expanded view all the good the present may bestow on the future, he associated others with himself, and became the founder of the American Antiquarian Society The gift of his great collections and library, the donation of land, and of a spacious edifice, an unceasing flow of bounty in continuous succession of benefactions, and ample bequests for the perpetuation and extension of the benefits he designed to confer on the public and posterity, are enduring testimonial of enlightened liberality The institution will remain, an imperishable monument to his memory, when the very materials of the hall reared by his generosity shall have crumbled

While his private charity relieved the distresses, his public munificence promoted the improvements of the town. The site of the County Court House was bestowed by him, and the building and avenues on the front constructed under his uncompensated direction No inconsiderable share of the cost of enlarging the square at the north end of Main Street, and erecting the stone bridge, was given by him The street bearing his own name, and the spot where the brick school house has been built, were his benefaction to the municipal corporation In the location and execution of the Boston and Worcester Turnpike, an enterprise of much utility at the period, he assisted by personal exertion and pecuniary contribution, and few local works for the common good were accomplished without the aid of his purse or efforts

In 1814, he received the honorary degree of Master of Arts from Dartmouth College that of Doctor of Laws was conferred by Alleghany College in 1818 He was member of the Historical Societies of Massachusetts and New York, and of numerous Philosophical, Humane, Charitable, and Typographic associations The appointment of Justice of the Court of Sessions was made by Gov. Gerry, Feb 21, 1812. the office was held until June 7, 1814, when it was resigned He was President of the Antiquarian Society from its foundation to his decease, April 4, 1831, at the age of 82 years.

While the institution of Freemasonry was prosperous, Dr Thomas attained its highest honors and degrees, and was long presiding officer of the Grand Lodge and Chapter of Massachusetts He attended and bore part in most of the consecrations, installations and high festivals of the association in the state, during his active years

The incidents of the life of Dr Thomas have occupied broad space in these poor annals His memory will be kept green when the recollection of our other eminent citizens shall have faded in oblivion His reputation in future time will rest, as a patriot, on the manly independence which gave, through the initiatory stages and progress of the revolution, the strong influence of the press he directed to the cause of freedom, when royal flattery and favor would have seduced, and the power of government subdued its action; as an antiquarian, on the minuteness and fidelity of research in the History of Printing; as a philanthropist, on the foundation and support of a great national society, whose usefulness, with the blessing of Providence, will increase through distant centuries.[1]

There have resided in Worcester, eighteen settled Clergymen: two Barristers: sixty-four Counsellors and Attorneys at Law: and thirty-one Physicians. Fifty-nine of the natives of the town have received education in the colleges. Of those born here, fifteen Physicians, twelve Lawyers, and ten Clergymen, have gone out to other places of settlement and professional employment.

Worcester has furnished good proportion of those who have held civil and judicial offices.

Of the natives or citizens of the town, previous to the war of independence, were: one Attorney General of the Province: three members of His Majesty's Council: one Mandamus Councillor: three Judges of the Court of Common Pleas: two Judges of Probate; three Clerks of the Courts: four Treasurers and four Sheriffs of the County: one Judge of the Supreme Court of New Brunswick: one Councillor, and one Clerk of the Assembly of that Province.

Since the Revolution there have been: two Governors of Massachusetts and one Governor of Maine: two Lieutenant Governors: two Speakers of

---

[1] Moses Thomas, father of Dr. Isaiah Thomas, married Fidelity Grant of Rhode Island: Their children were: 1, Elizabeth, born on Long Island, who married and went to the West Indies: 2. Peter, who resided at Hampstead, L. I. 3. Joshua, b. at Boston, March 3, 1745; m. Mary Twing of Brighton, and resided in Lancaster: 4. Susannah, married four times: last to Capt. Hugh McCullough, of Philadelphia: surviving him, she died Feb. 28, 1815, a. 69: 5. Isaiah, b. Jan. 19, 1749.

Dr. Isaiah Thomas, married Mary, d. of Joseph Dill, of the Isle of Bermuda, Dec. 25, 1769: Their children were, Mary Anne, b. March 27, 1772: was three times married; last to Dr. Levi Simmons: 2. Isaiah, b. at Boston, Sept. 5, 1773; m. Mary d. of Edward Weld of Boston; he was educated as a printer, and succeeded his father in business; he removed to Boston, where he died June 25, 1819. His children were: 1. Mary Rebecca, m. Pliny Merrick, Esq. of Worcester: 2. Frances Church, b. Aug. 12, 1800; m. William A. Crocker of Taunton. 3. Augusta Weld, b. Aug. 1, 1801; d. Aug. 19, 1822, at Taunton; 4. Caroline, b. Sept. 26, 1802; m. to Samuel L. Crocker of Taunton. 5. Hannah Weld, m. June 14, 1825, to Samuel L. Crocker of Taunton; d. November 22, 1827; 6. Isaiah, b. Dec. 11, 1804; d. Oct. 14, 1805: 7. Isaiah, merchant in New York; 8. William, merchant in Boston: 9. Edward Weld, b. Feb. 15, 1810; d. Oct. 5, 1810; 10. Edward Isaiah, merchant in New York: 11. Benjamin Franklin, lawyer in Worcester.

Dr. Thomas was married a second time to Mrs. Mary Fowle, d. of William Thomas of Boston, b. June 9, 1751; d. Nov. 16, 1818, aged 67: and again married, Aug. 10, 1819, to Miss Rebecca Armstrong of Roxbury.

the House of Representatives six Councillors and eleven Senators of Massachusetts. two Senators of New Hampshire one Secretary of the Commonwealth · one Treasurer of New York · one Attorney General of the United States: one acting Secretary of State. one Senator and eleven Representatives in Congress · one elected member of Congress under the Confederation one appointed Judge of the Supreme Court of the United States, who declined the commission one Judge of the Supreme Court of Massachusetts three Justices of the Court of Common Pleas of this State, and one of Alabama three Judges of Probate. and one Judge of the Orphan's Court of Alabama two Justices of the Court of Sessions two County Commissioners eight Clerks of the Courts and eight County Attorneys one District Attorney, two Sheriffs and three Treasurers of the County; five Justices throughout the Commonwealth, thirty-eight Justices of the Quorum, and eighty-one Justices of the Peace.[1]

[1] This estimate of the offices of the worthies of Worcester, accurate so far at it extends, is necessarily imperfect Many emigrants from this town, who have held honorable stations in other states, have not been included in the enumeration

Of those natives of the town, not educated in the colleges, who emigrated, and practised as Physicians, before unmentioned, were Samuel Rice of Athol, son of Samuel Rice William Young of Ipswich, son of William Young, Jacob Holmes of Leicester, son of Jacob Holmes, William Barler of Mason, N H son of James Barber and James McFarland of Rutland, son of James McFarland.

STATISTICS AND HISTORY.

—

CHAPTER XV.

Education. Common Schools. Centre District Schools. Private Instruction. Manual Labor High School. Mount St. James Seminary.

When the original committee of settlement secured the support of the worship of God, they made provision for the education of youth. At their first meeting, in 1669, when the untrodden wilderness spread over the territory of Worcester, it was agreed that a lot of land should be 'appropriated for the maintenance of a school and school master, to remain for that use for ever.' In the contract with Daniel Henchman, in 1684, this determination was affirmed; and it was enjoined, ' that care be taken to provide a schoolmaster in due season.' When surveys were made, after the permanent settlement, a tract of forty acres was granted for the promotion of this object.

The circumstances of the first planters long prevented the commencement of public instruction. The earliest municipal action on the subject, was April 4, 1726. In pursuance of a vote of the town, 'the selectmen agreed with Mr. Jonas Rice to be schoolmaster, and to teach such children and youth as any of the inhabitants shall send to him, to read and write, as the law directs,'[1] until the 15th of December. On the expiration of this term, it was peremptorily voted ' that the town will not have a school.' The period succeeding the commencement of the last century has been well described by one of the most discriminating of our local antiquarians,[2] as the '*dark age*' of Massachusetts. Every hand was busy in converting the forest into farms. A fluctuating currency scarcely served for the supply of the necessaries of life. The planters of Worcester, feeling the burden of sustaining elementary education without immediately realizing the resulting benefits, failed to give practical operation to the enlightened views of the founders. In this respect they could have shown the example of elder and more wealthy neighbors in extenuation of the negligence. Few towns about that time, escaped fine for contempt of wholesome laws. The grand jury admonished Worcester of its omissions of duty by presentment, and the sum of £2 8s. 6d. was raised in

[1] The Great and General Court of the Colony, in May 1647, stating as inducement, that, ' It being one chief project of Satan to keep men from the knowledge of the Scriptures, as in former times keeping them in unknown tongues, so, in these latter times, by persuading from the use of tongues, that so at least the true sense and meaning of the original might be clouded and corrupted with false glosses of deceivers: to the end that learning may not be buried in the graves of our forefathers, in church and commonwealth, the Lord assisting our endeavors,' ordered that every township within the jurisdiction, ' after the Lord hath increased them to the number of fifty householders,' should maintain a common school, and each town of one hundred families should keep a grammar school. A penalty for the neglect of these wholesome provisions, for quaint reasons, was established in 1671, increased by the statute of October, 1683.

[2] Lemuel Shattuck, Esq. in the History of Concord.

1728, to defray the charges of a prosecution, for want of schools, suspended on promises of amendment Benjamin Flagg, directly after, was employed as schoolmaster, and £14 granted for the annual stipend In April, 1731, considering ' that many small children cannot attend in the centre of the town by reason of the remoteness of their dwelling places, and to the intent that all may have the benefit of education,' districts were formed. Division lines, drawn from the middle of each exterior boundary, separated the town into north, south, east and west quarters, surrounding the central territory The mild sway and cheap services of females were sought, and the selectmen instructed, ' to procure a suitable number of school dames, not exceeding five, for the teaching of small children to read, to be placed in the several parts, as may be most convenient, and these gentlewomen to be paid such sum, by the head, as they may agree ' The terror of the law, in September following, produced a vote, ' to maintain a free school for a year, and to be a moving school into the several quarters.' In August, 1732, Mr Richard Rogers was engaged as teacher, and continued in that relation about eight years. The instructor of those days was migratory, revolving in his circuit round a centre not then fixed to a particular location Directions similar to this of 1735, abound ' Voted, That Mr Richard Rogers repair to the house of Mr. Palmer Goulding, there to keep school till further orders ' The inconvenience of temporary arrangements, induced the inhabitants, after long consideration and debate, and great doubt of the expediency of the measure, to resolve, May 15, 1735, ' that a school house be built at the charge of the town, and placed in the centre of the south half or as near as may be with conveniency, having regard to suitable ground for such a house to stand on, where land may be purchased, in case it falls on any particular property, provided the purchase may be made on reasonable terms ' The surveys of Col John Chandler, commissioned to measure under these instructions, and afterwards employed with new directions to find the intersection of a central line with the country road, not having indicated acceptable points, after five years of deliberation, it was determined to ' set up ' the first school house of Worcester ' between the Court House and bridge, below the fulling mill ' An humble edifice was raised at the north end of Main street, and nearly in the middle of the present travelled way, 24 feet long, 16 feet wide, and with posts 7 feet high, which remained beyond the close of the revolutionary war In 1740, £100 was granted for the support of schools, one half to be appropriated for the centre, and the other half divided among the quarters, ' provided the body of the town keep a grammar school the whole year, and save the town from presentment, and the skirts do in the whole have twelve months schooling of a writing master.'

It had been well and wisely ordered by the fathers of New England, that each municipal community of sufficient ability, should afford to youth the means of acquiring the languages The salutary effect of this regulation was little appreciated, and was even regarded as oppressive in times less enlightened than the present. In 1766, the representative was instructed to endeavor, ' that the law requiring a Latin Grammar School, be repealed, and that not

22

more than one such school should be kept in a county;' and, in 1767, to use his exertions to relieve the people from the great burden of supporting so many schools of this description, ' whereby they are prevented from attaining such degree of English learning as is necessary to retain the freedom of any state.'

The lower schools seem to have been sustained by liberal appropriations. In 1769, there were eight districts; the apportionment of the tax of £79 17s. in that year throws some light on the population and resources of the divisions.

Old Names.	Sums.	Old Names.	Sums.
Centre,	£19 1s.	Stone's,	£8 5s.
Tatnick,	10 10	Stowell's,	8 3
Bogachoag,	8 8	Curtis's,	7 11
Smith's,	9 8	Flagg's,	7 11

The sums raised by taxation for schools in different years, varied with the fluctuations of the currency to such extent that it is difficult to estimate accurately the real amount of expenditure. In 1727, the tax was £16 10s.: in 1730, £25: in 1740, £100 currency: in 1750, £46 10s.: in 1760, £75: in 1780, £76 16s.: in 1770, £3000 in continental bills.

It is not possible now to collect a perfect list of the school masters previous to the revolution. The figures prefixed to the names of the gentlemen mentioned below, show the time when their instruction commenced. 1725, Jonas Rice. 1729, Benjamin Flagg. 1732, James Wyman, Richard Rogers. 1733, Samuel Boutelle, Nathaniel Williams. 1738, Samuel Marsh. 1739, James Durant. 1744, James Varney. 1752, Henry Gardner. 1755, John Adams.[1] 1757, John Young. 1758, William Crawford. 1760, Micah Lawrence.

After the revolution, in 1785 and 1788, the town was presented by the grand jury for the neglect of its grammar school, and when it was maintained, it appears to have travelled around the centre, in the circle of districts, until 1808, when it became stationary.

In 1800, school houses were built in the several districts under the direction of a committee. The following table shows the dimensions, position, and cost of each.

Old names.	New names.	Feet square.	Expense.
Tatnick Quarter,	2,	25,	8270 27
Jones's,	3,	24,	270 27
Burbank's,	5,	22,	247 75
Baird's,	6,	22,	247 75
Gates's,	7,	20,	225 22
Fisk's Corner,	8,	22,	247 75
Burntcoat Plain,	9,	22,	247 75
Thaxter's,	10,	18,	202 70

Provision was made for the erection of two houses, not less than 22 feet square, in the centre, then containing one third of all the minors: one was

[1] Afterwards President of the United States. He was certainly employed one year, and probably more, while student at law with James Putnam.

built at the corner of the old burial place, and the other opposite to the building then the Unitarian Church, now the Franklin House.

Prudent and able committees have been elected annually by the town, who have had the supervision and visitation of the common schools in the manner directed by the statutes

The following statements illustrative of the condition of the schools, and the expenses of education, are derived principally from the returns in the office of the Secretary of the Commonwealth

	1834	1835	1836
Number of School Districts,	12,	12,	12,
Number of minors in all the districts,	2509,	2666,	3041
Males from 4 to 16 attending schools,	675,	622,	570,
Females,	494,	501,	636,
Average attendance in days,	924,	859,	1010,
Number attending private schools,	111,	100,	—
Winter schools, months,	96,	100,	88,
Summer schools, months,	111,	103,	87,
Instructors, Males,	12,	14,	11,
Females, instructing,	20,	21,	19,
Wages, average by months, Winter,	$17,	$21,	—
" " " Summer,	$9 ¼,	$16 ½,	—
Board per week, males,	$2 ½,	$2 ½,	$2½ ,
Amount raised for schools by tax,	$5535,	$5500,	$6270,
Expenses for furniture,	$500,	$550,	$550,
Tuition in private schools,	$2028,	$1500,	$1500.

The monies granted by the town for the support of schools are distributed thus from the whole tax is first deducted the amount assigned for the grammar school as an equivalent for the school being kept within the centre, the other districts receive two hundred and fifty dollars, equally divided: the residue of the whole sum is then apportioned according to the minors The mode of distribution will be seen from the following table six columns, after the first, show the number of persons under twenty one years of age, the six last the sum given to each district, in the year marked at the top of the column ·

	MINORS							MONIES.					
No	1831	1832	1833	1834	1835	1836.		1831	1832	1833	1834	1835	1836.
1	1058	1164	1256	1360	1524	1816		$978	$1012	$1039	$1299	$1402	$1670
2	151	146	135	146	138	144		166	149	131	162	119	155
3	200	227	221	225	232	293		210	220	205	237	234	292
4	98	112	96	103	83	104		118	120	102	131	98	118
5	106	103	108	111	106	99		123	112	112	128	120	113
6	81	72	66	70	73	71		99	85	77	89	89	88
7	66	78	73	84	112	101		86	83	83	102	125	115
8	138	88	102	104	98	93		138	99	107	121	112	108
9	95	75	81	75	72	90		95	88	89	94	88	105
10	62	59	59	55	65	42		62	74	71	79	82	61
11	54	61	55	59	55	59		50	76	68	79	73	77
12	—	59	104	117	108	129		—	74	108	134	122	141
	2109	2244	2356	2509	2666	3041		2125	2197	2195	2645	2697	3043

The following gentlemen, among others, have been employed in instruction here since the revolution, most of them in the Grammar School.

Dr Amasa Dingley, who died in New York   Rev. Thaddeus M. Harris, long clergyman of Dorchester .   Thomas Payson, afterwards teacher in Boston, and now of Peterborough, N. H. .   Roger Vose, counsellor at law in Walpole, N. H :   Silas Paul, sometime in the practise of the law in Leominster   Andrew Morton, lawyer, who died at Hampden, Me .   Calvin Park, Professor in Brown University: Isaac Gates, afterwards of the United States army .   Samuel Swan, practising law in Hubbardston .   Rev. Nathan Parker, late of Portsmouth, N. H.   Dr Jacob Bigelow, physician of Boston ,   Rev. John Nelson, of Leicester   Nathan Guilford, of Cincinnati, Ohio .   Ebenezer D. Washburn, of Mobile, Alabama   Levi Heywood   Rev Jonathan Going, now of the city of New York;   Jonathan Smith, now of Bath, N H   John Reed, son of John Reed, of Worcester ·   Thomas Fiske, who died at Charleston, S C   Benson C Baldwin, who died at Milford .   Leonard Worcester, late teacher in Newark, N. J.   George Folsom, now of New York.

Charles Thurber, B U 1827, son of Rev Laban Thurber, born in Brookfield, the present master of the Latin School, was elected to that office, March 27, 1832   The English School of the District, is under the charge of Warren Lazell, son of Deacon Daniel Lazell of Mendon, who was chosen as instructor, Feb 23, 1828.   Albion P. Peck, son of Dr Gustavus D Peck of Milford, was elected master of the second English School, June 22, 1835.[1]

CENTRE SCHOOL DISTRICT.

One of the earliest steps in the progress of the improvement of education in the Centre District, was in 1752, when the town, by their votes, consented, ' that the inhabitants of the centre, extending one mile and a half around the school house, should have allowed them their proportion of money for the support of schooling, provided they do, bona fide, keep a grammar school the whole year : and if their proportion of money will procure a master more than twelve weeks, the usual time they have of late had schooling, then any person may have liberty to send children afterwards.'   About this period, a school house, with two rooms on the floor, was erected by James Putnam, John Chandler, and other public spirited individuals,[2] and the deficiency of the grants for the support of instruction was supplied by subscriptions.   In 1769, the town gave to the proprietors of the grammar school, £6, ' they engaging that the school shall be free, for all persons in the town desirous of learning the languages '

All minor objects gave way to the intense interest and exhausting necessities of the revolutionary contest ; its stern excitement diverted attention, and

[1] The compensation paid to the instructor of the Grammar school, is $900   of the English school $700 · of the second school $400, annually   of the Apprentices school $32 monthly   of the Female High school $5 50 . of the Primary, Infant, and African schools $3 50, by the week   the assistants are paid at the rate of $1 the week

[2] This humble one story edifice was placed near the east side of Main street, south of the termination of the Boston Railroad, and surrounded with trees   During the revolution, it was converted into a dwelling, and remained, until modern improvement swept away the ancient house and the venerable elms that embowered its lowly roof.

its exigencies absorbed the whole available resources of the people all improvements were neglected; and education sunk low amid political commotion When peace revisited the land, an effort was made for the establishment of a system, perfected in after years, which might afford to the children of each citizen good and thorough education in their own homes An association was formed for erecting a school of high grade, with the real merits though without the ostentatious name of academy In 1784, Elijah Dix, Joseph Allen, Levi Lincoln, Nathan Patch, John Green, John Nazro, Palmer Goulding, and others, uniting in a joint stock company, procured a lease of the land on the west side of Main street on which the Centre School House now stands, and that building was erected in front of the position it now occupies A conveyance of the lot was obtained, Sept 29, 1787 The property had been divided into 100 shares, and each proprietor, by the terms of the deed, was to hold an amount of interest in the estate proportionate to his contribution for the purchase, under limitations securing the appropriation to the purposes of the fund

Two schools were opened in the new house by the proprietors, one for the common elementary studies, under Mr. Brown, the other for the highest branches of academic education, called 'The Seminary,' under the tuition of Mr Thomas Payson For a time they were sustained with great spirit The quarterly examinations, with the attraction of dramatic exhibitions were attended by a numerous audience In Aug 1787, the tragedy of Cato was played by Mr Brown's scholars, with brilliant success rivalled by the pupils of the seminary, in October following, by the recitation of original orations, forensic discussions, poems, and dialogues in Greek and Latin

As the children of the subscribers were removed to the colleges, or the preparation for professions or active business, the warm interest of the parents in the institutions declined, and with it the schools gradually sunk from the high ground on which they had been placed. In May, 1799, the building was advertised for sale at public auction, and in July, 1801, purchased by the inhabitants of the Centre District from its owners, at the cost of $950, including the expense of repairs

In the summer of 1823, a vigorous effort was made for the renovation of the decayed system. Dr. Bancroft, foremost in every good word and work, Jonathan Going, earnest and ardent in the promotion of improvement, Samuel M Burnside, author of the school law of 1827, Levi Lincoln, Otis Corbett, and Samuel Jennison, were the framers of that plan, whose successful operation has given occasion for just pride in the excellence of the schools of the district These gentlemen, from a committee 'to consider the interesting questions regarding the good of our children in the acquisition of knowledge,' submitted a report, Aug 22, 1823, published and distributed to all the families They declare their opinion, that for several years, the schools had generally fallen below the common standard, and would not bear comparison with many of the immediate neighborhood The evils so long endured, they attributed to false economy, in the employment of ill paid and incompetent teachers. The remedy was suggested, in the arrangement soon after adopted.

22*

and since continued, with the slight modifications pointed out by experience or required by the alteration of social condition. It was urged on the inhabitants, 'as they regarded parental obligations, as they loved their offspring, as they estimated their responsibility to God and their country, to cooperate unitedly and individually in the attainment of the great object.' The appeal was not in vain. The recommendations were confirmed, and liberal grants made for their execution. On the 31st of Dec. 1823, the first Board of Overseers was elected. They were Aaron Bancroft, Jonathan Going, Aretius B. Hull, Loammi Ives Hoadley, Levi Lincoln, John Davis, Theophilus Wheeler, Otis Corbett, Enoch Flagg, Benjamin Chapin, Samuel M. Burnside, and Frederick W. Paine; the heavy duty of carrying into operation the measures proposed, and sanctioned by the votes of the district, was devolved upon and faithfully discharged by them. The statement of the present condition will show the extent of their arduous and meritorious exertions, and the amount of resulting good.

Resort to the contingent aid of voluntary contribution having been found ineffectual and feeble, authority was obtained from the Legislature, Jan. 27, 1824, to bring the steady support of taxation for the support of schools. An additional act, Feb. 1826, authorized the notification of meetings, by an advertisement, signed by a majority of the overseers, posted on the meeting houses seven days previous.

A board of twelve persons, annually elected, have the duty of ascertaining the qualifications of teachers and the attainments of scholars ; prescribing the course of instruction ; establishing proper regulations ; investigating all complaints of parents, pupils, or instructors ; of the disbursement of monies ; the examination and supervision of the schools ; and of reporting in writing on the progress made during their term of office.

Ten permanent schools are arranged in regular gradation, and kept through the year, with such vacations only as the convenience of the teachers may require, or the discretion of the board permit.

Of the lowest grade, are the Infant Schools, first opened in 1830, receiving children at the earliest age at which they can derive benefit from public instruction.

Next are the North and South Primary Schools, receiving their pupils by promotion from the infant schools.

The pupils, when qualified, are advanced to the two Boy's English Schools, and to the Second Female School.

Highest in rank, is the Female High School, corresponding with the Latin Grammar School, to which promotions are made from the Primary schools.

There is an African School, for children of color, established in 1828, where all the useful branches of education are taught.

A school, first opened in 1828, has since been annually kept during the winter months, for apprentices and clerks, and such other boys as can attend only through a part of the year.

The instructors are required to keep a register, exhibiting an account of the conduct and proficiency of every pupil during each day. Monthly visitations are made by the overseers, and each scholar is then subjected to examination, and report of the result made to the board, at their stated meetings on the first Monday of every month.

It was originally proposed, that all the schools subject to the visitorial direction of the overseers, should be under the superintendence of the Grammar master, with the view, that some competent person, professionally devoted to education, should bestow that constant attention on the execution of the details of the system, which men engaged in the cares and occupations of life, could not give hour by hour. Dr Bancroft, the enlighted friend of youth, reporting for the committee of 1823, writes, ' the whole will form but one school, under the general superintendence of the board of overseers, and children will be advanced from class to class till they reach the highest. And in order to give strength and *unity* to the system, your committee are convinced, that the grammar master ought to have the superintendence of all the schools in the Centre House, and that the pupils shall be classed under his direction in such manner as to make the most economical use of time, without reference to the particular school to which they belong ' Difficulties resulting from the separate policy of the town and district, prevented the effect of an arrangement so judicious in its principle.

The following table exhibits the condition of the schools of the district in the month of September, 1836.

Schools.	Teachers.	Whole No	Boys	Girls	3 to 5	5 to 10	10 to 15	Over 15.
Latin Grammar,	Charles Thurber,	40	40	0	0	0	29	11
Female High,	Eliz B. Hamilton,	38	0	38	0	1	32	5
Second Female,	Jerusha Knight,	49	0	49	0	8	41	0
Boy's English,	Warren Lazell,	50	50	0	0	9	39	2
Second Boy's,	Albion P Peck,	53	53	0	0	24	29	0
North Primary,	Lois W Harrington,	63	0	63	0	10	23	0
South Primary,	Caroline M Corbett,	55	55	0	0	45	10	0
North Infant,	Mary S Ward,	75	39	36	33	42	0	0
Central Infant,	Abigail Pratt,	80	46	34	39	41	0	0
South Infant,	Martha S Hamilton,	53	29	24	23	30	0	0
New South Inft,	Rebecca S Cocs,	34	16	18	8	25	1	0
African,	Hannah C Perrin,	22	9	13	5	16	1	0

A recommendation from Dr Bancroft was adopted, Feb, 23, 1825, and it was ordered, ' that at two o'clock of the afternoon of the Saturday which closes the scholastic year, a public address be annually delivered in one of the houses for public worship, by some person appointed by the board ; the prominent objects of which shall be, to illustrate the importance of good education and the best method of acquiring and extending such an education , and give to the district assembled a just view of the manner in which their schools are and should be conducted. Let this address be followed by prayer Let proper measures be taken to insure a full audience from the District, and let the pupils of each school be seated together, with their teacher at their head. Further pageantry, the committee think, would be unnecessary and useless.' The beautiful thought of its benevolent author has had that observance which its origin deserved. Among the most interesting of festivals, has been the long procession of children, going up to the church, each April, with the plain unostentatious simplicity the founder of the ceremony designed, to hear the words of good counsel or admonition.

Those named below have made addresses on these occasions.

1825.	Aaron Bancroft,	1831.	Alfred D. Foster,
1826.	Samuel M. Burnside,	1832.	John S. C. Abbot,
1827.	Jonathan Going,	1833.	Frederick A. Willard,
1828.	Isaac Goodwin,	1834.	Stephen Salisbury,
1829.	Alonzo Hill,	1835.	Ira Barton,
1830.	Isaac Davis,	1836.	William Lincoln.

Such are the brief outlines of the plan, affording instruction from its lowest elements to its highest branches, beginning at the alphabet, advancing by regular gradations to the more elevated departments of learning, and affording to every citizen of the district the means of giving to his children all the education necessary for admission to the Universities, or desirable for the commencement of the engagements of business.

PRIVATE INSTRUCTION.

Although munificent grants sustained the great system of the common schools, instruction alike of lower and higher grade than they afforded, was required and has been supported at private charge, or undertaken by individual enterprise.

On the last day of March, 1791, Mr. Thomas Payson advertised his intentions to open a seminary for young ladies, 'as soon as the roads were more settled.' His experiment was brief, and probably unsatisfactory to himself.

Miss Hannah Spofford commenced a school on the same plan, in May, 1804. Her proposals afford data for estimating the extent of female accomplishments deemed desirable at that period, and the cost of their attainment. Reading, plain sewing and marking, were taught, for the compensation of two dollars the quarter: embroidery, ornamental work on muslin, writing, arithmetic, grammar, rhetoric, and the art of composition, could be gained for three dollars: painting in water colors and crayon, and filagree work, were charged at four dollars for the same period.

Mrs. Nugent succeeded this lady, adding in the Academy she opened in 1805, the exercises of geography, tambour work, landscape painting, and music.

Other instructors were here in later years. In 1823, an Academy for the instruction of youth in the highest branches of education, was commenced by the Rev. Benjamin F. Farnsworth, and continued about a year. A building was purchased, by an association, incorporated March 10, 1832, as the Proprietors of the Worcester Female Academy, and a school was kept by Mrs. A. M. Wells, during a year, and subsequently by Mr. John Wright. The corporation was afterwards dissolved, and the edifice sold.

Instruction of the most excellent cast has been given to young ladies, by

Dr John Park, for twenty years a teacher of distinguished reputation in Boston, who removed from that city to this place, in 1831 His classes have been so limited, as to admit of that oral communication which best imparts knowledge, and of the direct influence of a gifted mind, rich in learning and experience, to form pure moral and strong intellectual character

In the spring of 1836, a school of high grade for young ladies was commenced by Mr. Robert Phipps, which has been successfully continued In September, the pupils were 35

SUNDAY SCHOOLS.

Before 1816, beside the public religious instruction, there were recitations in a catechism prepared by Dr Bancroft, after the stated lectures, by the children of the second parish In May, of that year, a class of 25, soon increasing to 60, was formed by the Rev. Jonathan Going, in the Baptist society, and one of the first of the Sabbath Schools within the county of Worcester was established Almost simultaneously, the system which is exciting a happy influence on moral condition, was adopted by the first parish, and has been extended to the other societies

The number of scholars connected with the several churches, is stated in the latest published reports, as follows ,

First Parish,	300,	Calvinist Society,	235,
Second Parish,	170,	Union Society,	162.
Baptist Society,	250,		

The schools are generally under the direction of societies formed for their support, and are furnished with useful libraries collected by voluntary contributions

WORCESTER MANUAL LABOR HIGH SCHOOL.

At a meeting of a few individuals desirous of founding an institution for education in the interior, under the patronage of the Baptist denomination, in March, 1832, it was determined to raise $5000, as a foundation fund This sum was obtained, by subscriptions. principally within the county, and it was resolved, that the school should be placed in Worcester A committee was elected to effect the design, consisting of Isaac Davis and Otis Corbett of Worcester, Edward Phillips of Sturbridge, and Otis Converse of Grafton The details of the plan were wisely left to their discretion, under the general direction that the instruction should be of the first order ; that strict moral and religious character should be attained , and that every facility should be afforded for productive labor, to the end that education should be good, but not expensive

Among the most influential and zealous in the formation, development, and execution of this project, was Isaac Davis, Esq , who has been the President, and one of the most devoted in personal and pecuniary exertions, to the promotion of the prosperity of the Institution.

In November, 1832, a tract of twenty nine acres of land was purchased at the price of $75 the acre, and another lot of thirty one acres for $65 the acre, about half a mile south of the village The academic buildings were erected in 1833, at the expense of about $10,000. The trustees were incorporated Feb. 28, 1834, with full powers of visitation and government.

On the dedication of the seminary, June 4, 1834, an address was delivered by Rev. Frederic A. Willard, and religious exercises performed by Rev. Abiel Fisher. The school went into operation with about 30 scholars, under the superintendence of Silas Bailey, B. U. 1834. The second term, Amos W. Stockwell, A. C. 1834, was employed as assistant, succeeded the third term by Mr. Rhodes B. Chapman, who resigned in the fall of 1836, and Hervey S. Dale, B. U. 1834, was appointed teacher.

The institution has a library of about 500 volumes, and a philosophical and mathematical apparatus, was presented by Stephen Salisbury, Esq. one of the trustees. The studies pursued, are grammar, geography, rhetoric, book-keeping, arithmetic, algebra, geometry, surveying, the languages, intellectual and natural philosophy, and chemistry. The academic year is divided into four terms, of eleven weeks each, commencing on the first Wednesday in September, December, March, and June ; and each followed by two weeks of vacation. The charge of each term, for tuition in English studies, is $5, and in the languages, $7 : for rent of room and furniture, $2. Board in commons is furnished at the actual cost : the aggregate expenditure for provisions, servants and other necessary payments, being divided proportionably among the scholars.

It was the original design, not only to afford the means of the acquisition of knowledge by teachers, library, and apparatus, but to furnish such employment as would promote the health of the students, while it enabled them to defray some part of their expenses. During the period of agricultural operation, this has been provided. The farm and garden are cultivated by the students : if the full labor of a man is performed, eight cents the hour is allowed for the service, and the same ratio of compensation is adopted for less work. A report of the principal, in the autumn of 1835, states, that many of the students have been enabled to pay their tuition, and some, by industry, had discharged the bill for board : and adds, that those who had given evidence of the greatest improvement, on a then recent examination, had spent a portion of almost every day in active labor. The want of funds has yet prevented the erection of buildings and accumulation of capital, necessary for establishing branches of manufactures and mechanics, affording useful occupation during the inclement season.

The number of students in 1836, was 135 : among them, 18 from Worcester. The officers are : Isaac Davis, *President :* Otis Corbett, *Secretary :* Ichabod Washburn, *Treasurer :* Silas Bailey, *Principal :* Hervey S. Dale, *Teacher :* Joel Marble, *Steward :* Rev. Abiel Fisher, Joseph White, Rev. Otis Converse, Rev. Frederic A. Willard, Stephen Salisbury, Otis Corbett, Isaac Davis, Edward Phillips, Samuel D. Spurr, Pearley Goddard, Daniel Goddard, Ichabod Washburn, Joseph Converse, Joshua T. Everett, *Trustees.*

MOUNT ST. JAMES SEMINARY.

This institution, of very recent origin, was founded by Rev. James Fitton. Its buildings are situated on the northern slope of Pakachoag Hill, and are connected with a farm of about sixty acres of land   The government is vested in a President, Principal and Prefects, of the Catholic denomination   The course of instruction comprises the branches of practical education which qualify youth for usefulness, in the business of life   Pupils of the age of eight years are admitted   From the elementary studies of reading, writing, and grammar, they may proceed through courses of arithmetic, book-keeping, geography, astronomy, history, and composition   There are two scholastic terms in the year   one from September to March, the other from March to the middle of August   the first followed by one week, and the second by two weeks, of vacation   In the published statement, the expenses of support and tuition are estimated at eighty dollars per annum

The present officers are Rev James Fitton, President, and Joseph Brigden, Principal

---

CHAPTER XVI.

Population. Emigration Mortality Valuation Taxation. Support of the Poor Communication. Stages Manufactures Trade

POPULATION   Until within a few years, the inhabitants of Worcester have been principally employed in agriculture, and the population has increased slowly but gradually, until the commencement of works of internal improvement and the establishment of manufactures, which have given great and rapid accessions of numbers

The tables below show the numbers in the different years expressed

	1790		1800.		1810		1820	
Age	Male	Fem.	Male.	Fem	Male	Fem	Male	Fem
Under 10 years,	—	—	350	428	337	355	479	344
From 10 to 16,	494	—	178	162	186	182	171	188
From 16 to 26,	601	—	277	230	262	283	403	312
From 26 to 45,	—	949	213	245	242	234	319	325
45 and upwards,	—	—	175	170	207	231	218	270
Total,	1095	949	1193	1235	1234	1275	1590	15439

1830.

Age	Male	Fem	Tot.	Age	Male	Fem	Tot
Under 5 years,	300	280	580	From 40 to 50,	155	156	311
From 5 to 10,	218	218	436	50 to 60,	83	95	178
10 to 15,	188	209	397	60 to 70,	44	71	115
15 to 20,	258	229	487	70 to 80,	43	38	81
20 to 30,	537	428	965	80 to 90,	8	10	18
30 to 40,	260	251	511	90 to 100,	0	3	3
					2094	1988	4082

The number of free blacks in 1777, were 10: in 1790, 51: in 1800, 83: in 1810, 88: in 1820, 95: in 1830, 90.

In 1820, there are returned as engaged in commerce, 1: agriculture, 218: manufactures, 126: foreigners, 19.

The whole population in different years was as follows:

Years,	1763.	1776.	1790.	1800.	1810.	1820.	1825.	1830.	1835.	1836.
Pop.	1478	1925	2095	2411	2577	2962	3650	4172	6624 abt.	7500

EMIGRATION. The enterprize of the citizens of Worcester, and the want of profitable employment of industry at home, has, at different periods, led her natives to seek fortune in regions deemed more propitious. About 1730, a colony of the presbyterian planters went out to Worcester in New York. Soon after the war of the revolution, the town of Paris, in Maine, was founded by Levi Hubbard, and the brothers of the Stowell family, joining with him, have been among the useful and honored inhabitants of that town. Many other of the young plantations of that state derived accessions of numbers and worth from our community. Col. Josiah Brewer was the first settler of Cummington in Hampshire Co. Mass. Col. Timothy Bigelow, in 1780, became grantee of Montpelier: Col. Ephraim Doolittle, long resident here, commenced the cultivation of Shoreham; and Windsor, Chester, and Woodstock, all in Vermont, received additions from our citizens. Some were in Col. Putnam's expedition of 1787, to build cities in the then far West, and many went, after the war of 1812, to new lands. The county of Worcester has been like a hive of population, sending out swarms in all directions. The town has borne full share in this contribution to the good of others. The biographical notices of former pages show a portion of the talent thus bestowed.

MORTALITY. The favorable local situation of the town, the salubrity of the climate and healthful occupations of the people, have rendered the visitations of epidemic disease unfrequent.

Before the small pox had been disarmed of its fearful power of destruction, during the period when it spread over the country, hospitals were established in the town, to which whole families resorted for inoculation, in preference to awaiting the danger of taking the disease in the natural way. This malady prevailed generally in 1776, when the deaths here were 76.

In 1795, the dysentery prevailed, and between July and November, 44 children under five years, and 15 persons over that age, died here of that complaint. The number of deaths in that year, was 80; the average of five preceding years had been 24.

In 1810 and in 1813, a very malignant fever raged and created great terror in the county. Its destroying effect, though severe, was less fatal here than in other towns.

The bills of mortality have been imperfectly kept until recently. The following tables, collected with great labor, exhibit accurate results through the period they comprehend.

Years	Under 1.	1 to 5.	5 to 10.	10 to 20.	20 to 30.	30 to 40.	40 to 50.	50 to 60.	60 to 70.	70 to 80.	80 to 90.	90 to 100.	Unknown	Tot
1816	2	3	0	1	2	2	2	2	2	4	2	0	1	23
1817	3	5	4	4	5	5	4	2	3	4	3	1	6	49
1818	1	6	0	2	7	3	4	3	6	2	0	2	7	43
1819	4	5	1	2	8	2	1	3	3	3	3	2	14	51
1820	2	2	2	2	5	5	2	3	2	4	0	3	7	39
1821	3	2	0	2	4	2	3	1	8	3	0	0	7	35
1822	2	5	1	3	5	7	1	4	0	1	1	1	2	39
1823	3	6	2	4	4	4	4	3	2	2	3	0	20	57
1824	0	2	1	1	1	6	3	5	10	1	2	1	5	38
1825	3	4	1	0	1	4	3	3	3	2	1	0	18	43
1826	4	5	1	5	5	6	2	4	3	3	0	0	22	60
1827	3	5	1	1	5	3	1	1	1	4	6	1	14	46
1828	7	5	0	0	4	6	1	2	5	4	6	0	15	55
1829	5	11	2	2	4	1	5	4	5	2	3	0	5	49
1830	8	5	2	4	12	9	4	4	8	5	6	2	2	68
1831	9	6	10	3	10	5	5	5	4	10	7	0	0	74
1832	10	10	7	5	10	5	10	3	5	3	0	1	2	71
1833	14	13	1	3	8	1	11	4	4	2	7	0	0	68
1834	21	15	4	1	4	9	5	4	6	5	3	0	10	87
1835	20	10	5	10	12	10	4	5	6	2	3	1	17	105

	Jan	Feb	Mar	Apr	May.	June	July.	Aug	Sept.	Oct	Nov	Dec	Total.
1807	10	4	4	3	2	1	2	5	5	4	2	6	48
1810	0	0	3	5	7	5	3	4	5	4	1	2	39
1815	2	1	3	3	4	1	2	0	2	5	3	6	32
1820	6	5	2	1	4	1	2	3	5	5	2	3	39
1825	2	7	2	1	2	3	2	3	6	6	1	8	43
1830	5	7	9	4	4	4	8	8	7	8	1	3	68
1831	8	6	5	3	3	3	6	4	2	10	6	14	70
1832	4	6	7	7	6	4	7	7	8	2	10	3	71
1833	7	8	7	1	4	5	3	8	12	7	4	2	68
1834	8	8	4	7	3	5	9	11	5	10	7	10	87
1835	10	9	12	8	7	3	6	10	11	15	5	9	105

The deaths in other years, so far as the means of ascertaining the numbers are preserved, were. in 1775, 22 in 1776, 76 in 1778, 39 in 1779, 21. in 1780, 17: in 1781, 24 in 1782, 31 · in 1783, 28: in 1784, 38 in 1791, 22 · in 1792, 26 in 1793, 23. in 1794, 18. in 1795, 33 in 1796, 80: in 1797, 28 in 1808, 39 in 1809, 29 in 1811, 32. in 1812, 21. in 1813, 70 in 1814, 12.

The ratio of deaths to population in 1830 was 1 in 61: 1831, 1 in 61. 1832, 1 in 65. 1833, 1 in 70. 1834, 1 in 80. 1835, 1 in 63

There have been a few instances of extraordinary longevity John Young died June 30, 1730, aged 107 Sylvia, an African female, May 22, 1804, a 105 · Kesina Harris, Oct 27, 1832, a 102.[1]

VALUATION The following estimates of the principal articles of property

[1] Josiah Pierce, who died in 1806 a 85, left 14 children, 77 grand children, and 35 great grand children Kesiah Nichols died 1807 leaving 152 lineal descendants 7 children, 52 grand children, 86 great grand children, 7 great great grand children Col Benjamin Flagg, died Nov 1819, aged 95, leaving 4 children, 42 grand children, 83 great grand children.

23

are compiled from the returns of the assessors in the office of the Secretary of
the Commonwealth. On these documents the valuation of the state in successive years has been founded. Although the results cannot be considered
precisely correct, they approximate near to accuracy.

		1781.	1791.	1801.	1811.	1821.	1831.
Buildings,	Barns,	207	218	256	310	371	450
	Houses,	216	244	278	330	384	521
	Shops,	11	16	18	71	86	123
	Other Buildings,	32	49	110	146	221	372
Cider,	No. of barrels,	2063	2478	2999	3324	2114	—
Grain,	Barley, bushels,	—	—	359	289	625	575
	Corn,	—	—	13350	14112	17813	22272
	Oats,	—	—	6165	7228	11784	17645
	Rye,	—	—	4813	4164	5726	4261
	Wheat,	—	—	482	238	287	39
Hay,	English, tons,	—	—	1464	1683	2500	4249
	Meadow,	—	—	1393	1417	1204	1431
Land,	Tillage, acres,	1034	1193	1395	1745	1962	1925
	Mowing,	1074	1253	1754	2362	2882	3932
	Meadow,	1606	1574	1814	1856	1844	1751
	Pasture,	2881	4199	7469	7794	10560	10262
	Wood,[1]	14912	12213	5114	4874	3421	3730
	Unimproved,	—	—	4246	3918	1293	1072
	Unimprovable,	—	2166	907	316	857	72
	Covered by water,	—	—	90	396	388	448
	roads,	—	—	420	444	450	489
Live Stock,	Cows and steers,	778	1039	1063	1050	1101	1822
	Horses,	277	319	390	321	314	434
	Oxen,	365	407	513	391	488	614
	Swine,	212	671	687	565	717	698
Ratable Polls,		389	486	520	519	643	1109

The ratable polls have numbered as follows, in years not included in the
tables.

Years,	1777.	1778.	1780.	1793.	1803.	1813.	1823.	1833.	1834.	1836.
Polls,	438	440	460	490	508	599	715	1300	1312	1683

The aggregate value of the property of the town is inserted in a column below.

TAXATION. The following statement will furnish a comparative view of the
sums raised for public expenses in different periods. In addition to the town
taxes for the support of schools, large sums are assessed in the Centre District.

Years.	Total Valuation.	Total Taxes.	High-ways.	School Tax.	Public Worship.	County Tax.	State Tax.	Ratable Polls.
1800.	$296542	$3017	$1500	$1628	$808	$151	$962	530
1805.	443760	2130	2000	1300	875	238	1171	540
1810.	1476383	3213	2000	1500	1195	297	1049	518
1815.	1776635	4580	2000	1500	1443	219	1325	641
1820.	2015750	4715	2000	1700	2604	983	1181	626
1825.	2437550	6215	2000	2000	2458	485	—	881
1830.	2747800	8073	2000	2700	4868	1295	619	1018
1835.	3667250	15986	2500	3600	5480	1564	—	1570
1836.	3990950	24047	6700	5200	6435	1564	—	1683

[1] In 1781, 1791, the woodland and unimproved land are not distinguished.

The expenditures of the town during the year ending in March, 1836, were, as stated in the report for highways, $2445; repairs of bridges, $104, new roads, $965, schools, $3472; fire department, $800, new engine house, $1200, principal and interest of town debt, $3379 ' lighting streets, $311; poor establishment, $1404, poor not at the poor house, $453, compensation to assessors, $170, burials, $216, amounting with some contingent expenses, to $15,698. Of this sum, $527 has been repaid by allowance for support of state paupers, and $341 from other towns from individuals, or from pensions.

SUPPORT OF THE POOR. In the early years of the town, the charges for supporting those who by infirmity or misfortune were destitute of the means of subsistence, were inconsiderable. There was a general equality of pecuniary condition, and that common prosperity and independence resulting from industry, frugality and temperance, which either prevented indigence or relieved its wants. Those who needed aid, were sustained by the charity of neighbors, more blessed with worldly goods, freely contributing for their comfort. The first tax assessed for the support of the poor, seems to have been as late as 1757, when £5 4s were appropriated for that use. In 1763, it was voted, ' that a suitable workhouse be built for placing therein all persons that are, or may be, to be supported by the town, to be under the direction of the selectmen.' In 1772, a building for the same purpose was erected on Front street, 40 by 18 feet in dimensions, at an expense of £70. Little charities were often bestowed on the meritorious, so small as to be memorials of the compassion, rather than the munificence of the public. In 1766, £6 were raised to be disposed of in transporting a sick female to Stafford, and supporting her there while using the medicinal waters of the spring, ' she being one of the poor of the place, and laboring under great infirmity. In 1784, the selectmen were empowered ' to procure an anvil for Cato Walker and lend it to him, or let him it during their pleasure.' In 1807, it was determined to build an Alms House of brick. but after land had been purchased for the site, and materials for the structure, the plan was abandoned. Until 1817, the poor were supported by contracts with the highest bidder at public auction, in the manner usual in the country towns. In that year, the Jennison farm, situated on the great road to Boston, bordering on the upper end of Quinsigamond Pond, was purchased, with its comfortable mansion, for $5500, and a permanent home provided for the aged and infirm of our indigent citizens. This establishment, under the supervision of the selectmen, is confided to the charge of a superintendent, constantly residing with his family in the house, upon a salary of $350 annually, with board and rent, conducting the cultivation of the land, and ministering to the comfort of the numerous dependents placed by the swelling population and peculiar local situation of the town under his charge, as well as exercising good discipline over those committed by public authority to this institution, as a workhouse.

A building has been erected, affording suitable accommodations for the insane, and a hospital is to be established for relief from the occasional visitation from contagious disorders.

The following statement exhibits the condition of those supported by the charity of the town for two years

	1834	1835
Males,	42,	58
Females,	27,	23
Whites,	63,	75
Blacks,	6,	6
From 80 to 90 years of age,	6,	6
Above 90 years of age,	6,	6
Intemperate,	25,	28
Married,	24,	31
Born in Worcester,	31,	33
Foreigners,	9,	24
Unable to read or write,	5,	4
Blind,	2,	2
Idiotic,	5,	5
Insane,	4,	2
Whole number,	69,	81

The annual taxes for the support of the poor from 1762 to the revolution, would average £30.

COMMUNICATION Prior to 1755, there was a mail between Boston and Philadelphia A letter sent fiom one city to the other, was then three weeks on its way, and the writer could not have obtained an answer in less than about seven weeks A great reform took place in that year, and the speed was so accelerated, that the mails were delivered in fifteen days, so that the reply to the letter could be received in a month from its date The first stage on the route from Boston to New York, set up by J. and N. Brown, started June 24, 1772, and was intended to run once a fortnight. In the Boston Evening Post, July 6, 1772, patronage is solicited, and it is promised 'that gentlemen and ladies who choose to encourage this new, useful, and expensive undertaking, may depend upon good usage, and that the coach will always put up at houses on the road where the best entertainment is provided.' Notice was given, that 'the coaches will leave New York and Boston, on their next trip, on Monday, July 13, and arrive at each of those places on Saturday the 25th,' occupying thirteen days in going from one place to the other. The mail stage now goes from Boston to New York in 34 hours, and to Philadelphia in 44 hours. A person might reach the former city in 24 hours by public conveyance.

The stage was not continued to the revolution In 1774, the only regular communication of the town, was by a post, going once a week between Hartford and Boston, and occupying six days in the journey At that time, the mails were carried on horseback in saddlebags James Adams, who died at Charlemont, at advanced age, and a Mr. Hyde, were long employed on this route, and went through Shrewsbury, Worcester, Leicester, and Springfield.

Soon after the removal of the Spy to Worcester, Mr Thomas made extensive arrangements for its distribution. In June, 1775, a post rider set off each Wednesday at noon, who, by hard travelling, arrived at Cambridge the next forenoon, and at Salem by night Returning, he left Watertown as soon as Edes and Gill's Gazette was published on Tuesday, and reached Worcester in the evening On Wednesday, a post started for Providence, and came back on Saturday

The first Post Office of the town was established, Nov 15, 1775 under the charge of Isaiah Thomas, receiving and forwarding one mail from the west on Tuesday evening, and one from the east on Friday morning Nathaniel Maccarty, who had been apprentice to Mr Thomas, carried papers and letters to Fitchburg every Wednesday, thence distributed through the north part of the country

The condition of the roads rendered traveling slow, difficult, and dangerous, and intercourse was laborious, tedious, and expensive The mails were transmitted, as almost all passing was performed, on horseback. A journey of an hundred miles was a matter of greater preparation, apprehension, and toil, than one of a thousand would be now There were few vehicles of any description The first pleasure carriage which was in the town, is said to have been a chaise, owned by Daniel Waldo, sen , a merchant of Boston, who, after residing some time in Lancaster, removed to Worcester in 1782

The first effort to establish a stage, appears, from an advertisement, June 13, 1782, stating, that ' a gentleman in Boston, having a genteel coach and a span of horses, would be willing to be concerned with some trusty person capable of driving a stage between Boston and Worcester ' The proposal was not accepted But the project of making a regular communication did not long slumber Levi Pease, then of Somers, Conn , and Reuben Sikes,[1] then of Suffield, 'having furnished themselves with two convenient wagons,' began a business, Oct 20, 1783, which became most extensive One wagon started from the sign of the Lamb in Boston, every Monday morning, at 6

---

[1] LEVI PEASE, sometime of Somers, Conn , afterwards of Boston, became an inhabitant of Shrewsbury, where he died Jan 28, 1824, aged 84 During the revolution, he served under Gen Thomas, in the Northern department, and in supplying the army with provisions, was often exposed to great danger and hardship His activity and fidelity recommended him to Gen Wadsworth, and he was employed in useful service, connected with the operations of the South He kept tavern for some time in Somers, afterwards in Boston, and finally went to Shrewsbury, where he afterwards resided

He was the original projector, for some time the sole proprietor, and long a principal owner, of the stages between Boston and New York He entered on the enterprise not only unassisted, but discouraged by his friends , the scheme was considered visionary and ruinous , and the most judicious, regarded it as being at least a century in advance of the public wants

REUBEN SIKES, born in Somers, Conn July 16, 1755, went to Hartford in 1783, and after about two years residence removed to Wilbraham, where he remained about ten years was sometime of Suffield, Conn , and in May 1807, came to Worcester, and was long proprietor of the hotel, now the Exchange Coffee House Although much younger than Capt Pease, the industry, perseverance and enterprise, which marked his character, rendered him fit assistant in the execution of a plan, in its origin bold and hazardous He was extensively engaged in the establishment and management of stages, and after the retirement of his partner, was one of the largest proprietors of that property in New England He died August 19, 1824, aged 69, not long after his associate.

23*

o'clock, and stopped for the night at Martin's in Northborough : on Tuesday, going through Worcester, it rested at Rice's in Brookfield: on Wednesday, it advanced to Pease's, in Somers : and on Thursday reached Hartford. The other, leaving Hartford at the same time, and stopping at the same houses, arrived in Boston in four days. Passengers were carried for 4d. the mile. Mr. Thomas remarks, in the Spy of Oct. 30, ' Should these wagons be encouraged, it will be of much advantage to the public, as persons who have occasion to travel between, or to, or from, either of the places, may be accommodated on very reasonable terms, and will not have the trouble and expense of furnishing themselves with horses.' They *were* encouraged, and the enterprising proprietors, personally acting as drivers and conductors, set about improvements of their accommodations and arrangements. In May, 1784, they purchased new carriages : Pease, going from the Lion, in Marlborough street, Boston, lodged at Farrar's in Shrewsbury, and the next day exchanged passengers at Spencer with Sikes, who returned by the route of Springfield to Hartford. The customers found their way to New Haven, and thence took sloop navigation to New York. Industry, frugality, devotion to business, and sagacious management, soon made the wagoners and stage drivers wealthy proprietors and great mail contractors. They entered into an arrangement with Talmage Hall and Jacob Brown of Hartford, to extend the stage communication to New Haven, in Nov. 1784.[1]

In Jan. 1786, the energetic founders had established a line of stages from Portsmouth to Savannah, transporting the several mails. From Boston to Hartford, coaches left the inn of Levi Pease, opposite the Mall, every Monday and Thursday morning, at 5 o'clock : went to Worcester on the first day :

---

[1] The following interesting memoranda, transcribed from the New York Daily Advertiser of 1833, differ somewhat from the account in the text.

' In the year 1786, the first stage carriage that ever was established on the great post road between New York and Hartford, was set up by Jacob Brown, then a resident of Hartford, in the state of Connecticut, and commenced running between Hartford and New Haven. It was a carriage somewhat resembling the coaches of later times, but far inferior to most of them in workmanship and appearance, and was drawn by one pair of horses, which performed the whole journey through from one town to the other. The route was upon what is called the middle road, that is by Berlin, Wallingford, &c. and the journey occupied the day. At that time, for a large part of the year, a great proportion of travellers from the Eastward to the city of New York, took passage at New Haven, on board the sloops which plied between the two ports, and thus finished their journey by water. The passages varied according to wind and weather, from twelve hours to three days. A considerable part of the road between New Haven and New York, along the shore of the Sound, was extremely rough, rocky, and uncomfortable, and in fact in some places almost impassible for wheel carriages. After Brown's carriage had run for a year or two, or perhaps more, a man of the name of Hall petitioned the legislature of Connecticut for the exclusive privilege of running stage carriages on the road from New Haven through that state, to Byram river, which was granted, and the stages were established, and run for a number of years, when they passed into other hands. Not far from the same time, an exclusive privilege of running stage carriages from Hartford to the Massachusetts line, between Suffield in Connecticut and West Springfield in Massachusetts, on the great post road to Boston, which then passed in that direction, was granted by the legislature of Connecticut to Reuben Sikes, who for many years, in connection with Levi Pease, of Shrewsbury in Massachusetts, and probably with others, kept up the line through to Boston.'

on the next day to Palmer on the third to Hartford and in three days more arrived at New York This was the winter arrangement· in summer, the stages run with the mail three times a week, ' by which means,' say the owners, ' those who take passage at Boston in the stage which sets off on Monday morning, may arrive at New York on the Thursday evening following, and all the mails during the season will be but four days from Boston to New York ,' and a letter adds, ' by this unparalleled speed, a merchant may go from Boston to New York, and return again in less than ten days , which is truly wonderful ' The advertisement proceeds to remark, that ' it is the most convenient and expeditious way of travelling that can be had in America, and in order to render it the cheapest, the proprietors had lowered their price from 4d to 3d the mile, with liberty to passengers to carry 14 pounds weight of baggage ' In July, 1788, notice was given by Levi Pease, that after great expense and fatigue, he had completed the line of stages from Boston to New York , that the carriages which before were heavy and uneasy, had been hung upon springs, and would not fatigue more than a common coach and that to Nov 1, there would be three stages a week, and from that date to May 1, two the week

From this time onward, the speed of travelling and its facilities were increased almost beyond measure [1]

It would not be useful to detail further the steps in the progress of a branch of improvement, whose course may be so easily traced by inspection of the newspapers

Stages were placed on almost every road The lines which centred at Worcester, and went out and returned here in 1825, before canal or railroad affected this mode of conveyance, are thus enumerated there were stages, *daily* to Boston, Hartford, and New York, and to Oxford *three times a week*, 5 lines to Boston , 1 to Providence , 1 through Hardwick to Northampton ; 1 through Brookfield to the same town , 1 to Springfield , 1 to Keene , 1 to East Chelmsford 1 to Southbridge , 1 to Dudley , *twice a week*, there was a line to Providence , and there were *weekly* lines to Athol, to Richmond, N H and to Ashburnham. Post riders carried mails twice a week to Pomfret, Conn and weekly to Thompson, Conn. . others without mails went to Concord, Charlton, and Oxford.

In 1831, it was estimated that the average amount of travelling in stages between Boston and Worcester, was equal to 22,360 passages per annum, for which the lowest price of fare was two dollars, and the shortest time six hours

[1] The improvement in the rate of motion in England, has been as great as in the United States An advertisement of stage coaches in the Newcastle Courant of 1712, says, ' All that desire to pass from Edinbro' to London, or from London to Edinbro', or any place on that road, let them repair to Mr. John Baihe's at the Couch and Horses, at the head of Cannongate, Edinbro', every other Saturday, or to the Black Swan, in Holborn, every other Monday at both of which places, they may be received in a stage coach, which performs the whole journey in thirteen days, without any stoppage, if God permits, having 80 able horses to perform the whole stage ' A late English paper states that the Mail coach from Edinburgh to London has been through in 40 hours

The subjoined list exhibits an account of the different lines of stages in September, 1836, and the number of times each arrives and departs weekly.

Stage to		Weekly.	Stage to	Weekly.
Boston,	Mail,	7	Springfield,	6
"	Accommodation,	3	Northampton,	6
"	Springfield Mail,	3	Amherst,	6
Hartford,	Southern Mail,	7	Keene,	6
"	Tremont Line,	6	Brattleborough,	6
"	Citizens,	6	North Brookfield,	3
"	Telegraph,	6	Barre,	3
Providence,		6	Greenfield,	6
Lowell,		6	Millbury,	12
Norwich,		6	Leicester,	12

The stage books gave the total receipts of three lines for the year ending April 1, 1835, thus: from Worcester to Springfield $8,699: to Northampton $13,086: by the way of Amherst $3,131: amounting in the whole to $24,915. It was estimated that the number of passengers annually carried between Worcester and Hartford was 30,000.

MANUFACTURES. Before the revolution, and for a long period after its conclusion, the manufactures of the town were very inconsiderable.

Works for making potash were first established in the north part of the town, about 1760; buildings for similar purposes were placed on Lincoln street, by John Nazro, about ten years after: four more were erected at much later periods: but all have long since been destroyed.

The distillation of rye, to an extent not only sufficient for home consumption, but affording some surplus for exportation, was early commenced, but was not successful.

In 1780, an association was formed, for the purpose of spinning and weaving cotton. In February, it was stated in the Spy, that a subscription was making for defraying the expenses of a jenny. Mr. Thomas announces, under date April 30, that 'on Tuesday last, the first piece of corduroy made at the manufactory in this town was taken from the loom. Good judges speak highly of it, as superior to English. The carding machine, which is a great curiosity, as well as is the spinning machine, has been completed some time. In a little time it is hoped, the corduroys, jeans, &c. made in this town will be sufficient to supply the country.' The proprietors, it is said, in December, 'had lately erected buildings, and taken other measures to carry on business extensively. A large quantity of fustian, jean, and corduroy are for sale now, lasting longer, and retaining color and beauty better, than the foreign.' These articles, with the addition of 'federal rib and cotton,' were advertised by Samuel Brazer, in May, 1790. The site of the establishment was on the stream a short distance below the Court Mills. Want of profit or perseverance, induced the owners to forego their brilliant anticipations, and the manufactory edifice, removed to Main street, was long after known as the 'Green store.'

Paper was made by Mr. Thomas in 1794, on the Blackstone river. The mill then erected was afterwards leased and finally sold to Elijah Burbank, and the business, continued by him until 1834, has since been extended by the Quinsigamond Paper Company

A card manufactory was commenced by Daniel Denny in 1798

Peter and Ebenezer Stowell, in Oct 1804, commenced weaving carpets and plaids, and at one time, had six looms of their own invention and construction in operation They pursued, at the same time, the business of printing calicos, and built shearing machines, superseded in use, in latter days, by those of more perfect operation

Abel Stowell, carried on a very extensive manufacture of tower and church clocks, and many now remain to attest the value of his handiwork, and mark the hours of the present generation.

In 1803, Joshua Hale began the carding of wool in the south part of the town, and in 1810, erected a cotton factory, which, though of humble extent in comparison with the immense structures of the mill owners of the valley of the Blackstone, was considered a great enterprise a quarter of a century ago

During the last ten years the water power of the town has been made to have more than double the former capacity, by the establishment of reservoirs, and is susceptible of being increased to great extent by the same means

There are now 2 mills manufacturing broadcloths 6 making satinets· 1 for cotton sheeting and shirting 2 for satinet warps 1 for pelisse wadding 2 for paper. There are seven extensive establishments for building machinery . one wire factory an iron foundry and manufactories of sashes, doors, and blinds of lead aqueduct pipe . of paper hangings· of cabinet furniture· of chairs· of brushes of trunks and harnesses of ploughs of hats of shoes of watches of umbrellas : of cutlery of piano fortes and many other articles of utility or ornament The amount of production in the different branches of manufacturing industry is very great, and constantly increasing [1]

TRADE Where almost every hand and head is busy in some branch of industry, and employments are multiplied and various, it has been found impossible to state in figures the amount of capital employed, or the precise results on general wealth

Some aid is afforded in estimating the amount of business by the annual receipts of the Post Office. They are returned as follows

Years	1825	1826.	1827	1828	1829.	1830	1831.	1832	1833	1834	1835	1836.
Receipts	$713	844	961	1008	1141	1332	1338	1469	1743	2053	2294	2827

The number of dwelling houses, stores, and factories, erected in the town within the two last years, has been estimated to exceed three hundred the stores and warehouses actually occupied are upwards of ninety

The principal articles of import are grain, flour, lumber, coal, salt, lime, gypsum, oil, iron, lead, hardware, dry goods, groceries, paints, dye stuffs, cotton and wool: of exports, ship timber, bricks, machinery, wooden ware, castings, cotton and woolen goods, paper, shoes, chairs

[1] An effort has been made to ascertain the amount of manufactures of the town but sufficient information has not been obtained to make an estimate with accuracy Some details in relation to manufactures, trade, and business, will be found in the appendix

CHAPTER XVII.

Societies and Institutions. Medical District Society. Antiquarian Society. Agricultural Society. Historical Society. Atheneum. Banks. Insurance Companies. Savings Institution. Various Associations. Military Companies. Newspapers and Periodicals.

Many of the societies meeting, acting and having a kind of residence here, belong to the county or country, rather than the town : yet, they are so closely connected with Worcester, that they could not properly be passed by in its history.

WORCESTER MEDICAL SOCIETY. A medical association was first formed in the county of Worcester, August, 1784, of which Dr. Samuel Prentice was Secretary, but it soon died, leaving no records for the historian.

The Mass. Medical Society, intended to produce that harmony and mutual effort necessary to elevate the profession to the standing and usefulness which the interests of the community required, failed of its object, by the limitation of its members to eighty in Massachusetts and Maine, and the restriction on their consultations with any, except those who obtained the qualifications they required. By the exertions of Dr. Oliver Fiske, the most repectable and influential physicians of the county assembled, and formed the Worcester Medical Society, Dec. 18, 1794. Dr. John Frink of Rutland, was elected President, and Dr. Fiske of Worcester, Secretary. At an early meeting, a petition was preferred to the Legislature for incorporation, referred to a joint committee of physicians, and resulted in an arrangement to enlarge the numbers of the general society, and a proposal to create district associations. This system, removing the evils which had been felt, and mutually satisfactory, was carried into effect, and on the 26th of Sept. 1804, the Worcester District Society was organized. The succession of Presidents has been as follows : 1794, John Frink : 1804, Israel Atherton : 1806, Oliver Fiske : 1807, Thomas Babbitt : 1813, Abraham Haskell : 1814, Jonathan Osgood ; 1820, Abraham Haskell : 1825, Stephen Bacheller : 1830, John Green.

The Society have a very valuable library of about 400 volumes of works of professional use.

THE AMERICAN ANTIQUARIAN SOCIETY. This institution, having for its object the collection and preservation of materials for the history of the western continent, was founded by Isaiah Thomas, LL. D. In the preparation of his work on printing, he had gathered the relics of the departed centuries, with curious illustrations of the literature of former times, at an expense few antiquarians could have bestowed, and with diligence and care none other would have devoted. Feeling the good the experience of the past may convey to the future, it was his design to save the seeds of knowledge gathered in successive centuries, to yield their increase in those which may succeed; and by perpetuating the memorials of the present, to enable other generations to become wiser and happier by the experiments of their predecessors. Connecting with himself many friends of improvement and lovers of history, an association was formed by his exertions, incorporated by the Legislature of Massachusetts, Oct. 12, 1812. The centre building of Antiquarian Hall, erected at his expense, in 1820, with the land on which it stands, was presented by him to the society. The first volume of transactions, relating principally to the fortifications, mounds and antiquities of the extinct nations of the west, was published, in 1820, at his charge. On his decease, by munificent bequests, he provided for the support of the institution he had established, and for the promotion of its great purposes. In the second volume of transactions, published in Sept. 1836, are inserted, an extended and profound dissertation on Indian history and languages, by Hon. Albert Gallatin, and the Memoir of the Chistian Indians, by Daniel Gookin, so frequently referred to in former pages. The Library, estimated to contain 12,000 volumes, includes the collections of Mr. Thomas, a large portion of the books of the Mathers, many in the German language, bequeathed by Dr. Bentley of Salem, a vast mass of tracts and manuscripts, and the best series of American newspapers preserved in the country. There is a valuable cabinet illustrative of antiquities and natural history. Two stated meetings of the society are held annually : one in Boston, on the old election day in May; the other for the election of officers, in Worcester, in October, on the anniversary of the landing of Columbus. The number of American members is limited to 140 ; many distinguished foreigners are enrolled on the catalogue by honorary elections. The funds, amounting to about $22,000, are appropriated to the support of a librarian, the purchase of books, the exploration of antiquities, and the other specific purposes designated by the munificent donor. The institution has been managed on the most liberal plan : its collections have been kept open to the public freely, and have been much frequented by strangers and scholars.[1]

WORCESTER AGRICULTURAL SOCIETY. This most excellent institution was incorporated, Feb. 23, 1818.[2] At the first meeting, March 11, 1818, for the purpose of forming a fund to be sacredly appropriated for the promotion of agriculture, the contribution of five dollars was required from each member on admission. In December following, Levi Lincoln, Daniel Waldo, and Edward D. Bangs, were appointed a committee, to ask for legislative bounty, who presented a petition at the next session. In consequence of this application, and other similar memorials, the Act of Feb. 20, 1819, granted from

[1] These officers have been elected : *Presidents*; 1812, Isaiah Thomas : 1831, Thomas L. Winthrop. *Vice Presidents ;* 1812, William D. Peck : 1813, William Paine : 1816, Aaron Bancroft, Timothy Bigelow : 1821, DeWit Clinton : 1828, Thomas L. Winthrop : 1831, John Davis, Joseph Story. *Treasurers ;* 1813, Levi Lincoln : 1814, Isaiah Thomas, jr. : 1819, Nathaniel Maccarty : 1829, Samuel Jennison. *Corresponding Secretaries ;* 1812, Thaddeus M. Harris : 1814, Samuel M. Burnside : 1816, Abiel Holmes : 1826, William Lincoln, for domestic correspondence : 1832, Edward Everett, for foreign correspondence.

The late C. C. Baldwin, was librarian from April 1832, to his death in August 1835. Maturin L. Fisher, has been acting librarian since that date.

[2] Before the revolution, cattle fairs were held annually at Hardwick. The Shrewsbury Agricultural Society, and the Brookfield Association of Husbandmen, preceded the society of the county.

the state treasury, to each agricultural society, $200 annually for six years, for every thousand dollars of funds they had raised; with the limitation, that the sum thus drawn, should not exceed $600 the year. The full amount of the munificent appropriation of the government, since extended for a longer period, has been received by the association, and an amount nearly equal distributed in premiums, or applied to the payment of necessary charges. The exhibitions of cattle and manufactures, in the month of October, beginning in 1819, have been since continued with increasing interest. The festival has given one quiet spot among the conflicts of excited times, where all sects and parties have met to unite their efforts for the common good. Addresses on these occasions have been delivered by the following gentlemen:

Years.		Years.	
1819.	Levi Lincoln,	1828.	William S. Hastings,
1820.	Lewis Bigelow,	1829.	William Lincoln,
1821.	Jonathan Russell,	1830.	Ira Barton,
1822.	Nathaniel P. Denny,	1831.	Oliver Fiske,
1823.	Oliver Fiske,	1832.	Waldo Flint,
1824.	Isaac Goodwin,	1833.	Solomon Strong,
1825.	George A. Tufts,	1834.	Charles Allen,
1826.	Emory Washburn,	1835.	Stephen Salisbury,
1827.	Pliny Merrick,	1836.	James G. Carter.

The amount of funds and of monies paid as premiums, in years ending with the annual meeting in April, are as follows:

Years,	1820.	1826.	1827.	1828.	1829.	1830.	1831.	1832.	1833.	1834.	1835.	1836.
Funds,	$2955	4636	4880	5100	5378	5739	6036	6645	6942	7352	7683	7938
Premiums,	$434	492	687	536	414	417	391	464	476	476	480	494

The following officers have been elected; *Presidents*, 1818, Levi Lincoln, sen.: 1820, Daniel Waldo: 1824, Levi Lincoln; *Treasurer*, 1818, Theophilus Wheeler: *Cor. Secretaries*, 1818, Levi Lincoln: 1824, Oliver Fiske: *Recording Secretaries*, 1818, Abraham Lincoln; 1819, Edward D. Bangs: 1823, William D. Wheeler; 1834, Charles G. Prentiss; 1836, Edwin Conant.

THE WORCESTER HISTORICAL SOCIETY, incorporated Feb. 19, 1831, was formed for the purpose of collecting and preserving all materials necessary for compiling a full account of the history, statistics, and geography of the county. It requires, as evidence of qualification for membership, the publication of some work, or some practical exertion in aid of these objects. Hon. John Davis has been president since the organization.[1]

---

[1] The Centennial anniversary of the erection of Worcester county, was celebrated by this society Oct. 4, 1831. The first Court of Common Pleas was opened Aug. 10, 1731: and the Supreme Court of Judicature was held Sept. 22, 1731. It was deemed equally proper to commemorate either of the leading events of the first year of the century. Having regard to the attendance of the citizens, and from other considerations, the first day of the session of the Supreme Judicial Court in 1831 was selected, and the centennial anniversary of the sitting of that tribunal was commemorated, on Tuesday, Oct. 4, although the date was not precisely coincident with the return of the judicial term. The Address was delivered by Hon. John Davis, and, with a particular account of the ceremonies, is deposited in the Am. Antiquarian Society's Collections.

THE WORCESTER COUNTY ATHENEUM, was incorporated, March 12, 1830, with the intention of forming a full library for general use Thirty four proprietors purchased shares, at the price of twenty five dollars each, subject to an annual assessment of two dollars About 3000 volumes of works of general literature have been gathered, making a foundation for an extensive collection in future time The library is now kept in one of the rooms of Antiquarian Hall, appropriated for the purpose.

The Rev. George Allen has been President. Frederick W. Paine, Treasurer and William Lincoln, Secretary, from the organization

The WORCESTER BANK, was originally incorporated with a capital of $200,000, March 7, 1804, and its charter has been renewed, in 1811 and 1831. The first President was Daniel Waldo, sen chosen 1804, who declined the office in October following, when Daniel Waldo was elected his successor, and has since been at the head of the institution The Cashiers have been 1804, Levi Thaxter : 1806, Robert Breck Brigham . 1812, Samuel Jennison

The CENTRAL BANK, was incorporated March 12, 1828, with a capital of $100,000 Benjamin Butman was President to the autumn of 1836, when Thomas Kinnicutt was elected The Cashiers have been , 1828, Otis Corbett , 1829, George A. Trumbull 1836, William Dickinson

The QUINSIGAMOND BANK, chartered March 25, 1833, has a capital of $100,000 Its Presidents have been 1833, Alfred D Foster 1836, Isaac Davis Charles A Hamilton has been Cashier

The CITIZENS BANK, was incorporated April 9, 1836, with $500,000 capital, and went into operation in October following Benjamin Butman is President, Geo A Trumbull, Cashier, and Rhodes B Chapman, Accountant.

The WORCESTER MUTUAL FIRE INSURANCE COMPANY, was incorporated Feb 11, 1823 Its powers are vested in a president, treasurer, secretary, and eight directors, elected at the annual meeting on the second Wednesday of December The following has been the succession of the principal officers *Presidents* . 1824, Rejoice Newton ; 1831, Frederick W Paine ; *Secretaries* , 1824, Henry K. Newcomb, William D Wheeler . 1827, Isaac Goodwin 1832, Anthony Chase

The table below shows the extension and progress of its business

Years.	Amt each year	Total amt insured	Premiums received	Expenses	Losses	Cash Funds
1824	$153815	$153815	$2169 86	$610 79	—	—
1825	179786	333601	2675 56	392 65	—	—
1826	190304	523906	2815 00	295 90	—	—
1827.	135800	659706	2159 34	394 60	—	—
1828.	157643	817350	2374 71	317 27	$1800	—
1829	188009	1005359	3190 28	414 83	415	—
1830.	180353	1185712	2880 86	499 80	2414	—
1831	372352	1404249	4653 90	637 49	1000	$15885 11
1832.	478482	1702994	5973 43	808 00	325	21991 80
1833.	701933	2214623	9343 75	935 35	4850	26400 24
1834.	583449	2662272	8403 90	838 80	430	34904 31
1835.	778642	3283270	10750 62	1132 40	374	46603 50

24

As the association is formed for mutual security, and not for profit, there are strictly speaking no dividends. The average of amounts returned to the insurers on the expiration of policies, have been : in 1831, 77½ cents of each dollar paid as premium : in 1832, 82¾ : in 1833, 81½ : in 1834, 83 ½: in 1835, 90½.

The MANUFACTURERS MUTUAL FIRE INSURANCE COMPANY, founded on that principle of giving mutual security expressed by its name, was incorporated Feb. 25, 1834. Two millions of dollars were subscribed and are held as a fund, liable to assessment for losses. The company commenced business, Aug. 5, 1834, by issuing policies on the property of manufacturing establishments. By an act additional to the charter, the corporation were authorized to effect insurance on buildings, public and private, except dwelling houses not connected with manufactories, within the United States.

The statements below include the business of years ending Oct. 1.

Years.	Insured.	Premiums.	Expenses.	Losses.	Cash funds.
1834.	$381222	$3318	—	—	—
1835.	2063301	22352	$3140	$6712	$16160
1836.	5000000	48126	3016	19100	30686

The dividends of returned premiums in 1835, were 55½ : in 1836, 65½. The concerns are managed by a president, twelve directors, and a secretary. The former and latter have been these : *Presidents ;* 1834, David T. Brigham : 1835, Harvey Blashfield : *Secretaries ;* 1834, Edward H. Hemenway : 1835, Samuel Allen.

There is an agency of the Springfield Insurance Company in Worcester.

The WORCESTER COUNTY INSTITUTION FOR SAVINGS, was incorporated February 8, and organized April 17, 1828. A president, secretary, treasurer, twelve vice presidents, and twenty-four trustees, chosen at the annual meetings, have the general charge of the institution, and make examination of its concerns by monthly committees. The funds are loaned and invested by a board selected by the trustees. The statement annexed, shows the condition of this most useful institution in years terminating in April.

	1829.	1830.	1831.	1832.	1833.	1834.	1835.	1836.
Depositors,	105	251	400	678	913	1128	1442	1860
Deposites,	$6263	13645	32032	68994	109983	151797	202477	276388

It appears from the annual returns made to the Secretary of the Commonwealth, that the whole expenses of the institution, during the current year, when the funds have increased to nearly $300,000, were 8641, only. From the commencement, not a dollar of the investments have been lost.

Daniel Waldo has been President, and Samuel Jennison, Treasurer, from the organization. Isaac Goodwin was Secretary to August, 1832, and William Lincoln has held that office since.

The multitude of unchartered associations is too great for separate enumeration. There are societies for the promotion of sabbath schools ; of temperance ; of missionary purposes ; of moral reform ; of education ; of charity ; of science : there are others for mutual protection against the calamity of fire ;

for punishing depredations on orchards and gardens , for the prevention and detection of theft ; for improvement in music, and for many other benevolent or useful purposes   Among these, the Bible Society and the Lyceum are probably the only ones requiring particular notice

The AUXILIARY BIBLE SOCIETY was organized Sept 7, 1815   The settled ministers of the gospel in the county, of every denomination, are entitled to membership ex officio   The payment of one dollar annually constitutes a member while the contribution is continued, and of ten dollars gives the privileges for life   So well have the people of the county been supplied with the sacred scriptures, that during the first ten years of its existence, the society, furnishing the indigent in a population of about 80000 gratuitously, and seeking for those who are destitute, had distributed only 710 bibles, and 77 testaments   During this period, about $2000 had been collected.   In 1822, the association having become a branch of the American Bible Society, paid over $500 in one sum, and subsequently transferred to that noble institution a fund of $1000, which had been invested on interest   Within the last period of ten years, increased population and accessions of foreigners have rendered the distribution of the scriptures greater, and the better means and deeper interest of the charitable in the objects of the society swelled the donations   From the latest annual report which has been published, it appears that, for the year ending Oct 1, 1834, the receipts were $2353   the amount paid to the national society for the purchase of books $331 : and as free gift $1722   the number of bibles issued were 267, of testaments 683 [1]

WORCESTER LYCEUM.   This society was formed Nov 4, 1829, for mutual instruction and improvement.   The management of the common concerns is confided to a president, treasurer, secretary, and an executive committee of eight members, elected by ballot, at the annual meeting, first held in November, and recently on the last Thursday of March   Lectures are delivered on each Thursday evening during the months from October to March   Occasional courses on the sciences, have been given by distinguished teachers   During the first years of the association, classes were formed among the members for acquiring practical knowledge, and their exercises were pursued with pleasure and benefit

Membership is gained by any person of good moral character, on the payment of one dollar, at the commencement of the year ; by those from eighteen to twenty-one, on the annual contribution of seventy-five cents , and any one between the ages of twelve and eighteen years, on the deposit of fifty cents, becomes entitled to all the advantages and means of improvement of the institution

The Lyceum is possessed of a good chemical apparatus, and a well-selected library of about 500 volumes, beneficially and extensively used by the young

[1] The *Presidents* have been ; 1815, Joseph Allen   1822, Aaron Bancroft   1824, Jonas Kendall   1827, Levi Lincoln   1834, John Davis   *Treasurers*, 1815, Benjamin Heywood   1817, Samuel Allen   1820, William Jennison   1824, Charles Allen   1830, Benjamin Butman   *Secretaries*, 1815, Nathaniel Thayer   1818, Lemuel Capen   1819, Joseph Allen, of Northborough   1829, George Allen . 1832, Alfred D Foster

artizans and operatives of the village. By a provision of the constitution, no alienation of the property is to be made: to secure its preservation during any suspension of the society, the selectmen are authorized to deposit the collections with some incorporated literary institution of the town, to be held in trust, and transferred to some new association for similar purposes.

The number of members in 1830, was 276: in 1831, 126; in 1832, 191: in 1833, 171: in 1834, 181; in 1835, 190. But these numbers do not indicate the attendance; the great hall of the Town House has been thronged with a continually increasing crowd; and the institution, sustained by popular favor, has been an example of the successful diffusion of learning by the cheapest possible medium of communication.

The officers have been these: *Presidents:* 1829, Jonathan Going; 1832, John Park; 1836, Alfred Dwight Foster. *Secretaries:* 1829, Anthony Chase; 1832, Horatio L. Carter; 1833, Warren Lazell.

MILITARY COMPANIES. Soon after the garrisons of the first planters, formed from the neighborhood, ceased to be kept, a military company was formed to act against the Indian enemies, who had united themselves with the French, and retiring to a distance, made frequent invasions. Daniel Heywood was elected and long remained captain. There are some slight traces of its existence, in 1725, but it cannot be certainly stated that it began so early. In 1760, there were two bodies of militia, one numbering 59, and the other 48, under Capt. John Johnson and Capt. James Goodwin.

About 1783, the *Worcester Artillery* was formed, of volunteers, and William Treadwell[1] elected Captain. This corps, the oldest of the martial associations of the town, is now commanded by Capt. Josiah G. Perry, and has two six pounders granted by the state for its use.

The *Independent Cadets*, under Capt. Thomas Chandler, was formed during the war with France in 1798, and on its conclusion, was disbanded.

The *Worcester Light Infantry* paraded for the first time, in May 1804, under Captain Levi Thaxter. The commanding officers have been, Levi Thaxter, Enoch Flagg, William E. Green, Isaac Sturtevant, John W. Lincoln, Sewall Hamilton, John Coolidge, Samuel Ward, Artemas Ward, John Whittemore, Charles A. Hamilton, William S. Lincoln, Charles H. Geer.

The *Worcester Rifle Corps*, established in 1823, was disbanded in 1835.

The numbers doing duty in volunteer companies during 1835 and 1836, has been about 50; there are two large companies of militia, with a force of more than 200 men.

---

[1] Major William Treadwell, one of the most gallant of the officers of the army of the revolution, entered the service at an early age, and was distinguished for lion-hearted courage. He had an enthusiastic love of danger. Twice, when his own division was at rest, he obtained leave of absence and joined another corps on the eve of battle. While the shot of the enemy struck around him, the testimony of a cotemporary states, he would consider with the most deliberate coolness the direction of his own guns, look over the sights to give the best aim, and after the discharge, spring upon the cannon to see the effect. He retired with honorable scars and rank, to a condition of poverty, that drove him to despair, and died broken-hearted, April 14, 1795, aged 46.

NEWSPAPERS AND PERIODICALS

THE MASSACHUSETTS SPY, established in Boston by Isaiah Thomas, in July, 1770, was first issued in Worcester, May 3, 1775, and has preserved the series of its numbers unbroken to the sixty-fifth volume and year of its existence, having long since reached the venerable rank of the oldest paper in Massachusetts, where the printing of newspapers began   Daniel Bigelow and William Stearns, two gentlemen of the legal profession, became lessees, June 27 1776 finding the labors inconsistent with their appropriate business, they transferred the right of publication to Anthony Haswell, afterwards conductor of the Vermont Gazette, Aug 14, 1777 The press was resumed by Mr. Thomas in June, 1778, and retained until 1 02, when it was resigned to Isaiah Thomas, Jr   After some changes of ownership, in 1819, it was purchased by William Manning and George A Trumbull, and in 1823, John Milton Earle became editor, and has since continued the principal or sole proprietor

THE MASSACHUSETTS HERALD OR WORCESTER JOURNAL, a small paper of four quarto pages, was issued by Isaiah Thomas, Sept 6, 1783, and intended by the publisher, as a Saturday abridgement of his larger sheet   The advertisement states ' that if it should fail of being properly nurtured by the public, it will, as it is a *rib* taken from the *Spy*, be again replaced, without murmur or complaint ' Public patronage did not sustain the undertaking, and it was abandoned after the fourth number

AMERICAN HERALD and WORCESTER RECORDER   The Herald, which had been published in Boston during seven preceding years, was removed to Worcester, Aug 21, 1788, and issued on Thursdays, by Edward Eveleth Powers, who united the trade of bookseller with that of printer   The paper was decorated with an agricultural device, and bore the motto, ' venerate the plough', professed perfect impartiality in politics, promised intelligence in rural economy, and was marked by no distinct character   after two years and two months, it was discontinued.

THE INDEPENDENT GAZETTEER, the fourth newspaper of Worcester, was commenced Jan 7, 1800, and published by Nahum Mower and Daniel Greenleaf, until the 7th of October succeeding, when the partnership of the proprietors was dissolved, and the publication was continued by the latter, through two years   When this period was completed, the list of subscribers was transferred to the conductor of the Spy

THE NATIONAL ÆGIS, was established in support of the policy of Mr. Jefferson, amid the fiercest warfare of the great parties organized at the commencement of the present century   Subscriptions were obtained among the ardent politicians in the vicinity and in Boston, amounting to about $1200, for the purchase of a press and printing materials [1] Proposals, bearing internal evidence of the authorship of Hon Francis Blake, were sent out Sept 8,

---

[1] Among the subscriptions were these   Benjamin Austin, $150 , James Sullivan, $100 , James Prince, $100 , Jonathan L. Austin, $100 , Levi Lincoln, sen $100 , William Eustis, $45 ; William Jarvis, $45

24*

1801, detailing the plan afterwards executed in spirited manner by himself and others ; the paper was to be devoted to the defence of the national administration, and unceasing opposition to its enemies ; the last page, called " the Olio," was assigned as a separate department for literary essays, and selections. The first number appeared Dec. 2, 1801. Deriving its name from the arms of Minerva, the front exhibited the figure of the mythologic goddess of wisdom, grasping the spear in one hand, and resting the other on the shield, bearing the device of the gorgon's head, wreathed with olive branches. Mr. Blake, as editor, gave high character to the print, and many of the ablest writers of the county cooperated with its gifted conductor, to influence and direct public sentiment. This arrangement continued until 1804, when Mr. Blake retired. In December, 1805, the whole property was attached under a claim growing out of debts of the printer, Samuel Cotting, and the publication suspended. The democratic citizens, roused to exertion, procured new apparatus, which they vested in trustees, and the Ægis again appeared, Feb. 19, 1806, in deplorable dishabille for a time, but soon regained neatness and beauty. A new calamity occurred to interrupt its prosperity. On Sunday, the 6th of July, during the hours of worship, a part of the types were removed, and the sheets, impressed on one side, carried away by Cotting, who, on the next Wednesday, in his individual capacity, sent out the paper in handsome form, while the trustees of the subscription fund were scarcely able to communicate their misfortune. A curious state followed, realizing the confusion of external identity, imagined in the Comedy of Errors. Two papers were published in the same town, on the same day, claiming to be ' the true Ægis.' A contest painful to retrace ensued, disturbing the repose of the village, proceeding almost from words to blows in private discussion, and furnishing subjects for judicial investigation. The good sense of the community, for a time amused by the bitter feeling of the combatants, and the personal insult degrading pages which should have been devoted to common improvement, at length acted on the source of the commotion, and after a few months of infamous existence, the false print disappeared.

After some changes, the Ægis, in 1807, went into the hands of Henry Rogers, then late of Hartford, who was publisher until the close of 1824, when Charles Griffin became partner with him. In July, 1833, it was united with the Yeoman, and became merged with that print not long after.[1]

The MASSACHUSETTS YEOMAN was commenced Sept. 3, 1823, by Austin Denny, Esq., who continued to be sole or principal editor, proprietor, and

---

[1] Among the editors of the Ægis, at different periods, were Francis Blake, Edward Bangs, Levi Lincoln, Samuel Brazer, William Charles White, Enoch Lincoln, Edward D. Bangs, Pliny Merrick, William Lincoln, Christopher C. Baldwin, William N. Green.

A paper borrowing its descriptive appellation from the worst of reptiles, the Scorpion, came out July 26, 1809, and on successive Wednesdays, without the name of printer or publisher, resembling those abusive periodicals serving as safety valves to convey away the fermenting malignity of base hearts. Its existence was evidence of the unlimited freedom of the press, and its speedy suppression, an instance of the power of public opinion to restrain its licentiousness, and of the healthy tone of moral sentiment amid the violence of party hostility, crushing the slanderer under the weight of general contempt.

publisher, until his decease It was issued on Saturday In July, 1833, it was united with the Ægis, and in January following, the title was changed and the existence of the paper ceased.

The WORCESTER REPUBLICAN was established in 1829, by Jubal Harrington, and has been under the management of that gentleman, except during short intervals

The WORCESTER PALLADIUM succeeded to the Ægis and Yeoman. It was commenced in January, 1834, and has continued under the editorial care of Mr J S. C. Knowlton.

The WORCESTER WEEKLY MAGAZINE An act of Massachusetts, March, 1785, imposing a duty of two thirds of a penny on newspapers, and a penny on almanacs, which were to be stamped, was so unpopular from its very name, that it was repealed before it went into operation, and as a substitute, for the purposes of revenue, a tax was levied on all advertisements inserted in the public journals This was regarded by Mr Thomas as an undue restraint on the press He suspended the publication of the Spy during the two years the act was in force, and printed a periodical in octavo form, with the name at the head of this article, beginning in the first week of April, 1786, and ending the fourth volume on the last of March, 1788

The WORCESTER MAGAZINE and HISTORICAL JOURNAL, was published by William Lincoln and Christopher C. Baldwin, in 1825 and 1826 the numbers of the first volume were issued twice a month, and those of the second once a month It was intended to contain a particular history of each town of the county Notices of Templeton, Sterling, Shrewsbury, Leicester, Northborough, West Boylston, Paxton, and Lancaster, and a general view of Worcester county, were furnished by different writers. At the expiration of a year the work was discontinued

The WORCESTER TALISMAN, a literary and miscellaneous journal, consisting principally of selections, was published on Saturday, during the year after April 5, 1828, on an octavo sheet, forming one volume, by Messrs Dorr and Howland, and was continued to Oct 15, 1829, in quarto form, by John Milton Earle.

The FAMILY VISITOR, a religious quarto, was published weekly by Moses W Grout during a few months of 1832 ; but was soon discontinued.[1]

[1] Printing was formerly carried on by Isaiah Thomas to an extent, which, relatively to the general state of business at the period, was immense, and would be considered as great even in comparison with the rapid publication of recent years Seven of his presses were worked under his immediate direction, and the number of persons employed by him, in paper making, printing, binding, and the branches of bookmaking and selling, was about 150 There are in 1836, four printing offices

The books belonging to the societies and associations, number about 20,000 volumes · probably those in private libraries would exceed 50,000 volumes

The number of newspapers and periodicals circulated in the town, is greater than the whole amount printed in the state before the revolution In no community are the facilities of instruction and information greater , and there can be few where they are better improved

TOPOGRAPHY AND HISTORY.

CHAPTER XVIII.

Situation. Boundaries. Extent. Divisions. Streets and Roads. Turnpikes. Black-stone Canal. Railroads. Public Buildings. Public Lands. Burial Places. Face of the town. Ponds. Streams. Hills. Mines and Minerals.

SITUATION. Worcester, the shire town of the county, is situated 40 miles westward from Boston, 40 N. N. W. from Providence, 60 miles E. N. E. from Hartford, about 50 miles from Northampton, the nearest point on Connecticut river, and 394 from Washington. From the boundary of New Hampshire, in the shortest direction, the town is distant about 30 miles; from that of New York, about 70; from Rhode Island, about 20; from the tide waters of Boston Harbor, about 40 miles. Lines drawn on the map, intersecting each other at Worcester, Boston, and Providence, would form a triangle almost equilateral. The north latitude of Antiquarian Hall, ascertained by Robert Treat Paine, Esq. is 42° 16′ 9″: the west longitude, computed from observation on the annular eclipse of the sun in February, 1831, by that gentleman, in degrees, is 71°, 49′, in time, 4h. 47m. 16s.

The elevation above the ocean, as estimated by the engineer of the Blackstone Canal, at Thomas street, near the centre of the village, is 451 feet: the elevation of Main street above Charles street in Boston, is stated by Mr. Fessenden at 456 feet.

BOUNDARIES AND EXTENT. The town is bounded, on the north principally by Holden, touching at the northwest corner on Paxton, and at the northeast extremity of the line, on West Boylston; east by West Boylston and Shrewsbury, and for a short distance at the southeast corner by Grafton: south, by Millbury and Ward: west by Leicester, and at the southwest corner borders on Ward.

The area contained within these lines, is about thirty six square miles: or more exactly, 22842 acres; about 600 acres are covered with water: 700 used for roads; 1925 are estimated to be occupied as tillage; 5683 as mowing; 10262 as pasture; 3730 with wood; and about 1000 are unimproved.

DIVISIONS. The town is separated into twelve school districts, having permanent boundaries: the centre is marked 1: directly west is that designated 2: next south of this is 3: the others are numbered in regular succession, circling around the centre district, with the exception of 12, which was formed by partition of an original district, and lies between those distinguished as 9 and 10, disturbing the symmetry of the arrangement.

The principal village, so surrounded by hills that it is scarcely seen by the stranger until he enters its streets, has extended but little south of the territorial centre on which the founders seem to have designed it should be planted The description of Dr Dwight,[1] about 1812, has not ceased to be correct : 'the houses are generally well built frequently handsome and very rarely small, old, or unrepaired Few towns in New England exhibit so uniform an appearance of neatness and taste, or contain so great a proportion of good buildings, and so small a proportion of those which are indifferent, as Worcester '

Villages have grown up around the manufacturing establishments *New Worcester* is situated on the road to Leicester *Trowbridgeville*, on the road to Oxford *South Worcester*, on that leading to Ward the *Quinsigamond Village*, on the Millbury road . *Adams Square*, upon the old road to Lancaster · *Northville*, on the road to West Boylston.

STREETS The most ancient passage way through the town is Main street, used in 1674, and constantly traveled over since 1713 It is still the principal avenue of the town, extending about a mile from north to south It is broad and planted with fine shade trees [2]

Nearly contemporary with the permanent settlement, was the establishment by use, of a road from the Meeting House to Pine meadow, now Front street, of a path to the first burial place, over a part of Summer street . and the Lancaster way, through Lincoln street The roads now Salisbury, Pleasant, Green, and Grafton streets, existed at a very early period

Mechanic street was laid out in 1757. In 1806, Isaiah Thomas made and gave to the inhabitants the street called by his name It was planted through its whole length with poplars, perhaps fortunately destroyed, soon after, by some malicious person [3]

Most of the other streets have been opened within the last five or six years by individuals at their private expense, as the increasing population has rendered it desirable to occupy their lands for buildings

The length of roads within the town in 1826, was equal to 82 miles and 88 rods At present the extent would exceed 100 miles

TURNPIKES At the beginning of the century, great improvements were

---

[1] Dwight's Travels, i 366 Letter xxxvi

[2] The time when these beautiful ornaments of the village were first set, appears from an ordinance for their protection, April 7, 1788 · 'Whereas, a number of persons have manifested a disposition to set out trees for shade, near the meeting house, and elsewhere about the centre of the town, and the town being very desirous of encouraging such a measure, which will be beneficial as well as ornamental, Voted that any person being an inhabitant of this town, who shall injure or destroy such trees so set out, shall pay a fine not exceeding 20s for every offence to the use of the poor ' Other and more strict municipal regulations have from time to time been adopted for their preservation

[3] The following memoranda from the interleaved almanacs of Isaiah Thomas, Esq show something of the customs of the time '1806 October 6 finished work on the new street The selectmen came and surveyed it and laid it out in form. The Light Infantry company, under arms, commanded by Capt Flagg, marched through it, baled on the bridge, and discharged three vollies The gentlemen of the street prepared a large tub and two pails full of excellent *punch*, and the selectmen, at the request of those present, and in conformity to their own proposal, named the street Thomas street The Infantry company had as much punch as they chose to drink, and all present Three cheers were given, and the company marched off '

made in internal communication by the establishment of these highways. A corporation was chartered for building a turnpike to Stafford, in Connecticut, Feb. 15, 1806 : and March 17, 1806, the Worcester turnpike was incorporated. It was a favorite principle with the engineers of that time, that roads must be carried on a straight line between the points to be connected, without any deviation from the direct course to conform to the undulation of the surface. On this plan, the turnpike to Boston, going out from the north end of the village, went through a considerable eminence by a deep cutting, passed a deep valley on a lofty embankment, ascended the steep slope of Millstone hill, crossed Quinsigamond by a floating bridge, and climbed to some of the highest elevations of the country it traversed, when inconsiderable circuit would have furnished better and less costly route. These undertakings, of great convenience and utility in the period of their construction, have been more beneficial to the public than the proprietors.

The Worcester and Fitzwilliam Turnpike, incorporated June 15, 1805, was not completed : the Worcester and Sutton, March 3, 1810, and Worcester and Leicester, Feb. 29, 1812, were not commenced.

BLACKSTONE CANAL. The project of opening a navigable communication from the waters of Narragansett bay in Rhode Island, to the centre of Massachusetts, through the valley of the Blackstone, first engaged public attention in 1796. The author and patron of one of the earliest attempts to connect the interior with the seaboard, by a water highway, was the late John Brown of Providence. The whole weight of his wealth, intelligence, and zeal, were lent to the enterprise. Public meetings were held, and warm interest in the undertaking excited. In Rhode Island, a charter was obtained. The petition of inhabitants of Worcester county, praying for incorporation for the opening of ' inland navigation from the navigable waters near Providence, to the interior parts of Worcester county, and if feasible, to Connecticut river,' was presented at the May session of the General Court of the Commonwealth, in 1796. At the same time, a counter plan, which had the effect, if not the intent, of defeating the former, was started, of constructing a canal from Boston to the Connecticut river : the application for the Providence canal was refused, and the projectors, left without power to execute the work, were compelled to abandon the undertaking. Surveys were soon after made for the Massachusetts Canal, under the direction of Gen. Henry Knox, and with their conclusion terminated the exertions of the subscribers.

In 1822, by a general movement, the plan was revived and subscriptions opened for a survey, completed in October of the same year. Acts of incorporation were obtained for distinct companies in each state, subsequently united, July 5, 1825, under the name of the Blackstone Canal Company. In 1824, the excavation was commenced in Rhode Island; in 1826, the first earth was removed in Massachusetts, near Thomas street. The first boat which passed through the whole extent, arrived at the upper basin, Oct. 7, 1828.

Three Commissioners had been elected in each state, acting in cooperation during the construction : on the union, the same gentlemen were elected on

one board   they were Edward Carrington, Moses B Ives, and Stephen H
Smith of Providence, John Davis, John W Lincoln, and Sylvanus Holbrook
of Massachusetts For some time past, Thomas Burgess has had the sole direc
tion. The expense of the work was about $750,000 Of this amount more
than half a million of dollars was paid by the citizens of Rhode Island, and the
work, projected by the intelligence was principally executed by the capital of
our sister state

The canal has been more useful to the public, than to the owners . the
amount of transportation, however, has increased

The BOSTON AND WORCESTER RAILROAD was incorporated, June 23 1831.
The road, extending 44 miles eastward, is laid with a single track of edge
rails, on cast iron chairs, resting on wooden sleepers, bedded in trenches fi led
with stone The cost of construction has been $1500000, including land, la-
bor, cars, engines and buildings Passenger cars, go in each direction, three
times daily during the warm months, and twice in the cold season, except on
Sundays The time is from $2\frac{1}{2}$ to 3 hours, including stops at ten places the
fare has been $1,50, but in the autumn of 1836, was raised to $2 The freight
of merchandize from Boston to Worcester, by the ton, is $3,50 from Wor-
cester to Boston $3 A branch railroad is soon to be laid to Millbury

About a mile from the depot on Main street, the road passes through a
deep cutting of the slate rock, about 30 feet in its greatest depth, and extending about 30 rods The strata are almost perpendicular, and were removed
from their beds by a laborious process of blasting

The NORWICH AND WORCESTER RAILROAD COMPANY was incorporated
March 26, 1833 A charter had been previously obtained in Connecticut, for
the route within her jurisdiction, at the May session, 1832 By an act of
this Commonwealth, April 10 and of that state, May 1836, the two companies were united From Norwich to Worcester is 58 miles to Boston 102.
The work of construction is now advancing The capital stock is $1500000.

The WESTERN RAILROAD CORPORATION was established, March 15 1833,
for the purpose of building a railroad from the western termination of the Boston and Worcester Railroad to Connecticut River in Springfield, and thence
across the stream to the western boundary of the state, where it will connect
with railroads in progress, one to Albany, one to Troy, and one to Hudson
The stock of $3000000 has been subscribed, two thirds by individuals, and
one third by the state, and a portion of the road located,[1]

PUBLIC BUILDINGS. It is a curious circumstance, that the earliest provision for the erection of any county building, in a community of moral, order-
ly, and religious habits, should relate to the confinement of malefactors

At the first meeting of the Court of General Sessions of the Peace, Sept 2,
1731, it was ordered, that a prison should be built, and that, with his consent,

[1] A statement of the amount of transportation by the Canal and Railroad, will be found
in the appendix.

the house of William Jennison[1] should be used as a temporary gaol : a suitable *cage* was to be built in the back part, and the liberties of the yard were to extend 20 feet on the south side and east end.

In February following, the court ordered, ' that in lieu of the prison before appointed, the *cage* so called, already built, be removed to the chamber of the house of Daniel Heywood,[2] and be the gaol until the chamber be suitably finished for a gaol, and then the chamber be the gaol for the county, and the cage remain as one of the apartments.' Here the prisoners were confined until they were placed in the building erected in 1733,[3] 41 feet long, 18 feet wide, with 8 feet studs: the prison part was 18 feet square, made of white oak timber, set with studs, 4 inches thick and 5 inches broad. and floored, roofed and ceiled with two inch plank spiked together. A dungeon was stoned under : the other end, finished as a dwelling house, became part of the Butman tavern, and was destroyed by fire, Dec 23, 1824.

In 1753, a new gaol was built a few rods south of the former prison, 38 feet long, 28 feet wide, with 7 feet posts. The south end was studded with joist six inches square, set five inches apart, and filled between with stone and mortar. The top, sides, and floor, were covered inside and out, with oak plank, fastened with a profuse use of iron spikes, and doors, windows, and partitions were heavily grated.

Notwithstanding these precautions for security, many effected escape, and the wooden gaol becoming too infirm for the confinement of dangerous persons, a structure of massive granite, 64 by 32 feet, three stories in height, was ordered to be erected in Dec. 1784, on land granted by the Commonwealth, and £500 were appropriated for the expense. This was completed Sept. 4, 1788, and Mr. Thomas remarks, ' this is judged to be at least the second stone building of consequence in the Commonwealth ; none being thought superior except the Stone Chapel in Boston : that is built of hewn stone ; the stones of this are mostly as they were taken from the quarry. The master workman, Mr. John Parks of Groton, has acquired great credit for the ingenuity and fidelity with which he has executed the work. A great saving must be experienced from the new building, as, without some convulsion of nature, it is not probable that it will need any repairs, excepting the roof, for two or three centuries.' And he adds ' that the capaciousness of the building will make it answer for a work house, and save the county the expense of erecting one.'

The course of nature went on undisturbed, but the increase of crime and the improvements of discipline, prevented the permanency which was expected by the founders. The ' capaciousness ' was insufficient for modern use, and in April 1835, the gaol was transferred to the House of Correction : the land and buildings were sold, and the prison demolished.

COURT HOUSES. It was ordered, Aug. 8, 1732, that a suitable and convenient court house be built on land given by William Jennison, Esq., and a committee was instructed to inform those ' who had an interest in lands in the

---

[1] Occupied by Dr. Oliver Fiske in 1836. [2] Part of the buildings of the Central Hotel.
[3] On land of Stephen Salisbury, Esq. east of the south extremity of Lincoln street.

county, and especially in the town of Worcester, which, by that town's being
made the shire town, are greatly advanced, of the court's intention and to
know what any of them will be pleased to give towards building and adorning
the house ' This building, placed very near the site of the present edifice,
was of wood, 36 feet long, 26 feet wide, with 13 feet posts Until its completion, courts were held in the meeting house The address of Chief Justice
John Chandler, of Woodstock, delivered Feb 8, 1734, at the opening of the
Courts of General Sessions and Common Pleas, published in the Boston
Weekly Rehearsal, Feb 18, 1731, shows the ideas of beauty and magnificence
entertained in that period

Taking occasion to speak from ' some instances of the Divine Providence
remarkably favorable to us,' he says, ' It demands our observation and acknowledgment, . . that we are now entered into a new and beautiful
house, erected purposely for the reception and entertainment of the courts,
which for the future are to be held within the same, at the occurring seasons
thereof . an article that I know not the like in any county within this province, so soon after the constitution thereof, it being but about thirty months since
we held our first court ' . . ' It is our duty on this occasion, . . very
thankfully to acknowledge the good hand of God's Providence upon us, who
has stirred up and opened the hearts of sundry worthy gentlemen some of
whom live in other parts of the province, to be benefactors to us, by assisting
us in our infant state to erect and beautify so agreeable a house as we are in
the possession of, and which exceeds so many others in the province built for
the like service, in the capaciousness, regularity, and workmanship thereof
so that those who have business to be transacted here, may now and hence-
forth, be suitably and conveniently accommodated with room, while they attend the courts, without intruding on that which we have been necessitated
to use hitherto, though designedly built for another purpose To God be
the glory ascribed, as the unmerited effects of the Divine Favor to us notwithstanding which, our benefactors and their benefactions, should be very
gratefully remembered by us

After a few years, the edifice thus commemorated, was found to be too
small for the purpose of its erection, and a new court house was ordered to be
built March 16, 1751, of greater dimensions It was 36 feet by 40 in size,
and after being the temple of justice forty years, was converted into a dwelling house, and still stands at the intersection of Franklin and Green streets

The increasing business of the county requiring larger accommodations, the
present court house was commenced in 1801, and opened Sept 27, 1803.[1]

[1] In the charge of Chief Justice Robert Treat Paine, Sept 27, 1803, to the grand jury, he
says, ' We meet you with great pleasure at this first opportunity of our assembling with
you to attend the administration of justice within the walls of this magnificent building
On this occasion, we can but recollect what has been said, that when the proposal, in 1731,
was made, in General Court, for erecting this County, some great politician of that day,
[Gov Hutchinson,] objected to it, because, from the then appearance of the country, it
must be a great length of time before it would be an object for county jurisdiction , and
that there are some now, who well remember when the territory which composes this county, was, in many parts, but thinly inhabited, and but just emerging from a wilderness

25

The lower story is appropriated for county offices, the next contains the court room and lobbies for jurors.

The following inscription on a silver plate inclosed in a leaden box, with several ancient silver coins of Massachusetts, (shillings and sixpences,) and some modern money, was deposited in a cavity cut for the purpose in the lower corner stone of the hewn underpinning on the south east.

' The corner stone was laid Oct 1, 1801, by Isaiah Thomas, Esq who with William Caldwell, Esq. Sheriff of the County, and Hon Salem Towne, were appointed a committee for building and completing this (now intended) Court House The old Court House now stands two feet southeast from this spot, 1801 '

William Lancaster of Boston, was employed as master workman of the exterior, and Mr. Baxter, of the interior.

The cost of the court house, furniture for the public offices, and brick walls of the yard, with a part of the stone walls, iron railings, and embankments in front, was $17,830 ; an additional allowance was made to Mr Baxter, and the whole charges when completed were about $20,000.

The COUNTY HOUSE OF CORRECTION, first occupied in November, 1819, is situated east of the village, and not far from the Hospital The front of the building, a large and handsome structure 53 by 27 feet, is occupied by the keeper's family, except the north side of the basement, where three cells are appropriated for solitary imprisonment, and the punishment of the refractory, fortunately but little used The part used for confinement is in the rear of the keeper's apartments The plan of construction first adopted was found to be bad . the rooms were large, and several convicts were, from necessity, placed together ; so that sometimes, novices in crime were associated with veteran offenders, and the establishment, with all vigilance and fidelity of supervision, was more the nursery of vice than the school of reformation Impressed with the evils of this arrangement, the County Commissioners, in 1832, directed an alteration in conformity with a plan submitted by the Overseers, resembling that of the State's Prison in Charlestown. The whole interior was taken down, and another building erected within the exterior walls, divided into 40 cells, each 7 feet by 3 1 2 feet in size, 7 feet high, receiving light through iron doors properly made for the purpose, opening into the area around, which is warmed by stoves In the basement are three other rooms for confinement, and on the same floor with the kitchen is the

---

state of uncultivated roughness and until our happy revolution took place, its appearance was but small in comparison of what we now behold The grandeur of this building is a striking proof of that prosperity of the inhabitants, which flowed from the fruitful fountain, the revolution, and the good government and wholesome laws consequent upon it. And we also, can but consider it as strong evidence of the good disposition of the inhabitants, respecting social and political regulations , of their determination to support the constitution and government of this Commonwealth and the due administration of justice among them ; seeing they have made such ample provision therefor May these walls remain consecrated to the pure administration of Justice, here may the injured always find redress, the oppressed be relieved, and the disturbers of public peace and welfare be brought to condign punishment,'

sleeping apartment of the assistant keeper, placed so as to afford him inspection of the area in front of the cells, and security from injury by the prisoners in case of revolt.

In April 1835, a part of the building was appropriated for the county gaol and the two upper stories of cells, with the rooms above and below the kitchen, were occupied for that purpose. A brick building, 40 feet by 16, in the yard, connected with the house, furnishes workshops in the two lower stories; the third story, having six rooms, is used for the confinement of females. There is also a wooden building, which has been used for working stone. By a recent order of the County Commissioners, all persons confined in the House of Correction, able to labor, are to be constantly employed according to their ability; if not acquainted with any mechanic trade, they work at the shoe business. Under this system, it is probable, the convicts will not only be able to remunerate the expense of their support, but may form habits of industry and derive moral improvement.

The following statement shows the condition of the House of Correction during years, each ending in November.

	1833.	1834	1835	1836.
Committed for crime,	5	15	11	14
for correction,	58	57	62	58
Discharged in the year,	48	54	56	68
Remaining, Nov 1,	15	18	17	21

Among those now in the establishment, are 3 lunatics sent from the hospital, and 5 insane persons supported there by their friends, with the consent of the Commissioners.

John F. Clark has been keeper from the commencement. Nathan Heard and John W. Lincoln, are overseers.

LUNATIC HOSPITAL. This monument of the enlightened charity of the government of the state, is situated on a beautiful eminence eastward of the town. The buildings of the west front, erected in 1831, consist of a centre, 76 feet long 40 feet wide, and four stories high, projecting 22 feet forward of the wings, which extend to the north and south ninety feet each on the front and 100 feet in the rear, are 36 feet wide, and three stories high. This arrangement was adopted so as to secure free communication with the central structure, occupied by the superintendent, steward, attendants, and domestics, and to permit the ventilation and lighting of the long halls reaching through the wings. The ranges of apartments for the insane, 8 feet by 10, have each a window with the upper sash of cast iron and lower sash of wood, both glazed; on the exterior of the wooden sash is a false sash of iron, corresponding in its appearance and dimensions, but firmly set into the frame, giving the reality of a grate without its gloomy aspect. In 1835, a building 134 feet in length and 34 feet in width was attached to the southern extremity of the hospital, of equal height, and extending eastward at right angles with the front; in 1836, another edifice of the same magnitude, was placed at the north end. Three sides of a great square are now enclosed by these immense structures of brick. Provision is made for the diffusion of heat, the circulation of air, the supply of water, and the most judicious regulations promote the health and comfort of the inmates.

In this hospital, those are placed under restraint by public authority, who are so furiously mad, that their liberty would endanger the safety of the community. To feel its value, one must have heard the chained maniacs howling in the dungeons of the common gaols, in frantic excitement and hopeless misery, and seen the quiet of the great establishment where the insane receive every alleviation of their mental diseases, which fit accommodations, remedial treatment, and high skill can bestow.

The institution has been under the superintendence of Dr. Samuel B. Woodward since its commencement. Its statistics are fully detailed in the reports annually made by the Trustees to the Legislature.

CHURCHES. The first house appropriated for public worship, was built like the log huts of the planters, and placed near the intersection of Green street by Franklin street, about 1717.

In 1719, a meeting house was built, under a contract with Mr. Constable, as architect, on the site of the present South Church. It was of respectable dimensions, but had no tower. At first, the area of the interior, floored, but otherwise unfinished, was occupied by benches. In 1723, a pulpit was set up, and the space divided into long seats; and soon after, galleries were provided. In 1733, it was voted ' that the front of the gallery, the pulpit, and pillars, be colored and varnished, and the outside of the doors and windows; and the town thankfully accepts the £8 offered by Col. Chandler, towards the same; and being informed that Daniel Gookin, Esq. has been pleased to say, he would give something to said work, voted, that a committee be desired to know of him what he will give towards said coloring and varnishing.' In 1743 a spire was erected.

In 1763 the *The Old South Meeting House* was built, 70 feet long, 55 feet wide, with 28 feet posts, at the expense of £1542. There were 61 square pews on the lower floor. That esteemed the best, on the west side of the pulpit, and directly under it, valued at £9, was assigned to Hon. John Chandler, as an acknowledgment of his donation of £10 towards erecting the church. The highest price paid for pews was £9, the lowest £4 10s. In front of the pulpit, were two long pews, one for the deacons, the other for aged persons; and along the head of the central aisle, were seven slips, for the free seats of men and women, placed on opposite sides. There were three porches, at the south, east, and west entrances, and a tower on the north surmounted by a spire, 130 feet high.

In the day of small things, the purchase of a bell was an important matter. After many conferences, the town and county united their funds for the purpose, and in May, 1739, it was agreed, that the town would pay £60 towards procuring a bell weighing not less than 300 pounds, and half the expense of a frame for hanging it near a small tree, a little north of Capt. Daniel Heywood's, about midway between the meeting house and court house, ' to serve the town as well as the county.' In 1740, difficulties arose in completing the arrangements; the partnership was dissolved; the town paid £140 pounds for the whole bell, and it was placed in the steeple.

The bell now used, cast by Revere and Sons, in Boston, in 1802, weighing 1975 pounds, bears this inscription,

' The living to the church I call,
And to the grave I summon all.'

The tower clock was made by Abel Stowell, in 1800.

The *Old South Church* has been enlarged, and is now 90 feet long, and 55 wide, having a vestry at the south end.

Unitarian Church The first Meeting House of the Second Congregational Society, near Antiquarian Hall, on Summer street, was built by Ignatius Goulding and Elias Blake, on land given to the parish, June 16, 1791, by Charles and Samuel Chandler. It was a plain and neat edifice of wood. A bell was purchased, and a tower clock presented by Isaiah Thomas, Esq., both removed, and still used on the new church.

The new brick meeting house on Main street, was erected at an expense of about $13,000, on land purchased of Isaiah Thomas, Esq. at the cost of $4000.[1] The foundation was laid August 11, 1828, when an address was delivered by the Rev. Mr. Hill,[2] and religious services performed by the Rev. Dr. Bancroft.

This building is 75 feet from east to west, and 68 feet from north to south : the walls 31 feet in height, and the tower, surmounted by a cupola, 125 feet high. The floor is divided into 104 pews. It was dedicated Aug. 20, 1829. The highest price paid for pews was $337, the lowest, $80. This church has an organ purchased for $2,000.

The *Calvinist Church*, on Main street, built in 1823, and enlarged in 1834, is 93 by 57 : the height of the spire 130 feet. There are 94 pews on the floor, which have been sold from $116 to $200 each. An organ has lately been purchased for $1700.

The *Union Church*, on Front street, built in 1836, is 90 by 54 feet in size, including a vestry, with a spire 130 feet high. The organ cost $1200.

The *Baptist Church*, east of the common, rebuilt in 1836, is 79 feet long, 50 wide, and has a spire 138 feet in height.

Christ Church, on Temple street, built in 1836, the Catholic place of worship, is a neat structure of the Grecian Doric order, 64 feet by 32, fronting to the south.

The *Methodist Church*, on Columbian avenue, built in 1836, 66 feet long and 48 feet wide, with a spire about 100 feet high.

The CENTRE SCHOOL HOUSE, on Main street, built in 1792, is about 60

---

[1] The following inscription was deposited under the corner stone of its foundation. ' This house was erected by the Unitarian Congregational Society, Worcester, for the worship of the one God, through the mediation of Jesus Christ. Foundation laid August 11, 1828. John Quincy Adams, President of the United States. Levi Lincoln, Governor of Massachusetts. Rev. Aaron Bancroft, D. D. and Rev. Alonzo Hill, Pastors. Frederick W. Paine, Esq., Rejoice Newton, Esq., Deac. Alpheus Merrifield, Col. Samuel Ward, Capt. George T. Rice, Capt. Lewis Barnard, Pliny Merrick, Esq., Building Committee. Elias Carter, Peter Kendall, Master Builders.

[2] Published in the National Ægis, August 13, 1828.

25*

by 30 feet, and its four apartments are occupied by the primary and female school of the district

The BRICK SCHOOL HOUSE, on Thomas street, built in 1832, 67 by 30 feet, is appropriated for the Latin grammar school, and higher boys schools.

The TOWN HALL, a neat brick building of fine architectural proportions, built in 1825, at an expense of about $10,000, is 54 by 64 feet The basement is occupied for keeping fire apparatus, and for stores. A large hall on the first floor is used for town meetings, religious exercises, and public lectures There are two spacious and neat halls on the second floor An address was delivered at the dedication, May 2, 1825, by Hon John Davis

ANTIQUARIAN HALL The centre building, erected by Isaiah Thomas, in 1819, is 46 feet long and 36 feet wide, with a cupola. Wings were extended in 1832, each 28 feet long and 21 feet wide.

WORCESTER COUNTY MANUAL LABOR HIGH SCHOOL The Academy building is of brick, two stories in height, with a basement, and is 45 feet by 60 in exterior dimensions The first story affords a convenient recitation room, and a chapel which may contain two hundred persons. The upper floor is divided into twelve rooms ; one for the instructors · one for library and apparatus , and ten, neatly furnished, for the accommodation of students A mansion with proper outbuildings has been erected in the vicinity of the Academy for the residence of the superintendent and students

PUBLIC LANDS The lands granted for the support of schools and the ministry by the proprietors, were sold, from time to time ; the proceeds invested ; and the interest, and finally the principal, applied to the purposes of the original appropriation.

The land near the meeting house was early reserved for a training field, and has remained open for military exercise and public exhibitions The location of the Norwich Railroad across this tract, will impair its use as a square, and leave no spot of the common territory susceptible of being converted into an ornamented ground for the use of the crowded population.

August 27, 1733, the proprietors voted ' that 100 acres of the poorest land of Millstone Hill, be left common for the use of the town for building stones ' A subsequent grant was made of the territory to Daniel Heywood. The Supreme Court have determined, that a perpetual interest in the land for the limited use of taking stone, passed to the town by the first grant. and the fee of the soil, subject to this use, to the grantee, by the second.[1]

BURIAL PLACES. The most ancient burial place of Worcester was north of the intersection of Thomas street with Summer street It is now included in the enclosure around the brick school house, and the children of the present generation frolic over the remains of those whose graves were earliest made. Rachel, daughter of John and Jean Kellough, was the first person who died in the town, Dec. 15, 1717 The number of deaths which occurred from that date to the time when another cemetery was occupied, were 28

[1] Inhabitants of Worcester vs. William E. Green, Pickering's Reports, ii 425.

Among them were some of the founders and first settlers They were laid beneath old oaks, which long shadowed their place of rest

The burying place bordering on the common, was opened in 1730, when Ephraim Roper, accidentally killed in hunting, was interred there When this became too populous for new occupation, another place of sepulture was provided, in 1795, on Mechanic street, and now adjoining the Boston Railroad In 1828, a tract of eight acres was purchased on the plain, east of Washington square, which has since been divided by the railroad A tract of about 20 acres, half a mile westward of the village, was purchased in 1835, laid out as a cemetery, and is to be ornamented with a belt of shade trees There is a grave yard between South Worcester and New Worcester [1]

FACE OF THE TOWN The whole surface is undulating, swelling into hills of moderate acclivity, with gentle slope and beautifully rounded outline From the eminences, the prospect is of the wide-spread and highly improved fields of a fertile soil. Better description cannot be given of the valley of Worcester, than by adopting the words of a writer of high authority. 'Apart from human culture,' says Prof Hitchcock, ' this geographical centre of Massachusetts would present no very striking attractions to the lover of natural scenery. But this valley possesses precisely those features which art is capable of rendering extremely fascinating And there is scarcely to be met with, in this or any other country, a more charming landscape than Worcester presents, from almost any of the moderately-elevated hills that surround it The high state of agriculture in every part of the valley, and the fine taste and neatness exhibited in all the buildings of this flourishing town, with the great elegance of many edifices, and the intermingling of so many and fine shade and fruit trees, spread over the prospect beauty of a high order, on which the eye delights to linger. I have never seen, in a community of equal extent, so few marks of poverty and human degradation, as in this valley. and it is this aspect of comfort and independence among all classes, that enhances greatly the pleasure with which every true American heart contemplates this scene since it must be considered as exhibiting the happy influence of our free institutions '[2]

PONDS AND STREAMS Along the eastern boundary of Worcester, and partly within its territory, lies Quinsigamond Pond, sometimes called Long Pond, a beautiful sheet of water, which, in any other country, would be dignified with the name of *lake* It extends from north to south, in crescent form, about four miles in length, presenting, by reason of disproportionate breadth, the appearance of a noble river, with bold banks, covered with wood, or swelling into green hills There are twelve islands, varying in extent from a few square rods of surface to many acres Some of them, of singular

[1] The burial places have been heretofore enclosed in rude fences, and overgrown with wild grass and briars That strange taste, which disgraces the living, by placing senseless or inappropriate inscriptions on the monumental stones of the dead, has rarely left examples of its perversity here. Nor are there epitaphs distinguished by any singular merit, worthy of being transcribed

[2] Report on the Geology of Massachusetts, 100

beauty, are still clothed with their original forests. At the south end, the waters, with those of Half Moon, Round, and Flint's Pond, which are connected with Quinsigamond, flow out in a southeasterly direction into the town of Grafton, forming the stream anciently called 'Nipnapp River,' now the Little Blackstone, a principal tributary to the main stream. When the Blackstone canal was constructed, the ponds were raised by a dam, and made a reservoir for that work.[1]

The southern part of Quinsigamond and most of its fair islands, lie within the limits of Shrewsbury. The northern part is principally in Worcester.[2]

North Pond, situated in that part of the town indicated by its name, lies principally in district No. 12, and is the reservoir of the summit level of the Blackstone Canal. It is the source of the stream called in the old records, Danson's, Mill, and Bimelick Brook, which passes through the village on its way to join the Blackstone River. The original surface has been estimated at 30 acres; the dams and embankment raised around, now extend it to about 200 acres.

Bladder Pond has the shape described by its appellation. It is situated on the northeast part of Chandler hill, and contains five or six acres. The surface has been gradually diminishing, as the roots of vegetation have stretched themselves over its waters, forming a floating belt around, on which it would be dangerous to tread.

These are all the natural ponds within the territory of Worcester. Many have been created, by artificial means, for manufacturing purposes.

The valley of Worcester is drained through the channel of the Blackstone River, which is divided into branches, themselves subdivided, intersecting the whole territory with veins of water, so that there is scarcely a farm which has not rill, rivulet, or brook, within its boundaries. Beginning at the southwest

---

[1] An estimate of the quantity of water contained in this reservoir, between high and low water mark, exhibiting the extent of surface, has been kindly furnished by Henry Snow, Esq. of Shrewsbury, made from actual admeasurement by that accurate surveyor. Low water is estimated at 2 feet 10 inches above the bottom of the floom at the Irish Dam, for all waters below the neck of Quinsigamond, and 1 foot 5 inches above the bottom of the floom at that point, for all above.

	Surface. acres.	rods.	Depth. feet.	inches.	Cubic feet.
Above the old Road,	28	120	2	0	2501700
Quinsigamond,	437	06	3	3	61871398
"	17	31	2	3	1746415
Half Moon Pond,	14	155	3	3	2119126
"	2	00	2	3	196020
Flooded Meadow and River,	202	18	2	4	20542714
Round Pond,	6	50	3	3	893660
Flint's Pond,	45	147	3	3	6500717
"	36	125	2	0	3204382

Making 99379135 cubic feet, rejecting minute fractions. About 21 millions of cubic feet cannot be drawn down by reason of the back water from the pond of the New England Village Factory.

[2] A full description of this Pond will be found in Ward's History of Shrewsbury, in Worcester Magazine, ii. 8.

corner of Worcester, we meet the *Kettle Brook*, flowing southwardly into
Ward, and after a little progress further, we strike the main stream into which
this brook empties, returning to the north, and called on the ancient records
French River, till it reaches New Worcester, there it receives the waters of
Tatnuck Brook and of *Beaver Brook*, both coming from Holden, and joining
together before they unite to the river. After their junction, the river flows
eastward about a mile and a half, and was called *Halfway River*, to the point
where it receives the stream named on the proprietary records, usually *Mill
Brook*, sometimes *Danson's Brook*, and very rarely *Bimelick*. This tributary,
receiving *Weasle Brook* soon after it flows out from its source in North Pond,
goes in a southerly direction through the village; from the junction, the main
stream, swelled to a considerable volume, sometimes having the appellation of
Nipmuck River, but usually called *Blackstone*, flows by a southeasterly course
into Millbury.

Among the tributaries of Mill Brook, near the town *Pine Meadow Brook*,
bringing water from Bladder Pond, a minute stream, falls in near the Brew-
ery. and *Bear Brook*, scarcely larger, flows back of the brick school house
on Thomas street.

HILLS. Along the western boundary of the town, extends a chain of
rounded highlands, the seat of Indian villages of yore, called by the natives
Tataesset, and now known as Tatnuck. In the north part of the town is
Winter Hill, in district No 10 ; *Mount Ararat*, beyond North Pond, in district No. 12, and the ridge forming the northern wall of the valley, named on
the records *Indian Hill*. *Millstone Hill*, northeast from the town, is an immense quarry of granite, presenting a remarkable geological structure of layers, spread over each other in circular form like the coats of an onion. *Chandler Hill* lies east of the town, and *Oak Hill* southeast. Nearly south, and
forming one margin of the valley of the Blackstone, is *Sagatabscot*, where
Jonas Rice first built. Opposite, and across the river, is the huge mound of
Packachoag Hill, extending far into Ward. *Wigwam Hill*, is a rounded eminence on the western shore and near the head of Quinsigamond.

MINES AND MINERALS. About the middle of the last century, a mania
for mining prevailed, almost as ruinous as that for speculation an hundred
years later. Tired of the slow process of acquiring wealth by cultivating the
surface of the earth, its possessors were enticed to dig into its bosom for
treasures. The precious metals were the object of the search, and mining
operations, began almost simultaneously in Worcester, Sterling, Templeton,
and many other towns of the county, terminated, from want of science and
skill, in total failure.

In 1754, a vein of metal which was supposed to be silver, was discovered
near the head of the valley, about a mile north of the town. A company for
exploring the spot was formed by some of the most substantial inhabitants.
Furnaces and smelting houses were erected, and a cunning German employed
as superintendent. Under his direction, a shaft was sunk 80 feet perpendic-
ularly, and a horizontal gallery extended about as far through the rock, which

was to be intersected by another shaft, commenced about six rods north of the first opening. Among the masses, which within a few years laid around the scene of operation, were specimens of the ores containing a minute portion of silver, specks of copper and lead, much iron, and an extraordinary quantity of arsenic. When struck against steel, a profusion of vivid sparks are thrown out, and the strong and peculiarly disagreeable odor of the latter mineral emitted. On the application of heat, this perfume increases to an overpowering extent. The company expended great sums in blasting the rock, raising its fragments, and erecting buildings and machinery. While the pile of stones increased, the money of the partners diminished. The furnaces in full blast, produced nothing but suffocating vapors, curling over the flames in those beautiful coronets of smoke which still attend the attempt to melt the ore. The shrewd foreigner, in whose promises the associates seem to have placed that confidence which honest men often repose on the declarations of knaves, became satisfied that the crisis was approaching when it would be ascertained that the funds were exhausted, and that stone and iron could not be transmuted to gold. Some papers which exist, indicate that he pretended to knowledge in the occult sciences as well as skill in the art of deception. However this may be, he assured the company, that the great enemy of man had been busy in defeating their exertions, making his presence redolent in the perfumes of sulphur and arsenic. He obtained the sum of $100, and made a journey to Philadelphia, to consult with a person experienced in mines and their dæmons, for the purpose of exorcising the unsavory spirit of the crucible. He departed with a barrel full of the productions of the mine, but never returned to state the results of his conference. The proprietors abandoned the work, when they were waked by the reality of the loss from the dream of fortune, and afterwards destroyed the records of their credulity.

A much more valuable source of wealth is in the *Anthracite Coal*. A deposit of this mineral exists about two miles northeast from the town. It was long converted into a paint, under the name of *Black Lead*, and furnished a cheap and durable covering for roofs and for the exterior of buildings exposed to the weather. In 1826, it was partially explored and began to be worked by Col. Amos Binney. It was found to be a valuable combustible, suitable, even in the impure state presented by the upper strata, for furnaces and places where intense heat and great fires were required. Engagements of business, and local circumstances, induced him to suspend the prosecution of the undertaking. Since his decease, the mineral, which might be made to give motion to the wheels of manufacturing and mechanic industry to unlimited extent, has been permitted to rest undisturbed in its bed.

The rock in which the Worcester Anthracite occurs, is termed by Prof. Hitchcock, an imperfect kind of mica slate, and called by Humboldt, transition mica slate, having a moderate dip to the north east. Although the coal is considered by him as inferior to that of Pennsylvania and Rhode Island, its specific gravity is greater than that from those states. He expresses the opinion that ' it will be considered by posterity, if not by the present generation, as a treasure of great value, and adds, ' I can hardly believe, that a coal, which contains probably not less than 90 per centum of carbon, should not be employed, in some way or other, as valuable fuel."[1]

Beds of *clay* are abundant. In the north and west parts of the town, about four millions of bricks have been made from this material during the year.

Soapstone of good quality has been discovered, and a narrow vein was worked, in the south east part of Worcester, though not with success. Pots of this material, used by the Indians for cooking, are sometimes turned up by the plough.

Peat is found in many meadows and as the supply of wood is diminished, may be advantageously used as fuel.

Among the minerals of scientific interest are *Idocrase*, accompanied by small, pale green crystals of *Pyoxene, Epidote,* and *Garnets* of a wine yellow color, *Asbestus, Amianthoid, Plumbago,* and veins of *Pyritous Iron* were found in working the coal mine. *Carbonate of Iron, Arsenical Sulphuret of Iron,* massive and crystalized, and *Sulphuret of Lead,* were once abundant around the old silver mine. *Macle* sometimes occurs in argillaceous slate.

The quarry of granite on Millstone hill, has furnished building material for a century, and the excavation now extends over two or three acres. The rock is composed almost entirely of gray quartz and white foliated feldspar, with very little mica, and differs only from the sienite of Quincy in the absence of hornblende. The only distinct example of apparent stratification of granite found in the state, by Prof. Hitchcock,[2] was in this locality, and from the strata conforming on all sides to the slope of the land, being horizontal at the apex, and extending over the sides in concentric flakes, he infers that the hill is an enormous concretion. The rock is crossed by natural seams, dividing it into layers nearly parallel at the quarry, from one foot to two feet in thickness, and easily split by wedges. The surfaces are blackened with iron, which forms a crust on the exterior, called by the workmen 'the bark' from the admixture of the same metal in the composition, the faces of the blocks, when cut, become discolored on exposure to the weather.

A quarry is extensively worked on the south end of Sagatabscot hill, called the 'South Ledge.' The rock is of light color, of the geological character of *Granitic Gneiss,* entirely free from iron, wrought with facility, and often beautifully veined. The hewn fronts of buildings of this material on Main street, would advantageously compare in elegance with the marble edifices of the cities.

[1] Report on the Geology of Massachusetts, 55 [2] ib. 162

MISCELLANEOUS.

—

CHAPTER XIX.

Municipal Officers. Selectmen. Clerks. Treasurers. Representatives. Fire Department. Fires and accidents by lightning.

Selectmen chosen since 1722.[1]

Nathaniel Moore	1722, 25—30, [32—35, 40	Thomas Stearns	1748
Nathaniel Jones	1722, 23	John Chandler, jr.	1748—59, 61—[73
Benjamin Flagg	1722, 23, 26, 28, [34, 35, 37—40, 43—51	Daniel Ward	1752, 53
Jonas Rice	1722, 24, 28, 30, 32, [34, 35, 38, 40	Elisha Smith	1752
John Gray	1722, 24	John Curtis	1754, 55, 60
Henry Lee	1723	Nathaniel Moore, jr.	1754
John Hubbard	1723	Jonathan Lynds	1754
Benjamin Flagg, jr.	1723, 25, 30—[32	Timothy Paine	1754—63, 66—74
Gershom Rice	1724, 27, 31, 33, 36, [39, 46	John Boyden	1754, 65
James Taylor	1724, 26, 35, 39	Gardner Chandler	1754—56
Daniel Heywood	1724, 26, 27, 29, [31,34,35,38,40,42—46.48—53	Tyrus Rice	1755
Moses Leonard	1725, 26	Israel Jennison	1756—58, 61
James McLellan	1725	Josiah Brewer	1756, 62, 63
James Holden	1725, 29, 30, 33, 36	William Young	1757, 74—77
William Jennison	1727—31, 33, [35, 37, 38, 41	Asa Moore	1757—62
James Rice	1728	Daniel Boyden	1759, 62
Zephaniah Rice	1729	James Goodwin	1759
Palmer Goulding	1731, 37, 41, 43	James Putnam	1760
James Moore	1732, 36, 39, 41	Jonathan Stone	1760, 67, 68, 72, [75—77
John Stearns	1732, 36, 41	Jacob Chamberlain	1761
John Chandler	1733—35, 37—40, [42—53	Ephraim Doolittle	1763—66
Gershom Rice, jr.	1736	Samuel Miller	1763—65, 75, 81, 82
Joshua Child	1737	Jacob Hemenway	1764
Solomon Johnson	1742	Palmer Goulding	1764, 65, 71
Elijah Cook	1742	Samuel Mower	1765
Joshua Eaton	1742	Josiah Pierce	1765, 74—76
Thomas Wheeler	1743—45, 49—[51, 53, 73, 74, 79	Samuel Curtis	1766, 75, 90—94
John Chadwick	1744, 45	Benjamin Flagg	1766—77
Daniel Ward	1746—47	Micah Johnson	1769
Joshua Bigelow	1747, 67—73, 75, [78	Nathan Baldwin	1770
James Boyd	1747	David Bigelow	1776, 77, 79, 80, [83, 84
		Nathan Perry	1777, 81—83, 85—89
		Benjamin Stowell	1777
		John Kelso	1777
		Ebenezer Lovell	1778, 79, 84
		Robert Smith	1778, 79
		William Stearns	1778, 79
		Nathaniel Brooks	1778, 79, 84

[1] When this mark — is placed between the dates, it indicates that the person was elected in the successive years between one and the other.

John Green	1780	Nathaniel Stowell	1816—1821
Jonathan Rice	1780	John Flagg	1816—1820, 21, 27,
Joseph Barber	1780		[28, 33, 31
Edward Crafts	1780	Peter Slater	1818—1821
William McFarland	1781, 82	George Moore	1821—23
Samuel Brown	1781, 82	John Gleason, jr.	1822—25
John Gleason	1781, 82	Edward D Bangs	1823, 24
Joseph Allen	1783	Joel Gleason	1824
Joseph Wheeler	1783, 87—91	Otis Corbett	1825, 26, 39
Samuel Brooks	1784—93	John W Lincoln	1825, 26, 33—
Daniel Goulding	1784, 95, 96, 98		[35
John Chamberlain	1785—95, 97, 98,	Daniel Stone	1825, 26
	[1801, 02	Pliny Merrick	1827—29, 35
Jesse Taft	1785, 86	Thomas Chamberlain	1827—29
Daniel Band	1785—89	Frederic W. Paine	1827, 31
Samuel Flagg	1790—1805, 1807	Benjamin Butman	1828, 29, 31, 35
Benjamin Heywood	1792—97, 99,	Alpheus Merrifield	1829—32
	[1800	Lewis Chapin	1829, 35, 36
Nathaniel Paine	1794—1802	Asahel Bellows	1830
Phineas Jones	1796, 97	Lewis Barnard	1830
David Andrews	1798—1802	Henry Heywood	1831, 32
Ephraim Mower	1799—1810, 15—	Benjamin Flagg	1831
	[17	Luther Burnett, jr.	1831
Edward Bangs	1803—1808	Charles Allen	1832
Joseph Holbrook	1803—1806	Guy S. Newton	1832—35
Nathaniel Harrington	1803—1809	Jonathan Harrington	1832, 33
Nathan White	1806—1819	Alfred D Foster	1833
Thomas Nichols	1808—1815	Samuel B. Thomas	1834
Abraham Lincoln	1809—1824	Simon S. Gates	1835, 36
William Eaton	1810—1813, 20—	Ebenezer L Barnard	1835, 36
	[22, 25—28, 30	Thomas Kinnicutt	1836
John Gleason	1811—1815	Artemas Ward	1836
William Chamberlain	1814, 22—	E. H. Hemenway	1836
	[24	Thomas Harback	1836

Town Clerks since 1722.

1722	Jonas Rice	1781	Daniel Goulding
1723	Benjamin Flagg	1783	William G Maccarty
1724	Jonas Rice	1783	Daniel Goulding
1729	Zephaniah Rice	1787	Theophilus Wheeler
1730	Benjamin Flagg.	1792	Daniel Goulding
1731	Jonas Rice	1796	Leonard Worcester, protem
1753	Daniel Heywood.	1797	Daniel Goulding
1754	Timothy Paine	1800	Oliver Fiske
1764	John Chandler	1803	Daniel Goulding.
1768	Clark Chandler	1808	Enoch Flagg
1775	Nathan Baldwin.	1816	Levi Heywood.
1778	William Stearns	1818	Benjamin Chapin
1780	Nathaniel Heywood.	1833	Samuel Jennison
1780	Joseph Allen.	1836	Charles A. Hamilton

26

Town Treasurers since 1722.

1722	Daniel Heywood.	1775	Nathan Perry.
1723	Henry Lee.	1778	John Green.
1724	Daniel Heywood.	1780	William Gates.
1725	Nathaniel Moore.	1781	Nathan Perry.
1726	James Taylor.	1790	Samuel Flagg.
1727	Henry Lee.	1791	Benjamin Heywood.
1729	Nathaniel Moore.	1795	Samuel Chandler.
1731	William Jennison.	1798	Oliver Fiske.
1732	Daniel Heywood.	1799	Theophilus Wheeler.
1736	Gershom Rice, jr.	1803	Samuel Flagg.
1737	Palmer Goulding.	1808	Levi Lincoln, jr.
1739	Benjamin Flagg.	1815	James Wilson.
1741	John Chandler.	1829	Samuel Jennison.
1752	John Chandler, jr.	1830	Asa Hamilton.
1760	John Curtis.	1832	Charles A. Hamilton.
1761	John Chandler, jr.	1833	Charles G. Prentiss.

Representatives chosen since 1727.

Nathaniel Jones	1727	William Eaton	1822—25, 27—30
William Jennison	1728—30	Samuel Harrington	1823
Benjamin Flagg	1731, 43, 44, 46—	Otis Corbett	1824, 26—28, 30, 31,
	[51		[35
John Chandler, jr.	1732—35, 38,	John W. Lincoln	1824—26, 32—34
	[39, 52, 53	Samuel M. Burnside	1826
John Chandler	1736, 37, 40, 42,	Pliny Merrick	1827
	[63—65	Rejoice Newton	1828—30
Timothy Paine	1755—57, 59—62	Benjamin Chapin	1829
	[88, 89	Charles Allen	1829, 32, 33
Palmer Goulding	1741	Frederick W. Paine	1829
Ephraim Doolittle	1766, 67	Alfred D. Foster	1831—34
Joshua Bigelow	1768—74	Jubal Harrington	1831, 35
Ebenezer Lovell	1777	Lewis Chapin	1832, 33
David Bigelow	1777	Winsor Hatch	1832, 33
John Green	1777	Silas Brooks	1832
Ezekiel Howe	1777	John Flagg	1833, 34
Samuel Curtis	1778—85, 1802,	Thomas Kinnicutt	1834, 36
	[1804, 1806	Thomas Chamberlain	1834—36
Samuel Brooks	1786, 87	David T. Brigham	1834
Samuel Flagg	1790—98, 1805, 07	Samuel B. Thomas	1834
Levi Lincoln, sen.	1796	Thomas Harback	1835
Nathaniel Paine	1799—1801	Benjamin Goddard, 2d.	1835, 36
Edward Bangs	1803—11	Benjamin Flagg	1835
Ephraim Mower	1806—1810	William Lincoln	1835, 36
Nathan White	1808, 1812—15	Guy S. Newton	1835
Abraham Lincoln	1809—1823	John Coe	1836
William Eaton	1811—1813	David Wadsworth	1836
Levi Lincoln, jr.	1814—17, 20, 22	Ebenezer L. Barnard	1836
Edward D. Bangs	1810, 17, 20, 24	Edward H. Hemenway	1836

FIRE DEPARTMENT. By the Act of Feb. 26, 1835, accepted by the town, a fire department was established in Worcester. Engineers were appointed by the selectmen, who are authorised to exercise the same duties in relation to engine men as the selectmen before possessed, and the same power as to the extinguishment of fires before belonging to firewards

The Department was organized in May, 1835 nine engineers and three assistants were appointed There are six fire companies, attached to as many engines, with these numbers, names, and stations 1 Hero, at Quinsigamond Village 2 Rapid, at New Worcester · 3 Despatch, at Lincoln Square 4 Torrent, at the Town Hall 5 Extinguisher, in Goddard's Row 6 Lafayette, on Columbian Avenue The Hook and Ladder company have their apparatus on the common. Isaac Davis, Esq is chief engineer.

FIRES, AND INJURIES BY LIGHTNING.

1767, May 25 The dwelling house of Mr James Barber, and all his goods, were consumed The fire was occasioned by a defect of the oven

1778, Feb 21. A fire broke out in the house of Francis Cutting, but being timely discovered, was extinguished

1782, Nov 2 The blacksmith's shop of Ebenezer Chapin, was burnt

1784, July 10. The house of Bezaleel Stearns, in the Gore, was entirely destroyed The owner was at work in the fields at a distance, his wife, having put fire in the oven, went out on a visit to a neighbor On her return, dwelling, furniture, clothing, and every article of property had disappeared, and nothing but ashes remained

1786, Jan 26 The house of Capt Samuel Flagg, on the site of that now owned by Hon Charles Allen, was burnt to the ground in the night · the furniture was saved, but many articles of wearing apparel consumed. At this time there was no fire engine in town

1791, July 4. The pearlash works of Messrs Chandlers, on the farm, in 1836, of Abiel Jaques, Esq., took fire by reason of the excessive heat in the furnace the day preceding, but the progress of the flames was arrested without great injury

1793, Jan 4 The weaver's shop of Cornelius and Peter Stowell, with more than 2000 yards of cloth, and the stock for 700 yards more, were consumed The loss was estimated at £300

1798, March 19 The hatter's shop of Jacob Harrington was discovered to be on fire A brand had been left standing, being separated by burning, it fell on the floor, and communicated flames to the roof, which were subdued by great exertions

1799, June 26 During a severe tempest, resembling in violence the hurricanes of the West Indies, the lightning struck a building directly back of the Court House, then occupied by Isaiah Thomas, in which were stored the types for the 12mo edition of the Bible. The electric fluid, in four distinct veins, pervaded the whole structure, splintering spar and stud, scattering bricks and mortar, and bursting away boards, laths, and plastering.[1]

1801, May 22. In the immediate vicinity of the former injury, the lightning struck a large elm tree, close by the residence of Judge Edward Bangs, on Main street, owned in 1836 by Isaac Davis and William Pratt. One stream, descending from the tree, entered the house, broke two looking glasses, and the furniture, and passed through an apartment in which were seven persons, without doing them hurt. Another branch went to the adjoining house, and a female was rendered apparently lifeless for sometime by its effects. The third vein went down the trunk of the tree and expended its force in the earth.

1805, Aug. 11. The Court House, of loftier elevation than either of the buildings in the near neighborhood which had been struck, at length experienced a visitation of the same calamity. The lightning touched the front pediment, threw off the shingles, shivered the diamond glass of the large eastern window, shattered the venetian blind, and splintered the style of the great door.

1805, Nov. 6. The hatter's shop of Nathaniel Mower, on the site occupied in 1836, by the block of stores of Hon. Daniel Waldo, was destroyed by fire.

1811, May 20. A dwelling house of Silas Bigelow was burnt.

1815, Jan. 12. The loss occasioned by the burning of the carding factory of Earle and Williams, on the site of the Court Mills, was estimated at $4000.

1815, Feb. 18. The most destructive conflagration experienced in this town, broke out on the west side of Main street, amid the violence of a severe storm, when the depth of snow, strength of wind, and intensity of cold, cooperated to render the efforts to arrest its progress unavailing. The house, store, and merchandize of Samuel Brazer, and the dwelling house, bake house, and out buildings of Enoch and Elisha Flagg, were consumed. The aggregate loss exceeded $10,000. The inhabitants subscribed $2700, and $1800 were contributed in other places, for the relief of the principal sufferers.

1816, Feb. 15. A house, wheelwright's shop and barn of Nathaniel Flagg, 2d, and the store of Jonathan Knight, at Adams square, were burnt. Loss, $2000.

1821, May 2. The house of Daniel Chadwick, about three quarters of a mile north from the court house, was struck by lightning. The fluid, descending by the chimney, killed a dog on the hearth, but the inmates of the dwelling escaped uninjured.

1824, Dec. 24. The old Brown & Butman tavern house, north of Lincoln square, which had been unoccupied for three or four years, and then belonging to Stephen Salisbury, Esq., was set on fire by an incendiary, in the night, and destroyed.

1825, May 7. A large blacksmith's shop of Levi Howe was burnt, and a loss of $800 occasioned.

---

[1] A detailed account of the effects of this accident will be found in the Mass. Spy, July 3 and July 10, 1799.

1825, July 4 The new two story dwelling house of Moses Whipple, on Grafton street, was struck by lightning and consumed, with part of the furniture and the joiner's tools of its owner An apprentice who was working in a room occupied as a carpenter's shop, was stunned by the shock, and on recovering, found the apartment enveloped in flames Loss, $1500

1827, Feb 28 The lower paper mill of Elijah Burbank, about 50 feet in length, was set on fire by the spontaneous combustion of cotton waste, and the upper story, with a large quantity of stock, destroyed Loss $500

1827, April 11 The joiner s shop of Zenas Studley, on Prospect street, was burnt on Sunday afternoon. A barn adjoining was destroyed, and the dwelling house of Mr Stowell, near by, injured. Loss $1500.

1829, July 30 A barn of John and Abel Flagg, in District No 6, was set on fire by lightning, and consumed, with the whole crop of hay and a valuable horse

1830, Feb 6. On Saturday evening, the dwelling house and store of Oliver Harrington, in New Worcester, were burned

1830, Sept 5. On Sunday morning, about 3 o'clock, a fire broke out in the store in Goddard's block, occupied by George M Rice & Co. The interior, and the goods, insured for $6000, were burned The damage to the building was about $600.

1831, Jan 7. The hatter's shop of J P Kettell & Co was set on fire Loss $200

1831, Aug 19. The two story house and barn of William Stowell, in New Worcester, were burned

1832, March 11 A dwelling house on Mechanic street, owned by Luther Burnett, was set on fire, and destroyed Loss $700.

1834, Jan 27. The dry house of the woolen factory of W B. Fox & Co. took fire, but was extinguished Loss about $500

1834, Sept 11 The house, bake house, and barn, of Andrew March, at the corner of Main and School streets, took fire about midnight, and were destroyed. Loss $3500.

1835, Feb. 5 A small factory in the southwest part of the town, belonging to Ira Bryant, was burnt. Loss, $1500

1836, May 21. About 1 o'clock of the morning, flames broke out in the Baptist Meetinghouse, and spread so rapidly, that in little more than half an hour not a stick of timber of the church was left standing The origin was attributed to an incendiary.

Other inconsiderable fires, and accidents by lightning, have occurred. but the principal are enumerated.

26*

APPENDIX.

[See page 10]

I PETITION FOR A PLANTATION AT QUINSIGAMOND
October 8, 1665.

To the right worshipfull Governor, the deputy Governor, together with the worshipfull Magistrates, and the Deputies, assembled in General Court at Boston, 11th Oct 1665 The petition of Thomas Noyes, John Haynes, Josiah Haynes, of Sudbury, and Nathaniel Treadaway, of Watertown, Humbly Sheweth, That your Petitioners, having purchased several parcels of land without the limits of any Plantation, in the Wilderness, lying to the Westward of the Plantation called Maurlborrow, and the sayd lands being to the quantity of about five Thousand acres, by reason of distance from any plantation, is not so profitable to your petitioners as it might bee, and whereas, the sayd lands do ly in a very convenient place for a plantation, and other lands lying adjoining thereto, sufficient to make a plantation, which will be very beneficiall to the countrey, lying in the new and most direct way to Connectequot, neare unto Quansigamug Pond, and will be a meanes to advance the worth and benefitt of your Petitioner's lands, and make them more usefull to themselves, and more beneficiall to their posterity, which are many, the lands being very good, were they in a way of improvement, and divers friendes and neighbors being very desirous to enter upon the same, to whom it will probably be very beneficiall

Your Petitioners, from these and equivalent consideracons, are animated and incouraged to petition this honored Court, seriously to weigh the premises, and doe humbly intreat and desire, if in your wisdomes you shall see meet, a grant of a plantation, there to be sett up, and for that end, to appoint a committee to view the same, and lay out the bounds thereof, and for the settlement of it, which wee hope will bee both acceptable and beneficiall to the whole, and your Petitioners, as in duty bound, shall ever pray, &c,

Thomas Noyes   Josiah Haynes.
John Haynes   Nathaniel Treadaway

[See page 10]

II ORDER OF THE GREAT AND GENERAL COURT.
October 11, 1665

This Court, understanding by the Petition of Thomas Noyes, John Haynes, Josiah Haynes of Sudbury, and Nathaniel Treadaway, of Watertown, hereunto affixed, that there is a meete place for a Plantation, about ten miles from Marlborow, westward, at or neer Quansetamug Pond, which, that it may be improved for that end, and not spoiled by granting-uge of farms, in answer to the forsaid petition, This Court doth order, that there should be a quantitie of eight miles square layd out and reserved thereabout, in the Court's dispose, for a plantation, for the encouragement of such persons as shall appear, any time within three years from the date hereof, beeing men approved of by this Court; and that Capt Edward Johnson, Lieutenant Joshua ffisher, and Lieut Thomas Noyes, shall, and hereby are appointed and empowered to lay out the same, and to be payd by such persons as shall appear within the terme above expressed   The Deputies have past this with reference to the consent of our honored Magistrates hereto   William Torrey, clerk.

11 8, 1665

The Magistrates consent to a survey of the place petitioned for, and that Captaine Gookin doe joine with thise mentioned of our brethren the deputies, and make returu of their survey to the next General Court of Elections, who may take order therein as they shall see meete, then brethren the deputys hereto consenting   Edw'd Rawson, Sect'y

Consented to by the deputies.   William Torrey, Cleric

[See page 10]

III ORDER OF THE GREAT AND GENERAL COURT

MAY 15, 1667

Whereas, this Court, upon the petition of Ensigne Thomas Noyes and others, did nominate and appoint Capt. Gookin and some other Gentlemen, to view a place about tenn miles westward from Marlborough, at or about a place called Quansigamon Ponds, and to make report to this Court whether the place was capable of making a plantation (as it is informed to be), which work hitherto hath been neglected, through the death of Thomas Noyes and other impediments It is therefore ordered by this Court, that Capt Daniel Gookin, Capt Edward Johnson, Mr Samuel Andrew, Mr Andrew Belchar, senr or any three of them, be desired and empowered as a committee, to take an exact view of the said place, as soone as conveniently they cann, and to make a true report to this Court, whether it be capable to make a village, and what number of familyes (they conceive) may be there accommodated And if they finde it fitt for a plantation, then to offer unto this Court some meete expedient how the same may be settled and improved for the publie good, and this Court doth prohibit the laying out of any grants in the sayd place until the Comittee have made returne, which the Court would have done by ye next session of this Court if it may be

---

[See page 16]

IV FIRST INDIAN DEED.

JULY 13, 1674

Bee it known to all men by this present writing, that Wee, John, alias Horrawanuomit, or Quiquonassett, Sagamore of Pakachoge, and Solomon, alias Woonaskochu, Sagamore of Tatacssit, together with the consent of our kindred and people, and for and in consideration of twelve pounds of lawful money of New England, or the full value thereof, in other specie, to our content, within three months after the date hereof well and truly to be paid, and satisfied, and pt whereof, viz two coats and four yards of trading cloth, valewed at twenty six shill wee do acknowledge to have received in hand, as earnest, of Daniel Gookin senr of Cambr Esqr and of Daniel Hinchman, of Boston Brewer, in behalf of themselves and Capt Thomas Prentice, and Lt Richard Beers, and the rest of the Genll Court's Comittee, appointed for the management of a new plantation granted by the said Court, conteyning eight miles square, or the contents thereof, being to the westward of Marlborough, near Quansiquamond Ponds, and on each side of the Roadway leading towards Connecticott, Now know ye, yt wee, ye sd Jno and Solomon, Sagamores aforesaid, and upon the terms aforesaid, have bargained, sold, aliened, enfeoffed, and confirmed, unto ye sd Daniel Gookin, Thomas Prentice, Daniel Hinchman, Richard Beers, and ye rest of the people admitted, or to be admitted, by ye sd comittee to be inhabitants of yt new plantation, and to their heirs, executors, admrs, and assigns for ever, in fee simple, all and every pt of our civil or natural right, in all and singular the broken up land and woodlauds, woods, trees, rivers, brooks, ponds, swamps, meadows, mineralls, or any other thing, or things whatsoever, lying and being within that tract of land, conteyning eight miles square or the contents thereof, to be layd out by ye sd persons or their order in time convenient To have and to hold the premises, and every pt thereof, unto them the sd Daniel

Gookin, Thomas Prentice, Daniel Hinchman, and Richard Beers, and all ye rest of ye sd Inhabitants admitted or to be admitted planters there, and unto ym and yr heirs forever, freely and absolutely, without any lett, molestation, or disturbance, of us, or any of our kindred or people, or any claiming by, from, or under us, for evermore, as our heyrs or assigns, and wee do promise, upon the finishing ye payment, to make full and ample deeds and writings for the same, according to law   In witness of the truth hereof, wee ye said John and Solomon, alias Horrowanonitt and Wocannaskochu, have herennto set our hands and seals, this thirteenth day of July 1674.

Signed, Sealed and delivered }   Solomon, alias Woonnasakochu, seal and mark
in the presence of us,   }   John, alias Hoorrawanwit, mark and seal

    Onnamog, his mark, Sagamore of Occonomesett
    Namphow, his mark, Sagamore of Wamesett.
    Joseph Thatcher, of Chabanakonchoie, his mark
    Nosannowitt, his mark   Noah Wiswall, present
    Full payment rec'd August 20, 1676   D Gookin
This deed acknowledged by the Sagamores, before Daniel Gookin, Sen Assist   July 13.
Entered, 9   2.   83 by Thomas Danforth, R.

[See page 24]

V   ORDER OF COUNCIL TO CAPT EDWARD HUTCHINSON.

July 27, 1675

The Council, being informed that the Narraganset Indians are come down with about 100 armed men into the Nipmuck Country, Do order you, Capt Edward Hutchinson, to take with you Capt Thomas Wheeler, and his party of horse, with Ephraim Curtis for a guide, and a sufficient interpreter, and forthwith to repaire into those parts, and theie labour to get a right understanding of the motions of the Narraganset Indians and of the Indians of Nipmuck, and for that end to demand of the leaders of the Narraganset Indians an account of the grounds of their marching in that country, and require to understand the orders of their Sachems   And also, to demand an account of the Nipmuck Indians, why they have not sent down their Sagamore, according to their promise unto our Messenger, Ephraim Curtis. And further, let them know that we are informed, that there are some among them, that have actually joyned with our enemies in the murder and spoile made upon the English by Philip. And that Matoonus and his complices, who have robbed and murdered our people about Mendon, are now among them, And that we require them to deliver up to you, or forthwith bring into us, those our enemies, otherwise we must look at them to bee no friends to us, but ayders and abbetors, and unto all these things you shall require their expresse answer, and as soon as you have dispatched this affayre, you are to return home and give us an account   So desiring the Lord's presence with you, and in the prosecution of this affair, if you should meet with any Indians, that stande in opposition to you, or declare themselves to be your enemy, then you are ordered to ingage with them, if you see reason for it, and endeavour to reduce them by force of arms

---

[See page 25]

VI.   ORDER OF COUNCIL

Sept 15, 1675.

At a meeting of the Council, Sept the 15, 1675, It is ordered by the Council, that Ephraim Curtis, hath hereby liberty, together with such other English men as he shall procure, provided they be not less in number than thirty men well armed, the said Curtis with his company aforesaid, are allowed to gather and improve for their own use all the Indian Corn of the Indian Plantations of Pakchooge, Maanexit, Senexit, Noobsquesit,

Quanaticke, and Quatoositt, belonging to our enemies the Indians that are fled, provided allwais, they do not disturbe the praying Indians of Hassanamesit, Chabannokonkon, Manchage, Quantisit, and Magunkoog, that now are at Naticke, to gather and improve the Indian Corne growing upon those places, or any other Indian Plantations belonging to our Enemies, that are not above mentioned, alotted, and appointed for the sd Curtis and the English with him to improve, which the Council granted to the sd Indians by a former order

By the Council,   Edw Rawson, Sect'y

[See page 26]

VII. ORDERS AND INSTRUCTIONS FOR CAPT JOSEPH SILL

NOVEMBER 2, 1675

1 You are to take charge of the Souldiers raised from Charlestown, Watertown, and Cambridge, which are about sixty men, and being fitted and furnished with Armes Amunition, and Provision for a week, you are to march away forthwith to Naticke and there take such trusty Indian guides with you, as Corporal Whatson hath prepared for that purpose, and then march away, with all convenient speed, to Hassanamesit an Indian Plantation, near Nipmuck river, from whence you are to send intelligence unto Capt Daniel Henchman, who with his Company is to march to Mendon, informing him that you are ordered to join with him to pursue the Enemy whom we hear is come down to a place called Pakachooge, about 7 miles from Hassanamesit Northwest, and hath killed and surprised some of our neighboring Indians that were gathering Corn there, and as we have ground to fear hath lately attacked Marlborow.

2 Being joined with Captain Henchman, you are to be under his order, and jointly to seek out for the Enemy at the said place, or any other place where you can understand he is, and if you meet the Enemy you are to use your best skill and force to surprise, seize, kill, and destroy the Enemy, and to rescue and relieve any of our friends, either English or Indians, that are taken or injured by him

3 You are to be very carefull to send forth Scouts before you, to discover the Enemy's quarters, and if it may be, to come upon him in the Night

4 You are carefully so to march the men in the woods, that if it be possible to avoid, or shun, or search well before you go too near, all such places as Swamps or Thickets, where the Enemy use, with subtlety to lurk in Ambushment

5 You are in all your attempts and enterprise, to have your eyes and hearts lifted up to God in Christ Jesus, who is the Lord of Hosts and God of Armies, that he will give his presence with you, and assistance unto you, and your Company, in all your undertakings · not trusting or relying upon the arm of flesh, but upon the living Lord alone, from whose gracious blessings and presence all good comes.

6 And you are carefully so to demean yourself, in your consultation, that you may give your Souldiers a good example in piety and virtue, and so govern the Souldiers under your command that your Camp may be holiness to the Lord: and to this end, you have the Military laws printed and published, which are for your rule and direction in that matter

7 If you find a considerable quantity of Corn at Pakachooge, if you can save it, we give it you and your Souldiers, together with Capt Henchman and his Souldiers, for Plunder, so desireing the ever living Lord God to accompany you and your Company, with his gracious conduct and presence, And that He will, for Christ's sake, appear in all the mounts of difficulty, and cover all your heads in the day of Battle and deliver the blood thirsty and cruel Enemy of God and his People into your hands, and make you executioner of his just indignation upon them, and return you victorious unto us who commit you and your Company unto God, and remain

These orders and instructions by the Council

                                        E R [Edward Rawson]

November the 2d—1675.

[See page 32]
VIII   SECOND INDIAN DEED.

FEBRUARY 12, 1677.

Bee it known to all men by these presents, yt we, Anthony, alias Wunaweshawakum, and Abagail his wife, only Daughter and Heyr of Pannasunet, late of Quansicamund, deceased , also Nannuswane, widdow and relict of the said Pannasuned , also Sasomett, and Quassawake his wife, sister to the said Pannassunitt, for and in consideration of full satisfaction in trucking cloth and corn, paid to and received by us, from Daniel Gookin, Esq Capt. Thos Prentice of Cambr and Capt. Daniel Henchman of Boston, pd unto us and each of us, have bargained and sold, alioned, enfeoffed, and confirmed, and by these presents do bargaine, sell, alien, enfeoffe, and confirm, unto the said Daniel Gookin, Thomas Prentice, Daniel Henchman, for ye use of themselves, and all other their parners and associates yt are and shall be admitted Inhabitants and planters, upon a township granted unto ye sd Daniel Gookin, Tho Prentice, Daniel Hinchman, by a General Court of Massachusetts, at a place between Marlborough and Brookfield, called by the Indian Name Quansicamond Ponds, conteining ye contents of eight miles square, with all the lands, woods, meadows, watercourses, mineralls, or any other matter or thing, within the said tract which in naturall right belonged to us, or any of us, and posses'd of, by the said Pannasunet, Sagamore, or his heirs or kindred wtsoever To Have and To Hold all the lands, both woodland and brokenup lands, and all ye apurtenances, as aforesaid, to ym the said Daniel Gookin, Thomas Prentice, Daniel Henchman, their heirs and associates, yt shall and may duely and legally possess and sett down upon their lands and plantations, and to their heirs, executors, administrators, or assigns, for evermore, and the said Anthony, alias Wannoshanuhannitt, and Abagail his wife, daughter and only heir to Panasunet, and her mother Nannaswane, and Sasuet and his wife, Sister of Panasunet, being all Indians, and Natives, and Inhabitants, they and their ancestors, of that place and tract of land at Quansicamond Ponds, have good and just naturall right and interest in the said land, and do freely and absolutely sell and alien all the premises aforesaid, unto the said persons and their heirs forever, warranting ye lawful sale herein made, for us, our heirs, executors and administrators, or from or by any person wtsoever In witness whereof we have hereunto set our hands and seals, this sixth day of the 12th Mo. 1677.

Signed, Sealed and delivered   Anthony, Signed and Sealed
   in presence of us,   Abagail, Signed and Sealed
      John Elliott   Nanswan, Signed and Sealed
      Nathaniel Gookin.   Sasomet, Signed and Sealed.
      Waban, his mark   Quasonoit, Signed and Sealed.
      James Speen
      Simon Betoghom

This deed acknowledged by all ye subscribers, and sealed this 6 of Febr 1677, before me,
                                        Daniel Gookin, Senr Assist.

Entered, 9 2. 83. by Tho Danforth R

[See page 33]
IX.   ORDER OF THE GREAT AND GENERAL COURT
1679.

For the greater comfort and safety of all people who are intending to resettle the villages deserted in the late war, or the planting any new plantation within this jurisdiction It is ordered by this Court and the authority thereof, that no deserted town or new plantation shall be inhabited, till the people first make application unto the Governor and Council, or to the County Courts within whose jurisdiction such plantation is, and the Council or County Court are hereby ordered and empowered, to appoint an able and discreet committee, at the charge of the people intending to plant, which Com are ordered and empowered to view and consider the place or places to be settled, and give directions and orders in writing, under their hands in what form, way, and manner, such town shall be settled and erected , wherein they are required to have a principal respect to nearness and conveniency of habitation for security against enemies, and more comfort for christian communion and enjoyment of God's worship, and education of children in schools, and civility, with other good ends , and all such Planters are hereby enjoyned to attend and put in practise such orders and directions as shall be given by such committee, upon the penalty of one hundred pounds fine to the Country, to be inflicted upon them by order of the Council, or County Court, for their neglect or refusal to attend this order

---

[See page 134]

X VOTES IN WORCESTER FOR GOVERNOR SINCE 1780.

Date	Candidates		Candidates		Date	Candidates		Candidates	
1780	Hancock	56	Bowdoin	20	1809	Lincoln	221	Gore	147
1781	Hancock	48	Bowdoin	04	1810	Gerry	220	Gore	142
1782	Hancock	29	Bowdoin	14	1811	Gerry	210	Gore	137
1783	Hancock	49	Bowdoin	08	1812	Gerry	241	Strong	165
1784	Hancock	30	Bowdoin	12	1813	Varnum	233	Strong	175
1785	Bowdoin	85	Dana	33	1814	Dexter	235	Strong	194
1786	Bowdoin	43	Cushing	02	1815	Dexter	226	Strong	201
1787	Hancock	111	Bowdoin	67	1816	Dexter	249	Brooks	202
1788	Hancock	92	Gerry	87	1817	Dearborn	248	Brooks	191
1789	Hancock	78	Bowdoin	37	1818	Crowninshield	205	Brooks	174
1790	Hancock	51	Bowdoin	20	1819	Crowninshield	230	Brooks	184
1791	Hancock	68	Dana	01	1820	Eustis	234	Brooks	158
1792	Hancock	21	Phillips	19	1821	Eustis	191	Brooks	166
1793	Hancock	31	Gerry	31	1822	Eustis	191	Otis	182
1794	Adams	55	Cushing	38	1823	Eustis	266	Otis	182
1795	Adams	70	Gerry	04	1824	Eustis	298	Lathrop	222
1796	Sumner	102	Adams	42	1825	Lincoln	284	Morton	09
1797	Sumner	83	Sullivan	37	1826	Lincoln	201	Lloyd	40
1798	Sumner	81	Gill	01	1827	Lincoln	327	Jarvis	06
1799	Sumner	119	—	—	1828	Lincoln	161	Morton	12
1800	Gerry	140	Strong	35	1829	Lincoln	203	Morton	15
1801	Gerry	127	Strong	59	1830	Lincoln	503	Morton	142
1802	Gerry	144	Strong	88	1831	Lincoln	299	Morton	107
1803	Gerry	151	Strong	101	1832	Lincoln	361	Morton	148
1804	Sullivan	150	Strong	86	1833	Davis	478	Morton	153
1805	Sullivan	194	Strong	109	1834	Davis	582	Morton	160
1806	Sullivan	219	Strong	135	1835	Everett	416	Morton	291
1807	Sullivan	221	Strong	134	1836	Everett	577	Morton	317
1808	Sullivan	213	Gore	133					

[See page 131]

XI NOTICE OF DANIEL SHAYS

[It was accidentally stated in the note to page 151 that a sketch of the life of this individual would be found in the Appendix The necessity of performing a promise inadvertently made, is the only reason for its appearance here]

This individual acquired an unenviable notoriety which imparts some degree of interest to the incidents of his life He was born in Hopkinton, in 1747 , the son of parents not in affluent circumstances, he worked with Mr Brinley, a respectable farmer of Framingham The activity and energy of his youth promised at maturity more desirable elevation than he attained That his education was neglected, is apparent from his official letters, bidding defiance alike to government, grammar and good spelling Just before the revolution, he removed to one of the towns beyond Connecticut river, and afterwards resided in Pelham When the war commenced he entered the army at the age of twenty eight, with the rank of Ensign, in Capt Dickinson's company, in Col Benjamin Ruggles Woodbridge's regiment

His ambition, activity, and the plausible manners covering the want of acquirements, joined with personal intrepidity, obtained promotion, and in 1776, he was appointed lieutenant in Col. Varnum's regiment. At a time when the line peculiarly needed reenforcement, he was detached on the recruiting service, with the promise of some suitable reward for the enlistment of twenty men. For this purpose he visited his native state, and his unwearied exertions were crowned with ample success. When the complement assigned to him was filled, a plan suggested itself for grasping honor and pay at once. Finding the pulse of patriotism beat high, and the young men of New England were ready to devote themselves for their country, he continued his enlistments. Insinuating address and bold representations, produced impressions of his ability and influence, easily turned to his own advantage, and by holding out expectations of indulgence to those who should serve under his command, a company was raised, on the condition that he should be their captain. With these men he returned to the camp, where they were mustered. When the inspector was about to distribute them to different corps, Shays produced the enlistment papers; pointed to the condition which held them to serve under himself alone; and requested the appointment of Captain. The necessity of the times prevented the sacrifice of so many recruits, and after indignant remonstrances, it was deemed expedient to yield to his demands. The commission was promised, and issued after long delay, in Sept. 1779, to relate back to Jan. 1, 1777. Such is the account tradition gives of his military rank. The honors, ill won, were not long worn. He was discharged Oct. 14, 1780, at Newark, in New Jersey, from Col. Rufus Putnam's regiment.

The deficiency of honorable sentiment in his mental constitution, may be inferred from a characteristic incident. Lafayette had presented, in 1780, to each of the American officers under his immediate command, an elegant sword. Such pledge of regard from the patriot chief, a soldier with a spark of generous feeling, would have cherished as his dearest possession, and transmitted to his posterity as an heirloom of inestimable value. Shays sold the gift of his commander for a few dollars.

After being disbanded, he retired to Pelham, and lived in obscurity. Bankrupt in fortune and in fame, Shays was ready to embark on the flood of any desperate adventure. Without the energetic decision or enlarged conceptions, the strong spirit or the bold daring, which befit a leader, by some accident, he was elevated to the command of the insurgents. Of capacity too humble to direct the movements of an army in those moments when the force of talent makes itself felt by triumphant results, and turns even obstructions into encouragements, he was weak, vacillating, and irresolute. It was providential that the physical power of the arm of rebellion had so feeble a head to direct its blow.

With the first shade of adversity, he made indirect overtures to the agents of government, to abandon his comrades to their fate, on assurance of personal safety; and when his base propositions were rejected, and promises of indemnity and pardon were offered to his followers, his persuasions induced them to reject the proffered mercy and retain the arms of hopeless controversy, to purchase by their sacrifice security for himself.

When the insurrection was crushed, he retired to Vermont. After the lapse of a few years, the general of the rebellion passed through the streets of Worcester, which he once entered at the head of an army, and received assistance from those whose homes he had threatened with desolation.

At length he removed to Sparta, in New York. As a pensioner of the United States, he derived his daily bread from the government, whose forces he had encountered in arms. Declarations filed in the department of war by himself, show that his family consisted of an aged wife, and that he lived in extreme poverty. He died Sept. 29, 1825, aged 78. [o]

However much the honor and integrity of Daniel Shays were questioned, his courage was never disputed. He was in the battle of Bunker's Hill, at the capture of Burgoyne,

---

[o] He married Nancy Haven, a widow. The schedule of his property in 1820, filed in the pension office, exhibits a condition of almost utter destitution. It is as follows:

1 mare, $25: 1 old saddle, $2 50: 1 bridle, 50: 1 old cutter, $5: 1 old axe, 62½ cents: 1 hoe, 62½ cents; 1 table, $3: 3 chairs, $1 12½: 1 old scythe and snath, 1 12½: 1 old pail, 12½ cents: 1 large bible, $1: amounting to $49 62.

and at the storming of Stony Point ; was under Lafayette, and did good service in many bloody encounters. A severe wound, received during the revolution, was honorary testimonial of intrepidity. When Shepard and himself met at Springfield, the former addressed him by the title of general : Shays instantly demanded an explanation, declaring that he claimed no rank but that of captain, and added, laying his hand on his sword, that if different designation was given, he should consider it insult, and would exact immediate satisfaction on the spot.

An aged inhabitant of Hopkinton, who was schoolmate of the rebel captain, states that he was born on the farm in that town, still called the 'Shays place,' situated on Saddle Hill, about two miles west of the meeting house ; that he made his home there principally until he removed with his father, to a place beyond Connecticut river, which, as is supposed, was Great Barrington. The estate where his early youth was passed, has long been deserted as a human habitation, and the forest which has overgrown the forsaken orchard is interspersed, at regular intervals, with aged apple trees.

An estimable and respected clergyman relates, that soon after he began to preach as a candidate, he was employed at Pelham : on the first Sunday of his visit there, he observed a very well dressed gentleman, with a military air, enter the meeting-house : immediately, every pew door from the bottom to the top of the aisle was thrown open, and he was received with the most respectful salutations : this distinguished person was Daniel Shays, who had just returned to that town, with the pardon of the government, and lived upon the west side of the east hill. The next day, Shays called on the clergyman, and held long discourse about his labors and sufferings. He said he had been entirely deceived in respect to the feelings of the people : that he received assurances that if he would collect an hundred men, and march in any direction, multitudes would flock to his standard. Relying on these representations, he began his march with a small force, but found he produced little sensation and that few joined him : at night, he thought it necessary to preserve the appearance of military organization and to mount guard, and ordered a man to stand sentry ; 'no I won't,' was the reply to the commander, 'let that man, he is not so sick as I be': the second man refused, desiring him to take another who was stronger, and the chief of the insurrection found himself without authority at the head of a tumultuary army.

A soldier of the rebellion, who had fled from Springfield to Pelham without stopping, and hid his gun under the barn floor, asked Shays why he did not stand his ground ? The reply was, 'you know, if I had, I must have stood alone.'

The clergyman describes Shays as an agreeable and intelligent person, and the day he spent with him as one of the most interesting of his life.

These particulars have been obligingly communicated by Samuel B. Walcott, Esq., of Hopkinton.

XII. STATEMENTS IN RELATION TO THE TRADE, MANUFACTURES, EMPLOYMENT AND BUSINESS OF WORCESTER,

TRADE. The following excellent abstract of the transportation on the Blackstone Canal, stated in tons, has been prepared by Mr. Eddy, the collector, and was politely furnished by Thomas Burgess, Esq., of Providence.

To	1831.	1832.	1833.	1834.	1835.
Worcester	4300	4400	4663	5336	4694
Millbury	876	1140	1316	1533	1375
Grafton	968	1019	1174	909	736
Northbridge	1026	920	1280	428	534
Uxbridge	964	1184	1059	1497	1534
Millville	601	555	610	252	295
Blackstone	986	814	540	528	359
Waterford	386	660	540	469	120
Woonsocket	3139	3304	2564	1158	1965
Manville	377	193	366	71	417
Albion	225	156	149	12	291
Kelleys	275	37	—	—	35
Lonsdale	462	1800	1274	558	807

27

From					
Worcester	868	890	848	826	739
Millbury	360	223	171	187	183
Grafton	289	158	236	110	158
Northbridge	1624	1821	1208	542	233
Uxbridge	1755	3276	1500	2617	1470
Millville	94	52	221	5	15
Blackstone	279	195	245	226	127
Waterford	11	59	60	64	5
Woonsocket	291	259	135	86	303
Manville	10	63	—	—	61
Albion	23	20	1	1	41
Kelly's	99	298	191	—	255
Lonsdale	—	6	134	79	51

The amount of tolls collected on the Blackstone Canal has been as follows:

In 1828	$1000,00	In 1831	$14944,67	In 1834	$16464,45
In 1829	8606,00	In 1832	18907,45	In 1835	14433,08
In 1830	12016,82	In 1833	17545,10	In 1836	11500,00

The following are the principal articles transported on the Canal.

Years.	Coal. Tons.	Iron. Tons.	Cotton. Bales.	Wool. Bales.	Corn. Bushels.	Salt. Bushels.
1834	2759	635	3829	2100	24698	19631
1835	3148	840	3590	3151	8618	18223
1836	3044	567	3494	2048	25174	11095

	Flour. Barrels.	Molasses. Gallons.	Oil. Gallons.	Gypsum. Tons.	Leather. Tons.	Wood. Cords.
1834	21158	68519	49957	—	364	1500
1835	16278	58823	43137	—	292	825
1836	10025	22389	39024	582	220	1185

BOSTON AND WORCESTER RAILROAD. The following statement of the business of this road has been communicated by Nathan Hale, Esq.

From July 1 to Dec. 31, 1835, the receipts were as follows:

For Transportation of passengers	$72912,12
Freight	18828,21
Net Income	51272,67

The whole number of passengers conveyed on the road within the six months, was 72,-558, making the average of 460 the day: of these, 37700 travelled over the whole road, and the remainder were taken up or set down at one of the stopping places between Worcester and Boston. The number of trips was; with passengers 757, in the average time of 2h. 50m.; and with freight cars, 533.

The whole amount received from Dec. 1, 1835, to Dec. 1, 1836, was

For conveyance of passengers	$118233,44
Freight	59836,93—$17807,37

The freight carried out from Boston, was 5771 tons; brought in, 1190 tons.

The passengers to and from the places mentioned below, in the same period, were,

Brighton and Angier's corner	3219
Newton	403
Needham and Natick	1061
Framingham and Hopkinton	3424
Southborough and Westborough	2807
Grafton	2771
Worcester	11161—24847

A large amount of fare was taken in the cars where the places were not entered.

The number of stores in Worcester, in 1836, was as follows: for groceries 16: dry goods 16: crockery 2: hardware 3: iron 1: wool 3: flour and grain 4: coal 2: provisions 4: fruit and confectionery 6: drugs and medicines 4: dye stuffs 2: books and stationery 3:

music and umbrellas 1 hats and furs 5 shoes and leather 6 dresses and millinery 5:
jewelry and watches 4 cabinet furniture 2 carpet warehouses 2 drapers and tailor's
shops 5

There are 4 banks 3 insurance offices an insurance agency and 1 printing offices

A statement of the condition of the manufactures and mechanic industry of any town,
exhibiting the aggregate amount of capital invested, the number of hands employed, the
sums paid for labor, and the annual quantity and value of production in each department,
would be alike interesting and useful For the purpose of presenting this view of the
prosperity of Worcester, circular letters were distributed among those engaged in different branches of business, soliciting information Acknowledgments are due to several
gentlemen, who kindly furnished full answers to the inquiries but, unfortunately, some
have felt reluctant, even for such general purpose to communicate facts and many, under
the pressure of their engagements, have not found time for any reply The results obtained were so incomplete, that in forming an estimate of the whole, it would have been
necessary to substitute conjecture for certainty, in filling up many intervals. As the
whole value of such statistics depends on that degree of accuracy which it was impracticable to attain, after much labor and trouble bestowed by others, the compiler has been
reluctantly compelled to leave the accomplishment of an object so desirable, to those who
may be more fortunate in their effort for obtaining materials.

III EXECUTIONS

As Worcester has been the seat of the Courts of justice, these dreadful exhibitions have
taken place here The following are all the executions which have occurred within the
county since its foundation 1737, Nov 26, Hugh Henderson, alias John Hamilton, for
Burglary 1768, Oct. 20, Arthur, a negro, for Rape. 1770, Oct 25, William Lindsay, for
Burglary 1778, July 2, William Brooks, James Buchanan, Ezra Ross, and Bathsheba
Spooner, for the murder of Joshua Spooner of Brookfield 1779, Nov 11, Robert Young,
for Rape 1783, June 19, William Huggins and John Mansfield, for Burglary 1786, Aug
17, Johnson Green, for Burglary 1793, Oct 31, Samuel Frost, for the murder of Elisha
Allen of Princeton 1825, Dec 7, Horace Carter, for Rape No one of these criminals
were natives of Worcester, and but three were born within the county.

IV FESTIVALS FOURTH OF JULY

The anniversary of national independence has usually been celebrated in this town
The gentlemen named below have delivered orations the addresses of those designated
by a star, have been printed.

1791	°Edward Bangs	1816	°John Davis,
1795	°Joseph Allen	1817	°Pliny Merrick
1796	°Francis Blake	1818	*Austin Denny
1797	°Oliver Fiske	1819	°Edward D Bangs
1798	°Samuel Austin	1820	Charles H Warren
1799	Pelatiah Hitchcock.	1822	Jonathan Going
1800	°Edward Bangs	1823	Francis B Stebbins
1801	°Isaac Story	1824	William Lincoln
1802	°Zephaniah S Moore	1825	Richard H Vose.
1803	John W Caldwell	1826	Charles Allen
1804	°William Charles White	1827	Thomas Kinnicutt
1805	°Daniel Waldo Lincoln.	1829	John Davis
1808	°Estes Howe	1830	Peter C Bacon
1810	°Levi Heywood	1831	Samuel M Burnside.
1811	°Samuel Brazer		Edwin Conant
	°John W Hubbard.	1832	George Folsom
1812	°Francis Blake	1833	ˡEdward Everett
	°Enoch Lincoln	1834	Franklin Dexter
1813	Thomas Snell	1835	[Boston & Worcester Rail Road
1814	°Rejoice Newton.		opened]
	Edwin A White	1836	Benjamin F Thomas
1815	°Peleg Sprague.		

Jme. Bigelow.

HISTORY

OF

WORCESTER,

MASSACHUSETTS.

FROM 1836 TO 1861.

WITH

INTERESTING REMINISCENCES

OF

THE PUBLIC MEN OF WORCESTER.

BY CHARLES HERSEY.

SAVE THE LITTLE THINGS — NAMES, DATES, AND FACTS; COLLECT THE LOOSE SEEDS;
DRIVE YOUR LAND MARKS, AND PASS DOWN THE CURRENT OF TIME.

WORCESTER:
PRINTED FOR THE AUTHOR,
BY HENRY J. HOWLAND.

CONTENTS.

HISTORY OF WORCESTER.

From 1836 to 1861.

— ◆ —

INTRODUCTION.

Although it might be a task and a tax on the industry of one individual, to compile the history of Worcester from its first settlement in 1664 to 1836, a period of one hundred and seventy-two years, without authentic records, and without a living man to gain any thing of by tradition, yet the work has been accomplished, and the public has been favored with the history of the Town from its first attempt at settlement to 1836, by William Lincoln, Esq., whose indefatigable labors have done more for the history of Worcester than any man now living. Upon the death of Mr Lincoln, who was then styled the living historian of Worcester, the humble compiler of the following pages saw the necessity of some one to keep the records whereby the history might in after years be pursued with accuracy. Such a record, to some extent, the compiler has kept, and believing that a continuation of the history of the City ought to be made as often as once in twenty-five years, has come to the conclusion, at the earnest solicitation of many friends, to offer the following pages as the History of Worcester from 1836 to 1861.*

— ◆ —

GENERAL HISTORY.

From the time that Lincoln's History closes to the present, we have enjoyed almost one uninterrupted season of prosperity. Property has increased more than four fold; mechanical and manufacturing interests have more than quadrupled, churches and school houses have been reared in the morning and evening of the same day, the Town has become a City, third in wealth and importance in the Commonwealth; the Fire Department has risen from infancy

* By the kindness of Hon Levi Lincoln, the owner of the copy right of Lincoln's History, am permitted to reprint the same, which forms the first part of this volume

to manhood, and is now second to none; the water power has been immensely augmented by the building of new dams, and flowing of large reservoirs of almost worthless land; the city has not suffered from any visitation of epidemic disease; water has been introduced; gas courses its way from Lincoln square to New Worcester, giving light as it passes along; new streets have been laid out; lamp posts have been erected; societies for moral and religious instruction have been formed; facilities of communication have been more than doubled by railroads and omnibuses; and taxes have been light, as they always will be in the community that reverences God and educates its children. Probably there is not a town or city in New England, if there is in the Union, which can be said to have at the same time so good a round of schools and school-houses, and a rate of taxation not exceeding eight dollars upon a thousand.

INCREASE OF POPULATION. — In 1836, the number of inhabitants was 7,500. The following table will show the increase from time to time to the year 1860.

1840 — 7,497.	Lost	3.	1845 — 11,556.	Gained	4,059.
1850 — 17,049.	Gained 5,493.		1855 — 22,284.	"	5,235.
			1860 — 24,983.	"	2,697.

We see from the above, that the largest gain in five years was from 1845 to 1850, and that the city gained, from 1850 to 1860, 7,934, which is a larger number than any other town has in this county. When we consider the great disaster by fire which took place in June, 1853, called the Merrifield Fire, and the general depression of business in 1856 and 7, we think the growth of Worcester has been very respectable.

Selectmen chosen since 1836 to 1848.

Isaac Davis	1837	Lewis Chapin	1839, 40, 41
Luther Burnett, Jr.	1837	Wm. A. Wheeler	1840, 41
Nathaniel Stowell	1837	George T. Rice	1840
Joseph Converse	1837	Albert Curtis	1840, 41
Benjamin Flagg	1837	Henry W. Miller	1841, 42, 43, 44,
Jubal Harrington	1837		[45
Samuel Banister	1837	Henry Goulding	1842
John W. Lincoln	1838, 39, 43, 44,	Darius Rice,	1842, 43, 44, 45,
	[45	Wm. Barber	1842
F. W. Paine,	1838, 40, 41, 42, 43,	Edward Earle	1843, 44, 45, 46
	[44, 45, 46, 47	Jonas Bartlett	1846
Charles Blair	1838	Samuel Davis	1846
Thomas Chamberlain	1838, 39	Eben'r H. Bowen	1846, 47
John P. Kettell	1838, 39	Horatio N. Tower	1847
Stephen Salisbury	1839	Albert Tolman	1847

Representatives since 1836 to 1848.

William Lincoln	1837, 38, 39, 40	Benj. F. Thomas	1841
Guy S. Newton	1837	John Hammond	1841
Emory Washburn	1837	Nathaniel Brooks	1842, 43
Nathan Heard	1837, 38, 39	Fitzroy Willard	1842, 43
Eben'r L. Barnard	1837	Alex. H. Bullock	1844, 46, 47, 48
Stephen Salisbury	1838, 39	John M. Earle	1844, 45
Lewis Chapin	1838, 39, 40	Darius Rice	1844, 45
Simon S. Gates	1838	Ira M. Barton	1845
Ichabod Washburn	1838	Peregrine B. Gilbert	1846, 47, 48
Charles Allen	1839	Daniel Waldo Lincoln	1846
John Wright	1839	Samuel Davis	1847, 48
Thomas Kinnicutt	1840, 41, 42, 43		

Representatives since 1848.

1849 — Peter C. Bacon, Albert Tolman, Charles White.

1850 — John M. Earle, Albert Tolman, Charles White.

1851 — John M. Earle, Edward Earle, Benjamin Flagg, John F. Gleason, Charles Washburn.

1852 — Isaac Davis, John M. Earle, John F. Gleason, George F. Hoar, Putman W. Taft.

1853 — Henry W. Benchley, George W. Gill, Edward Lamb, Eli Thayer, Charles White.

1854 — Eli Thayer, Henry W. Benchley, George W. Gill, Edward Lamb, Henry H. Chamberlin.

1855 — Harrison Bliss, Elijah B. Stoddard, Putman W. Taft, George W. Russell, John H. Brooks.

1856 — William T. Merrifield, George F. Thompson, Dexter F. Parker, John B. D. Cogswell, Stephen P. Twiss.

1857 — Alexander Thayer, Dexter F. Parker, James S. Woodworth, O. H. Tillotson, Albert L. Benchley.

1858 — Albert Tolman, Henry C. Rice, Charles B. Pratt, George Chandler, Marcus Barrett.

1859 — Benjamin F. Otis, Samuel A. Knox, Henry C. Rice, Joseph Pratt, Timothy S. Stone.

1860 — Dexter F. Parker, Joseph D. Daniels, Patrick O'Keefe, Alexander H. Bullock, Benjamin F. Otis.

1861 — Delano A. Goddard, Samuel Souther, Joseph D. Daniels, John L. Murphy, Alex. H. Bullock.

CHURCHES AND MINISTERS.

1. OLD SOUTH.—Rev. Rodney A. Miller was the pastor of this Church in 1836, having been ordained June 7th, 1827, and dismissed by a mutual council, April 12th, 1844, after a long and successful ministry in this place of almost seventeen years. Accompanying the act of dismission on the part of the council, was a formal testimony, of the most satisfactory character, as to his moral worth and ministerial efficiency.

Since his dismission as pastor of the Old South Church, he has resided in Worcester, and has preached occasionally to destitute churches. He was elected overseer by the Board of Harvard College in 1843, and continued one year.

In 1852 he was elected by the legislature to the same office, and continued in office four years. In 1856 he was elected to fill the unexpired term of Hon. Abbot Lawrence, which was four years, making in all nine years.

He was member of the first or visiting committee of the University, including the last year's appointment, nine years in succession.

After a vacancy of nearly one year in the pastoral office, the Rev. George P. Smith, of South Woburn, (now Winchester,) having received and accepted a call, became the eighth pastor of the Church, and was installed March 19th, 1845. The sermon on this occasion was delivered by the Rev. Thomas Snell, D. D. of North Brookfield.

Mr. Smith was born in Salem, Mass., on the 11th of February, 1814, and was a graduate of Amherst College of the class of 1835, and of Andover Theological Seminary of the class of 1840.

Mr. Smith died at Salem on the third day of September, 1852, in the thirty-ninth year of his age, and in the eighth of his ministry in Worcester. By his kind and affectionate spirit he endeared himself to the people of his charge, and a large circle of friends, by whom his death was deeply lamented.

On the 13th day of December, 1852, the church and parish with great unanimity invited the Rev. Horace James, of Wrentham, Mass., to become their pastor and minister. Mr. James accepted the invitation, and was installed on the 3d day of February, 1853, on which occasion the sermon was preached by Rev. Edwards A. Park, D. D., of Andover. Mr. James, the present pastor, is a native of Milford, Mass. He graduated at Yale College in 1840, and pursued a course of theological study at New Haven and Andover.

He married Helen Leavitt, daughter of Gen. David Leavitt, of Boston. Mr. James was absent from his people five months in the spring and summer of 1858, on a tour in Europe.

Mr. James having been appointed chaplain of the 25th regiment of Massachusetts Volunteers, left his people October 13th, for his new field of labor.

2. SECOND PARISH, (FIRST UNITARIAN) — This church and society was under the charge of Aaron Bancroft, D D , as senior pastor, and Rev. Alonzo Hill, as junior pastor, in 1836 Rev Dr Bancroft died August 19th, 1839, in the 84th year of his age, and fifty-fourth of his ministry. He died beloved and respected by all who had the pleasure of his acquaintance.

An organ was introduced into the church October 25th, 1836 Their second meeting-house was burned, August, 1849, and the third, standing on the same site of the one destroyed, was dedicated March 26th, 1851 Their chapel was dedicated December 12th, 1852 The third bell having been broken on the 4th of July, was replaced by another October 5th, 1853. The old organ having been sold, a second was introduced May 10th, 1855

Rev Dr Hill, the present pastor, was overseer of Harvard College from 1851 to 1854, received the degree of D D in 1851, was absent from his charge in Cuba in the winter of 1837-8, and in Europe eight months in 1856

Dr Hill has published, since 1836, the following Sermon at the interment of Rev Dr Bancroft, August 22d, 1839 ; Sermon at the interment of Rev Dr. Thayer, June 28th, 1840 , Review of Messrs Edwards and Sears' Sermons on Rev Isaac Allen, Christian Examiner, Sept. 1844 , Article on Rev. Jonathan Farr, Christian Examiner, Nov. 1846 , Sermon preached in Boston, May 27th, 1847, on Christian Communion, Sermon in Monthly Miscellany, October, 1848 , Article on Rev Hiram Washington, Christian Examiner Sermon on General Taylor, National Ægis, July 31st, 1850 , Sermon preached in the Ancient meeting-house, Hingham, Sept. 8th, 1850 , Sermon at the dedication of the New meeting house, March 26th, 1851 , Sermon on the 25th anniversary of his ordination, March 28th, 1852 , Discourse on the death of Hon John W Lincoln, October 10th, 1852 : Address before the Worcester North-East Temperance Union, Sterling, April 13th, 1853 , Sermon on the death of Hon John Davis, April 25th, 1854 , Address before the Alumni of Leicester Academy, August 7th. 1855 , Address before the Guardians of the Orphan's Home, February 5th, 1857 , Discourse commemorative of Hon Thomas Kinnicutt, January 31st, 1858 , Speech before the Antiquarian Society on Mr Prescott, February 10th, 1859 , Commemorative Discourse on Rev. Samuel Clark, Uxbridge, December 11th, 1859

This church has been constituted seventy-four years, and Dr Hill is its second pastor He has officiated in the sacred office thirty-three years May the day be far distant when the people of his charge shall lose his valuable services Their house of worship stands upon Court House Hill, about four rods south of the new Court House, and is built of brick, covered with mastic drawn in squares representing granite For symmetry, externally and internally, this church will compare favorably with any in this Commonwealth

3. FIRST BAPTIST. — Rev Jonathan Aldrich was pastor of this church in 1836 Their meeting house was burned May 21st, 1836 , the origin of the fire was attributed to an incendiary The house of worship erected on the site of that which had been burned, was dedicated in 1836, and Mr. Al-

drich preached on the occasion from the words, "Holiness becometh thy house, O Lord, forever." Ps. 73 : 5.

This house is built of wood, and is furnished with an elegant organ, presented by Hon. Isaac Davis, and surmounted with a spire 138 feet high, with a bell weighing 2200 lbs., and is situated on Salem street, a little east of the old Common. Mr. Aldrich was dismissed from this church, May, 1838; and when he left Worcester the church passed the following commendatory resolution : "That we hold his character as a vigilant peace-maker and able pastor in the highest estimation; and acknowledge our obligations ever to be grateful to the giver of every good and perfect gift, that we have been permitted to enjoy his faithful ministry."

Mr. Aldrich has for several years acted as agent of the American Baptist Missionary Union, residing in Worcester, where he died January 19, 1862, aged 62.

In April 1839, Rev. Samuel B. Swaim assumed the pastoral relation with this church, and continued the pastor until May, 1854, serving them faithfully and acceptably for fifteen years.

Mr. Swaim is a native of New Jersey. He was graduated at Brown University in 1830, and at Newton Theological Seminary in 1833. He was first settled over the First Baptist Church in Haverhill. In 1835 he was invited to fill the Theological professorship in Granville College; he occupied this position about two years.

Rev. J. D. E. Jones received and accepted a call of the church, March 7, 1855, and commenced his labors with the church in April. He continued with the church as pastor until May, 1859, when he was chosen Superintendent of Public Schools in this city.

August 30th, 1860, the ordination of Mr. Lemuel Moss took place, as the sixth pastor of this church. The council convened at 9 o'clock, A. M., in the vestry of the church, over which Rev. Dr. Pattison, of Worcester, presided.

The services at his ordination were as follows : Reading of the scriptures by Rev. J. D. E. Jones, of Worcester; introductory prayer by Rev. J. Aldrich, of Worcester; sermon by Rev. J. R. Scott, of Yonkers, N. Y.; ordaining prayer by Rev. Dr. Pattison, of Worcester; charge to the candidate by Rev. Dr. Robinson, of Rochester Theological Seminary; right hand of fellowship by Rev. H. L. Wayland, of Worcester; charge to the church by Rev. Dr. Warren, of Boston; closing prayer by Rev. Dr. Fisher.

Rev. Lemuel Moss was born in Boone county, Kentucky, December 27th, 1829; he worked nine years at the printing business in Cincinnati, Ohio, and was married, December 1851, to Miss Harriet Brigham. In September 1853, he took up his residence in Rochester, N. Y., to prosecute his studies for the ministry. In July 1858, graduated from the University of Rochester, and in July 1860, from the Rochester Theological Seminary.

4. CENTRAL CHURCH, (2d CONGREGATIONALIST.)—This church was under the pastoral care of Rev. David Peabody, which continued until the autumn of 1838, when Mr. Peabody's request, (on account of ill health,) for

dismission was laid before the church for their action, and the following resolutions were adopted :

" Resolved, That this church entertains a high sense of the value of the ministerial labors of the Rev. Mr. Peabody, and of his faithful discharge of all the duties resulting from his connection with us, and that we do most sincerely regret the occurrence of an event which seems likely, for a season at least, to deprive the church of Christ of his services as a pastor.

" Resolved, That we do most cordially sympathize with the Rev. Mr. Peabody and his companion in this visitation of divine providence, and most earnestly pray that his health may be restored, and that he may be useful and happy in the situation in which he has been called to labor."

On leaving Worcester, Mr. Peabody was appointed Professor of Rhetoric in Dartmouth College. This office he held until within a few weeks of his death, which occurred October 17th, 1839, at the age of thirty-four years and six months.

The church being left vacant by the transfer of Mr. Peabody to Hanover, Rev. Seth Sweetser was called to become their pastor, and having accepted the call, was installed over them December 19th, 1838. Mr. Sweetser is a native of Newburyport, and a graduate of Harvard University, in the class of 1827. He pursued the study of theology in the Seminary at Andover. He was a missionary to a feeble church two years in Gardiner, Me., and ordained pastor of the same, November 23d, 1836 ; which office he held until November 8th, 1838, when he came to Worcester.

Mr. Sweetser received the degree of D. D. from A. C. If a celebrated divine could say of Dr. Sweetser, now more than nine years since, that " his ministry here, of more than twelve years, has been both laborious and pleasant, vigilant and successful," what shall the historian of to-day say of him, more than that he is the same laborious, pleasant, vigilant, and successful pastor he was at that time.

5. FIRST METHODIST EPISCOPAL CHURCH. — Their first house of worship, built in 1837, stood at the corner of Exchange and Union streets. At the dedication of this house, Rev. Joseph Holdich, D. D., preached the sermon. The house cost $4150, and was destroyed by fire February 19th, 1844. After the loss of their house of worship, they were obliged to return to the Town Hall, where they first commenced services as a religious society. The year following, (1845,) a portion of this church was set off and organized into the "Laurel street Methodist Episcopal Church." The Park street Society erected their house of worship in 1844-45 ; it was dedicated August 16th, 1845, when Rev. Bishop Janes preached the sermon. It stands on the south side of the old Common, on Park street, from which the church takes its name ; it is built of brick, and is 72 by 50 feet, surmounted with a cupola, and cost rather more than $10,000.

Rev. John T. Burrill was the pastor of this church in 1836. He ministered to this people with great acceptance two years, which is the longest

28

time allowed by the Methodist Conference. Rev. James Porter followed him,
and remained with the church one year. Rev. Jotham Horton was here one
year, and afterwards labored in the vicinity of Boston. Rev. Moses L. Scudder
followed Mr. Horton, remaining two years. He was followed in Worcester
by Rev. Miner Raymond, who began his labors here in 1841, and closed them
in 1843 ; on leaving here he was stationed in Boston, and thence transferred
from the itineracy to the Wesleyan Academy at Wilbraham, Mass., as principal of that institution.

Rev. Charles K. True, D. D., succeeded Mr. Raymond in the pastoral
supervision of this church. Mr. True is a graduate of Harvard University.
In 1849 he was honored by his Alma Mater with the degree of Doctor in
Divinity. On leaving Worcester he was stationed in Charlestown, Chelsea,
and Lowell, and afterwards appointed Professor of Polite Literature in the
Wesleyan University at Middletown, Ct. He was followed in the pastoral care
of this church by the Rev. Amos Binney. Mr. Binney was with this people
two years. These were years of peculiar interest to the church. A part of
their number was set off to form a second interest. A new house of worship
was erected, more spacious and convenient than their former one. After
leaving Worcester, Mr. Binney was the Presiding Elder of the Charlestown
District. He was followed here by the Rev. Jonathan D. Bridge, who during
the two years of his ministry was a successful pastor. He was subsequently
Presiding Elder of the Worcester District, after a pastorate in Roxbury,
Boston and Malden. His successor in Worcester was the Rev. Loranus
Crowell. Mr. Crowell remained in Worcester but a single year, and was
transferred to Boston, as pastor of the Bromfield street Church in that city.
He was graduated at the Wesleyan University in Middletown, Ct., in 1841.
Rev. Nelson S. Cobleigh was Mr. Crowell's immediate successor. He was
graduated at the University in Middletown with the class of 1843. Mr. Cobleigh is President of M'Kendree College, Illinois, at this date. The Rev. L.
A. Mudge, was the next pastor of this church, who served very acceptably for
the term of two years. Rev. D. E. Chapin was his successor, who also served
two years. Rev. F. H. Newhall, Rev. Chester Field, and Rev. J. H. Twombly, have also served this church two years each.

Rev. John W. Dadmun, the present pastor, was born in Hubbardston, in
this county, in 1819. He received his education at Wilbraham Seminary,
and commenced preaching at the age of nineteen years. He preached in
Boston four years previous to his connection with the church in this city.* He
has compiled and published the following works : 1. " Revival Melodies: "
this work is of great interest ; eighty thousand copies was sold the first year
of its publication. 2. " The Melodeon : " this is a valuable collection of
hymns and tunes, original and selected, adapted to all occasions of social wor-

* Mr. Dadmun married for his first wife, Miss Lucy Ann, daughter of Beriah Smith, of
South Wilbraham, Mass., in 1842. She died April, 1844. His second wife was Miss
Martha Jane, daughter of Wm. S. Rogers, Esq., of South Hampton.

ship 3. "The Æolian Harp " this is a collection of hymns and tunes for Sunday schools and Bands of Hope. 4. "Army Melodies : " original and selected hymns and tunes adapted to the army and navy.

6 FIRST ROMAN CATHOLIC — Rev. James Fitton was the pastor of this church in 1836 They at that time had a small house of worship on Temple street , this house was built in 1834 ; it has been succeeded by St John's Church. the largest structure of the kind in the city ; it is 136 feet in length and 65 feet in breadth, of Roman Doric style of architecture.

The Rev A. Williamson succeeded Mr Fitton He was from Baltimore, and a student of the Propaganda of Rome Having accomplished his services here, he gave place to the Rev. Matthew W Gibson He took charge of the " Worcester Mission in 1844, and remained here until March, 1856 He is by birth an Englishman, and received his education partly in England and partly in Rome, in the College of the Propaganda. Mr Gibson was a powerful working man while the pastor of this church He built both of the Catholic churches in this city, and many others in this county and state. Rev J A McAvoy was appointed his assistant, a native of Ireland , he was educated in Trinity College, Dublin and had the reputation of great learning Ill health prevented him from performing the labors expected of him here, and induced his resignation in 1847 , on his retiring from the office as assistant, Rev John Boyce was stationed here as associate pastor with Mr Gibson. Mr Boyce is by birth an Irishman, was educated at the Royal College of Maynooth, Ireland. Previously to his entering upon this field of labor, he ministered to the Catholics in Eastport, Maine. He still remains the pastor of this church, with Rev P. J O'Reilley as assistant pastor Mr Boyce, under the name of " Paul Peppergrass,' has published the following " Shandy Maguire," an excellent story of Irish life " The Spæwife," and " Mary Lee " He is an agreeable writer of fiction

7 UNION CHURCH, (3D CONGREGATIONALIST) — This church was organized February 3, 1836, with sixty-three members. Twenty-seven of these were from the First Church, and nineteen from the Calvinist Church. Their house was dedicated July 6th, 1836 Rev. John Nelson preached the sermon on the occasion and Rev George Allen offered the dedicatory prayer This house is of brick, 90 feet in length and 45 in width, and is situated on Front street, on the north east side of the common. The house is surmounted by a well proportioned spire, and has a fine toned bell, and an organ, which is one of Stevens' best.

Their first pastor was Rev Jonathan E. Woodbridge, who was installed November 24th, 1836. On this occasion Rev. Parsons Cooke preached the sermon , installing prayer by Rev Samuel Gay , charge by Rev. John Nelson, D. D ; right hand of fellowship by Rev J D. Farnsworth , address to the people by Rev Josiah Clark. Mr Woodbridge had been settled before over the church in Ware Village When he had labored in Worcester about one year, a difference of opinion arose between him and a majority of his society as to the expediency of opening the church edifice to anti-slavery lecturers. Believing that the action of the society was such as to diminish his influence, and impair his usefulness, he asked his dismission, and was accordingly dismissed February 14th, 1838, with the following testimonial: " The council feel great pleasure in recommending Rev. Jonathan E. Woodbridge to the churches as a minister of highly respectable talents and learning, of sound doctrinal views, of amiable character and devoted piety,— a minister qualified by nature, by education and the grace of God, to be greatly useful in any field of labor to which divine providence may call him."

On his retiring from his labors in Worcester, Mr. Woodbridge was principally engaged in editorial labors in connection with the New England Puritan, and afterwards the Puritan Recorder.

Rev. E. Smalley succeeded Mr. Woodbridge as pastor of this church. He was installed in office on the 19th day of February, 1838. On that occasion Rev. John Nelson offered the introductory prayer; Warren Fay, D. D., preached the sermon; Rev. Horatio Bardwell made the prayer of installation; Jacob Ide, D. D., gave the charge to the pastor; Rev. George Allen presented the right hand of fellowship; Rev. Francis Horton addressed the people; and Rev. Rodney A. Miller offered the concluding prayer. Before Mr. Smalley's settlement here, he was nine years associate pastor with Nathaniel Emmons, D. D., of Franklin.

Dr. Smalley at his own request was dismissed from the charge of this church May 10th, 1854, and soon became the pastor of the 3d St. Presbyterian Church, Troy, N. Y., where he died July 30th, 1858. Upon the receipt of the news of the death of Dr. Smalley, the Union church, at a meeting held August 1st, passed the following among other resolutions: " Resolved, That his long continued ministrations to this people were attended with signal success to our spiritual edification and improvement; that as in time past we were accustomed not only to respect him as an accomplished gentleman and scholar, but to honor him as an eminent divine, and to love him as a sympathizing friend, a wise counsellor and a faithful minister of the Gospel of Christ; and in time to come it will be our pleasure to cherish the memory of his exalted virtues and excellencies of character, as well as his labors of love for the people of his charge. Voted, That two of the deacons of this church be appointed to attend the funeral of Rev. Dr. Smalley. Deacons Washburn and Chapin were appointed."—Church Record, p. 152.

Rev. Ebenezer Cutler, the third pastor of this church, was installed Sept. 6th, 1855, and still continues to officiate in that office. On this occasion Rev. A. Dean, Jr., of Newbury, Vt., preached the sermon; Rev. L. I. Hoadley offered the installing prayer; charge to the pastor by Rev. S. Sweetser, D. D.: right hand of fellowship by Rev. H. James; address to the people by Rev. J. W. Cross; concluding prayer by Rev. George Bushnell. Mr. Cutler was born in Royalston, Mass.; graduated at the Vermont University in 1845, and at the Andover Theological Seminary in 1848. Married E.

Jane daughter of John Charlton, Esq , of Littleton, N H , July 25, 1849
Ordained pastor of the First Congregational church at St Albans, Vt , March
6th, 1850 , dismissed July 10th, 1855 Mrs Cutler died June 5th, 1859
married Marion C , daughter of the late Rev. William Eaton, of Hardwick,
January 10th, 1861

8 PLEASANT STREET CHURCH, (2D BAPTIST.) — This church was organized December 28th, 1841. The Rev John Jennings preached the sermon
on that occasion; Rev Abisha Samson offered the consecrating prayer ; and
Rev. Samuel B Swaim expressed the fellowship of the churches The church
was constituted with ninety-eight members, eighty-nine of whom were recommended from the First Baptist Church About one hundred members were
added to the number in a single year after their organization The church
worshipped in the Town Hall until January, 1844 , on the 4th of that month
the new house of worship which they had erected was dedicated to the special
service of Almighty God , the pastor, Rev John Jennings, preached on that
occasion from the words, " Worship God ; " Rev. Mr. Bronson, from Fall
River, offered the dedicatory prayer The house is pleasantly situated, neat
and commodious In consequence of its location the church voted, just before
entering it for worship, that thereafter they would be known as the " Pleasant Street Baptist Church " It is situated on the north side of Pleasant,
some six rods from Main street, and is built of brick, surmounted with a
cupola ; as yet they have no bell This church has no society, all business
being transacted by the church, by whom also, as an organization, the church
edifice is owned

Rev John Jennings was their first pastor He entered upon his labors
here early in 1842, and for nearly eight years he was the acceptable and
respected pastor of the church It then appeared to him expedient to discontinue his pastoral relations, and, on the first of July, 1850, he retired from the
position he had filled so honorably to himself and useful to others. He still
remained in Worcester for a season, acting as an agent of the American Tract
Society Mr Jennings is a native of Danbury, Ct ; he was graduated at the
Newton Seminary in 1834 In September of that year he was ordained
pastor of the First Baptist Church in Beverly. January 10th, 1836, he became pastor of the Baptist Church in Grafton , he sustained that connection
nearly six years When he left that church, he brought with him to his new
relation the following testimonial · " We trust also that many souls have been
converted here through your instrumentality, and that your labors in Grafton
have, under God, caused many rejoicings in heaven , and we also by this cer-
tify to those with whom in the providence of God you may be placed, our
fellowship for and attachment to you as a minister of the Gospel, and our
hearty commendation of you as such to the churches generally '

Rev Charles K. Colver was the second pastor of this church , he entered
upon his duties here on the 14th of September, 1850 Mr Colver pursued
his collegiate studies at Brown University, and his theological studies at
28*

Newton. Previous to his coming to Worcester, he was pastor of the Baptist Church in Watertown. His connection with the Pleasant street Church he held nearly four and a half years, during which time, though no powerful work of grace was manifest, the moral strength of the church increased; a debt of long standing was diminished by several thousand dollars; through his efforts mainly, and by some of the members, one of the best organs in the city was placed in the church. The accessions by baptism during the period of his pastoral labors, were the same as during the corresponding period immediately prior to his pastorate.

After a little more than four years of labor he received an offer of a voyage to Valparaiso, and his failing health, with the advice of friends, induced him to accept the offer. After making known his determination to the church, he devoted the time before he should sail in the most earnest endeavors to diminish the church debt, which efforts were crowned with success.

Mr. Colver was a faithful pastor, a bold and fearless preacher, a devoted, conscientious, consistent Christian, and a firm and faithful friend. With him to determine that a course of action was right, was to enter upon that course without " conferring with flesh and blood." He was a ripe scholar, and the light of learning was all brought to bear upon the elucidation of divine truth.

Rev. D. W. Faunce was the third Pastor of this church. He continued here about six years; during his ministry about two hundred were added to the church. Mr. Faunce was born at Plymouth, Mass., in 1828; graduated at Amherst College in 1850; pursued theological studies at Newton, and entered the ministry in 1853. He is at the present time Pastor of the Baptist church in Malden.

August 30th, 1860, the Rev. James Judson Tucker was ordained as the fourth pastor of this church. The sermon was preached by Rev. J. Girdwood of New Bedford; the ordaining prayer by Rev. Dr. Robinson of Rochester Theological Seminary; the charge to the pastor was given by Rev. Dr. Hovey of Newton; Rev. Lemuel Moss (who had the same day been ordained as the pastor of the First Baptist church,) gave the right hand of fellowship; Rev. J. D. E. Jones gave the charge to the people. The exercises closed with prayer and benediction by the pastor.

Rev. James Judson Tucker, was born in Halifax, Vt. October 6th, 1827; he graduated at Williams College in 1854, and at Rochester (N. Y.) Theological Seminary in 1860.

9. UNIVERSALIST. — There was no Society of this denomination in Worcester until 1841. A Church was formed in connection with the Society, November 21, 1843. The Rev. S. P. Landers was the first minister; he commenced his labors with them at the time of their organization, and continued his ministry here until March, 1844.

Rev. Albert Case was Mr. Landers' successor; he labored here more than four years. On retiring from Worcester he engaged in other business, and is not now preaching.

Rev O H. Tillotson was installed as pastor of this Church on the 27th of June, 1849 He is a native of Orford, N H He left the office of pastor in August, 1852, and after a short time spent in the study of the law, he entered into practice with Hon Henry Chapin He left Worcester again to engage in the ministry in 1859, and is now settled in Stafford, Ct Rev Mr Tillotson was a man greatly beloved by the people of his charge, and highly respected by his fellow citizens He represented the city in the Legislature in the year 1858

Rev. Mr Adams was installed as Mr Tillotson's successor in April 1853, and closed his pastoral services June 1st, 1860 Mr Adams was a man greatly beloved by his people, and highly respected in this community.

Rev L M Burrington succeeded Mr Adams as pastor, September 1st, 1860 He is a native of Vermont, he received his education at St Johnsbury, Woodstock, and at the University of Vermont at Burlington; he pursued his professional studies at Woodstock and Boston, under the care of Rev A A Miner, and was first settled in Reading in March, 1858 He married Miss Elizabeth M Brewster, of Woodstock, Vt, in June, 1859

10 ALL SAINTS CHURCH, (EPISCOPAL.) — There was an effort made in 1835 to establish the Episcopal Church in Worcester Services were held in the South Town Hall The first clergyman that officiated was the Rev Thomas H Vail; after a few months, services were suspended, and the hopes which had been entertained of establishing the church permanently in Worcester, were for the time disappointed

In 1843, another effort was made under the care of Rev F. C. Putnam, who, in a short time, was succeeded by the Rev Henry Blackaller

In 1847, under the Rectorship of the Rev George T Chapman, D D, the church edifice was built and dedicated to the Triune God by the Rt Rev Manton Eastburn, Bishop of the Diocese. From that time services have been regularly held, and the number of worshippers has gradually increased

The Rev George T Chapman, D D, did valuable service for the Church here, as well as the Church at large, by his unanswerable sermons in favor of the ministry, doctrines and worship of the Protestant Episcopal Church, that the truth lay between the two extremes of Romanism on the one hand, and Puritanism on the other. Hundreds have been reclaimed to her fold by reading these sermons

Rev George Clark succeeded Dr. Chapman in 1847, and his health failing, he resigned in 1849 He was succeeded by the Rev Nathaniel T. Bent, who labored acceptably and successfully until 1852, when he resigned and accepted a call to the Church at New Bedford After a short time he returned and established a school for young ladies at "Herbert Hall," where after a few years of valuable labor he died in 1856

He was succeeded by the Rev Archibald Morrison, who after four years was succeeded temporarily by the Rev Wm H Brooks, both of whom labored assiduously for the welfare of souls, when in 1858, th Rev. A. C. Patterson assumed the Rectorship, but on account of ill health, soon resigned, and the Rev. E. W. Hager from the Diocese of California, was called to the Rectorship of the parish in 1859.

The parish after years of change and discouragement now ranks among the first in the Diocese of Massachusetts, and is rapidly on the increase, — favorably attracting the attention of the citizens of Worcester, and by her prosperity cheering the hearts of friends far and near.

Mr. Hager was born April 27th, 1819, in Skaneateles, N. 'Y.; he was married in 1843, to Mary Jane Huxtable, of Skaneateles; he received his theological education at the Theological Seminary at Gambier, Ohio; and was ordained by Bishop McIlvaine in 1849.

11. LAUREL STREET, (2D METHODIST.) — This Church was duly organized July 20th, 1845; until February 1849 they held their meetings in such lecture rooms and halls as could most conveniently be procured; on the 27th of that month their new house on Laurel street was by public religious exercises consecrated to the especial honor of Almighty God, the Father, Son and Holy Ghost; the Rev. Stephen Olin, D. D., preached on that occasion. The house is a neat structure of wood, and will accommodate a growing congregation. They are known as the " Laurel Street Methodist Episcopal Church." Their first pastor was Rev. Richard S. Rust. He entered upon his labors July 1st, 1845. Diligent in the performance of his duties and devoted to his charge, he was acceptable as a preacher, and soon won the confidence and affection of his people. His ministry was short; elected to be principal of the "New Hampshire Conference Seminary," at Northfield, N. H., he accepted the appointment and was released from his prior engagements in February, 1846.

He was succeeded by Rev. J. W. Mowry, who came to Worcester with more than an ordinary reputation for ability and success in the Gospel ministry, and his services were such as not to disappoint the expectations which his coming had excited. His labors among his own people gave him a high place in their estimation, while his courteous bearing towards those of a different denomination awakened respect for him as a man and a Christian gentleman.

Rev. George Dunbar was his successor. He commenced his ministry here in April 1847. He was indefatigable in his exertions to secure the erection of their new house of worship. At the end of two years he was transferred to another field of labor, and his place was supplied in April, 1849, by the Rev. Francis A. Griswold.

Mr. Griswold's services were highly appreciated by those whom he served, and he was followed in the year 1850 by Rev. Cyrus L. Eastman, whose services were very acceptable and successful.

In the year 1851, Rev. Wm. Mann was appointed pastor of this Church, and continued in that relation two years. Owing to Mr. Mann's ill health he was unable to preach most of the time, and the pulpit was for the most part supplied by Rev. David H. Higgins. In his pastoral intercourse with his people Mr. Mann was very useful and much beloved.

In 1853 Rev. Joseph W. Lewis was stationed over this church. Mr. Lewis was a man of sterling worth, and his labors were successful.

In 1854, Rev. J. W. Mowry, of Wilbraham, Mass., a former pastor of this church, resumed his labors with this people, continuing with them for a period of one year.

In 1855, Rev. H. W. Warren, a graduate of the Wesleyan University at Middletown, Conn., was appointed to the charge of this Society, it being his first field of ministerial labor. Mr. Warren was a man of superior talent and scholarship, and labored very acceptably for the period of two years. He was then removed to Boston.

In the year 1857 Rev. Ichabod Marcy was appointed pastor of this Church. He labored very ardently and successfully both for the temporal and religious interests of the Society. Through his efforts the debt on their church edifice, which had long embarrassed the Society, was removed, and during a revival which was experienced many were added to the Church, who have since proved themselves to be worthy members.

In 1858, Rev. Samuel Kelley was appointed to this charge, and by the most unceasing pastoral labors and public efforts made many very warm friends, not only in his own Society but also in the city. In the spring of 1860, Mr. Kelley was removed to Newburyport, and Rev. J. C. Cromack was appointed in his stead; under the labors of Mr. Cromack the Society enjoyed great prosperity until the breaking out of the civil war in April 1861. In August following Mr. Cromack volunteered and was accepted as Chaplain to the 19th regiment Mass. Volunteers, and resigned his connection with the Society.

Rev. Jefferson Hascall, of Shrewsbury, who had long been favorably known as a Presiding Elder, was appointed to supply this Society during the remainder of the Conference year. Mr. Hascall is regarded as one of the most able and eloquent ministers of the Methodist Episcopal Church in New England, and at the time of our writing, (October, 1861,) he is regarded with great favor by his congregation, and is laboring with good prospects of success. Mr. Hascall was born in Thompson, Ct., and has been in the ministry many years.

12. CHURCH OF THE UNITY, (2D UNITARIAN.) — This church was formed in 1845, and in the latter part of that year and the beginning of the next, the edifice was reared and completed. Its location is eligible, its style of architecture tasteful, and its whole arrangement commodious and agreeable. It was dedicated to the worship of God, April 28, 1846. Itroductory prayer by the Rev. Mr. Clark of Uxbridge; prayer of dedication by Dr. Hill of Worcester; sermon by Dr. Dewey of New York; closing prayer by Rev. Mr. Wilson of Grafton.

On the first Sabbath in June, the Church passed the following resolves: "That this church has united for all means and purposes of Christian sympathy and fellowship, Therefore, Resolved, That an invitation be given to all persons present, to partake with us of the Lord's Supper."

Rev. Edward E. Hale was their first pastor. He was ordained April 29th, 1846. Rev. S. K. Lathrop of Boston, preached the sermon; Rev. Calvin Lincoln of Fitchburg, (now of Hingham,) made the prayer of ordination; Dr. Hill addressed the people; Rev. Ephraim Peabody of Boston, gave the charge; and Rev. John Weiss of Watertown, presented the right hand of fellowship. Mr. Hale is a native of Boston, and the second son of Nathan Hale of that city. He prepared for College at the Boston Latin School, entered Harvard College in 1835, and was graduated in the class of 1839. Rev. Dr. Palfrey and Rev. S. K. Lathrop of Boston, were his instructors in theology. In 1844 he preached several months in the city of Washington. In the spring of 1845, he first preached in Worcester. July 27th, 1856, Mr. Hale left this church to take charge of a church in Boston.

Rev. Rush R. Shippen was Mr Hale's successor. He was installed December 22, 1858. On that occasion Rev. James Freeman Clarke preached the sermon; Rev. Edward E. Hale offered the prayer of consecration; Rev. Rufus P. Stebbins gave the charge; Rev. Alonzo Hill, D. D., gave the right hand of fellowship; address to the people by Rev. John F. W. Ware.

Mr. Shippen was born in Meadville, Pa., January 18th, 1828. Attended the Alleghany College, (a Methodist institution,) at Meadville, and afterwards the Unitarian Theological School at the same place. He was ordained November 11th, 1849, and immediately took charge of the Unitarian church at Chicago, Ill., and remained there until July 1, 1857. After spending one year at Meadville he came to Worcester. Mr. Shippen married Miss Zoviah Rodman, of Oriskinny Falls, near Utica, N. Y.

13. SALEM STREET CHURCH, (4TH CONGREGATIONALIST.) — This Church was organized June 14th, 1848. On that occasion the Rev. E. Smalley preached the sermon; the consecrating prayer was offered by Dr. Nelson of Leicester; Dr. Sweetser gave the address to the church; the right hand of fellowship was given by the Rev. George P. Smith of the Old South.

The number constituted was one hundred and thirty three. About eighty of these were members of or regular worshippers with the Union Church, nearly thirty from the Calvinist Church, and the remainder mostly from the Old South Church. Their new house, which had been erected on Salem street, (from which they take their name,) was dedicated December 12th, 1848. Rev. Dr Sweetser preached the sermon; Rev. E. Smalley offered the prayer of dedication; and Rev. George P. Smith offered the concluding prayer. On the day following, Rev. George Bushnell was ordained their first pastor. Their house of worship is one of the largest in the city, conveniently arranged and attractive, and is built with brick.

At the ordination of Mr. Bushnell the introductory prayer was made by Rev. E. Smalley of the Union Church; sermon by Dr. Bushnell of Hartford, brother of the candidate; ordaining prayer by Rev. William P. Paine, of

Holden ; charge to the pastor by the Rev Dr. Nelson, of Leicester , right hand of fellowship by Rev Leverett Griggs, of Millbury ; address to the people by Rev J. W. Cross, of West Boylston , concluding prayer by Rev. Mr Corning, of Clinton Mr Bushnell is a native of Washington, Ct , was graduated at Yale College in 1842. He pursued his theological studies at the seminaries in Newburn and New Haven

Mr Bushnell having been chosen Superintendent of Public Schools by the City Council, asked a dismission from his relation as pastor, January 7th, 1857, and was dismissed by a mutual council, over which Rev Seth Sweetser, D D , presided, January 27th, 1858

December 29th, 1857, the Church and Society extended a call to the Rev. Merrill Richardson to become their pastor, by a vote in the Church of yeas 28, nays 23 ; and in the Society of yeas 24, nays 20. Mr Richardson accepted the call by his letter dated Terryville, Ct , January 7th, 1858, on a salary of fifteen hundred dollars, and two Sabbaths a year He was installed the same day that Mr Bushnell was dismissed, and still officiates in that office, to the entire acceptance of his numerous congregation

Mr Richardson was born in Holden, Mass , in 1812 ; graduated at Middlebury College, in 1835, studied theology in New Haven, and was settled in Terryville, Ct., in 1841. His first wife was Emily Allen of Middlesex, Vt. His second wife was Eunice Terry, of Terryville, Ct He labored two years in the Holden Teacher's Institute, and edited the School Journal, in Ct

14. CHAPEL AT LUNATIC HOSPITAL — In 1837 a chapel was erected for religious worship, and on the 8th of November in that year, it was solemnly dedicated to that purpose ; on the day of dedication about one hundred and twenty-five inmates were present It was the first assemblage that had ever taken place to so great an extent, and was a most interesting meeting

Rev Luzerne Rae, was the first regular chaplain employed to officiate in this Hospital. His term of service commenced in October, 1838, and was completed in September, 1839 He was well qualified for the place, and his labors were highly appreciated

Rev Julius F Reed, followed Mr Rae, and remained the chaplain until October 1st, 1840 His services were no less acceptable than had been those of his predecessor.

Rev George Allen succeeded Mr Reed, and continued to officiate as chaplain more than seventeen years Mr. Allen is a native of Worcester He graduated at Yale College in 1813 , in 1823 he settled as pastor of the church in Shrewsbury ; he was dismissed from that church in 1839, with cordial attestations to his ability and scholarship, his fidelity and success. With what success Mr Allen was able to perform the duties of his office will appear by the annual reports of the Superintendent, one only will we quote, from the Eleventh, p 86, " His performances are judicious and very acceptable to our congregation ; they are always interesting, and often eloquent and forcible expositions of religious truth. His views of all subjects are given with great freedom, and yet with such propriety and delicacy as to offend none and satisfy all." Since Mr. Allen left, the place has been occupied by different individuals, although none permanently.

Rev. Mr. Samuel Souther officiates now as its chaplain, to the satisfaction of all who are interested.

15. JAIL CHAPEL. — In connection with the County House and Jail located in Worcester, a convenient room, through the praiseworthy exertions of the Hon. John W. Lincoln, (who was then the High Sheriff of the county,) was set apart and fitted up for religious worship. The place was opened with appropriate religious services, and is known by the name of " Jail Chapel ; " there is also a Sabbath school for the especial benefit of the prisoners. The effect of this arrangement has been happy. Rev. George Dunbar, then pastor of the Second Methodist Church, was the first chaplain in this connection. He found here an attentive audience, and often had evidence that the truths of the Gospel are well fitted to reach the heart even of those who have become hardened by long-continued habits of transgression. He was followed by Mr. Francis Le Baron. Mr. Le Baron was the minister at large in Worcester, sustained principally by the Second Church and the Church of the Unity. Rev. Wm. T. Sleeper, Rev. Warren Burton, Rev. David Higgins, and Rev. Samuel Souther, have all served very acceptably as Chaplains in this department of labor, and Mr. Souther still continues with satisfaction to all.

16. EVANGELICAL CITY MISSION. — This Mission has been established about ten years. The experiment thus far has been most gratifying. Some years since, benevolent individuals were impressed with the conviction that there was great need of such a Mission ; and the Rev. Mr. Fox was employed for six months. He was not permitted to continue by reason of death. His memory is still precious to many. Deacon Moses Bingham, who had been licensed to preach by the Worcester Central Association, was Mr. Fox's successor. Deacon Bingham's first Annual Report showed that he had been indefatigable in his duties ; and evidence is not wanting that his exertions have been much blessed.

In 1853 Rev. Wm. T. Sleeper, from Andover Theological Seminary, commenced missionary labors, which were continued with great success for three years. From the first, those interested in the Mission had felt the need of a place of worship, and in 1854, through the liberality of Dea. I. Washburn, a tasteful Chapel was erected on Summer street, corner of Bridge street, with a tenement attached for the missionary's residence. The structure is an ornament to that part of the city, and one of the many proofs of the public spirit and generosity of its founder.

Rev. Samuel Souther succeeded Mr. Sleeper, February, 1857. continuing in the service of the Mission till September, 1860. As a part of his labors, an Industrial School was gathered and sustained at the Chapel. reaching at times two hundred children in attendance ; a field of effort in which all good citizens most warmly sympathize, and to support which many gave their hearty assistance. Outside of the above named organization, missionary labor has been acceptably performed by Rev. Messrs. Burton and Le Baron.

17. FRIENDS. — The number of families in Worcester who belong to the Quakers, is not large; in 1847, they erected a tasteful and commodious house of worship on the corner of Oxford and Chatham streets, and on the first of January, 1848, it was opened for public worship. They have meetings regularly on the Sabbath, and also on other days of the week. They have no settled pastor, but from time to time enjoy the ministrations of some of the regularly authorized preachers of the denomination. Their meetings are characterized by quiet and decorum. Some of their speakers have the reputation of being very eloquent.

The principal supporters of this meeting are among our most worthy and respected citizens, whose habits of life and intercourse with society are as unobjectionable and unobtrusive as the religion they profess.

18. SECOND ADVENT. — As early as 1840, individuals in Worcester were interested in what was called the "Second Advent;" preaching that the time was drawing near when they anticipated the second coming of Christ for a personal and visible reign on earth. Their numbers and zeal increased, and in 1850, they organized a Church, and since that period they have had for their spiritual teachers, Elder J. Shipman, formerly settled in New Hampshire; Elder George Needham, Elder J. S. White, Elder D. T. Taylor, and Elder Albion Ross, who is the present pastor. Mr. Ross was born in Nobleboro, Me., in 1825; he married Miss Irena D. Stephens of Lowell, Mass. This church worship at Warren Hall, and have adopted the following as their creed:

"We the undersigned, 'who are looking for that blessed hope and the glorious appearing of the great God and our Saviour Jesus Christ;' Titus 9: 18; Hebrews 9: 8: that we may walk in harmony, and more effectually advance the cause of our Saviour on earth, and spread the light of divine truth, live in peace with all Christians, and all men as far as in us lies, and labor for the conversion and' salvation of sinners, and lead a life of holiness and devotion to God; — agree to receive the Scriptures of the Old and New Testaments as the rule of our faith and practice, believing that reference to their sacred teachings will be sufficient to guide us in all the duties of life, as the members of the body of our Lord Jesus Christ."

19. ST. ANNE'S, (SECOND CATHOLIC.) — St. Anne's Church, East Worcester, Shrewsbury street, was commenced by Rev. M. W. Gibson, in 1855, and completed by Rev. Jno. J. Power, its present pastor. Rev. Jno. J. Power was born in Charlestown, this State, in 1828. After having passed through the public schools of his native place, began his college course in Holy Cross College this in city. Graduated in 1851. Pursued his Theological studies for one year in Montreal, Canada; continued the same studies

29

during three years in France at Aix. Was ordained priest in 1856. Placed in his present position, as pastor of St. Anne's, August 1856. Mr. Power has been one of the School Committee for four years, and is now serving out a term of six years as director of the Public Library.

20. CHURCH OF CHRIST. — This Church was divided and set off from the Advent Church, and worship in the Thomas street Chapel. They are denominated " Disciples of Christ, and sometimes called Campbellites. They consider immersion into the name of the Father, Son, and Holy Spirit, after a public, sincere, and intelligent confession of the faith in Jesus, as necessary to admission to the privileges of the kingdom of the Messiah, and as a solemn pledge, on the part of Heaven, of the actual remission of all past sins, and of adoption into the family of God."* Their distinctive feature, and that which distinguishes them from all other sects, is that they believe immersing the body, or baptism, will save them in the kingdom of God ; and that without this, no one can be saved in that kingdom.

21. ZION METHODIST, (COLORED.) — This Church was organized in 1846, and their house of worship was dedicated by Rev. C. Rush. Rev. Alexander Posey was their first pastor ; he was succeeded by Rev. Levin Smith, in 1849, who remained in charge about one year, when the church came within the cognizance of local preachers until re-organized in 1853, and Rev. J. A. Mars became their pastor. Mr. Mars proved himself to be a worthy and laborious pastor, and a man highly respected by his people and this community. Their place of worship was burned in June, 1854, in connection with the Merrifield fire; another was built on Exchange street in July, 1855, and dedicated by Rev. Mr. Raymond. Mr. Mars was succeeded by Rev. R. R. Morris in 1857 ; he was a deacon under Elder Mars one year, and became Elder himself in 1858. He was succeeded by Rev. P. Ross in 1859, who occupied that position one year, and was succeeded by Rev. Joseph Hicks in June 1860, who still remains its pastor.

Mr. Hicks was born at Long Island, N. Y., in 1818. He has preached in Bridgeport, Ct., New Haven, Hartford, Middletown, Providence, R. I., and New Bedford, Mass. Mr. Hicks married Miss Riley, of New York. He is a man of great energy, and is doing good service in his position. He has almost cleared the church of debt, and is exerting a salutary influence among his people.

This Church is not under, or in any connection with the Methodist Episcopal Conference as the other three are in this city. They belong to the " African Methodist Zion Church in America," and are controlled by their own Conference.

22. 3D METHODIST. — The Third Methodist Episcopal Church in this city was organized at New Worcester in April, 1860. Its first pastor, Rev.

° Hayward's Book of all Religions, page 62.

Daniel Dorchester, A M, was born in Duxbury, Plymouth county, Mass., but received his education at the "Norwich Academy," and the Wesleyan University, at Middleton, Ct. He was married April 15th, 1850, to Miss Mary P. Davis, daughter of Mr Henry Davis, of Dudley Mr Dorchester has been about fourteen years engaged in the work of the Christian ministry, which time has been spent chiefly in Connecticut

In the spring of 1855 he was elected to the Connecticut Senate, in which body he served as the Chairman of the Committee on the Humane Institutions of the State He was appointed Chairman of the Board of Commissioners on Idiocy, whose duty it was to investigate into the number and condition of the idiots in the State, and their susceptibility of improvement, and make their report to the next Legislature

This new church has commenced with favorable indications Its membership is small, but much united, numbering at first but thirty-one, it increased to sixty-three, during the first year. A very interesting and promising Sabbath School has been organized under the efficient superintendence of Mr John Dean, late of Providence, R I. The school embraces about one hundred and seventy members

A congregation of about two hundred persons assemble every Sabbath in Union Hall, for religious services A lively interest is manifested by all the religious denominations residing in that part of the city, in the progress and success of this enterprise, and pecuniary contributions are freely made by them in aid of the Society   *

23 GERMANS —The Germans resident in Worcester number not far from four hundred They are mainly employed in the manufacturing establishments of the city

The following account of their social and religious history and condition, was communicated to the author of this volume by Mr Jacob P. Weixler

The first religious services in the German language held at Worcester, took place in May, 1853, at the Park street Church, and were conducted by Rev S F Zimmermann, of Philadelphia. The occurrence of this service awakened in some of the Germans a desire for the establishment of a church among them. Accordingly, on a subsequent Sabbath, a number of persons met for the purpose of organizing a Society for mutual religious instruction. This body met in private houses

During the spring of 1855, subsequent to the completion of the Mission Chapel erected by the munificence of Dea I Washburn, a desire was felt for the institution of services of a more formal and public character, and the free use of the Chapel was most kindly tendered for that purpose [It is not known to the author of this volume whether the proposal for these religious services proceeded from within or from without the Germans resident in Worcester] The Moravian Missionary Society, located at Bethlehem, Penn, appointed Rev Jacob Leonard Rau, to labor in Worcester. He was accordingly installed with appropriate services, conducted by Rev Charles F. Seitel,

Secretary of the Society. A subscription was opened among the American friends of the Germans for the support of the missionary. Messrs. Morrison, Salisbury, Washburn, Davis, and Thurber, were the chief subscribers. Some of the churches of the city also took up collections in aid of this people. A subscription for the same purpose was opened among the German population. After laboring with great faithfulness but with many discouragements for about two years, Mr. Rau was appointed by the Society to labor in Provi- dence, where he still resides. Rev. W. Geyer was then appointed to labor in his place, residing in Norwich and preaching in Worcester one Sunday in a fortnight. The services connected with his installation were conducted by Rev. Mr. Schultz of Bethlehem. After laboring for a year with much fidelity, though amid many obstacles, Mr. G. suspended his labors, and no public religious services have been held since his departure.

The Germans in Worcester have their organizations, viz: an order of " Hungarrie," similar in design to the Odd Fellows, formed for charity and mutual aid, established in 1853, and now possess a capital of about $500; one Lieder Krantz or Singing Society, and one Gymnastic Society.

SPIRITUALISTS. — This sect, or class of worshippers, hold regular meetings in the city on the Sabbath, and other days of the week, and among them are some of our most respectable citizens. They claim to receive their inspiration from the spirits of the departed through different processes of communication. Some are " knocking " mediums, some " tipping," some " writing," and some spirits communicate through " trance " mediums. The Bible to a cer- tain extent is discarded.

————

MINISTERS NOT CONNECTED WITH CHURCHES AS PASTORS, AND WHO ARE NOT MENTIONED ELSEWHERE.

Rev. Robert Everett Pattison, D. D., was born in Benson, Vt., August 19th, 1800. At the age of sixteen he emigrated with his father's family to the western part of New York, designated the Holland Purchase. He was fitted for College at Wyoming Academy — then called Middlebury Academy — and entered Amherst College in the autumn of 1822 ; graduating with the class of 1826.

On coming to Massachusetts for his collegiate education he brought letters of introduction to the late Dr. Going, and for several years spent portions of each year in this city, enjoying the friendship and counsels of that venerable man, to whom so many young men have been indebted for judicious counsel and encouraging sympathy.

After having spent a few years in teaching — first as tutor in Columbia College, D. C., and afterwards as Professor of Mathematics, &c., in Waterville College, Me , he received a license to preach in the First Baptist Church in this city, and was soon after settled as pastor of the First Baptist Church in Providence, R. I , being the immediate successor of the late Dr Stephen Gano He was pastor of this church about eight years.

For three years he was one of the secretaries of the Baptist Board of Foreign Missions, Boston. He has been between eight and nine years President of Waterville College, which place he resigned in consequence of impaired health, in 1858. At present Dr Pattison has the charge of the Oread Institute for Young Ladies in this city — conducted chiefly by members of his own family

He received the honorary degree of Doctor of Divinity from Brown University at the Commencement of 1839 Nearly thirty years of his life has been devoted to teaching Besides frequently contributing articles to our periodical literature and religious magazines, he is the author of several published addresses, and of a Commentary (Explanatory, Doctrinal, and Practical,) on the Epistle to the Ephesians

The late wife of Dr. Pattison was Frances, the youngest daughter of Deacon James Wilson of this city

Rev David Metcalf was born in Lebanon, Conn , Nov. 27, 1795 , graduated at Yale College in 1819 approbated to preach the Gospel by the Windham Association, in May, 1823 ; attended the Theological Lectures in New Haven, in 1827–8 , was ordained pastor of the Congregational Church, May, 1829, and dismissed in the autumn of 1832 He continued to preach as stated supply in different places in Massachusetts, New Hampshire and Ohio, till 1840, and on account of a bronchial affection only occasionally since. He came to Worcester in 1853. and since then has written and published a work on Moral Obligation

Thomas Wentworth Higginson, son of Stephen Higginson and Louisa Storrow, was born in Cambridge, Mass , Dec 22, 1823. Graduated at Harvard College in 1841, and at the Cambridge Theological School, in 1847, having spent part of the intervening period in teaching and in private study , was ordained in 1847 as minister of the First Religious Society in Newburyport, retaining that position until 1850, when he resigned it. In 1850 he was the candidate of the Free Soil party to represent the District in Congress, but was defeated In 1852 he was invited to become minister of the newly-organized " Free Church " of Worcester, and removed thither for that purpose. He has since resided in Worcester, having resigned his office in 1858, in order to devote himself to literary pursuits He was married, in September, 1847, to Mary Elizabeth Channing, daughter of Walter Channing, M D , of Boston. Mr Higginson is the author of various pamphlets and magazine articles, especially in connection with the Atlantic Monthly

Rev Henry A. Eaton, Universalist, formerly settled in Cambridge, Milford, Waltham and Meriden, Ct Mr Eaton died May, 1861

29*

Rev. J. D. Baldwin was graduated and studied theology at New Haven. After preaching several years in Connecticut, was editor and publisher of the " Republican," a weekly newspaper, issued at Hartford, Conn. In 1852 became editor of the Boston "Daily Commonwealth," and was editor of that paper after its name was changed to " Evening Telegraph." Mr. Baldwin purchased the Spy establishment in 1858.

Rev. Albert Tyler was born in Smithfield, R. I., Nov. 16, 1823. Received ordination from the Union Association of Universalists at its session in Warren, in 1851, and became pastor of the Universalist church in Oxford, Mass., 1852, and remained there two years. In 1854 accepted the call of the First Universalist Society in Granby, Conn., and remained there six years. In 1860 became pastor of the Universalist church in Quincy, Mass., remaining there but one year. He returned to this city, where he formerly resided, and is now engaged in the printing business.

Rev. Chester Newell graduated at Yale College, and studied theology at Alexandria, Va., and entered the Navy of the United States as chaplain, in 1841. He was obliged to leave his post on account of ill health in 1857, and retired on three-fourths pay. On the breaking out of the present war Mr. Newell tendered his services to the Secretary of the Navy, but on account of feeble health was exempted from active service. He married in 1851 Miss Sarah Z., of Philadelphia, daughter of Mr. James Hall, formerly of Shrewsbury, Mass.

Rev. William H. Sanford, born in Belchertown, Feb. 14, 1800; graduated at Harvard College, 1827; ordained at Boylston, Oct. 17, 1832; dismissed Sept. 1857, and removed to Worcester Sept. 1857.

Rev. John Toulmin, born in Preston, county of Lancashire, England, 1811, son of John Toulmin. Commenced preaching in England, removed to this country in 1845, and was ordained deacon in 1854, by Bishop Baker, of the M. E. Church, and ordained Elder in 1858.

Rev. Zephaniah Baker, born in Dudley, July 7th, 1815; ordained 1837; projected and published, some time, the Gospel Messenger at Providence, R. I., from 1840 to 1843, afterwards the Providence and Worcester Journal. Settled over the Fifth Universalist Society in New York city, from 1846 to 1849, which charge he was obliged to relinquish on account of bronchial difficulty, whereby the use of speech was denied him. Mr. Baker took charge of the Worcester Free Public Library in February, 1860.

Rev. James R Stone, graduated at Brown University in 1838; preached in Wickford, R. I., North Stonington and Hartford, Ct., and at Providence, R. I. Mr. Stone came to Worcester in 1860, and took charge of the Worcester

Academy, which office he now holds. He married, first, Miss Sarah A. Gilmore, of Providence, R. I., she having died, he married, second, Miss Gertrude E. Stelle of New York city.

Rev. Llkanah Andrews Cummings was born at Parkman, Me., January 31, 1821, graduated at Waterville College, 1847, and at the Newton Theological Institution, 1850, was ordained pastor of the First Baptist Church, Amherst, Mass., May 8, 1851. United with several gentlemen in calling the first meeting, which was held at Amherst, Dec. 3d, 1853, to consider the question of founding, in Massachusetts, a college for females. This College receiving a charter from the General Court, April, 1854, Mr. Cummings was elected Financial Secretary, and, until the present time, has labored in its establishment with unabated zeal. He removed to Worcester, where the College is located, in March, 1855. In Nov. 1852, he married Emily S. Spicer of Rochester, N. Y.

Rev. Job B. Boomer, born at Fall River in 1793; commenced the ministry in 1819, and was ordained over the Second Baptist church in Sutton, and after an honorable dismission, which took place April 11, 1841, and was again settled in West Brookfield in 1841, he remained there about four years, and afterwards preached for the First Baptist Church in Sutton three years. He supplied the Second Church one year, he then went to North Uxbridge and supplied that church one year. He came to Worcester in 1852, and is now supplying the 2d Baptist Church in Sutton. He married in 1818 Miss Nancy, daughter of Deacon McClellan of Sutton.

Rev. Joseph B. Brown was born at Thompson, Conn., in 1806, was educated at Wilbraham, Mass., and entered the ministry in 1831, labored with the M. E. Church about eleven years in this State, he then united with the Second Baptist Church in Newport, R. I.; after this he became pastor of the Baptist Church in Lonsdale, R. I. He then assumed the agency of the American Baptist Board of Foreign Missions, where he labored until his health became impaired. He married Lydia, daughter of Percy Jenkins, of Nantucket, Mass.

The Rev. A. D. Spalter, late Rector of St. John's Church, Wilkinsonville, Mass., was ordained to the ministry of the Protestant Episcopal Church, by the Rt. Rev. J. H. Hopkins, D. D. LL. D., of the Diocese of Vermont.

Rev. Werden P. Reynolds was born at Canaan, N. Y., in 1788, he was ordained pastor of the Baptist Church in Rupert, Vt., in 1811. In 1825 he became the pastor of the Baptist Church in Manchester, Vt., and continued its pastor thirty years. In 1857 he removed to this city, and is now engaged in preaching the Gospel at the Mission Chapel as assistant with Rev. Mr. Souther, and at the Poor Farm, and elsewhere. For fifty-seven years Mr. Reynolds has not drank a single drop of ardent spirits except in medicine and has *never* in his life spoken a profane word, and never since his ordination failed to preach on account of ill health.

LAWYERS.

Levi Lincoln remained a member of Congress until he resigned in 1841; was appointed by President Harrison in that year Collector of the port of Boston; in 1844 was elected to the State Senate and served two years, the last year he was president of that body; in 1848 was elected first Mayor of the city, and served one year, since then has mainly retired to private life. He has been chairman of the Commissioners of Hope Cemetery since the organization of that Board.

Henry Chapin was a graduate of Brown University of 1835; he was the son of Elisha Chapin, born in Upton, in the County of Worcester. After leaving college Mr. Chapin studied law from 1835 to 1838, a part of the time in the office of Hon. Emory Washburn in Worcester, and a part in the law school at Cambridge. He commenced practice in Worcester in July, 1838. In 1839 he married Sarah R. Thayer, a daughter of Joseph Thayer, Esq., of Uxbridge. In 1845 he represented the town of Uxbridge in the Massachusetts House of Representatives; in 1846 removed to Worcester and practiced law in partnership with Hon. Rejoice Newton for two years. In the year 1848, upon a reconstruction of the Insolvency system, he was appointed by Gov. Briggs sole Commissioner of Insolvency for the County of Worcester. In 1849 he was elected Mayor of the city of Worcester; held the office for two years, and was re-nominated, but declined a re-election. In 1851 was nominated for the Massachusetts Senate, but declined. In 1853 was elected from Worcester a delegate to the Constitutional Convention. In 1855 was appointed by Gov. Gardner a Commissioner under the Personal Liberty Law, and accepted the appointment. In 1856 was unanimously nominated for Congress by the Republicans of the Ninth Congressional District, but declined the nomination. In 1858, upon a new organization of the Courts of of Probate and Courts of Insolvency, by which the jurisdiction of both Courts is vested in one judge, Mr. Chapin was appointed by Gov. Banks to the office of Judge of Probate and Insolvency, which he now holds. Since Mr. Chapin commenced business he has applied himself diligently to the duties of his profession, and has been too much occupied by a laborious and extensive practice to engage in political life except as an incidental necessity, preferring the comforts of a quiet home, to the restless artificial life which seems to be too often incidental to political office.

Peter C. Bacon was born in Dudley, Mass., Nov. 11, 1804; was the son of Jepthah Bacon, Esq. He graduated at Brown University in the class of 1827;

road law at New Haven Law School, also in the office of Davis and Allen, of Worcester, and Ira M Barton of Oxford, and George A Tufts of Dudley He was admitted to the bar in September, 1830, and practiced law in Oxford twelve years; removed to Worcester January 1, 1841, where he has been in the practice of the law ever since Mr Bacon was elected a member of the House of Representatives to represent the city of Worcester in the General Court the first year of its organization, in 1848, and was elected Mayor of the city in 1851 and 1852 The degree of Doctor of Laws was conferred on him by Brown University in 1857.

John S C. Knowlton has been the editor of the Palladium from its first number to the present time, about twenty-eight years. He was the 4th Mayor of the city, in 1853-4 In 1857 he was appointed Sheriff of the County, and holds that office at this time The author places this notice of Mr Knowlton in the chapter with the Lawyers for two reasons. first, he has been one of the Mayors, and the order would not be complete without, second, being the sheriff of the county, the presumption is that he hears as much law as any of the lawyers

George W Richardson was the son of John Richardson of Newton; was born in Boston, and studied law with Hon. P. Merrick, was admitted to the bar and began practice here in 1834 He was commissioned by Gov. Davis in 1841 as Aid to the Commander-in-Chief of Massachusetts; was appointed in 1853 by Gov Clifford Sheriff of the County of Worcester, which office he held for three years, was chosen President of the City Bank of Worcester at its organization in 1854, which office he now holds, was chosen Mayor of Worcester in 1855 and 1857, was appointed Bank Commissioner of Massachusetts by Gov Gardner in 1857, which office he held about one year and resigned. Mr Richardson graduated at Harvard College in 1829.

Isaac Davis still continues in the profession of the law, was Mayor of Worcester in 1856, 1858, and 1861; was a member of the State Senate in 1843 and 1854, member of the House of Representatives in 1852, and of the Executive Council in 1851 Elected a member of the Constitutional Convention to revise the Constitution of Massachusetts in the year 1853, appointed a member of the State Board of Education in 1852, and held that office for eight years Appointed by the Secretary of War one of the Board of Visitors to examine the institution at West Point in 1855, and was chosen President of the Board of Visitors. Appointed Assistant Treasurer of the United States by the President, which appointment Mr Davis declined The honorary degree of LL D was conferred on him in 1846, by Columbia College, Washington, Brown University conferred on him the degree of LL D in 1860 Mr Davis holds many offices in business, literary, scientific, and benevolent institutions

Alexander H. Bullock, son of Rufus Bullock, born at Royalston, Mass., March 2d, 1816; graduated at Amherst College in 1836, read law with Hon. Emory Washburn and at Harvard Law School, admitted to the bar in 1841, for several years in partnership with Hon. Thomas Kinnicutt; in 1844, married Elvira, daughter of Col. A. G. Hazard, of Enfield, Conn. In 1841 was appointed one of the aides de camp of Hon. John Davis, then Governor of Massachusetts, was a member of the House of Representatives from Worcester in 1845, 1847, 1848, 1861, and elected for 1862. Chairman of the Judiciary Committee in 1848 and 1861, a Senator from Worcester County in 1849; appointed Commissioner of Insolvency in 1853, and Judge of Insolvency for the County of Worcester in 1856, and resigned the office in 1858. Mayor of the city of Worcester in 1859.

William W. Rice was born at Deerfield, Mass., March 7th, 1826, son of Rev. Benjamin Rice, and graduated at Bowdoin College in 1846; was preceptor in Leicester Academy from September, 1847 to September, 1851; he then came to Worcester and studied law with Hon. Emory Washburn; was admitted to the bar, May, 1854; appointed Special Justice of the Police Court, April, 1855; Judge of Insolvency for the County of Worcester, February, 1858; Mayor of Worcester for the year 1860.

P. Emory Aldrich was born in New Salem,—attended the public schools till he was sixteen years old, and then became a teacher,—went through the usual preparatory course of studies, at Shelburne Falls Academy; after which, in the fall of 1837, he went to Virginia, and was there engaged in teaching until 1842; completed in the meantime a pretty extensive course of classical and mathematical studies, and began the study of law, which he continued at the Cambridge Law School eighteen months during the years 1842 and '43. He then returned to Virginia to fulfill an engagement in the school with which he had been formerly connected. Was admitted to the bar on examination at Richmond, Va., in 1845, but did not commence practice there. In December, 1845, he returned to his native state, entered the office of Messrs. Chapman, Ashmun & Norton, of Springfield, as a law student, and remained there six months, and while there was admitted to the bar, and was then a few months in the office of F. A. Brooks, Esq., in Petersham. In December, 1846, he commenced practice in Barre, in company with N. F. Bryant, Esq. This connection continued two years. Soon after his removal to Barre, he became the editor and subsequently proprietor of the Barre Patriot, which paper he edited, and published, for about three years. In 1853, he was elected to represent the town of Barre, in the convention held that year for the revision of the State Constitution. In May of the same year, he was appointed district attorney, by Governor Clifford, for the Middle District; which office he still holds, having been twice elected, since the office was made elective, in 1856. In the spring of 1854, he removed from Barre to this city, and opened an office here. In Jan. 1855, he formed a law partnership with Hon. P. C. Bacon, which

till continues   In December, 1861, he was elected Mayor of this city for
he year 1862

Pliny Merrick continued Attorney for the Commonwealth until 1843, and
vas then appointed Judge of the Court of Common Pleas   in 1848 he re-
igned that office.   During the two succeeding years he was president of the
Worcester and Nashua Railroad Company and devoted most of his time to its
business , he was, however, to some extent engaged in professional service.
t was during this period he was counsel for professor Webster on his trial
or the murder of Dr George Parkman   In 1850 he was a senator for the
County of Worcester in the State Senate.   December 31, 1850, he was a
econd time appointed a Judge of the Court of Common Pleas   In 1853
vas appointed one of the Judges of the Supreme Judicial Court, and still
holds the office.   Judge Merrick removed from Worcester to Boston in 1855,
where he still resides.

Charles Allen was senator of the Commonwealth in 1855, 6, and 7   repre-
sentative in 1840, was Commissioner of Massachusetts with Hon Abbot
Lawrence, and Hon John Mills, at the treaty of Washington, relating to the
North Eastern Boundary of the United States in 1842, same year he was
appointed Judge of the Court of Common Pleas, and resigned in 1844,
Elector of President and Vice President in 1844; nominated Judge of the
Supreme Judicial Court, but declined the appointment, in 1847   Mr Allen
was a member of the 31st and 32d Congress of the United States , and was
appointed Chief Justice of the Superior Court for the County of Suffolk in
1858, and accepted the appointment of Chief Justice of the Superior Court of
the Commonwealth at its organization in 1860   Declining a seat on the
bench of the Supreme Court, he was a member of the Constitutional Convention of 1853.   He was also a member from Massachusetts of the Peace
Congress at Washington in 1861

Emory Washburn, in 1841 and 1842, was a member of the Massachusetts
Senate   In 1844 he was appointed Judge of the Court of Common Pleas, and
resigned in December, 1847   In 1853 he was chosen Governor of the Commonwealth, and served one year   In 1856 was appointed Professor of Law
in Harvard University, and still retains that office.   Gov. Washburn removed
from Worcester to Cambridge in the autumn of 1856, where he still resides.

Benjamin F Thomas was a member of the House of Representatives for
Worcester in 1842, and appointed Commissioner of Bankruptcy the same
year   He was appointed Judge of Probate in 1844, and resigned in 1848,
he same year was chosen Elector of President and Vice President, and was
Secretary of the Electoral College   In 1853 Judge Thomas was appointed
one of the Justices of the Supreme Judicial Court, and resigned in 1859, and
soon after removed to Roxbury, and commenced the practice of the law in

Boston. In June, 1861, he was elected representative to Congress from the Third District, to fill the place of Hon. Charles F. Adams, who had been appointed minister to the Court of St. James.

Ira Moore Barton was commissioned Judge of Probate, February 22, 1836, and resigned October 1, 1844; in 1840 he was chosen one of the Electors of President and Vice President. In 1844 he entered into a law copartnership with Hon. Peter C. Bacon of Oxford, which continued until 1849, when Mr. Barton sailed for Europe. In 1846 he was one of the representatives of Worcester in the General Court. Judge Barton is a counsellor of the American Antiquarian Society, and a member of the New York and the Wisconsin Historical Societies.

Maturin L. Fisher was Post Master of Worcester, from 1839 to 1849. He then removed to Farmersburg, Clayton County, Iowa. Elected to the Senate of Iowa in 1852 and 1856. He was president of that body in 1854 and 1856. In 1857 elected superintendent of Public Instruction of the State, and was appointed Loan Agent of the State in 1861, both of which offices he now holds, with honor to himself, and profit to his constituents. Mr. Fisher married Miss Caroline A. Pratt, daughter of Dr. L. Nathan Pratt, of Worcester.

J. C. B. Davis was born in Worcester, Dec. 29th, 1822, graduated at Cambridge in the class of 1840, was admitted to practice in Worcester, March term C. C. P.,1844—was appointed Secretary of Legation at London by General Taylor in 1849, and entered on duties of the office in August of that year; was charge d'affaires ad interim from August to October, 1849, remained Secretary till Dec., 1852, when he resigned; resided in London during the year 1853, having since been a resident of New York, where he is now practicing law.

Dwight Foster, son of Alfred Dwight Foster, born in Worcester, December 13th, 1828, graduated at Yale College in 1848. Studied law with Messrs. Barton & Bacon, at Worcester, with Samuel C. Perkins, Esq., at Philadelphia, and at the Harvard Law School; was admitted to the bar in Dec., 1849. He has since pursued his profession in this city, and has been associated in partnership with the following gentlemen: Peter C. Bacon, Benjamin F. Thomas, James E. Estabrook, and George W. Baldwin. He married Aug. 20th, 1850, Henrietta P., daughter of Hon. Roger S. Baldwin, of New Haven, Connecticut. In the year 1854, he was aid de camp of Hon. Emory Washburn, then Governor of Massachusetts. In the year 1858, from February to July he was Judge of Probate of the county of Worcester. In November 1860, he was elected Attorney General of Massachusetts, which office he now holds.

Charles W. Hartshorn was born at Taunton, Mass., October 8, 1814; graduated at Harvard College in 1833; was admitted to the bar, March 9, 1837;

commissioned Master in Chancery, July 2, 1844; appointed Clerk of the Supreme Judicial Court, October 6, 1847, held the office for five years, and declined a re-appointment.

Charles Devens, Jr., the eldest son of Charles and Mary (Lithgow) Devens, was born at Charlestown, in the county of Middlesex, April 4, 1820. Mr. Devens graduated at Cambridge in 1838, and afterwards pursued the study of the law in the school at Cambridge, and in the office of Hubbard and Watts of Boston. He was admitted to the bar in 1840, and commenced the practice of law at Northfield in the county of Franklin, and removed thence in 1844 to Greenfield in the same county, where he practiced in partnership with Hon. Geo. T. Davis until 1849. Mr. Devens represented the county of Franklin in the State Senate during the years 1848 and 1849, where he served on the Committee of the Judiciary during both years, and during the latter year as chairman of the joint Committee on Militia. In 1849 he was appointed by President Taylor Marshal of the United States for the District of Massachusetts, which office he held until his resignation in the spring of 1853. Mr. Devens resumed the practice of the law in May, 1854, establishing himself in the city of Worcester, where in 1857 he formed a partnership with George F. Hoar and J. Henry Hill, Esqs., which continued until 1858, when Mr. Hill retired from the partnership, and Messrs. Devens and Hoar have since practiced together. During the years 1856, 7, and 8, Mr. Devens was the City Solicitor of Worcester. He was appointed Colonel of the 15th Massachusetts regiment in 1861, and is now in the field doing good service for his country.

Elijah B. Stoddard was born in Upton, June 5, 1826, son of Colonel Elijah Stoddard; graduated at Brown University in 1847; studied law with John C. B. Davis, Esq., at Worcester, and was admitted to the bar, June 18, 1849. He commenced business with John C. B. Davis, under the firm of Davis and Stoddard, and on the dissolution of that firm, formed a partnership with Hon. Isaac Davis, which continued until 1855. He represented the city of Worcester in the Legislature in 1856; succeeded John H. Matthews in the office of District Attorney, and held the same for about six months. He was President of the Common Council in 1858. In 1856 he was appointed a staff officer by Major General Augustus Morse, and in 1858 was elected the first commander of the Third Battalion of Rifles. He was appointed aiddecamp to Governor Banks in 1860. Col. Stoddard married, 16th June 1852, Mary E., eldest daughter of Hon. Isaac Davis.

George F. Verry, born at Mendon, this county, July 14th, 1826; commenced the study of the law in the office of H. D. Stone, May, 1849; was admitted to the bar at Worcester, Sept. 8th, 1851; commenced practice of law in Worcester in the of autumn that year; formed a copartnership with H. D. Stone, July, 1852, which continued till July, 1857; since which time has practiced law.

John W. Wetherell, graduated at Yale College in 1844, and at the Law School of Harvard University in 1846. Studied law for a few months in the office of Barton & Bacon at Worcester, where he was admitted to the bar, in the autumn of 1846. In January 1847, he opened a law office in Worcester, where he has continued in the practice of his profession. In 1858, he married Hester, daughter of Hon. Rejoice Newton, of Worcester. He was appointed aiddecamp to Governor Andrew in 1861.

S. B. I. Goddard was born in Shrewsbury, Mass., September 5th, 1821. He pursued his studies preliminary to entering College, in the Grammar School in Worcester; graduated at Amherst College in 1840, and commenced the study of law immediately after in the office of Hon. Isaac Davis; was admitted to practice at the bar in Sept., 1843; and has since been engaged in the practice of law in Worcester.

Joseph Mason, a native of Northfield, Mass., and a son of the Rev. Thomas Mason, late of that place, was born March 16th, A. D. 1813. He studied law with Hon. Samuel C. Allen, of Northfield, also at the Law School in Cambridge, and in the office of Hon. Emory Washburn, at Worcester. He was admitted to the bar at Worcester, Sept. 6th, A. D. 1837, and immediately commenced the practice of law, in Westborough, where he remained till the following spring, and then removed to Templeton, and resumed there the practice of law. In the spring of the year 1846, Mr. Mason removed to Worcester, and practiced law here till Oct. 1852, when he was appointed clerk of the Judicial Courts, for this county, and has since held that office.

George Frisbie Hoar, son of Hon. Samuel Hoar of Concord, and Sarah, daughter of Roger Sherman, of Connecticut; born at Concord, Mass., August 29, 1826. Graduated at Harvard University, 1846; studied law in the office of his brother, Judge E. R. Hoar, at Concord, from Sept., 1846, to Sept., 1847; in the Law School of Harvard University, from Sept., 1847, to Aug., 1849; in the office of Judge B. F. Thomas, at Worcester, from Aug., 1849, to Dec., 1849. Admitted to the bar, Dec., 1849, then opened an office in Worcester. June 8th, 1852, went into partnership with Hon. Emory Washburn, which partnership continued till Jan. 8th, 1854, when Mr. Washburn became Governor of the Commonwealth. In partnership with Hon. C. Devens, Jr., and J. Henry Hill, Esq., from Jan. 1st, 1857, to Dec. 1st, 1858, and since the latter date with Hon. C. Devens, Jr. Representative in the General Court, and chairman of committee on probate and chancery in 1852; Senator and chairman of judiciary committee, in 1857. Married March 30th, 1853, Mary Louisa Spurr, daughter of Samuel D. and Mary A. Spurr, who died Jan. 30th, 1859.

Francis H. Dewey, eldest son of Hon. Charles A. Dewey, was born at Williamstown, Mass., July 12, 1821; graduated at Williams College in 1840;

studied law at the Yale and Harvard Law Schools, and at Northampton with Hon Charles P Huntington, prior to May, 1842, when he entered the office of Hon. Emory Washburn, in Worcester, with whom he completed his studies He was admitted to the bar, June, 1843, and formed a connection in business with Mr Washburn, which was dissolved by the appointment of the latter as judge of the Court of Common Pleas in July, 1844. Mr Dewey continued alone, having a large and successful practice, till September, 1850, when he formed a co-partnership with Hartley Williams, Esq, which has continued till the present time In November, 1846, he married Frances A, only daughter of John Clarke, Esq, of Northampton, she deceased March 13, 1851 he married, April 26, 1853, Sarah B, daughter of Hon. George A. Tufts of Dudley. In the fall of 1855, Mr Dewey was chosen a member of the Massachusetts Senate; was the republican candidate for the presidency of the Senate, and was chairman of the judiciary committee, with this exception he has not been engaged in political life, but has devoted himself to the duties of his profession

Charles G. Prentiss was appointed Register of Probate in July, 1837, and held that office with honor to himself until 1859, since then has practiced law in this city.

Edward Mellen was born in Westborough, in the county of Worcester, the 26th of September, 1802, graduated at Brown University in 1823, was admitted to the bar in Middlesex on the 11th of December, 1828 Opened an office on the same day in East Cambridge, where he remained for only a short time He removed to Wayland on the 22d day of October, 1830, where he remained in practice till the time of his appointment to the bench of the Court of Common Pleas, which took place November 17th, 1847 He was appointed Chief Justice of that Court in June, 1855 This office he retained till the 1st day of July, 1859, when the Superior Court took the place of the Court of Common Pleas—a court which had been in existence from the earliest times after the colonization of this country. After his retirement from the bench, he opened an office in Worcester, in August, 1859

William A Smith graduated at Harvard University in 1843; was the son of John A Smith of Leicester, Mass, fitted for college at Leicester Academy; studied law with Emory Washburn and Francis H. Dewey; admitted to the bar September 2d, 1846 When the office of Assistant Clerk of the Courts for the county of Worcester was established, in April, 1850, he was appointed by the Supreme Court, and has filled the office by successive appointments to the present time

John A Dana was born at Princeton in this county, March 10, 1823, entered Yale College in 1840, graduated in 1844; taught school two years in Pennsylvania, during which time read law in the office of Hon Wm Strong, now one of the Justices of the Supreme Court of that State. In October, 1846, resumed the study of the law in the office of Barton and Bacon, and was admitted to the bar at Boston, January 21, 1848. Opened an office in Worcester, February 1, 1848 ; has practiced law in this city since. November 26, 1860, married Eliza Henshaw, youngest daughter of Hon. Isaac C. Bates, late of Northampton.

William Austin Williams, the son of George Williams, was born in Hubbardston, August 29th, 1820. He entered the office of Francis A. Brooks of Petersham ; afterwards spent eighteen months at the Law School of Cambridge, and finished his studies in the office of W. A. Bryant of Barre, and of John C. B. Davis of Worcester ; was admitted to the bar in 1848. He commenced the practice of the law in the office of Otis Bridges, and in June following formed a connection in business with him, which continued one year ; since then he has been in the practice of the law alone. Mr. Williams has been a member of the Board of Aldermen two years ; was City Solicitor one year ; aid to Gov. Boutwell two years ; Worcester Commissioner of Insolvency since 1859.

A. McF. Davis was born in Worcester, December 30, 1833 ; son of Hon. John Davis, late of Worcester. Appointed a midshipman in the U. S. Navy, March, 1849. Went one cruise up the Mediterranean, and resigned in Sept. 1852. Entered Lawrence Scientific School in 1852 ; graduated in 1854. Studied law in the office of Eaton, Davis, and Tailer, New York, and in Columbia Law School ; was admitted to practice in New York, May 9th, 1859. Admitted to the bar of Massachusetts, and commenced practice in Worcester the same fall.

Henry C. Rice, son of Oliver Rice, was born at Millbury, in Worcester county, August 22, 1827. Graduated at Brown University, September, 1850 ; studied law with Bacon and Foster of Worcester, and commenced the practice of the law at Worcester in November, 1852. Member of the Common Council in the years 1858 and 1861 ; Master in Chancery and Notary Public ; Representative to the General Court from Worcester in the years 1859 and 1860. Married Josephine Allen, daughter of Hon. Charles Allen of Worcester, April 23, 1861.

William S. Davis was born in Northboro' in 1832. Graduated at Harvard University in 1853, and was admitted to practice in 1855.

Charles M. Ruggles was born in Providence, R. I., July 25, 1835. Studied law with Hon. Emory Washburn and Devens and Hoar, and at Dane Law School, Cambridge. Admitted to the bar in Worcester at the March term of the Superior Court, 1860, and commenced the practice of the law in said city in September, 1860.

Appleton Dadmun was born in Marlboro', Massachusetts, graduated at Amherst College in 1854, read law in the office of Hon Henry Chapin, and was admitted to practice in 1857

Francis L. King was born in Charlton, May 29th, 1834; commenced the study of the law with James G Madden of Monmouth, Warren county, Ill, April, 1856; admitted to the Illinois bar, August, 1857, graduated at Poughkeepsie Law School in 1858; entered the office of Beach and Bond, Springfield, Mass the same year, admitted to the Massachusetts bar, February, 1859, at Worcester, and commenced the practice of law.

Adin Thayer was born December 5th, 1828, at Mendon, was the son of Caleb Thayer, of Mendon, studied law with Hon Henry Chapin, admitted to the bar and commenced the practice of the law in Worcester, September, 1854, holds the office of Trial Justice

David L Morril, born at Goffstown, N H, June 2d, 1827, son of Hon David L Morril, late of Concord, N H, graduated at Dartmouth College, in 1847, studied law with Hon. Ira Perley and Hon Asa Fowler, of Concord, N H, commenced the practice of law in Winchendon in Sept, 1850, afterwards in West Brookfield, and removed to the city of Worcester, in March, 1860

Charles A Holbrook was born at Grafton, in this county, Dec 6th, 1827, and received as thorough an education as could be obtained in the schools in the vicinity studied law with Lorenzo Leland, Esq, and afterwards entered the office of Calvin E Pratt, Esq, of this city, and was admitted to the bar, Dec, 1857, when he formed a copartnership in business with Mr Pratt, which continued for about one year He is now practicing in his profession in this city with success

George Swan, son of Samuel Swan, Esq, of Hubbardston, born June 8th, 1826, graduated at Amherst College, studied law with Hon Benjamin F. Thomas, admitted to practice in 1848, and still remains in Worcester

John D. Washburn, born in Boston, March 27th, 1833, son of John M Washburn, now of Lancaster, graduated at Harvard University in 1853 Studied law with Hons Emory Washburn and George F Hoar, at Worcester; commenced practice of law in Nov, 1856, at Worcester Married, June 5th, 1860, Mary L, daughter of Charles L. Putnam of Worcester.

Stephen P Twiss, the son of James J Twiss, was born in Charlton in this county, May 2d, 1830, graduated at the Dane Law School at Cambridge in 1852, afterwards studied in the office of Davis and Stoddard in this city, was admitted to the bar in 1853, and has since that time practiced here In 1857 he represented the city of Worcester in the Legislature

30*

Hartley Williams was born in Somerset county, Maine, August 12, 1820; he studied law with Hon. Francis H. Dewey; was admitted to the bar in September, 1850, and at the same time formed a partnership with Mr. Dewey, which has continued to the present time. He was a member of the Board of Aldermen of the city of Worcester in 1854; was elected Commissioner of Insolvency in 1856, and to the Senate of Massachusetts in November 1861. He married Rachel R., daughter of David Harris, Esq., of Industry, Maine.

Thomas Kinnicutt graduated at Harvard University in 1856; was born in Worcester, July 13th, 1835, son of Hon. Thomas Kinnicutt. In Oct. 1852 made a voyage to Calcutta, returning through Europe. Studied law in the office of Devens, Hoar and Hill, Worcester, and took the degree of LL. B. at the Harvard Law School, Cambridge; commenced the practice of law in Worcester, September, 1860.

Edward L. Davis, son of Hon. Isaac Davis, was born in Worcester, April 22, 1834; graduated at Brown University in 1854; studied law with Isaac Davis, E. B. Stoddard, and at the Cambridge Law School; was admitted to the bar in March, 1857.

J. Henry Hill, son of Elias H. Hill of Petersham, studied law with Charles Allen and Judge Thomas; admitted to the bar in March, 1844, commenced practice in Barre, April, 1844; returned to Worcester in July same year, and then formed a connection with Judge Thomas, which connection continued until Oct., 1848; was alone in business until Jan. 1st, 1857, and was then a partner with Gen. Devens & G. F. Hoar for two years, since then alone; was appointed Justice of the Quorum, Sept., 1854; Master in Chancery in Dec., 1850; appointed Notary Public in 1853; Secretary of Worcester Institution for Savings in 1854.

William Sumner Barton, son of Ira Moore Barton of Worcester, born at Oxford, Mass., Sept. 30, 1824; graduated at Brown University, Providence, R. I., in 1844; a member of Harvard Law School in 1845; was admitted to the bar at Worcester, December, 1846, and practiced law in partnership with his father, (Judge Barton,) and Hon. Peter C. Bacon, at Worcester.

Thomas W. Fox, born at Worcester, near the old red mills, May 24th, 1835, graduated at Brown in 1856; graduated at the Law School in Cambridge, 1858, with the degree of LL. B.; admitted to practice at Boston, Jan. 17th, 1859.

Franklin Hall, son of Deacon Luther Hall of Sutton, in this county, born May 2d, 1820, educated at Westminster Academy. Studied law in the office of Barton & Bacon; admitted to the bar in 1846, and has practiced since, in this city. Married Elizabeth J., daughter of Parley Goddard, of this city, June 17th, 1856.

Abraham Garland Randall was born Jan 19th, 1804, in Manchester, in this state, son of Rev Abraham Randall He prepared for College at Westford and Phillips Academies ; entered Yale College in 1822, and passed his Freshman year, when he left and entered the Sophomore of Harvard Before and after he went to College he taught a district school in his native State, and while in College he kept the Grammar School in this city during one winter term. He finished his studies in College in 1826 He was then preceptor of the Academy in Middleboro', Plymouth county, two years He studied law with Hon Wilkes Wood of Plymouth, William Draper, Esq . of Marlboro , and with Hon John Davis, and Hon Charles Allen, of Worcester , admitted to the bar, 1831, opened, same year, an office in Millbury , continued in Millbury until 1860, since then, has practiced in this city Mr Randall has been appointed by the loyal states and territories, commissioner to take the proofs and acknowledgments of deeds, to take depositions, to administer oaths, make affidavits, powers of attorney, &c

Henry D. Stone, born in Southbridge His early education was bestowed on him by a charitable association with direct reference to the ministry He fitted for college at the Worcester Academy, and graduated at Amherst College, and commenced the study of the law with Messrs Barton and Bacon of Worcester ; he has practiced in this city for several years , at one time he was a leading criminal lawyer at the Worcester bar He has since retired from practice.

George Webster, son of Gen George Hobbs, born in Worcester, March 22d, 1838, was educated at the schools in this city and Norwich University, Vt. Studied law with E. B. Stoddard, Esq , was admitted to the bar, and commenced practice in Uxbridge in this county in 1860 He is lieutenant in the Worcester Light Infantry He married Chloe F , daughter of David Taft, Esq , of Uxbridge

Samuel Nelson Aldrich, was the son of Sylvanus B Aldrich, born in Upton, Mass ; graduated at Brown University , studied law with E B Stoddard, Esq , and on being admitted to the bar removed to St Louis, Mo., and entered into the practice of the law there

James E Estabrook, son of Col James Estabrook, born in this city, Oct 29th, 1829 ; graduated at Yale College, 1851, read law with Judge Thomas, and admitted to practice in 1854.

There are some other lawyers who have practiced law here, some of whom have left the city permanently, others have gone to the war, and a few decline to have their names mentioned in this connection.

George Chandler

Joseph Sargent, son of Col Henry Sargent of Leicester, was born in Leicester, December 31st, 1815 He entered Harvard University in 1830, and
graduated in 1834 He studied medicine with Dr Edward Flint in Leicester
in 1834 and 1835, in Boston with Dr. James Jackson and his colleagues in
1835, 1836, and 1837 , attended medical lectures in Boston in 1835 and
1836, and in Philadelphia in 1836 and 1837 He took his degree of M D
at Harvard University in 1837, and immediately entered upon office as House
Physician at the Massachusetts General Hospital In 1838 he went to Europe
and pursued his medical studies chiefly in Paris till the spring of 1840, when
he returned to America and opened his office in Worcester late in May of that
year. He was married to Emily Whitney of Cambridge, September 27th,
1841. In March 1850 he visited Europe again for professional improvement,
and was absent till the 30th of December , since which time he has continued
in practice among us

Pierre Bazile Mignault, son of Louis Mignault, was born in the parish of
Chambly, Canada East, August 28th, 1818 He took his medical degree at
the medical school of Harvard University, in the spring of 1846 He took
an office in Boston, Mass , where he remained a few years , he removed to
Worcester in the spring of 1848, where he continued in the practice of medicine In the fall of 1858 he went to Europe to visit the hospitals and recruit
his health, and returned the following year, since which time he has continued
in practice in this city His grandfather, Bazile Mignault, was driven from
Acadia, N S , by the English, in company with many others of his countrymen of French descent, in 1763, and afterwards served two years as a volun-
unteer in the American army during the revolutionary war, and probably in
Lafayette's division.

Henry Sargent, son of Col Henry Sargent, was born in Leicester, Nov 7,
1821 He entered Yale College in 1837, and graduated in 1841 He studied
medicine with his brother, Dr Joseph Sargent, in Worcester, in 1841 and
1842 , in Boston with Dr Bowditch and his colleagues in 1842 and 1843 ;
and in Philadelphia with Dr Gerhard in 1843 and 1844. He continued his
studies with interruptions of ill health till 1847, passing about two years of
the time in Europe, and mostly in the hospitals of Paris In 1847 he took
his degree in medicine at Cambridge and commenced practice here In May,
1849, he married Catherine Dean Whitney, who died in September of the
same year Dr Sargent's health was never good after his illness contracted
in the study of anatomy in 1844, and he was obliged repeatedly to withdraw
from the laborious practice of his profession, visiting Europe again in 1851,
and again in 1854 He died in April, 1858, and was buried at Mount
Auburn in Cambridge He was an excellent physician and an upright man

Dr George Chandler continued his duties of Assistant Physician in the
State Lunatic Hospital until May 2, 1842, when he resigned to take the

Superintendence of the Asylum for the Insane at Concord, N. H., which he did October 1, 1842. This Asylum had then just been erected, upon a plan submitted by him. During this vacation in his labors he had married Miss Josephine Rose, daughter of Joseph W. Rose, of Antigua, W. I., by his wife Harriet Paine, daughter of Dr. William Paine of Worcester, Mass. The Asylum at Concord became under his superintendence self-sustaining, and successful in the benefits it conferred upon its inmates. In the fall of 1845 Dr. Chandler resigned his charge of the Asylum, and on the first of July, 1846, succeeded Dr. Samuel B. Woodward as Superintendent of the State Lunatic Hospital at Worcester. This institution continued, during the ten years of his superintendence of it, overflowing with patients. With a capacity for only about three hundred, the number registered on its books reached at one time, five hundred and sixty-eight. He resigned the superintendence in July, 1856, and has since resided in the city of Worcester, which honored him with a seat in the Legislature in 1859, and in her city councils as one of her Aldermen.

Rufus Woodward, the second son of Dr. Samuel B. Woodward, was born in Wethersfield, Ct., October 3, 1819. He graduated at Harvard College in the class of 1841, and took his degree in the medical school of Harvard College in 1843. He commenced practice as Assistant Physician in the State Lunatic Hospital in Worcester, where he remained five years. He then went to Europe to complete his studies, and remained two years, and on his return, resumed practice in this city in June, 1850.

J. Marcus Rice was born in Milford, N. Y., in 1828; he married Mrs. Elvira M. Dodge, daughter of Sylvanus Pratt, of Oxford, in 1861. The author cannot give a full account of Dr. Rice's education, or the commencement of his practice in Worcester. Suffice it to say that he has been a practitioner here, and the city physician for several years, and is now surgeon for the 25th regiment, and is doing good service.

Albin J. Eaton was born in Ashburnham, Mass., June 19, 1809; graduated at Pittsfield in 1836. For about sixteen years had extensive and successful practice in New Hampshire and Massachusetts; came to this city in 1851, and for several years has been out of practice. In March, 1838, married Delight Stow, of Fitzwilliam, N. H.

Dean Towne was born in Windsor, Vt., Feb. 7, 1810; graduated at the Academy of Medicine, Castleton, Vt., in 1833; married Sally D. Sibley, daughter of Francis Sibley, Esq., of Oxford, January 9, 1851. He is now mainly out of practice.

Thomas H. Gage, eldest son of Dr. Leander Gage, of Waterford, Maine, was born at Waterford, May 22, 1826. He took his medical degree at the

...dical school of Harvard University in 1852, and commenced the practice of his profession at Sterling, in this county, in the spring of 1853. He moved to this city in 1857, where he now resides

Seth Rogers was born February 13, 1823, in Danby, Vt., graduated in medicine at Castleton College, Vt., in the autumn of 1849; was previously a student and assistant of Dr. Joel Shew in the practice of Hydropathy, and joined him in New York city during the winter of 1849 and 1850. Came to Worcester in the spring of 1850, and entered upon general practice. In the following autumn established the "Worcester Water Cure," which still remains under his medical superintendence. This institution has always been conducted on liberal, or eclectic principles, though water has been the ruling agent in the management of chronic diseases. He went to Paris to study in the hospitals in the autumn of 1852, and returned to practice again in the spring of 1854; in the spring of 1855 became a Fellow of the Massachusetts Medical Society, in the autumn of 1858 sailed for Rio Janeiro, S. A., and from there to Havre, France, and there spent four months again in the Paris hospitals. Dr. Rogers married Miss Hannah Mitchell, daughter of Jethro T. Mitchell, of Middletown, R. I.

Peter E. Hubon was born in the town of Loughrea, county of Galway, Ireland. Acquiring an early hatred of monarchial and an early love for democratic institutions, he induced his parents to allow him to immigrate to this country at the age of fifteen. In 1854 he commenced the study of medicine at the Fort Edward Institute, under the direction of Dr. Miller, lecturer on physiology. In 1855 he became a student of Prof. J. H. Armsby, of the Albany Medical College, with whom he remained as private pupil until he graduated in June, 1858. He at once commenced practice in Springfield, Mass., but not succeeding to his wishes he removed to Worcester in October of the same year. In 1859 he became a member of the Massachusetts Medical Society, in 1860 a Fellow of the Botanical Society of Canada, a Society of Queen's College, Kingston, and in 1861 was elected City Physician of his adopted city, which office he now holds.

S. F. Haven, Jr., born May 20, 1832, in Dedham, Mass.; graduated at Harvard College in 1852; studied medicine three years at the Medical School in Boston, and spent about two years in France and Germany, preparing for the specialty of diseases of the eye. After keeping an office a few months in Boston, he established himself in Worcester in the spring of 1858.

R. L. Hawes, son of Amos Hawes, of Leominster, born March 22, 1823; graduated at Harvard University Medical School in the spring of 1846, and commenced practice in Worcester in the spring of 1846, and continued practice about two years.

Samuel Flagg, son of Samuel Flagg, was born in Worcester, and fitted for college at Leicester Academy, and graduated at Dartmouth College in 1839; studied with Dr. Twitchell of Keene, N. H., and commenced practice here. At this time he is in the 25th regiment as hospital steward.

Henry Parker, son of William Parker, born in Worcester in 1786; studied with Dr. Eaton of Dudley, and Dr. Green of Worcester, and attended medical lectures in Boston. Commenced practice in 1811, at Grafton, and continued there about forty-six years, and removed to this city where he now resides. Dr. Parker married first, Catharine, daughter of Lemuel Davis, Esq., of Holden; second, Maria N. Norris of Salem.

Armet B. DeLand, son of Charles M. DeLand, born in Brookfield in 1823, studied in Worcester with Dr. Geo. A. Bates, attended medical lectures at Pittsfield, Castleton, and Charleston, S. C. Graduated in 1845, and commenced practice in Worcester, where he still continues. Married Clara M., daughter of Stephen Tallman.

Oramel Martin, born in Whitingham Vt., July 21st, 1810; studied medicine and received his degree at Pittsfield; commenced practice in New Braintree; in 1845-6, visited Europe, pursued his studies in the hospitals at Paris; removed to Worcester, 1850. Dr. Martin was appointed one of the commissioners to investigate the cattle disease in 1860. In 1861, he was surgeon to the Third Battalion Rifles from this city, and spent the summer mostly at Fort McHenry; in August, of the same year, he was appointed brigade surgeon, and is still in the army.

Merrick Bemis was born in Sturbridge, Mass., in 1820; studied medicine in the office of Dr. H. Gilmore, in Brookfield, and Dr. Winslow Lewis, in Boston, and graduated at the Medical School in Castleton, Vt.; came to Worcester in 1848; was employed as Assistant Physician at the State Lunatic Hospital, under the superintendence of Dr. Geo. Chandler, and was appointed Superintendent of the Hospital in 1855.

Frank Horton Rice was born in Rowe, Mass., in 1831. Studied medicine with Dr. S. Clapp, in Pawtucket; graduated at Woodstock, Vt., in 1854; came to Worcester in 1855, and has since been employed as Assistant Physician at the State Lunatic Hospital.

Henry Conant Prentice was born in Northampton, Mass., 1832; graduated at Harvard College, 1834; studied medicine with Drs. D. & J. Thompson, in Northampton; graduated in medicine, at the Berkshire Medical Institution, 1857; came to Worcester in 1858, and has since been employed as Assistant Physician at the State Lunatic Hospital.

Joseph N Bates commenced the study of medicine in the spring of 1829 with his father, Anson Bates, M. D., of Barre, attended lectures at Dartmouth college in the autumn of 1829 and 1830, also at Bowdoin, Me, and graduated at Dartmouth in the autumn of 1831, subsequently attended the lectures of the University of Medicine at Philadelphia · commenced practice in the autumn of 1832 at Barre, where he remained until 1856, when he came to Worcester. Joined the army of the United States as surgeon of the 15th regiment of Mass Volunteers, August 6th, 1861

George A Bates, son of the late Dr Anson Bates of Barre, Worcester county, Mass, born in Barre, commenced the study of medicine with Joseph N. Bates, M. D. of that town, attended lectures at the Berkshire Medical College, in the autumn of 1840 and 1841. In 1842, entered the office of Dr. Marshal S Perry and associates of Boston, and graduated at the Medical College of Harvard University in March, 1844; commenced practice in Barre the same year, and in April, 1845, removed to Worcester and continued in practice until 1856, when he removed to Washington, D C., and was succeeded in practice by Joseph N Bates, M. D, of Barre In August, 1861, he returned to Worcester to fill the place of his brother who enlisted as surgeon of the 15th regiment of Massachusetts Volunteers

Henry Clarke, son of Benjamin Clarke, was born at Marlboro', Mass, Oct. 3d, 1824; he took his medical degree at the medical school of Harvard University in the spring of 1850; he then went to Europe and continued his professional studies at Paris and Vienna until the autumn of 1851, when he returned to this country and commenced the practice of medicine in Worcester. In 1854 he was married to Rebecca F Foster, daughter of Hon Alfred Dwight Foster of this city. In the spring of 1861, he again went to Europe for the purpose of spending a few months in the hospitals and of recruiting his health, he returned in the autumn of the same year and resumed practice in this city

Benjamin F. Allen was born in Mendon, March 1829; graduated at the Medical Department of Yale College in 1859, commenced practice in this city in 1860. Dr. Allen married Elizabeth V., daughter of Joseph P. Emerson, of Parsonsfield, Maine.

ECLECTIC.

Frank H. Kelly is a native of New Hampton, N. H.; at the academical institution of which town he fitted for college He pursued the study of medicine at the medical department of Harvard College, and at the Eclectic Medical College of Cincinnati, Ohio, and at the latter institution was graduated in the year 1851. Commenced the practice of his profession in Worcester the same year, and from that time to the present, has enjoyed an enviable reputation as a physician. He is at this time President of the State Eclectic Medical Society, and a member of the present city council.

H. W. Buxton was born in Merrimack, N. H., May, 1809 ; studied at Nashua, and commenced practice at Haverhill, Mass., in 1836 ; removed to this city in 1850, where he still resides. He married first, Rebecca L., daughter of Thomas Munroe, Esq., of Nashua, N. H. She having died, he married Miss Lydia M., daughter of Elijah Harrington of Shrewsbury.

John A. Andrews, was born in Hopkinton, Mass., September 30, 1802 ; took his degree of doctor in medicine at the Southern Botanic Medical College, Forsyth, Georgia ; commenced the practice of medicine in Smithfield, R. I., in 1834 ; in 1836 removed to Worcester, and is still in practice here.

Edwin Schofield, son of John W. Schofield, was born at Oldham, England, and came here in early childhood ; commenced the study of medicine in 1850 ; attended the first course of lectures at the American College, Philadelphia ; second, third, and last course were attended at the Worcester Medical Institution, and graduated June, 1855. Since which time has practiced at Pawtucket, R. I., and Mason Village, N. H. He married Miss Mary Jane Moore, of Barre, daughter of Horace S. Moore.

HOMEOPATHIC.

L. B. Nichols was born in Bradford, N. H., in the year 1816 ; entered Brown University in 1839, and graduated in 1842. After a period spent in teaching, he continued his medical studies, and received the degree of M. D., as an allopathic physician, at the Philadelphia College of Medicine. He commenced the homeopathic practice of medicine, in the city of Worcester, in 1849. He married Miss Lydia C. Anthony, daughter of James Anthony, Esq., of Providence, R. I., in the year 1843.

J. E. Linnell was born at Orleans, Barnstable County, Mass., June 9, 1823 ; educated at Amherst College ; studied medicine with the late Dr. T. J. Gridley, Amherst ; received medical diploma at Dartmouth College, in 1844 ; commenced practice in the spring of 1845, at Prescott this state ; removed from there to East Douglas, in the spring of 1847 ; from East Douglas, came to Worcester on the first day of Jan. 1855. Married, Nov. 27th, 1848, Miss Fanny A. Graves, of Sunderland, Mass.

Dr. Bugbee was in practice here in 1853-4, and removed to Warren, Vt., and died there in 1859.

Joseph Birnstill was in practice here from 1844 to 1847, and removed to Boston, where he still resides and is in practice.

THOMSONIAN

Franklin Barnard was born May 17, 1809, at Harvard, Worcester county, Mass., educated by Dr. Samuel Thomson, the father and founder of the Thomsonian system of practice, commenced the practice of this system in Boston, in 1836, in Worcester, in 1840, where he still resides

---

FEMALE PHYSICIANS.

Mrs S Goodwin, wife of Martin Goodwin, born in Townsend, Vt., 1808. In 1849 she commenced practice in this city as a midwife Mrs Goodwin has had great success in her department of practice, having attended 2113 cases since her practice in Worcester commenced.

Mrs. M W Geralds, wife of S W Geralds, and daughter of deacon John Foss of New Durham, N H, attended the medical lectures in Boston and Worcester, commenced practice at Concord, N. H, removed to this city in 1851, and has been in successful practice here since. She is a physician and midwife

Mrs B R. Clark, physician and midwife, born in Mason, N H, daughter of Hubert Russell, and wife of Joel C Clark, attended the Eclectic schools in Worcester and Boston; received her medical degree from the Pennsylvania Institute, in Philadelphia, in 1861, and commenced practice in this city, where she still resides.

In addition to the above, there have been from time to time, several other practitioners here, who have not remained for any length of time, and therefore will not appear in this chapter.

BANKS OF WORCESTER.

WORCESTER BANK.

Of the one hundred and seventy-seven Banks now existing in Massachusetts, the Massachusetts, Union, Boston, Gloucester, and Plymouth, were in operation in 1803.

At a meeting of a number of gentlemen, at Barker's tavern, in Worcester, December 18th, 1803, Isaiah Thomas, Esq., being chosen moderator, it was voted : That it is the sense of the gentlemen present that it would be advantageous to the County of Worcester to have a Bank established at Worcester ; that a subscription be opened, and that Benjamin Heywood, Francis Blake, Isaiah Thomas, Dr. William Paine and Daniel Waldo, Jr., be a committee to superintend the subscriptions, prepare a petition to the Legislature to be signed by the subscribers, and notify a meeting of the subscribers to be holden at a suitable time after the subscription is closed.

At a meeting duly called by this committee, held April 10th, 1804, it was reported that the subscription amounted to 2615 shares ; and a charter, dated March 7th, 1804, incorporating Daniel Waldo, Isaiah Thomas, Daniel Waldo, Jr., Benjamin Heywood, William Paine, Stephen Salisbury, Nathan Patch, William Henshaw, Francis Blake, Nathaniel Paine, Elijah Burbank, and their associates, as the President, Directors and Company of the Worcester Bank, was accepted. The capital authorized was one hundred and fifty thousand dollars, and the charter was to continue until the expiration of eight years from the first Monday in October next following.

The charter having been accepted, Daniel Waldo, Benjamin Heywood, Samuel Flagg, Isaiah Thomas, Daniel Waldo, Jr., Theophilus Wheeler, and Samuel Chandler, were chosen Directors, and the organization was completed April 12th, 1804, by the choice of Daniel Waldo as President, and Daniel Waldo, Jr , as Secretary of the Board of Directors, to officiate as such until a Cashier is chosen.

In conformity to a vote of the stockholders, they proceeded at once to cause the erection of "a brick building, three stories high, having in the front two belts of marble," on the site now occupied by the Central Exchange. It contained, besides the banking rooms, a hall for the meetings of the stockholders, and a tenement which for many years was occupied by Mr. Waldo. It was sold in 1834, and destroyed by fire in 1842. The Bank continued to occupy it, however, as long as it stood, and leased rooms in the Exchange Building which succeeded it, until 1851, when the Worcester Bank Block, on Foster street, was erected.

On the 11th of May, 1804, Levi Thaxter was elected Cashier, and Robert

Breck Brigham, Accountant, " upon the condition that they enter themselves at some Bank in the town of Boston to be instructed at their own expense in the duties of their respective offices by persons to be approved by the Directors of this Bank, the salary of each to commence on the first day of September, 1804, provided they respectively produce a certificate from the person by whom he has been instructed that in his said instructor s opinion he is fully competent to execute the duties of his office "

At the next election of Directors, October 3d, 1804, Daniel Waldo, sen , declined a re-election , Daniel Waldo, Jr , was elected President, and so continued until his decease July 9th, 1845 He attended a meeting of the Directors on the evening of the 8th, in usual health, and early on the next morning was suddenly removed from his wide sphere of duty and usefulness During a period of forty-one years his services were gratuitously rendered to the Bank. He presided with singular talent and uniform courtesy over the deliberations of the Directors, watched over, protected, and advanced its interests with untiring vigilance, and was to every director and officer a wise counsellor, a kind assistant and friend. He was succeeded, July 16th, 1845, by Stephen Salisbury Mr Thaxter resigning the Cashiership, has been succeeded by Robert Breck Brigham, elected March 12, 1805, resigned 1812 Samuel Jennison, Jr , elected August 25, 1812, resigned 1816 , Levi Lincoln Newton, elected September 22, 1846, resigned 1847 , William Cross, elected June 29, 1847 Mr Jennison s connection with the Bank covered a period of more than thirty-six years, he having held the office of accountant from April 17, 1810, until his election to the Cashiership Being thus identified with its history, it would be incomplete without a recorded acknowledgment of the ability, the despatch, the undoubted integrity, and the unsparing labor with which he performed his official duties, while his efficient services were accompanied and adorned by his cultivated intellect, his simple and genial manners, and his moral worth

Anticipating the expiration of the charter in October, 1812, the stockholders, at a meeting May 1, 1811, voted to petition the Legislature for its renewal. The importance of the institution, and the manner in which its operations were conducted, are thus set forth in the petition :

" In pursuance of the vote of the stockholders, the Committee appointed to now most respectfully represent, That the Worcester Bank was incorporated by an act passed May 7, 1804, with a capital of one hundred and fifty thousand dollars. In the spirit of the act, the whole sum was actually paid in and deposited in the vaults of the Bank before a single discount was attempted. From that, to the present time, a scrupulous regard has been had to the management of the institution upon the strict, and known, and approved principles of banking The specie capital has been exclusively appropriated to the redemption of the bills issued upon it The bills, in every instance, have been redeemed upon demand, and with a promptitude and cheerfulness which has left nothing for just complaint to the applicant The accommodation of the Bank has been alike extended without partiality or prejudice to every

31*

individual whose occasions have required and whose responsibility has justified the credit of a loan. The stockholders themselves have been among the smallest borrowers of the Bank. As they had no other inducement, so they have received no other consideration for the investment of their money, than its security and the legal interest it has borne.

" In its operation the Bank has been attended with all the advantages which could have been anticipated at its incorporation. With a very restricted capital, and from its local situation exposed to repeated drafts, it has, notwithstanding, uniformly maintained a character and credit, which, among the country banks is almost peculiar to itself. It has increased the wealth, the resources, and the business of the County of Worcester; it has facilitated the progress of useful arts and manufactures; it has aided in the establishment of others, which, otherwise, would have languished for want of capital. It has been highly beneficial in the common intercourse of business, by rendering credit less necessary, and thereby it has diminished the number of lawsuits. It has enabled the prudent farmer to extend his improvements by anticipating the value of his crops. These are among the most obvious of its effects; but to every class of people, and to every kind of business within its influence, it has communicated some share of benefits. It has given spirit to enterprise, and patronage to laudable exertion. Had its capital been greater, the accommodation to the public would have been proportionably increased. The demand for money within the County has constantly exceeded the ability of the Bank to loan, and the recent establishment of many manufactories for various useful branches of business has for some time past greatly augmented the number of applications. The arrangements of the Bank are better, and more generally understood, and the confidence of the community is becoming daily more attached to the institution.

" The evils resulting from the expiration of the charter without renewal are too many and too obvious to escape the discernment of the Legislature. A considerable proportion of the debts are with the yeomanry of the County. More than one hundred and seventy thousand dollars is usually due to the Bank. The embarrassments, the perplexity, and the positive distress which would be produced by a sudden demand of this amount, are incalculable. Suits would be indefinitely multiplied, and an immense sacrifice of property must be the inevitable consequence.

" Your petitioners therefore do request that the charter of said Bank may be renewed, and that the Corporation may be allowed to increase the capital stock to a sum not exceeding four hundred thousand dollars."

The application, however, was unsuccessful; and the committee reported that although " a petition was presented to the Legislature at the May, 1811, and January, 1812, sessions, in which the importance of the institution to this part of the country was fully represented, Mr. Lincoln, Jr., employed as agent to support the application, and every other step taken to insure its success, the conflicting interests of the members of the Legislature prevented any thing being done."

At the May session of 1812, the application was again renewed, and in addition to the reasons before given, the Committee state, "your petitioners are authorized in the assurance that the existence of the Bank, and the continuance of its accommodations, are indispensable to the preservation of these important interests. So solicitous indeed was the public mind on the subject of a renewal of the charter at the last session of the Legislature, that petitions for that object were spontaneously preferred from almost every important town in the County. To these unbiased testimonials to the credit of the corporation and its salutary operations your petitioners would respectfully refer On this subject there are no conflicting claims Men of all classes, parties, and situations in the County are satisfied with the present application, and without discrimination are engaged in its success. Your petitioners, therefore, in view to a perfect ability for the accommodation of this western section of the Commonwealth, pray that, with a renewal of the charter, they may be allowed to increase their capital stock "

A new charter was granted June 22d, 1812, and the capital was increased to two hundred thousand dollars It was renewed in 1831, and again in 1850, by the general acts of those years. Its charter expires January 1st, 1870

Under an Act of the Legislature, passed May 21, 1851, the capital was increased to two hundred and fifty thousand dollars, and under an Act passed April 28, 1853, to three hundred thousand dollars

The Bank pursued the even tenor of its way, carrying a loan but little in excess of its capital, and holding a specie reserve nearly as great as its circulation, until, in 1820, a system for the redemption of country money at par in Boston, was devised. At that time the minimum charge for discount on country bills was from 1-4th to 3-4ths per cent The money accumulated in the Boston Banks, and became a dead deposit until redeemed by the country Banks, which was then a slow and insecure process, as the specie, mostly silver, must be received by a special messenger in exchange for the bills, when presented at the Bank counters, and transported to Boston, to be again procured there by the country Banks and transported back again. To remedy these evils, and with an avowed intention of regulating the currency of New England, the Suffolk Bank proposed to receive at par the bills of such Banks as should keep a deposit with it for that purpose It is easy to see that the community was greatly benefitted by this arrangement, as it was relieved from the brokerage on a large sum of money, and that the Suffolk Bank, by means of these deposits, obtained a large addition to its working capital It is equally easy to see that to the country Banks, many of which already had open accounts with the Boston Banks, for the purpose of facilitating the increasing mercantile interests, it was advantageous, inasmuch as the risk, expense, and necessity of keeping more than a small percentage of specie in their vaults was obviated The experience of thirty-five years has proved the wisdom of the "Suffolk Bank system," and its incalculable benefit to the currency and business of New England But the scheme at first met with strong opposition, not only from the country Banks, but from some of the Boston Banks, which declined

to compensate the Suffolk for receiving country bills from them, which was a
part of the plan, and those which established the association were stigmatised
as " *The Holy Alliance.*" Remembering, doubtless, " the conflicting interests,"
which so nearly extinguished the Worcester Bank in 1812, Mr. Waldo was
one of its most determined opponents. All overtures for an arrangement
having been rejected by him, an occurrence took place on the 26th of July,
1826, which is clearly described, with the opinions of the project then prevailing, in the following statement which was published by Mr. Waldo on behalf of the Directors.

" A transaction of an unexpected and extraordinary character having occurred within the last two days, which is calculated, and doubtless was intended,
injuriously to affect the credit and management of the Worcester Bank, the
Directors feel called upon to publish a statement of facts, and to submit to
the knowledge and judgment of the public the conduct of those who have been
agents in the concern.

" Soon after the opening of the Bank on Wednesday morning, July 26th, a
person representing himself to be in the employ and under the direction of
the Suffolk Bank in Boston, presented two packages of bills, amounting as he
said to $48,000, and demanded the redemption in specie. He was promptly
and undisguisedly informed that the bills would be received, but as the sum
was greater than had been anticipated, being more than one half the whole
amount of bills of the Worcester Bank in circulation, the Bank was not prepared to redeem the whole with specie from the vaults, but having a deposit
in Boston, the Cashier would give a draft for the balance, payable at sight, or
would despatch a messenger, to return immediately with the money ; and in
the meantime the Directors would pay for all the expenses and inconvenience
for this short delay, rendered necessary by the journey to the city. From the
agent of the Suffolk Bank it was distinctly understood that he was to carry the
specie directly to Boston, for which purpose he had a team with him. It was
therefore represented to him that this Bank had a deposit exceeding $39,000
of their own proper money in the New England Bank, that the specie would
be as early in the possession of the Suffolk Bank by accepting the proposed
draft as it could be placed there by transportation from Worcester, in addition
to which the useless and idle labor of a double removal, first here and then
back, would be avoided. No doubt was expressed by the agent of the truth
of this representation. On the contrary he offered, under his instructions and
in conformity with them, to accept a draft, if the Directors here would engage
in future to redeem their bills and make their deposit at the Suffolk Bank, so
as to secure to that institution the advantage of our constant and large deposits. This proposition the Directors rejected. It had been made before
to them under circumstances, and with accompanying conditions, which, in
their opinion, were both humiliating and dishonorable. They had heretofore
been urged to become the brokers of the Suffolk Bank in collecting and depositing with that institution the bills of other banks, and they had been
offered immunity to their own corporation from *runs* and *drafts* at the price of

a violation of precedent engagements, or of a departure from an honorable and scrupulous system of regular and legitimate banking. It was therefore with firmness that the Directors determined to yield nothing to the spirit of unjustifiable coercion. The agent of the Suffolk Bank was told that no negociation of the kind could be effected. He was immediately paid in specie $28,000, and was informed that at the opening of the Suffolk Bank the next morning, and probably before he could reach Boston, the balance would be offered at their counter.

Our Cashier was forthwith despatched to execute this purpose, and it was our hope and expectation, that it would have been satisfactory. What then was our astonishment, at three o'clock next day, to be addressed by a Sheriff, charged with a special writ of attachment to secure upon the real estate of the Corporation, the above mentioned balance of $20,000, upon a writ too, made in Boston at the instance of the directors of the Suffolk Bank, after an interview with them by our Cashier, with the money in his possession to satisfy the claims, and forwarded by an express through the country, at the rate of ten miles an hour, to attach real estate, in security for the payment of bank bills, for which the specie was offered before the process issued!

We will only add, that the Worcester Bank was never in a more solvent state, and ready for a comparison with other banks, even the Suffolk Bank to prove with what fidelity to the Institution, and security to the public, our concerns have uniformly been managed. We have reason to complain of the utmost disingenuousness on the part of the directors of the Suffolk Bank, That they did not distrust the solvency and punctuality of the Worcester Bank. is conclusive from the fact that they instructed their agent to receive a draft, if we would consent to pay the tribute of our own independence, and become brokers to them in future. They artfully devised this surprise upon us. Heretofore they had been in the habit of sending an amount of $6000 or $7000, whenever they had received it, and as frequently as once in a week or fortnight. About four weeks since, they made a draft to that amount. Where then was this sum of $18,000, now presented? Has it been collected by runners and agents through the country? Or has it been carefully accumulated for the present occasion?

The Suffolk Bank and its managers, and the friends of such measures of hostility to the country banks, as solvent as their own, as prudently and honorably, if not as cunningly managed, these promoters of jealousy between town and country, have the short-lived enjoyment of the paltry gratification of exciting suspicion of our Institution. We have now tendered them the specie, for all the bills they presented. And in future, on our own counter, dollar for dollar, carefully told and counted, they shall receive it.

To the public we need offer no assurances. The credit we have maintained is not forfeited. Our doors have never been closed. Our paper will be redeemed with specie, whenever and by whom demanded. Our business is not interrupted. Our discounts will not be suspended, or the more restricted."

The affair, however, was not yet ended. The writ was returnable at the

October term of the court, and peremptorily declining to receive the specie elsewhere than at the counter of the Worcester Bank, the Suffolk Bank claimed, as damages, interest at the rate of 24 per cent. per annum, until the bills should be redeemed. Mr. Jennison, after making the tender of $20,000, with one day's interest, deposited that sum in the New England Bank, subject to the presentation of the bills there, and so notified the Suffolk Bank. The case was argued by Samuel Hubbard for the Suffolk, and Lemuel Shaw for the Worcester, and was decided in March 1827, when the sufficiency of the tender was sustained. This result was considered a signal triumph by the opponents of the Suffolk Bank system.

For many years the loans, upon the then "strict, and known, and approved principles of banking," were upon notes, with one or more sureties, payable in fifty-seven days and grace, and duly attested. When due, a payment of one fourth part of the original loan was required, and the balance was renewed. No loans were made for a less sum than fifty dollars, or renewed for a less sum than twenty dollars. Notes remaining unpaid for eight days after maturity, were invariably handed to the solicitor for collection. When sued, and the action entered in court, the principal debtor or debtors were debarred from having a new loan, until six months after the settlement of the debt, and when a suit was continued in court, or judgment obtained, the by-laws provided that the principal debtor or debtors, shall *never* after have a note discounted. Loans were also occasionally made on pledge of the stock of the bank, and on bond and mortgage, the latter running for one year, with interest payable at the expiration of that time. The practice of discounting business paper, did not prevail to any extent, until so lately as 1835.

Among the curiosities of the ancient record book are these:

"Voted, that each and every director, who shall be absent at the hour appointed for any meeting, and does not produce a satisfactory reason therefor, shall forfeit and pay to the use of the directors present at the meeting, the sum of twenty-five cents."

"All mistakes made by the officers of the bank, must be discovered and stated before the persons concerned leave the bank, or they *cannot be inquired into* or allowed."

A large proportion of the stock of this bank, has always been held by charitable, savings, and other corporations, trustees, &c., who desire a safe and permanent investment. For many years, the dividends, though regular, were small. For the past twelve years, they have never been less than eight per cent. per annum. The reserve after declaring the dividend in April 1861 was about twenty-five per cent.

The present Board of Directors is as follows:

Stephen Salisbury,	. . .	first elected, October 1st, 1832.
Levi Lincoln, ...	" "	" 3d, 1810.
Rejoice Newton, ...	" "	" 6th, 1817.
George T. Rice, ...	" "	" 3d, 1825.
Benjamin F. Heywood, . .	" "	" 3d, 1831.
Dwight Foster, ...	" "	" 11th, 1856.
Russell L. Hawes, . . .	" "	" 10th, 1857.

CENTRAL BANK.

By an act approved by the Governor, March 12th, 1828, William Eaton, L. W Stowell, Isaac Davis, T. A. Merrick, David Stowell, Pliny Merrick, William Jennison, Daniel Heywood, Gardiner Paine, Samuel Allen, Jr , Levi A Dowley, Benjamin Butman, Asahel Bellows, Daniel Goddard, Isaac Goodwin, Artemas Ward, Anthony Chase, and their associates, successors and assigns, were created a corporation, with a capital of one hundred thousand dollars, by the name of the President, Directors, and Company of the Central Bank.

The first recorded meeting of stockholders was held on " Tuesday, the 5th of May, 1829, at the dwelling house of Joseph Lovell, Innholder," Samuel M. Burnside, chairman, Emory Washburn, secretary   Seven Directors were chosen, viz : Benjamin Butman, Pliny Merrick, Lewis Barnard, John Davis, Isaac Davis, Simeon Burt, Daniel Heywood   Benjamin Butman chosen President, May, 1829, resigned August, 1836 , Thomas Kinnicutt chosen President, August, 1836, died January 22d, 1858 , John C Mason chosen President, January, 1858, now in office   Otis Corbett was chosen Cashier May 1829, resigned November, 1829 , George A Trumbull, chosen Cashier November 1829, resigned October, 1836 , William Dickinson, chosen Cashier October, 1836, resigned October, 1850 , George F Hartshorn, chosen Cashier October, 1850, resigned October, 1856 , George C Bigelow, chosen Cashier October, 1856, died May 12, 1859 ; George F Hartshorn, chosen Cashier May 24, 1859, and now in office

The Bank commenced business in a building erected by Dr John Green, (No 100 Main street,) and remained there until June, 1853, when it was removed to the rooms now occupied in Harrington Block, corner of Main and Front streets.

July, 1848, the capital was increased to $150,000 ; October, 1853, to $250,-000 ; July, 1854, to $350,000

The annual dividends have been as follows . 1830, 1831, 1832, 1833, 7 per cent. ; 1834, 6 per cent , 1835, 1836, 7 per cent , 1837, 6 1-2 per cent , 1838, 6 per cent. ; 1839, 7 per cent. : 1840, 1841, 1842, 1843, 6 per cent., 1844, 5 per cent ; 1845, 1846, 6 per cent., 1847, 7 per cent ; 1848, 6 1-2 per cent., and an extra dividend of 9 per cent ; 1849, 1850, 7 per cent.; 1851, 1852, 1853, 8 per cent , and an extra dividend of 12 per cent , 1854 to 1858, 8 per cent. ; 1858 to 1861, 7 per cent.

QUINSIGAMOND BANK.

Incorporated March 25th, 1833, with a capital of $100,000   The capital has since been increased to $250,000

The Presidents have been elected as follows · A. D. Foster, April 27th, 1833, Isaac Davis, October 3d, 1836, William Jennison, October 13th, 1842, William Dickinson, (pro tem,) October, 1853, Isaac Davis, October 9th, 1854, who now holds that office.

Charles A. Hamilton was Cashier, from its first organization, to October 6th, 1853, when J. S. Farnum was chosen, who still remains its Cashier.

Elected April 17th, 1833, first directors, Samuel D. Spurr, F. W. Paine, Isaac Davis, A. D. Foster, Levi A. Dowley, Emory Washburn, and Samuel Damon.

CITIZENS BANK.

Was incorporated, April 9th, 1836, with a capital of $250,000. In 1844, the capital was altered to $150,000.

The Presidents have been elected as follows: Jan. 8th, 1836, Benjamin Butman; Oct. 1st, 1838, Nymphas Pratt; Oct. 7th, 1839, Pliny Merrick; Oct. 10th, 1842, F. T. Merrick; Nov. 5th, 1860, F. H. Kinnicutt, who now holds the office. Oct. 3d, 1836, Geo. A. Trumbull was elected Cashier, and held the office until Oct. 6th, 1858, when John C. Ripley was chosen, who now holds that office.

Directors, elected Oct. 3d, 1836, Benjamin Butman, Harvey Blashfield, Pliny Merrick, William Lincoln, Ebenezer Aldrich, Edward Lamb, Nymphas Pratt, F. W. Paine, Calvin Willard, F. T. Merrick, John H. Richardson, J. A. Hovey.

MECHANICS BANK.

Incorporated April 21st, 1848, with a capital of $100,000. In 1850, the capital was increased to $150,000. In 1851, the capital again increased to $300,000. Increased again in 1852, to its present capital, $350,000.

The presidents have been elected as follows:

July, 1848,	Alex. DeWitt,	June, 1858,	Henry Goulding,
Oct., 1855,	F. H. Dewey,	Oct., 1859,	Alex. DeWitt,
Oct., 1857,	Alex. DeWitt,	Oct., 1860,	Harrison Bliss.

July, 1848, Parley Hammond was chosen Cashier, and held the office until July 10th, 1854, when S. Berry was chosen, who now holds that office.

DIRECTORS: Henry Goulding, George T. Rice, Wm. T. Merrifield, F. H. Dewey, W. M. Bickford, Charles Washburn, Harrison Bliss, E. H. Bowen, Alphonso Brooks.

CITY BANK.

The City Bank of Worcester was incorporated in March 1854, with a capital of $200,000, and commenced business in September of same year, in a room in Harrington's block, corner of Main and Front streets; but was shortly removed to the present rooms, corner of Main and Pearl streets, in a building built and owned by Calvin Foster. (This building was the first one built in Worcester county, with an entire iron front, and was considered as a great undertaking at the time of its erection.)

The capital stock has since been increased to $400,000. George W. Richardson has been President, from the organization of the bank to the present time. Parley Hammond was first Cashier, and served till Oct. 1857, when Nathaniel Paine, the present Cashier, was chosen. The first board of directors, chosen in May, 1854, consisted of George W. Richardson, George Bowen, Henry Chapin, Calvin Foster, Lewis Barnard, W. B. Fox, Jr., and H. N. Bigelow. In Oct., same year, Charles Thurber and George M. Rice were added to the board.

WORCESTER COUNTY INSTITUTION FOR SAVINGS.

The Worcester County Institution for Savings was incorporated February 5, 1828. Hon. Daniel Waldo was the first President, and held the office to the time of his death, July 9, 1845; Hon. Stephen Salisbury was then elected President, and has held the office since. Samuel Jennison was the Treasurer from the organization of the Institution, to October, 1853, at which time Charles A. Hamilton was elected, and has held the office since.

At the time the former Treasurer resigned his office, the deposits amounted to $1,473,312 15, and the number of depositors was, 8,760.

In April 1861, the deposits amounted to $2,742,833 50, and the number of depositors was 12,408, giving an average of $218 17 to each.

Board of Investment—D. Waldo Lincoln, John C. Mason, A. H. Bullock, Stephen Salisbury, and the Treasurer and Secretary, ex officio.

Secretary—J. Henry Hill. Treasurer—Charles A. Hamilton. Assistant Treasurer—Edward Hamilton. Clerk—James P. Hamilton.

Twelve Vice-Presidents and twenty-four Trustees, constitute the Board of Trustees; they have the general charge and superintendence of the business of the Institution, and their duties are performed by monthly Committees, consisting of one Vice President and two Trustees, who are to "Attend at the Office of the Institution on the first Saturday next after the termination of each month, at nine o'clock, A. M., to examine the Books for the preceding month."

MECHANICS SAVINGS BANK.

The Worcester Mechanics Savings Bank was incorporated May 15th, 1851. The Hon. Isaac Davis was chosen its first President, and was reelected till January 4th, 1855, when he resigned, and Hon. Alex. DeWitt was elected, and held the office till Jan., 1859. He was succeeded by Hon. J. S. C. Knowlton, who now holds the office.

Parley Hammond, Esq., was chosen the first Treasurer, and held the office till July 10th, 1851, when he was succeeded by Henry Woodward, who now holds the office.

The Board of Trustees is composed of the President, Secretary, and twelve Trustees.

The present Board of Investment are Harrison Bliss, and T. W. Hammond, Esq., with the President and Secretary, who are ex officio members.

The number of depositors, on the last Saturday of June, 1861, was 2702, and the amount of deposits, $704,273,99; giving an average to each depositor of $260,65.

32

WORCESTER FIVE CENTS SAVINGS BANK.

This Bank was chartered April 7, 1854; commenced receiving deposits July 1, 1855. It is open daily to receive deposits. It will receive any sum, from five cents to one thousand dollars. Interest at the rate of five per cent., paid semi-annually, or added to the principal. Extra dividend every five years. The smallest sum entitled to receive interest is three dollars.

OFFICERS FOR THE YEAR 1861. — *President* — Charles L. Putnam. *Vice Presidents* — George W. Richardson, William N. Green, D. S. Messinger, Charles Paine, G. W. Russell, Emory Banister. *Trustees* — J. M. C. Armsby, J. S. Farnum, John B. Shaw, James B. Blake, Rufus Carter, George W. Wheeler, Edward W. Lincoln, James Green, C. B. Metcalf, C. H. Fitch, Nathan Washburn, Horace Ayres. *Auditors* — Emory Banister, James B. Blake. *Financial Committee* — Geo. W. Richardson, C. L. Putnam, D. S. Messinger, E. B. Stoddard, James Green, C. Harris. *Treasurer* — Clarendon Harris. *Secretary* — E. B. Stoddard.

INSURANCE COMPANIES OF WORCESTER.

WORCESTER MUTUAL FIRE INSURANCE COMPANY.

Incorporated February 11th, 1823. Its powers are vested in nine Directors. The following has been the succession of the officers: *Presidents* — 1824, Rejoice Newton; 1831, Fred. W. Paine; 1852, Anthony Chase. *Secretaries* — 1824, H. K. Newcomb; William D. Wheeler; 1827, Isaac Goodwin; 1832, Anthony Chase; 1852, Charles M. Miles. The dividend has averaged from 75 to 80 cents on each dollar paid as premium.

PEOPLE'S MUTUAL FIRE INSURANCE COMPANY.

Incorporated March 23, 1847. Officers in 1847: *President* — E. H. Hemenway. *Secretary* — O. Harrington. *Treasurer* — E. H. Hemenway. *Directors* — E. H. Hemenway, George Bowen, James H. Wall, Amos Brown, James Estabrook, Geo. A. Dresser, Warren Lazell, H. N. Tower, Joseph Pratt, Joseph Boyden, Warren Hunt, Jonathan Warren, Henry A. Denny, James W. Jenkins, John Edgell.

Officers in 1861: *President* — Henry Chapin. *Secretary* — A. N. Currier. *Treasurer* — Samuel H. Colton. *Directors* — Henry Chapin, Joseph Pratt, Horatio N. Tower, Joseph Boyden, James H. Wall, John C. Mason, Jonathan Luther, Henry Goulding, Edward Earle, Samuel H. Colton, E. L. Brigham, Timothy S. Stone, Dwight Foster, Charles W. Freeland, Ichabod Washburn.

MANUFACTURERS' MUTUAL INSURANCE COMPANY.

Incorporated March 1855. Directors and Officers: *President* — A. H. Bullock. *Secretary* — P. Hammond. *Directors* — A. H. Bullock, Paul

Whitin, John Gardner, Esek Saunders, F. H. Dewey, George M. Rice, S. L. Hodges, E. E. Manton, James Read, H. N. Bigelow, George Blackburn, George Hodges, Jr., John E. Bacon, Edward Atkinson, Joseph T. Whiting.

MERCHANTS AND FARMERS MUTUAL FIRE INSURANCE COMPANY.

Incorporated in 1846. Officers and Directors: *President* — Isaac Davis. *Secretary* — John D. Washburn. *Directors* — Isaac Davis, Alex. H. Bullock, William Dickinson, Charles L. Putnam, E. B Stoddard, Clarendon Harris, Alex. DeWitt, John Brooks, Joseph A. Denny, John S. Adams, Henry H. Stevens, John D. Washburn. Office 98 Main street.

BAY STATE FIRE INSURANCE COMPANY.

The Bay State Fire Insurance Company commenced business on the first day of January, A. D. 1861. It has a cash capital paid in of $104,300. It is in a healthy condition, and is under the management of the following Directors, who are well known to the public: Stephen Salisbury, Alexander H. Bullock, Charles L. Putnam, George T. Rice, Francis H. Dewey, Lewis Barnard, Francis H. Kinnicutt, George W. Richardson, Calvin Foster, Josiah H. Clarke, Isaac Davis, William Claflin, Jacob Edwards, Jr., George Hodges, Jr., Sullivan Fay, Aaron C. Mayhew, Royal O. Storrs, Charles G. Stevens, Edward B. Bigelow, Cheney Hatch. Charles L. Putnam, Esq., for many years Secretary of the Merchants and Farmers Mutual Insurance Company of this city, is the President, and Edward R. Washburn, lately of Boston, is the Secretary. The office of the Company is in Clark's Block, corner of Main and Mechanic streets.

STATE MUTUAL LIFE ASSURANCE COMPANY.

This Company was incorporated in 1844, and has a cash capital and accumulation of $177,619,00. The officers for 1860 and 1861, were Hon. Isaac Davis, President; Hon. E. Washburn and Hon. J. Brooks, Vice Presidents; Clarendon Harris, Secretary; Wm. Dickinson, Treasurer. Medical examiners in Worcester, Dr. B. F. Heywood, Dr. Joseph Sargent.

INSURANCE AGENCIES.

S. A. HOWLAND, is agent for a number of Insurance Companies in Boston and vicinity, Rhode Island and Connecticut, including the Manhattan Life Insurance Company of New York; aggregate capital represented, over $3,000,-000; office in the Central Exchange, on first floor, rear of Post Office.

WILLIAM S. DENNY, is agent for a number of Massachusetts, Rhode Island and Connecticut Insurance Companies. Office in Clark's Block, 257 Main st.

SAMUEL H. COLTON is agent for many of the popular Insurance Companies in New England and New York. Office 229 Main street.

JOHN G. KENDALL is agent for the Springfield Fire and Marine Insurance Company, and others.

A. N. CURRIER is agent of the Massasoit Insurance Company, Springfield, Mass. Office 229 Main street.

A. H. BULLOCK, is agent for several companies in New York, Connecticut and Rhode Island. Office in Waldo Block.

LUCIUS BEACH is agent for several Insurance Companies. Office No. 2 Warren Hall, Pearl street.

FIRE DEPARTMENT.

An act to establish a Fire Department in the Town of Worcester passed the Legislature of this Commonwealth, February 25, 1835. The first Board of Engineers were Lewis Bigelow, John F. Clark, Isaac Davis, Francis T. Merrick, George T. Rice, Nathan Heard, Lewis Thayer, Samuel Ward, and Ichabod Washburn. At the first meeting of the Board, May 2d, 1835, Isaac Davis, Esq., was elected chief engineer, Lewis Bigelow, assistant to the chief, and Ichabod Washburn, clerk.

The following table shows the officers of the Board of Engineers since 1835: 1836, Isaac Davis, Esq., chief, Ichabod Washburn, clerk, Capt. Lewis Bigelow, assistant chief; 1837, Gen. Nathan Heard, chief, Ichabod Washburn, clerk, Capt. Lewis Bigelow, assistant chief; 1838, Nathan Heard, chief, Ichabod Washburn, clerk, Samuel D. Spurr, assistant chief; 1839, Nathan Heard, chief, Clarendon Wheelock, clerk, Samuel D. Spurr, assistant chief; 1840, Henry W. Miller, chief, Clarendon Wheelock, clerk, James Estabrook, assistant chief; 1841, Henry W. Wilder, chief, Clarendon Wheelock, clerk, Joseph Pratt, assistant chief; 1842, Henry W. Miller, chief, Joseph Pratt, clerk, William Leggate, assistant chief; 1843, same as last year; 1844, Henry W. Miller, chief, Clarendon Wheelock, clerk, James S. Woodworth, assistant chief; 1845, Joel Wilder, chief, S. G. Pratt, clerk, Freeman Upham, assistant chief; 1846, same as last year; 1847, same as last year; 1848, Joel Wilder, chief, E. G. Pratt, clerk, Frederick Warren, assistant chief; 1849, Joel Wilder, chief, F. Warren, clerk, Osgood Bradley, assistant chief; 1850, Erastus N. Holmes, chief, F. Warren, clerk, Joel Wilder, assistant chief; 1851, Erastus N. Holmes, chief, Sewell Thayer, clerk, Joel Wilder, assistant chief; 1852, Erastus N. Holmes, chief, Alzirus Brown, clerk, Joel Wilder, assistant chief; 1852-3, E. N. Holmes, chief, A. Brown, clerk, T. Raymond, assistant chief; 1853-4, E. N. Holmes, chief, Charles Hersey, clerk, B. E. Hutchinson, assistant chief; 1855-6, L. W. Sturtevant, chief, Horatio Dolliver, clerk, S. H. Porter, assistant chief; 1856-7, L. W. Sturtevant, chief, E. G. Watkins, clerk, S. A. Porter, assistant chief; 1857-8, L. W. Sturtevant, chief, E. G. Watkins, clerk, S. A. Porter, assistant chief; 1858-9, L. W. Sturtevant, chief, E. G. Watkins, clerk, S A. Porter, assistant chief; 1859-60, S. A. Porter, chief, L. W. Sturtevant, clerk, L. R. Hudson, assistant chief; 1860-61, L. R. Hudson, chief, A. T. Burgess, clerk, E. N. Keyes, assistant chief; 1861-2, Alzirus Brown, chief, E. A. Harkness, clerk, E. B. Lovell, assistant chief.

DOCT. JOHN GREEN 3ᴰ

FROM THE LIFE-SIZE STATUE BY B.H.KINNE

IN THE PUBLIC LIBRARY.

WORCESTER LYCEUM AND LIBRARY ASSOCIATION

This Association was formed in August, 1852, under the name of the Young Men's Library Association, "its object being the improvement of the young men of the city of Worcester, by affording them intellectual and social advantages, by the maintenance of a Library, Reading Room, and such courses of Lectures and Classes as may conduce to this end." Any male citizen of Worcester could become a member by the payment of one dollar into the treasury. In November, 1852, an arrangement was made by which this Association purchased the furniture and took the room occupied by the Young Men's Christian Association, (an Association just started in Worcester,) and the first meeting for the choice of officers was held at this room, in Worcester Bank Block, on Saturday, December 18, 1852. At this meeting Francis H. Dewey was chosen President, and George W. Bentley, Vice President, George F Hoar, Corresponding Secretary, Nathaniel Paine, Recording Secretary, and H. Woodward, Treasurer; there was also a Board of thirteen Directors chosen.

In January 1853, an appeal was made to the public for aid in carrying out the object of the Association, and a subscription was started for the purpose of raising funds to purchase a library. Over $1300 was raised in this way, besides generous donations of books, so that the Association commenced its third year with over seventeen hundred volumes in its library. In March, 1853 the Association was incorporated by act of the Legislature, and officers were elected under that act in April

Through the active exertions of Rev E E Hale, then pastor of the Church of the Unity, a Natural History Department of the Association was organized in April, 1854, and has since continued a permanent department of the Association The meetings are held twice a month, except during July and August, and have been of great interest to those who attend A cabinet was commenced by the transfer of the collection of the "Worcester Natural History Society," in possession of the American Antiquarian Society, to this Department, since which time it has been largely increased by donations from its members and others The officers of the Natural History Department for 1862, are Rufus Woodward, President, H A Marsh, Secretary, Nathaniel Paine, Treasurer, and eleven Curators. This association, under the name of the Worcester Natural History Society, are now occupying rooms in the Free Public Library building

In the year 1855, a union of the "Young Men's Rhetorical Society," (an association of young men formed in 1849, for the improvement of its members in writing and public debate,) was made to this Association, and their library of some hundred volumes transferred to its rooms. The articles of agreement making this union were revoked in 1859 by the mutual consent of both parties

In December, 1855, Dr John Green placed his large and valuable miscellaneous library in the rooms of the Association, to be used by them as a consulting and reference library, for a term of not less than five years. The num-

32*

ber of volumes thus placed in the hands of the Association was about five thousand, many of which were very rare and valuable.

In 1855 a union of the Worcester Lyceum (formed in 1829,) was made with this Association, and by a special act of the Legislature the name was changed to "The Worcester Lyceum and Library Association," which it still retains. This union increased the Library of the Association some two thousand volumes, making, besides the Green Library, about four thousand volumes the exclusive property of the Association.

In November 1859, the Association lost by death their very efficient and much esteemed librarian, Mr. John Gray, who had served in that capacity since the foundation of the Library. A special meeting of the Directors was called at once, and a committee appointed to confer with Dr. Green in relation to the selection of a new librarian.

At an adjournment of this meeting, held November 26, this committee reported : "The Worcester Lyceum and Library Association having existed under its present name four years, and its Board of Direction having made annual reports, it would ill become us, since the important changes that have recently taken place, not to give a brief account of our stewardship.

Financially, we found the Association in good condition, but as heretofore the Library department has not been self-sustaining — owing more especially to our receipts being cut off at the very season when they are ordinarily the largest. This was occasioned by the prospect that the Library would soon be made a free one, which has now taken place, the same having been transferred to the city. This in connection with the well-known Green Library has unquestionably been the immediate nucleus for the Free Library, and we doubt not our citizens are favored with this boon several years earlier than they would have been, had these not been offered as they were.

The following are the proceedings immediately connected with this transfer.

That an interview had been had with Dr. Green, in which he expressed a readiness and desire to present the Green Library to the city, as the foundation of a Free Public Library. That subsequently, the committee had visited the Mayor, who expressed much gratification at Dr. Green's liberality, and cordially entered into the plan.

The following preamble and resolution were then adopted :

"Whereas Dr. John Green has indicated to a committee of the Directors of the Worcester Lyceum and Library Association, a desire to give his Library to the city, on such liberal conditions that the Directors believe it best that the public should receive the gift :

"Resolved, that the Directors recommend that the Library of the Association be transferred to the city, provided suitable appropriations and arrangements are made for its reception."

It was voted to send a copy of the same to the Mayor, which was done, and the action of City Council was as follows, viz.

In the Board of Aldermen, Monday evening, Dec. 5th, Mr. Lincoln offered the following resolutions, which were passed, and concurred in by the Common Council.

" Whereas a communication has been received from his Honor the Mayor, laying before the City Council the proposed donation of large and valuable libraries to the city, by Dr. John Green and the Lyceum and Library Association :

" Resolved, That the City Council have received the communications from Dr. John Green, and the Lyceum and Library Association, with a grateful and profound sense of the importance of the subject, and of the magnitude of the gifts which are proposed to be conferred upon the city.

" Resolved, That the several communications be referred to the joint standing committee on education, with instructions to report suitable resolutions in recognition of these municipal endowments, and to recommend what action the City Council should take in the premises. And, that said committee be requested to confer with Dr. John Green and the Lyceum and Library Association, for the purpose of learning their views and wishes concerning the whole subject."

On December 16, at a special meeting of the Association, called for that purpose, it was voted, on motion of Mr. N. Paine, that the Association accept and adopt the resolutions passed by the Board of Directors, at their meeting, held November 23, and that the Board of Directors have full power to carry out any arrangements that may be necessary under the resolves, including the transfer of the Library. Also, that the Secretary be authorized to transmit to the City Government the doings of the meeting.

As a result of this, the following resolutions were ultimately passed and transmitted to our organization.

CITY OF WORCESTER.

In City Council, December 23d, 1859.

Resolved, That the City Council, for and in behalf of the City of Worcester, hereby tender to the Worcester Lyceum and Library Association, their grateful acknowledgment of the generous offer made by said Association, to transfer to the City their large and valuable Library, to become a part of the Public City Library; and that the same be and hereby is accepted in the name of the City, in the faith that it shall be set apart for the use contemplated by the donors.

Resolved, That a copy of the foregoing be transmitted by the City Clerk to the Lyceum and Library Association, in proof of the acknowledgment of their public-spirited munificence. A Copy.

Attest, SAMUEL SMITH, City Clerk.

Thus was finally consummated, what had from the first been the desire and hopes of the originators and friends of the Library Association, a Public Library open freely to all citizens, and the Association had been kept for about eight years, to form a nucleus for such Library. The number of volumes thus transferred to the city, amounted to more than 4500. With these was transferred a large part of the edition of a new catalogue, just printed, thus saving the city that expense.

This Association still keeps up its organization, and has a course of lectures during the winter months. The present officers of the Association are, Edward Earle, President; George Chandler, Vice President; J. S. Rogers, Secretary; R. Hammant, Treasurer; T. W. Higginson, Nathaniel Paine, Henry Chapin, Daniel Tainter, Albert Tolman, Trustees.

From 1852 to 1861, the Presidents have been, F. H. Dewey, G. F. Hoar, Henry Chapin, T. K. Earle, I. M. Barton, Edward Earle. Vice Presidents, G. W. Bentley, W. Cross, H. J. Holmes, Nathaniel Paine, Daniel Tainter, P. L. Moen, Edward Earle, George Chandler, D. Tainter. Recording Secretaries, Nathaniel Paine, Thomas Earle, H. A Hill, A. Cary, J. S. Rogers. Corresponding Secretaries, G. F. Hoar, E. E. Hale, Horace James, T. W. Higginson. Treasurers, H. Woodward, J. H. Walker, L. L. Harding, R. Hammant.

WORCESTER GAS LIGHT COMPANY.

Perhaps no event in the history of a city is more indicative of its prosperity and enterprise, than the introduction of illuminating gas in its public streets, and in the stores and dwellings of its citizens ; we cannot therefore omit a passing record of the establishment of this company, whose birth typifies an era so marked in the city's progress.

Early in the spring of 1849, at the suggestion of Dr. Joseph Sargent, Hon. Isaac Davis and George T. Rice, Esq., met him at the house of the latter, to consider the expediency of forming a company, and establishing works for the supply of illuminating gas to the citizens of Worcester ; the necessary measures were then taken to obtain subscribers for an amount of capital necessary to proceed with the undertaking.

Sufficient encouragement having been given to warrant the success of the enterprise, a meeting of the subscribers to the stock of a Gas Light Company proposed to be formed in Worcester, was held May 4th, 1849, and " Charles W. Hartshorn, Russell L. Hawes and Warren Lazell, were appointed a committee to procure such facts as they can, relative to the subject of introducing gas into the city of Worcester, to report at an adjourned meeting."

At a meeting of the subscribers held June 12th, 1849, the report of a committee appointed at a previous meeting, consisting of William A. Wheeler, Warren Lazell, Alex. DeWitt, Joseph Sargent, R. L. Hawes, and John W. Lincoln, reported that they had contracted with Messrs., Blake & Darracott of Boston, to erect works for the manufacture and supply of Coal Gas, in accordance with the plans and specifications submitted by them, for the sum of forty thousand dollars.

June 22d, 1849.—The subscribers to the capital stock of forty-five thousand dollars, thirty in number, met and adopted a set of by-laws for the Worcester Gas Light Company, and completed their organization by the election of the following officers.

John W. Lincoln, President.   George T. Rice, Charles W. Hartshorn, John H. Blake, Charles Thurber, Directors. William Cross, Treasurer. Warren Lazell, Secretary.

June 27th, 1849. — The Board of Directors chose Warren Lazell as Agent of the Worcester Gas Light Company, which office he filled until Jan. 17th, 1852, at which time James B. Blake was elected as Agent of the Company, and Superintendent of the works.

The construction of the Gas Works on Lincoln street was commenced in July, 1849, and they were completed, and gas supplied to the citizens of Worcester, in the month of November following. The length of distributing pipes laid was about 2¼ miles, and were located in the following streets. Main, (from Lincoln square to Austin street,) School, Thomas, Exchange, Foster, Front, Pearl and Elm streets, from Chestnut street to the house of Levi Lincoln.

The number of consumers of gas in the city, January 1st, 1850, was 102. The amount of gas consumed in the year 1852, was about 2,000,000 cubic feet.

A charter having been granted by the Legislature of 1851, a meeting of the Stockholders was held, June 12th, 1851, and having duly accepted the charter, the officers chosen June 22, 1849, were re-elected and assumed their duties, in corporate capacity.

In 1853, the gradual increase of the consumption of gas in the central part of the city, rendered additional storage room necessary ; a location was obtained on Green street, near Fox's mill, and a suitable gas holder and building were erected for the purpose. An extension of the company's building on Lincoln street to facilitate the manufacture of gas, was accomplished in 1854.

The consumption of gas in the city having been greatly increased through the yearly extension of street mains, and the addition of consumers, it became necessary in the year 1860, to enlarge the works. It was thought best to do this in such a manner as to provide for the city for many years to come; accordingly, plans were adopted, involving almost a re-construction of the works, in such a manner, as not only to supply the best quality of illuminating gas, but also to obviate any possible objection to their location. A new chimney 135 feet high was erected, with ample ventilating flues. The main building on Lincoln street was extended from 90 feet, to 250 feet : the most approved machinery for the manufacture and purification of gas was introduced, a new gas holder of a capacity of sixty thousand cubic feet was constructed, and the general character of the works improved in every manner, at a cost of about forty thousand dollars.

The length of distributing pipes laid in the streets of the city, Jan. 1st, 1861, was 12½ miles, and extend from the house of F. W. Paine on Lincoln street, to the house of Albert Curtis, New Worcester, a distance of nearly three miles from north to south, and from the Female College, Providence street, to the house of D. W. Lincoln, Pleasant street, a distance of nearly 1½ miles from east to west.

The number of meters used by consumers of gas January 1st, 1861, was 1041. The amount of gas consumed in the year 1860, was about twelve and a third million cubic feet. The estimated number of burners in the city, is 10,253. The number of public street gas lights, is 163. The amount of capital invested by this company in real estate, gasworks, pipes, meters, &c., January 1st, 1861, was about $189,000.

The officers of the company, for the year 1861 :

George T. Rice, *President : Directors*—Joseph Sargent, Russell L. Hawes, John C. Mason, Alexander H. Bullock, Edward W. Lincoln, Dwight Foster. William Cross, *Treasurer and Clerk.* James B. Blake, *Agent and Superintendent.*

WORCESTER POST OFFICE.

In order to show the increase of business in this office, the author will insert a letter from James Wilson, Esq , son of James Wilson, late Post Master of this city ; it is directed to Emory Banister, Esq., dated Cincinnati, Ohio, April 25th, 1859:

" On an examination recently of the papers of my late lamented father, I find the enclosed account current, with the Post Office Department, rendered by him *half a century ago.* Thinking you might feel interested in knowing the extent of the business transacted in the Post Office at Worcester at that early period, and contrast it with the present operations of the office, I concluded to send it to you."

An account current, showing the amount collected by James Wilson, Postmaster. from January 1st to April 1st, 1809, was $178,80½ ; the amount collected by Emory Banister, just fifty years from the above date, from January 1st to April 1st, 1859, was $4183,00 ; the number of letters sent from the office by Mr. Wilson, 1809, must have been about 4400 ; the number sent by Mr. Banister, 1859, was 497,872 ; drop letters received during that year was 25,936, making in all, letters put into the office, for one year, 523,808, and 501,450 letters received from other offices, to be delivered.

Emory Banister was appointed Postmaster, May 1st, 1854, retired from office, July 1st, 1861.

John Milton Earle, is Mr. Banister's successor, and now holds the office.

GRADUATES OF COLLEGES, NOT MENTIONED ELSEWHERE.

William E. Green is the oldest native-born citizen, now living in Worcester, and the oldest member of the Worcester Bar. The following interesting reminiscence of Mr. Green and his family, was communicated to the author by Hon. William N. Green, his eldest son, who is now the Chief Justice of the Police court, Worcester.

The children of William E. Green, Esq., after a separation of some twenty five years, assembled for a family reunion, on the fifteenth and sixteenth of September, A. D. 1861, at the old ancestral manor of "GREEN HILL."

The venerable ancestor, now in his eighty fifth year, hale and active, attended public worship at the Central Church, Rev. Dr. Sweetser's, on the afternoon of the 15th, with his ten children.

On the 16th, the children all assembled at "Green Hill," and remained together in social converse during the day, and in the evening were joined by a circle of relatives and friends.

This family reunion is the more remarkable, from the widely distant places of business and residence of the family, and their long separation from the paternal mansion.

Their names, and places of residence are as follows:

Hon. William N. Green, Worcester, Mass.; Lucy M. Green, New York City; Mary R. Green, New York City; Julia E. Green, Worcester, Mass.; Dr. John P. Green, Copiapo, Chili, South America; Hon. Andrew H. Green, New York City; Dr. Samuel F. Green, Batticotta, Ceylon, East Indies; Lydia P. Green, Worcester; Oliver B. Green, Esq., Chicago, Illinois; Martin Green, Esq, Peshtigo, Wisconsin.

These ten, are the children of William E. Green, by his first three wives, and another child died in infancy. The father is now living with his fourth wife.

Rejoice Newton, several years ago, relinquished his professional occupation, and now, within a few months of 80 years of age, enjoying the most perfect state of health, spends his time reading and superintending his farm, an employment he always loved. He has been a member of the State Senate two years.

Stephen Salisbury, President of the Worcester Bank, &c.

Daniel Waldo Lincoln was educated a lawyer, and is not now in practice. He represented the town in the Legislature, in 1846, and was Alderman in 1858 and 1859. Mr. Lincoln has been President of the Worcester County Horticultural Society. He is now engaged in his extensive Nursery and Green House.

William S. Lincoln, has retired from the practice of the law. He has been

City Marshal, and is now President of the Worcester County Agricultural Society.

Edward W. Lincoln, born Dec., 1820 ; graduated at Harvard University in 1839 ; admitted to the bar in Illinois. Postmaster of Worcester from May 1849, to May 1854. Been editor of the National Ægis, and the Daily Bay State. At present, is secretary and librarian of the Worcester County Horticultural Society.

George Jaques, graduated at Brown University, 1836 ; son of Abiel Jaques ; was a teacher in Virginia, 1838—1840, and has subsequently been a resident of this city.

Charles W. Holbrook was born in Holden, May, 1828 ; graduated at Williams College, Mass., in the class of 1851. Was principal of a Classical High School in Greensboro, N. C., six years. Returned home, and taught in the North, three years, and has since been in the book business in this city.

Charles Francis, son of Pliny Holbrook, born in Bellingham, Mass., April 1, 1832 ; graduated at Brown University in 1855 ; ordained pastor of the Baptist church, Tariffville, Ct., February 13th, 1859, where he still remains.

John Green, son of James, was born in Worcester, April 2d, 1835 ; graduated at Harvard College in 1855 ; member of the Lawrence Scientific School at Cambridge, chemical department. In 1856 spent two years in the medical schools in Europe, and is now in practice in Boston.

Samuel Swett Green, son of James, graduated at Harvard College. He is now a member of the Divinity School at Cambridge.

James Green, brother of the above, senior in Harvard College.

Charles E. Simmons, son of John Simmons, was born in Worcester in 1834 ; entered Madison University in 1857, and was obliged to leave in 1859 on account of his eye sight and ill health. Mr. Simmons enlisted into the 21st regiment, and is now hospital steward.

Addison Prentice was born, June 13, 1814, at Paris, Me.; studied law in his native town, and was admitted to the bar there in 1839 ; practiced four years in Lee, Me., and removed to Worcester in 1847 ; practiced about three years and retired, and since then has been engaged as an artist and engraver.

Daniel Waldo Haskins came to Worcester in 1848, was graduated at Amherst College in 1858, and is now in the law office of Peter C. Bacon and P. Emory Aldrich.

Samuel Swan was born in Leicester, May, 1778 ; graduated at Harvard College in 1799. He is the oldest member of the Worcester bar except one, (Wm. E. Green.) He always had the reputation of being an *honest* lawyer.

Prof. James Bushee, born in Smithfield, R. I., October, 1805 ; graduated at the Friends' Institution, Providence; commenced teaching in Fall River in 1830, took charge of the Smithfield Academy in 1833, and remained there twenty years, when he removed to Worcester, and has since been engaged in teaching, and is now at the head of the Young Ladies Institute

Rev. William A Bushee, son of the above, was born in Smithfield, R I, January, 1831, graduated at Yale in the class of 1856, and the Theological School in 1858 He is now teacher in the Highland School in this city.

Everett Wilson Pattison, son of Dr Pattison, born at Waterville, Maine, 1838, graduated at Waterville College in 1858, came to Worcester in May, 1860, and read law with Bacon and Aldrich, and is now Lieutenant in the Second Regiment, Mass. Volunteers

Eli Thayer was born in Mendon, Mass, in 1819, fitted for college at the Worcester Academy, and graduated at Brown University in 1841, having supported himself during the time by teaching, gardening, sawing wood, &c. He was afterwards principal of the Worcester Academy, and founder of the Oread Institute In 1854 and 55, he was representative in the General Court. In 1854, was Alderman of this city. While in the Legislature, he originated the plan of "organized emigration" as an antidote for the threatened enslavement of Kansas. In 1857 and 1859, he was elected representative to Congress, and served the two terms with considerable distinction.

Werden Reynolds, son of Rev. Werden P Reynolds now of Worcester, Mass, and Emme daughter of Asa Reynolds of Granville N Y Born at Rupert, Bennington county, Vt, May 1st 1813 Selected, at an early age, the profession of teaching, and was educated for that vocation Graduated at Middlebury College, Vt, 1839 From that time till July, 1855, was constantly engaged in teaching, being employed as Principal, successively of the Franklin Academy, Cong Collegiate Seminary, Holley Academy, and Whitehall Academy, all in the state of New York. In Aug, 1855, moved from Whitehall, N Y to Worcester, Mass, and commenced publishing the Daily Transcript in company with E R Fiske and his brother-in-law, Z K Pangborn In Aug, 1856, was appointed associate principal with William S. Green, of the Worcester Academy In Aug, 1859, was elected President of of the Ladies Collegiate Institute, and entered upon the duties of the appointment, at the commencement of the winter session in December following. July 16th, 1840, while Principal of the Academy at Malone, N. Y., married Emeline, daughter of Amariah H Wood of that place.

John Green Burbank was born in Fitchburg, Mass, August, 1819; entered as Cadet at West Point Military Academy in 1837, graduated in 1841, was engaged in the Florida war until 1846, was in several battles in Mexico, and was mortally wounded in the battle of Molino del Rey, September, 1847, and died two days after. His remains were interred in the Rural Cemetery in May, 1848.

OBITUARIES, FROM 1837 TO 1861.

Dr. Oliver Fiske died in Boston, January 25th, 1837, aged 74 years. He was for many years a prominent citizen of Worcester.

Capt. Nathaniel Brooks died February 3d, 1838, aged 97. Capt. Brooks passed 70 years of his life in this town, and for nearly half a century was connected with the Old South Church.

Edward D. Bangs died April 21st, 1838, aged 48 years.

John Hubbard died Nov. 10th, 1838, aged 67. Mr. Hubbard attended a religious meeting at the Baptist Vestry, and as usual led in prayer, and in a few minutes after breathed his last.

Deacon James Wilson died in Cincinnati, Ohio, February 5th, 1841, aged 78 : for many years postmaster of this town, and first deacon of the first Baptist Church.

Deacon Moses Perry died March 12th, 1842, aged 80. He was deacon of the First Church many years, and a valuable citizen.

Frost Rockwood died March 9th, 1842, aged 88. Mr. Rockwood was a good man, and a consistent Christian. In the year 1800 he abandoned the use of ardent spirits, and for more than 42 years kept his pledge.

Elder Luther Goddard died May 25th, 1842, aged 81. He was a skillful watchmaker, and well known in this county as a Baptist minister.

Paul Gates died January 11th, 1843, aged 85.

John Adams died September 23d, 1843, aged 82.

William Lincoln, Esq., died October 6th, 1843, aged 42 years. He was the author of " Lincoln's History," which forms the first part of this volume.

Judge Nathaniel Paine died October 7th, 1840, aged —. He was for many years Judge of Probate for this county.

Henry Paine, son of Hon. Nathaniel Paine, died April 24th, 1844, aged 39.

Gardiner Paine died January 27th, 1854, aged 55. Mr. Paine was a military man ; for several years he was major in the old 6th regiment.

Daniel Waldo died July 9th, 1845, aged 82.

Joseph G. Kendall died October 2d, 1847, aged 59. Mr. Kendall was Clerk of the Courts, and one of our most honored and *beloved* citizens, and a man of good talents, of refined and cultivated taste, and of uncommon purity of character.

Levi Lincoln Newton, son of Hon. Rejoice Newton, died October 21st,

1847, aged 27 years. Mr Newton was a young man of sterling integrity and honor, and eminent social affections, and purity of character

Dr Samuel Woodward died at Northampton, January 3d, 1850, aged 64 He was for many years the Superintendent of the Lunatic Hospital in this city.

Gen Ebenezer L Barnard died July 8th, 1850, aged 45.

Southworth Howland died June 8th, 1855, aged 78 He was born in Barnstable, Mass, and resided over fifty years in West Brookfield, and the last ten years in Worcester In 1809, he made the first artificial leg ever made in this country, for Maj Phinehas Upham of West Brookfield, and for over twenty years was the sole manufacturer in America specimens of his work being still in use in all parts of the country He was an early and zealous advocate of temperance, having in 1815, published and distributed, at his own expense, an edition of Rush's celebrated Essay on the effects of ardent spirits. He was never confined to the house a day by sickness

William Eaton died May 4th, 1859, aged 92 years Mr Eaton was a grandson of Adonijah Rice, who was the first male child born in Worcester.

Lewis Barnard died April, 1855, aged 75. He was the largest cattle dealer in the county

Artemas Ward died Nov., 1850, aged 75 Esq. Ward was Register of Deeds from 1821 to 1846, a period of 25 years, which office he filled with honor to himself, and satisfaction to all concerned.

Simon Gates died Feb 1849, aged 93 Mr. Gates was never from home more than two or three nights at a time, during his whole life, except when his country called him to its service in the revolutionary struggle. He died in the same house and room he was born in

Deacon Nathaniel Brooks died Nov. 3d, 1850, aged 53; for several years deacon of the first church

Abiel Jaques, graduated at Harvard University, 1807, born at Wilmington, Mass, March 7th, 1780, died here Oct 7th, 1852. Was Preceptor of a Nautical Academy at Salem, in 1809–1810, and, for many years afterwards was engaged as a teacher in Watertown, Newton, Brooklyn, (Conn) Uxbridge, &c, &c Subsequently devoted himself to land surveying and civil engineering, which, with the care of his farm, continued to occupy him until a short period before his death.

John W Lincoln died Oct., 1852, aged 64. Mr. Lincoln was closely identified with the history of the town and county, for nearly forty years. In all the relations of life, he secured the confidence and respect of his associates He was a true and steadfast friend.

The following account of Winthrop Chandler, has been kindly furnished by Dr George Chandler of this city, who is a descendant of the Chandlers who flourished so conspicuously in this town now more than one hundred years ago   Dr Chandler has also furnished the author with a fine engraving of his ancestor, which is placed in this connection.

Winthrop Chandler, the painter, was son of Captain William Chandler of Woodstock, Conn, born 6th of April, 1747, old style, married Mary, daughter of Rev Charles Gleason, of Dudley, Mass, and died at the residence of his brother Theophilus Chandler, in Thompson, Conn, 29th, July 1790.

He studied the art of portrait painting in Boston, and some of his likenesses in oil, are yet in Woodstock and Thompson, Conn, Worcester and Petersham, Mass   The likenesses of his wife and of himself, by his own brush are in the keeping of his son, Winthrop Hilton Chandler, Esq, at Avon, N Y

In the last years of his life, he resided at Worcester, Mass, and in his leisure from portrait painting, which at that day was in its infancy in this country, he sought the means of sustaining his family in house painting, and for that purpose had a shop near the building erected for the manufacture of cotton and linen, east of the Common

The Worcester Spy of August 19th, 1790, speaks of him thus —"Died at Woodstock, Conn, Mr Winthrop Chandler of this town,—a man whose native genius has been serviceable to the community in which he resided.   By profession he was a house painter, but many good likenesses on canvas, shew he could guide the pencil of a limner   He left a manuscript, that discovered that he had merit as a botanist   Many plants, the growth of his native county, are in his manuscript not only well delineated, but are accurately and botanically described   The world was not his enemy, but as is too common, his genius was not nurtured on the bosom of encouragement.   Embarrassment like strong weeds in a garden of delicate flowers, checked his usefulness and disheartened the man.

John Davis died April, 1854, aged 67   The author can give no better eulogium of Gov Davis, than to quote the words of his venerable pastor, Rev. Dr Hill, on the occasion of his funeral   "There are times when we prefer to sit silent and meditate   There is a presence before which human lips are dumb, and the tongue refuses to speak   There is such a spectacle before us to-day, that human speech cannot add to its power.   He who once spoke to us in tones that we always loved to hear, is now silent forever."

Thomas Kinnicutt died Jan'y, 1858, aged 58.   Judge Kinnicutt had been an selectman, representative and senator in the General Court, speaker of the House of Representatives, trustee of the State Lunatic Hospital, a vice president of the Worcester County Institution for Savings, for a long time president of the Central Bank, and for several years Judge of Probate for this county.

Samuel M Burnside died July, 1850   Mr Burnside was an eminent lawyer, and a strong-minded man

Alfred Dwight Foster died August, 1852, aged 52.   Mr Foster was one of our most respected citizens   He held many important offices of trust, the duties of which were discharged with ability and fidelity

George Lincoln, son of Hon Levi Lincoln, was born in Worcester, Oct 19, 1816 After a preparatory education at Leicester Academy, he entered Harvard University in 1832 In his second college year, preferring an active business life, he availed himself of an opportunity to accompany a family relative and friend, who was in command of a valuable ship, on a voyage to India Returning with success, and a fondness for such employment, after some short interval, he made a second voyage, in another vessel to India, taking some interest in a mercantile adventure Upon the return passage from Batavia, the captain died, and much of the charge of the ship and cargo devolved upon young Lincoln Most of the crew were down with sickness, and the vessel in distress put into a Dutch port, where she was unladen and the ship and cargo disposed of. From thence, after many delays, Mr Lincoln found his way, through France, to his own country. Upon his arrival home, learning that the government was about to increase the army for the suppression of the Seminole war in Florida, a service which had not been either very successful or desirable, he solicited a commission, and upon examination, with the approval of Gen Scott, and Mr Poinsett, Secretary of War, he was appointed second lieutenant in the 4th regiment of Infantry, and immediately entered upon active duty On the 18th of September, 1840, he was promoted to be a first lieutenant, and transferred to the 8th regiment, specially selected for the command of the gallant Colonel Worth, in the final effort for the termination of the long-continued and obstinate conflict with the Indians In this service, Lieut Lincoln was placed in command of a detachment of mounted men, and for his good conduct was highly complimented in regimental orders After the close of the war with the Seminoles, he was occasionally detached upon the recruiting service, but generally was with detachments of his regiment in different camps, as the exigency of the service required the disposition to be made of the troops The breaking out of the Mexican war found him stationed at Tampa Bay, in Florida, from whence he marched with the first forces to meet the enemy. He was engaged, and greatly distinguished himself, in the hard-fought battles of Palo Alto and Resaca de la Palma, in the latter of which he saved the life of a prostrate brother officer, in a personal conflict with two Mexican soldiers, who were about transfixing him with their bayonets. On the 8th of July, 1846, he was appointed Assistant Adjutant General with the brevet rank of Captain, and with directions to report in person to Major General Taylor In the terrible battle of Buena Vista, he was attached to the staff of General Wool, and while gallantly bearing his orders, in the hottest of the fight, he was fatally pierced by two musket balls and instantly killed The most fitting tributes to his character and memory are to be seen in the General Orders, which report the events of the conflict, and the touching testimonial of the commanding officer of the brave Kentucky Volunteers, his associates in the campaign, extracts from which are appropriately inscribed upon the family Monument in the beautiful Rural Cemetery in this city, at the base of which, his remains, removed from their temporary grave near the battle field, now repose

33*

"We have to lament the death of Captain George Lincoln, Assistant Adjutant General, serving on the staff of General Wool, a young officer of high bearing, and approved gallantry, who fell early in the action." — *Major Gen. Taylor's Official Report.*

"I lost my Assistant Adjutant General, Captain Lincoln, who was as brave, gallant, and accomplished an officer as I ever knew. He fell in the execution of my orders, and in the attempt to rally our men." — *Brigadier General Wool's Report.*

"By his noble bearing and kindness of heart, he won our affections completely. We looked upon him as upon a brother, and when we were leaving the country, we could not consent to leave his remains behind us." — *Major Frye, surviving commanding officer 2d Kentucky Volunteers.*

On the 16th of February 1847, only seven days before his death, he had been promoted to a full captaincy in the line, but which commission he never received.

Deacon Alpheus Merrifield died Jan., 1853, aged 73. He was Deacon of the Second Church for many years, and Secretary of the Board of Overseers of the Poor. He was a valuable citizen.

Benjamin Thayer died March, 1852, aged 70.

Benjamin F. Newton died March, 1853, aged 32. Mr. Newton possessed excellent abilities, and was one of our most promising young lawyers. He was universally esteemed for his suavity of disposition and high moral integrity.

Deacon John Bixby died July, 1853, aged 82. Mr. Bixby was deacon of the first church for many years.

Professor Calvin Newton died August, 1853, aged 52. He was President of the Worcester Medical Institution.

John H. Matthews died July 20th, 1856. Mr. Matthews was at that time District Attorney for this district.

Thomas Chamberlain died Sept, 1855, aged 72. He had filled most of the military offices, from corporal to major general, with the highest honor to himself, and satisfaction to those under his command. Gen. Chamberlain was the first President of the Common Council, and Crier of the Courts for many years, all of which duties he discharged with ability and faithfulness.

George C. Bigelow died May, 1859, aged 29. Mr. Bigelow was Cashier of the Central Bank about three years, and died while in office. He was a young man of promise, and his loss was severely felt in this community.

John Gray, was born in Boston, December 5, 1798; graduated at Brown University in 1823; was admitted to the bar, but never practiced to any extent. He edited a paper in Brooklyn, Conn., in 1832 and 1834. In 1838 he removed to Newburyport, Mass., and opened a bookstore; removed to

Worcester in 1847, and was chosen Librarian of the Young Men's Library Association, which office he retained until his death, in November, 1859. Mr Gray was respected by all, and rendered very efficient service in the formation of the Library from which sprung the present Free Public Library

Gideon Paine died September, 1853, aged 67   Mr. Paine was one of Worcester's best farmers, and an honest man

Samuel Gates died October, 1853, aged 76.

Rev John F. Burbank died November, 1853, aged 42.   He was an efficient man in the City Council and School Board, and pastor of the Baptist Church in Greenville, Leicester

Elisha Flagg died December, 1853, aged 74.   Mr Flagg built the Flagg Block that was burned, on the site of the present Flagg Block.

William Barber died February, 1854, aged 59.   He was a very worthy citizen

Albert Brown died September, 1854, aged 51.   Mr Brown came from Providence, R I, in early life, and opened a tailoring establishment here, and was at the head of it until his death

Peter Rich (colored) died October, 1854, aged 93   Mr Rich was an honest and industrious citizen.   He worked for Mr Waldo and Gov Lincoln, and for Messrs Rice and Miller, almost his whole life.   He was employed by Messrs Rice and Miller for more than twenty years.   He was a mechanic, and when he had a job of ditching to do in water, he would make for himself a pair of wooden boots, which answered a very good purpose.

Samuel Sturtevant died April, 1855, aged 82, a very worthy man

Oliver Harrington died November, 1855, aged 50.   Mr Harrington died lamented by all who knew him

Charles Warren died February, 1856, aged 72.   He was the agent for the building of Warren Block, on Pearl street, hence its name.

Silas Brooks died March, 1856, aged 83   Mr Brooks was Crier of the Courts for many years prior to Gen Chamberlain

Walter Bigelow died May, 1857, aged 82   Mr Bigelow was a very worthy citizen, and a nephew of Col Timothy Bigelow of revolutionary fame

Jesse W Goodrich died June, 1857, aged about 50   He was an uncompromising advocate of temperance, and was the editor and proprietor of the Worcester County Cataract, and the Massachusetts Washingtonian   He died a temperance monomaniac

Moses Clement died October, 1857, aged 75.   Mr Clement was a worthy citizen and an excellent mechanic

Oliver H Blood, M D, died, April, 1858, aged 57.   Dr. Blood was a graduate of Harvard University

John Sutton died September, 1858, aged 68

Matthew Gray died September, 1858, aged 75.

FIRES.

It is not considered by the author necessary to enumerate all the fires and alarms that have occurred since 1836, but some of the most disastrous will be noticed.

In 1838, February 20th, the house, barn, and chair factory of Alvin Wait, was burnt : the family escaped with only the clothes they had on.

In 1838, August 22d, the large machine shop of Henry Goulding & Co., in School street, was consumed. This was the most destructive fire at the time that had ever been in Worcester.

In 1842, May 12th, the extensive Railroad Car Manufactory of Bradley & Rice was burned, together with a large blacksmith shop, and nearly all their contents. Loss, $20,000.

In 1842, May 31st, the large barn with the cow house and sheds adjoining, together with a valuable yoke of oxen, belonging to Horatio Gates, was burned.

In 1842, July 18th, the extensive machine shop and lumber house adjoining, and the satinet factory, owned by Albert Curtis, occupied by Metcalf and Barbour, were burned.

In 1843, April 6th, the Worcester Bank, Post Office, and two printing offices, were burned. See Spy, April 8th, 1843.

In 1844, February 19th, the first Methodist Church was burned.

In 1844, May 29th, a large wooden building at the corner of Main and Mechanic streets was destroyed. The same ground was burned over three years before.

In 1845, January 1st, a large store at Washington Square, owned by F. W. Paine, Esq., was burned.

In February, 1846, the brick school house at Northville was burned.

In May, 1848, the house of Tyler P. Curtis was burned.

In February, 1854, Flagg's Block was burned. This was a most destructive fire ; it broke out at midnight, when the thermometer was below zero. Loss about $50,000.

In 1854, June 14th, the most disastrous fire that ever occurred in this city, called the Merrifield Fire ; loss about *a half a million dollars*. For full particulars see Daily Spy, June 15th, 1854.

In 1852, July 14th, the Catholic College building was nearly all destroyed.

November 22d, the County House, damage trifling to the building, but four men were smothered to death.

In 1858, October 8th, the factory of Albert Curtis, New Worcester. Loss, $2,600 ; fully insured.

November 2d, the factory at Jamesville, owned by the Messrs. James. Loss, $5000 ; fully insured.

OLD MEN OF WORCESTER

The following is a list of the men now residents of Worcester who were born in the last century, with the exception of those mentioned elsewhere, and some who decline giving their ages : others may be omitted by the author through mistake.

Nam	Date of birth		Place of birth
Allen, Samuel,	Nov	1789,	Worcester
Allen, George,	Feb	1792,	Worcester.
Allen, Charles,	Feb	1797,	Worcester
Aldrich, Paine,	Jan	1791,	Swanzey, N H.
Aldrich, Eben,	April,	1785,	Uxbridge
Abbot, Asahel,	April,	1769,	Lebanon, N H
Bullard, Aaron B. W	April,	1800,	Buckland
Bowles, Thomas,	June,	1788,	Ireland
Bancroft, Timothy,	May,	1798,	Auburn
Bond, Joseph,	Nov	1784,	Boylston
Bancroft Peter M	Feb	1779,	Auburn
Brown, Sylvanus,	Sept	1794,	Webster
Bond, Jeremiah,	Oct	1800,	Leicester.
Brown, William,	Aug	1797,	Pawtucket, R I
Braman, Biadish,	July,	1795,	Norton
Bryant, Ira,	Feb	1791,	Leicester
Blanchard, William,	Nov.	1799,	Brookfield
Butman, Benjamin,	March,	1787,	Worcester.
Boice, John F	Nov	1798,	Rutland.
Barber, Silas,	March,	1785,	Worcester
Barker, Samuel D.	Sept	1793,	Arundill, Me
Brown, Willard,	July,	1790,	Douglas
Brown, Felix,	Dec	1796,	Charlton
Brown, Benj H	Dec	1799,	Spencer
Bullard, Herman,	Oct	1796,	Medway
Barton, Ira M	Oct.	1796,	Oxford
Curtis, Oliver,	Nov.	1791,	Sharon
Curtis, Edward,	July,	1795,	"
Curtis, Joseph,	June,	1798,	"
Chase, Anthony,	June,	1793,	Paxton
Clark, John F ,	April,	1790,	Hubbardston
Connell, James B ,	Dec	1790,	Ireland.
Croney, Henry,	Aug	1787,	Northbridge.
Corbett, Otis,	July,	1782,	Milford
Culver, Joshua,	Dec	1782,	New London, Ct.

Names.	Date of birth.	Place of birth.
Collier, Ebenezer,	May, 1786,	Oxford.
Conant, Hervey,	June, 1796,	Dudley.
Combs, Corral,	Feb. 1790,	Northbridge.
Caldwell, Seth,	Dec. 1791,	Barre.
Chapin, Lewis,	May, 1792,	Worcester.
Cobleigh, Henry,	May, 1800,	Dummerston, Vt.
Campbell, James,	July, 1790,	Worcester.
Congdon, Samuel,	Nov. 1793,	Portsmouth, R. I.
Clapp, Luther J.,	Jan. 1795,	Templeton.
Childs, Benj. N.,	March, 1796,	Rutland.
Corey, John,	Oct. 1792,	Ashburnham.
Cox, Ebenezer,	May, 1791,	Hardwick.
Davis, Isaac,	June, 1799,	Northboro'.
Dorr, Enos,	Aug. 1799,	Brookfield.
Dana, Caleb,	Dec. 1797,	Princeton.
Dexter, John B.,	June, 1797,	Millbury.
Donald, John Mc,	Dec. 1785,	Liverpool, Eng.
Drury, Ephraim,	June, 1793,	Boylston.
Day, Jonathan,	Jan. 1799,	Dudley.
Earle, John Milton,	April, 1794,	Leicester.
Estabrook, James,	Sept. 1796,	Holden,
Earl, Charles,	June. 1790,	Leicester.
Elder, James,	June, 1795,	Worcester.
Flagg, Samuel,	April, 1784,	Holden.
Flagg, Abel,	Oct. 1780,	Worcester.
Fuller, James,	Aug. 1798,	Savoy.
Faden, Samuel Mc,	Dec. 1781,	Ireland.
Fenno, Wm. D.,	Dec. 1798,	Worcester.
Foster, Samuel,	May, 1779,	Holden.
McFarland, Ira,	Oct. 1785,	Worcester.
Flagg, Samuel D,	Dec. 1789,	Boylston,
Flagg, Benjamin,	June, 1790,	Worcester.
Felton, ———	Sept. 1792,	Barre.
Gates, David R.	March, 1799,	Worcester.
Goddard, Ezra,	June, 1783,	Rutland.
Goddard, Parley,	Jan. 1787,	Shrewsbury.
Gates, Asa,	Feb. 1788,	Worcester.
Green, Wm. E.	Jan. 1777,	Worcester.
Goddard, Isaac,	March, 1800,	Royalston, Vt.
Green John,	April, 1784,	Worcester.
Goodwin, John,	Sept. 1796,	Holden.
Goddard Daniel,	Feb. 1796,	Shrewsbury.
Goss, William,	Nov. 1779,	Mendon.
Goddard, Benjamin,	May, 1791,	Royalston.

Names	Date of birth		Place of birth
Gorham Huram,	Aug	1799.	Hardwick
Gates Andrew,	May,	1799,	Worcester
Gates, Henry,	Aug.	1797,	Worcester
Gates, Levi,	Nov.	1790,	Worcester.
Green, Benjamin,	Feb.	1789,	Watertown
Greenhelgh, ——	Dec	1799,	England
Goodnow, William,	April,	1798,	"
Gleason John,	——	1779,	Worcester
Howland, S A.	Sept	1800,	West Brookfield
Heisey, Charles,	June,	1800,	Worcester
Hill, Alonzo,	June,	1800,	Harvard.
Heywood, Henry,	Aug	1785,	Worcester
Holbrook, Micah,	Aug	1794,	Princeton
Harkness, Nathan,	Feb	1800,	Leicester
Hammond, John,	Aug	1789,	Rutland
Heywood, Benjamin F,	April,	1792,	Worcester
Howe, Levi,	Jan	1792,	Shrewsbury
Harrington, William,	Feb.	1788, .	Worcester
Hill, Richard,	Feb	1780,	York, Me
Hadwin Charles,	Jan.	1797, .	Newport, R. I
Harritt, William,	Jan	1784,	Baltimore, Md.
Harrington, Lawson,	May,	1780,	Worcester.
Hector, John,	May,	1791,	Grafton
Harris, Clarendon,	Sept	1800,	——
Holbrook, Pliny,	Dec	1798,	Bellingham.
Harrington, Daniel,	—— ——,		Worcester.
Jones, John,	July,	1786,	Worcester.
Jones, David,	March,	1787,	Leominster,
Johnson, Luther,	May,	1788,	Worcester.
Johnson, John,	Sept	1787,	Worcester.
Johnson, Micah,	May,	1794,	Worcester
Jennison, William,	Jan	1789,	Oxford,
Kettell, John P	Jan	1797,	Boston
Kendall, Smith,	Sept.	1793,	Unadilla, N Y.
Katied, Patrick,	Dec	1799,	Ireland
Lincoln, Levi,	Oct.	1782,	Worcester.
Lovell, Cyrus,	Nov.	1790,	Worcester.
Lovell, David,	Nov	1786,	Worcester
Lamb, Isaac,	Dec.	1800,	Spencer.
Luvay, Thomas,	June,	1795,	Athol
Lester, John,	June,	1770,	Baltimore, Md
Loring, Israel,	Nov	1774,	Boston
Lovering, John,	Dec	1771,	Holliston
Moore, Ephraim,	June,	1778,	Leicester.

Names.	Date of birth.	Place of birth.
Mason, Lyman L.	March, 1800,	Thompson, Ct.
Murray, Henry,	Sept. 1800,	Ireland.
Mills, Richard,	Oct. 1795,	Needham.
Morse, J. C.	Sept. 1799,	Woodstock, Vt.
Moore, Nathaniel C.	Oct. 1800,	Worcester.
Mann, John,	Sept. 1790,	Mendon.
Merrick, Francis T.	—— 1791,	Brookfield.
Mann, William W.	Aug. 1787,	Needham.
Morton, David,	June, 1786,	Whately.
Miller, Henry W.	Sept. 1800,	——
Moore, Levi,	Oct. 1788,	Worcester.
McArkey,	—— 1788,	Ireland.
Nichols, Joseph,	Dec. 1799,	Westboro'.
Nichols, Charles P.	1794,	Oxford,
Newton, L. D.	Dec. 1797,	West Boylston.
Newton, Rejoice,	Oct. 1782,	Greenfield.
Newcomb, Henry K.	Oct. 1796,	Greenfield.
Nourse, Stephen,	March, 1793,	Bolton.
Newton, Ezra,	Nov. 1774,	Shrewsbury.
Nelson, Jonathan,	July, 1783,	Milford.
Powers, Patrick,	March, 1797,	Ireland.
Paine, F. W.	May, 1788,	Salem,
Parker, Henry,	Nov. 1786,	Worcester,
Pattison, Robert E.	Aug. 1800,	Benson, Vt.
Pond, John F.	May, 1798,	Franklin.
Perry, Samuel,	Nov. 1796,	Worcester.
Prentiss, Charles G.	Oct. 1798,	Leominster.
Parsons, Solomon,	Oct. 1800,	Leicester.
Pratt, Joseph,	Jan. 1799,	Foxboro'.
Parkhurst, N. R.	Jan. 1800,	Milford,
Patch, Wm. W.	Jan. 1795,	Worcester.
Parker, Robert,	July, 1799,	Salem.
Quirk, Michael,	Dec. 1757,	Ireland.
Rawson, Deering J.	Aug. 1798,	Uxbridge.
Redican, James,	Feb. 1800,	Ireland.
Rice, Sewell,	Nov. 1799,	Princeton.
Rice, Curtis,	June, 1795,	Boylston.
Rice, Jabez,	June, 1793,	Oakham.
Rich, Peter,	Nov. 1793,	Boston.
Reed, Benjamin,	May, 1781,	Milford.
Rice, Darius,	July, 1800,	Putney, Vt.
Raymond, James,	March, 1796,	Weathersfield, N. H.
Rice, Geo. T.	Feb. 1795,	Brookfield.
Stone, Elisha J.,	Nov. 1791,	Hopkinton.

Names	Date of birth		Place of birth
Stone, Uriah,	June,	1795,	Oxford North Gore
Stephens, Reuben,	Dec.	1779,	Sturbridge.
Swan, Samuel,	May,	1778,	Leicester.
Salisbury, Stephen,	——,	1798,	Worcester.
Simmons, John,	Nov	1800,	Dighton
Shepard, Paul,	Dec.	1777,	Sudbury.
Sprague, Lee,	Feb	1798,	East Douglas.
Siven, Jonathan,	Aug	1778,	West Woodstock, Ct
Sever, William,	——	1790,	Worcester.
Trumbull, Geo. A ,	Jan.	1791,	Petersham
Tarbox, Daniel,	April,	1772,	Biddeford, Me.
Thayer, Lewis,	Jan	1797,	Bellingham.
Taylor, Samuel,	Sept	1778,	Ashby
Tooker, Josiah,	——	1794,	Goshen, N. Y.
Valentine, Gill,	Sept	1788,	Hopkinton.
White, Luther,	Aug.	1795,	Worcester.
Weixler, J P ,	July,	1798,	Germany.
White, James,	Feb.	1798,	Pomfret, Vt
Williams, Lemuel,	June,	1783,	New Bedford.
Wesson, Rufus,	Feb	1786,	Brookfield.
Washburn, Charles,	Aug.	1798,	Kingston
Washburn, Ichabod,	Aug	1798,	Kingston
Willington, Nahum,	——	——,	——.
White, Benjamin,	May,	1788,	Worcester.
Wilkins, John,	June,	1798,	Ireland.
Willard, Calvin,	Dec.	1784,	Harvard
Wheeler, Elisha,	Nov.	1797,	Plainfield, Vt
Wood, A J	——	1788,	Watertown.
Willard, John,	——	——,	——
Wood, Jonathan,	May,	1792,	Lunenburg.
Wheeler, Wm. A.	March,	1798,	Hardwick

34

EDUCATION.

PUBLIC SCHOOLS.

The public schools in Worcester, have long enjoyed a very high reputation for excellence; and many of them are well deserving that reputation. They are fifty-five in number, taught by seventy-five teachers, and located in all parts of the city, to accommodate all the children within its boundaries. Those in the center and New Worcester are graded, and admission to their advantages is obtained by application to the Superintendent, at his office in the City Hall. The schools are under the general charge of a Committee of twenty-four, eight being elected for each year and serving three years, whose deliberations are presided over by the Mayor. Besides the supervision of the Committee, the schools have the benefit of the entire services of the Superintendent, Rev. J. D. E. Jones, which have proved most useful and efficient, as well as economical.

PRIVATE SCHOOLS.

Private schools of various grades, abound in the city. Among the more prominent of these are Mr. Metcalf's "Highland School," for boys, on Salisbury street; Mr. Lombard's "Salisbury Mansion School," Lincoln Square; Rev. Dr. Pattison's "Oread Institute," on a romantic eminence west from the City Hall; the Worcester Academy, located in the old Antiquarian Hall, Summer street, Rev. J. R. Stone, principal,—Professor Bushee's Young Ladies Institute, in Clark's Block, and Mr. Eaton's College of Commerce, Science and Literature, in Bank Block,—which are wholly or partially boarding schools of high grade, and receive many scholars from abroad. There are besides, several private schools for smaller scholars, which are well sustained.

Misses Robinson and Gardner's School of Design and French Institute, in Clark's Block, is a valuable addition to our educational advantages, and is meeting with encouraging success.

THE COLLEGE OF THE HOLY CROSS,

Situated on the beautiful eminence known as Mt. St. James, is designed exclusively for the education of young persons of the Catholic faith. Rev. James Clark, S. J., is President; and he is assisted by a full board of Professors.

THE FEMALE COLLEGE,

On Union Hill, was established and opened for students on the first of Sept., 1856, and now has about 100 students. It is intended to furnish for young women the advantage of a full classical and collegiate education; and the expenses are materially reduced by the performance of the domestic duties of the boarding department, by the pupils. Werden Reynolds, the President, is assisted by a full board of teachers. Rev. Joseph Smith, Steward. Rev. E. A. Cummings, Financial Secretary. Rev. J. M. Rockwood, Recording Secretary.

THE WORCESTER RHETORICAL SOCIETY,

Incorporated in Oct., 1853, meets every Tuesday evening in South Warren Hall, "for mental and moral improvement, by means of Essays, Debates, and various Rhetorical exercises." Clark Jillson, Corresponding Secretary; the other officers are chosen quarterly.

FRANKLIN LITERARY SOCIETY,

Organized in October, 1859. Object, mental and moral improvement, by Debates, and Rhetorical exercises —Officers chosen quarterly. Meets Friday evenings, at Franklin Hall, 263 Main street.

VARIOUS ASSOCIATIONS.

THE WORCESTER COUNTY HORTICULTURAL SOCIETY.

The preliminary steps toward the formation of this society — which was incorporated March 3d, 1842 — were taken early in the autumn of 1840. On the 19th of September of that year, several gentlemen desirous of associating themselves together for the purpose of advancing the science and encouraging and improving the practice of horticulture, made their first organization by the choice of the following officers:

President, Dr. John Green; *Vice Presidents*, Dr. Samuel Woodward, Stephen Salisbury; *Recording Secretaries*, Benjamin Heywood, L. L. Newton, J. C. B. Davis; *Corresponding Secretaries*, William Lincoln, Dr. Joseph Sargent; *Trustees*, Dr. John Park, Isaac Davis, E. F. Dixie, S. D. Spurr, Thomas Chamberlain, Nathaniel Stowell, A. D. Foster, Lewis Chapin, J. G. Kendall, Emory Washburn.

The Society's first Exhibition was held on the 13th, 14th and 15th of October, 1840, the 14th being "Cattle Show" Day. Since that time, with the exception of the year 1861 — which was remarkable for the general failure of the fruit crop in this vicinity — the Association has had its annual exhibitions simultaneously with those of the Worcester Agricultural Society.

From fees of membership and other sources the Association had already accumulated funds to a considerable amount, when, by the generous bequest of the late Hon. Daniel Waldo, an accession of three thousand dollars was made to its treasury. The little fund thus acquired and steadily augmented by its annual interest and the profits of the exhibitions, finally enabled the Society to erect that fine building on Front street, known as "Horticultural Hall." The cost of this edifice far exceeded the resources of the Association: The investment, however, proved a profitable one, and the indebtedness of the

Society is gradually diminishing from year to year, three thousand dollars of it having been discharged at one time through the munificent liberality of Hon. Stephen Salisbury, who was one of the founders, and who has ever been, — whether as President or other officer, — one of the most efficient members and patrons of the Association.

The Society has a valuable and well-selected Library, consisting of treatises upon subjects interesting to horticultural readers. Among the books are many which are chiefly useful for occasional reference, but which contain a great deal of information not readily to be found elsewhere.

The Society's Exhibitions have been eminently successful. Indeed, it is not too much to say that the splendid displays of fruits, flowers, and floral decorations in Horticultural Hall, have been second to none of the attractions which bring so many visitors to the city during the annual "gala week" of the county. Through the agency of these exhibitions an immense amount of information, particularly in regard to the cultivation of fruit, has been diffused throughout the central portions of the commonwealth. The flourishing condition to which the Society has now attained, — so gratifying for the present and so encouraging for the future, — place it among the institutions of which Worcester county has a right to be proud.

WORCESTER COUNTY MECHANICS ASSOCIATION.

This Association provides a course of Lectures each winter, and the use of a choice library of more than 1400 volumes, besides other valuable privileges, to its members. Richard Ball, President; Phineas Ball, Secretary; A. Marsh, Treasurer.

The Mechanics Hall, erected by this Association, is one of the most spacious and beautiful in New England, and will furnish seats for about 2400 persons. There are eight entrances to the hall, and six stair cases communicating with the floor below. Washburn Hall, in the same building, is a very accessible and convenient Hall for an audience of five or six hundred persons. Dea. Z. E. Berry, Janitor.

WORCESTER CHILDREN'S FRIEND SOCIETY.

This Society still continues its efforts to "rescue from evil and misery such children as are deprived of their natural parents," and provides for them at its Home on Shrewsbury street, until homes are found for them in suitable families.

FEMALE EMPLOYMENT SOCIETY.

This is another public Institution of much value. Its design is to furnish work, chiefly sewing, at fair prices, to the industrious poor, finding a market for the various articles manufactured.

WORCESTER MECHANICS MUTUAL LOAN FUND ASSOCIATION.

A Corporation for the aid of mechanics and other workers in securing homes, by the regular monthly investment of small sums. A. L. Burbank, Secretary.

WORCESTER AGRICULTURAL SOCIETY.

Wm S Lincoln, President; Charles M Miles, Treasurer, John W. Washburn, Corresponding and Recording Secretary

The Society has nearly twenty acres of land on Highland street, west of the Court House, for the accommodation of its Annual Exhibitions, (including a half-mile trotting course) on which is erected a spacious hall Its annual exhibition is now fixed by law on the first Tuesday of October.

REV. THEOBALD MATHEW TOTAL ABSTINENCE SOCIETY

John Fahy, President, Richard O'Flinn, Vice President, Edward Leahy, Treasurer, John Quinn, Secretary, Committee, Thomas Butt, Thomas Crowley, Wm Millea, Edward Cunningham, Michael Garvey.

ST JOHN'S CHRISTIAN DOCTRINE ASSOCIATION,

Devoted to the promotion of Sunday School instruction in St. John's Church, in Worcester Robert Laverty, President; Thomas L. Magennis, Recording Secretary.

WORCESTER CATHOLIC LIBRARY AND DEBATING ASSOCIATION

Object. Mutual Improvement. John McDonald, President; H. McConville, Secretary, S. Dodd, Librarian.

AMERICAN ANTIQUARIAN SOCIETY.

Library in Antiquarian Hall, Lincoln Square, Worcester President, Hon Stephen Salisbury, Vice Presidents, Rev Wm Jenks, D D, Hon. Levi Lincoln, LL. D ; Secretaries, Jared Sparks, LL D , Foreign; Hon Benj F. Thomas, LL. D , Domestic; Hon. A H Bullock, Recording, Treasurer, Hon Henry Chapin, Committee of Publication, Samuel F. Haven, Esq , Rev. E E Hale, Charles Deane, Esq. , Librarian, Samuel F. Haven, Esq.

WORCESTER MOZART SOCIETY

This is a Musical Association, composed of the principal professors of music and members of the several choirs of the city The society meets for the rehearsal of sacred music, &c , at Temperance Hall, every Monday evening during the winter, and occasionally favors the public with concerts A L. Benchley, President, A Firth, Vice President, E H. Frost, Conductor , J. A Dorman, Secretary and Treasurer; S Brown, Librarian

THE WORCESTER TEMPERANCE LEAGUE.

This is a new Association, whose object is to promote, by all proper means, total abstinence from the use of intoxicating liquors as a beverage. Any person may become a member by signing the pledge ; and all over sixteen years of age, who pay annually at least 50 cents, may vote at its meetings The officers elected in October last are as follows President, Hon William W. Rice, Vice Presidents, Rev Dr A Hill and S. Sweetser, Dr. Geo Chandler,

33*

Hon. Dexter F. Parker, P. L. Moen, Edward Earle; Secretary, Rev. Horace James; Treasurer, Albert Tolman; Directors, the Secretary and Treasurer, *ex officio*, and Rev. J. H. Twombly, Rev. H. L. Wayland, Charles Ballard, Abraham Firth, Wm. Mecorney, Geo. W. Russell, S. R. Heywood.

WORCESTER GYMNASTIC CLUB.

Consists of forty members. Established in 1858. The club has a gymnasium in Foster's Block, opposite the Railroad station. Transient subscribers also admitted. Regular classes at 5 and 8 P. M. daily. T. W. Higginson, President; Dr. O. F. Harris, Vice President; L. H. Bigelow, Secretary; C. W. Gilbert, Treasurer; Samuel H. Putnam, R. H. Southgate, and Edward A. Rice, Executive Committee.

SONS OF TEMPERANCE.

Worcester Division, No. 39, meet every Thursday evening at their rooms on Foster street.

Rainbow Division, 117, meet every Tuesday evening on Foster street.

New Worcester Division, No. 149, meet at Union Hall, New Worcester, every Friday evening.

The officers of these Divisions are elected quarterly.

FREE MASONS.

There are in Worcester, Morning Star and Montacute Lodges, Worcester Royal Arch Chapter, Hiram Council of Royal and Select Masters, and Worcester County Encampment of Knights Templar.

ODD FELLOWS.

The Quinsigamond Lodge of Odd Fellows meet every Monday evening at Masonic Hall, Waldo Block.

REGISTRY OF DEEDS.

When Artemas Ward, Esq., resigned the office of register in 1846, Alexander H. Wilder, who had been a clerk in the office for about twenty-three years, was chosen, and qualified in his stead, and has held the office till the present time.

When Mr. Wilder came into the office, there were four hundred and thirteen volumes of records, including the period (from 1731 to 1846) of one hundred and fifteen years.

There are now six hundred and fifty volumes, so that in fifteen years now last past, two hundred and thirty-seven volumes have been made; more than one third of the whole number now in the Registry of Deeds, showing a very great increase in the business of conveyancing in the county of Worcester.

The greatest number of deeds ever recorded in this office in any one year, was in 1855; in that year, there were 10,979 deeds and other instruments recorded.

DEDICATION OF THE BIGELOW MONUMENT

The services at the dedication of this beautiful structure is of so much importance in our local history, that the author has concluded to insert the contents of a pamphlet compiled by Rev Andrew Bigelow, D D , of Boston, a grandson of Colonel Timothy Bigelow.

—

PREFACE.

It is good to commemorate brave deeds in the cause of God, of country, or of humanity. It is a homage due to the heroic dead, and it re-acts for the benefit of the living It is peculiarly meet in times like these. Revolutionary memories should be precious Examples fitted to stir and re animate the flame of patriotism have special claims to prominent remembrance

The courage and self-sacrifices of the earlier champions of our freedom and independence bequeathed lessons to their sons What the former achieved, the latter are expected to guard and maintain The sculptured stone, which tells of the valor of the sires, is an empty honor, considered in reference to themselves They have passed beyond the reach of human applause. Posthumous ovations avail them not The value the significance is with their children. To them, indeed, monuments are silent monitors, richly eloquent in the teachings of a bygone age Too few of these have been reared to the memory of the intrepid fathers and founders of our civil liberties May they be multiplied! May the tablets inscribed with their venerable names, their heroic deeds, or the scenes of their struggles and achievements, be reverently read and pondered ! And may the lessons conveyed be fraught with quickening incentives, illustrated by the generous self-devotion, the constancy and courage, — under the sternest calls of public exigency, — both of the present and each future generations !

By a fortunate coincidence, altogether contingent, the completion of the monument in honor of the Revolutionary services of Colonel TIMOTHY BIGE-LOW occurred in the month of April, this present year, — an era destined to new and momentous interest in our national annals The ceremonies of dedication were generously undertaken by the municipal government and citizens of Worcester. It was decided that they should be celebrated on the ever-memorable NINETEENTH, — the opening date of the War of Independence Arrangements were made to such effect, and the preliminary notices sent abroad, before the outbreak of the mad and wicked rebellion which was so soon to burst upon the land. Sumter, though beseiged, had not been bombarded. It was hoped that the frenzy of the insurgents would pause, — that it would stop, — ere that last base outrage, content with the insult of a bare bravado. But the hope was delusive. The fort was assaulted, and its chivalrous little garrison compelled to succumb to the overwhelming odds combined against it.

Washington was next threatened. An alarum sped through the land. The mighty heart of our people, — the loyal heart of the indignant North, — at length profoundly roused, fiercely burned to avenge the affront, and curb and punish such insufferable wrong. Troops were hurried to the capitol, — Massachusetts, as always, foremost in the van. Her sons were everywhere arming. Worcester responded to the first drum-beat, — her gallant soldiery rallying promptly to the call, — their ranks daily swelling, and new companies formed, with a zeal and impetuosity almost embarrassing amidst the multifarious correspondent demands found needful at the hour. All were animated by a common impulse, — eager to battle for their country's imperilled rights, — impatiently awaiting the signal of departure for the defence of the national metropolis — all panting to join, nay, rather to lead, in the advancing movement.

These stirring scenes and incidents occurring during the eventful week of April 12-19,* naturally so engrossed the minds and hearts of all, that the expediency was questioned of attempting any public display on an occasion of such comparatively trifling moment as that detailed in the following record. On maturer reflection, nevertheless, it was deemed so accordant with the spirit of the crisis, so intrinsically suggestive, and of such kindling, awakening influences bearing upon the juncture, that it was resolved to adhere to the arrangement previously devised, and carry out the programme, so far as practicable in the altered condition of the times.

A public celebration in honor of the completion of the BIGELOW MONUMENT was accordingly held; and the dedication of a structure to the memory of a brave Revolutionary Chief, with its formal transfer to the future guardianship of the authorities of his native town, as a beacon memorial to the present and after times, was solemnly inaugurated with the imposing ceremonies described in the ensuing pages. The account is presented substantially as given in the "Worcester Daily Spy" of Saturday, April 20, from the pen of D. A. Goddard, Esq., assistant editor; some additions being made, with fuller sketches of several of the speeches than could conveniently appear in the columns of that journal.

One feature, it should be added, in the pageant of the day, although not

* News of the terrible onslaught in Baltimore, at the date last named, on the Massachusetts Sixth Regiment, in its struggle and triumphant passage through that city, did not reach Worcester till the afternoon of Friday, an hour or two later than the close of the ceremonies of the day. Of course, no allusion could be made to the event by the speakers on the stand.

wanting, had less of the brilliancy anticipated, owing to the inexorable necessities of the times. The military — of whom a fuller display had been promised, comprising the entire *élite* of Worcester — were in general too busily employed in the duties of drill and equipment, under an expectancy of an immediate march to the seat of war, to take part in the parade of procession. One company, enrolled in the valiant Sixth Regiment, had started two days before to aid in the defence of Washington, and, at the very hour of the exercises in consecration of the Monument at home, were bravely fighting their way through Baltimore. They were honorably represented, notwithstanding, by the senior members of their corps, the elder exempts of the Worcester Light Infantry alone numbering about one hundred. They made a fine appearance.

—

BIGELOW MONUMENT.

"Before noon, on the 19th of April, 1775, an express came to town, shouting as he passed through the street at full speed, 'To arms! to arms!—the war's begun!' His white horse, bloody with spurring, and dripping with sweat, fell exhausted by the church. Another was instantly procured, and the tidings went on. The bell rang out the alarm, cannon were fired, and messengers sent to every part of the town to collect the soldiery. As the news spread, the implements of husbandry were thrown by in the field, and the citizens left their homes, with no longer delay than to seize their arms. In a short time, the minute-men were paraded on the green, under Captain Timothy Bigelow. After fervent prayer by Rev. Mr. Maccarty, they took up their line of march to the scene of conflict."[*]

The remarkable event to which the above reminiscence relates, was appropriately commemorated in Worcester, yesterday, April 19th, by the dedication of an elegant and costly monument, erected to the memory of TIMOTHY BIGELOW, by his great-grandson, Colonel T. Bigelow Lawrence of Boston. It was the eighty-sixth anniversary of the battle of Lexington,—the opening scene of the revolution. Our streets were early thronged with spectators. Many buildings, private and public, were decorated with the national colors, and every thing indicated a unanimous sentiment of devotion to the Union, and respect for the memory of its founders.

The procession, preliminary to the exercises of the day, was formed at eleven o'clock, adjacent to the Central Park. Halting at the mansion of his honor Mayor Davis to receive the invited guests and other distinguished citizens there assembled, its progress was resumed. In the first carriage were seated Mayor Davis, Colonel Lawrence, Tyler Bigelow, Esq., of Watertown, (nephew and son-in-law of Col. Timothy Bigelow,) George Tyler Bigelow, Jr., son of the Chief Justice. They were followed by a carriage containing Ex-Governor Lincoln, Rev. Dr. Bigelow, and Hon. John P. Bigelow, Ex-Mayor

[*] Lincoln's History of Worcester.

of Boston. The past Mayors of Worcester, and guests of the city, occupied the remaining carriages. The procession was arranged as follows : —

National Band.
Past and exempt Members of the Worcester Light Infantry, bearing the Colors of the Company ; D. Waldo Lincoln, Captain.
Highland Cadets.
Committee of Arrangements.
City Government.
Invited Guests.
Joslyn's Band.
Assistant Marshal.
Chief-Engineer Fire department.
Yankee Engine-Company, No. 5.
Ocean Hose-company, No, 2.
Father Mathew Temperance Society.
German Turners.
Citizens.

Altogether, the show was brilliant. Advancing through the central street, — Worcester's fair Broadway, beautifully draped, its sidewalks and houses filled with gazers, — the cortege moved on its line of march. The route was in the following order: through Main, Highland, Harvard, Chestnut, Elm, West, Pleasant Streets, to the head of Main Street again, thence to the Old Common ; completing the march about noon.

At twelve o'clock, a salute of thirty-four guns was fired. The procession forming in a square around the stand, General George H. Ward, Chief-Marshal, announced Mayor Davis as President of the day. Among the notabilities on the platform, besides the gentlemen elsewhere named, were the Hon. Rejoice Newton, Stephen Salisbury, Esq., Hon. Dwight Foster, Hon. George F. Hoar, Major-General Hobbs, Colonel Stoddard, Charles Hersey, Esq., Walter Bigelow, Esq., Abbott Lawrence, Esq., with others. After a voluntary performed by Joslyn's Cornet Band, an appropriate and impressive prayer was offered by Rev. Dr. Hill. The following song, written for the occasion by C. Jillson, Esq., was next sung by the Glee Club, under the direction of Albert S. Allen, by whom the music was composed : —

We come to day, with solemn tread,
To consecrate an earthly shrine,
And raise this column o'er the head
Of hero, patriot, and divine,—
A hero in his country's cause ;
A patriot on the lists of fame ;
Divine, because an honest man
Can justly own no other name.

A thousand other men have died,
Who toiled for fame, and sought renown ;
But no one knows their resting-place,
On hill, in valley, or the town.
But here the humblest of them all
Beneath this beauteous column lies;
His dust has unto dust returned ;
His spirit, to the upper skies.

Here, ages hence, when Spring-time comes
With laughing footstep o'er the hills;
When Nature lifts her wintry hand
From all the valleys and the rills,—
Shall generations yet unborn
Beside this marble column stand,
And mingle with the dust their tears
For one who loved his native land.

Colonel LAWRENCE was then introduced, and spoke as follows:—

MAY IT PLEASE YOUR HONOR,—Actuated by the wish to perpetuate, in a suitable manner, the memory of one whose name has ever been reverently cherished by his descendants, I informed your Municipal Government a year and a half ago of my desire to erect a monument, upon your Central Park, over the remains of Colonel Timothy Bigelow. That desire was recognized in the kindest manner by the prompt passage of a resolve authorizing the Mayor to set apart the lot in question, and to dedicate it for ever to this purpose. For the cordial response thus given, permit me now to return my most sincere thanks. The work is completed; and at the request of your citizens, I am here to consign it, in a formal manner, to the custody and safe-keeping of yourself and your successors.

Little did I expect, however, to witness this imposing civic ceremonial, and the vast assemblage here collected. But I cannot be surprised, when I remember that the regiment commanded by Colonel Bigelow, so distinguished for its gallantry and prowess on many of the hardest-fought fields of the Revolution, was recruited solely from the yeomanry of the county of Worcester; and seeing as I do around me the descendants of the men who followed him to Cambridge, fought by his side under the walls of Quebec and on the plains of Saratoga and Monmouth, endured with him the trials and terrible sufferings of Valley Forge, and participated with him in the crowning glories of Yorktown.

I feel that the tribute paid to-day, and on this anniversary, is not to the memory of one man alone, but to the Revolutionary sires of Worcester,—an ancestry of which we may well be proud. May I venture to hope, that in the present dark and trying hour of our country's life, this monument may serve to sustain and stimulate our patriotism, by recalling to memory the public spirit, the courage and the sacrifices, so nobly displayed for the cause of liberty during the Revolution, by the soldiers of the gallant old Fifteenth Regiment of the Continental Line!

Mayor Davis responded as follows:—

Colonel Timothy Bigelow Lawrence: Sir,—You have caused to be erected on our Central Park a monument to the memory of one who was foremost among the citizens of this place in the great acts of the American Revolution.

This civic procession, this large concourse of people, are assembled here to commemorate your generosity to the memory of one of those heroes of the

American Revolution. This very moment — as you have well said, sir — and this very occasion should admonish us to rally in support of the principles, to express anew our admiration of the character, and our gratitude for the lessons of wisdom and patriotism, bequeathed to us by those who fought the battles of the revolution, and laid the foundation of our liberties. They are fixed stars in the firmament of great names ; shining, without twinkling, with a clear and beneficent light.

Sir, allow me, as the chief executive officer of this city, in behalf of all its citizens, to thank you sincerely for this splendid tribute to the memory of one of our bravest and most cherished citizens. With great pleasure, I accept, in behalf of the city, the custody of this chaste and magnificent monument, which will forever mark the spot where repose the remains of Colonel Timothy Bigelow. To him and his associates — who, at the expense of treasure, a contempt for peril, a prodigality of blood as pure as ever flowed from mortals, of which we can form no adequate conception — we owe a debt of gratitude for giving liberty and equality to this nation. You, sir, with a noble liberality, have placed over the grave of your ancestor a memorial which will commemorate his heroic virtues till the last succession of earth's inhabitants.

My poor thanks for this act of your munificence are weak and feeble when compared with the untold thousands who shall hereafter gaze upon this structure, and breathe forth their thankfulness to him who so nobly commemorated the deeds of the mighty dead.

Eighty-six years ago this day, news reached this place that the British were on their march to Concord to destroy the military stores in that place. Captain Timothy Bigelow instantly assembled his company near the spot where we are now standing, and marched with all possible despatch to meet the enemy. This was the beginning of the Revolution.

When Washington, the Father of his Country, arrived at Cambridge, and took the command of the American troops, he reviewed them by companies. Having reviewed the company of Capt. Bigelow, he remarked to him, " This is discipline indeed." In 1775-6, he was Major under Gen. Arnold in the expedition against Quebec, in which the hardships and sufferings of the army mock all description. He commanded the Fifteenth Continental Regiment at the capture of Burgoyne and other battles. He was a member of the Provincial Congress. He continued in the public service till the independence of the Colonies was established. He returned to his native place, poor in property, but rich in honor. His descendants have done much to sustain and perpetuate the liberties he fought to establish ; and now, after more than seven decades of years since his death, a great-grandson of the deceased, prompted by noble feelings of patriotism, with princely liberality, has erected over the remains of his heroic and patriotic ancestor a monument worthy of the good and great man. As the friends of liberty in all coming time shall look on it and read its inscriptions, it will call to their minds a generation of heroic, brave, and noble men, who pledged their lives, their fortunes, and their sacred honor, in the great cause of freedom, equality, and brotherhood. In behalf of all the friends of liberty, I again thank you for this act of your munificence."

The venerable Ex-Governor LINCOLN was next introduced, as one who had a distinct personal recollection of Colonel Bigelow. He said, —

Mr. Mayor, — In respectful submission to your authority, I answer to your call, that I may show by my presence here, rather than by any speech, the deep personal interest which I feel in this occasion, and my respect and reverence for the character of him, whose public services this costly and beautiful structure, before which we now stand, and these imposing observances in which we have engaged, are designed to commemorate. In the dedication of the monument by fervent prayer and thanksgiving; by the expressive and touching address of our noble friend, whose abounding munificence, prompted by a sense of filial duty, and a just pride of ancestry, has placed it upon these consecrated grounds, committing it forever, for preservation and care, to the gratitude of the city; and with your official response, so appropriate and so eloquent, in behalf of your fellow-citizens, and as their authorized representative, gracefully acknowledging the benefaction and accepting the trust, — the purpose for which we assembled, seems to me, to have been most fully and happily accomplished. I know not what more the proprieties of the occasion could demand. For myself, I have nothing, of word or of thought, which can add to the satisfactions of the hour; nor, if I would, have I the strength, or the voice, to reach the listening ear of this thronging multitude. And yet, sir, as you have kindly said, it may be expected of me — one of the few, the very few, of the living, who have ever looked upon the person of Colonel Bigelow — that I should give such reminiscences of him as I have, imperfect and unimportant though they be. A little longer, and there will be none to utter these personal remembrances.

My impressions of Colonel Bigelow are such only, as are made upon the mind of a child, in the presence of mature and perfect manhood. From family connection, there was frequent intercourse and association between him and those of my own kindred; and I well recollect, as though it were of yesterday, his general appearance, — his tall, erect, and commanding figure, his martial air, his grave and rather severe countenance, his dignified and earnest address. I cannot doubt the respect and deference with which he was universally regarded; for it was among the most positive injunctions of the antiquated district schoolmistress to the boys of my day, enforced even by the fear of the rod, that we should always "pull off our hats to Parson Bancroft and Colonel Bigelow." At the time of his death, and for many years after, I often heard him spoken of as the gallant old soldier, and the thoroughly accomplished officer; and now, after the lapse of seventy-one years from his burial, in the same vernal season of the fragrance of the budding flower, and the gushing melody of birds, I stand, an aged man, again at his grave, to remember and to honor him.

I know of no record of the life of Colonel Bigelow which even approaches

35

the character of a biography. In Lincoln's "History of Worcester" is contained, probably, the best notice of him which can be found; but this, from the more general object of the work, and the time when it was prepared, is necessarily stinted and meagre. It is there related that, "with a taste for military life, he was deeply skilled in the science of war; " that "the troops under his command and instruction, exhibited the highest condition of discipline;" and of his regiment, that "a braver band never took the field, or mustered to battle. High character for intrepidity and discipline, early acquired, was maintained unsullied to the close of their service;" and, "when Colonel Bigelow left military life, it was with the reputation of a meritorious officer."

The accomplished and eminent historian Bancroft, in enumerating the forces sent against Quebec in the autumn of 1775, names among the officers of rank "Timothy Bigelow, the early patriot of Worcester."

These testimonials to the merits and services of Colonel Bigelow have the singular and affecting coincidence of having been rendered by the sons of two of his most distinguished fellow-townsmen, associates, and friends, — the elder Lincoln, and the elder Bancroft. How simple and appropriate these tributes to his worth! how beautiful this brief summary of his character! how suggestive of the virtues alike of the civilian and the soldier! Timothy Bigelow, the early patriot of Worcester, — a braver man never took the field, or mustered to battle. High character for intrepidity and discipline early acquired, and maintained unsullied through seven years' military service, — what more pertinent inscription for his tombstone? — tributes of cotemporaneous renown, transferred from the "fleshly tables of the heart" to the ever-enduring marble of the monument.

Colonel Bigelow was a type of a generation, now passed away. Of such, in patriotism and valor, were the corps of *Minute Men* under his command, and the *Train Band* of the brave Capt. Benjamin Flagg, who alike, on the 19th of April, 1775, of which this day is the anniversary, at the horseman's cry, "To arms!" hastened, with no delay but for prayer and a benediction, to join their brethren of Lexington and Concord in resistance to tyranny and the oppressor's sword. Such was the townsman and friend of Bigelow, the intrepid and beloved Capt. Jonas Hubbard, his inferior only in rank, his companion and comrade in the dreadful winter's march through the wilderness to the siege of Quebec; who, in the midst of hardships and privations almost unequalled in the experience of human suffering, uttered the noble declaration, "I do not value life or property, if I may secure liberty for my children; " and who, when mortally wounded, at the foot of the ramparts, in the storming of the fortress, said to his men who sought to remove him from the field, "I came to fight with you: I will stay here to die with you." Such too, *at this time*, are the gallant young men of our own city and state, who, with alacrity, on the first summons, have buckled on the armor, in defence of all which is dear to freemen. Oh, that now, — now, in this most portentious and perilous crisis of our country's destiny — there were men like these, *in all parts of this land*, to uphold this nation; to defend and protect the Government and its institutions; to preserve, and transmit to posterity, those great political, civil, and social privileges and blessings which the present generation received and have enjoyed, as an inheritance, through the wisdom, and patriotism, and valor, of the founders of the Republic! They were, indeed, men of stern integrity and public virtue, of elevated aim and lofty principle, unselfish and self-sacrificing; with whom, a sense of honor was not lost in personal ambition, nor fidelity to duty sunk in subservience to party; men devoted to the people's service, and the country's welfare.

May this monument, erected to the honor of one of Liberty's noblest sons, instruct us in the priceless value of the glorious achievements of our ancestors! May it be made admonitory to our own high duties and momentous responsibilities! — so that the disruption of our national Union, if dissevered it must be, shall never become a reproach to our supineness or indifference, nor the destruction of our liberties brought about, by our debasement, or our follies."

At the close of Governor Lincoln's address, the chairman called for a speech from the Rev. ANDREW BIGELOW, D. D., of Boston, grandson of the old Colonel. Dr. Bigelow rose, and said, —

"Mr. Mayor and Gentlemen, — In compliance with your call, I cannot withhold a word, chiefly to express the emotions of gratitude shared by me in common with other descendants of an ancestor whose monument is this day publicly dedicated, in view of the honors paid to his memory by yourselves in your official capacity, and the citizens at large of this great outpouring community. I am touched, profoundly touched, by such tokens of respect to the name and character of one, who, distinguished as he was in his day, has been separated from the present living age by the space of two entire generations.

Threescore years and ten — nay, eleven — have passed away since his ashes were laid to rest where they have quietly reposed in their late humble but not forgotten sepulchre; during which period, new races have sprung into active and stirring life, and Worcester, the beautiful village of his time, has grown up to its present expansion, — a teeming hive of wealth and industry, — a fair and flourishing, a rich and populous city.[*] But the demonstration of this day, this hour, attest that his memory still lives, — green in the hearts of a people who have come after, and that it is still cherished with filial and affectionate veneration.

Yet, in honoring him, the heroic dead, Worcester, though unconsciously, honors herself. He, Colonel Bigelow, was her own child. Here he was born and bred; here he lived and moved and wrought, — never absent from his native precincts, save at his country's call to other fields and less lovely scenes; and here, at length, he died, — bowed not so much by the weight of years, as the waste and wear, the toils, hardships, and sufferings, endured in the same sacred cause. He was a type, a noble type indeed, of the gallant

[*] Matre pulchra, Filia pulchrior.

spirits here in Worcester who rose cotemporaneously with himself. Sparta, we forget not, had other sons than he; but none, — I dare hope for your ready assent in claiming, — none more worthy than himself. His enthusiasm — springing from the impulses of a warm, generous nature, dauntless as it was wise, thoughful and prescient — quickened, no doubt, to a brighter glow the flame of patriotism in many sympathetic breasts; and, whilst firing the brave, it roused the torpid, nerved the weak, and emboldened the timid. The force of his character — from all which I have heard and have been able to learn of its weight and influence, confirmed by the testimonies so emphatically and eloquently borne by my honored friend, the Nestor who has last addressed you — was such as could not fail to impress itself upon all within the reach of its spell. It reminds me of a saying left on record from an earlier age, of Thomas Randolph to Cecil, Lord Burleigh, during the stormy crisis of the Scottish Reformation, alluding to the fiery energy of the brave, indomitable old John Knox: "Where your honor exhorteth us to stoutness of heart, I assure you the voice of one man is able, in an hour, to put more life in our souls than six hundred trumpets continually blustering in our ears."

This much may be accorded to the worth of a progenitor whose marble on yonder mound denotes the last resting-place of his earthly remains; but the marble itself (as has been so justly and so modestly intimated by my young kinsman, in his opening address), — the marble itself, the Monument this day consecrated, stands, and will remain to future generations, a memorial, not alone of his personal services and prowess, but of the public spirit, the unflinching bravery, the self-sacrificing patriotism, of those sires in common, his fellow-townsmen, — the men, co-eval with himself, who joined heart and hand in the days which emphatically "tried men's souls."

But, sir, the times we are thrown upon — sad to say — may prove quite as momentous in experience, and as memorable in coming history, as the era, long past, which we here commemorate. What was achieved by the stormy and victorious struggles of the Revolution now remains to be preserved and defended. We have an enemy almost at our gates, an enemy crowding to our very borders, — a crafty and unscrupulous, a treacherous and insolent foe, — led on by a band of rebels and conspirators; men false to their duty, their country, and to God, yet true to their traditions, the hereditary counterparts (worthy legatees) of the old toryism of 1775–6; men whose fields and broad acres, whose fair plantations, were scoured and rid of a foreign oppressor by the bayonets of Northern men and Northern regiments. Yes, alas! we have such an adversary at this hour to cope with, threatening not only our national liberty, but our national existence. Our country, mother of us all; our country, dear, weeping form, — daughter of struggle, born amidst conflicts, rocked by the storms and tempests of Revolutionary battle, — OUR COUNTRY turns, with anxious eye, to her offspring for help and succor in this dark hour of her unlooked-for extremity. And shall she turn and look to them in vain? No, not here: no, not to Worcester. By the memories of the past, by the bones of her fathers, by the precious relics of the Chief whose valor is this day recalled, again do I say, No! Let all other hearts faint and falter, those of Worcester will never droop nor quail. Her sons will be faithful and true. Already she has sent forth an advance, now moving to the fight; and others, all emulous, are eagerly mustering. A thousand swords are leaping from their scabbards. A thousand muskets are ready to be shouldered by her chivalrous youth, and borne to the embattled field, for their country's honor and avengement;—never to be laid down till the land itself shall be purged from the foul viperous brood too long and too indulgently hugged to its bosom; never to be laid down till the black war-cloud now lowering upon our land shall be triumphantly dispersed; never to be laid down till not only Worcester, but Boston and Washington alike, with all the other aggrieved and insulted cities of our land, shall be shielded from the hazard of future menace and aggression. And then, and not till then, will Worcester's gallant sons again sit down beneath the laurels of a final and crowning victory."

The Hon. JOHN P. BIGELOW, Ex-Mayor of Boston, another grandson of Colonel Timothy Bigelow, was next called up. He declined making a speech; but, after some amusing and piquant remarks (roundly applauded,) he presented to Mayor Davis, in behalf of the city, a package of a dozen ball-cartridges made for the regiment from Worcester and vicinity in the Revolutionary War, being a sample of those used at Still Water and Saratoga. He said he had tried some of the powder that very morning; and it flashed brightly, after being kept eighty-four years. He knew of no more appropriate place of deposit for this Revolutionary relic than Worcester, so renowned for its patriotic and firm devotion to the principles of liberty and union.

Hon. BENJAMIN F. THOMAS was introduced as a grandson of the political associate, cotemporary, and friend of Colonel Timothy Bigelow, Isaiah Thomas, senior. He spoke in substance as follows:—

I thank you, Mr. Mayor, and fellow-citizens, for this kindly greeting and welcome. I rejoice to look again on these familiar faces, and to hear once more the voices that stirred the blood of my early manhood.

Mr. Mayor, it is good for us to be here. The place and the day are full of blessed memories. The noblest lessons of wisdom, of self-denial, and of self-sacrifice, come to us from the grave of this "village blacksmith," sagacious statesman, prudent and gallant commander, devoted patriot,—chevalier of nature, whose chivalry was illustrated in breaking, and not in forging, the chains of human bondage. Well may this beautiful monument crown his resting-place. Well may the gratitude, the munificence, and the eloquence of his descendant, and the sympathies of this thronging multitude, unite to do him honor. Three generations come up to bless him.

"How sleep the brave, who sink to rest
With all their country's wishes blest!"

Fellow-citizens, it is good for us to be here; and here, by the graves of our fathers,—with their spirits hovering around us, a cloud of witnesses,—to give
35*

ourselves anew to the cause and to the country for which they nobly lived or
nobly died. The day of trial has come again: it may be of darker, sterner,
severer trial than that of our fathers. We are to save for our children what
our fathers bought for us, and at the same price of toil, of treasure, and of
blood. The cry to-day, in the streets of this beautiful city, is that which,
eighty-six years ago, startled the quiet village,—"To arms!" So be it. To
arms! The leaders of this rebellion have appealed to the last arbitrament of
States. It is well for us. The first gun that boomed against Sumter, startled
a great people from the grave of its lethargy as with the trump of the arch-
angel. It was the beginning of the end. The bells that pealed in Charleston
over the lowering of the Stars and Stripes, rang out the death-knell of the
" Southern Confederacy."

It will cost us a long, severe, and bitter struggle; but this rebellion must
be utterly crushed out. There is for us no hope of freedom, of peace, of safety
even, till this work is fully done. Seven years of war were spent in the purchase of our freedom; seven more of toil in giving it organic and national life.
If seven years of toil and blood are spent in securing it,—in our national redemption,—they will be wisely, divinely spent, with the blessing of God and
all coming generations of men. Let us to-day, in God's name and in the name
of humanity, devote ourselves to the work.

Judge Thomas having concluded, TYLER BIGELOW, Esq., of Watertown,
nephew of the Revolutionary colonel, was last presented. His appearance
produced a sensation. With the weight of eighty-three years upon his shoulders,
he stood firm and erect as in manhood's early prime. His remarks, delivered
with great energy, were few and pithy. He said that,—

So late was the hour, so fully had the exigencies of the occasion been met
by the able and eloquent remarks and addresses of the gentlemen who had
preceded him, he would not further exhaust the patience of his fellow-citizens,
but forego any extended remarks he had contemplated. He wished simply to
relate an interesting reminiscence, or anecdote, of his late uncle, which he had
received many years since from a member of his family, that would illustrate
his character, and exhibit the spirit and ardor with which he entered upon
and persevered in the great drama of the Revolution.

When the news of the destruction of the tea in Boston Harbor reached
Colonel Bigelow, he was at work in his blacksmith's shop, near the spot now
called Lincoln Square. He immediately laid aside his tools, proceeded directly to his house, opened the closet, and took from it a canister of tea, went to the
fireplace, and poured the contents thereof into the flames. As if feeling that
every thing which had come in contact with British legislative tyranny should
be purified by fire, the canister followed the tea; and then he covered both
with coals. So well known and determined were his opinions on the great
questions of the day, he returned to his labors without deigning a word of explanation or apology to any one.—Such, also, was his zeal and ardor in the

great cause of the times, that he appeared, on the morning following the battle of Lexington, at the head of his company of *minute-men*, on the public square in Watertown, April 20th; having marched them there, upwards of thirty miles, during the evening and night subsequent to that event.

Music by the band succeeded the address of the last-named speaker,—the Marseillaise being performed with admirable skill and effect. A benediction by the Rev. Dr. HILL, concluded the public exercises of the day.

The gentlemen specially invited to the dedication of the monument were recipients in the morning of the hospitalities of His Honor Mayor Davis; and, after the close of the ceremonies, were entertained at an elegant banquet given by Governor Lincoln.

APPENDIX.

The Monument itself, of which the dedicatory ceremonial is recorded in the foregoing pages, claims a notice.

It occupies a conspicuous position at the northerly front of the ancient cemetery,—an inconsiderable but beautiful elevation, planted with trees, overlooking and now forming a part of the Central Park, better known as the Old Common, of Worcester. The spot of the original grave of Colonel Bigelow is included within the area allotted to the structure, some two or three yards to the right of the centre. It was necessarily disturbed by the alterations requisite in preparing and shaping the ground-plot for the edifice. The remains were carefully exhumed, incased in a metallic casket, and removed to their new receptacle beneath the base of the monument.

They were found remarkably well preserved, considering the long period of their interment; the hair, which was abundant, being in singular freshness. They indicated a tall and robust frame, above the average stature, correspondent with the traditionary reports of the person of Colonel Bigelow, as having exceeded six feet in height.*

The site of the monument is a space of twenty feet to a side, enclosed with a light iron fence, on a granite plinth with trefoiled piers. From this, a slope of grass is formed to a solid block of granite, nine feet square, upon which the monument is erected.

The design is in the style of the English Gothic of the thirteenth century,

* It has been described as six feet and two inches.

and the material is white Italian marble. The pedestal is ornamented at
its angles with carvings of ram's-heads, and bears on its sides the following
inscriptions :—

On the front, in raised capital letters, —
TIMOTHY BIGELOW.

On the right face, in sunken letters, —

Born
Aug. 12, 1739.
Died
March 31, 1790.

On the rear, —

In memory of
The Colone' of the 15th Massachusetts Regiment
Of the Continental Army
In the War of Independence,
This monument
Is erected by his great-grandson,
Timothy Bigelow Lawrence,
Anno Domini 1861.

On the left face are the words, —

QUEBEC.	MONMOUTH.
SARATOGA.	VERPLANCK's POINT.
VALLEY FORGE.	YORKTOWN.

Above the pedestal, the monument diminishes in size ; but from each of its
four sides trefoiled canopies project, supported on columns whose capitals are
elaborately carved with various designs, their bases resting on the shelving top
of the pedestal. Above the canopies, the shaft again diminishes in size. It
assumes an octagonal figure, and is surmounted with a foliated cross ; the
total height being thirty feet.

The monument was designed and superintended by George Snell, Esq.,
architect, of Boston. The granite work was executed by the Granite Railway
Company ; and the marble, imported from Tuscany, was chiseled by Messrs.
Wentworth and Co., Boston.

Such a structure, though a memorial of the past, is usually a custodian for
the future. On the Friday previous to the celebration (April 12,) the customary formality took place of depositing sundry articles and documents, of more
or less value, in the Bigelow Monument. It was performed in the presence
of Mayor Davis and other city officials, of Ex-Governor Lincoln and distinguished citizens, besides several members of the Bigelow Family, specially
represented in the lineal descent by Messrs. Andrew and John P. Bigelow,
and Colonel Lawrence. The articles consigned were enclosed in a pair of
strong, double boxes of tin and copper, firmly soldered, and placed beneath
the marble base of the monument. The latter (the base) is composed of four

1776
Timᵒ Bigelow

massive pieces, so constructed as to leave a central space between the block of granite on which the structure stands and the die of the pedestal surmounting it above. Within the cavity, the boxes were stored. Appended is a list of their contents : —

A parchment containing the following record : " This monument to the memory of Colonel Timothy Bigelow, a hero of the American Revolution, was erected by his great-grandson, Colonel Timothy Bigelow Lawrence, of Boston, A. D. 1861. Isaac Davis, Mayor of the city of Worcester ; John A. Andrew, Governor of Massachusetts ; Abraham Lincoln, President of the United States. — George Snell, architect, Boston."

History of Worcester. By William Lincoln. Published by Moses D. Phillips & Co., 1837.

Reminiscences of the Military Life and Sufferings of Colonel Timothy Bigelow. By Charles Hersey.

A plan of the old cemetery upon which the Bigelow Monument is erected. By Gill Valentine.

History of the First Church (Old South) in the city of Worcester, this eleventh day of April, A. D. 1861 ; with its pastors and officers from its organization in 1716, and a catalogue of its members at the present time. By Caleb Dana.

Massachusetts Weekly Spy, vol. 90, No. 15, April 10, 1861.

Three Daily Spys, vol. 16, Nos. 85, 86, 87, April 10, 11, 12. By J. D. Baldwin & Co., proprietors.

Ægis and Transcript, vol. 24, No. 14.

Daily Transcript, vol. 11, Nos. 81, 82, 83, April 9, 10, 11. By W. R. Hooper.

Worcester Palladium, vol. 28, No. 15, April 10, 1861 ; and vol. 25, No. 51, containing interesting matter. By J. S. C. Knowlton.

Worcester County Democrat, vol. 1, No. 37, March 30, 1861.

Worcester Daily Times, vol. 2, No. 60, April 3, 1861. By Moses Bates.

Franklin Advertiser, vol. 1, No. 1, 1861, with specimens of beautiful cards.

Worcester Directory for 1861. By Henry J. Howland.

The Heart of the Commonwealth. By Henry J. Howland.

Daily Spy, Aug. 31, 1860 ; Home Statistics. By Samuel Smith.

Massachusetts Spy, Sept. 26, 1860, containing the valuation and taxation of Worcester ; census statistics of Worcester by wards ; number of inhabitants, dwellings, and families ; by Samuel Smith.

A piece of the Charter Oak.

Daily Spy, of Feb. 12, 1861 ; Birth Statistics, containing the total number of births, number in each month, number of males and females, number of American and of foreign origin, with full particulars. By W. A. Brigham.

A package of ancient and modern relics ; viz., the New England States cents, United States cents and half cents, Washington medals, Washington button, Massachusetts volunteer militia and infantry buttons. By W. A. Brigham.

Medal of President Lincoln, and one of Hon. John Davis.

City Document, No. 14 : Inaugural Address of Hon. W. W. Rice, Mayor of the city of Worcester, Jan. 2, 1860 ; with the annual reports of the several city officers for the municipal year ending Jan. 2, 1860.

Inaugural Address of Hon. Isaac Davis, Mayor of the city of Worcester, to the City Council, Jan. 1, 1861.

Report of the School Committee of the city of Worcester for the year 1860. By Rev. J. D. E. Jones, superintendent of schools.

A beautiful steel engraving of the Worcester Hospital ; likewise a large document containing the records of the founders, and names of all the officers, of the institution, from the commencement to the present time. By Merrick Bemis, M. D.

Journal of the Prince of Wales' tour in America in 1860, by G. D. Engleheart, Esq., secretary of the Duke of Newcastle.

Printed pedigree of the Bigelow Family.

Appleton's Railway and Steam-navigation Guide, published in New York and London;
American Weekly Traveller, Boston, April 13, 1861; Boston Semiweekly Advertiser,
April 13, 1861; Boston Herald, April 12, 1861; Boston Courier, April 12, 1861; Daily
Atlas and Bee, April 12, 1861; Boston Journal, April 12, 1861; Boston Daily Adver-
tiser, April 12, 1861; New York Times, April 11, 1861; New York Herald, April 11,
1861; New York Independent, April 11, 1861; Home (weekly) Journal, New York,
April 13, 1861; Vanity Fair, do., New York, April 13, 1861; Harper's Monthly, New
York, April 13, 1861.

Coins of United States, one dollar, half a dollar, quarter of a dollar, ten cent piece, five
cent piece, two three cent pieces, three one cent pieces, 1860, one cent of 1861.

Ball cartridges made by the soldiers of Colonel Bigelow's command, at his barn in Worcester, 1777.

Lock of the hair of Colonel Timothy Bigelow.

Also the following original manuscript letters of Colonel Bigelow:

Oct. 25, 1775.
On that part of the Kennybeck called the Dead River,
97 miles above Norridgewalk.

DEAR WIFE, — I am at this time well, but in a dangerous situation, as is the whole detachment of the Continental Army with me. We are in a wilderness, nearly one hundred
miles from any inhabitants, either French or English; and but about five days' provisions,
on an average, for the whole. We are this day sending back the most feeble, and some
that are sick. If the French are our enemies it will go hard with us; for we have no
retreat left. In that case, there will be no other alternative between the sword and
famine. May God, in his infinite mercy, protect you my more than ever dear wife and my
dear children!

Adieu! — and ever believe me to be your most affectionate husband,

TIMO. BIGELOW.

CHAUDIER POND, Oct. 28, 1775.

DEAR ANNA, — I very much regret my writing the last letter to you, the contents were
so gloomy. It is true, our provisions are short (only five pints of flour to a man, and no
meat); but we have this minute received news that the inhabitants of Canada are all
friendly, and very much rejoiced at our coming, and a very small number of troops in
Quebec. We have had a very fatiguing march of it; but I hope it will soon be over. The
express is waiting; therefore must conclude.

I am, dear wife, with unlimited affection, your faithful husband, TIMO. BIGELOW.[2]

° Beautiful as is the monument to the memory of Colonel Bigelow, a loftier and more durable one stands in the State of Maine. It is a mountain bearing his name, near the head
of the Kennebec, a few miles distant from the place of encampment recorded under date
of the former of the two letters printed above. He was the first white man who ascended
it. It was for purposes of exploration, when in command of a detachment of Arnold's
army en route to Quebec, as intimated in the same letters. There was, of course, no chart
of the wilderness. The pathless forest lay beyond. It was important to ascertain the
character of the region, and the trending of the great natural landmarks, in advance.
Colonel Bigelow (then a Major) undertook, sua sponte, whilst his troops were halting at the
foot of a steep mountain, its laborious ascent. It is a towering and rugged eminence,
or rather apex of an alpine range, difficult to climb at the present day. Few attempt it.

The achievement of Colonel Bigelow was thought so remarkable, that the peak was called
and afterwards familiarly known as Bigelow's mountain. The name of mount Bigelow
was thence introduced into our maps, and, extended since to the entire ridge, is stamped
in memoriam.

The documents subjoined pertaining to the earlier history of the Monument have an importance entitling them to a place in this connection : —

[SEAL.]   CITY OF WORCESTER, ⎫
        In City Council, Dec. 23, 1859. ⎰

Resolved, That leave be granted to Timothy Bigelow Lawrence to erect a Monument over the remains of Colonel Timothy Bigelow ; and that the Mayor be empowered to designate a suitable lot for that purpose, where the said remains now lie, — the same not to include the remains of persons of any other family ; and that said lot be forever appropriated and devoted to said purpose.

  A copy of record. — Attest :   SAMUEL SMITH, *City Clerk.*

CITY OF WORCESTER.

Whereas, by a resolve of the City Council, passed Dec. 23, A. D., 1859, leave was granted to Timothy Bigelow Lawrence to erect a Monument over the remains of Colonel Timothy Bigelow ; and, by said resolve, the Mayor was empowered to designate a suitable lot for that purpose, where said remains now lie, — the same not to include the remains of persons of any other family ; and it was further resolved, that said lot be forever appropriated and devoted to said purpose —

Now, in pursuance of the authority in me so vested, I, Alexander H. Bullock, Mayor of the city of Worcester, have designated, and do hereby designate, for the purpose aforesaid, the following-described lot, being twenty feet square, and being section number four of the second division, as laid down on the plan of the cemetery on the Common, dated October, 1853, made by Gill Valentine. Said section has a stone monument at its south-east corner, and contains grave number seven, being the grave of Timothy Bigelow, but does not include the remains of any other person.

And I hereby for ever dedicate and appropriate said lot to the purpose aforesaid.

In witness whereof, I have hereunto set my hand, and affixed the seal of the city of Worcester, this thirtieth day of December, in the year of our Lord one thousand eight hundred and fifty-nine.

         A. H. BULLOCK, *Mayor.* [SEAL.]

—

The following officials constituted a Committee, on the part of the City Government of Worcester, to take action on the measures deemed suitable for a public notice, by inaugural exercises, at the erection of the Bigelow Monument ; viz. : —

His Honor Mayor Davis ; Messrs. George Hobbs and Charles B. Pratt, *Aldermen ;* Messrs. Walter Bigelow, Frank H. Kelley, and M. S. McConville, *Councilmen.*

Annexed are the names of twenty-five gentlemen, chosen by the citizens at large to co-operate with the Committee of the Municipal Government in making arrangements for a due observance of the occasion aforesaid, viz. : —

Hon. Levi Lincoln, *Chairman :* Messrs. Stephen Salisbury, A. H. Bullock, Rejoice Newton, J. S. C. Knowlton, George F. Hoar, Henry Chapin, George W. Richardson, W. W. Rice, Gen. George H. Ward, Dr. George Chandler, Fitzroy Willard, T. L. Nelson, H. N. Tower, Charles Hersey, Rev. Dr. Hill, Rev. Horace James, Albert Tolman, Joseph Mason, F. H. Kinnicutt, William A. Wheeler, John M. Goodhue, Edwin Bynner, Carter Whitcomb, George W. Bentley.

It was at first proposed by the Committee of Arrangements that an oration should be delivered on the day of celebration, and that a suitable gentleman be invited to perform the office. The Hon. George Bancroft, of New York, was selected, and addressed on the subject. The following is the correspondence which passed : —

WORCESTER, MASS., March 22, 1861.

Hon. GEORGE BANCROFT.

My dear Sir, — You are probably informed, that, with the consent of the authorities of this city, T. Bigelow Lawrence, Esq., a great-grandson of Colonel Timothy Bigelow of Revolutionary fame, is about to erect a monument to the memory of his ancestor on the site of his grave, in the old burial ground near the Common. This act of filial duty and reverence is proposed to be celebrated by impressive and appropriate ceremonies, in which the government and citizens of the place will unite with Colonel Lawrence, on the 19th of April next, — the anniversary of the battle of Lexington. The monument, when in position, will be a costly and beautiful structure, worthy its commemorative purpose, and greatly ornamental to the city. At a meeting of a large Committee of Arrangements for the occasion, it was the spontaneous and unanimous expression of desire, that you should be solicited to add that interest to the day, by an address, to which no one else could so effectually contribute. It seems to them to be a service most eminently becoming your friends and fellow-citizens of your native town earnestly to ask from you. Born in their midst; cherished, loved and honored by them, not only in your own person, but in the memory of your father, — long their instructor and guide, — they would see in your compliance with their wishes, renewed cause of obligation and grateful regard. Besides, as the eminent historian of the country, will you not give the seal of your recognition to the services of one of its most heroic defenders?

The Committee will be greatly obliged by an answer at your earliest convenience.

With faithful esteem and respect, your obedient servant,

LEVI LINCOLN,

In behalf of, and by the unanimous request of, the Committee.

36

NEW YORK, March 25, 1861.

My dear Sir, — I am to-day made very happy by your assurance, that the great affection I bear my native town is met by an honorable place in their regard; but neither my health nor my engagements will permit me to be with you on the 19th of April, though I heartily join in every tribute to the sons of liberty in Worcester, who were by none exceeded in their devotion to the cause of liberty and their country.

Very truly, and with affectionate respect, your obliged,

GEORGE BANCROFT.

Governor LINCOLN.

In consequence of the disappointment to secure the presence and eloquent voice of Mr. Bancroft on the occasion proposed, and the brief interval remaining before the time fixed for the dedication of the Monument, other arrangements were made by the Committee, and the plan of celebration adopted which was carried out in the manner and form detailed in previous pages.

—

Allusion is made in an antecedent page, at the introduction of the name of Judge Thomas, one of the speakers of the day, to the friendship which subsisted between his ancestor, the elder Isaiah Thomas, and the subject of these notices. It was, indeed, a close and tried one. They were "true yoke-fellows;" each alike active in defence of a common cause, — the rights of the people, and the liberties of the old Colonies. They employed different weapons, — one wielding the sword: the other a pen, of scarce less potency in the popular movement.

Colonel Bigelow was the senior of Mr. Thomas by nearly ten years. An ardent Whig, foremost of the *élite* of Worcester in opposition to the tyranny of the British Crown, and of course to the little clique of Tories, not wanting in the town, — few in number, but swelling in self-conceit, looking down on the people as a plebeian class, — Colonel Bigelow cast about for auxiliaries to aid in the work of unflinching resistance. A press was needed. Mr. Thomas, then editor and proprietor of the "Massachusetts Spy," printed in Boston, was invited to Worcester. He had been placed on the honorable list of the "suspects;" and, in the early spring of 1775, was proscribed. He was compelled to flee; the last number of his paper, in Boston, being issued April 6, 1775. Mr. Thomas gladly availed himself of the proffered shelter and stand presented by the eligible opening at Worcester. The removal of his press and types was an affair of some difficulty, requiring caution in the management. Colonel Bigelow undertook the task. With the aid of a couple of assistants, choosing a dark night, the press with its *materiel* was secured by him, and, conveyed to a landing near Barton's Point, was ferried to Charlestown. Thence transported to Worcester, it was set up and worked, at the beginning, in a basement room of the Colonel's house. The first appearance of the "Spy" next after, and therewith the first printing executed in

Worcester, was on the 3d of May next following. The paper proved, as before, an instrument of mighty energy, acting as a powerful lever on the sentiment and spirit of the times. Subscriptions flowed in. A suitable office was shortly obtained, and the sheet, under its new title of the "Massachusetts Spy, or American Oracle," was spread abroad everywhere. Its tone lost none of its boldness. The loyalists gained nothing from their prior attempts to muzzle and silence it. It spoke like a trumpet. The weekly articles by its conductor were impatiently awaited by the public, and read with avidity. The name of Isaiah Thomas, as the exponent of his paper, soon became, throughout New England, familiar as a "household word;" and the Worcester Massachusetts Spy remains to this day, as at the outset of its career, the faithful "oracle" of the rights asserted and the principles maintained by both its original publisher, and his confidential friend and coadjutor, Colonel Bigelow.

Following upon the arrival of the press in Worcester, a bright, burly boy, or rather a stout, vigorous youth, apprenticed to Mr. Thomas, appeared, — the late Benjamin Russell, afterwards familiarly known as "Major Ben," of the Boston "Columbian Centinel," — a man who attained to a distinguished and honorable position in the community; whose newspaper, like that of his famous master, acquired at a later day, and long exerted, a wide and commanding influence; and who lived to become the veteran of the craft, as personally he ever was a bright and shining ornament of his profession.

Young Russell was made an inmate of the family of Colonel Bigelow, where he found a welcome home, and was treated with the regard and affection of a child and brother.

Between him and the eldest son of the Colonel — also conspicuous in another walk, in after-life, as an eminent lawyer (the Hon. Timothy Bigelow, of Groton and Medford) — a warm attachment sprung up, which ripened subsequently into the closest intimacy, never broken, never jarred, till the death of the latter severed the tie. Mr. Bigelow deceased in 1821, at the comparatively early age of fifty-four. Major Russell survived to be an octogenarian. He was several years older than his friend.

An anecdote is told by the Rev. Andrew Bigelow, illustrative of the impression made on a stranger by the personal appearance and bearing of his grandfather, the Colonel, when in the prime of manhood. His informant was an aged parishioner, surviving a few months after the date of Dr. Bigelow's settlement in Taunton, nearly thirty years ago, — a man of bright memory, naturally a cool, observant mind, and who dwelt much on the reminiscences of earlier days. At his first interview with his pastor, the old gentleman inquired of the latter if he had an ancestor in the Revolutionary Army, — an officer of the Massachusetts Line. Being satisfied on those points, he was asked, in turn, the special reason of his queries. "Guess I have seen him," was the reply. "When and where?" next followed. Shaking the ashes from his pipe, as he sat in a big chair beside the chimney-corner, the old man said, "Well, you must suppose, that after the fight at Lexington, when the *milish* was called out, we all wanted to know what chaps they were to face the enemy, — them ' red-coats,' as we called the regulars, — in case of more scuffling. So I said to neighbor ——, (Sam was his given name,) ' Let us tackle up, and go and see the fellows about Boston' " — (*a la* " Captain Goodwin "). " He agreed, and we hitched team, and started off. We went to Cambridge, saw Ward's camp, and fetched up at Watertown. Our Congress (Provincial), they told us, was sitting there, then.

" Next morning, standing outside the tavern, many people coming and going, I spied a couple of officers walking up. One of them was a tall man, stepping very handsome; had a firm, quick gait, and no swagger. He was speaking to the other quite earnest, and looked, somehow, serious." — " Tall, you say ? " — " Yes : he was a six-footer, and something more ; carried himself straight; was broad-chested, not spare. I remember he was rather dark-*complected*, but with a good brown color on his cheeks ; his hair a jet-black, very full, and clubbed behind, — the fashion of those times." — " Any thing more ? " — " Well, I watched his eyes : they were very bright ; blackish, or thereabouts ; saw them plain, as he passed by and went into the house." — " And what of his companion ? " — " Don't remember," said the old man ; "nothing particular about him. When they had got in, I asked a countryman, standing by, who that tall officer was. He said, 'Major Bigelow : Major Bigelow of Worcester.' I looked at friend Sam. He eyed me mighty sharp. I knew what he wanted: so I told him the name of the gentleman. ' Well, neighbor Jo,' said he, ' what think you of that big fellow ? ' " — The old man stopped in his narrative (he was slow of speech), gave another nudge to the bowl of his pipe, lifted his eyebrows as if the distant scene, neighbor Sam and all, were again before him, then turned to his listener, and concluded : " I told Sam ——, ' Sam,' says I, '*that man will fight.*' — ' Guess so, too,' said Sam, ' right smart.' " *

The honors paid to the memory of Colonel Timothy Bigelow, by the public celebration held at the dedication of his Monument, were no barren formalities, restricted to the grateful recognition of a venerated name. Occurring at a crisis the most momentous in our national annals since the War of Independence, when all that was gained by the triumphs of the Revolution was suddenly and wickedly imperilled, they combined, with the traditionary reminiscences awakened, to lend a deeper and more powerful impulse to the indignant spirit of patriotism then stirred afresh among the citizens of Worcester and its neighborhood.

By a communication before us from His Honor Mayor Davis, under date of Sept. 27, in which he states that " the Monument has attracted great atten-

---

° The Colonel came of a fighting stock. His father, Daniel Bigelow, one of the original settlers of Worcester, was a soldier in the Canadian-French War.

tion, and thousands, and tens of thousands, have visited it," we learn " that it has excited in numerous minds a noble spirit of patriotism, and has induced many to volunteer in sustaining the Constitution and the Union. Since the Monument (he adds) was erected on our Central Park, more than five thousand men have left that Park in defence of the glorious institutions which Colonel Timothy Bigelow and his brave compeers fought to establish."

When addressing the officers and soldiers of the Fifteenth Regiment of Massachusetts Volunteers, a few weeks previously, near the grave of Colonel Bigelow, we gather also, from an animated report which has reached us, that His Honor invoked the troops in fervid strains " to imitate the self-sacrificing, the noble daring, the heroic spirit, of Colonel Timothy Bigelow and his brave associates of the Fifteenth Regiment of the Revolution."

" If," said the Mayor, with thrilling emphasis, — " if that valiant Colonel and his comrades, who now sleep near us, could hear your martial tramp, it would be music in their ears; and methinks their immortal spirits are looking down from the battlements of heaven, beckoning you on to sustain and uphold the liberties which they fought to secure.

Again: at the presentation of a beautiful stand of colors, from the ladies of Worcester, to the Fifteenth Regiment of Volunteers, on the 8th of August, the Hon. George F. Hoar, who spoke in their behalf, when tendering the gift to the colonel and officers of the corps, introduced his speech by saying.—

" I am deputed by the ladies of Worcester to present to you this banner. Eighty-four years ago to day, there was mustering in these streets the first Regiment ever raised in Worcester County for actual warfare,— the Fifteenth Regiment of the Massachusetts Line. What hard-fought fields at Monmouth and Trenton, what sufferings at Valley Forge, what glory and victory at Saratoga and Yorktown, have made that name famous, history has recorded; and now that, for the second time, Worcester County sends out to battle a full regiment of her sons, by a coincidence too appropriate to be called accident, the name which your fathers rendered illustrious has been allotted to you. What they won for us, it is yours to preserve for us."

Colonel Charles Devens, jun., in receiving the colors, responded with deep feeling in like stirring and sympathetic strains: —

" There is, indeed, a remarkable coincidence, as you have so well said, in the name of the regiment which I have the honor to command; being numbered the same as that commanded, during the Revolutionary War, by Colonel Timothy Bigelow, over whose remains yonder proud monument was three months ago erected with such inspiring ceremonies. It is, indeed, a most fortunate omen. I trust that some of the spirit which animated our ancestors has descended upon the present sons of Worcester County, and that they will be able to render an equally good account of their labors. I know they stand ready to defend that flag, as much dearer than life as honor is dearer; that they will 'not suffer a single star to be obscured, or a single stripe erased,' from that glorious symbol of our national union. I am unable to predict as

36*

to our return; yet this symbol shall be returned to the ladies of Worcester untarnished. Defeat, disaster, and death may come to us; but dishonor never."

Eloquent words, and nobly answered; as witnessed by the subsequent intrepid bearing of the heroic colonel and the regiment under his command, — a regiment which, whilst inheriting the prestige of the name, most worthily asserts its title to the distinction, and proudly emulates the honors, of the brave old FIFTEENTH of the Continental Line.

The city of Worcester has now upwards of one thousand men in the service of the country. At the date of the Revolution, the County altogether contained a population estimated at twenty-five thousand souls. The Fifteenth Continental Regiment, commanded by Colonel Timothy Bigelow, was raised from both town and county. At the present time, the City alone, comprising about the same number of inhabitants as the shire collectively in the Revolutionary contest, sends forth, as above remarked, more than a thousand troops to the field, to wage battle in defence of all that we hold most dear, — against the parricidal foes of our common rights so audaciously assailed, of the glorious temple our civil liberties and the sacred ark of the Constitution.

Truly it may be said, that not alone in "ashes" — the buried ashes of our fathers — live the *ancient* fires. They glow with equal warmth and intensity in the bosoms of their sons.

Certainly, at least, it is shown, that the "heart" — the brave HEART of our goodly Commonwealth — has lost none of its pristine vigor. It is still firm in its beatings, responsive to the throbbings of its sturdy youth. Long may it quicken with unabated ardor and strength, — the noble energy as redeveloped, now, in the maturity of its manly prime!

All homage to heroic Worcester! — Ever honored be her sons!

MILITARY.

WORCESTER LIGHT INFANTRY

This old Company, chartered in 1804 by a special resolve of the Legislature, bearing the signature of Harrison Gray Otis, as Speaker of the House of Representatives, and approved by Caleb Strong as Governor, upon the petition of Levi Lincoln, Jr , Joseph Blake Caldwell, Levi Thaxter, John Nelson, Jr , Daniel W Lincoln, and thirty two others, still exists to illustrate its early history by new acts of patriotism

The commanding officers since 1837 have been, Henry Hobbs, 1837 Dana H Fitch 1837; D Waldo Lincoln, 1838,–9,–40 , Ivers Phillips, 1841 , Henry W Conklin, 1842; Joseph B Ripley, 1843 , Edward Lamb, 1844–8 , Levi Barker, 1849 , Edward Lamb, 1850–1 , Charles S Childs, 1852 , Samuel P Russell, 1853–4 , George W Barker, 1854 , George F Peck, 1855 , Edward Lamb, 1856–7, Harrison W Pratt, 1858–62 The present commander is the 29th Captain in regular succession

On the 6th of February, 1861, orders were issued from headquarters directing the commanders of the Volunteer Militia, to fill their companies to the full number required by law, (fifty-six privates,) and to prepare for active duty in defending the national capital

On the 16th of April, at nearly midnight, orders were received for the Light Infantry to proceed to Boston without delay The company left town the following morning, and in a little more than twelve hours after receiving the summons, reported at the State House with ninety-six men, afterwards increased to one hundred, being the strongest company among the three months' men of Massachusetts The Infantry was attached as the left flank company to the Sixth Massachusetts Regiment under Col Edward F. Jones

Receiving arms, equipments and overcoats, the company left Boston in the evening , was with the regiment in its famous passage through Baltimore, April 19th, where the first blood of the insurrection was shed, and were the first armed troops to reach Washington, where they were quartered in the Senate Chamber, and served the full term of three months alternately at Washington, Annapolis and Baltimore

Of the members of the Light Infantry who served during the three months' campaign, twelve afterwards enlisted as officers, and twenty-seven as non-commissioned officers and privates, in various other companies and regiments, to serve during the war.

WORCESTER GUARDS

This company organized in 1840 under the name of " Harrison Guards," and was a Light Infantry company Within a few years it has been changed to a rifle company, and is attached to the Third Battalion of Rifles It was in the first three months service under the command of Capt. A B R. Sprague.

THE WAR.

Over eight hundred men have left Worcester for the war, among which are some of our best citizens, not only officers, but privates. These have mostly gone in the Sixth Regiment, Third Battalion of Rifles, Fifteenth Regiment, Twenty-first Regiment, and the Twenty-fifth Regiment.

The following is a list of the names of the officers belonging in Worcester to the SIXTH REGIMENT: H. W. Pratt, Captain; George W. Prouty, F. S. Washburn, J. W. Denny, D. F. Parker, Lieutenants.

THIRD BATTALION OF RIFLES: Major, Charles Devens; Adjutant, John M. Goodhue; Surgeon, Oramel Martin; Quartermaster, J. E. Estabrook; Quartermaster Sergeant, George F. White; Sergeant Major, N. S. Liscomb; Co. A, Captain A. B. R. Sprague; Lieutenants, Josiah Pickett, George C. Joslin, O. Moulton and E. A. Harkness; Co. C, Captain, M. S. McConville; Lieutenants, M. O. Driscoll, M. J. McCafferty, Thomas O'Neal, and M. Melaven. Most of the officers and privates of the Third Battalion, after their first three months were out, enlisted again, and are now in different positions in the army, as will be seen.

FIFTEENTH REGIMENT.

Colonel, Charles Devens, Worcester; Lieut. Col. George H. Ward; Adjutant, George W. Baldwin; Quartermaster, Church Howe; Surgeon, Joseph N. Bates; Asst. Surgeon, S. Foster Haven, Jr. Captain John M. Studley, Co. D; Capt. George C. Joslin, Co. I; 1st Lieut. Edwin P. Woodward, Co. D; 1st Lieut. Thomas J. Spurr; 2d Lieut. John S. Hall, Co. D.

TWENTY-FIRST REGIMENT.

Quartermaster, George F. Thompson; Capt. Thomas S. Washburn; 2d Lieut. William H. Valentine.

TWENTY-FIFTH REGIMENT.

Lieut. Col., Augustus B. R. Sprague; Major, Matthew J. McCafferty; Adjutant, Elijah A. Harkness; Surgeon, J. Marcus Rice; Chaplain, Horace James; Captains, Josiah Pickett, Albert H. Foster, Thomas O'Niel, Lewis Wageley, Orson Moulton, J. Waldo Denny; 1st Lieutenants, F. E. Goodwin, George S. Campbell, William Daly, Henry M. Richter, David M. Woodward; 2d Lieutenants, Merritt B. Bessey, George H. Spaulding, Henry McConville, Fred. A. Wiegand, James M. Drennan.

The following is a list of the killed, wounded and missing, and those who have died in the army, belonging to Worcester.

Lieut. Col. George H. Ward, wounded at Ball's Bluff in the leg severely; leg amputated below the knee.

Lieut. J. W. Grout, killed while swimming the river at Ball's Bluff.

Horace E. Brooks, wounded at Roanoke Island in the ankle, badly.

David B. Bigelow, wounded at Roanoke Island in the thigh ; not dangerous.

George E. Barnard, wounded at Ball's Bluff in the leg; not dangerous.

Corporal Charles A. Upham, died with fever at Richmond.

Ralph T. Finney, wounded at Ball's Bluff in the thigh ; not dangerous.

Charles W. Adams, died with fever at hospital in Washington.

Sargeant Benj. Taft, died at Salisbury, N. C., from exposure.

John W. Smith, killed at Ball's Bluff.

John F. Stafford, killed at Ball's Bluff.

Charles Goff, killed at Ball's Bluff.

Stillman L. Commins, not heard of, probably killed in the river at Ball's Bluff.

David Sever, wound in the arm, not dangerously.

George E. Curtis, died at Roanoke Island from the effects of measles.

Charles Bartlett, wounded slightly.

HOTELS.

EXCHANGE HOTEL.

This is the oldest public house in Worcester : its first name was the " United States Arms." It was at this house that Washington breakfasted on his way to Boston, in 1789. In 1807 Reuben Sikes opened the house and kept it as a stage house for many years. Under the wise and judicious management of Mr. Sikes, this house became the most popular of any house in the State out of Boston : it was called " Sikes' Coffee House," " Sikes' Stage House," &c. In 1825 Gen. Lafayette put up at this house and took breakfast, on his way to Boston, to assist in the laying of the corner stone of the Bunker Hill Monument. Samuel B. Thomas kept the house several years, when its name was " Thomas's Temperance Exchange Coffee House." At this time, as the name indicates, it was a thorough-going and consistent temperance house, and has maintained that reputation to the present time. The estate is now owned by Misses Clara and Sarah Sikes, daughters of Mr. Reuben Sikes, who now occupy rooms in the house, and board with Mr. Samuel Banister, who is now the landlord of the house. This house is principally sustained by jurymen, witnesses, and other persons attending the Courts, together with families and other boarders.

LINCOLN HOUSE.

This house is owned by James H. Wall and the heirs of the late E. H. Hemenway. It is situated on the west side of Main street, its front 128 feet by 70 wide, four stories high, with wings extending back on Elm and Maple streets, 168 feet, and three stories high. It contains about 130 rooms, besides a large number of stores and other rooms. It is kept as a first class hotel by E. T. Balcom.

BAY STATE HOUSE.

This is the largest public house in Worcester, and one of the most popular in the commonwealth. It is owned by a corporation, and is situated on the east side of Main street and north side of Exchange street, forming a front on Main of 100 feet, and on Exchange of 170, four stories high on Main and five on Exchange street, containing 165 rooms. It is under the management of Warner Clifford, who has had the control of the house since its erection in 1854.

FARMER'S HOTEL.

This hotel belongs to the heirs of Joseph Barnes, and is occupied by J. G. Witherby. This house is kept on strict temperance principles, and is situated on the North side of Mechanic street.

WALDO HOUSE.

This house is situated on Waldo street; it formerly stood on the site of the Mechanic's Hall, and was built and occupied by Hon. Daniel Waldo as his mansion. Since its removal it has been kept as a hotel; it is now kept by Thomas Tucker as a temperance house.

WASHINGTON SQUARE HOTEL.

This estate is owned by the Boston and Worcester Railroad Corporation. It is situated near the depot of the Western Railroad, and is kept by Elliott Swan as a temperance house.

CITY HOTEL.

This hotel is situated on the east side of Main street; it was the first brick building in Worcester, except a small store owned by Mr. Waldo, which has long since been torn down. It has long been kept as a public house, and is now under the management of William Whitney.

NEWSPAPERS AND PERIODICALS.

WORCESTER DAILY TRANSCRIPT.

The "Daily Transcript," the first daily paper ever published in Worcester county, was issued in Worcester on the 9th day of June, 1845, by Julius L. Clarke as editor and proprietor, Mr. Clarke having been for the two or three previous years, connected with the editorial department of "The Christian Citizen." In the latter part of the same year, a weekly journal, entitled, "The Bay State Farmer," was commenced in connection with this paper, and both were subsequently discontinued; he, soon after, commencing the publication of another daily paper, "The Worcester Telegraph," which was continued till the spring of 1849 In the beginning of 1851, the Transcript was again resumed as a daily, in connection with a weekly issue of the same, Mr Silas Dinsmore being its publisher, and Mr Clarke once more becoming its editor ; the paper having been in its first years an independent journal, but now entering the political arena, as an advocate of the principles of the whig party. In 1852, Mr Charles L Stevens, of Barre, was also associated with the editorial department of the paper ; but in 1855, it changed hands, Mr William R Hooper becoming its purchaser, and subsequently its editor, in 1857, Mr Hooper having purchased ' the National Ægis,' in the autumn of the latter year connected that journal also with the " Weekly Transcript, ' the two papers, the " Worcester Daily Transcript, ' (now an evening paper,) and the weekly " Ægis and Transcript," being published at the present time under his proprietorship and direction, and both being devoted to the republican party

WORCESTER DAILY SPY.

The first number of the " Worcester Daily Spy," was issued July 1st, 1845, by John Milton Earle, editor and proprietor Its publication has been continued, in connection with the " Massachusetts Spy " down to the present time In 1850, Mr Earle associated with himself Mr Thomas Drew, Jr, who, since 1845, had been an associate editor of " The Christian Citizen,' the two continuing their connection till 1859 In the beginning of the latter year, Messrs Earle and Drew retired, and Messrs S S Foss of the Woonsocket (Rhode Island) Patriot, and Moses Farnum of Blackstone, became the purchasers and publishers of the Daily and Weekly Spy A few months afterwards, however, the last named parties disposed of their interest to J D Baldwin & Co, who continue the publication of the two papers at the present time, both being in the interest of the republican party

OTHER DAILIES

Several other efforts have been made to establish daily papers in Worcester, but have been discontinued after the lapse of a brief period Among these, were " The Evening Journal," published during portions of the years 1854-5, and edited by Mr Dexter F Parker " The Daily Bay State," also an evening paper, commenced in September, 1856, and continued about one and a half years also the " Worcester Daily Times," commenced in July, 1860, but discontinued after a few month's existence The last paper was edited and published by Moses Bates

The Weekly Times is published as a Democratic paper by T W Caldwell.

THE CHRISTIAN REFLECTOR,

Was commenced in 1838 It was conducted by a board of managers of fifteen of the Baptist denomination, seven clergymen and eight laymen It was edited by Rev C P Grosvenor, and was a strong Anti-Slavery paper It continued a few years, and was then sold and merged with the Christian Watchman, which is now printed in Boston.

THE CHRISTIAN CITIZEN,

Was commenced in 1844, by Elihu Burritt, who was editor and proprietor. It was a weekly paper, devoted to the advocacy of religion, peace, anti-slavery, education, and general information. It was published seven years, a part of which time T. W. Butterfield was associate publisher, and Julius L. Clarke and Thomas Drew at different times aided in the editorial and business departments. It was not in its last years a pecuniary success, but for a time exerted a great and favorable influence, especially in the cause of peace. Mr. Burritt was a remarkable man. He was born in New Britain, Conn., Dec. 8, 1811, and served an apprenticeship at blacksmithing. Afterwards for several years he continued to work as a journeyman most of the time, devoting several hours each day to the study of languages, in quite a number of which he became proficient. He came to Worcester to secure the advantages of the Antiquarian Library. His mode of employing his time may be seen in the following extract from his diary for one week:

"*Monday*, June 18, headache; forty pages Cuvier's Theory of the Earth, sixty-four pages French, eleven hours forging. *Tuesday*, sixty-five lines of Hebrew, thirty pages of French, ten pages of Cuvier's Theory, eight lines Syriac, ten ditto Danish, ten ditto Bohemian, nine ditto Polish, fifteen names of stars, ten hours forging. *Wednesday*, twenty-five lines Hebrew, fifty pages of astronomy, eleven hours forging. *Thursday*, fifty-five lines of Hebrew, eight ditto Syriac, eleven hours forging. *Friday*, unwell; twelve hours forging. *Saturday*, unwell; fifty pages Natural Philosophy, ten hours forging. *Sunday*, lessons for Bible class."

About this time he was introduced to the public as "the learned Blacksmith," by Gov. Everett, and the fame thus acquired soon led to a demand for his services as a writer and lecturer. In the winter of 1842, he lectured successfully sixty-eight times. His published translations and writings would make up a formidable list, while his health was kept up by daily exercise at the anvil. After commencing the Citizen, he devoted himself largely to the cause of Peace and Universal Brotherhood, both in this country and in England, where he went in 1846, and remained several years. He now resides in his native town.

THE WORCESTER COUNTY GAZETTE,

Was established January, 1845, to advocate the principles of the "Liberty Party" in politics, by Rev. R. B. Hubbard, some time Principal of the Latin Grammar school in the centre district, and the nominee of his party for representative in Congress in the campaign of 1844. It was printed by Jonathan L. Estey, whose office was in Paine's block, corner of Main and Pleasant streets. In July following Mr. Estey formed a partnership with Dudley C. Evans, and Estey & Evans assumed the publication of the Gazette. Mr. Hubbard's connection with the paper continued to the close of its publication in Worcester, March, 1847, though Messrs. Estey & Evans conducted its issue mainly from June, 1846. The paper took from its commencement equal rank with the Spy, Ægis, and Palladium, of that time, and enjoyed a large patronage from the public. Its subscription list was finally sold to the Boston Emancipator.

Estey & Evans printed the first daily paper in Worcester,— the Transcript, by Julius L. Clark, Esq.,— during the first six months of its existence. They also printed the American Pulpit, for Rev. R. S. Rust, at one period. Mr. Evans died in New York city, being at the time foreman to Baker, Godwin & Co. Mr. Estey has entered the active duties of the christian ministry in the New England Conference of the M. E. Church.

WORCESTER PALLADIUM.

This paper was commenced in 1834, and has been under the editorial care of J. S. C. Knowlton. The first four years of the existence of this paper it advocated the old National Republican or Whig principles. About 1838, this paper became connected with the Worcester Republican, a Democratic paper, edited by Jubal Harrington, (who had occasion to leave Worcester at rather short notice.) The Palladium then became the Democratic organ of the county, and continued such until 1854, and since that time it has advocated the principles of the Republican party. It is an able and well-conducted weekly paper.

The WORCESTER WATERFALL and the WORCESTER COUNTY CATARACT and WASHINGTONIAN were all devoted to Temperance, and all merged in one paper before the close of their existence. Each of them exerted a salutary influence in their turn. These three papers were mainly conducted by Jesse W. Goodrich, Esq., as proprietor and editor.

THE SUNDAY SCHOOL GAZETTE

Was commenced under the patronage of the Unitarian Sunday School Society, in 1849, by A. Hutchinson & Co., and published once in two weeks. Rev. Edward E. Hale was editor for several years, succeeded by Rev. S. G. Bulfinch of Dorchester, followed after one year by Rev. W. H. Cudworth of East Boston. It was printed by H. J. Howland for eleven years, after which it was removed to Boston. Its circulation was in that time increased to 9500.

THE LITERARY GEMINÆ.

In June, 1839, the publication of this monthly periodical of forty-eight pages was commenced by Elihu Burritt, and continued one year. One half of each number was filled with the "choicest morceaux of French literature," in their original language.

THE ADVOCATE OF PEACE.

This organ of the American Peace Society, was edited and published in Worcester during the year 1847, by E. Burritt. It was a monthly of thirty-two pages.

37

THE WORCESTER ALMANAC, DIRECTORY, AND BUSINESS ADVERTISER.

In 1829, Mr. Clarendon Harris published a "Village Directory" of Worcester, containing the names, &c., of the owners and occupants of buildings on the thirteen streets then existing here, to accompany a map published by him. It occupied ten small pages. In 1843, A. W. Congdon issued a Business Directory of Worcester, printed in Boston. In 1844, the regular annual publication of a full Directory of the place, was commenced by Henry J. Howland, under the title at the head of this article. It was an 18mo. of 108 pages, and contained the names, residences, and business, of over 1200 persons, besides a calendar and much other useful information. It was intended from the first for general circulation among the people, and its very low price (12½ cents) secured for it a large sale, amounting in several years to six thousand copies a year. The number of names has increased every year till the present, and now exceeds 7000. It is still continued by its founder, who is now the oldest Directory publisher in New England.

PUBLIC BUILDINGS.

THE CITY HALL has been greatly enlarged, and adapted to the wants of the city. The lower part contains the Mayor and Aldermen's room, another for the Common Council, a third for Police Court, offices of the City Treasurer, City Marshal, City Clerk, and for the City Messenger. The upper story contains the large City Hall with its ante rooms, and the office of Superintendent of Schools. The basement is occupied as a Police and Watchman's office, Lock-up, Meat Market, &c.

THE OLD COURT HOUSE has been removed a few feet to its rear, and refitted. The Criminal Courts are held in it: it also contains the office of the Sheriff, and the offices of the Court of Probate and Insolvency.

THE NEW COURT HOUSE, standing a few rods south of the above named, is a most substantial fire-proof edifice: it was built in 1845, of Quincy granite. In it the civil terms of the courts are held, with numerous ante rooms for the jurors, and for consultation. The lower floor is occupied by the Register of Deeds office, the Clerk and Treasurer's office. This house cost about one hundred thousand dollars.

AMERICAN ANTIQUARIAN HALL. This building stands at the corner of Court and Highland streets, a few feet north of the old Court House: it is built with brick and is fire proof. It contains a very large Library Hall, and the office of the Librarian on the second floor. The first floor is occupied for the storing of old miscellaneous works; in this room is stored, also, the old printing press of its illustrious founder, Isaiah Thomas, Esq.

AGRICULTURAL HALL was built by the Worcester County Agricultural Society, on their ground a little west of the Court House. It contains a large

Hall for the Society Meetings, and their Public Dinners at their Annual Fairs, besides a tenement for the Superintendent of the grounds; also, in the basement, a room for the storage of their fencings, and other articles.

THE MECHANICS HALL. A short notice of this building is given on page 396, in connection with the Mechanics Association, but it is deemed of too much importance to omit a more full description of it in this connection. This splendid building is located on the lot long occupied by the residence of the late Daniel Waldo, on Main street.

The building has 100 feet front, and is 70 feet in hight from the side-walk to the top of the cornice; the pediment or triangular part over the entablature, rises 16 feet higher, making the whole 86 feet.

The basement and the first floor measure 145 by 100 1-2 feet. On the first floor there are four stores, each 78 by 18 feet, and in the rear of these are two other stores, each 61 by 32 feet, and communicating with the two centre stores which front on Main street. Between the two centre stores is the main entrance, which is 21 feet wide for a distance of 32 feet, as far back as the two principal stair cases, and is 9 feet wide the remainder of the distance through the whole floor, thus communicating with the rear entrance, and the two rear flights of stairs leading to the upper floors. The front stair-cases are each 6 feet in width.

Upon the second floor in front, are five offices, each 24 feet by 20; next in rear of these, are two library rooms, each 36 feet by 25, and communicating with the offices and each other, by passage ways between them; next in rear of the libraries, a passage way, 20 feet wide, and extending entirely across the building, communicates with the stair-cases from below, and with Washburn Hall. This room is 80 feet by 50, and with the ante rooms, each 15 feet by 11, occupies the remainder of the second floor, to the rear of the building.

The third floor is devoted to the great hall and its appurtenances. The hall will measure 128 feet by 80, and 40 feet in hight: allowing each man 2 1 2 square feet, this hall contains standing room for *four thousand five hundred men*; at the eastern end is the speaker's platform, 40 feet by 20; at the western end are two large ante rooms, and over them the galleries, which also extend along each side of the entire hall; the galleries on the side are 9 feet in width; there are six stair-cases leading out of the hall to the floors below; the finish and decorations of the interior are panel work overhead with columns and arches at its sides. It is thoroughly lighted and ventilated, and is one of the most beautiful halls in the country. The style of architecture of the building is the Corinthian, and the appearance of the whole will challenge the admiration of all. Elbridge Boyden, architect; H. N. Tower, superintendent; Tilley Raymond, carpenter.

PUBLIC LIBRARY, situated on Elm street, owned by the city, cost $80,000, and is occupied by the Librarian, Natural History Society's Collection, Green or Reference Library, and Farmers' Club and Library. This is a fine edifice of brick, a few rods from Main street, and is well arranged and adapted to the purposes for which it was built; it was erected in 1860, during the administration of Hon. W. W. Rice as Mayor.

LUNATIC HOSPITAL. This building has been greatly enlarged since 1836, and is now probably the largest building in New England, if not in the United States, occupied for that purpose.

HORTICULTURAL HALL, on Front street, was erected in 1851. The building is forty by one hundred feet, built with brick and the front finished with mastic.

WORCESTER THEATRE, adjoining the above, built in 1850, by William Piper: it is forty-six by one hundred and twenty-five feet, built of brick. It is calculated to seat 1200 persons. This building is more ornamental to the city than profitable to its enterprising proprietor.

COLLEGE OF THE HOLY CROSS, is situated on the northern slope of Packachoag Hill, and is connected with a farm of ninety-six acres. It was mostly burnt in 1852, but has since been rebuilt.

LADIES COLLEGIATE INSTITUTE, was formerly the Medical College. It is situated on a commanding eminence, on Union Hill, and is an edifice of great taste. The best view of the city is had from this building of any in the city.

THE ALMS HOUSE, connected with the poor farm, situated on Lincoln Street, near the Shrewsbury line, is a large brick edifice, sufficient to accommodate more paupers probably than will be in Worcester for many years to come. It was built during the administration of Mayor Knowlton, in 1854.

NUMEROUS OTHER HALLS, some of which we will record. Brinley Hall, in Brinley Block on Main street. Waldo Hall, on Pearl street. Temperance Hall, on Foster street. Union Hall, at New Worcester. Lyceum Hall, at Tatnuck.

THE CHURCHES have been mentioned elsewhere, except the Third Baptist, which was omitted in its place, under the head of "churches and ministers," by mistake. This church is at the corner of Main and Herman streets. It was built in 1855, and is a fine edifice of brick. The church was formed 1853, and the house was dedicated in January 1856. The sermon on the occasion was preached by Rev. Dr. Wayland of Providence, R. I. Rev. H. L. Wayland, the son of Dr. Wayland, was ordained the Pastor of this church, at its commencement, and continued to labor with them until the summer of 1861, when he left them and joined the seventh Connecticut Regiment as Chaplain. Mr. Wayland was born in Providence, R. I., and graduated at Brown University.

RAILROADS.

The Boston and Worcester, the Norwich and Worcester, and the Western Railroads, mentioned by Mr. Lincoln, are all in successful operation.

The Providence and Worcester Railroad was incorporated in March 1844.

The Worcester and Nashua, was incorporated in March, 1845, and the Worcester and Fitchburg in April, 1846; all of which are doing a large and profitable business. Persons starting from Worcester to any point may take the Rail, from this city. A Horse Railroad was incorporated by the Legislature of the State in 1861, to run from Lincoln Square to Leicester line, through Main street to New Worcester, and thence through Leicester street to the line of the town of Leicester. This Road is not as yet built.

CEMETERIES.

HOPE CEMETERY, on Webster street (New Worcester,) is owned by the city. It contains more than fifty acres, and has fine natural advantages, and is an attractive place of resort for citizens and strangers. Lots vary in price from five to forty dollars, and a portion of the lots are free.

THE RURAL CEMETERY, on Grove street, is the property of a corporation. Constant improvements are going forward there, quite creditable to the good taste of those having charge. It is managed by a Board of Trustees, over which Hon. Levi Lincoln presides as President.

CATHOLIC CEMETERY, situated on Sutton street, is a beautiful field of about twelve acres. Many of the lots are beautifully laid out and ornamented with trees and shrubbery. It is owned by the Catholic church.

37*

REMARKABLE EVENTS.

On the first day of January, 1859, our citizens were startled by one of the most singular and destructive explosions ever known in this community; the Engine House on Pleasant street, occupied by Eagle Hose Company No. three, and as a storage house for Engine No. four, became filled with gas from some leak in the pipes, and a little fire remaining of the fire the day before ignited it, and the building with its contents were blown to atoms in a moment. Most of the buildings in the vicinity were more or less damaged. Glass broken, doors shaken from their places, and whole buildings damaged. Fortunately no lives were lost. Damages $2500 to Engine House and contents, the total damage about $6000.

July 22d, 1859, — A terrific explosion took place at I. Washburn & Co.'s wire factory. The large steam boiler, thirty feet long and four feet in diameter and weighing about five tons, attached to their powerful engine, exploded with tremendous force, shattering the engine house into atoms; injuring sev ral workmen, but killing none. So immense was the force of the explosion, that the ponderous boiler was carried about two hundred feet into the air, and more than a quarter of a mile distant, and driving itself into the earth to the depth of four feet. The explosion produced a dull heavy sound, and was not very extensively heard.

FREDERICK WARREN, City Marshal of Worcester, was accidentally shot in his office on the 10th of November, 1858, by Henry W. Hendricks, Esq., of Charleston, S. C. Mr. Warren was 49 years of age, and was son of Charles Warren, late of this city. In his vocation he had few equals, and in this section of New England no superior. He was *the* detective officer of Western Massachusetts, and a worthy and upright man.

EXECUTION.

Thomas Barrett of Lunenburg was executed in the Jail yard by John W. Lincoln, Sheriff, for the murder of Ruth Holton, Jan. 3d, 1845.

LONGEVITY.

Mr. Ebenezer Mower died February 14th, 1861. He was the oldest native of Worcester, aged 100 years and four months; he was born on the old family homestead in Tatnuck.

Mr. Mower was a remarkable man to remember events; he could recollect the raising of the old South Church, in 1763, when he was but a little more than three years old. He recollected the marching of the minute-men under Captain Bigelow in 1775, and his death in 1790. As Mr. Mower's father was a royalist, he never engaged in the struggle of the revolution, although it was his desire to do so. In the election of President, the November before his death, and when he was past 100, he attended meeting and cast his vote for Abraham Lincoln.

ACKNOWLEDGMENT.

The Author is under lasting obligation to Hon. LEVI LINCOLN, for permission to reprint Lincoln's History, which forms the first part of this Volume. Also, to Hon. ISAAC DAVIS, Hon. PETER C. BACON, Hon. GEORGE F. HOAR, and ALBERT CURTIS, Esq., for material aid. Had it not been for this permission and aid from these friends, the enterprise would have failed. Also, to the Clerk and Treasurer of the city, to the Clerks of the several churches, and to all others who in any way have aided me, even by an encouraging word, I would tender my sincere acknowledgments.

INDEX.